D1461106

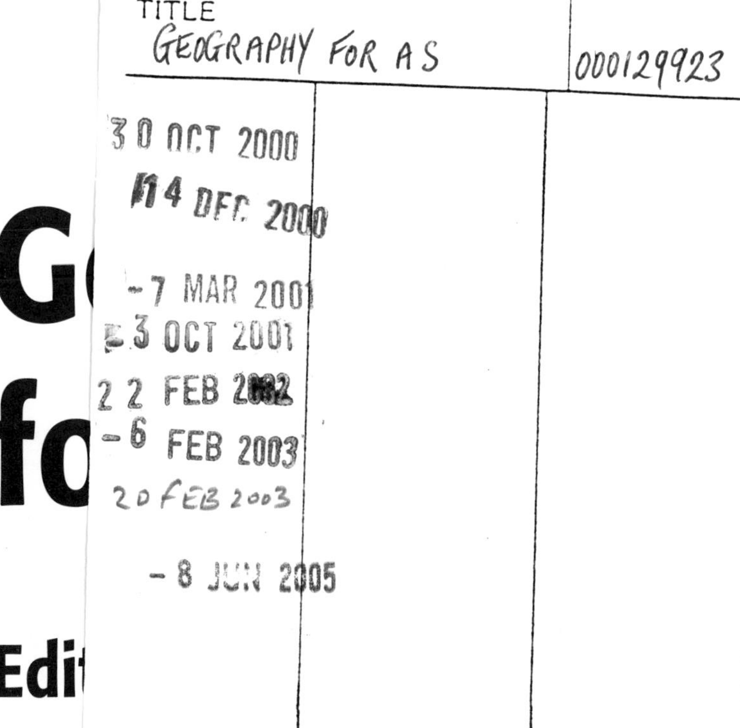
30 OCT 2000
14 DEC 2000
-7 MAR 2001
3 OCT 2001
22 FEB 2002
-6 FEB 2003
20 FEB 2003
-8 JUN 2005

G

fo

Edi

CAMBRIDGE
UNIVERSITY PRESS

* 000129923 *

This book is dedicated to the memory of Vincent Bunce (1958–1999)

PUBLISHED BY THE PRESS SYNDICATE OF THE UNIVERSITY OF CAMBRIDGE
The Pitt Building, Trumpington Street, Cambridge, United Kingdom

CAMBRIDGE UNIVERSITY PRESS
The Edinburgh Building, Cambridge CB2 2RU, UK http://www.cup.cam.ac.uk
40 West 20th Street, New York, NY 10011-4211, USA http://www.cup.org
10 Stamford Road, Oakleigh, Melbourne 3166, Australia
Ruiz de Alarcón 13, 28014 Madrid, Spain

First published 2000

Printed in the United Kingdom at the University Press, Cambridge

Typeface System QuarkXPress®

Typeset in Minion 11pt/15pt

A catalogue record for this book is available from the British Library

ISBN 0 521 78609 6 paperback

Design, page layout and artwork illustrations by Hardlines, Charlbury, Oxford.

The cover photo shows an aerial view of an island village, Cebu, in the Philippines.
By courtesy of Stone

Contents

Preface

This book has been prepared especially to support OCR's Advanced Subsidiary GCE in Geography, Specification A. It has been written by a team of experienced teachers and academic geographers who have paid close attention to the range and standard of work required for the Advanced Subsidiary qualification while, at the same time, attempting to ensure that the study material provides a sound and interesting basis for further work at Advanced and Advanced Extension levels.

You will find that the book is arranged to mirror the module structure of the specification and that, where possible, the subheadings within each chapter match the divisions of the modules given in the specification. Chapters 1 to 4 are concerned with Module 2680, *The Physical Environment*, and deal in turn with the four sections set out in the specification covering hydrological systems, ecosystems, the atmosphere and the lithosphere. Chapters 5 to 9 are devoted to Module 2681, *The Human Environment*, and explore systematically each of the main topics within the sections on population and rural and urban settlement. Chapter 10 provides advice and guidance on carrying out the enquiry required for Module 2682, *Geographical Investigation.*

Throughout the book emphasis has been placed on the fundamental ideas and relationships which characterise the topics specified in the modules. Chapters 1 to 9 each open with a statement of the key themes explored within it. Examples and case studies are introduced at a range of scales from local to global. Each chapter also contains a range of extension tasks enclosed within an Activity box. These tasks are closely related to the nature of the topics under study and are designed to help you develop some of the geographical skills and techniques that are an integral part of the subject at GCE Advanced level.

Key Skills

At the same time as developing geographical skills, some of the tasks in the Activity boxes provide opportunities for you to practise those *key skills* which are intended to help you improve your own performance in education and training, and later on in work and life in general. Many of the exercises will enhance your competence in communication, the application of number and the use of information technology; there are also some opportunities for working with others and problem solving. Module 3, Geographical Investigation, offers most scope for the formal assessment of these skills. It provides a suitable context in which to demonstrate your ability in several skill areas and, in the cases of *Application of number*, *Information technology*, *Working with others* and *Problem solving*, to meet the requirement that competence must be assessed through a piece of work that is both complex and substantial. The investigation might also be used to provide the evidence that you have met some of the requirements for the *Improving own learning and performance* skill.

Note: terms described in the Glossary are highlighted in **colour** when they are first mentioned in the text.

Contributors to this book

Editor

Clive Hart, Education Consultant

Authors

John Bailey, University of Bristol
Jane Dove, St Paul's Girls' School, London
Karen Holdich, St Mary's School, Ascot
Alistair McNaught, Peter Symonds' College, Winchester
Garrett Nagle, St Edward's School, Oxford
Alisdair Rodgers, School of Geography, Oxford University
Kevin Stannard, Eton College, Windsor

1 Hydrological systems

KEY THEMES

- ✔ Within the global hydrological cycle, the distribution of water between the main stores is uneven; the volume of water suitable for use by people is only a very small proportion of the total.
- ✔ Drainage basins, whatever their scale, are finely balanced systems involving complex links between inputs, outputs, stores and flows.
- ✔ Local hydrological cycles involve exchanges of water which, from time to time, may become unbalanced, creating floods or periods of water shortage.
- ✔ Human activity has a profound impact on hydrological systems: whenever land use is changed, local hydrological cycles will be affected, but not always as expected.

The global hydrological cycle

Origin and significance

Tom Robbins – a US novelist – once wrote 'Human beings were invented by water as a device for transporting itself from one place to another'. Whilst this may not be strictly true, he certainly had grasped some of the significance of the relationship between human beings and water. More than 75 per cent of our body weight is water. We depend on water for drinking, and it is a vital component of everything we eat. The landscapes we live in are fashioned by water, rocks are recycled by its actions, and Earth's climate is strongly influenced by the interaction of water with solar energy. Unique among the planets, Earth is a planet of water. It is just the right distance from the Sun to host water in all three states – icy solid, watery liquid and steamy vapour.

There is still some debate as to the origin of Earth's vast water supplies, but the main source seems to have come from volcanic activity outgassing steam from molten rock. Recent research into near-Earth asteroids and comets has suggested that small fragments of comets (a few metres wide) entering the Earth's atmosphere could have a significant long-term effect in 'topping up' our planet's water supplies, but for the most part we can consider Earth's global water supplies as constant.

Global scale: inputs, outputs and stability

Any system consists of essentially four components: inputs, outputs, stores and transfers, as shown in Figure 1.1. At the global scale, the inputs and outputs are negligible, so the Earth's water supply can be regarded as a 'closed system'. The main activity is the transfer of water backwards and forwards from one store to another whilst the overall system remains in balance.

Global-scale stores

The main stores in the global hydrological cycle are shown in Figures 1.2 and 1.3. Note particularly how the global water supply is very

Figure 1.1
A system model

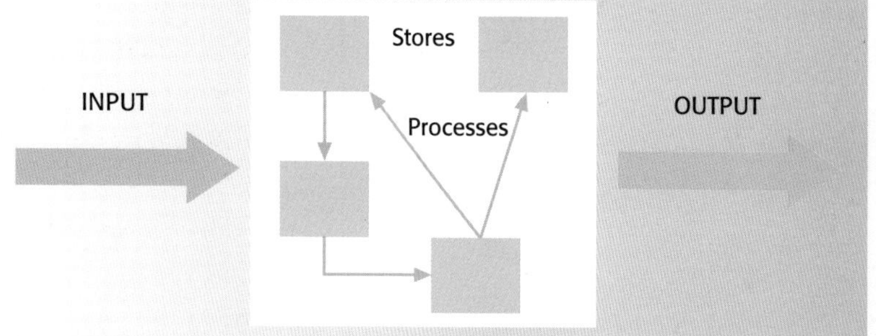

unevenly distributed between stores, and that the sources we rely on for human use (lakes, rivers and shallow groundwater) form only a small proportion of the total.

Figure 1.2 plots the percentage of each source of global water as a sphere. Seen in this light the world's rainfall and river supplies seem a fragile and vulnerable resource. These stores vary in their usefulness to humans. Freshwater stores closer to the surface – such as lakes, rivers and shallow groundwater – have the advantage of easy access but the disadvantage of being easily polluted. They are also smaller stores and may prove less reliable in the long term. The larger stores, such as deep groundwater, ice caps and seawater, are often not economically viable to exploit. But economics change. What is uneconomic one year may prove to be economic as demand rises or if alternative supplies become more expensive.

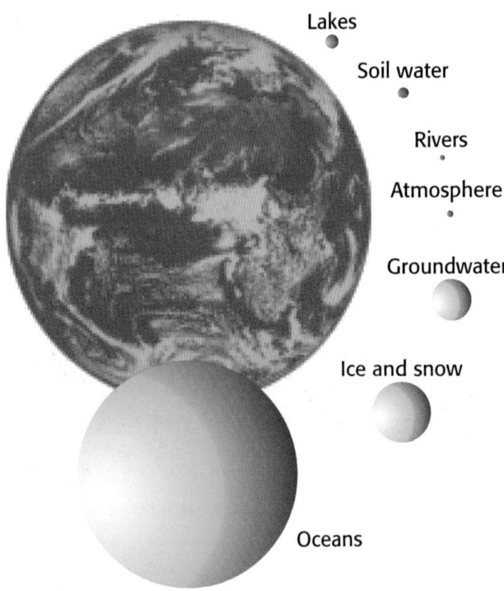

Figure 1.2
The Earth's water stores. The volume of each sphere is proportional to the percentage of global water contained in the store. Shallow and deep source groundwater have been combined in this figure. Notice how small lakes and rivers are in relation to the total store.

Activity

Assess each of the stores in Figure 1.3 in terms of its potential for human use, by allocating a score from 5 (good) to 1 (poor) to each store for the following criteria:

- Suitability of water for human use
- Proximity to population centres
- Need of treatment
- Vulnerability to pollution
- Volume available
- Alternative economic uses, e.g. recreation, transport

Figure 1.3
Global water stores

Store	Volume (million km^3)	% of total
Oceans	1370	97.25
Ice caps and glaciers	29	2.05
Deep groundwater (> 750 m)	5.3	0.38
Shallow groundwater (< 750 m)	4.2	0.30
Lakes	0.125	0.01
Soil moisture	0.065	0.005
Atmosphere	0.013	0.001
Rivers	0.0017	0.0001
Biosphere	0.0006	0.00004
Total	**1408.70**	**100.00**

Global-scale processes

Water moves between the stores by a variety of transfer processes as illustrated in Figure 1.4. From the data on the diagram it is clear that there are broad differences between the oceans and the land in terms of their **water balance**. Across the world's oceans, evaporation exceeds

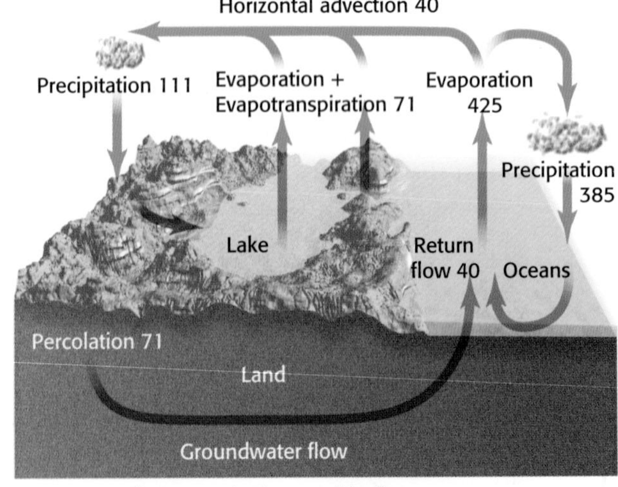

Figure 1.4
The global water cycle

precipitation because high wind speeds over the open sea create above-average rates of evaporation. Over land the reverse tends to occur, with precipitation exceeding evapotranspiration. The excess precipitation over land is returned to the seas by rivers and groundwater flow.

Whilst the broad water balance between ocean and land can be readily distinguished, variations from region to region mean that any one area of the globe has its own distinctive hydrological 'regime'. Figure 1.5 shows the regional water balances on a continental or oceanic scale.

On a global scale, **evaporation** depends mainly on temperature and the availability of water. Not surprisingly, evaporation rates are greater over oceans than over land owing to the abundance of water available. There are also strong latitudinal influences on evaporation. Figure 1.6 shows two major patterns in the Atlantic – a strong north–south gradient and an equally strong west–east gradient. The first is explained by the way temperature varies with latitude: hot near the Equator and cold near the poles. The second results from the circling of vast ocean currents which move clockwise in the northern hemisphere and anticlockwise in the south. These push warm water polewards along the western side of the oceans and slide cool water Equatorwards along the eastern edge of the oceans. Evaporation of water therefore varies from place to place. It also varies with time, being higher in the summer months and lower in the winter months.

Like evaporation, **transpiration** depends on temperature and the time of year. It also depends on plant types. In forested regions of the world, transpiration rates can be very high, making a major contribution to the local

	Evaporation (E)	Precipitation (P)	Water balance (P – E)
Ocean areas			
Atlantic	1240	890	-350
Indian	1320	1170	-150
Pacific	1320	1330	10
Continental areas			
Africa	430	690	260
Asia	310	600	290
Australia	420	470	50
Europe	390	640	250
North America	320	660	340
South America	700	1630	930

Units = millimetres per year

Figure 1.5

Global water balance for major ocean and continental areas

Activity

1 On a map of the world, plot the evaporation and precipitation figures for each region as bar charts, using colours to distinguish between evaporation and precipitation.

2 Describe the general pattern observed.

3 Suggest reasons why Australia and South America are so different from the other continental regions in terms of their overall water balance *(Hint: Use an atlas to consider the types of climate present or absent in each case.)*

Figure 1.6

Temperature patterns in the Atlantic Ocean. Global temperature patterns determine global evaporation rates – a major component of the hydrological cycle. This image shows the influence of both latitude and ocean currents in controlling temperatures. Orange and yellow represent warm water; blue and pink show cooler water.

hydrological cycle. In semi-arid areas where there is limited vegetation, transpiration rates are lower. Like evaporation, transpiration is a seasonal process, being strong in the summer and much weaker in the winter.

Precipitation shows an even bigger variation on a global scale. The type of precipitation, its timing, intensity and distribution, can vary from region to region and from season to season. Figure 1.7 is a typical satellite image showing the major precipitation bands along the Equator and at the polar fronts. Between these bands are the arid and semi-arid zones, which are seen as large cloud-free areas near the tropics. Looking at the image of Africa it is clear that evaporation and precipitation are unbalanced – some areas having more of one than the other. Seasonal variations complicate the balance still further. Figures 1.8a and b show the different locations of precipitation in January and July. The water balance clearly varies from place to place and from time to time, and may have an important impact on river flow.

With all water imbalances at the regional level, questions arise as to what keeps the system going, and what corrects the imbalances?

Figure 1.7
Satellite image showing major cloud and precipitation zones

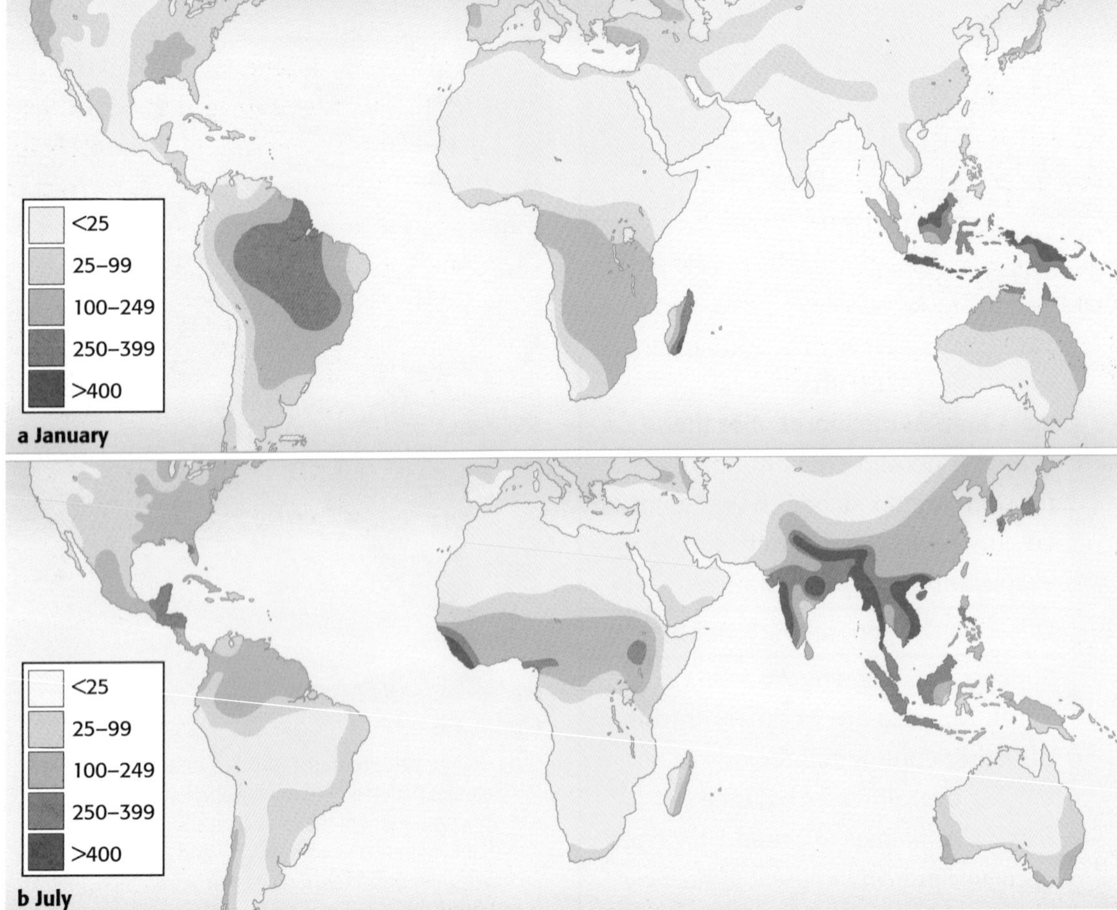

Figure 1.8
World precipitation patterns

> **Activity**
>
> From the two maps in Figure 1.8, identify and name three countries where there are strong seasonal contrasts in the precipitation input to the water balance. Use an atlas to compare and contrast the annual temperature variations at each location. How do temperature patterns relate to the rainfall patterns?

Two main processes correct the imbalances: **runoff** and **global wind patterns** transport water over vast distances from one place to another. And, as Tom Robbins noted, people play a small part in the process too.

Implications for societies

The imbalances in the global water cycle are of more than scientific interest. As standards of living improve in the developed world, and populations increase in the developing world, the demand for more water will become harder to satisfy. Many water resources are 'transboundary', crossing through several countries. Users located upstream can have a major negative impact on their downstream neighbours. It is possible that major international conflicts will develop over water rights in the early part of the 21st century. Areas already experiencing tension include the countries of the Middle East, North Africa and south-west Europe. Add to this pressure the increasing problems of water pollution – of both surface water and groundwater supplies – and it is clear that providing clean, usable water will be a major social, economic and political challenge in the years ahead.

The hydrological cycle on a local scale

Drainage basin definitions and models

In its simplest form, a drainage basin is the area of land contributing water to a particular stream. The boundaries, or **watersheds**, of drainage basins are the relatively high areas of land that separate one basin from the next, as illustrated in Figure 1.9. Rain landing on one side of the watershed line will end up in one river while rain landing on the other side will end up in the neighbouring basin. Drainage basins can be of almost any size. The Mississippi basin is an example of a drainage basin on a subcontinental scale. By contrast, even the smallest headwater tributary occupies its own definable basin area. The term 'catchment area' can be used interchangeably with 'drainage basin'. Figure 1.10 shows the drainage basin concept applied to the River Esk in North Yorkshire. The map illustrates the way drainage basins can be 'nested' one inside the other. Each sub-basin responds individually to rainfall but also contributes to the combined flow of the larger basins within which it lies. Every drainage basin of any size is therefore a distinctive assembly of nested, interacting sub-basins taking rainfall and routeing it through a unique version of the hydrological cycle to generate stream flow. It is probable that no two drainage basins are alike. Although the components of many drainage basins may well be similar, they will interact in different ways to produce a range of unique situations in the way they respond to rainfall.

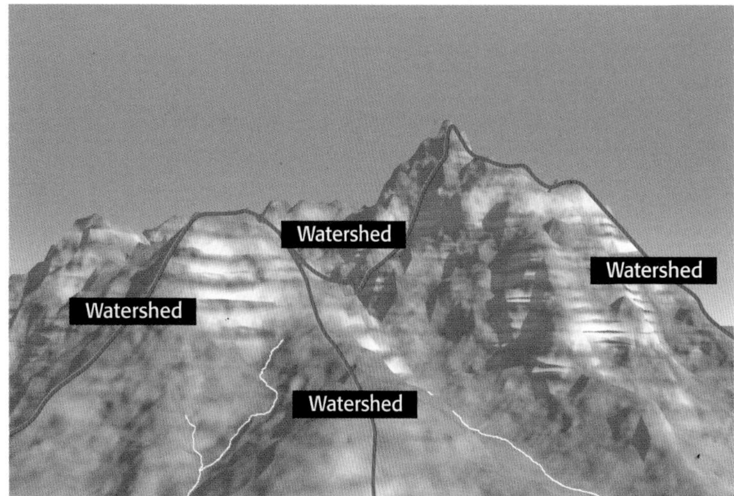

Figure 1.9

In this area of high relief, the watersheds can be seen as the boundary ridges between neighbouring drainage basins.

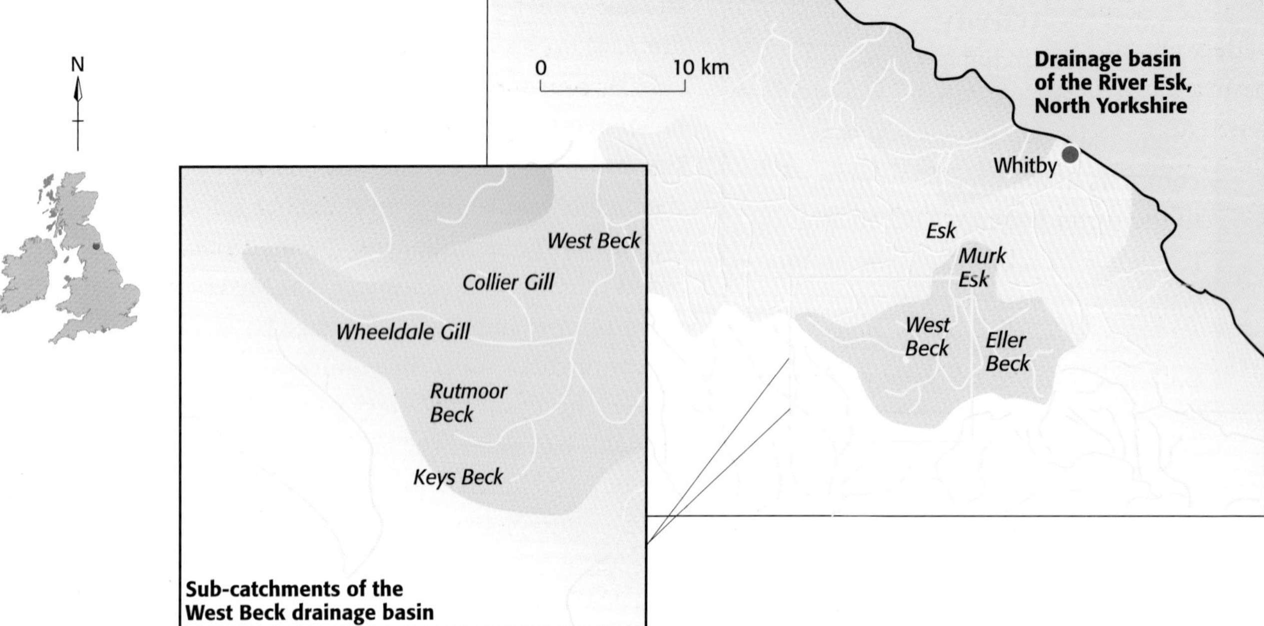

Figure 1.10

The map shows the drainage basin of the River Esk. Within this basin are several smaller drainage basins, including that of West Beck (inset map).

Activity

1 Make a copy of Figure 1.10. Identify the main sub-catchments of the River Esk system and sketch their locations on your copy (the Murk Esk has already been done for you).

2 Study the enlarged diagram of the West Beck drainage basin. With a partner, attempt to identify the total number of catchments (big and small) on the main diagram.

Local versus global hydrological cycles – an overview

The local hydrological cycle differs from the global cycle examined earlier. The global cycle is a closed system where there are minimal inputs and outputs. Its main feature is simply the recycling of water from Earth's surface to the atmosphere and back via precipitation, runoff and evapotranspiration. In contrast, the local hydrological cycle of a drainage basin is an **open system**, which means that in addition to the recycling of water within the basin, there are exchanges of water with areas outside the basin. A storm might bring in water from a source hundreds of miles away. Runoff or evaporation will remove water from the basin and deliver it many miles downstream, or downwind.

Figure 1.11 illustrates the main differences between the global and local hydrological cycles.

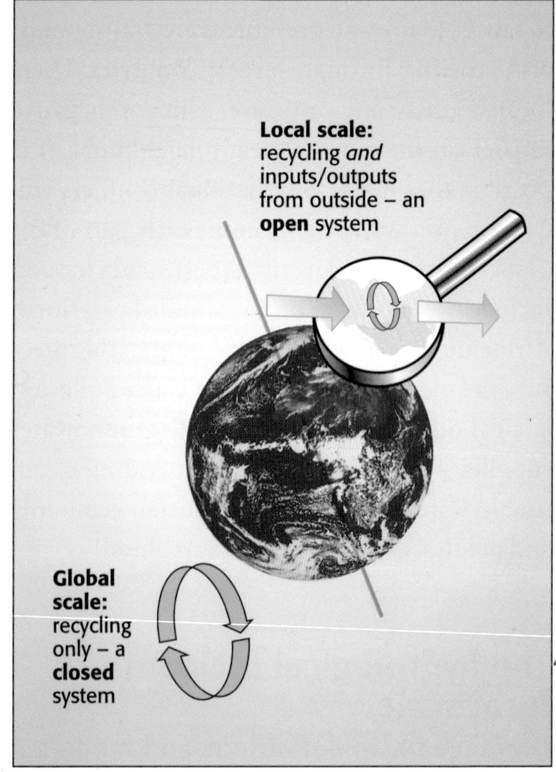

Figure 1.11

The hydrological cycle: global and local scales

The open nature of the local cycle allows great variety in both the total volume of water in the basin and the distribution of water through the different stores. It is the scale and pattern of this distribution which makes the management of rivers so interesting and challenging.

The drainage basin water balance

At drainage basin level there are three key influences:

- the nature of the local hydrological cycle (inputs, outputs, processes and stores)
- the nature of the drainage basin (steepness, size, geology, land use, etc.)
- the impacts (both deliberate and accidental) of human activity on drainage basins.

These three influences overlap and interact with one another to change the water balance in the drainage basin. They also operate at different scales within different-sized drainage basins.

The local hydrological cycle

The local hydrological cycle can be expressed as a simple equation:

Inputs = Outputs (+) or (–) change in stores

Figure 1.12 summarises the inputs, outputs, stores and processes in a drainage basin hydrological cycle. Figure 1.13 illustrates the relationships between these factors on a small scale.

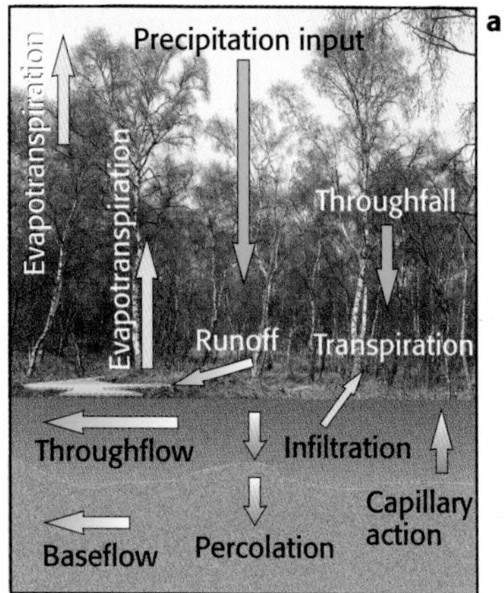

Figure 1.13
The hydrological cycle at the local scale

Figure 1.12
Inputs, outputs and stores in the local hydrological cycle

Inputs	Outputs	Stores	Flows
• Precipitation • Interbasin transfer • Interbasin transfer (artificial)	• Evaporation • Evapotranspiration • Runoff/overland flow • Interbasin transfer (natural) • Interbasin transfer (artificial)	• Atmosphere • Vegetation/ interception • Surface • Soil • Groundwater • Channel	**Vertical** • Throughfall • Stemflow • Infiltration • Percolation • Capillary action **Lateral** • Runoff • Throughflow • Interflow • Baseflow

Mainly related to climate ←- → **Mainly related to basin character**

Inputs to drainage basins

Precipitation

Key aspects of precipitation are illustrated in Figure 1.14. The **cause** of precipitation is air cooling. Air always contains moisture, even on a dry day. The moisture is normally held as an invisible gas, water vapour. When the air cools below a particular temperature (the dew point) it can no longer hold water as vapour, and it condenses to become liquid water. The dew point temperature depends on the amount of water in the air. Air with a large amount of water vapour only needs to cool a little to become saturated. Air with little water vapour has to cool down a lot before its vapour condenses. A further vital ingredient of precipitation, and one that is easily overlooked, is dust. Water vapour condenses directly around dust particles, which are known as **condensation nuclei**. It follows, therefore, that clouds form most readily when there is a plentiful supply of dust particles in the air. Urban areas are dustier and dirtier than rural areas, so drainage basins in urban areas may experience enhanced rainfall compared with rural catchments of similar size.

There are five main ways in which air cools to create condensation and cloud:

1 Air rises over high land (relief or orographic rain).
2 Air rises over adjacent cool air masses (frontal rain).
3 Air rises as a result of localised heating (convectional rain).
4 Air flows over cold surfaces (**advection fog**).
5 Air cools as a result of night-time radiation at the Earth's surface (dew and radiation fog).

Note that the presence of clouds does not necessarily indicate precipitation. Their absence, however, always indicates a lack of precipitation!

Many drainage basins experience precipitation caused by more than one of the above sources, but when comparing one basin with another it is important to recognise that different precipitation types have different impacts on the local hydrological cycle.

The **nature** of precipitation varies with location. Rain, sleet, hail, snow, fog and dew are all different forms of precipitation. Drainage basins in high latitudes and high altitudes experience more rain, sleet and snow. In other localities fog can be an important form of precipitation. High up in the forests of Mauna Loa, Hawaii, for example, fog-drip from trees accounts for 65 per cent of the annual measured precipitation input. Lowland basins may experience more in the way of convectional rainstorms. The nature of the precipitation will influence the basin hydrological cycle. For example:

- winter snowfall disrupts relationships between input and output – a large snow input may produce no output for many weeks until it melts
- broad bands of frontal rain may affect the whole drainage basin, whereas localised convectional storms might only affect some sub-catchments
- intense convectional rain is more likely to create floodwaters than prolonged frontal drizzle.

Precipitation **intensity** varies with the origin of the precipitation. Frontal rain in Britain brings drizzle with intensities as low as 0.5 mm/h and more moderate rainfall of up to 3 mm/h as the warm front passes over. These figures are small compared with convectional rainfall, which can yield more than 25 mm/h. Extreme quantities can be produced when rainfall is created by more than one mechanism, for example a frontal

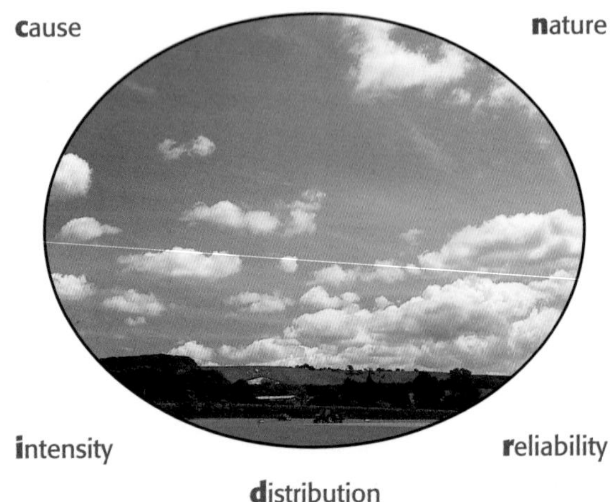

Figure 1.14 Model of precipitation. (A useful mnemonic for remembering the components of the model is *d-r-i-n-c*.)

system passing over high ground in summer at the end of a heatwave. Different rainfall intensities have different impacts on stream flow and on the hydrological cycle.

Just as precipitation shows global variations in space and time, so its **distribution** may vary both spatially and temporally across drainage basins. Even across a small region, such as Britain, differing annual precipitation totals (Figure 1.15) and differing seasonal distribution of precipitation (Figure 1.16) can cause adjacent drainage basins to experience widely varying precipitation inputs.

Precipitation **reliability** can vary from area to area. 'Reliability' measures the extent to which 'average' figures are actually observed. Two basins may have the same average precipitation, but one may have a more consistent and reliable regime whilst the other experiences very wet years and very dry years. One way in which precipitation reliability can be measured is by calculating the **variability** within a set of measurements taken over a substantial number of years. When the values for the UK are plotted (Figure 1.17), it is clear that the highland areas of the west experience most variability. These are the areas exposed to the most extreme weather conditions to be found in Britain, so they experience a wide range of extreme precipitation, from heavy snowfall to intense rainfall to drought.

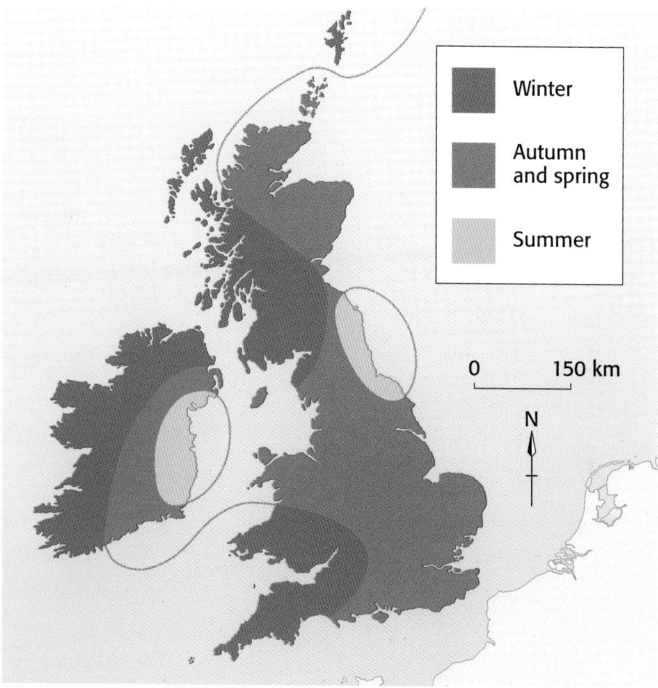

Figure 1.16

Season of maximum precipitation in the British Isles

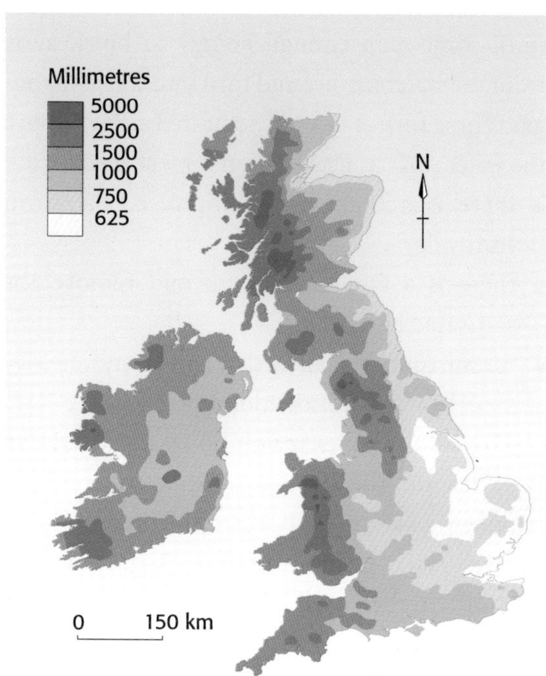

Figure 1.15

Annual precipitation in the British Isles

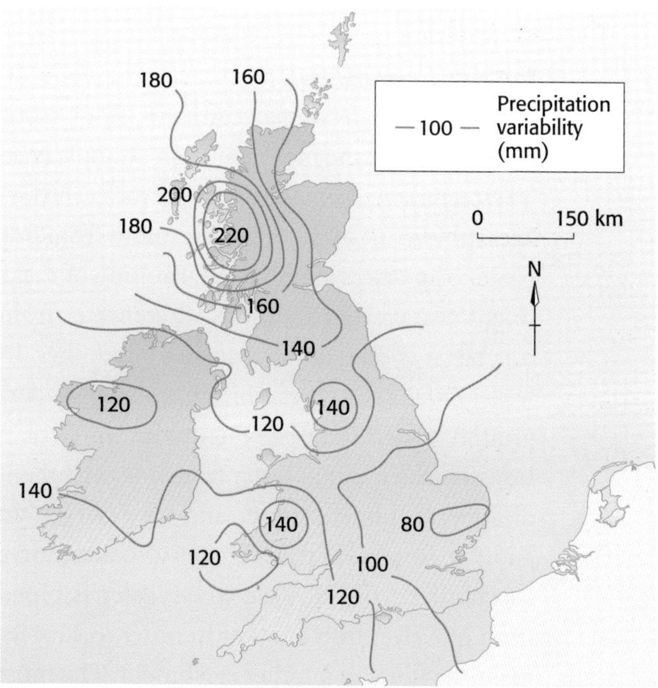

Figure 1.17

Precipitation variability in the British Isles

> ### Activity
> Using a copy of Figure 1.18 as a base map, create three overlays using information on Figures 1.15, 1.16, and 1.17. Use the overlays to describe the differences you might expect between the seasonal flows of the four rivers named on Figure 1.18.

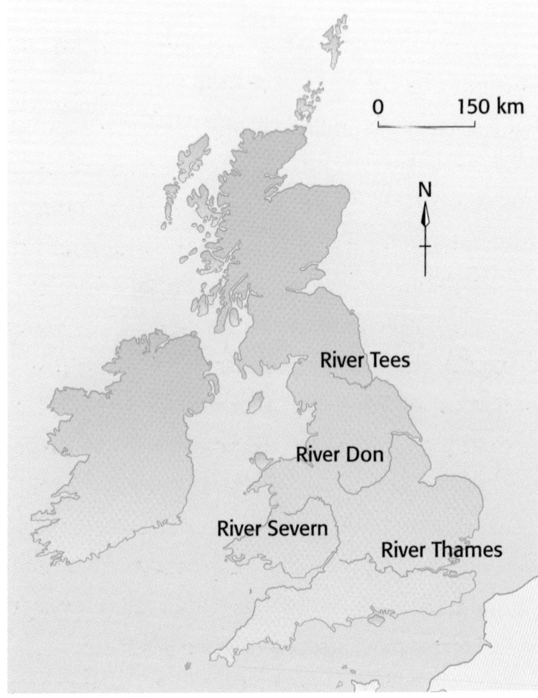

Figure 1.18
Selected UK drainage basins

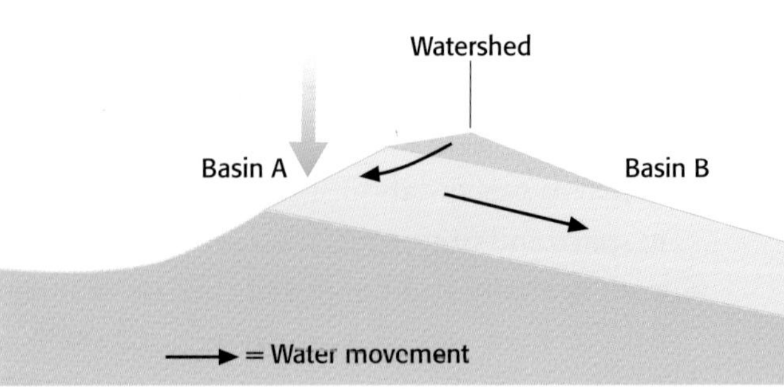

Figure 1.19
Interbasin transfer by natural processes

Interbasin transfers

Interbasin transfers can occur naturally or artificially. In nature the most common example is on an escarpment where the dip of the rocks encourages movement of water underground from one basin to another (Figure 1.19). Faulting of rocks might also create conditions where water from one basin is diverted to a spring in another. In well-jointed rock types which encourage underground water flow, very complex interbasin transfers can occur as water from one catchment disappears underground and re-emerges in another. Interbasin transfers can also occur on a substantial artificial scale when water is piped from one river into another in order to supplement the flows in another catchment. The most common reason for doing this is to provide water for public use. The Liverpool metropolitan area can import up to 205 million litres per day from the Vyrnwy basin in Wales, 380 million litres per day from the River Dee catchment, and 80 million litres per day from the Rivington reservoirs on the edge of the Pennines. These quantities represent huge artificial inputs into the hydrological cycle of an urban area.

Outputs from drainage basins

Evaporation

Evaporation is the transformation of liquid water back to its gaseous water vapour form. The main influences on evaporation are illustrated by the model shown in Figure 1.20. Solar radiation heats water, exciting the molecules until some gain enough energy to break away from the water surface and turn into water vapour gas. These form a layer of saturated air just above the water surface. Evaporation is most effective if:

- there is a high energy input, e.g. a warm sunny day
- there is a wind to stir up and remove the saturated layer of air
- the surrounding air is dry, and so more easily absorbs water from puddles, ponds or wet soil.

The amount of evaporation taking place also depends on the nature of the surface. The simplest case is evaporation from an open water surface. Evaporation rates from soils can be both higher and lower than evaporation from water bodies. Saturated soil can have a higher evaporation rate because the exposed surface area and the supply of water are greater – see Figure 1.21.

Transpiration

Plants use water to transport nutrients from the soil to leaves, stems and branches. Small pores on the leaf called stomata open to allow evaporation of moisture through the leaf pores. This biologically induced evaporation creates a complex pressure gradient which draws nutrient-filled soil water into the plant from the soil. The total surface area of leaves on a tree is considerably greater than the land area under the tree, so transpiration is an extremely effective way for water to leave the soil and re-enter the atmosphere. In a dense forest, over 60 per cent of water loss is by transpiration. In semi-arid areas, where the topsoil dries out, transpiration forms the major pathway for water to return from the soil to the atmosphere. Like evaporation, transpiration is influenced by heat energy, wind speed and existing humidity in the air.

Transpiration is also influenced by the nature of the vegetation. Stomata open and close on a diurnal (24-hour) cycle, so transpiration is high in the day but low at night, and some plants control stomatal opening when water supplies are limited. Overall, transpiration rates are difficult to predict since they vary with temperature, wind speed, air humidity, time of day, plant type and soil moisture availability.

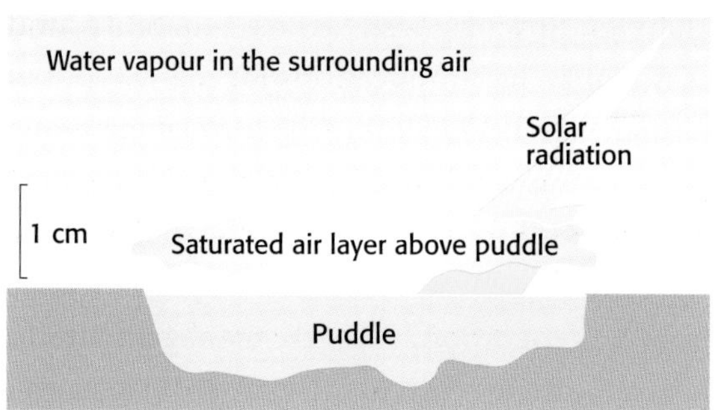

Figure 1.20
Evaporation principles

Evapotranspiration

In practice, evaporation and transpiration take place side by side across the majority of land surfaces; few areas are entirely bare or entirely vegetated. This joint process is called **evapotranspiration**.

Two types of evapotranspiration can be distinguished – **potential** and **actual**. Potential evapotranspiration is the maximum possible level of evapotranspiration given the characteristics of the vegetation, the availability of heat energy, atmospheric humidity, wind speed and, crucially, the availability of water. If the surface soil layer has dried out (although there may still be water deeper in the soil), the amount of evapotranspiration taking place will be much reduced and, as a consequence, the level of actual evapotranspiration will be much lower than the potential level.

Measuring evapotranspiration is extremely difficult. Potential evapotranspiration can be estimated using formulae to take account of energy, windspeed, etc. Actual evapotranspiration can be measured using a lysimeter. A **lysimeter** is a large-scale measuring device for calculating water balance – Figure 1.22. A plot or section of vegetation is grown in a large permeable soil tank which sits in a bigger impermeable drainage tank. Rainfall input is measured using a standard gauge. Losses through the soil can be recorded from the drainage outflow channel. The only other losses are due to evapotranspiration, and these can be recorded by measuring the change in weight of the soil tank. Whilst lysimeters are

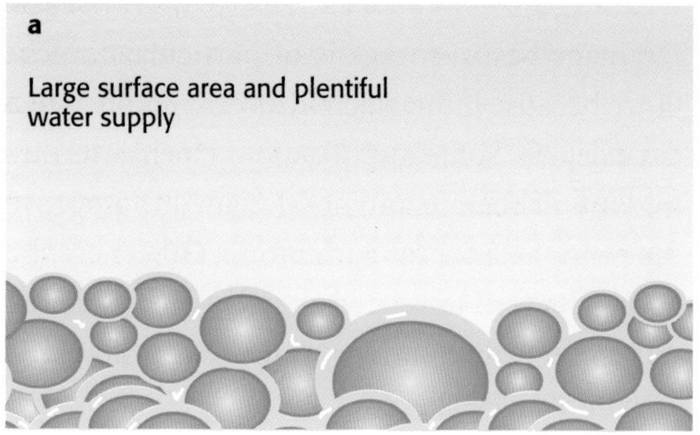

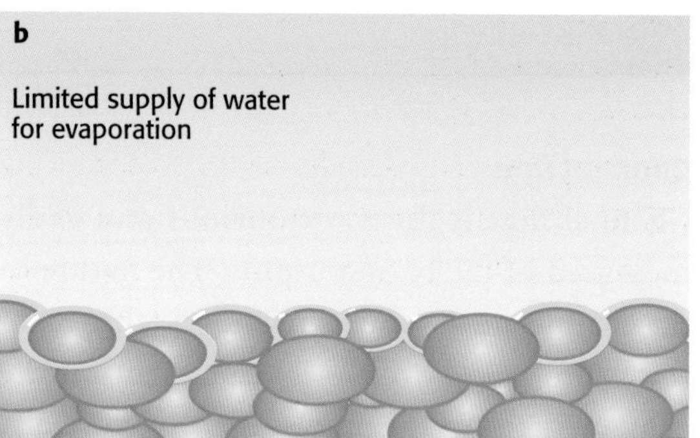

Figure 1.21
Rates of evaporation:
a from saturated soil **b** from unsaturated soil

an ingenious approach to the problems of measuring actual evapotranspiration, they are expensive and may be unrepresentative of real conditions. There are obvious technical difficulties in using lysimeters to calculate water balances for forests!

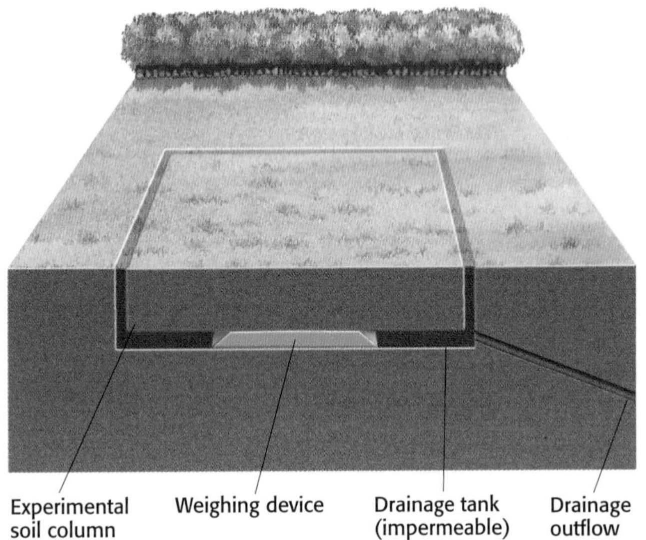

Figure 1.22
Measuring water balance using a lysimeter

> **Activity**
>
> Imagine you are trying to work out the water balance of a garden. You will have to measure rainfall input, evaporation output and any change in the level of soil and vegetation storage over several months. Suggest some of the difficulties you might encounter in:
>
> **a** finding a reasonably accurate measure of rainfall for the whole area
>
> **b** deciding how, where and when to measure evaporation rates and
>
> **c** deciding how, where and when to measure interception rates on the vegetation.

Channel flow

Channel flow is the most obvious and easily measured of the basin outputs. The nature of the channel flow – and its relation to the rest of the hydrological cycle – is dependent on the characteristics of the drainage basin, especially

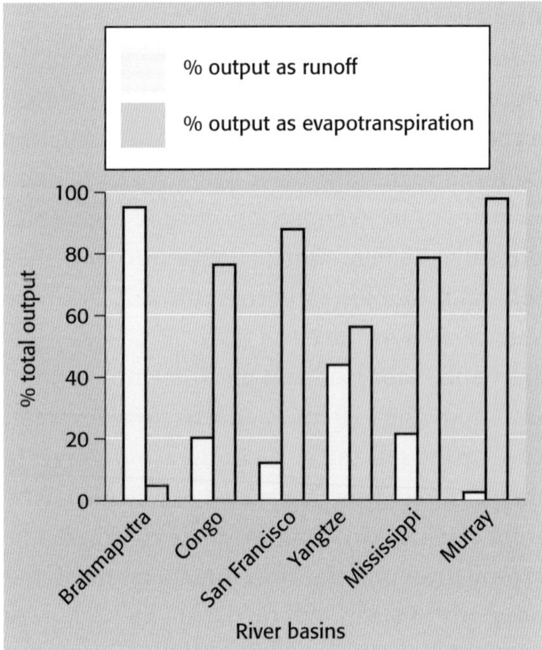

Figure 1.23
Runoff : evapotranspiration ratios for some major river basins

its water stores, and on the nature of the local climate. Both these themes are explored in more detail later. Channel flow may represent a small proportion of the drainage basin water cycle (e.g. River Murray, Figure 1.23) or a large percentage (Brahmaputra River, Figure 1.23). The amount of water being evacuated through channel flow, as well as its reliability and seasonality, has implications for many types of human activity, including the management of a regular supply of water for drinking, industrial cooling, industrial processes, irrigation supply, transport, waste disposal and hydro-electric power generation. Flood management to protect settlements and infrastructure may also be an important consideration.

Drainage basin stores

Drainage basin storage is of particular importance because human activities can modify it to a large degree. Some modifications (such as terracing) are deliberate and are designed to improve the water balance for agriculture. Others are the by-products of unrelated activity (such as deforestation or urbanisation) which have unforeseen and unintended effects.

Interception store

Water rarely lands directly on bare surfaces. More commonly, falling rain will first strike vegetation – the leaves and branches of trees, for example. A significant amount of water can be stored in this way, and everyday experience tells us to shelter under a tree during rain because the canopy will intercept and store the water. The amount of water stored by interception depends on several factors:

- Precipitation type, e.g. snow, rain and hail behave differently in terms of generating interception or runoff.
- Precipitation intensity, e.g. light rain and heavy rain produce different levels of interception and runoff.
- Precipitation duration, e.g. short showers and prolonged rainfall produce different effects in the basin.
- Nature of the vegetation, e.g. grass and woodland respond differently to rainfall events.
- Time of year, e.g. different seasons influence the water cycle differently.
- Agricultural land use – different crops have different impacts on interception, see Figure 1.24.

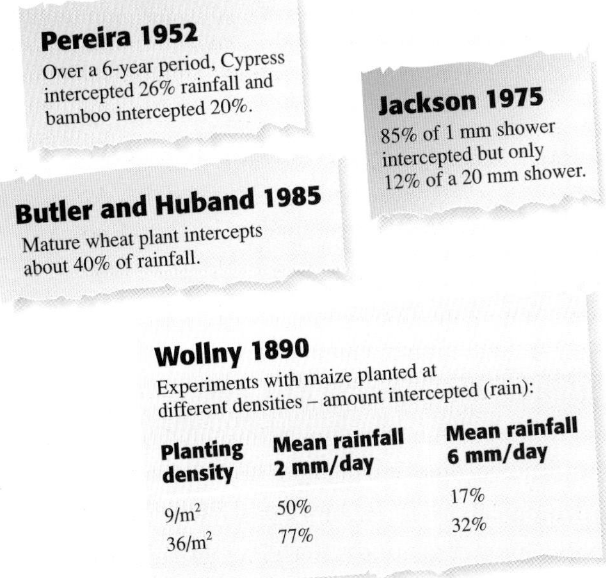

Pereira 1952
Over a 6-year period, Cypress intercepted 26% rainfall and bamboo intercepted 20%.

Jackson 1975
85% of 1 mm shower intercepted but only 12% of a 20 mm shower.

Butler and Huband 1985
Mature wheat plant intercepts about 40% of rainfall.

Wollny 1890
Experiments with maize planted at different densities – amount intercepted (rain):

Planting density	Mean rainfall 2 mm/day	Mean rainfall 6 mm/day
$9/m^2$	50%	17%
$36/m^2$	77%	32%

Figure 1.24
Results of selected interception experiments

Activity

Use the data in Figure 1.24 to describe and explain the range of factors influencing interception rates.

Surface store

The soil or bedrock surface is an important store for water. Typical surface water stores include puddles, ponds, lakes and wetlands. Surface storage is a major source of water for human use. It is easy to access and may serve multiple purposes, for example recreation, fishing, transport. The amount of surface storage available depends on:

- rock permeability – impermeable rocks allow large surface stores, but where there are permeable rocks water is stored underground.
- relief – even quite gentle slope-angles allow water to drain away; flat areas or basins are needed to create large surface stores.

By building dams or creating terraces it is possible to engineer large surface stores from otherwise unpromising relief. Whilst surface storage is very useful for human purposes, it is also prone to human mismanagement. The Aral Sea is a classic example. Here, since 1960, human interference in the rivers supplying water to the Sea has caused its volume to shrink by 70 per cent and to divide into two lakes. Between 1990 and 1992, the total area of the two lakes fell from 36 500 km^2 to about 33 650 km^2 – a reduction of almost 4 per cent per year.

Soil store

While people depend on surface and groundwater stores for drinking water, soil storage is essential for our food because water stored in the soil maintains plant life. Soil storage is highly variable, being completely saturated after heavy prolonged rain but drying out after a few weeks with little rain. Farmers often try to alter soil moisture to suit crop needs. Drainage can reduce excess soil moisture, whilst irrigation tops up any soil moisture deficiencies. Soil moisture is important for maintaining stream flow in dry conditions and reducing runoff totals in storms.

Soil moisture storage depends on several factors, including:

- soil depth
- soil texture (e.g. sand, silt, clay – a sandy soil has reasonable-sized pores between each grain, as shown in Figure 1.25)
- soil structure (e.g. a good crumb structure as shown in Figure 1.25 produces lots of additional storage space between the peds)
- land use and management practices – using heavy machinery on wet soils can destroy the soil structure leaving a much reduced soil store.

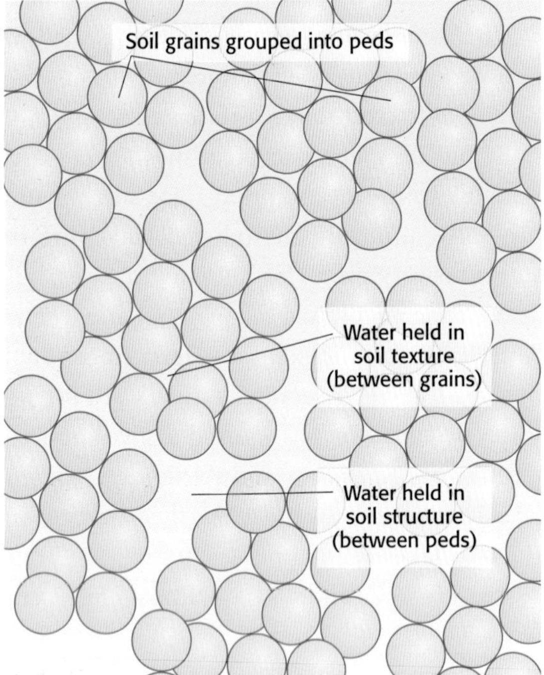

Figure 1.25
The effect of soil texture and structure on the transmission of water. A fine-grained soil texture can produce a large volume of tiny pores which transmit water very slowly.

Groundwater store

Water in the soil may pass deeper into the groundwater store as long as the underlying parent material is a suitable aquifer. An **aquifer** is a rock that can hold water. This contrasts with an **aquiclude** – a rock that cannot. Many drainage basins are underlain by aquifers. The presence of an aquifer in a drainage basin has a profound effect on the hydrological cycle of the basin. Excess water can be absorbed during times of high rainfall and later released during times of low rainfall. Figure 1.26 shows some of the main features of the groundwater store in a basin. The water table represents the boundary between the saturated rocks underneath and the unsaturated rocks above. The water table reflects a subdued version of the overlying relief. Where the water table meets the ground, water emerges onto the surface. It may emerge at a specific point as a spring or – more commonly – may simply leak more or less invisibly from the river bank into the river. The water table rises and falls throughout the year, depending on the local water balance. When the water table rises, river levels also rise and streams will start to flow from springs higher on the hillside. After a period with little rain, the water table will fall, river levels will drop and only the lowest springs in the valley will flow. After prolonged drought the water table may drop below the level of the river channel and the river will dry up completely.

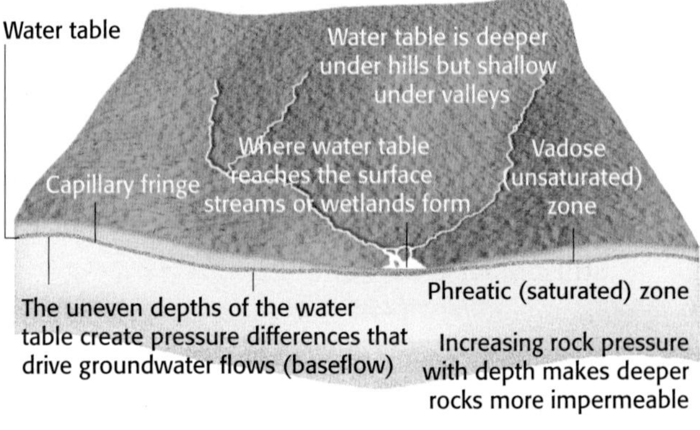

Figure 1.26
The main features of groundwater storage in a basin

Human uses of a river have a big influence on groundwater levels. By abstracting water for domestic, industrial or agricultural use, the hydrological cycle is short-circuited. Where people extract groundwater it is essential they pay close attention to recharge. **Recharge** takes place naturally when winter rain exceeds evaporation and runoff rates, but if demands on an aquifer are high, extraction may exceed natural recharge and the reservoir will continue to dwindle. This is known as 'groundwater mining'. In coastal areas this process often leads to 'saltwater intrusion' as saline groundwater under the sea bed migrates inland to replace the diminishing freshwater supply. In London, a century and a half of water extraction has lowered the water table by 60 m in the central area (Figure 1.27).

Activity

1 What will be the impact of the changes shown in Figure 1.27 on
a stream flow in the drainage basin
b shallow water-supply boreholes and
c the structural stability of buildings?

2 For 1850 and 1980, draw a cross-section along the diagonal line to show the change in water table shape over the 130-year period.

To avoid the problems caused by over-extraction, water resource management now focuses on the much more active integration of groundwater and surface water. Groundwater is still extracted for human use (and increasingly to maintain river flows for conservation purposes). But the opposite also occurs. Groundwater is topped up in times of high river flow by creating 'recharge basins' where diverted water can sink back into the reservoir. Figure 1.28 shows an old recharge basin in the Triassic sandstone aquifer of Nottinghamshire.

One example of highly managed basins where the 'normal' water balance is modified and regulated by human activity, is the Lancashire Conjunctive Use Scheme (Figure 1.29), which was developed to provide water for the communities of central and south Lancashire. The scheme exploits the Triassic sandstones in the Preston area, together with surface water stored in reservoirs within the Wyre and Hodder catchments. Water is also transferred from the River Lune, near Lancaster, to top-up the flow of the River Wyre and provide water for public supply from an intake

Figure 1.28
An artificial recharge basin in the Triassic sandstone aquifer of Nottinghamshire

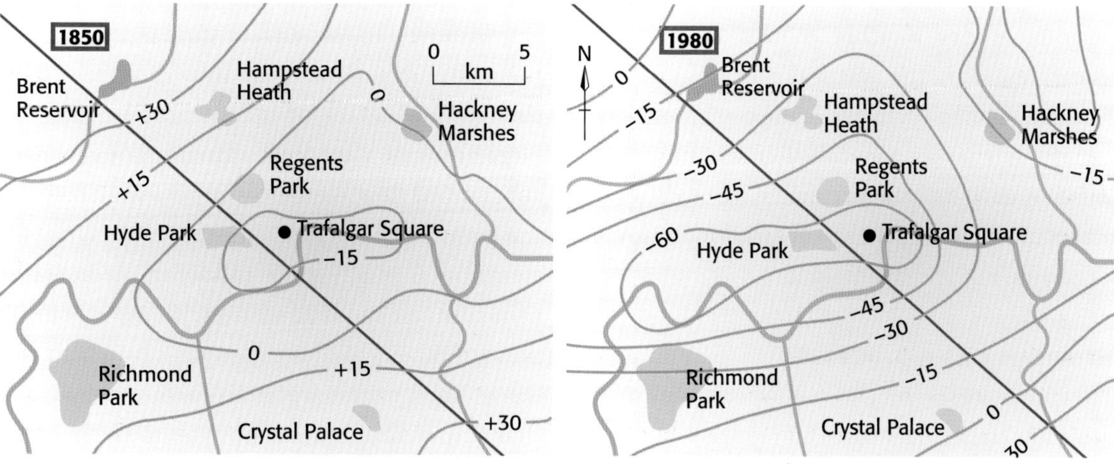

Figure 1.27
Water table changes in the London Basin as a result of over-extraction

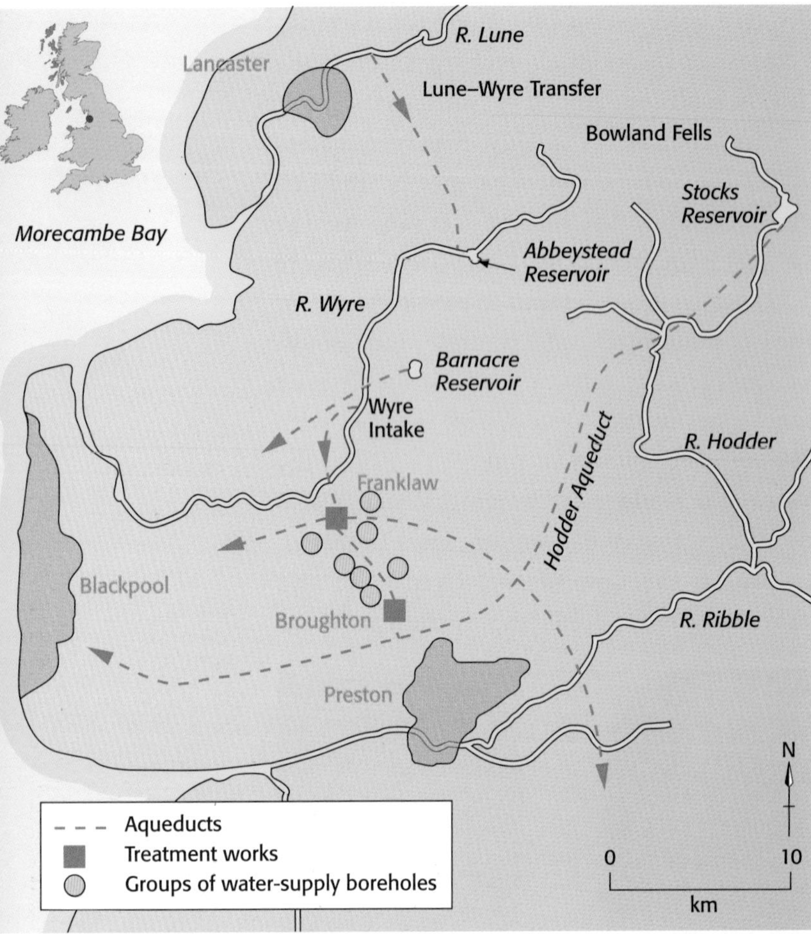

Figure 1.29

Lancashire Conjunctive Use Scheme. A highly controlled scheme such as this completely alters natural hydrological cycles within basins in order to maintain reliable supplies of water for human consumption in large metropolitan areas.

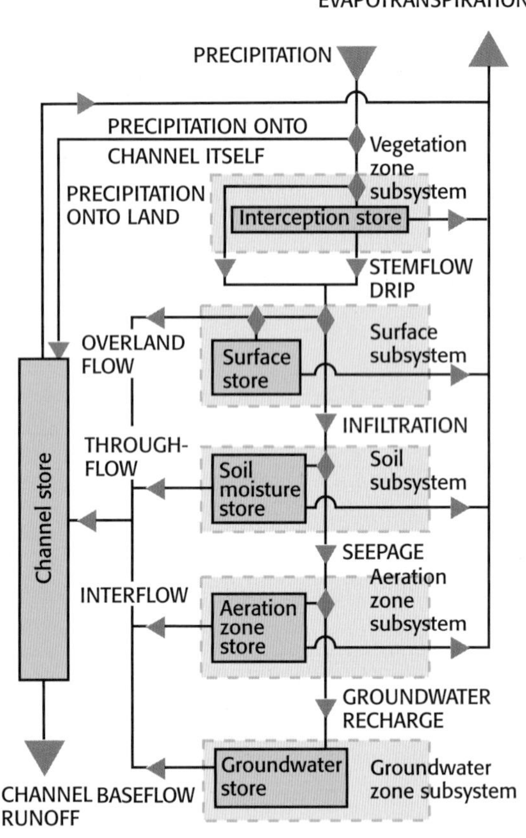

Figure 1.30

Model of a local drainage basin

at Garstang. The Triassic sandstones (up to 500 m thick), are tapped by over 40 boreholes, each yielding between 1 and 6 million litres/day. Groundwater is also discharged into the River Wyre to top-up the flow during extended periods of dry weather. Whilst this scheme interferes with the natural workings of the Hodder, Ribble, Wyre and Lune catchments, the benefit is that as a combined scheme it can balance deficits and surpluses from different places at different times of year, allowing a very large output to be maintained.

Drainage basin processes

The processes – or flows – operating in the drainage basin are shown in Figure 1.30. Each process transfers water from one store to another. Water may take long or short pathways through these complex routeways. Changes occurring in the drainage basin (for example land use changes) can alter the balance of water along the pathways.

Atmosphere, vegetation and surface transfers

Once the leaves of plants have intercepted precipitation from the atmospheric store, water is transferred to the surface store by one of two methods. **Stemflow** is the flow of water down the trunk of a tree or the stem of a plant. On large trees in a tropical climate this can be a substantial flow – erosion gulleys may form at the base of the trunk. In temperate climates stemflow is much more moderate and creates thin films of moving water with no erosional power. **Throughfall** is the process by which wet leaves shed excess water to form water drops that drip through the canopy onto the ground surface. These drops are both more and less erosive than the unhindered rain: more erosive because the drop size is larger than a typical raindrop; less erosive because the drop is falling a small distance, so has a low velocity compared with rain. Tall trees, however, can result in 'drip' erosion due to the large droplet size combining with a fairly high terminal velocity. The amount of stemflow and throughfall generated depends on the nature and size of the interception store. Studies have shown higher rates of throughfall in broad-leaved woodlands compared with coniferous woods because the flat leaves of broad-leaved trees allow water beads to collect into drops. Conifers, however, hold individual water beads on individual needles so it is much harder for larger drops to collect as throughfall. It is not surprising that interception losses are 1 to 2 times greater in a coniferous woodland. Much of the water intercepted by trees fails to reach the surface and soil stores, and evaporation returns it to the atmosphere. From a hydrological viewpoint, water returned to the atmosphere is not necessarily lost water because a remoistened atmosphere is likely to create new rain. In the Amazon basin, recycling of water by forest evapotranspiration has succeeded in maintaining moist conditions 2000 miles from the sea. Deforestation in Amazonia will only serve to reduce rainfall in the interior, making it vulnerable to desertification.

Transfers between surface, soil and channels

Once on the surface (in a puddle, pond or lake), water has three options: go up, go down, or go sideways. Evaporation can return water directly to the atmosphere and will do so where the land surface is impermeable and flat. Most land surfaces are neither impermeable nor flat, so water usually seeps into the soil as infiltration. **Infiltration** is a key factor in the drainage basin. The balance between runoff, throughflow and baseflow is first influenced by the soil's infiltration rate.

Water moves into the soil under the influence of two main forces: gravity, and capillary action (the suction effect of dry soil). When rain first lands on dry soil, the top few centimetres of soil quickly become saturated. Below the top layer of wetted soil the moisture content remains moderate. Here water is being 'passed on' down through the soil profile and there is no net build-up of water. As rainfall continues, the depth of wetting increases but the actual percentage of water in the subsoil changes little, as seen in Figure 1.31. The three diagrams show

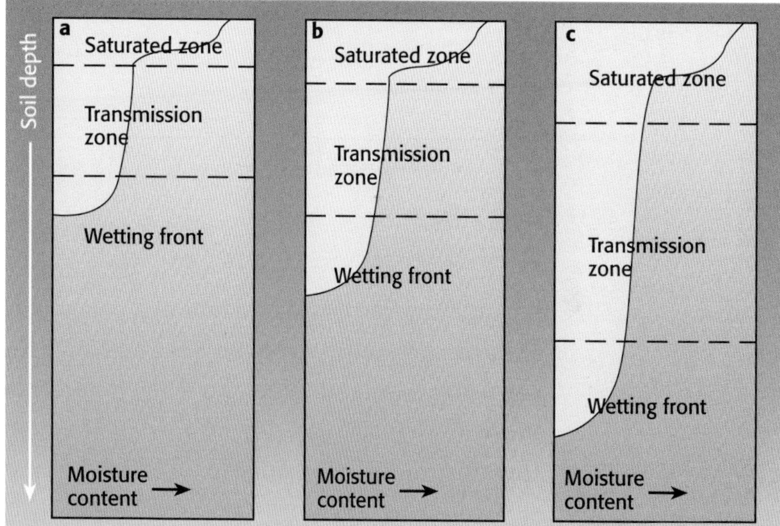

Figure 1.31 Water infiltrating a soil profile over three time periods

progressive wetting of the soil, but the maximum moisture content at any one level in the soil has remained unchanged. This means that infiltration can continue at a steady rate for a long time and build up substantial soil moisture stores. Figure 1.32 shows typical infiltration curves, demonstrating how the rate of water soaking into the soil remains constant after an initial high saturation period. Infiltration rates depend on a number of factors, including:

- soil storage (e.g. soil texture and structure)
- presence of vegetation
- previous rainfall
- land use – infiltration rates vary between 57 mm/h on permanent pasture to 6 mm/h on bare ground where rainsplash clogs soil pores with a fine crust
- slope angle and the shape of the landscape.

Once infiltration has resulted in water being absorbed into the soil profile, it will move downwards under gravity. In general terms, soil

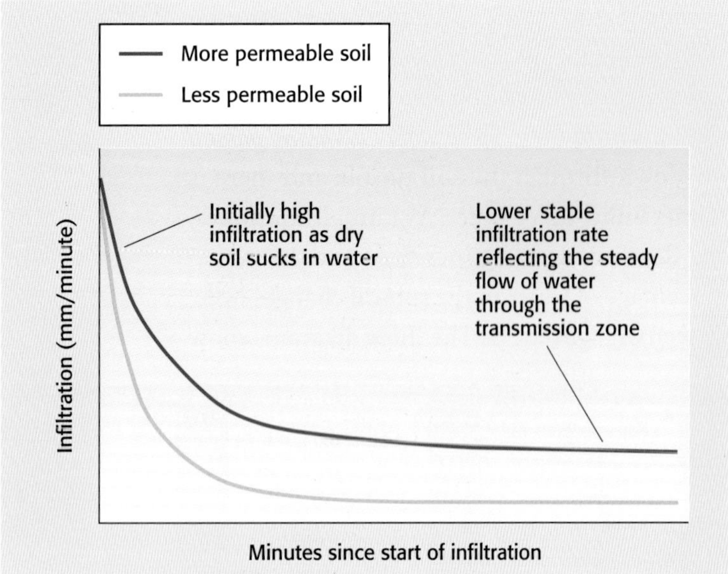

Figure 1.32
Typical infiltration curves

becomes more compacted and less permeable with increasing depth, so there is a tendency for soil water to migrate sideways when it becomes more difficult to go downwards. Water will therefore move downslope, parallel to the land surface – a process known as **throughflow**. This water flows at speeds of 0.005 to 0.3 m/h, depending on the slope of the land and on the texture and structure of the soil. Some soils with a high vegetation content have small underground 'pipes' where subsoil water is channelled along old root systems or shrinkage cracks in the soil. Water flowing in these pipes is called **pipeflow** and can reach much higher speeds of 50 to 500 m/h, and can almost be regarded as a form of surface runoff, if a rather unusual one. Throughflow from the drainage basin delivers water to streams on a medium timescale – perhaps tens of hours through to tens of days.

Throughflow delivers water from the soil store to the base of slopes, but there are other losses from the soil system. **Capillary action** moves water from wet areas of the soil to dry areas. After rainfall the surface of the soil may dry out and set up a moisture gradient moving towards the surface. Once near the surface, evapotranspiration can return the water to the atmosphere. **Percolation** also removes water from the soil system by draining it more deeply from the soil into the vadose zone, and ultimately to the water table. On sloping land, this deeper percolating water will still be inclined to migrate sideways as well as downwards. The lateral movement of water in the vadose zone (between the soil water above and the groundwater underneath) is termed **interflow**. Interflow provides a source of water to river channels that is slower than throughflow but faster than groundwater flow. Figure 1.33 shows the subsoil transfers and the ways in which they relate to surface flow.

Surface runoff or **overland flow** occurs when the rainfall input exceeds the capacity of the soil to accept infiltrating water. This form of flow is the fastest of them all, travelling up to 500 m/h towards the nearest stream channel system to which it supplies an intense, but short-lived, pulse of water. Strangely, overland flow can occur when conditions suggest it should not. Typical rainfall intensities in Britain, for example, are only 0.5 to 3 mm/h in 'normal' frontal rainfall. Even for bare, crusted soil, infiltration rates are much higher than these rainfall intensities, suggesting that overland flow is unlikely to occur except in severe thunderstorms when intensities greater than 25 mm/h can be experienced. Yet overland flow can often be seen taking place, with thin sheets of water running over the soil. The answer to this apparent contradiction is intriguing. Overland flow is generated from very small areas of the drainage basin. Figure 1.33 shows a 'shedding site' and a 'converging site'. The shedding site (a hill top or spur) will always be draining water out sideways as fast as it can infiltrate. In a converging site – a hollow or valley – the opposite occurs. Water draining from the upslope area fills the pore spaces in the soil, creating very high moisture levels. Research suggests that converging sites produce 5 to 10 times more water per unit slope width than shedding sites, so that even moderate rainfalls

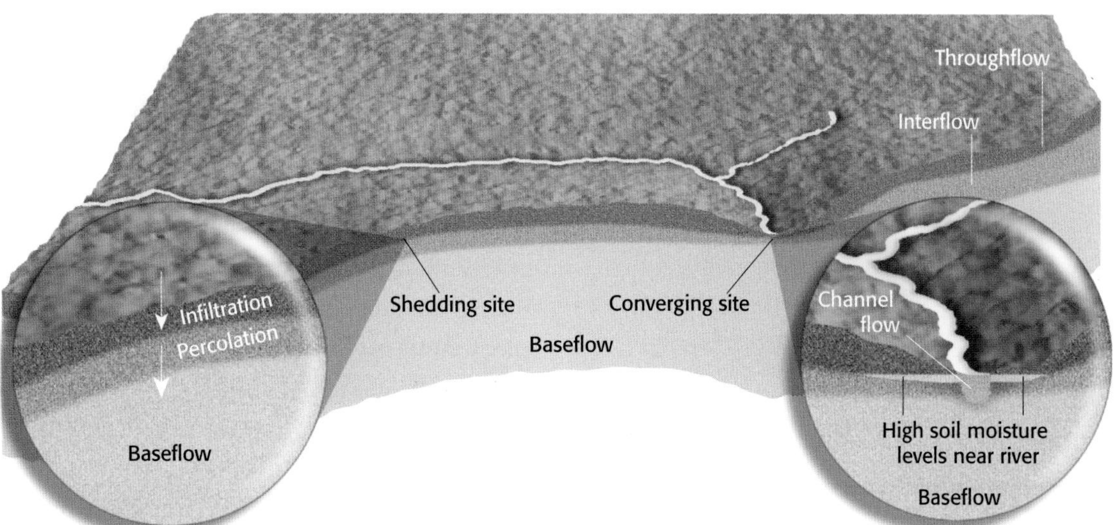

Figure 1.33
Subsoil transfers and their relation to surface flow

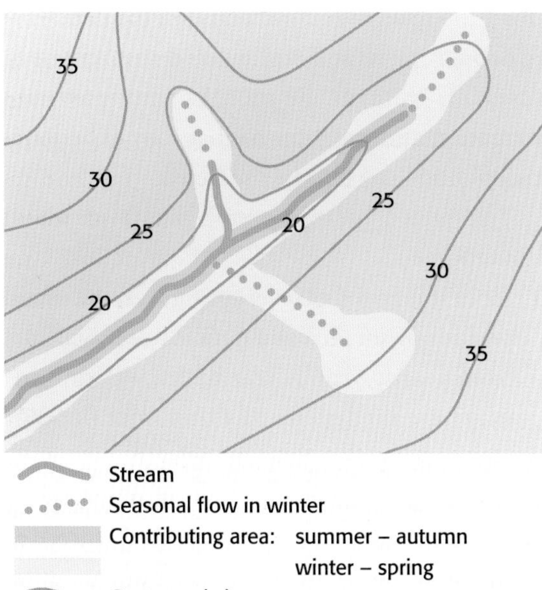

Figure 1.34
A dynamic watershed

can create overland flow in these particular areas. This is known as the partial area concept – only part of the basin is producing runoff, a form that is called **saturated overland flow** to distinguish it from the much rarer **infiltration excess overland flow** which might occur in severe thunderstorms.

Drainage basins are therefore dynamic in three dimensions, producing different amounts of water in different volumes from different depths and different areas. There is also a fourth dimension to their complexity – time. After a dry spell, areas contributing to runoff after a storm will be small and confined to the already wet zones near rivers. A fresh storm arriving a few days later will deliver its rain onto an already wetted landscape, so new, larger areas will contribute runoff to the stream. The previous state of the basin – known as the antecedent conditions – will have a big influence on the river's tendency to flood. In the UK most flooding takes place in late winter, by which time large proportions of catchment areas are already wet. This antecedent moisture helps to produce overland flow (Figure 1.34).

Baseflow is the final transfer process that takes water from the groundwater store to the stream. Water is stored in the rocks in one of two ways: in pore spaces or in cracks and joints. Sands, gravels and sandstones are porous whereas limestone is a pervious rock, holding water in subterranean cracks, joints and even caves. Some rocks such as chalk are both porous and pervious. A rock that allows the passage of water can be described as permeable. Water movements can be extremely varied in flow rate. Well-jointed limestones can move groundwater at speeds of 10 to 500 m/h. In a sandstone the flow speed is between 0.001 and 10 m/h. The best-developed water tables are found in porous rock. Limestones with joint-controlled cave systems may have an extremely complex 'water table', with underground streams criss-crossing one another in a three-dimensional maze.

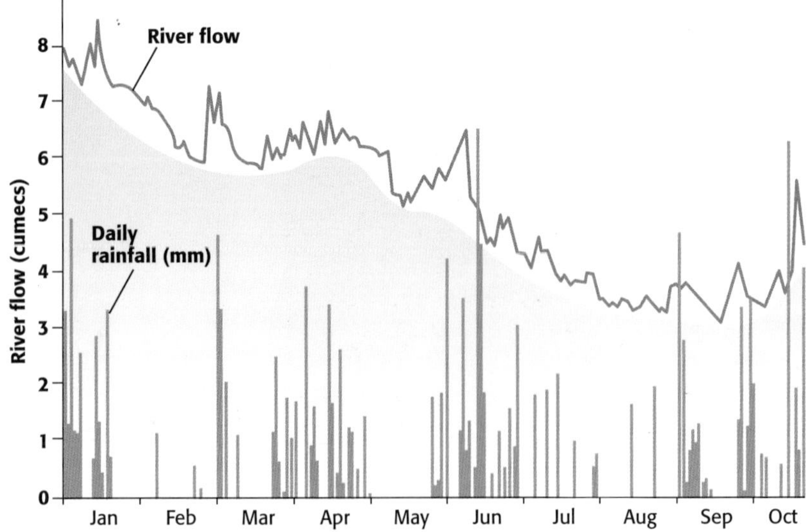

The shaded blue area represents the contribution of baseflow.

Figure 1.35
Importance of baseflow in maintaining flow between periods of rainfall: River Itchen (Hampshire), 1998

From a water supply perspective the natural baseflow rates reflect the **transmissivity** of the aquifer and determine the rate at which water can be pumped from boreholes. Underground water is the preferred water source for water companies because the volume is so large compared with a surface reservoir, and the water is less vulnerable to pollution. From a hydrological point of view the significance of baseflow is that it maintains the river flow during dry periods. Figure 1.35 shows the baseflow component shaded in blue. Notice that in May, with virtually no rainfall for a month, river flow only dropped by about 15 per cent because baseflow kept supplying excess water from previous wet months.

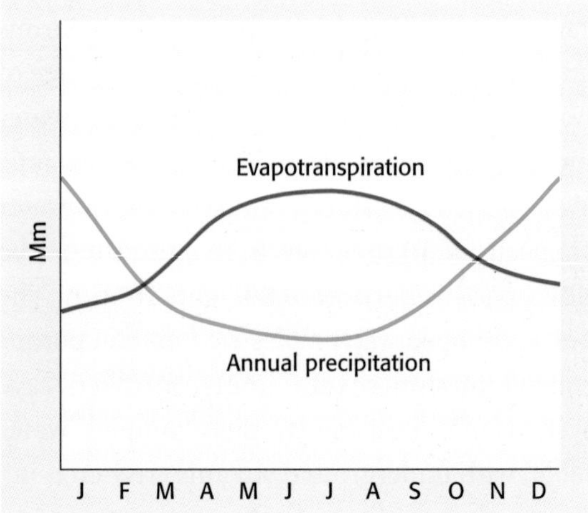

Figure 1.36
The basic water balance graph

Rainfall–discharge relationships

The water balance as a graph

You have already been introduced to the idea of a water balance on both local and global scales. From a practical point of view, farmers and water supply managers need to be able to understand the likely availability of water at any time in the year without having to resort to large amounts of precipitation and evapotranspiration data. Water balance information can easily be shown using a **water balance graph**, as illustrated in Figures 1.36 and 1.37. The water balance graph is a plot of average monthly precipitation and evapotranspiration. By examining the relative balance between the two, what is happening to soil storage and runoff can be assessed. In turn, the months that may need irrigation and the months that may experience risk of flood can also be predicted.

The water balance graph has two major limitations:

1 Since it is based on average figures, the actual periods of surplus and deficit water will vary from year to year. A year with a wet summer may have no deficit and experience flooding in autumn rather than late winter.
2 By relying on monthly figures, daily imbalances are ignored. For example, Figure 1.37 suggests that there will be no surplus water for runoff in the months of August and September, but whilst the total monthly rainfall may have been low in August it may have been delivered in a single storm lasting only 4 hours. Such rainfall intensities can produce flash floods which are much more common in summer than winter because convectional processes in the atmosphere create thunderstorms in the hot summer months.

Despite these limitations the water balance graph is a useful concept for illustrating broad differences between locations. It also explains how areas like the Sahel in Africa can have a large annual rainfall deficit yet be perfectly capable of supporting agriculture for a limited period of the year – see Figure 1.38a.

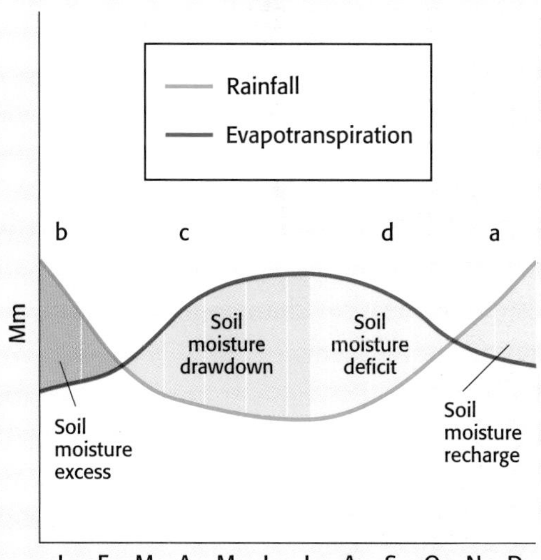

a In northern temperate climates the water year starts in October when the stores are at their lowest after summer and early autumn. This is the time of year when precipitation starts to rise as evaporation drops. Excess precipitation is used to fill up the soil stores, so relatively little generates runoff directly.

b By midwinter the stores are full of water and the groundwater stores are replenished. Precipitation is still high whilst evaporation is low in the cold weather. Excess precipitation is likely to generate excess runoff, and this is the season of river flooding in Britain.

c In early spring temperatures start to rise, increasing evaporation rates. Precipitation is falling at this time so that a net deficit in water occurs. Plants continue to grow and streams continue to flow because there is still plenty of moisture in the drainage basin stores.

d By midsummer the storage has been largely used and there is a large net deficit of moisture. Farmers may need to use irrigation at this time and water supplies will be low unless water has been stored in reservoirs or extracted from deep aquifers.

Figure 1.37 The water balance graph interpreted

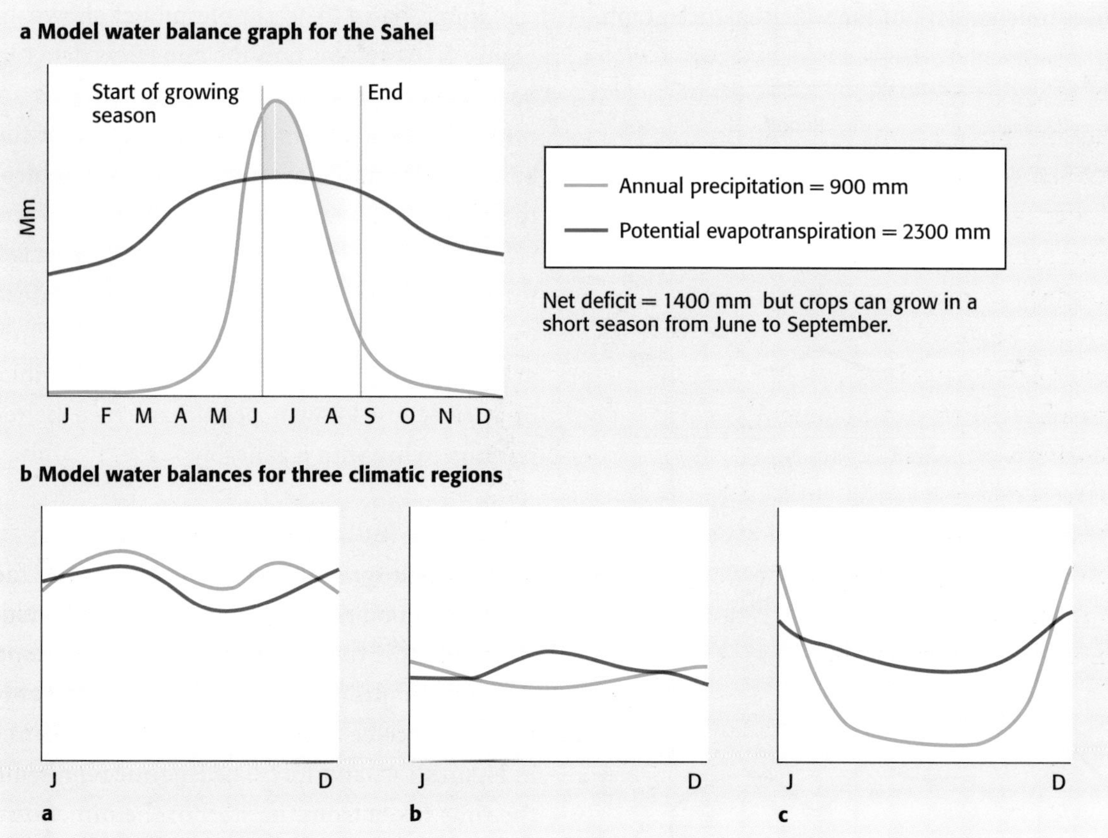

These locations include a southern hemisphere semi-arid region, an equatorial region, and a temperate oceanic region.

Figure 1.38 Water balance graphs

Activity

Examine Figure 1.38b. First match each graph to the global climatic region it is most likely to represent. Make copies of the graphs and, with reference to Figure 1.38a, shade and label the approximate areas representing soil moisture recharge, drawdown, excess and deficiency. Describe and attempt to account for the key differences between these three regions.

Careful examination of a water balance graph can give a lot of information about the nature of the climate and hydrology of an area. Few water balances look exactly like the model but the principles still apply. Where rainfall is higher than evaporation runoff should be higher. Where the difference is slight or reversed, runoff should go down. Figure 1.39 shows the water balance (and the resulting runoff patterns) for three major rivers. How closely river flow reflects the changing water balance may depend on additional factors such as basin permeability and basin relief. The graph of a river's flow over time is known as a **hydrograph**. These graphs have all sorts of uses independent of the water balance graph.

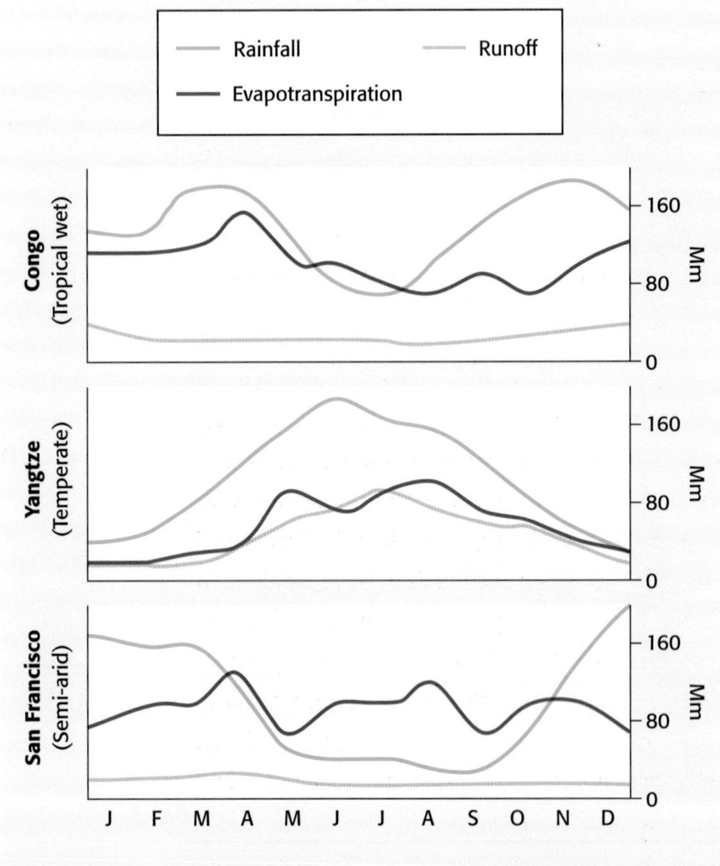

Figure 1.39
Water balance graphs for selected world river basins

Types of hydrograph: introduction

Water is delivered to the stream by the many routeways of the hydrological cycle. The amount of water flowing in the stream is known as the **stream discharge**. It can be expressed directly as a volume of water flowing down the channel (measured in cubic metres per second or 'cumecs') or indirectly by taking the total volume of water over a time period and calculating its equivalent depth averaged across the whole basin area. In general the direct method is used for measuring and analysing short term changes in flow related to individual flood events.

The **storm hydrograph** or **flood hydrograph** shows the river's response to a single rainfall event such as a passing storm. An **annual hydrograph** shows the variation of streamflow across the seasons, and this is more likely to be expressed as millimetres equivalent across the whole basin. The simple model shown in Figure 1.40 explains how the same flow data can be expressed either in terms of cumecs or millimetres equivalent per square metre of the basin. Hydrographs are important geographical tools because they express the character of the river – either its 'average' character represented through the annual hydrograph, or its response to specific events portrayed by the storm hydrograph. If both the average and extreme behaviour of a river are known, people are in a better position to live with it amicably.

The storm hydrograph

Storm hydrographs are valuable tools for analysing flood risk and water supply potential. Ironically it is rivers that are prone to flooding that are also prone to drought. Some key terms used to describe a storm hydrograph are found in Figures 1.41 and 1.42. The **lag time** represents the time taken from the start of the rain to the peak of the streamflow. Lag time is important in estimating the arrival times of expected floods. It has an inverse relationship with the hydrograph peak flow. Streams with long lag times have smaller peaks and vice versa. The **rising limb** can also be defined as the zone of rapid increase in discharge after a rainfall event. This is nearly always a steeper curve than the **falling** (or **recession**) **limb** because the rising limb

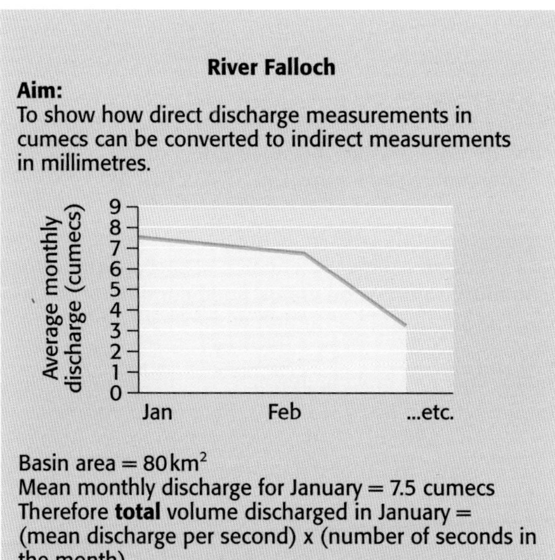

Figure 1.40
Converting between discharge measurements

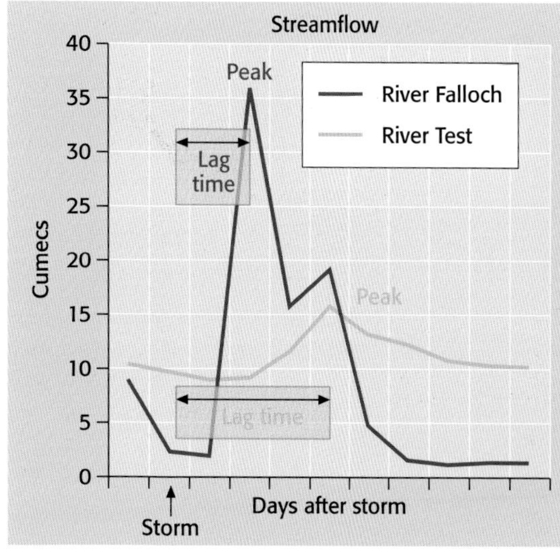

Figure 1.41
Comparative hydrographs for the Falloch and Test rivers

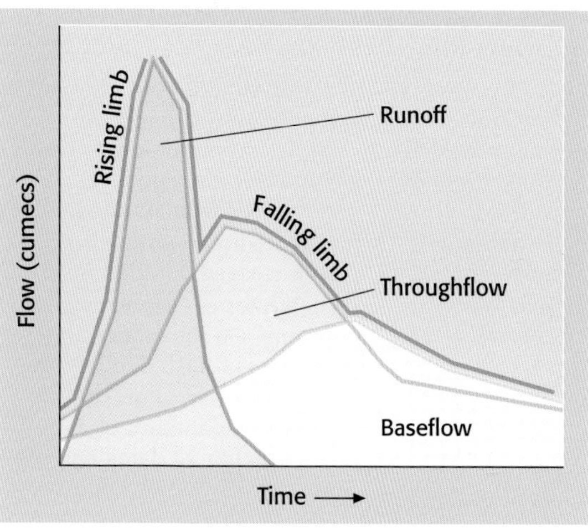

Figure 1.42
Hydrograph components

tends to have a fast runoff component whilst the falling limb is maintained by the slow drainage of throughflow and baseflow. In Figure 1.41 it is clear that the Falloch has a steep rising limb (representing a large component of runoff) which produces a high peak in a short lag time. Owing to a lack of storage in the drainage basin (this is a wet mountainous catchment draining hilly impermeable rocks in Scotland) the falling limb drops rapidly because there is very little throughflow or baseflow to sustain river flow for a long period. From a water supply point of view the Falloch is far from ideal. Floods are common, producing high sediment loads and dirty water, but in drier weather the flow diminishes to zero. The exact shape of the hydrograph varies for every river, with both the nature of the rainfall and the nature of the river basin. The Falloch has a 'flashy' hydrograph – rapid responses to rainfall and little storage capacity. The Test, by contrast, has a much flatter response reflecting a high storage capacity – much vegetation, thick permeable soils and a permeable bedrock.

Water enters stream channels by several different routes: runoff, throughflow and baseflow. Since these different routeways conduct water at different speeds the river ends up with different flows arriving one after the other and – usually – overlapping each other, as shown in Figure 1.42. This explains a common observation that the falling limb of a hydrograph may have a second peak reflecting the later arrival of throughflow or baseflow. The River Falloch hydrograph shows a clear secondary peak two days after the runoff peak.

There are many variables influencing the storm hydrograph. Some of these are fixed and predictable whilst others are dynamic and variable. Some relate to the nature of the precipitation while others depend on the character of the drainage basin. Figure 1.43 lists the key variables in alphabetical order.

Figure 1.43
Factors influencing the storm hydrograph

Factor	Characteristics
Area of basin receiving rainfall	Larger basins have smoother hydrographs because it is more likely that only part of the basin is receiving rain at any time. Flood waves are modified as they travel downstream through 'non-flood' areas. Small basins are often flashier because 100% of the basin experiences the same weather at the same time – see Figure 1.41 (Falloch = 80 km^2; Test = 1040 km^2).
Bedrock permeability	Permeable bedrocks produce flatter hydrographs since there is higher storage capacity to absorb rain. A common exception is Carboniferous limestone which absorbs water into underground cave systems where it can move rapidly and create flood conditions downstream (see Figure 1.47 – South Tyne). The subdued hydrograph of the Test is influenced by a large permeable catchment (Figure 1.41).
Direction of storm movement	A storm moving upstream has less impact than one moving downstream. In the latter case the rainfall source is moving downstream with the flood wave, so there is maximum likelihood of flooding.
Drainage basin shape	Elongated basins supply small amounts of water for a long time, reducing the size of the flood wave. More circular basins drain water more rapidly to the stream, creating bigger flood waves.
Drainage basin size	Larger drainage basins have more subdued responses to floods because they may be experiencing different climatic conditions in different tributaries. Small basins can be entirely inundated by a storm, creating a rapid flood response. This factor contributed to the Lynmouth flood disaster in north Devon in 1952.
Drainage density (total stream length in relation to the area of the basin)	Runoff moves much more rapidly once it has reached a stream. A dense stream network allows overland flow to reach a stream channel more quickly. High densities and high flood risk often go together; see Figure 1.47 – Dulnain flow peaks (low drainage density) compared with South Tyne peaks (high density).
Duration of precipitation	A short-lived storm is less likely to fill all drainage basin stores than a prolonged storm, so increased duration of rainfall leads to increased flood risk.
Evapotranspiration rates	High rates of evapotranspiration produce lower flood risks by removing water from the system. On the other hand, high evapotranspiration rates occur in hot weather when the chances of flash flooding from thunderstorms are increased.
Land use and human activity	Deforestation, afforestation, urbanisation and agriculture all have major impacts on the storage capabilities of a drainage basin. In addition to these 'accidental' impacts, the construction of dams and reservoirs strongly influences hydrographic responses. The hydrograph for Beverley Brook, a small urban catchment near Wimbledon Common, shows a high baseflow topped up by drainage from houses and occasional flashy spikes where urban storms have created sudden flood surges in the river (Figure 1.44).
Precipitation intensity	If precipitation intensity exceeds infiltration capacity overland flow is generated. Prolonged drizzle will produce a slower rise in discharge than a short intense storm. The nature of the stream's hydrograph becomes complicated by the fact that a storm may deliver different intensities of rainfall in different parts of the basin (Figure 1.45).
Precipitation type (snow, drizzle, rain)	Different types of input create different hydrograph responses. Snow is significant in creating a delayed response until thaw begins.
Pre-existing soil moisture levels	Rain landing on already saturated soils will quickly generate overland flow, encouraging a short lag time and a rapid rise to a high peak. This was a contributory factor in the Lynmouth floods.
Previous weather	In addition to the influence of previous rainfall on soil moisture levels, previous weather can cause soil to crust, reducing its permeability. Hot, dry weather encourages a crust to form and frosty winter weather reduces permeability.
Relief and topography	High slope angles encourage rapid runoff and discourage deeper percolation. Highland areas flood more easily than their lowland equivalents. This was also a factor in the Lynmouth floods.
River network	The arrangement of stream junctions can exaggerate flood peaks. If tributaries are staggered, small flood waves pass along in an orderly sequence. If many tributaries join the main river at a single point, the waves can combine to cause much larger floods.
Season	Season controls the water stores. Heavy rain at the end of winter is likely to cause more flooding than heavy rain at the beginning of winter. This was a factor in the Easter floods of 1998 in the Northampton and Peterborough areas of the UK.
Soil permeability	Permeable, well-drained soils offer high storage potential and discourage overland flow and 'flashy' flood hydrographs.
Soil thickness	Thick soils offer larger storage volume than thin soils.
Vegetation type and cover	Forests create the best conditions for water storage and act as natural flood defences by inhibiting overland flow. Deforestation was a major factor in the disastrous Central American floods caused by Hurricane Mitch in November 1998.

Activity

Consider the 19 factors listed in the left-hand column of Figure 1.43 and classify each one according to whether you think it is dynamic or fixed in nature. Record your decisions by entering each factor in the appropriate cell of an enlarged version of the following grid. Which category of factor predominates?

Factor category	Basin characteristic	Climate characteristic
Dynamic		
Fixed		

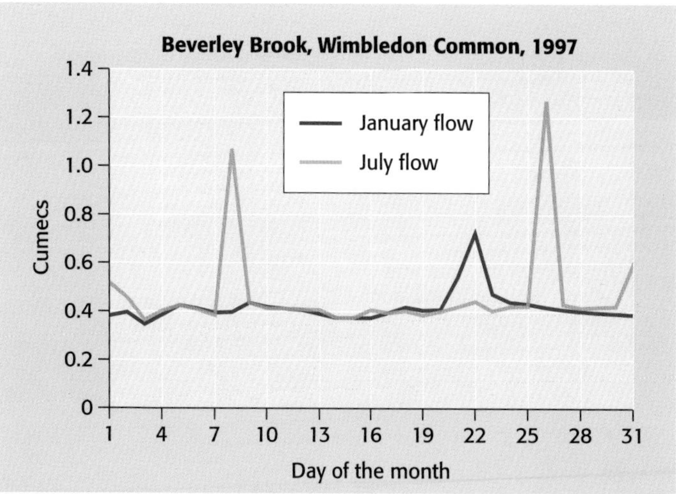

Figure 1.44
Daily flow variations in an urban catchment

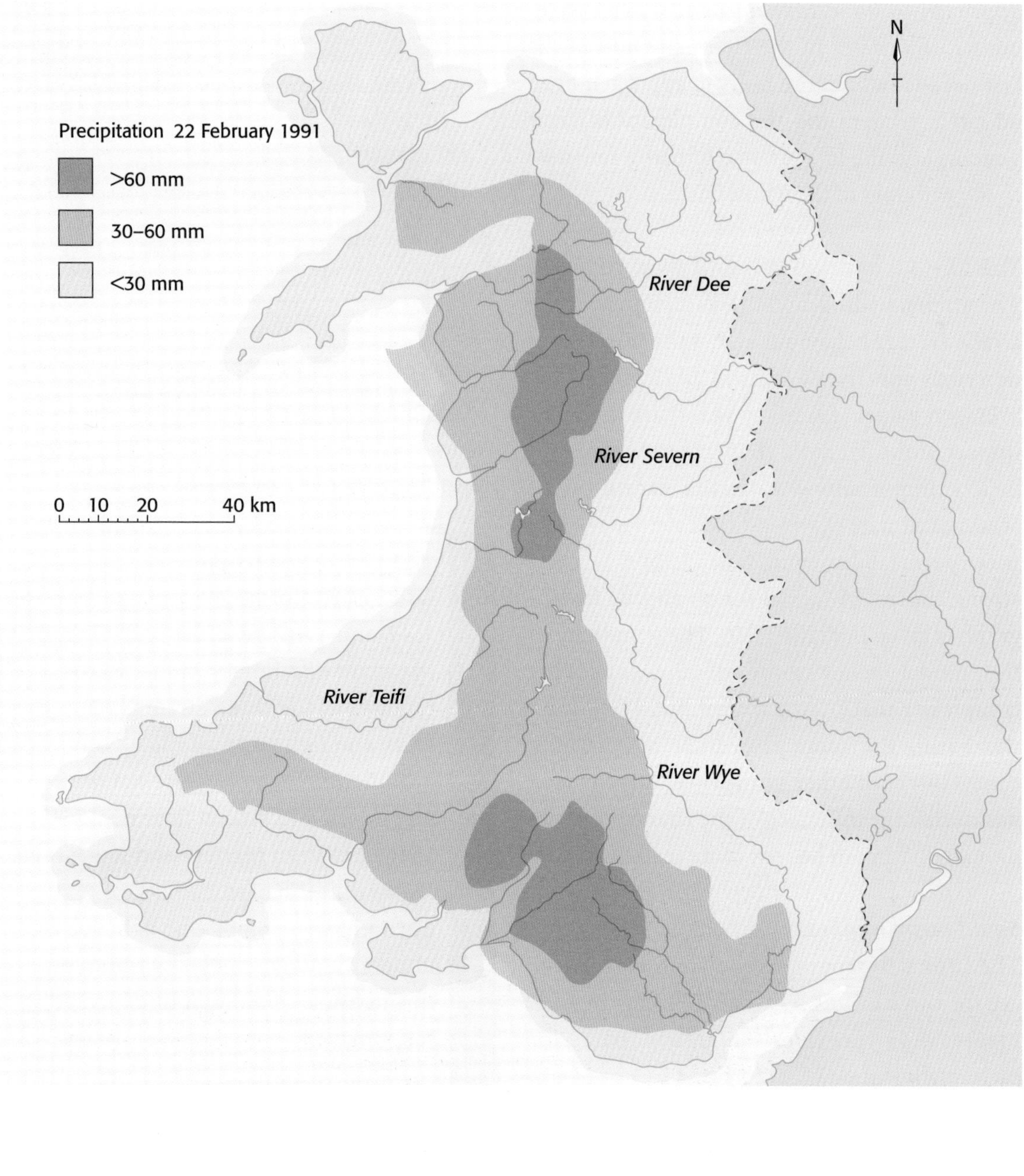

Figure 1.45
Variations in rainfall intensity across individual drainage basins. Notice how the tributaries of the main rivers vary in the intensity of rain received.

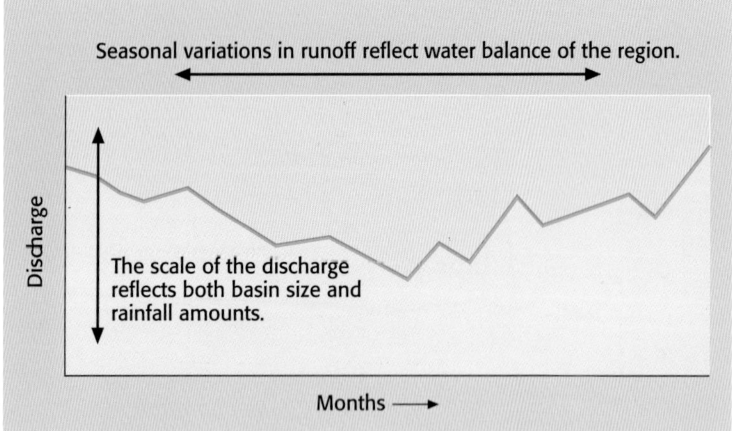

Figure 1.46
Model of the annual hydrograph

From both Figure 1.43 and your own table, it will be clear that flood behaviour is complex and difficult to manage. For many years the approach to flood management was to try to contain the water in the channel. Only in the last decade has a more holistic approach been adopted, recognising the complexity of river systems and the importance of being sensitive to the workings of the whole basin.

The annual hydrograph and river regimes

The annual hydrograph draws a picture of the river's average behaviour across the seasons – it describes the river's 'personality'. Since only averaged values (for many years) are used, the impact of the dynamic elements in Figure 1.43 is less important – with the exception of seasonal climate changes. Fixed elements – like rock permeability and basin slope – exert strong control. A model for an annual hydrograph is given in Figure 1.46. The simplicity of the model belies some of the intriguing complexity that occurs in real life. The bigger the basin, the more the different variables cancel out each other's influence. It is in small basins that the influence of the character of the drainage basin can be seen more readily.

Small basin regimes

The annual hydrographs shown in Figure 1.47 are for three basins less than 300 km^2 in area. Figure 1.48 provides summary data for each catchment.

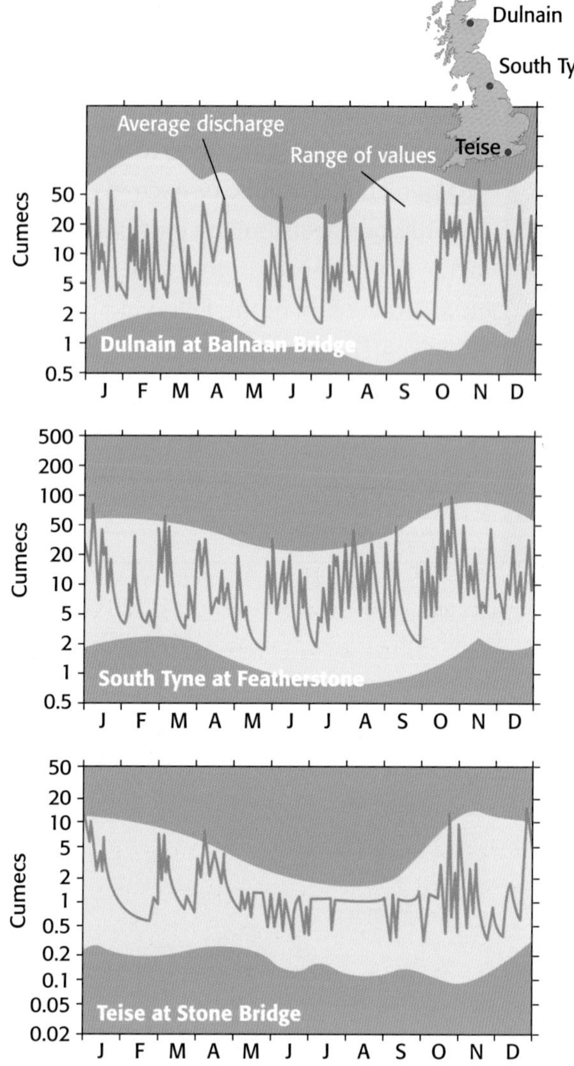

Figure 1.47
Annual hydrographs for three small UK basins

Activity

Using the information in Figures 1.46, 1.47 and 1.48, describe and explain the main differences in the flow regimes of the three streams. Quote facts and figures to support your arguments. Include reference to the steepness and size of flow peaks, the range between highest and lowest, etc. (Note that the permeability of Carboniferous limestone is based on underground channel flow rather than throughflow, making it unexpectedly responsive.)

	Dulnain	South Tyne	Teise
Average rainfall (mm)	1004	1358	800
Average runoff (mm)	682	1030	304
Basin area (km^2)	272	322	136
Average slope (m/km)	10	10.6	3.2
Stream frequency (junctions per km)	0.5	2.8	1.4
% of catchment area built up	0.02	0.08	0.5
Geology	Impermeable granite and metamorphic rock	Carboniferous limestone	Sands and impermeable clays
Management	Unmanaged upstream of gauging station	Unmanaged upstream of gauging station	Runoff reduced by abstraction for public water supply; reservoir upstream used to regulate summer flows

Figure 1.48
Summary data for three river basins

Large basin regimes

Whilst we can compare the small basins in Figure 1.48 and contrast their regimes on the basis of catchment characteristics, they all share a similar climate: moderate temperatures, and well distributed rainfall with a winter maximum. World climatic regions form an important basis for classifying river regimes of large catchments. Figure 1.49 shows the annual hydrograph for a selection of basins located in regions with a temperate continental climate, a monsoon climate, a subarctic climate, a semi-arid climate and a savannah climate. The basins occupy and drain huge areas of land which experience different conditions at different times. The result is a final hydrograph which ends up being a composite of many smaller tributary hydrographs.

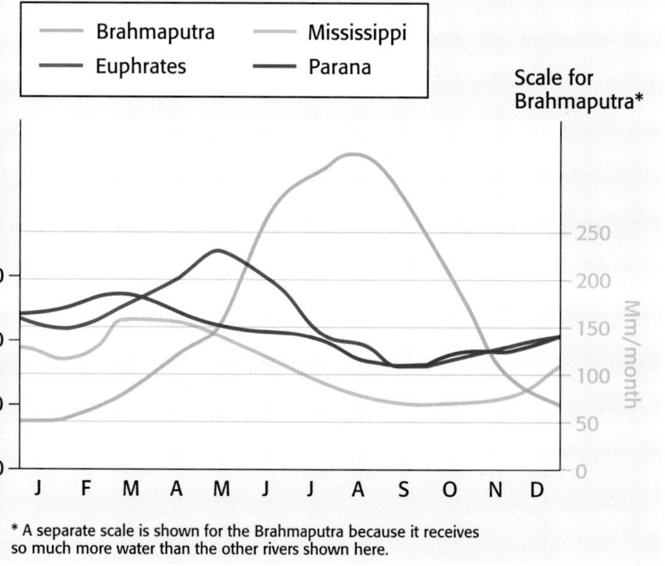

Figure 1.49
Selected world river regimes

> **Activity**
> On a world map outline, locate the basins named in Figures 1.39 and 1.49 and sketch the hydrograph for each one onto your world map. Use climatic data from an atlas to help explain the hydrograph shapes.

Humans and hydrological processes

Humans have a profound impact on the hydrological cycle and rivers. Some activities – such as reservoir construction – are planned and intentional. Others – like urbanisation – have unintended consequences. Figure 1.50 shows a range of ways in which the basin hydrological cycle can be influenced by people. Whenever land use changes, the local hydrological cycle is affected. Even seemingly insignificant factors such as a farmer's crop choice can influence microclimate. Figure 1.51 shows ground-level temperatures under a two different crop types over a three month period. The average temperature difference was 1°C. The effect of one field being a degree warmer than its neighbour may not have a huge influence on the local hydrological basin, but scaled over thousands of hectares the water balance could be changed.

Figure 1.50
Human impacts on elements of the hydrological cycle

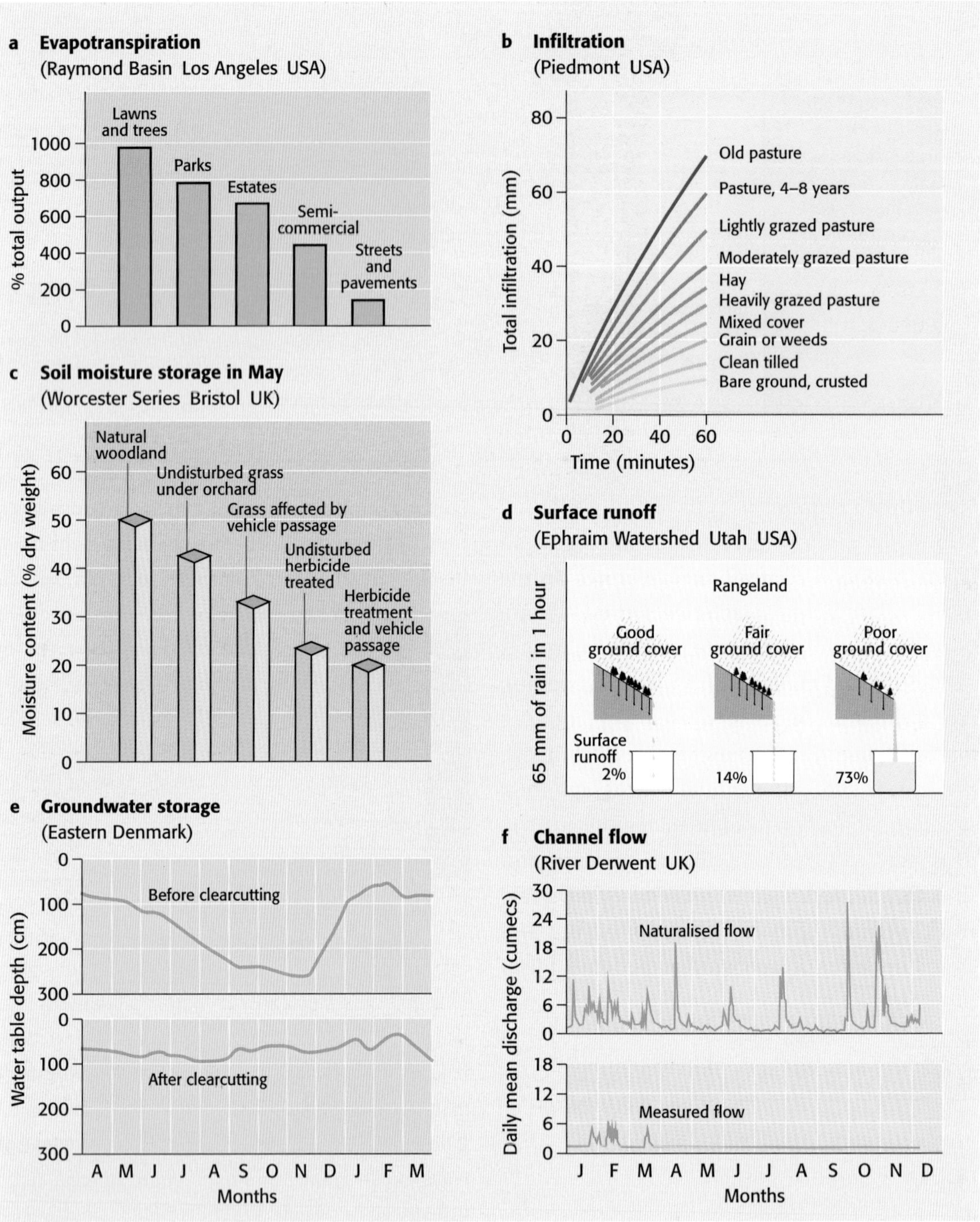

a Evapotranspiration
(Raymond Basin Los Angeles USA)

% total output
1000
800
600
400
200
0
Lawns and trees
Parks
Estates
Semi-commercial
Streets and pavements

b Infiltration
(Piedmont USA)

Total infiltration (mm)
80
60
40
20
0
Old pasture
Pasture, 4–8 years
Lightly grazed pasture
Moderately grazed pasture
Hay
Heavily grazed pasture
Mixed cover
Grain or weeds
Clean tilled
Bare ground, crusted
0 20 40 60
Time (minutes)

c Soil moisture storage in May
(Worcester Series Bristol UK)

Moisture content (% dry weight)
60
50
40
30
20
10
0
Natural woodland
Undisturbed grass under orchard
Grass affected by vehicle passage
Undisturbed herbicide treated
Herbicide treatment and vehicle passage

d Surface runoff
(Ephraim Watershed Utah USA)

65 mm of rain in 1 hour
Rangeland
Good ground cover
Fair ground cover
Poor ground cover
Surface runoff 2%
14%
73%

e Groundwater storage
(Eastern Denmark)

Water table depth (cm)
0
100
200
300
Before clearcutting
0
100
200
300
After clearcutting
A M J J A S O N D J F M
Months

f Channel flow
(River Derwent UK)

Daily mean discharge (cumecs)
30
24
18
12
6
0
Naturalised flow
18
12
6
0
Measured flow
J F M A M J J A S O N D
Months

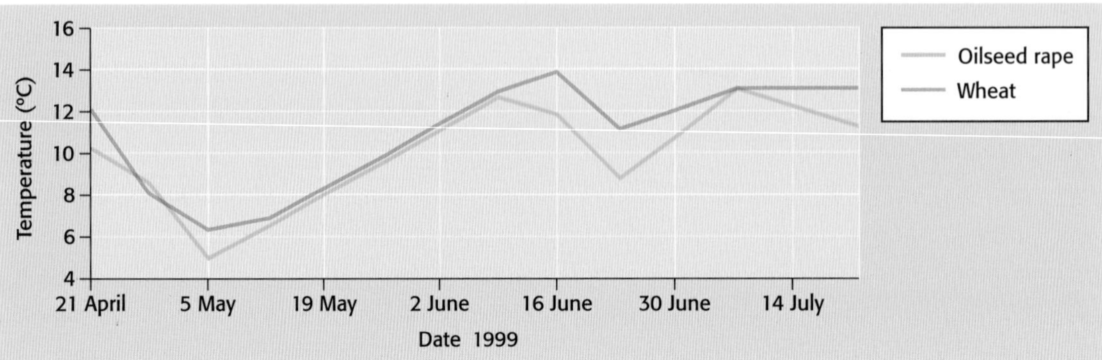

Figure 1.51
Influence of crop type on ground-level temperatures

Activity

1 For diagrams A–F in Figure 1.50, describe what the data is showing and explain your observations using the following terms:

- evapotranspiration • capillary action • water table • percolation
- infiltration • throughflow • soil structure • runoff • rainsplash
- surface storage • interception storage

2 Examine the list below showing potential human impacts on the hydrological cycle. Draw a model of a local drainage basin (see Figure 1.30) in the centre of a page, and use arrows to link the following human activities to the main part of the cycle which they influence. There may be different answers according to the arguments you use!

Artificial recharge	Reservoir construction	Street drainage	Air pollution
River diversion	Soakaways	Weirs	Cloud seeding
Irrigation	Waste water disposal	Field drainage	Forest clearance
Soil conservation	Global warming	Crop rotation	Global warming
Wells and boreholes	Afforestation	Ploughing	Soil erosion
Weirs	Roof gutters and downpipes		Seepage from water supply systems

3 Figure 1.52 shows two contrasting agricultural scenes, before and after harvest. On a sketch of each, identify and explain the likely differences in hydrological factors. Consider temperatures, wind speeds, shading, infiltration and interception.

Figure 1.52 Agricultural practices and hydrological variables:
a mature-crop wheatfield, just before harvest
b a field being ploughed or harrowed

Human vulnerability

There is one overriding motivation for understanding water balances and rainfall discharge relationships. The more we measure and monitor the more we can recognise changes and understand their causes. The more we understand the more we can reduce human vulnerability to floods and droughts.

Flood prediction

In broad outline there are three tools that are useful for flood prediction, all of which require long-term measurements.

1 **Recurrence intervals** (or return periods) are used to determine the probability of floods of a given size occurring. If all the recorded floods on a river are put in rank order, the recurrence interval for any one of them is easily estimated. In broad terms a place with a 100-year record will have some large, medium and small floods in the list. The biggest flood is counted as the '100-year flood' and the second biggest as the '50-year flood' (since that level was only reached and exceeded twice in the 100-year period). In practice a slightly more complex formula is

used, as shown in Figure 1.53. The advantage of this method is the simplicity with which the probability of a certain size of flood occurring can be estimated. Once the recorded floods are ranked it is a simple matter to graph them as in Figure 1.54, and to estimate the return period for a flood of a given size or vice versa. Hence, if a bridge with a design life of 100 years is to be built, the estimated size of the largest flood which it will have to cope with can be obtained from the graph. Obviously the accuracy of the return period will depend on the length of the flood record, and some basins have few records. A shortage of data need not be a problem, however. Basins with similar characteristics can be grouped and all their records pooled to give a fairly accurate set of data. Using this method, the data obtained in one basin can be supplemented by data from others. For example, if 20 basins have data covering 20 years, the pooled data is equivalent to 400 years of recording – enough for a good probability estimate. The big disadvantage with return periods is that they cannot predict timing of an event. A bridge built to withstand a 100-year flood could be swept away by the 500-year event a week after opening!

Recurrence interval $= \frac{n+1}{m}$

where: n = the number of years on record
m = the rank of the flood being considered.

In the example the biggest flood to have occurred has a recurrence interval of: $\frac{99+1}{1}$
i.e. 100 years.
The second biggest is the 50-year flood; the third is the 33-year flood; and so on.

Example

Rank	**Flood size** (cumecs)
1	50
2	42
3	31
4	20
etc.	

Total length of record was for 99 years.

Figure 1.53
Calculating the recurrence interval of a flood

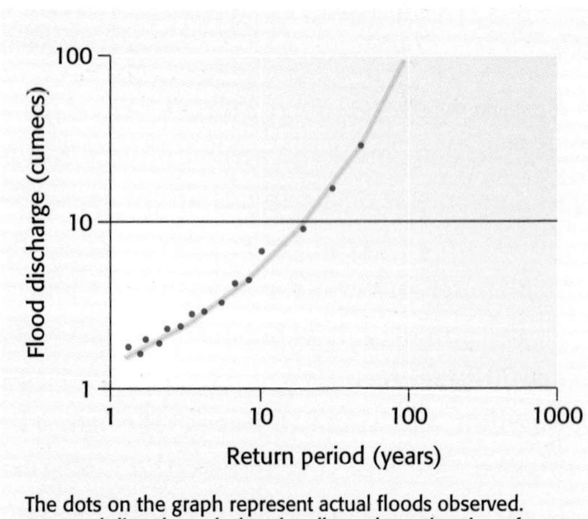

The dots on the graph represent actual floods observed. A smooth line through the plot allows the estimation of return periods not yet observed.

Figure 1.54
Return period graph

2 **Hydrograph analysis** is another tool for flood prediction. By analysing a series of storm hydrographs for a basin it is possible to derive estimates for the behaviour of the river for storms of different sizes.

3 **Real-time monitoring** allows hydrologists to follow the progress of flood waves down rivers, provided the river has a series of monitoring stations where automatic measurements are relayed to a central flood control office. This is the most accurate method of prediction used on large rivers such as the Mississippi, but it is expensive and difficult to set up, especially in large, complex or remote basins.

Flood protection

There are three basic approaches to flood protection for a populated area:

- increase storage upstream
- increase speed of output downstream
- separate people from the river channel.

Each of these approaches has its advantages and disadvantages, as summarised in Figure 1.55.

Approach	Methods	Advantages	Disadvantages	Examples
Increasing storage in the basin	Dams and reservoirs	Large storages easily created with multiple benefits, e.g. hydro-electric power, fish farming, recreation.	Loss of agricultural land and possible re-settlement issues. May silt quickly. Disruption to river regime and river ecosystems. Vulnerable target in event of terrorism and war.	Three Gorges Project, Yangtze River, China Colorado River, USA
	Terracing	Reduces overland flow by up to 90%. Reduces erosion (and therefore silting) and increases area of farmland.	Labour-intensive to create and maintain.	Tennessee River, USA Yangtze River, China
	Channel widening	Can be combined with landscaping to improve ecology and amenity value.	Involves compulsory purchase of riverside land – often with high visual, historic, agricultural or housing value.	River Lyn, Lynmouth, Devon River Colne, West London
	Afforestation	Reduces overland flow, increases throughflow. River flows are less extreme. Multiple benefits, e.g. timber, recreation, ecology.	Labour intensive. Long time lag between start of project and benefits being produced.	Yangtze River basin, China
Increasing output from the basin	Canalisation Dredging Channel re-shaping	Short cuts through long meanders evacuate water faster, reducing flood levels.	Faster-flowing water may increase flood build-up in downstream locations. River ecosystems disrupted. River channel may become unstable.	Blackwater River, Missouri, USA Rivers Ouse, Nene and Welland (Fens area of England)
Separating people from rivers	Levees	Natural levees can be reinforced relatively easily to contain most floods.	Deposition of silt no longer takes place on floodplain but in the channel, raising the level of the river bed and increasing the risk of future floods. If levees are over-topped the floodwater cannot drain back into the river, so floods may last longer. Can be expensive to monitor and maintain.	Mississippi River, USA Yangtze River, China River Thames, London
	Diversions	Relief channels can be used for other purposes (e.g. recreation) during non-flood conditions. Little impact on normal river ecology and hydrology.	Creates artificial barrier to urban growth.	San Francisco River, USA
	Strategic retreat – deliberate movement of people away from risk areas	Solves flood risk for all time with no ongoing maintenance costs. Retains river character.	Expensive initially – depends on suitable alternative locations being available. Politically unpopular.	Valmeyer, Mississippi, USA Yangtze River, China

Figure 1.55

Flood protection methods

Case Study : The Yangtze – a large-scale temperate river basin

The Yangtze River in China is one of the most significant rivers in the world. It is the deepest (150 m in some gorges), it is the third longest (6300 km), it has the fourth biggest discharge (34 000 cumecs), and the ninth biggest drainage area (1 959 000 km^2). It also has one of the highest flood death rates – nearly 1 million deaths in 1881 alone. The Yangtze has come to the world's attention in recent years after catastrophic flooding in 1998, and during the building of a highly controversial dam project, the Three Gorges.

Figure 1.56 shows the location and topography of the Yangtze basin. Figure 1.57 summarises some key data on the Yangtze. The Yangtze's hydrology is extremely complex. Its sheer size makes it difficult to monitor and model. Whilst most of the Yangtze experiences a temperate climate, the timing of rainfall varies across the basin and the pattern of water flow is complicated by the interaction of tributaries from different regions. The overall regime consists of a series of flood peaks from spring to summer (Figure 1.39) but these vary with the timing of (i) spring snowmelt (ii) the monsoon (iii) tropical cyclones. Flooding on the Yangtze is particularly significant because the river basin includes some of the most productive and densely settled regions of China. The fertile floodplains produce 70 per cent of China's rice crop, 40 per cent of its grain, and the water produces 50 per cent of the country's freshwater fish. A third of China's billion people live in the Yangtze basin, so understanding the river and managing it effectively are essential. The factors influencing the hydrology of the Yangtze are summarised in Figure 1.58.

Figure 1.56
The Yangtze Basin

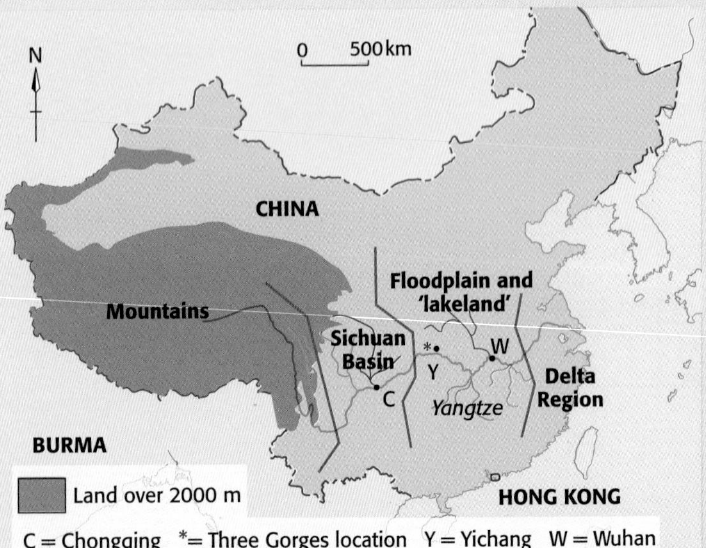

Activity

1 Take four separate sheets of plain A4 paper. On each sheet draw a simple sketch of the Yangtze basin (see Figure 1.56). Using one sheet per region, first highlight the region within the basin and then, referring to Figure 1.58, annotate your sketch to show the key issues influencing the management of the Yangtze.

2 Writing in the style of a newspaper report, produce two contrasting articles of no more than 500 words each. One should take the view that the Chinese government is successfully managing the Yangtze; the other should argue the opposite.

The 1998 Yangtze floods

A total of 400 million people live in the Yangtze basin. In 1998, 45 per cent of them (180 million people) were affected by floods: 4000 died and over 18 million were evacuated from their homes. Nearly 7 million homes were destroyed and over 5 million hectares of crops were lost. The overall cost was estimated to be US$ 26 billion. The cause was freak weather associated with an El Niño event. China experienced an unusually warm year (Figure 1.59). Early and rapid snowmelt combined with an early and wet monsoon to create huge water flows. The situation was worsened by high silt levels in the river resulting from deforestation in the upper Yangtze, and by bureaucratic corruption diverting funds from river defences to office development! Owing to the complex network geometry of the Yangtze,

Factor	Mountain section	Sichuan to Three Gorges	Floodplain section	Yangtze Delta
Typical discharges (m^3/s or cumecs)	2000	14 900	24 000	34 000
Major sources of precipitation	Snow	Monsoon	Monsoon and tropical cyclones	Monsoon and tropical cyclones
Vulnerability (i) Physical factors	Steep slopes, rapid snowmelt.	Large inputs from tributaries.	Silting of channels leading to floods; large inputs from tributaries.	Silting of channels (delta grows 15 m/yr); disruption by tropical cyclones.
(ii) Human factors	Deforestation of upland forest areas (nearly half of China's remaining native forest is in the upper Yangtze).	Over 5 million people live in the vicinity of the river or its tributaries. Major agricultural producer. Coalfields, iron ore deposits, oil and gas fields support large industries and heavy manufacturing industries.	Over 4.5 million people live in the vicinity of the river or its tributaries. Major inland port, commercial centre and iron/steelworking centre.	Over 17.6 million people live in the low-lying delta region. Major port and commerce area with manufacturing industry (e.g. fertilisers, textiles, vehicles). Major agricultural production with 8–11-month growing season.
Responses to flood threats	Upper Yangtze forest shelter belt planted. Tighter legislation controlling timber felling being introduced.	River diversion channels (since 500 BC!). Small-scale dams on some tributaries. Early warning system with 30 automated meteorological stations set up in 1998–99. Middle Yangtze forest shelter belt planted. Terracing in the foothills of the Sichuan basin. Dynamiting rapids in the gorges to speed flow of water. Levees to protect urban areas. Gezhouba dam near Yichang is the first dam to be built (1970) on the Yangtze and is a major source of HEP. The Three Gorges project (see below) started in 1993.	Many levees and dykes to contain water. Natural lakes used for flood storage and artificial storage basins created (e.g. Shashi = 920 km^2). Regular dredging needed to keep the river from silting. After disastrous flooding in 1954, government improved 3400 km of levees and 30,000 km of relief channels to divert water to storage ponds.	More than 1500 km of levees. Dredging of main channels, draining of swampland. Improved warning from automated weather and flood monitoring networks in upstream regions.
Problems remaining	Enforcing legislation in a remote area.	Earthquake threat to dams in this seismically active area. Levees prevent floodwater draining back to river.	Lake silting reduces storage capacity. Levees prevent floodwater draining back to river.	Threat of 'multiple event disaster' if river floods coincide with tropical cyclone storm surge. Levees prevent floodwater draining back to river.

Figure 1.57 Yangtze facts and figures, by basin section

several flood peaks continued in succession from August to September. Water from one peak was still on the floodplain when the next peak arrived. Floodwater was up to 6 m deep in many places, and many evacuees in the middle Yangtze spent more than eight weeks living in tents on the very tops of embankments.

The future

The Chinese government is putting most of its hopes (and US$ 28 billion) into the Three Gorges project, which was started in 1993. The project is designed to create a 634 km long lake behind a 175 m high dam. If the project is successful it will allow regulation of the river

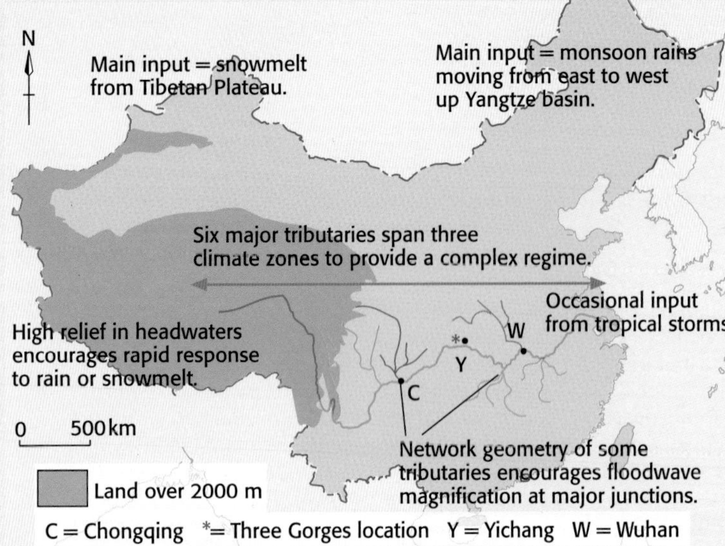

Figure 1.58
Yangtze hydrology

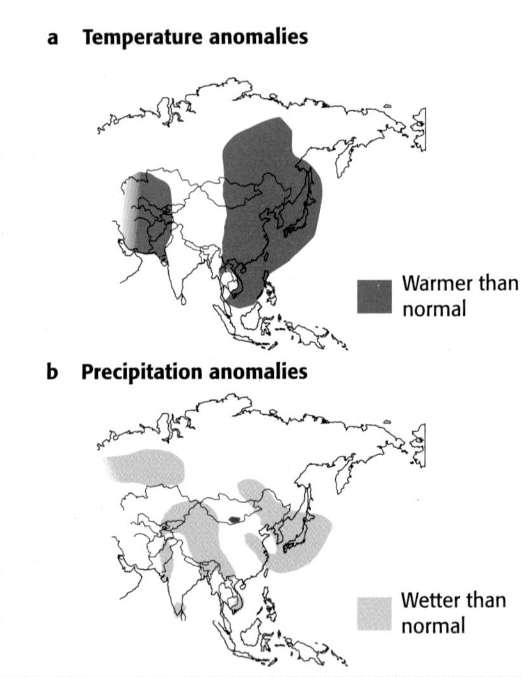

Figure 1.59
Temperature and precipitation anomalies, March 1998 to February 1999

downstream of the dam, protecting 10 million people. The financial savings from flood reduction could be enormous. Hydro-electricity production will supply 10 per cent of the total needs for central and eastern China. A giant canal system will bypass the dam, and the treacherous Three Gorges will be transformed into a 'ship-friendly' lake allowing ocean-going vessels access upriver as far as Chongqing. Access on this scale will create new economic opportunities for the whole Sichuan basin.

Opponents of the dam argue that the problems will outweigh the benefits. The dam will permanently flood the homes of 1.3 million people. It will increase the flood risk in upstream areas by encouraging the slower waters to deposit silt in the river channel. The new opportunities for Chongqing as an inland port could be wiped out by the port silting up. The dam will do nothing to protect the delta area from flooding associated with tropical cyclones; nor will it help areas in the floodplain when monsoon rains create floods in the tributaries *downstream* of the dam. Sedimentation behind the dam is likely to reduce its capacity to regulate floodwaters. At the same time, the reduction in the silt load of the water flowing downstream of the dam will increase its erosive power and add to its ability to undermine existing levees. The absence of regular downstream flooding will deprive the land of free nutrients and irrigation. Riverside ecosystems will be permanently altered. It is worth noting that the energy production of the dam would not be needed if Chinese industry was more energy-efficient. Nonetheless, whatever the arguments, the government is forging ahead with the project and opposition is strongly discouraged.

In March 1999 the government announced further plans to reduce flood damage in the Yangtze basin. Two million people living in vulnerable areas are to be moved from the floodplain. This figure is in addition to the 1.3 million being displaced by the Three Gorges Dam itself. In a country where only 10 per cent of the land is cultivable and over 60 per cent of the population are farmers, there are important questions to ask about where they will go and what they will do. There is no doubt that the Yangtze is a formidable force; Chinese planners are also a formidable force. Only time will tell which poses the greatest threat to the well-being of ordinary citizens in the Yangtze basin.

2 Ecosystems

Key Themes

- Over time, ecosystems evolve through clear developmental stages in response to the physical environment; human intervention may upset this sequence, both intentionally and unintentionally.
- The essential characteristics of individual ecosystems can be explained in terms of energy flow and the production of biomass.
- The cycling of nutrients between the various components of ecosystems is an essential process in their development and sustainability.
- Ecosystems vary in robustness and require different approaches to their care and management.

Ecosystems defined

An **ecosystem** is a group of organisms (plants, animals and bacteria) which interact with one another and with the environment so that material is exchanged between the living and non-living parts of the system. Ecosystems vary in size from large-scale **biomes**, such as equatorial rainforests, to individual hedgerows. Understanding how an ecosystem works involves studying two key components: energy flows and nutrient recycling. It is also important to recognise the influence of soils and human impact on ecosystems if they are to be sustained as healthy and productive habitats for plant and animal life. Ecosystems are not equally robust. Tropical rainforests are readily damaged and may never recover their original form despite the size and strength of the trees involved. By contrast, while grassland ecosystems may initially appear more vulnerable, they are remarkably resilient and able to recover strongly from damaging natural forces and the pressures of human activity (Figure 2.1).

Figure 2.1
Two contrasting ecosystems:
a a tropical rainforest
b a temperate grassland

Energy flows in ecosystems

The energy which powers all ecosystems comes from solar radiation. Light from the Sun is absorbed by chlorophyll in green leaves and, in the presence of water and carbon dioxide, produces carbonates and oxygen. This process is called **photosynthesis**. The oxygen is given off into the atmosphere, whereas the carbonate is used by the plant for respiration and for growing new tissue or **biomass**. New growth means the plant increases in size, produces more leaves, a thicker stem and longer roots. The rate at which an ecosystem accumulates biomass, together with the energy used up for respiration, is called **gross primary productivity**. If respiration is excluded, then the term **net primary productivity** is used.

Plants, or **autotrophs**, are the only organisms that can create organic matter from inorganic substances such as water, air and sunlight. As **primary producers** they are the first link in a **food chain** (Figure 2.2). The plant tissue is consumed by plant eaters, herbivores or **primary consumers**, which in their turn are eaten by carnivores or **secondary consumers**. The secondary consumer group may in turn be consumed by tertiary consumers. All consumers can be regarded as **heterotrophs**.

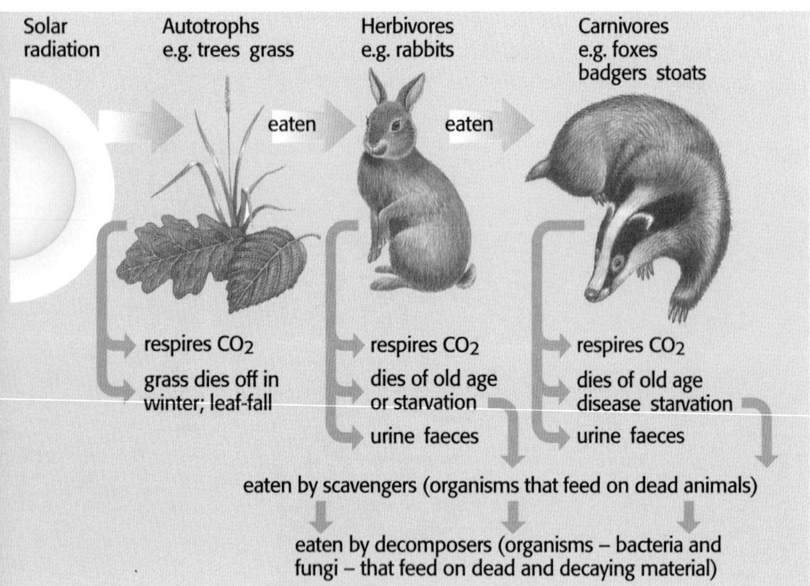

Figure 2.2

Example of a simple food chain with internal energy losses

The food chain can therefore be seen as a sequence in which organisms at each level become the food source for the next highest member in the line. Each step in the food chain is called a **trophic level**. Attempts have been made to quantify the biomass and the amount of energy at each level by constructing **ecological pyramids** as in Figure 2.3. Most ecological pyramids are this shape, but not exclusively. The amount of total energy available becomes smaller from one trophic level to another because:

- energy is lost at each level through respiration, defecation, chewing and mating
- not all the plants or herbivores are eaten – some die naturally or from starvation
- animals expend energy looking for and catching food.

Although the total number of organisms becomes smaller, the animals often become larger because size is important in successfully catching prey. Food chains do not usually consist of more than five levels. The reasons for this are controversial, but one suggestion is that the progressive reduction in food supply at each level acts as a control.

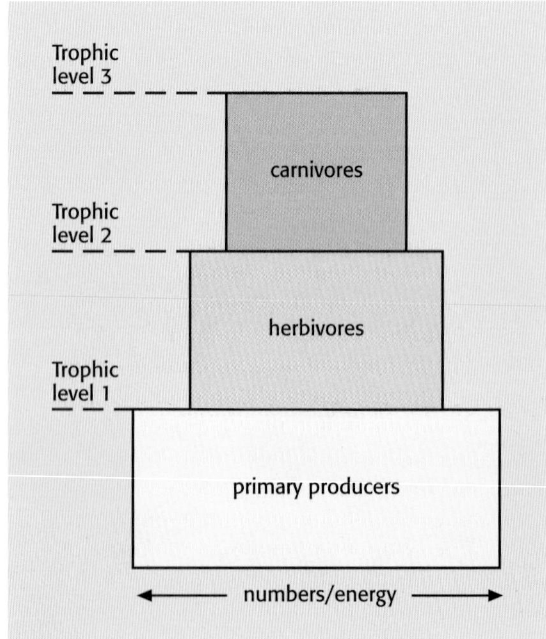

Figure 2.3

Ecological pyramid

Trophic levels and food chains are much-simplified models of reality. They have been criticised because they ignore the facts that:

- each animal has a particular feeding pattern, for example cattle and sheep graze at different levels
- some animals are **omnivores**
- some animals are herbivores when young but later become carnivores
- some animals move across the trophic levels on a seasonal basis.

An improved model is a **food web**, but this approach still ignores the importance of individuals within it, and does not record losses in energy (Figure 2.4). Left to themselves, food chains and webs become self-regulating. If all the green matter is eaten the herbivores begin to die of starvation, which in turn reduces the size of the carnivore population. This sequence gives the chance for the green matter to recover. Human activities, however, often interfere with energy flows. For example, hunting, poaching, conservation, overgrazing, forest clearance and human trampling all have direct effects on ecosystems. More indirectly, pollution can damage ecosystems, while people can disturb animal breeding patterns and upset the balance between numbers.

Activity

1. Define the following terms: **a** biomass, **b** trophic level, **c** gross primary productivity, **d** secondary carnivore.
2. Work out and explain *three* reasons why energy is lost up the food chain.
3. Identify from the food web in Figure 2.4 **a** a primary producer, **b** a herbivore, **c** a secondary carnivore.
4. What effect would a decline in the owl population in Figure 2.4 have on the food web in the short term and in the longer term?

Nutrient cycling

In addition to sunlight, plants also need water, warmth and a range of nutrients including carbon, nitrogen, oxygen, hydrogen, calcium, magnesium, potassium, sulphur, phosphorus and trace elements. At any one time nutrients can be thought of as being stored in the soil, biomass, or litter (dead leaves, stems and grass). Figure 2.5 shows where these nutrients come from and how they are recycled. The size of each store, or pool, reflects the volume of nutrients stored in it. The width of each arrow, or flow, indicates the relative volume of nutrients being transferred.

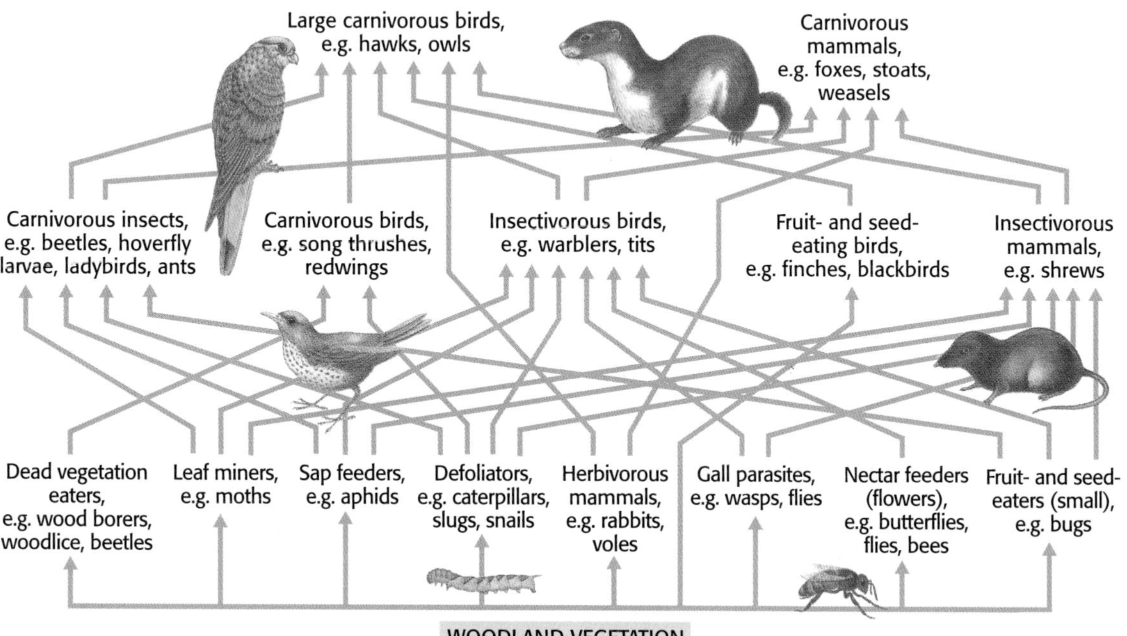

Figure 2.4 A woodland food web

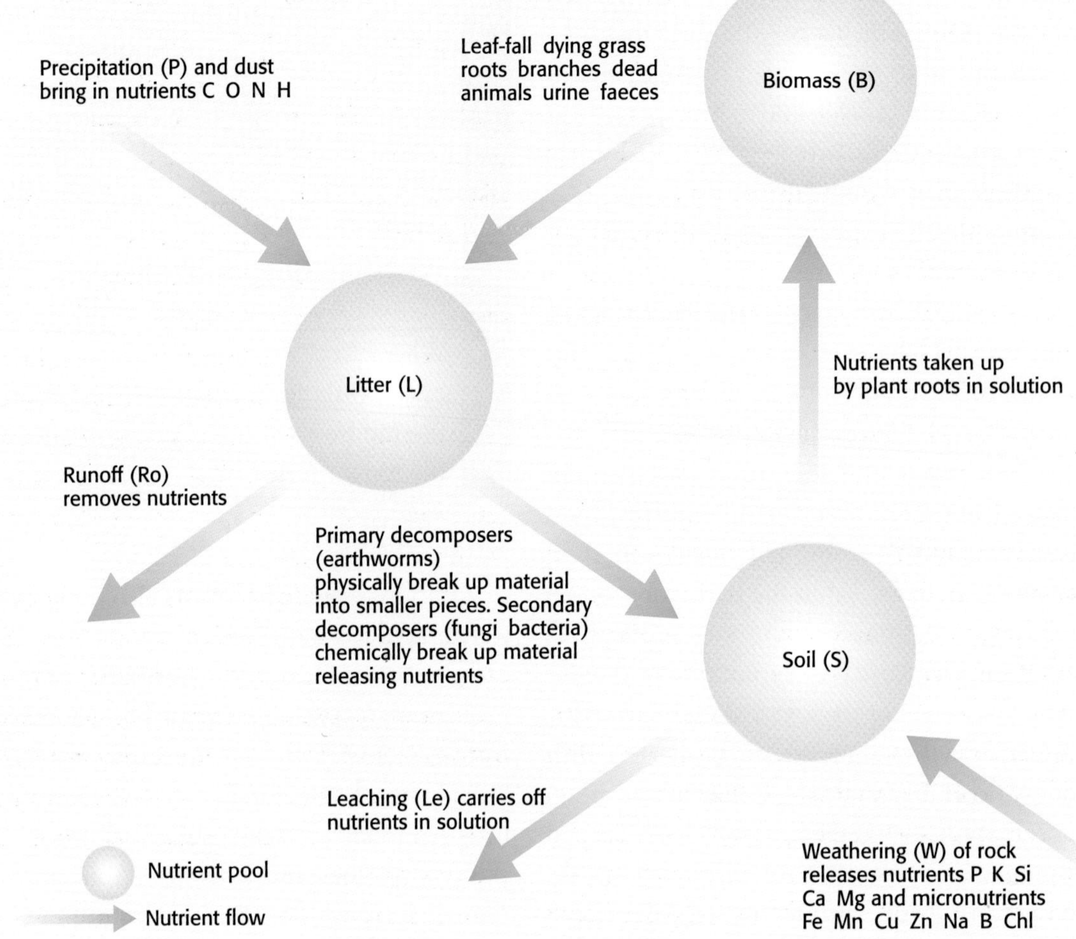

Figure 2.5
Nutrient recycling

Within the soil compartment, nutrients dissolved in water can be taken up by plant roots in solution, but they can also be easily carried down through the soil. Nutrients locked in soil mineral fragments are unavailable to plants until they are released by weathering. Nutrients attached to the surface of **clay and humus complexes** are the most important because they are not easily washed out and can be taken up by the plant roots through a process called **cation exchange** (Figure 2.6).

Clay humus complexes have surfaces which are negatively charged and to which are attached positively charged ions, or cations, of calcium, magnesium, potassium and sodium. These substances are all valuable plant nutrients, collectively referred to as **basic cations**, or just **bases**. Plant roots also have negatively charged surfaces to which are attached positively charged

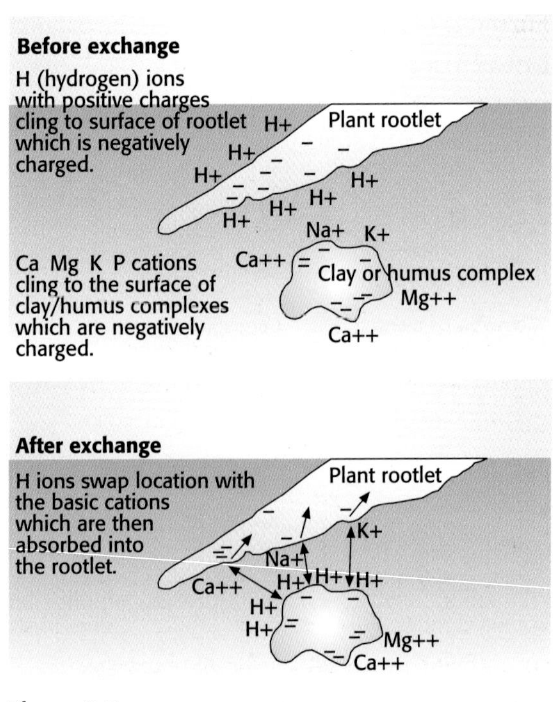

Figure 2.6
Cation exchange

hydrogen ions. Cation exchange occurs when plant roots exchange their positive hydrogen ions for the basic cations on clay humus complexes. The bases are then absorbed upwards though the roots to feed the plant.

The ability of soil particles to retain nutrients on their surfaces for plant use is called their **cation exchange capacity** (**CEC**). CEC is high in clay soils and even higher in soils with a large humus content, which explains why organic soils are very fertile. In contrast, sandy soils have a very low CEC because few bases are attached to their particle surfaces.

Human impacts on nutrient cycles

Human activities can alter nutrient cycles in various ways. Grazing livestock contribute urine and faeces which decomposers can convert to **humus**, but nutrients are lost when the animals are slaughtered. Crop harvesting removes nutrients, although some losses can be made good by adding **organic matter** and fertilisers.

Organic matter or farmyard manure (FYM) breaks down to release nitrogen, phosphorus and potassium. FYM also helps soil particles, or **peds**, to stick together to form **soil structures**. Furthermore, it has surfaces to which nutrients can become attached, and it acts as a sponge holding water that otherwise might be lost via overland flow and **leaching**.

Nitrate, phosphate and potash fertilisers all raise soil fertility. Nitrogen is a very important nutrient for plant growth because it helps to make protein and encourages green leaves and shoots to form. In nature the nitrogen cycle is in balance, but if the land is cropped, shortfalls can be made good using fertiliser. However, adding too much nitrogen causes toxicity; plants turn yellow and growth is stunted. Moreover, nitrate is very soluble and therefore can easily be leached through the soil. Unless a plant takes up this fertiliser quickly it can enter streams and rivers causing **eutrophication**.

Phosphorus is derived from weathered rock or by burning biomass. Both are slow processes and where farming is intensive, fertilisers are used to make up the balance. Phosphate fertiliser helps roots and seedlings to grow. Unlike nitrate, phosphate does not wash out so easily and it becomes firmly attached to clay humus complexes. However, in very acid or alkaline conditions it becomes insoluble, which means that plant roots cannot take it up.

Potash makes protein and increases plant resistance to frost and disease. It is released when rocks are weathered or vegetation is burnt, but losses are high because this element is very soluble. There is also a tendency for plants to take up more than they need, which results in potash being lost to the system when crops are harvested.

Liming can improve nutrient content and soil fertility. The addition of calcium and magnesium reduces soil acidity which in turn promotes biological activity because earthworms and bacteria do not function in acid conditions. Liming also improves the soil structure because calcium helps to bind the peds together.

Afforestation and deforestation also modify nutrient content and recycling. The impacts of deforestation are shown in Figure 2.7.

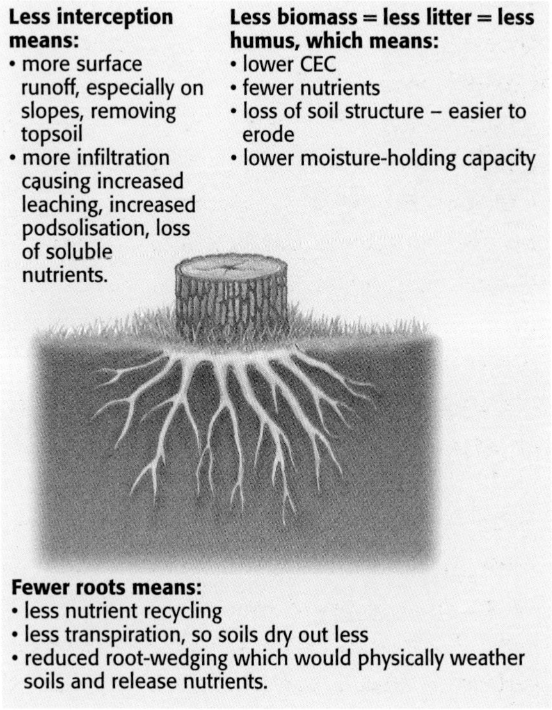

Figure 2.7 Impacts of deforestation

High ozone concentrations and acid rain can also indirectly damage nutrient cycles in coniferous forests. Acid rain falling on naturally acidic soils reduces the **pH** to the extent that iron and aluminium become soluble and too toxic for the trees. Moreover, leaching of potassium and magnesium from the soil under acid conditions adversely affects the trees. Typically, species such as Norway spruce suffer from chlorosis (yellowing) of the needles, defoliation, loss of vigour, slower growth and greater vulnerability to insects.

Case Study: Bradfield Wood, Suffolk

Bradfield Wood in Suffolk illustrates some of the human impacts on nutrient recycling. Bradfield Wood is an ancient deciduous woodland near Bury St Edmunds in Suffolk, and it is currently managed by the Suffolk Wildlife Trust (Figure 2.8). It contains a variety of tree species including ash, maple, hazel, lime, elm, birch, alder, oak and hawthorn. Coppicing is still practised in order to provide a woodland resource and also to encourage plant species such as oxlip, anemone and wood spurge. Hazel is coppiced every 8–12 years and used for making hurdles, whereas other species including ash, oak, birch and alder are cut every 20–25 years and used for firewood, poles, fencing, and the wood ash for pottery glazes. The variety of tree and plant species in the woodland at different stages of growth makes the site popular with visitors and educational groups. The site includes a visitor centre and car park.

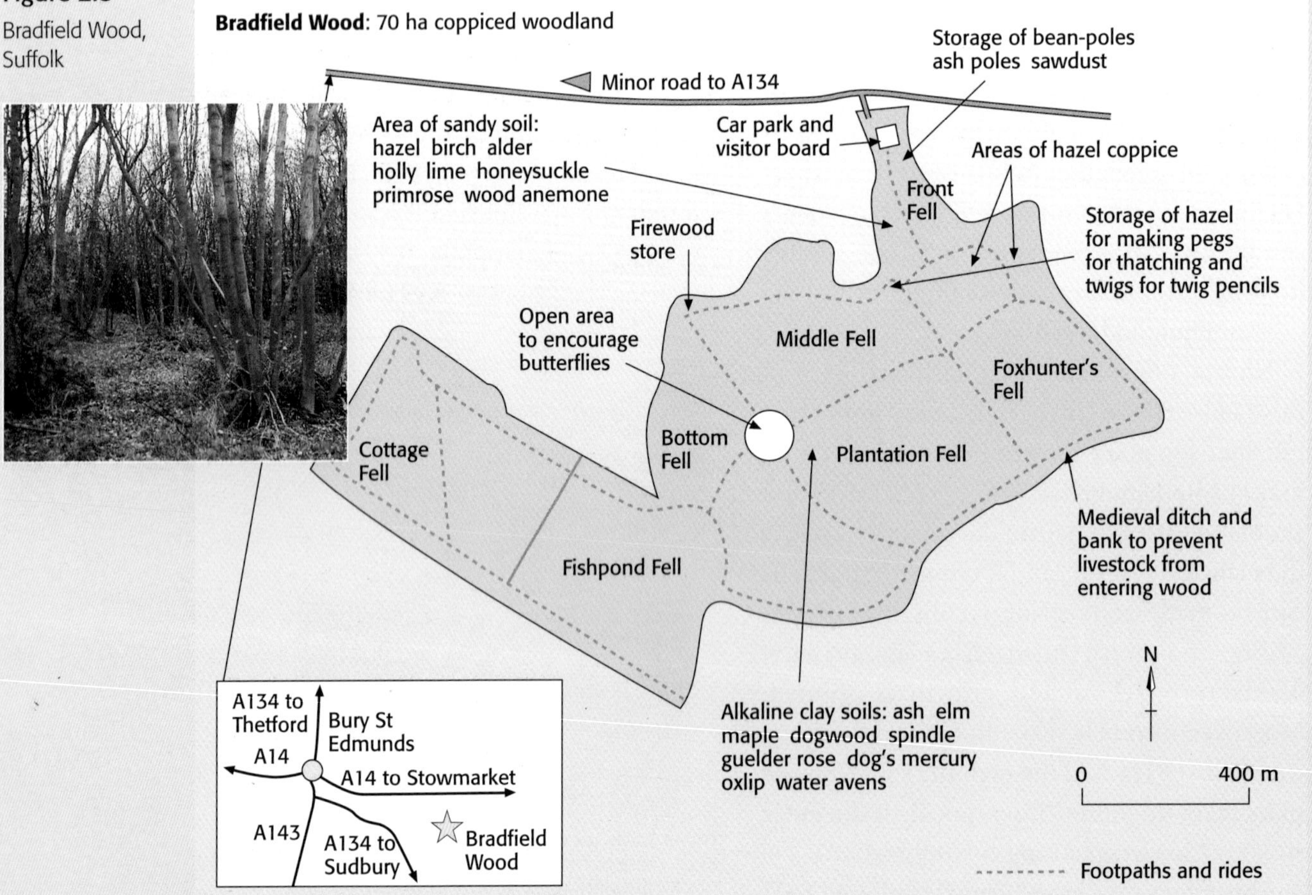

Figure 2.8 Bradfield Wood, Suffolk

Activity

1 What effects might coppicing have on the nutrient cycle in the short term and the longer term?

2 What would be the nature of the impact on the nutrient cycle if heavy sheep grazing were to be allowed in the wood?

3 Imagine that the Suffolk Wildlife Trust decided to extend the wood by planting more trees. Can you suggest three possible changes in nutrient recycling? Refer to Figure 2.5 to help you with this task.

The deciduous forest ecosystem

Temperate **deciduous forest** occurs only in the northern hemisphere in west and central Europe, north-east USA and parts of Japan. It covered much of south and east Britain before clearance for agriculture took place. The deciduous habitat of the dominant trees is a seasonal response to what is called 'physiological drought', which occurs when the roots encounter difficulty in extracting water from cold soils. In response, the trees shed their leaves in order to reduce water loss by transpiration.

Deciduous woodlands typically consist of four or five layers of vegetation. Oak, ash and hornbeam often form the tree layer, below which are shrub, field and ground layers (Figure 2.9).

Figure 2.9 Structure of a deciduous woodland

The vertical structuring is a consequence of the availability and competition for light. In spring, primroses, followed by celandines, wood anemones and then bluebells flower before the tree foliage becomes too dense. Temporary changes can occur when wind-throw, old age and fire produce clearings. Initially light-seeking species such as annual grasses and willow-herb thrive. Gradually the gaps are colonised by birch, which provides shade in which oak seedlings can become established. Eventually, oak overtops and shades out birch which in turn may itself be shaded out by beech. The dense foliage of this tree shades out the shrub and field layers below.

This ecosystem is rich because of the variety of plant species within it, which in turn create a variety of animal habitats. Mice feed on hazelnuts, caterpillars consume leaves, jays eat acorns, woodpeckers feed on grubs, and hedgehogs eat invertebrates. Holly-berries provide winter food. Feeding patterns vary seasonally, for example woodmice feed on insects, nuts and fruits, depending on what is available at the time. In winter hedgehogs hibernate, whereas other species migrate, or stay in a dormant stage as eggs or larvae. Trees provide nests for woodpeckers, while brambles provide cover for badgers and rabbits.

Nutrient cycling in the deciduous forest

As shown in Figure 2.10, the largest pool is the biomass because of the long-term immobilisation of nutrients within trunks, branches and stems, a feature of all woodland. Runoff is reduced because of interception by the canopy and the undergrowth. Precipitation is matched by leaching. Litter is fairly rapidly broken down by animals in two stages. Firstly the primary decomposers (millipedes, beetles and earthworms) attack the litter and break it down into smaller pieces. In the second phase these fragments, together with the faeces of these litter animals, form the food for the secondary

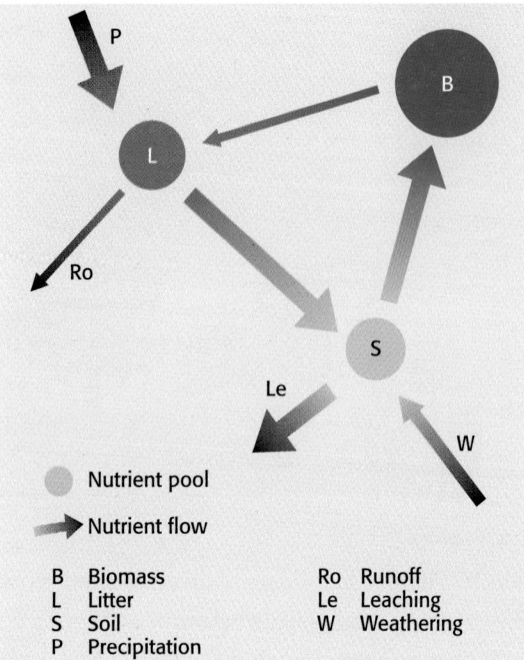

Figure 2.10 Nutrient recycling in a deciduous forest

decomposers (mites and springtails) which further commute organic material. Wet material is also broken down by bacteria and fungi. The loss of mineral matter through leaching is made good through inputs derived from precipitation and rock weathering.

Human impact on deciduous woodland

In the past, deciduous woodland was coppiced (i.e. cut near to the base to allow stools to regenerate as slender poles – see Figure 2.8) for timber and charcoal. Hazel was used for fence-poles. Beech trees were often introduced for aesthetic reasons and pines provided homes for birds of prey. Highgate Wood, an area of urban woodland in London, is a good illustration of the human impact on a deciduous ecosystem.

Case Study: Highgate Wood, north London

Highgate Wood is a 28 ha ancient hornbeam woodland located on hills in north London and largely underlain by impermeable London Clay (Figure 2.11). In addition to hornbeam, the wood contains oak, birch, rowan, hawthorn and the ancient wild service tree. Until the 19th century the woodland was used as a resource. Hornbeam was coppiced and used for fuel,

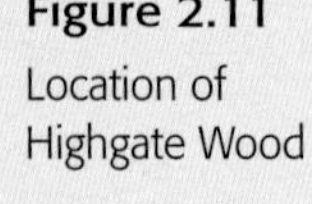

Figure 2.11 Location of Highgate Wood

while oak was used for timber and tanning. Newly coppiced hornbeam areas were enclosed to prevent cattle from grazing on the new shoots. In 1885 the Corporation of London took over the wood and managed it for recreation and conservation. Undergrowth was cleared which allowed public access; trampling followed and prevented plant regeneration. Leaves were burnt and the lower branches of trees were cleared. As a consequence of these actions the wood became an urban park – a closed tree canopy with little understorey. The traditional show of colour in the spring was lost and there were fewer bluebells and wood anemones.

In 1967 the cutting back of undergrowth, the removal of dead wood and the burning of leaves ceased. Instead, there was limited planting of native flowers such as meadowsweet and herb robert. Rhododendrons and non-native species were replaced by holly, hawthorn, elder and, in wetter areas, willow and guelder rose. In 1969 it was decided to diversify the woodland by planting Douglas fir, western hemlock, Norway spruce, Corsican pine, red oak, Turkey oak and Norway maple. In addition, some areas were fenced and planted with beech, while others were planted with oak, hornbeam and hazel. The aim, it seemed, was to turn the woodland into an arboretum containing a variety of trees.

By 1977 a report questioned this policy. It suggested that beech was better suited to lighter, drier soils and that its dense canopy shaded out plants beneath it. Conifers suffered from atmospheric pollution, gave little shelter to birds, and did not like the clay soil. Moreover, fencing off large areas had encouraged heavy trampling in other parts of the wood. The report recommended planting native species such as oak, holly, hornbeam, cherry and rowan. It suggested fencing off smaller areas and growing holly and hawthorn near the woodland edge to screen the wood from the road.

Some beech and pine have since been replaced by oak and hornbeam. Today the aim is to create different-aged stands by thinning out old trees which have become too tall and spindly (particularly a problem now that the hornbeams are no longer coppiced) and fencing off other cleared areas to allow regeneration to take place. In this way a variety of habitats will be created; fungi and invertebrates will thrive on dead wood; butterflies will live in the open spaces; and the mature trees will provide homes for nesting birds.

Activity

1 From the case study of Highgate Wood, summarise the main ways in which humans have **a** reduced, **b** increased species diversity over time.

2 With reference to Figure 2.11:
a calculate the area of the wood and suggest how this might limit species diversity
b identify the land uses which surround the wood – in what ways might these uses influence the ecosystem within the wood?

Soils and soil profiles

All soils are composed of varying amounts of organic matter, mineral particles, water and gas (CO_2). Cross-sections through soils are known as **soil profiles** and these are divided into a number of layers called **horizons**. Figure 2.12 is a generalised example of a soil profile, but not all soils have so many layers. The main factors influencing soil profiles are climate, parent material or rock type, time, relief, vegetation, and animal and human activity.

Climate

Warm temperatures and high precipitation increase weathering processes, whereas cold, dry conditions retard these activities.

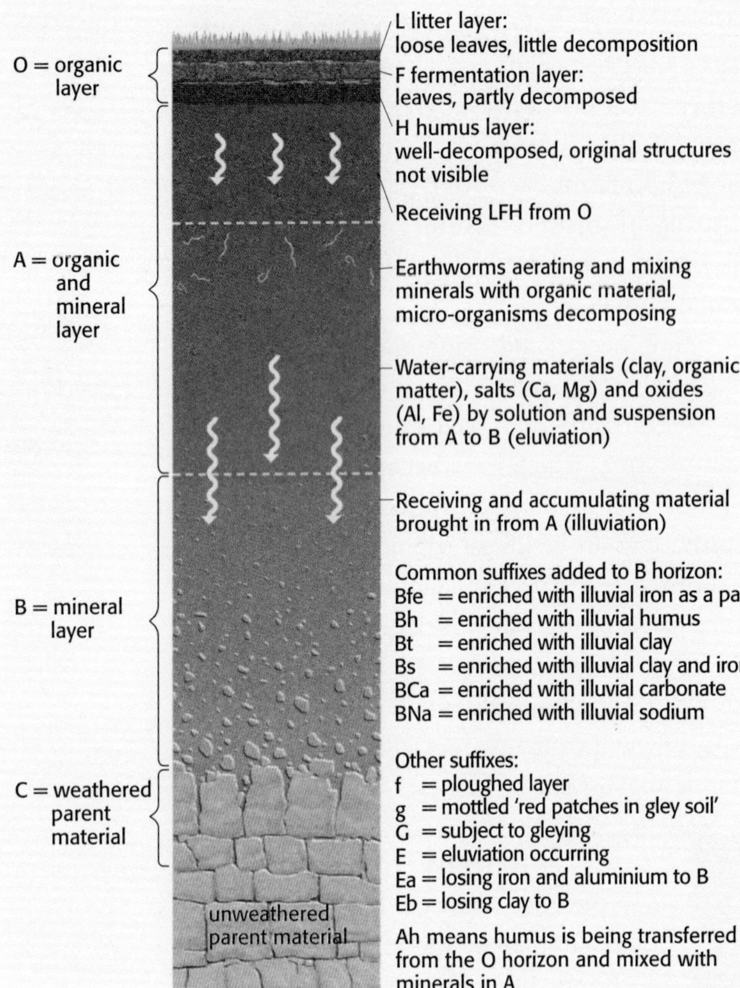

Figure 2.12 Generalised soil profile

Consequently, soils in tropical rainforests are very deep, whereas those in the tundra are shallow. High temperatures increase biological activity, a process that is well demonstrated by the rapid decomposition of organic matter in tropical rainforests. In contrast, decomposition is slowed up under cool conditions. In areas where precipitation is greater than evapotranspiration, the process of **podsolisation** occurs through the removal, or leaching, of nutrients down the profile. Where evaporation exceeds precipitation, the process of **salinisation** leads to the deposition of salts on the surface of the soil. Climate also influences the nature of the vegetation, which in turn determines the type and amount of humus in the soil.

Once a soil has developed sufficiently to be in equilibrium with its climatic conditions it is said to be mature. Soil types that closely match the distribution of the world's major climatic zones are called **zonal** soils. Examples of zonal soils studied in this chapter are **podsols** and **brown earths**. Podsols coincide with cold temperate climates and commonly support coniferous forests. Brown earths are associated with cool temperate climates and deciduous forest cover.

Podsols

In Britain podsols are found in the cooler, wetter upland areas of the north. Figure 2.13 shows a typical podsol soil profile.

Podsols are easily recognised by a light ashen layer a short distance below the surface and distinct darker horizons below. Acidic conditions are produced because precipitation exceeds evaporation so that bases are leached down the profile. The boundaries between the horizons are very distinct because the acidic conditions limit earthworm activity which would normally mix the soil.

The ashen appearance of the Ea horizon results from the fact that just about everything is lost from this layer. Soluble bases such as calcium and magnesium, clay and organic matter are removed by **eluviation** and re-deposited, or **illuviated**, in the B horizon. Humic acids, acting as **chelating agents**, attack the clays to release iron and aluminium which are carried down the profile and redeposited. Iron and aluminium sesquioxides (hydrated oxides and hydroxides) also become soluble in the very acid conditions and are also carried down the profile by podsolisation. The Ea horizon is structureless because nearly all the 'glues' that normally bind the peds together have moved down the profile and, in addition, the high acidity slows down those bacteria that usually secrete organic gums.

Podsols also occur where coniferous or heathland vegetation produces a type of humus called **mor** which decomposes to release humic acids and few bases. Alternatively, they may be found where the soil is freely or excessively drained, as on relatively

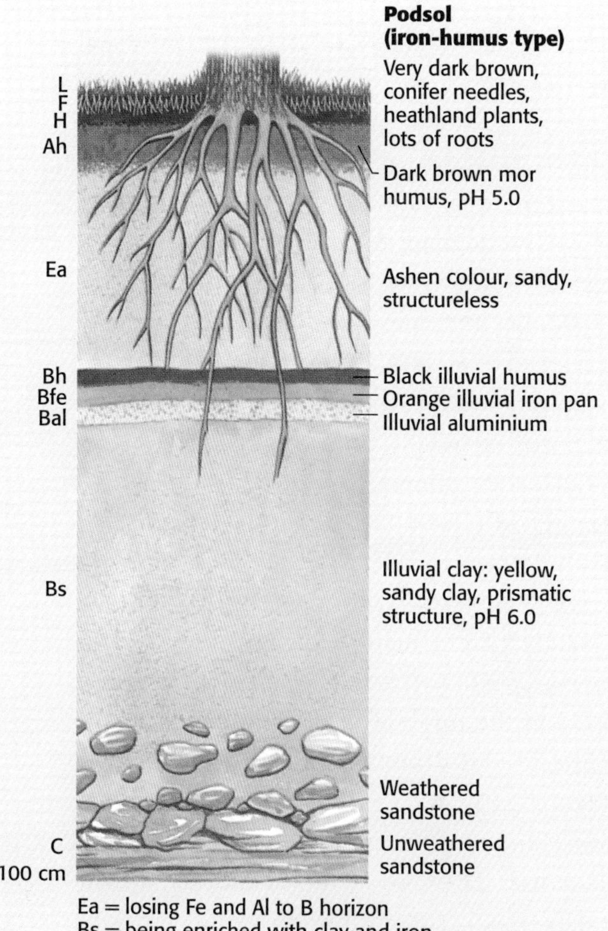

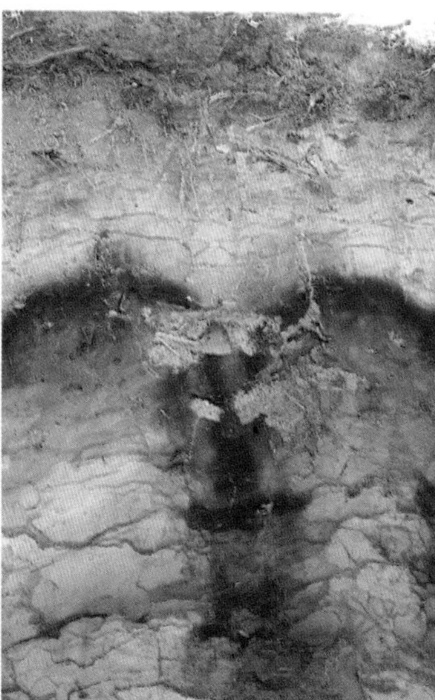

Figure 2.13
A typical podsol soil profile

steep slopes, where bases are readily carried downhill. They can also occur where the underlying rock type weathers to produce infertile soil with few bases, for example granite and sandstone.

Podsols are naturally infertile, but they can be improved by adding fertiliser or lime and by deep ploughing to break up the iron pan. Their low nutrient status has resulted in their use for coniferous plantations, and some heathland areas with podsol soils have been given over to recreation or military training.

Brown earths

The more temperate climate of lowland Britain was originally covered in deciduous woodland which produced brown earth soils. Figure 2.14 shows a typical brown earth

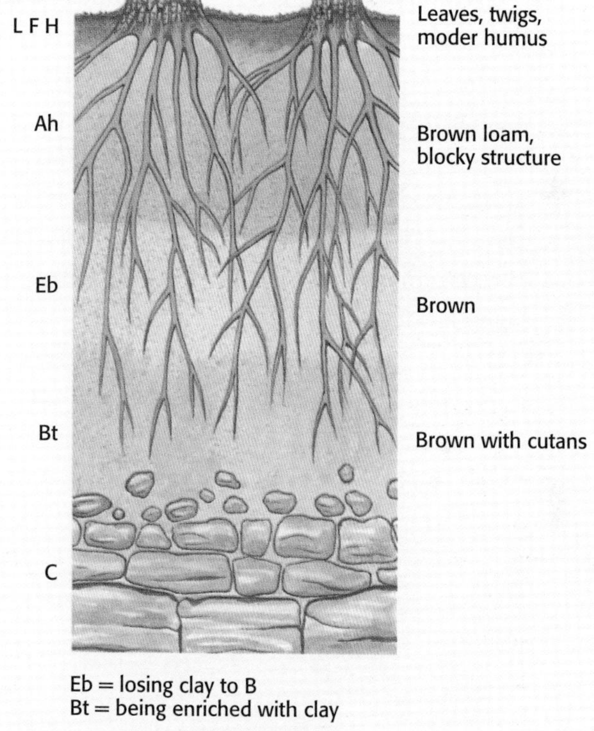

Figure 2.14
A typical brown earth under deciduous forest

profile. The soil horizons are less distinct than those in a podsol because:

- the environment is less acidic, which encourages more mixing activity by earthworms
- grass and tree roots recycle nutrients, thus preventing them from being carried down the profile
- the humus does not produce the humic acids that encourage podsolisation
- precipitation is lower and evaporation higher, which together help to reduce the leaching of nutrients down the profile.

The slightly acidic environment in the forest encourages clays to be removed and carried in suspension from the A horizon to the B horizon in a process called **lessivage**. The clay is often redeposited as a skin, or cutan, lining the walls of pores and old root channels. The humus formed under deciduous forest is called **moder**.

Brown earths often produce quite fertile soils because of their organic and clay content. They are often slightly acidic, a situation which can be improved by liming. With more intense leaching they can grade into podsolic brown earths.

Parent material

Parent material influences soils in a variety of ways. Granite tends to weather slowly, producing a shallow profile. Sandstones often weather to produce red-coloured soils, whereas those developed over chalk are alkaline and often pale in colour. Granites and sandstones are associated with generally infertile and acidic soils because their minerals, predominantly quartz, weather to release few nutrients. In contrast, clay weathers to release relatively fertile clay humus complexes.

Sandy parent materials produce soils that have a coarse texture. The large pore spaces between the mineral particles allow water to infiltrate and drain rapidly through the soil (Figure 2.15). As a result, in drought conditions, sandy soils are poor at holding water for plant use. They also dry out quickly, which makes them susceptible to wind erosion. However, in spring they warm up quickly, allowing plant growth to start early. Rapid

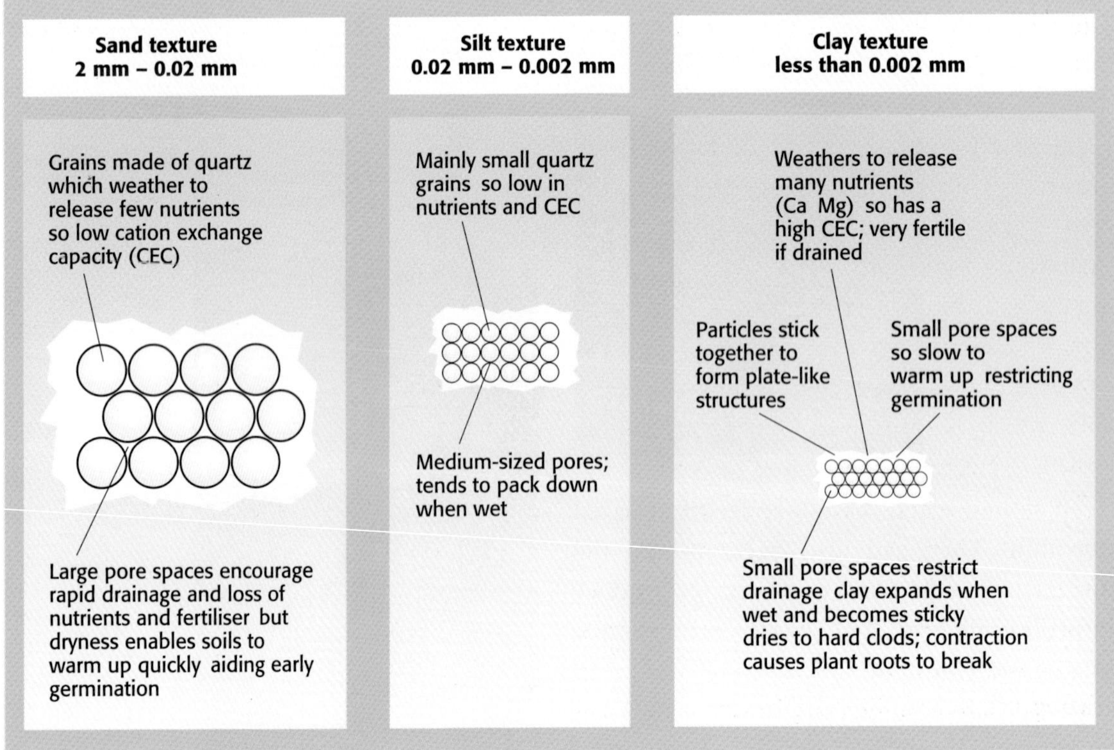

Figure 2.15 Features of sand, silt and clay soils

drainage also means that any fertilisers, unless they are taken up quickly by plants, are at risk from being lost by leaching down the soil.

By contrast, clay soils are composed of very small particles. The tiny pore spaces between the particles prevent water from entering the soil quickly, but once infiltration takes place, surface tension retains the water for some time. Consequently, prolonged rainfall causes clay soils to become waterlogged, which prevents plant roots from breathing and micro-organisms from decomposing organic matter. In spring, therefore, clay soils can be wet and cold, which delays germination. Waterlogging is further encouraged because the individual clay particles stick together to form larger **platy structures** which impede drainage. However, if clay is drained it often produces a very fertile soil because the particles weather to release lots of plant nutrients. In summer, clay soils may dry out to form hard clods, often causing finer plant roots to break.

Intrazonal soils

Within the main soil zones, local factors may override climatic influences to create soils of a different or **intrazonal** character. Examples include rendzinas developed on chalk and limestone, and gley soils in waterlogged areas.

A typical **rendzina** profile consists of a dark-brown organic layer directly overlying weathered limestone (Figure 2.16). The profile is shallow for two key reasons. First, the weathering of limestone and chalk is chiefly by solution, which leaves few insolubles to build up as a mineral layer. Secondly, chalk is highly permeable, which has the effect of limiting grass growth to create only a thin humus horizon.

The Ah horizon is rich in bases because weathering releases calcium from the C horizon, and the grass litter breaks down to form a well-decomposed, alkaline **mull** humus. In the past rendzinas were popular for sheep grazing, but today ploughing has brought much of this land under cultivation.

Gley soils have a distinctive blue colour, and occasionally come out in red blotches! Their colouring is the result of a process called gleying. Waterlogging produces anaerobic conditions which cause bacteria to turn to iron compounds for their supplies. In so doing they convert, or reduce, red ferrous iron compounds into their soluble, ferric state, turning the soil blue. However, when waterlogging is reduced, and the larger pore spaces crack and root channels again receive air, the iron is oxidised back

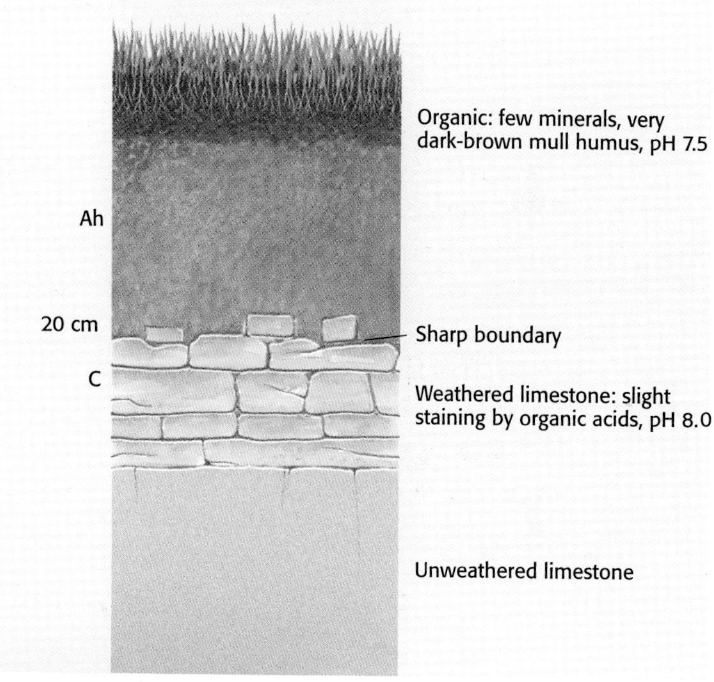

Figure 2.16
A typical rendzina soil profile

to its red ferrous state, giving the soil a mottled appearance.

Groundwater gleys can form when normally permeable soils such as alluvium on floodplains experience a period of heavy rainfall so that the water-table rises (Figure 2.17). Surface-water gleying can also occur above impermeable parent materials such as clays. Although gleys present farmers with problems, they are often very fertile if they can be drained or deep-ploughed.

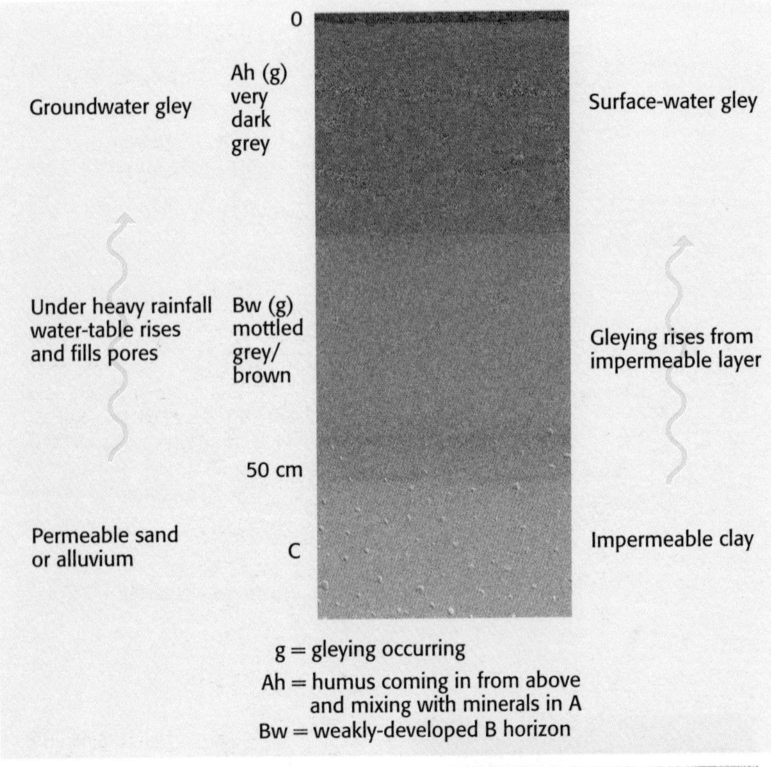

Figure 2.17
A gley soil profile

Time

Soils take time to develop, and profiles gradually become deeper and horizons more distinct. Not all old soils are deep, however. For example, desert soils have shallow, immature profiles because weathering processes are slow. Young soils that have not had the time, or the right conditions, to form a deep profile with a B horizon are called **azonal** soils. Typical examples are those found on newly-formed sand dunes or on recently-deposited alluvium.

Relief

With increasing altitude, high rainfall encourages leaching and low temperatures inhibit the decomposition of organic matter. These conditions may lead to the formation of **peat**. In the northern hemisphere, south-west-facing slopes experience reduced leaching because they are often warmer and drier than those that face towards the north-east. Slope angle controls the movement of water through the soil profile and may lead to the formation of a **catena** or soil association. In this situation well-drained podsols are likely to develop on the steeper upper parts of slopes, whereas gleys may be found at the base if the land is waterlogged (Figure 2.18).

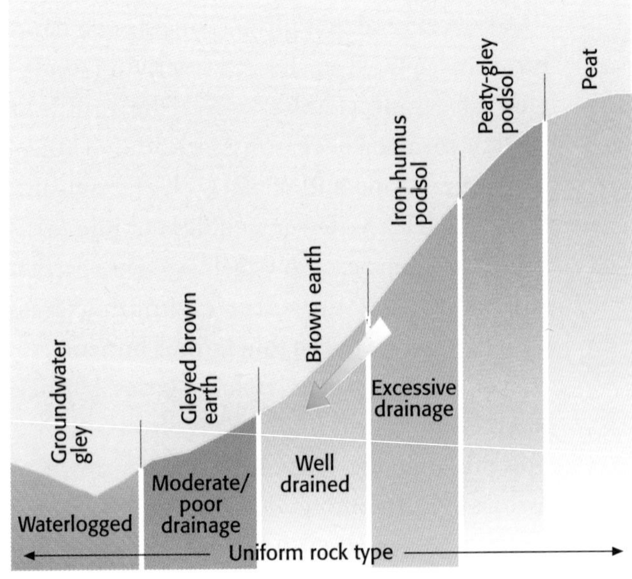

Figure 2.18
A typical catena sequence

Vegetation

Plants influence the volume and nature of soil humus. Tundra vegetation produces less humus than deciduous forests. Coniferous forests produce mor humus, deciduous forests are associated with moder, and grassland produces a deep, black, well-decomposed mull humus. Plant roots also help physically to break up the parent material.

Animals

Bacteria, fungi, actinomycetes and earthworms all physically and chemically break down litter and faecal material to produce humus. Figure 2.19 shows how earthworms, insects and burrowing animals all help to aerate and mix the soil. Soil aeration is important because plant roots give off carbon dioxide, which, if it builds up in the soil, restricts growth. Normally this gas gradually diffuses back into the atmosphere, but in warm weather the greater rates of plant growth and respiration can lead to an excessive accumulation which, in fine-textured soils, will reduce root growth and microbiological activity. Animals can also trample and compact the ground, destroying soil structures in the process.

Figure 2.19

Processes creating the regolith

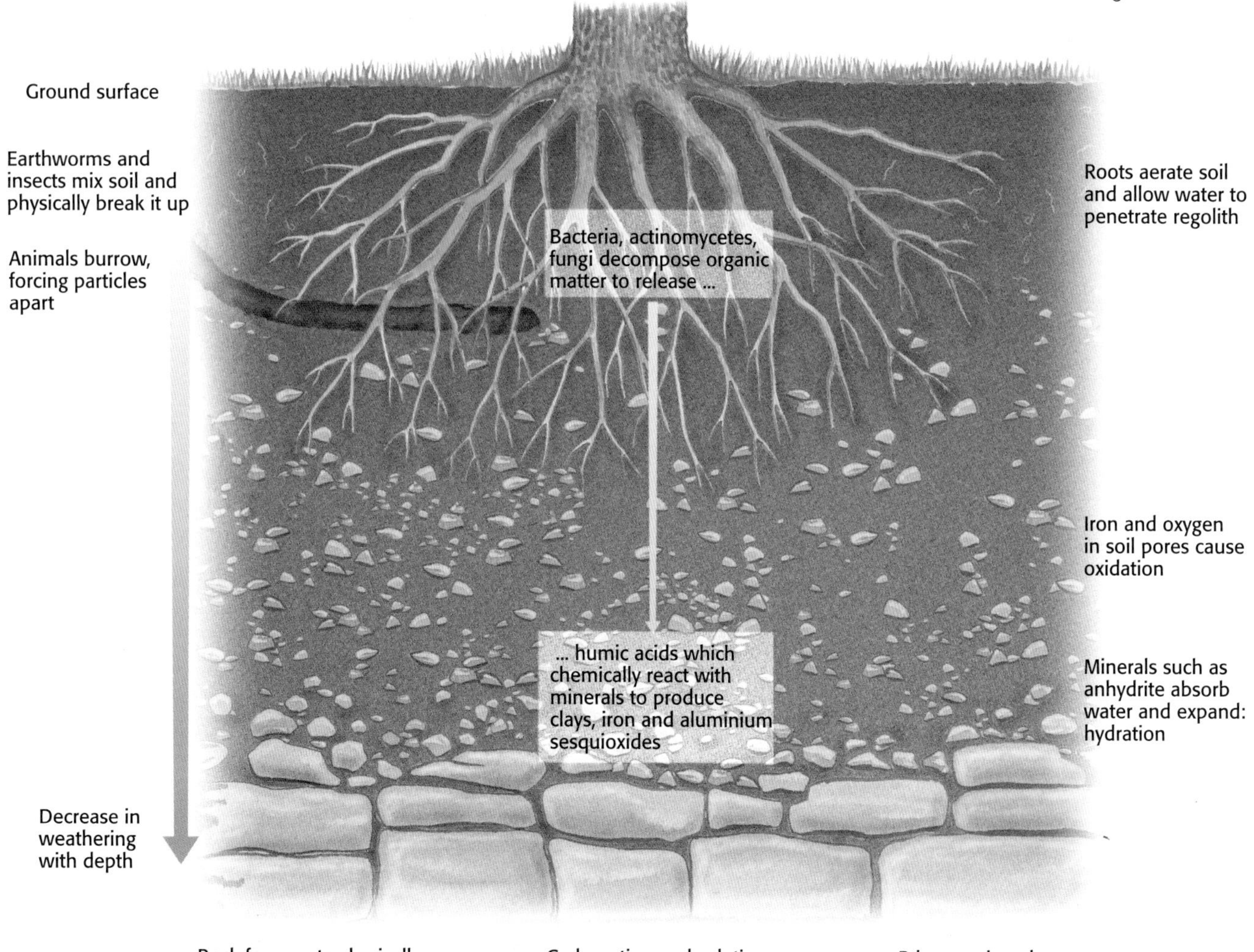

Activity

1 With the help of Figure 2.12, briefly describe the differences between the O, A, B and C horizons.

2 Produce a diagram showing the interactions between the main factors influencing a soil profile.

3 In what ways would a cold climate with low rainfall influence the weathering and biological processes shown in Figure 2.19?

4 Suggest why:
a bowling greens are (i) underlain with sandy soils and (ii) regular fertilising and watering is necessary
b cricket wickets are (i) underlain by clay while the rest of the field is sand and (ii) the covers need to be put on the wicket quickly when it rains.

5 How would you classify a soil recently formed on a newly-exposed lava flow?

6 Suggest why some soil profiles are shallow.

7 Using appropriate terms and referring to the processes you have studied, explain the features of the rendzina shown in Figure 2.16 and the gley soil in Figure 2.17.

Human activity and soils

All soils can be modified by human activity, especially by ploughing, draining and irrigation. Farm machinery may compress and damage soil structures, especially when they are wet. All peds lose a certain amount of stability when they are wet, but some soils can recover with their structures intact, whereas others deform so that the pore spaces between the peds are lost. At worst, serious soil erosion can result from the careless use of soil or from a failure to employ sensible soil management practices. The risk of soil erosion may be reduced by **contour ploughing**, terracing, **strip cultivation**, and the planting of **cover crops** and shelter belts.

Ploughing and harrowing break up compacted surfaces and help to create **crumb structures** which, while they improve soil drainage and are easy to cultivate, increase the risk of the soil being blown or washed away. Ploughing can also break up an iron pan further down the profile that would otherwise interrupt the downward movement of water. However, repeated ploughing at the same depth can create a plough pan – a hard layer of smeared soil which encourages waterlogging and prevents root penetration. Ploughing can also bury humus too deep for crops to use. In east Devon, for example (Figure 2.20), centuries of pastoral and arable farming have so modified the profiles of podsols and brown earths that litter has been removed and ploughed layers created. High acidity has been offset by liming using marl, ground-up limestone and calcified seaweed. Soil erosion has also occurred on some slopes. An early solution was to cart the soil by pack-horse from the base where it had accumulated, back to the top of the hill again! More recently, the most infertile soils have been planted with softwoods.

Light, sandy soils benefit from irrigation, but if irrigation occurs without drainage in hot climates it can cause human-induced, or secondary, salinisation, as in parts of west Africa where rice is now the chief staple crop. Rice has gained in popularity over millet and sorghum because it is tastier and quicker to cook. In Senegal, the rice-growing areas were once stretches of tidal land adjacent to the Senegal River. They have now been sealed with a barrier and the water needed to flood the fields for the rice crop is diverted from the river. The difficulty is that the river water first readily absorbs the salt from the originally saline soil, and then evaporates, leaving behind hard salt crusts. Further east, in southern Mali, irrigation of paddy fields alongside the Niger River has occurred without proper drainage and has

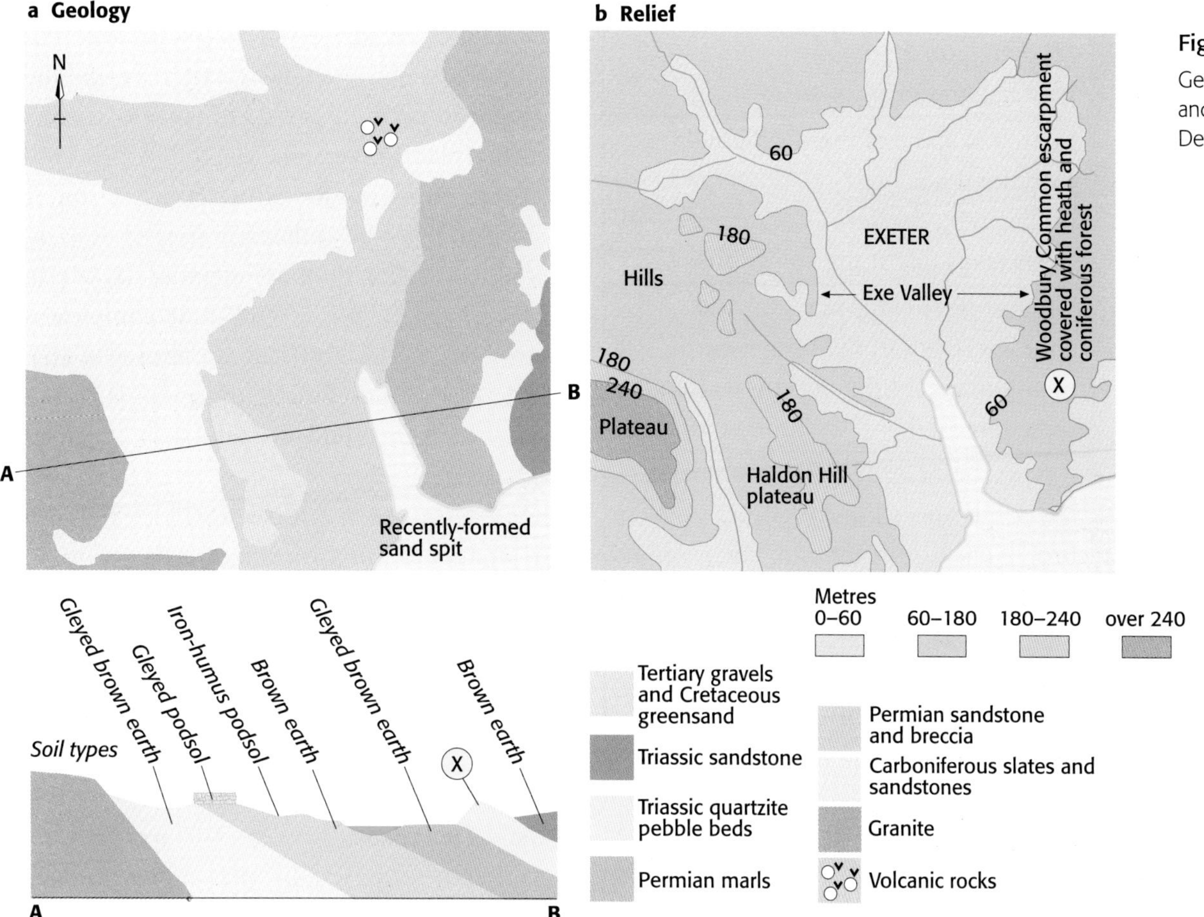

Figure 2.20
Geology, relief and soils of east Devon

caused the water-table to rise 17 m to within 3 m of the surface. Within this 3 m zone, salinisation has resulted in highly saline soils.

Draining waterlogged soils removes excess hydrogen ions from clay and humus complexes so that basic cations such as calcium can become attached. However, if drains are laid at too great a depth, excessive water loss will result in nutrients being lost. Sometimes drainage is inappropriate. For example, draining highly acidic coastal soils in Guangdong Province of southern China has resulted in extreme sulphate acidity and soils with a pH value of 3.5. As a consequence, crops grown on these soils suffer from iron and aluminium toxicity, and a deficiency in phosphorus. Draining peat soils creates particular difficulties in that the soil dries, shrinks and is then easily blown away.

Poor management practices such as deforestation, overgrazing, intensification of agriculture and **monoculture** can all result in the loss of topsoil through encouraging wind and water erosion, as has occurred in parts of northern Nigeria. In the Hadejia Nguro floodplain, near Kano, local people have acquired a taste for wheat, rather than the less nutritious millet and sorghum. Land has been cleared to grow wheat but the soils here are sandy, rich in iron and salt, but lacking the organic matter needed to support this nutrient-demanding crop. Consequently, once the soil has been cultivated, nutrients are lost and cannot be replaced with fertiliser because it is too expensive. Moreover, without humus the soil loses its structure and is easily blown away. One solution would be crop rotation, but in less economically developed countries the increasing pressure to grow cash crops often results in the reduction, or even elimination, of the fallow period.

Activity

Study Figure 2.20, which shows the geology and relief of east Devon.

1 In area X some of the deciduous woodland has been cut down and replaced by coniferous plantations. In what ways might the soil change?

2 Suggest *three* ways in which the characteristics of the brown earth might change if the deciduous trees were removed and the land cultivated.

3 Catenas frequently develop on the Carboniferous slates. Well-drained brown earth soils form on steep valley sides grading into gleyed brown earths and eventually gleys on the valley floor. Suggest *two* ways in which human activity might modify such a catena.

4 Suggest *two* ways in which ploughing might change the podsols developed on the Haldon Hill plateau.

5 Produce a concept map using the following terms as labels to show the ways in which ploughing might change a soil profile:
- erosion
- iron pan
- waterlogging
- weathering
- infiltration
- soil structure
- compression
- roots
- ploughing.

6 What techniques might be used to control topsoil losses on slopes?

Ecosystems over time

The ways in which ecosystems change over time can be illustrated by studying patterns of colonisation, competition and dominance occurring within a plant succession. The following examples are illustrations of a **xerosere** and a **halosere**. 'Xerosere' is the term used to describe a plant succession developing under dry conditions. An example is a sand dune complex or **psammosere**. The term 'halosere' is used to refer to successions developing under saline conditions such as are found on a saltmarsh.

The psammosere succession

The first species in this **primary succession** are often sea sandwort and sea rocket. They appear on the strand-line at the back of the foreshore where they obtain their nutrients from seaweed decomposing on the strand-line (Figure 2.21). The number of different species in this **pioneer community** is small because conditions are harsh. The plants have to survive periodic covering by saltwater, shifting sands and exposure to high winds. The beach sand is high in calcium carbonate from shell fragments and in sodium chloride from sea spray. To adapt to this **xerophytic** environment, many plants store water in their leaves or stems (succulents). Most plants are also short-lived and have rapid germination rates.

The pioneer species, which are eventually outcompeted, prepare the ground for the next community by providing organic matter and shelter. In this way the vegetation is helping to

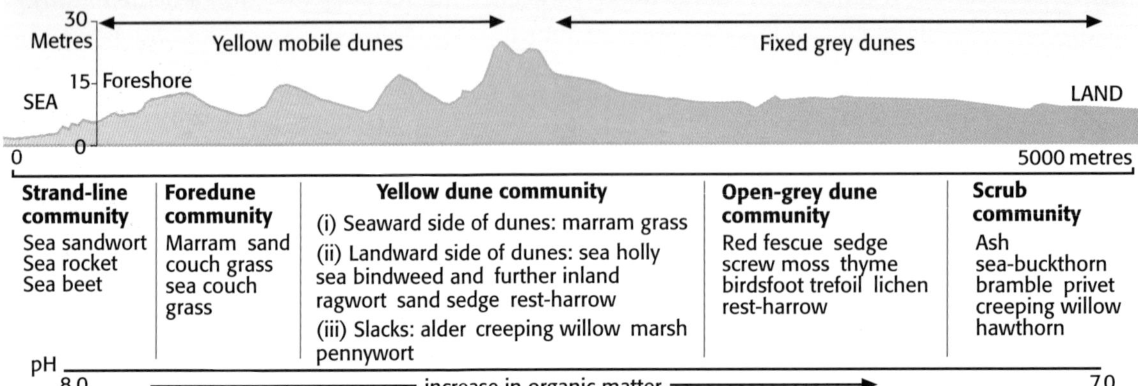

Figure 2.21 Cross-section through a psammosere: Braunton Burrows, north Devon

bring about an **autogenic succession**. The plants trap sand blown across the foreshore, encouraging mounds to form. The mounds eventually join up to form embryo dunes. On these dunes the next community becomes established. Plants with long roots, such as sea couch grass and marram grass, trap and stabilise the sand and for these reasons they are known as major sand dune builders. Like the strand-line community they have developed a number of mechanisms for surviving drought (Figure 2.22). When these plants die they add organic matter to the soil which provides nutrients for the next community and also acts as a sponge to trap moisture. They also have root nodules or rhizomes which support bacteria that are able to fix atmospheric nitrogen in the soil. Such **legumes** are valuable in raising soil fertility.

With the passage of time, new embryo dunes form in front of existing dune ridges and eventually deprive the latter of fresh supplies of sand. Between the dune ridges damper areas, or **slacks**, develop which contain water-loving plants such as willow.

As the vegetation continues to develop on the dune, the diversity of species increases. Grasses such as marram are replaced by a more complete cover of mosses and lichen. The pH declines because as vegetation accumulates and decomposes, it produces organic acids. The pH also declines, because rainwater leaches minerals and organic matter down through the soil. Eventually scrub species such as bramble and blackthorn replace the lichen and moss community on the old grey dunes. These plants are themselves eventually replaced by trees; the vegetation begins to form distinct layers and food webs become more complex. When the trees become established, a slight decline in diversity often occurs because some groundcover plants are shaded out.

The sequence of replacement thus described is called a **plant succession** or **sere**. Each group of plants within the succession is called a **seral community**. Eventually a stable situation is reached producing a **climatic climax community**.

Climax communities once formed can experience short-term changes. For example, when

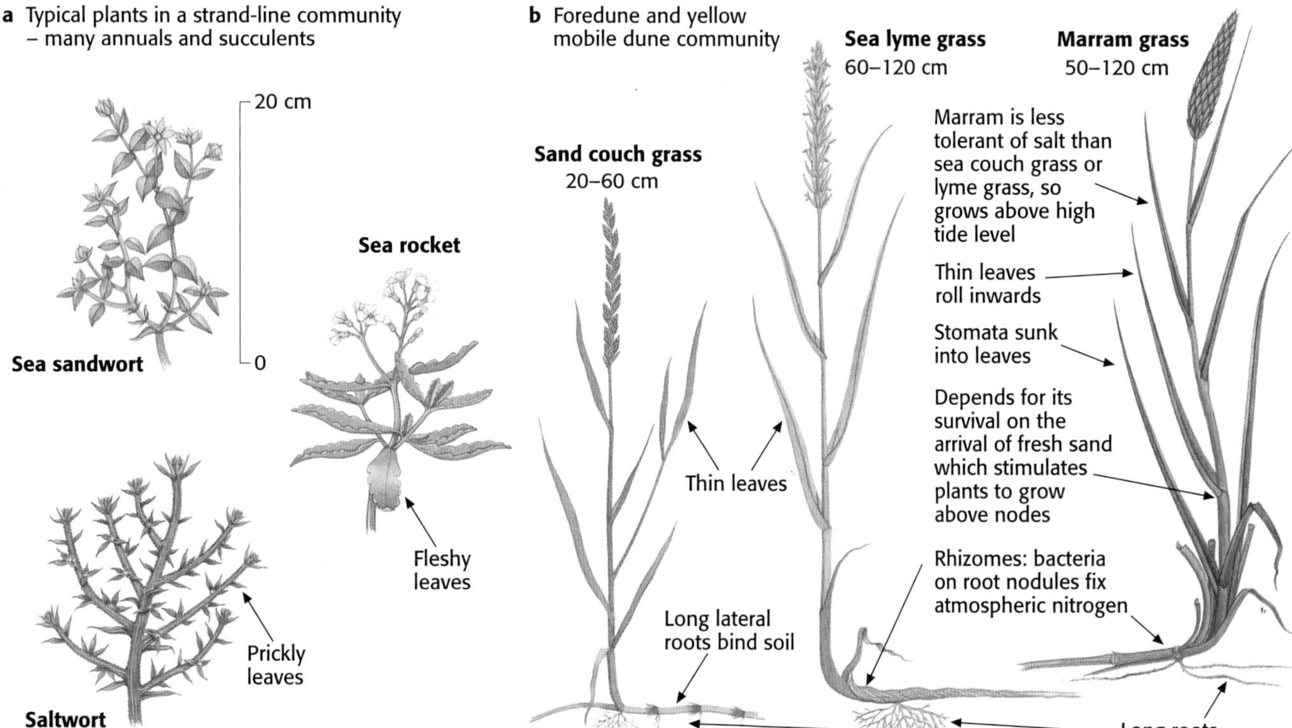

Figure 2.22
Typical plants in a psammosere

Activity

1 Define the following terms:
a pioneer community
b plant succession
c autogenic succession
d climax community.

2 With the help of Figure 2.21, suggest how plants are adapted to drought in the yellow mobile dune community.

3 With reference to Figures 2.21 and 2.22:
a suggest why marram is found on the mobile dunes, but not on the old grey dunes
b give *two* reasons why the soil pH declines inland
c suggest why the legume, birdsfoot trefoil, is valuable in the sequence
d give *two* reasons why humus is valuable in a psammosere.

an old tree dies in a wood it allows light to reach the forest floor where herbs and grasses can then develop. These plants are eventually shaded out by new tree seedlings. Climatic change can bring about longer-term changes in climax vegetation. Outside influences, such as volcanic eruptions, grazing animals or human interference can also bring about allogenic successions

Human modifications to sand dune ecosystems

Human activities can change psammoseres in a variety of ways. For example, marram is often planted on sand dunes as a means of stabilisation (Figure 2.23).

Older dunes are sometimes planted with conifers or upgraded for pasture. Vegetation cover may be reduced through grazing (Figure 2.24) and by visitor pressure, particularly trampling, and sand may be removed for the construction industry.

Figure 2.23
Sand dunes stabilised by marram grass and fencing

Figure 2.24
Sheep grazing on already worn sand dune vegetation cover, in Lincolnshire

Case Study: Braunton Burrows, north Devon

Human impact on a psammosere is well illustrated by the large sand dune complex of Braunton Burrows in north Devon (see Figure 2.21). In plan view, a series of large sand dune ridges, separated by intervening slacks, runs from north to south, as shown in Figure 2.25.

Until 1954 the dunes were heavily grazed by rabbits, which reduced the grass and sedge cover, exposing the underlying soil to erosion. Once the vegetation cover was lost the wind quickly removed the sand to form small hollows or **blow-outs**. When the rabbit population was reduced by myxomatosis the scrub community invaded. The dunes are privately owned and in the past some scrub has been cleared to create pasture for sheep. These animals maintain the grass sward and prevent scrub from re-invading. The open ground is a popular habitat for birds such as the wheatear and stonechat. Some scrub is maintained and this supports a community of reptiles, skylarks and warblers.

During the Second World War the sand dunes were used for army training, and tanks damaged the dunes. The area is still closed for ten days a year for army training. The area has become popular for recreation, particularly since improvements were made to the A361, the North Devon Link Road. Heavy visitor pressure has led to the formation of blow-outs, and this has been countered by planting the dunes with marram grass. Four-wheel drive vehicles occasionally drive illegally through the dunes onto the beach, adding to management difficulties.

Humans have been responsible for introducing new plant species into the sequence, such as sea-buckthorn. This plant was originally planted to stabilise the northern end of the dunes. It has since spread over the dunes, smothering other species.

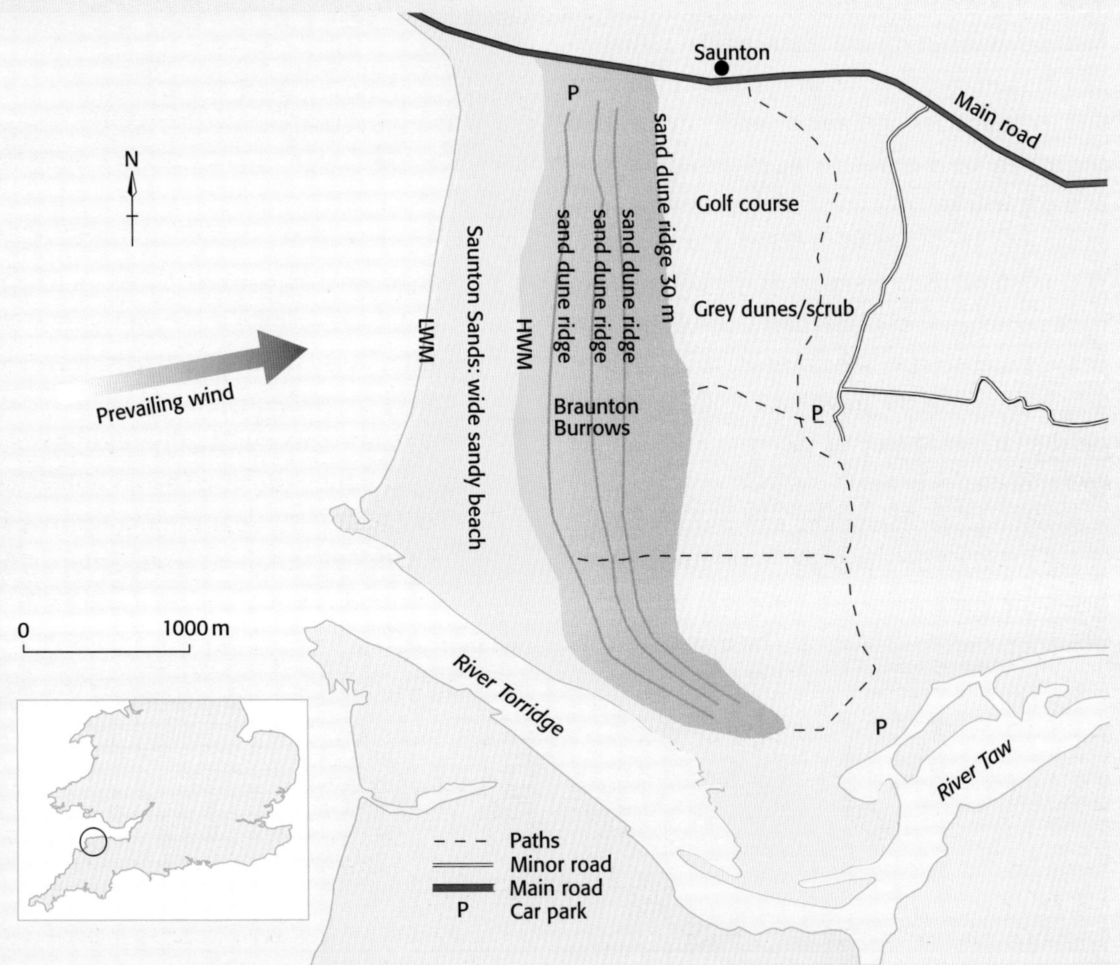

Figure 2.25 Braunton Burrows: location and main features

Activity

1	Why is the foredune plant community particularly susceptible to damage by vehicles?
2	On Figure 2.25, locate *two* areas where you think visitors might cause the most damage to the dunes, and suggest how the damage might be reduced.
3	Identify *two* current uses of the old grey dunes.
4	Why is it important to maintain some areas of scrub?
5	Burning is a cheaper method of clearing scrub than cutting. Can you suggest any drawbacks of this method?
6	Suggest why the slacks should not be allowed to dry out.

The saltmarsh succession

Saltmarsh forms on mudflats in tidal estuaries and in shallow coastal waters, often behind spits and bars. Species type and diversity depend on the nature of the underlying material (known as the **substrate**), the angle of slope, waves, tidal range and inputs of fresh water. For example, saltmarsh on the west coast of the UK tends to have more grass species than that on the east coast because the substrate is more sandy. Stages of saltmarsh growth are well illustrated on the landward side of the sand and shingle spit at Blakeney in north Norfolk.

Mud and fine silt brought in by incoming tides is deposited on the mudflats. At the lowest level, below the true saltmarsh, eel-grass (a marine plant) becomes established. The first terrestrial species to appear is annual glasswort, also known as marsh samphire, a succulent that can withstand twice-daily tidal saltwater inundation and shifting muds (Figure 2.26). Its roots help to stabilise the mud, while seaweed entwined around its stems helps to entrap further sediment. This pioneer species prepares the ground for the next community to appear. With increased sedimentation, low marsh is replaced by high marsh communities. Each community in the sequence improves conditions for the next one by trapping sediment. This sequence raises the level of the marsh above the tides and also allows rainwater to leach salt from the developing soil. Plant communities help to dry out the marsh through transpiration, and they also

Figure 2.26
Annual glasswort – a pioneer in a saltmarsh succession

contribute organic matter which raises nutrient levels. The full succession is shown in Figure 2.27.

This linear vegetation sequence is modified where creeks cross the marsh and where small enclosed saline basins called **saltpans** form. Sea purslane is common on raised banks bordering the creeks because this environment provides the plant with well-drained, aerated, nutrient-rich soil. Saltpans are often occupied by low marsh plants such as glasswort and sea aster.

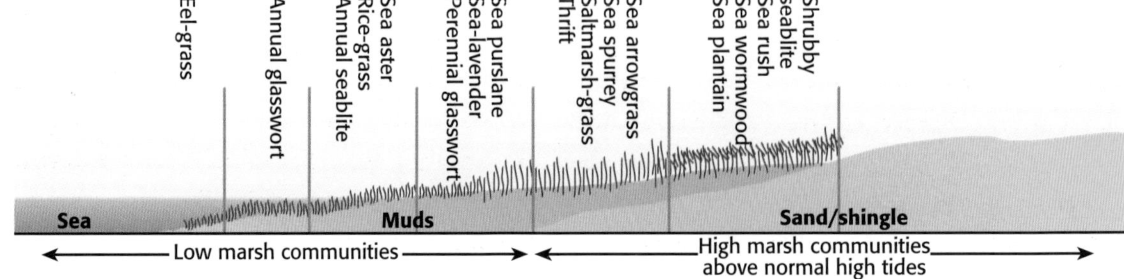

Figure 2.27
Typical saltmarsh communities on the north Norfolk coast

Human impacts on saltmarsh ecosystems

Upper saltmarshes have been lightly grazed by cattle for centuries. This practice has diversified plant communities and increased the redshank bird population which appears to thrive on lightly-grazed marsh.

However, where saltmarshes have been upgraded for improved pasture, or reclaimed for cultivation, plant communities and associated invertebrates such as cockles and crustaceans have been destroyed. Brent geese which graze on eel-grass, together with oystercatchers and plovers that feed on the mudflats, have also lost their habitats. Even where clearance has not been complete, losses have occurred because drainage has altered water-tables. Moreover, cultivation of land around saltmarshes has introduced nitrates, causing eutrophication.

More recently, the recognition of saltmarshes as efficient forms of natural sea defence has led to a reassessment of their worth. As a consequence, saltmarshes have been successfully re-established in localities in Essex, and further schemes are proposed for north Norfolk. Such proposals have, however, met with opposition because some embanked marshes have since evolved into brackish and freshwater nature reserves which would be lost if saltmarshes were re-established.

Industry as well as agriculture has modified saltmarshes. For example, the extraction of marl clays for brick-making from the Meadow estuary in the late 19th century destroyed saltmarsh there. More recently, oil refineries and power stations have been built on reclaimed marsh in several estuaries, and around the Severn estuary heavy metals carried in the atmosphere from smelters have accumulated in marsh sediments and adversely affected saltmarsh plant communities. Offshore dredging and marina construction increases the volume of suspended sediment, and this also interferes with saltmarsh development. In recent years rice-grass, a plant originally introduced by people to Southampton Water, has appeared in many UK saltmarshes. It has successfully competed with other low marsh species, reducing plant diversity. Attempts have been made to remove it by spraying and cutting but recently some natural die-back has occurred, the reasons for which are uncertain.

Activity

1 Name the type of succession shown in Figure 2.27.

2 Give *three* reasons why species diversity increases in the upper marsh.

3 Suggest *two* consequences for the saltmarsh community of **a** heavy grazing and **b** reclamation for agriculture.

4 Glasswort is often gathered for human consumption. Why should this practice be controlled?

Other plant communities

Sometimes events can prevent successions from reaching their climatic climax and a **subclimax** community will develop. For example, an avalanche may sweep down a mountainside destroying trees in its path, or a lightning strike may burn off an area of forest. In both cases the arresting factor is natural, and the effect only temporary. Once the arresting factor has been removed, a **secondary succession** will develop which may eventually change to a climax community.

Successions can also be arrested by human interference. For example, an area of climax tropical rainforest may be cleared and cultivated for a few years and then, as soil exhaustion sets in, abandoned. Again a series of **subsere communities** develops which are eventually replaced by climax rainforest.

Where the arresting factor is more long-lasting in its effect, a permanent **plagioclimax community** develops. Many, though not all, British heathlands fall into this category because they are believed to be the product of human activity – that is, they are **anthropogenic** in origin.

3 Atmospheric systems

KEY THEMES

- ✔ The global Earth–atmosphere energy budget provides the basic framework for studying weather phenomena at the global, regional and local scales.
- ✔ Surpluses and deficits of atmospheric energy between lower and higher latitudes are made good by a range of transfer processes that have a direct influence on the variability of surface weather conditions.
- ✔ Local energy budgets play an important role in influencing local weather conditions, although large-scale influences may override them.
- ✔ The detailed analysis of atmospheric energy budgets enables the influence of human activity on weather and climate to be better understood and the impact of weather and climate on human activity to be more accurately managed, especially at the local scale.

The atmosphere is vital to all of us since without an atmosphere of good quality we could not survive for more than a few minutes. The atmosphere, and the weather systems within it, influence almost all forms of human activity, especially agriculture, communications, water supply and shelter. While many branches of science involve the study of the atmosphere and its processes, the particular contribution of geography is a very practical one. Geographers seek to understand and explain the part played by the atmosphere as a component of the wider environment in which all human activity takes place. In recent years the search for a better level of understanding has become increasingly significant, since it is clear that while the atmosphere influences people, people are now influencing and modifying the atmosphere in a growing variety of ways. Some of these modifications, such as those which cause global warming and damage to the **ozone layer**, are a real threat to our current way of life.

There is a great deal of material readily available to help our understanding of both the weather and its longer-term counterpart, the climate. Newspaper and television presentations, meteorological fax services, specialised radio broadcasts and telephone lines offer a wide range of up-to-date information which can be matched against personal observations and predictions. Most recently, numerous high-quality meteorological sites have been developed on the World Wide Web. Two particularly informative sites are those of The Meteorological (Met.) Office and the Dundee Satellite Receiving Station, whose home pages are shown in Figure 3.1. Both these sites, and others to which they lead, provide a rich supply of interesting and useful data, including satellite images.

The Earth–atmosphere system

The broad structure of the atmosphere is shown in Figure 3.2. The zones are based on the changes in temperature which occur with increasing altitude. The **troposphere**, whose upper limit is the **tropopause**, is the most important layer in terms of the weather, partly because it contains almost all the moisture to be found in the atmosphere. Above the tropopause the stratosphere is the zone where most of the ultraviolet radiation from the Sun is absorbed. What the diagram does not reveal is the atmosphere's most outstanding characteristic – the colossal amount of energy present within it. A single major weather system can contain as much energy as a large city consumes in a year.

An important property of both the Earth and the atmosphere is that on average their temperatures are remarkably constant, showing only minor variations from year to year. Similarly, the Earth's wind systems remain broadly constant in their velocity patterns from year to year, with little sign of either speeding up or slowing down. Together, these two pieces of evidence suggest that over a period of several years the energy received from the Sun must be broadly equivalent to the energy that escapes from the atmosphere into space. The same kind of balance also exists between the Earth's surface and the atmosphere, since again there is no overall change of temperature, either increase or decrease. These balances are the foundation of the energy budgets which exist within the Earth–atmosphere system.

In basic terms, the Sun gives out energy in all directions. A proportion of this energy reaches the outer part of the Earth's atmosphere and then penetrates it to reach the surface. Solar energy travels in the form of radiant energy, or **radiation**, which is a common part of everyday life. For example, except in the case of cable television, both radio and television signals reach us by a stream of radiation transmitted through the atmosphere. While all such radiation streams consist of the same form of energy, they may be distinguished by their wavelength. Wavelength depends on the temperature of the radiating body: the hotter the body the shorter will be the wavelength of its radiation. This relationship is very important in the study of the atmosphere. Since the Sun is very hot (around 6000°C) it emits shortwave radiation which can pass through a clear, cloud-free atmosphere with little or no interruption on its way to the Earth's surface. It is important to note that solar

http://www.sat.dundee.ac.uk/

The Dundee Satellite Receiving Station, Dundee University, UK, maintains an up-to-date archive of images from NOAA and SeaStar polar orbiting satellites. Images from geostationary satellites covering the whole Earth are also available. Registration is **free** and the images are **free**!

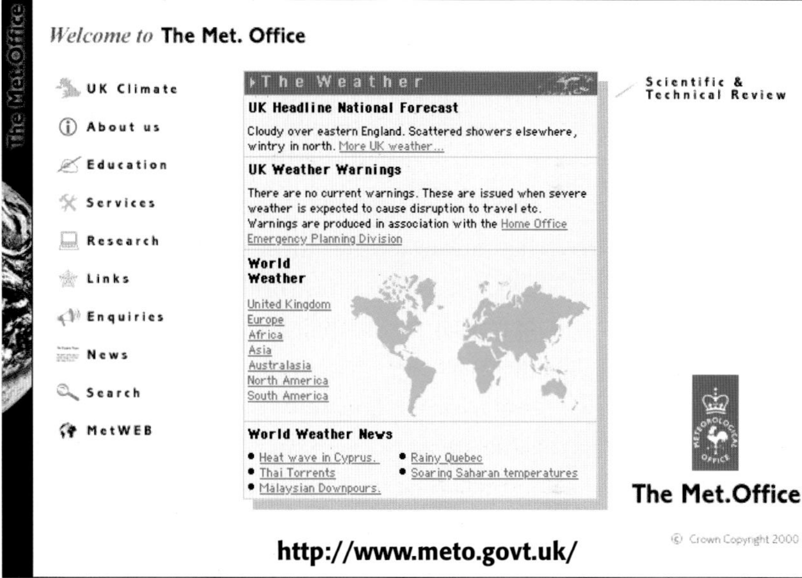

Figure 3.1

Two Internet sites providing information about weather and climate

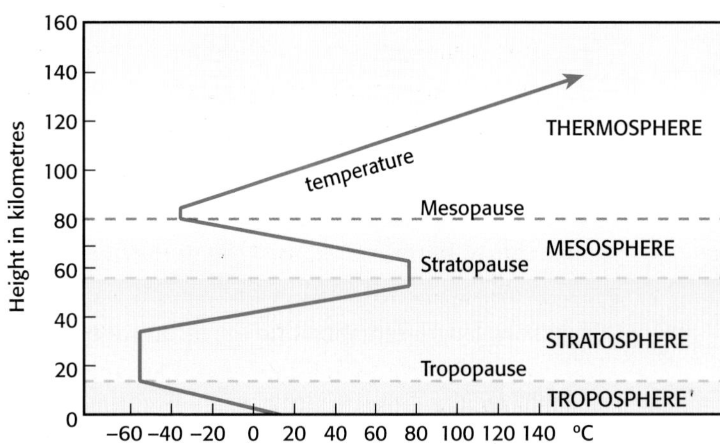

Figure 3.2

The basic structure of the atmosphere

radiation scarcely heats the troposphere and stratosphere as it passes through them.

Solar radiation that reaches the surface of the Earth is absorbed or soaked up by it. Whenever energy is supplied to an object, its temperature is likely to increase, and so the Sun's energy heats whatever surface it reaches, whether land or sea, road or forest. Although solar energy does not heat the atmosphere directly, the warmed surface of the Earth in contact with the air does have a heating effect. The atmosphere, then, is heated from below – another essential fact in understanding many atmospheric phenomena. There are three processes by which the warmed surface heats the atmosphere. They are **radiation**, **convection** and **conduction**.

Radiation and the greenhouse effect

Radiation is the most important warming process. As the surface of the Earth, at an average temperature of 16°C, is a great deal cooler than the Sun, the wavelength of Earth radiation is much longer. Longwave radiation cannot pass as easily through the atmosphere as shortwave radiation. Much of it is absorbed and some is re-radiated back to Earth. Eventually this absorbed energy is returned to space, but not before it has been stored for long enough to raise the temperature of the atmosphere. This process is commonly known as the **greenhouse effect**, since the atmosphere behaves like the glass in a greenhouse in letting the Sun's energy through but not allowing the radiant energy from the objects inside to escape (Figure 3.3). However, the gradual increase in temperature of those objects results in the emission of radiation with a progressively shorter wavelength which will be able to pass through the glass to the outside air. Such a rise in temperature leading to shorter wavelength radiation and the escape of energy is an example of what is known as a **forcing effect**.

Clouds play an important role in regulating the Earth's radiation exchanges, and in reflecting the sun's radiation back into space. The influence of cloud will depend on its type and its height. An example is given in Figure 3.4 of the influence of different cloud types on radiation exchange in the atmosphere.

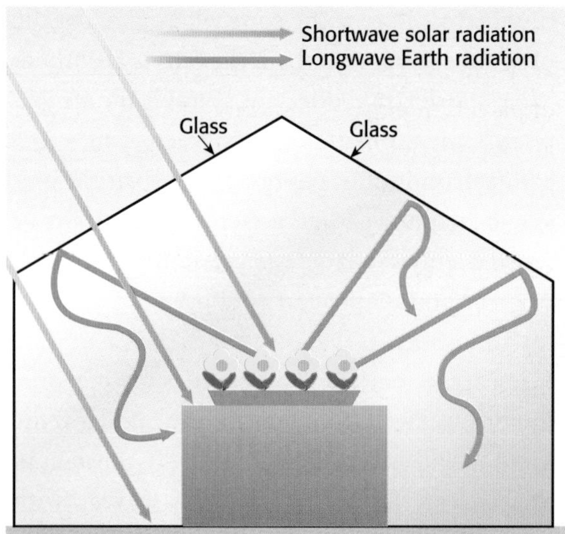

The glass of a greenhouse acts in a manner similar to that of the atmosphere. Like the atmosphere, it is largely transparent to solar radiation, which passes through it to be absorbed by objects inside the greenhouse. As these objects heat up, they give off longwave radiation which cannot pass back out through the glass. This energy is therefore trapped and the temperature within the greenhouse increases.

Figure 3.3
The greenhouse effect

Convection and conduction

The other two processes of convection and conduction are illustrated in Figure 3.5, along with radiation. **Convection** is the vertical movement of a parcel or pocket of air which is at a different temperature from its surroundings. The most common form of convection is the upward movement of a parcel of warm air. Hot-air balloons (see Figure 3.6) work on this principle. As the air within the balloon is heated it becomes less dense and lighter than the surrounding air, enabling it to rise and to lift the balloon with it. In a similar manner, glider pilots search for naturally rising streams of warm air, called thermals, in order to gain altitude quickly. Thermals develop over patches of ground which have absorbed more solar radiation and become warmer than the surrounding land. In turn these warm patches raise the temperature of the air in contact with them, and cause it to rise.

Convection in the atmosphere illustrates a very important principle about the behaviour of parcels of air. Any portion of the atmosphere at a different temperature (or level of **humidity**) from the air around it will tend to remain separate rather than mix with its surroundings. This phenomenon is usually known as 'the conservative behaviour of air masses'. Whether the air involved is a tiny parcel measured in fractions of a cubic metre, or a vast mass many million cubic metres in size, the principle is the same. There will always be some mixing, but it will often be slow and take place only at the margins of the air parcel.

Conduction refers to the transfer of energy by contact between the molecules, or tiny particles, that make up a substance. When they receive energy and their temperature rises, individual molecules move more vigorously, thereby increasing the number of contacts with their neighbours and transferring energy in the process. This lively movement can be likened to the jostling of people in a crowd: the jostling is transferred by increasingly frequent contacts between each person. A real example occurs when a soil surface is heated and the energy passes down to the subsoil by conduction.

Figure 3.7 on page 62 summarises the basic pattern of radiation exchange in the Earth–atmosphere system. The key points are:

- solar energy reaches the Earth in the form of shortwave radiation
- the atmosphere is almost transparent to shortwave radiation
- solar radiation heats the Earth's surface and this in turn heats the atmosphere from below
- the Earth gives out longwave radiation which is absorbed and delayed before it returns to space (without this delay and absorption the atmosphere would be too cold for us to exist)
- by reflection, clouds in the atmosphere play a very important role in reducing both the amount of solar radiation reaching the Earth's surface, and the amount of energy loss caused by radiation from the surface.

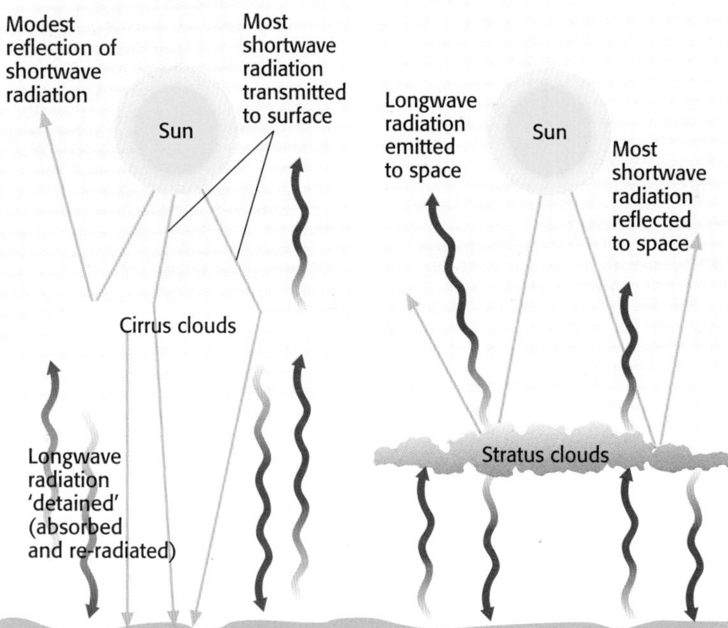

Figure 3.4
Different cloud types and their effect on radiation exchanges

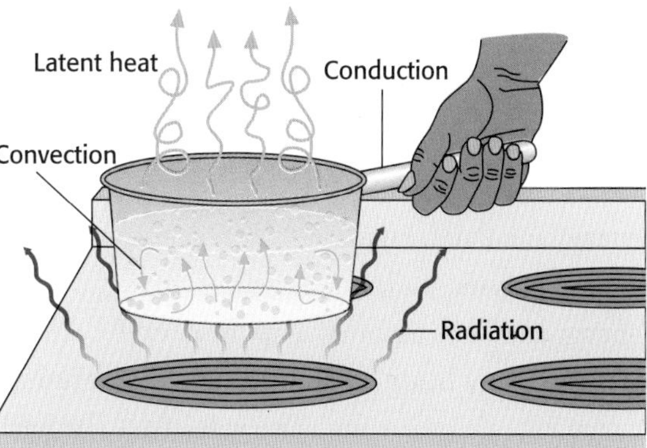

Figure 3.5
Heat energy transfer processes

The global energy budget

Over many years meteorologists have worked to develop more detailed analyses of the energy flow within the Earth–atmosphere system and, in particular, to assign values to the amounts of

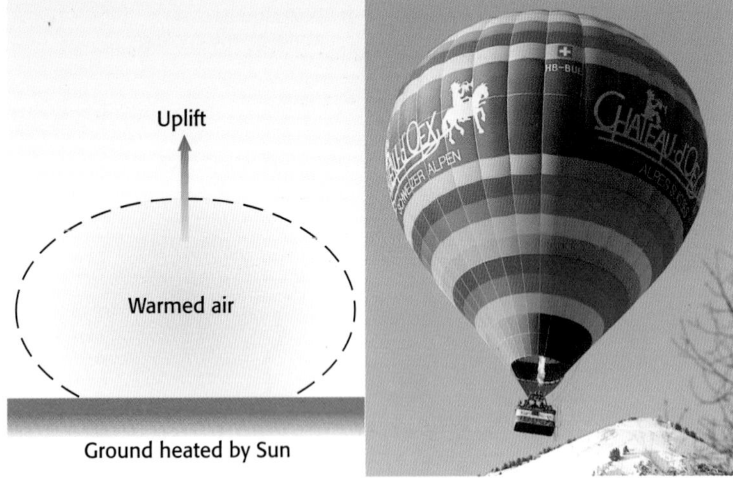

Figure 3.6
The hot-air balloon as an example of convection

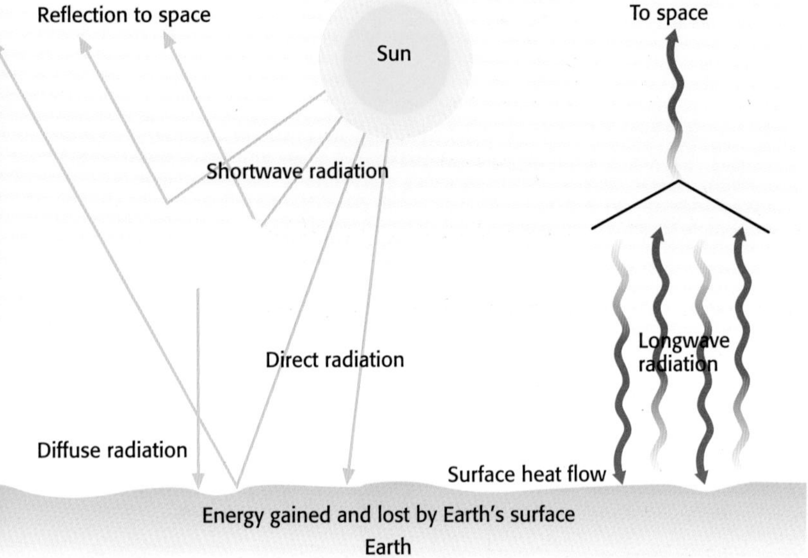

Figure 3.7
Simplified pattern of radiation exchange in the Earth–atmosphere system

energy involved. Figure 3.8 is an example of one such analysis. It links together many of the energy transfers that make up the overall budget.

All energy budgets should be considered to carry a 'health warning'. The values are the best estimates available. Although satellites have increased the quantity and quality of the information at our disposal, there are still areas of uncertainty. In practice, the budget only balances over a long period of time, never over a short period. There is a long way to go before such budgets can be regarded as accurate representations of reality.

The Earth–atmosphere system budget is best viewed as consisting of three main exchanges:

1 shortwave radiation exchanges
2 longwave radiation exchanges
3 other exchanges which occur through 'non-radiative' processes.

The energy flows associated with these three exchanges are shown on Figure 3.8.

Shortwave radiation exchanges

Conventionally, the total solar energy arriving at the outer edge of the stratosphere is treated as having a value of 100 units. Its subsequent distribution is complex.

- In the stratosphere, 3 units of very shortwave radiation, described as ultraviolet radiation, are absorbed by the gas ozone. This absorption is believed to be very important to us, since it prevents too much ultraviolet radiation from reaching the Earth's surface. It is argued that without this 'umbrella' the increased amount of ultraviolet radiation would cause damage to our skin and eyes, and also to plants. Measurements of ozone concentrations indicate that there is currently less ozone available to absorb ultraviolet radiation than previously, partly because of damage caused by gases called freons which have been added to the atmosphere through various forms of industrial and commercial activity.
- 25 units of the solar radiation pass directly through the atmosphere to the Earth's surface. In a cloud-free and clean atmosphere this amount would be much larger and is likely to vary from place to place and from time to time. The value of 25 units is a general one covering the whole of the Earth–atmosphere system.
- 18 units are absorbed by dust, impurities and gases in the atmosphere.
- 3 units are absorbed by clouds, and 21 units are reflected back by them. After multiple reflections 10 units continue down to the surface.
- Scattering is a process in the atmosphere where the smallest atmospheric constituents and particles intercept shortwave radiation

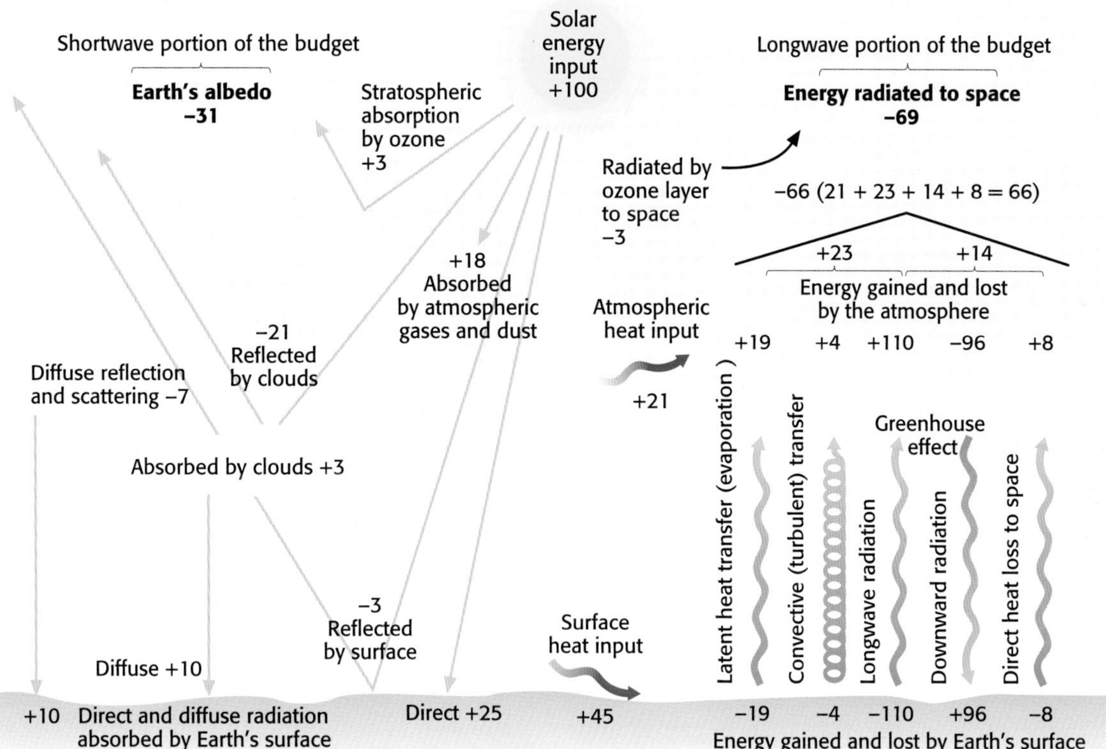

Figure 3.8 The Earth–atmosphere energy budget

and become tiny sources of radiation themselves. Scattering in the atmosphere results in 7 units being returned to space and 10 continuing down to the surface.

Overall, 31 units of the shortwave radiation budget are reflected back into space, forming a substantial proportion of what is known as the Earth's **albedo**, or total reflectivity. Of the balance of 69 units, 3 are absorbed by the stratosphere, 21 are absorbed in the troposphere, and 45 units are absorbed at the surface. The total input of 100 units is thus accounted for.

Longwave radiation exchanges

The total longwave budget originates from the 69 units derived from the shortwave budget. Radiative and non-radiative processes are involved in the longwave budget.

Radiative exchanges

Longwave radiation itself accounts for the direct return to space of 46 energy units derived from the shortwave budget. The distribution of these return units is as follows:

- 3 units of ultraviolet radiation returned by the ozone layer
- 21 units returned from within the atmosphere itself
- 8 units returned directly to space from the Earth's surface
- 14 units through the greenhouse effect.

The greenhouse effect within the atmosphere involves large longwave energy exchanges. A total of 110 units from the ground are absorbed by the atmosphere and 96 units are returned to the surface. The balance of 14 units returns to space. In recent years, scientists have detected an apparent warming of the atmosphere, which suggests that the balance of energy in the energy budget is less perfect than was originally believed. It seems that some of the 14 units are retained in the atmosphere, leading to an accumulation of energy which raises atmospheric temperatures. It is this imbalance which lies behind concerns about **global warming**, a process caused by people changing the gaseous composition of the atmosphere by adding substances such as carbon dioxide and methane in ever-increasing quantities.

Non-radiative exchanges

This category of exchanges involves air movements and the properties of water, and accounts for the remaining 23 units of the total longwave budget.

- Measurements have shown that convection and other air movement processes account for the transfer of 4 units from the surface to the atmosphere. Eventually this energy is returned to space as longwave radiation.
- The behaviour of water, however, plays a much larger part, although it is not hard to imagine why it is difficult to establish a precise value. Water has the remarkable property that it can exist as a liquid in the form of either raindrops, cloud droplets, fog or dew; as a gas in the form of water vapour; or in its solid form as ice. Even more remarkable is the fact that it can change states in a very short time. For example, on a cold night water in its liquid state, perhaps as a puddle, can be quickly converted into its solid ice form. The following morning when the temperature rises, it will first return to its liquid state and, if conditions become warm enough, it may be converted again through the process of evaporation into its gaseous water vapour form. The key point is that each of these changes of state involves energy; Figure 3.9 shows just how much.

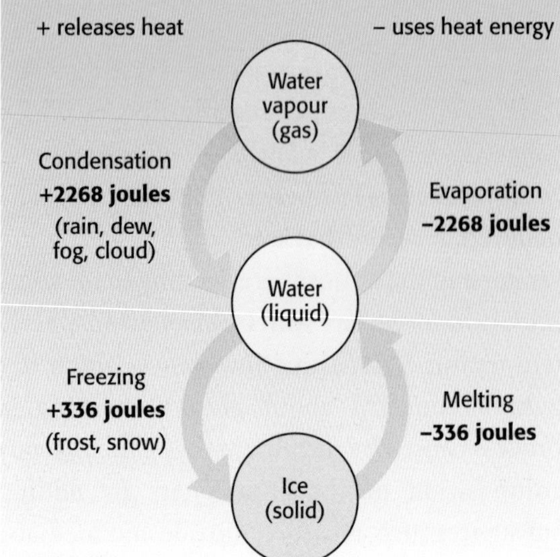

Figure 3.9 Changes of state of water, and the energy required

Melting and evaporation are processes that require the addition of heat energy, but when condensation and freezing occur this same energy is given up in the form of **latent heat**. Averaged out across the planet it is estimated that the net outcome of all the changes in the state of water is the transfer of some 19 units of energy from the Earth's surface to the atmosphere, which again are returned to space as longwave radiation.

While Figure 3.8 illustrates that an overall balance exists between the solar energy input and the energy losses from the surface and the atmosphere – and that all 100 units reaching

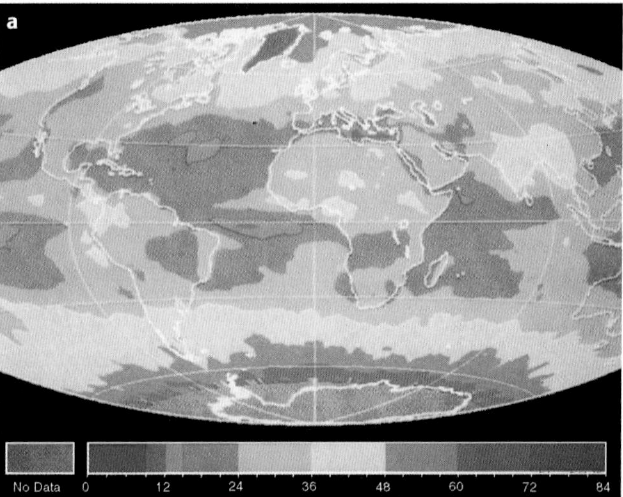

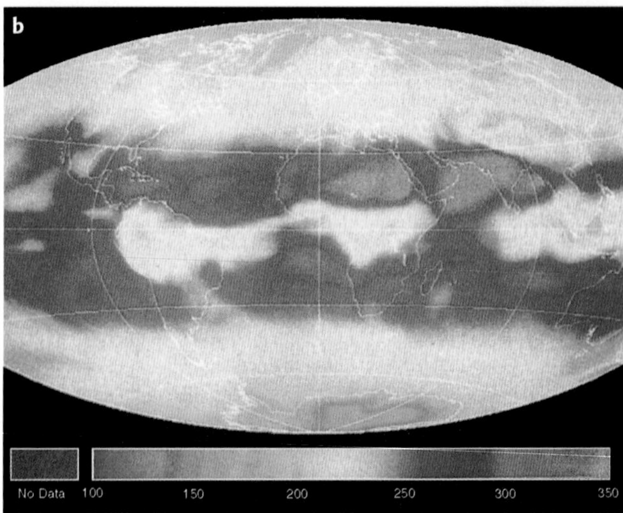

Figure 3.10 Global variations in albedo and longwave Earth radiation:
a albedo in July (*albedo* = percentage of incoming solar radiation reflected back into space)
b longwave radiation from the Earth

the Earth–atmosphere system from space are eventually returned – the values cited in the budget are averages for the Earth as a whole. By contrast, the satellite-derived images shown in Figure 3.10 reveal quite clear global variations in the observed values for reflection and long-wave radiation, and demonstrate the difficulty of producing single representative values for each part of the energy global budget.

Activity

1 Examine closely the satellite images presented in Figure 3.10 and, with the aid of an atlas, attempt an explanation of the patterns shown.

2 Study Figure 3.11, which shows the main cloud types occurring in the atmosphere. Using the information given in Figure 3.4, and with reference to your general knowledge of the weather, draw up a simple graph to show how the loss of longwave energy radiation from the Earth's surface to the higher parts of the atmosphere might vary according to cloud type.

Energy budget variation with latitude

When the global energy budget is broken down into 10 degree latitudinal strips, as in Figure 3.12, a clear pattern emerges. In terms of the radiation received and emitted by each strip, those between 0° and 40° gain more than they lose, while from 40° to 90° more is lost than is gained. Since, with time, the 0–40° zone does not become hotter and hotter and the 40–90° zone does not become colder and colder, a transfer mechanism must be at work to maintain the balance between them.

The black line on Figure 3.12 has been added to show how much energy needs to be transferred polewards at each latitude in order for the balance to be maintained. In the 0–10° strip the excess amount of energy will be matched by a similar excess on the other side of the Equator; thus movement towards the poles starts from this region. Further away from the Equator, for example in the 20–30° strip, the total excess energy to be transferred will consist of the excess for the strip itself plus the excesses which have reached it from the two strips nearer the Equator. As the curve on the graph shows, the greatest amount of energy transfer occurs in the

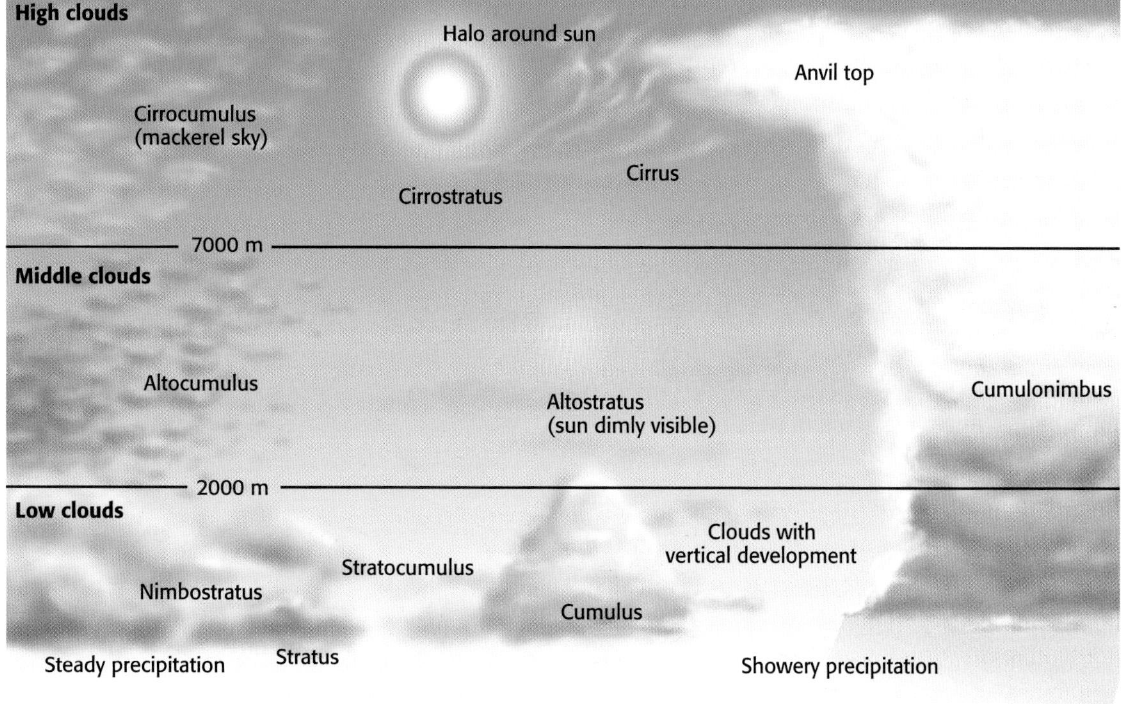

Figure 3.11 Basic cloud types showing their typical altitude and vertical dimensions

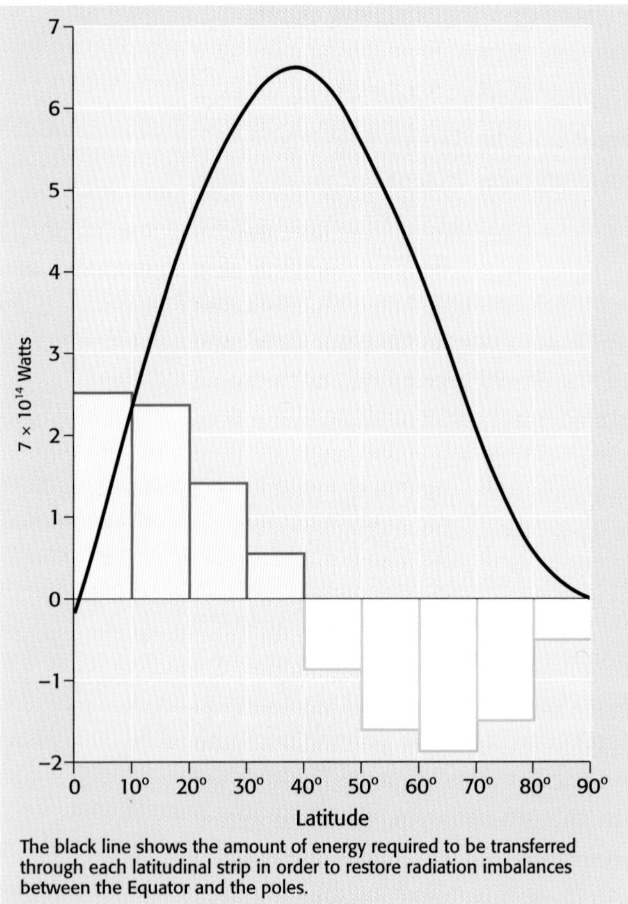

Figure 3.12
Energy surpluses and deficits by latitudinal strip

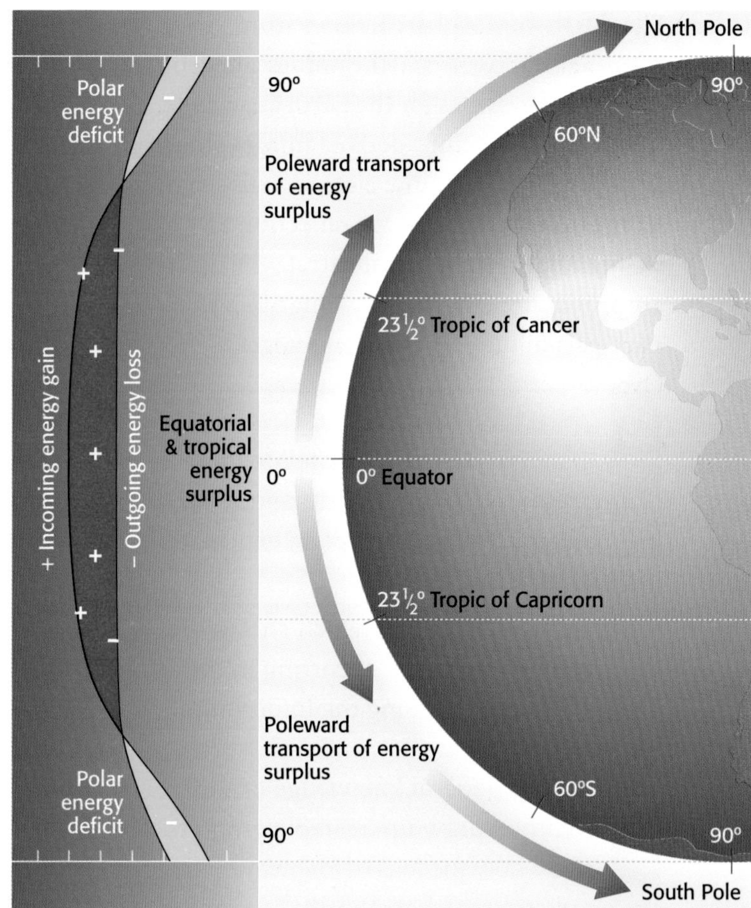

Figure 3.13
Energy budget by latitude: a pictorial representation

30–40° strip through which all the excess energy from latitudes nearer the Equator must pass on its passage towards the pole. Beyond 40° north, however, the energy flow is reduced since there are deficits of radiant energy in each latitude strip. In making good these deficits the flow is progressively reduced as the pole is approached. Overall the pattern is one of a huge transfer of energy which peaks in middle latitudes. This is shown pictorially in Figure 3.13.

Three key mechanisms are responsible for these energy transfers. **Ocean currents** play a major role. The Gulf Stream, part of the North Atlantic Drift system, provides an example from the northern hemisphere (Figure 3.14). In moving to the north, the energy stored in the warm water of the current is transferred polewards.

The other two mechanisms are atmospheric and reveal themselves in a variety of ways.

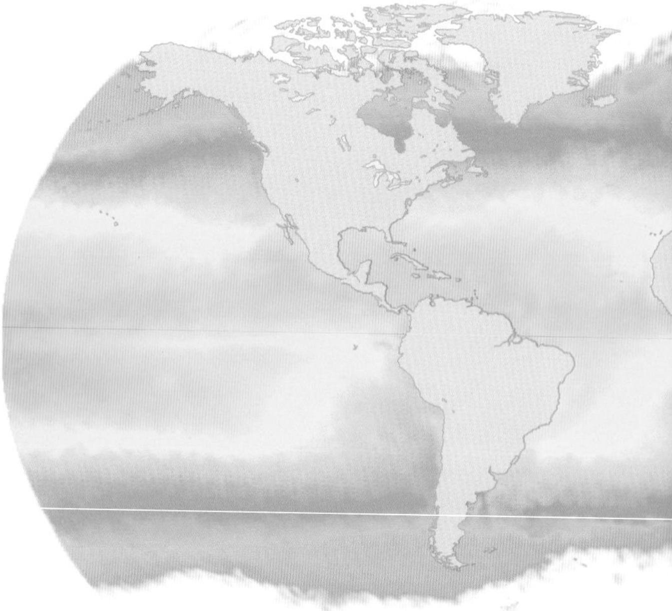

Figure 3.14
Satellite image showing the warm waters of the Gulf Stream moving north along the east coast of North America – an example of energy transfer in the oceans

First, the **general circulation**, shown in Figure 3.15, acts as the broad framework for the atmospheric transfer of energy, with major flows of warm air towards the poles and cold air towards the Equator. Secondly, large transfers are also achieved by clearly identifiable **weather systems**, the most noticeable of which are the vortexes or great swirls in the atmosphere which vary in form from place to place. Over the British Isles, for example, **depressions** are major swirling weather systems which play an important part in the energy transfer process. **Anticyclones** are less dramatic in their behaviour, but they are also responsible for energy transfer.

Depressions – a mid-latitude vortex

The underlying causes of atmospheric features such as depressions are complex, but the sequence of events from inception to their end

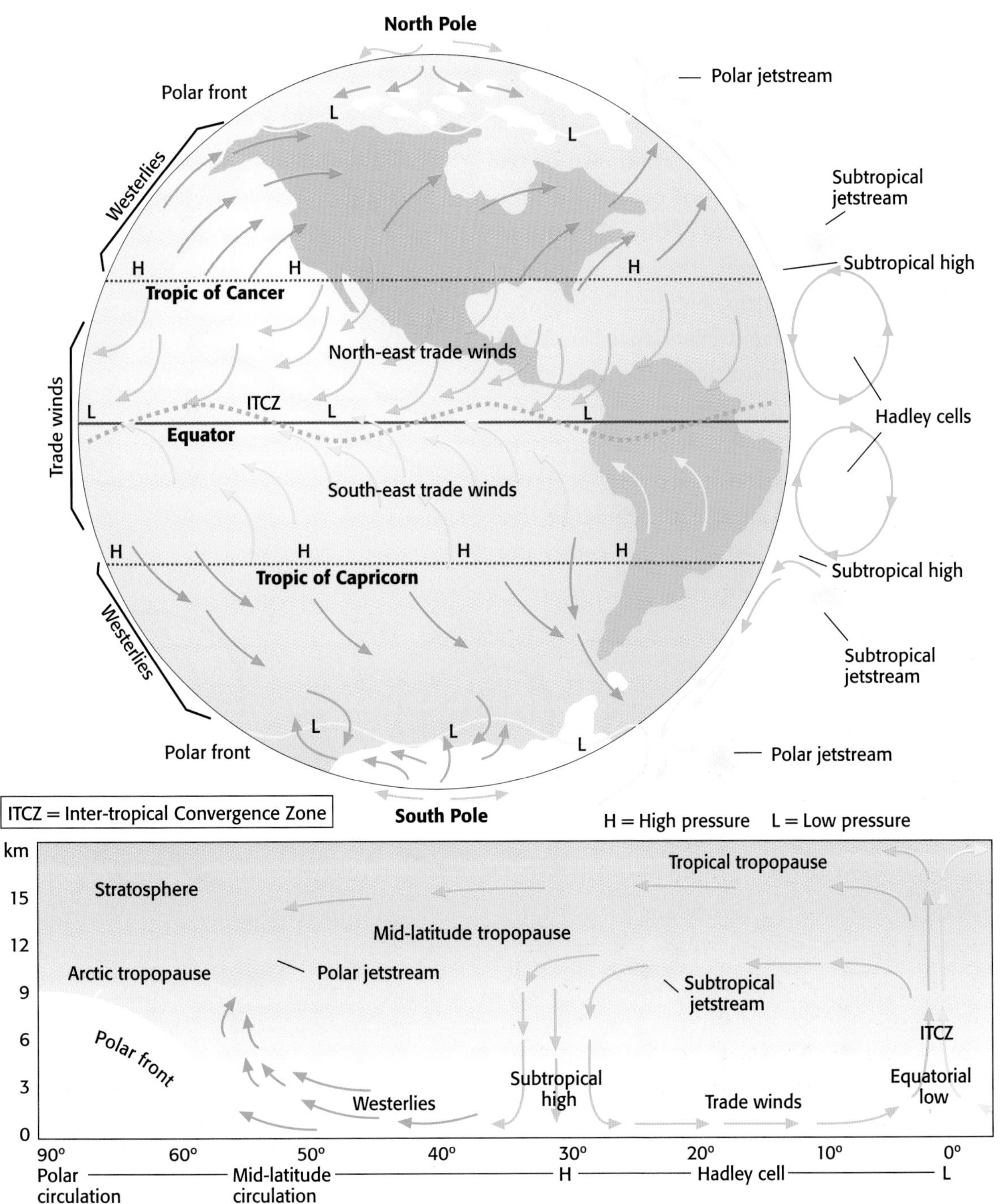

Figure 3.15 Simplified diagram of atmospheric circulation

is clear, and is shown in both plan and section in Figure 3.16. The diagrams comprise a generalised representation; reality is less clear-cut. Depressions are low pressure features because lighter warm air rises over denser cold air, thus lowering the air pressure at ground level. They, and other similar features, occur in many parts of the world. There are considerable variations, not only in terms of their size but also – and of more importance – in their intensity.

The concept of a front as the dividing line between air masses of different characteristics is fundamental to all meteorology, and particularly to the understanding of depressions. Although on the weather maps commonly used for forecast purposes fronts are shown in the positions they happen to occupy on the ground, in reality they exist in three dimensions (Figure 3.17). They can also take on a wide variety of spatial forms. Figure 3.18 shows a range of frontal shapes experienced over the British Isles at different times; the wide variation in form is readily apparent.

In Figure 3.19 it can be seen that a northern hemisphere depression in its early stages is little more than a kink in the dividing line between warm tropical air to the south and cool polar air to the north. In our latitudes this dividing line is commonly referred to as the **polar front**. Originally it was believed that depressions were *explained* by the development of the kink in the polar front. It is now known that the process is more complicated and that conditions in the upper atmosphere are of major significance in the formation of low pressure features such as depressions. Satellite images have shown that depressions are often

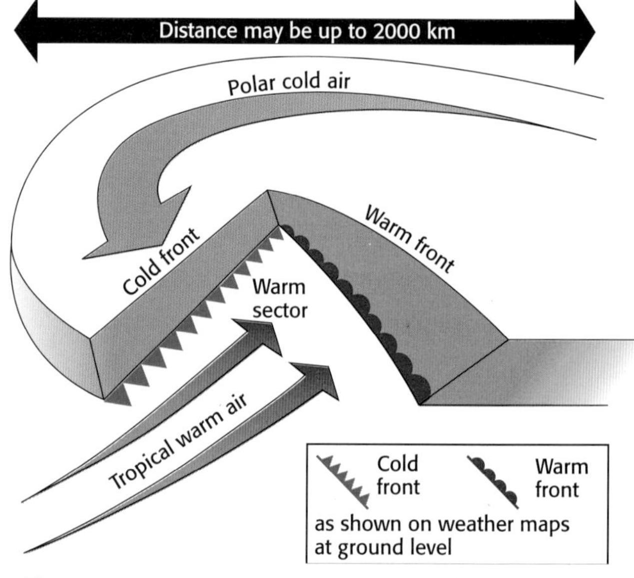

Figure 3.17
A depression in three dimensions

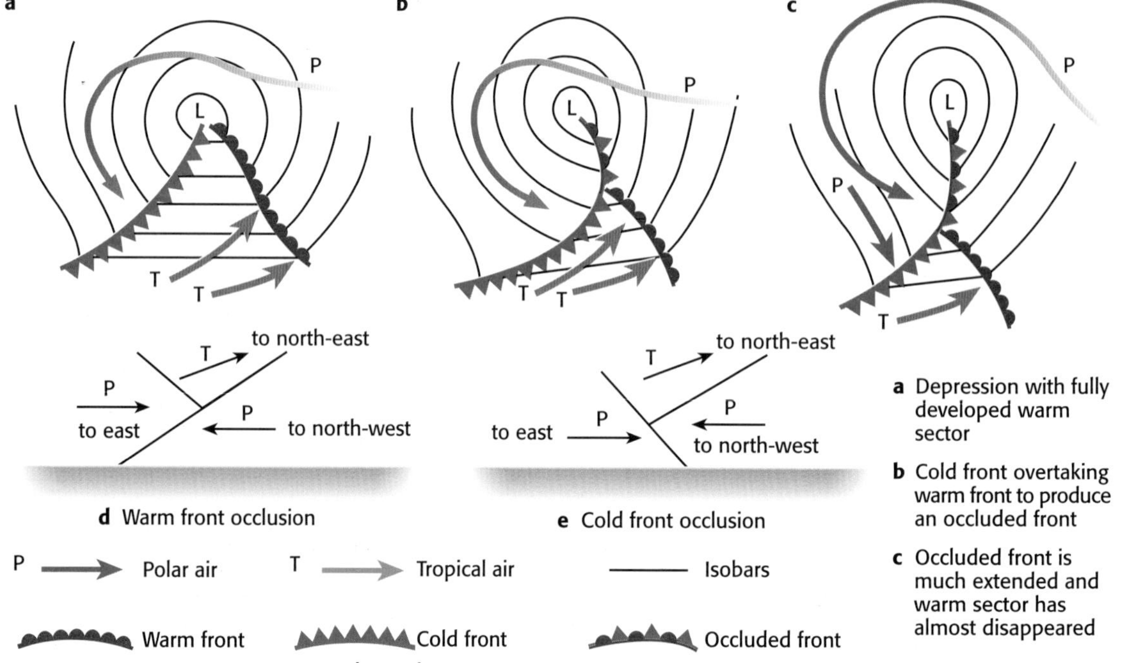

Figure 3.16
Frontal history of a depression

linked to upper air features, especially high-velocity airstreams in the upper atmosphere. These streams, with maximum velocities of nearly 500 km/h, are known as **jetstreams**. They can meander through the upper atmosphere as waves, but they are not always continuous and often bifurcate. Jetstreams themselves are a consequence of the very strong temperature gradients that exist between tropical and polar air, and as such play their own part in transferring atmospheric energy – from south to north in the northern hemisphere.

As the depression grows, warm air from the south moves north to create the eventual warm sector of the depression while the cold northern air moves southward. Depression fronts are associated with distinct weather patterns, some of which are shown in Figure 3.20. Generally the

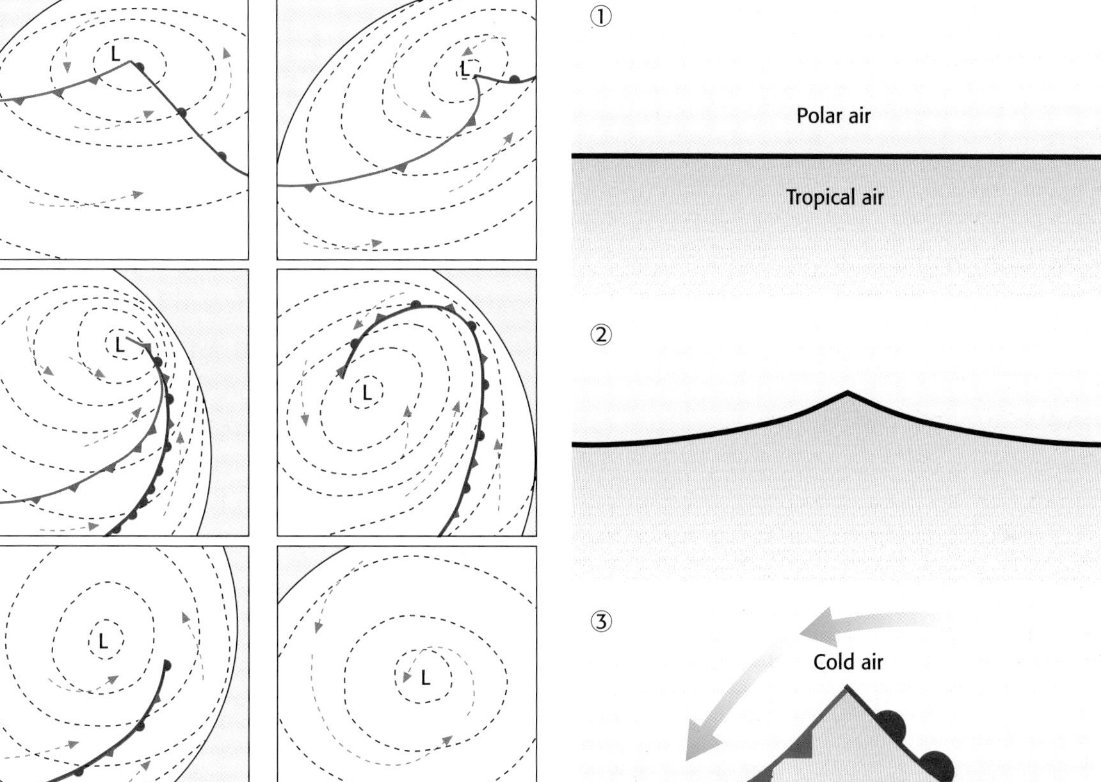

Figure 3.18
Frontal patterns over the British Isles

Figure 3.19
The development of a frontal kink

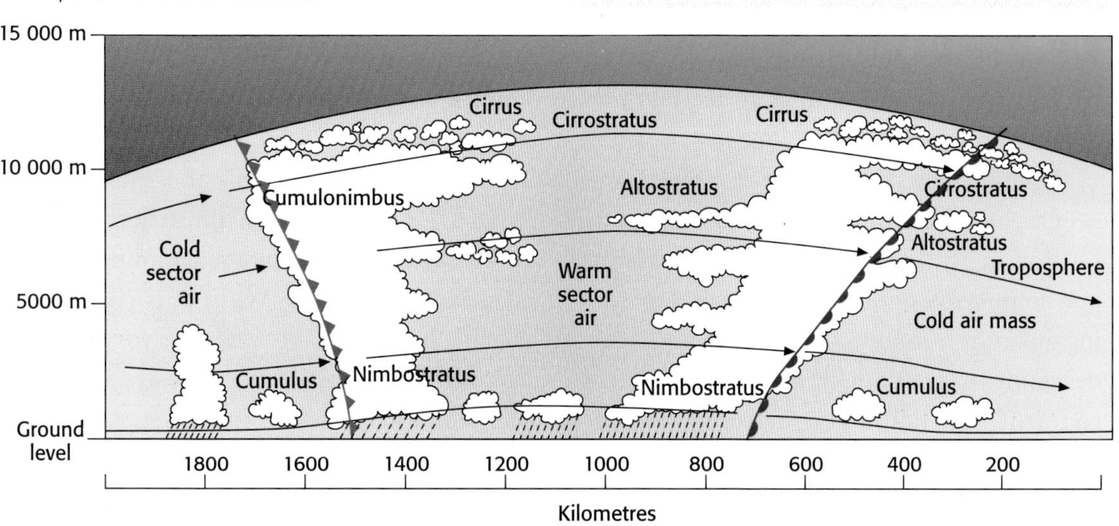

Figure 3.20
Weather associated with a depression and its frontal system

weather associated with depressions is unsettled and very variable. Much of this variability can be explained by reference to locations on the ground. Depending on their location relative to the track of the depression, different places will experience air masses with different characteristics, often in quick succession.

It is frequently remarked that the most outstanding characteristic of the weather of the British Isles is its variability. Although our weather lacks the extremes of high and low temperatures, aridity and rainfall found in other parts of the world, it does have extreme variability. Figure 3.21 shows the different air masses that can overlie the British Isles. Their temperature and humidity characteristics have been acquired from the surfaces over which they were previously located. When an air mass moves to another location it will retain those characteristics, and although they may change as new and different surfaces are encountered, the rate of change will be slow. An air mass that moves from the Tropics to the British Isles will still have the temperature and humidity characteristics of the Tropics on arrival, although it is modified in the lower layers close to the ground. Figure 3.22 illustrates the changes that may occur in a tropical air mass moving north and a polar air mass moving south. Such changes can create pronounced weather effects. For example, a polar air mass warmed at its base is likely to contain currents of rising air owing to the heating effect. This rising air will become cooler with altitude and may well produce clouds and rain.

Variability in the weather is important to geographers for a number of reasons, two being outstandingly important. First, the variability and complexity of our weather makes forecasting difficult. Secondly, it adds to the difficulty of designing many of the features of the built environment, such as bridges, roads and buildings, because wide variations in conditions have to be allowed for.

Anticyclones

Anticyclones consist of large masses of warm air moving north or cold air moving south, and are the second major family of atmospheric features which affect the weather of the British Isles. Their principal feature is descending air, which creates high barometric pressure at ground level. In winter, anticyclones are characterised by cold masses of air from the north and in summer by warm masses of air from the south-west.

Both types play a major role in atmospheric energy transfer, but since anticyclones tend to consist of one large air mass, they do not exhibit the complexities associated with depressions, such as the fronts. In Figure 3.23, summer and winter anticyclones are shown over the British Isles. Wind direction, wind speed, temperatures and cloud cover are indicated by the conventional symbols used on weather charts. As descending air has little of the turbulent uplift associated with low pressure systems, the weather brought by anticyclones is generally settled and precipitation is less common.

Local energy budgets

Weather and climate can be studied at a range of scales. The study of the global energy budget is the largest scale that concerns geographers. At the other end of the spectrum, investigations into the weather at the scale of individual plants may be important for people such as crop producers. Although the range of scales encountered in nature is a continuous one, three divisions have been recognised for practical purposes: **macro-** or large scale, **meso-** or middle scale, and **micro-** the smallest scale. Figure 3.24 illustrates the dimensions and some of the weather phenomena commonly associated with each scale. While it is common for local climates to be referred to as 'micro-climates', this practice is not always helpful and can lead to confusion. Strictly speaking, local climates lie between true micro-climates and meso-climates.

Air mass	Characteristics
Maritime Polar	Cold or rather cold at all seasons, especially on windward coasts, and clear nights inland. Unstable. Cumulus and cumulonimbus clouds. Bright intervals and showers. Clouds and showers die out inland at night and in winter.
Maritime Returning Polar	Temperature close to seasonal normal. Instability decreasing. Cloud types various, but spreading out; stability characteristics increase the farther south the air has been before recurving northwards.
Maritime Tropical	Mild or very mild in winter, rather warm and close in summer, warm in eastern districts. Stable. Dull skies and drizzle common on windward side, with low stratus cloud enveloping hills in fog, but clearing on lee side. Mists and fogs inland in winter and at night, when wind is light and sky clears. Some sea fog and coastal fog in Channel and western approaches in spring and summer.
Continental Tropical	Mild or very mild in winter, warm or very warm in summer. Unstable in upper layers; stable below, especially in winter. Cloud amount seems to depend very much on details of air's path, e.g. which mountains it has passed over or avoided, and length of Mediterranean, Atlantic and North Sea crossings. Stratus cloud types in winter, but in summer cumulus and occasionally high-level thunderstorm cloud. Commonly hazy.
Continental Polar	Cold or very cold in winter, warm in summer. Unstable, especially in lower layers, except near windward coasts in summer. Cloud cover depends greatly on details of air's path, e.g. air from Baltic and North German Plain is cloudier than air that has crossed hills and mountains farther south; northern air commonly brings skies overcast with stratocumulus cloud, especially in winter when it clears only west of Welsh and English mountains and Scottish Highlands; cumulus or cumulonimbus clouds, with breaks, develop on longer North Sea crossings to Scottish east coast. All associated cloud types are inclined to give occasional light sleet or snow in winter. In summer all inland districts experience a good deal of clear sky and warm sunshine; eastern coastal districts experience sea fogs (haars) and low temperatures with low overcast grey skies of stratus cloud, which sometimes clear completely in afternoon. Often somewhat hazy at all seasons.
Continental Arctic	Very cold or severe in winter, cold in spring and early summer. (This air mass is rare in high summer; when it does occur it is almost indistinguishable from Continental Polar air, and may be warm.) Unstable in lower layers. Cloud and weather characteristics similar to Continental Polar at all seasons, though in winter and spring precipitation is more likely to be snow. Visibility is clearer than with Continental Polar and sometimes extremely clear.
Maritime Arctic	Cold at all seasons, very cold in winter when weather may become severe if this air stagnates over the country. Unstable. Cloud types and behaviour resemble Maritime Polar, but showers are likely to be sleet, snow or hail in winter and spring. Leeward districts get long periods of clear sky. Extremely good visibility and beautiful blue opalescence of distant view are distinctive characteristics.

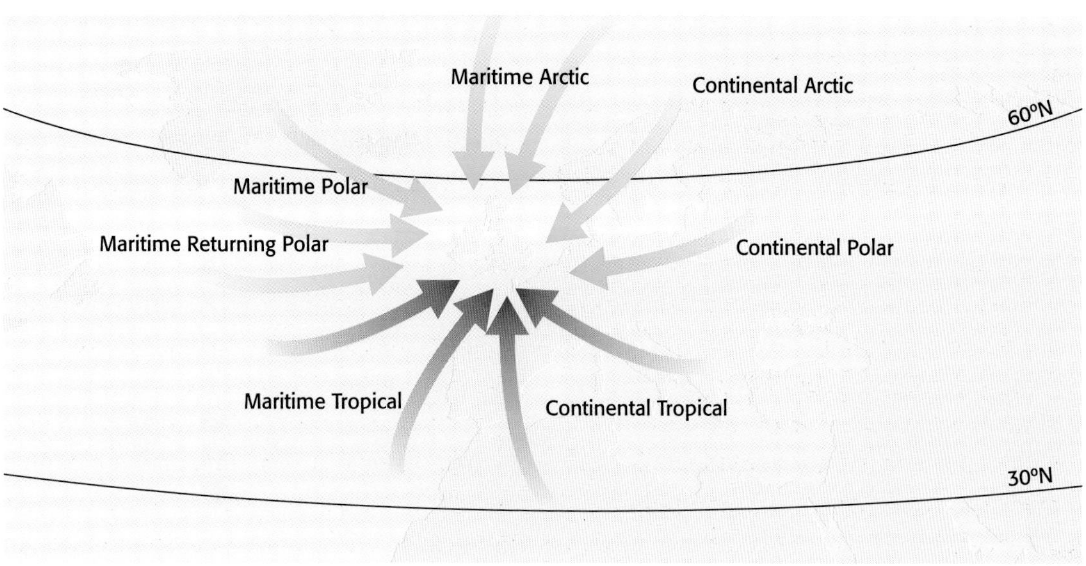

Figure 3.21

The characteristic air masses affecting the British Isles and the paths they commonly follow

In the real world it is not so much the exact divisions between the scales that are important as their interdependence. The icing of roads offers a good example because it can exert a strong influence on communications. The smallest or micro-scale factors affecting road icing include the composition of the road material

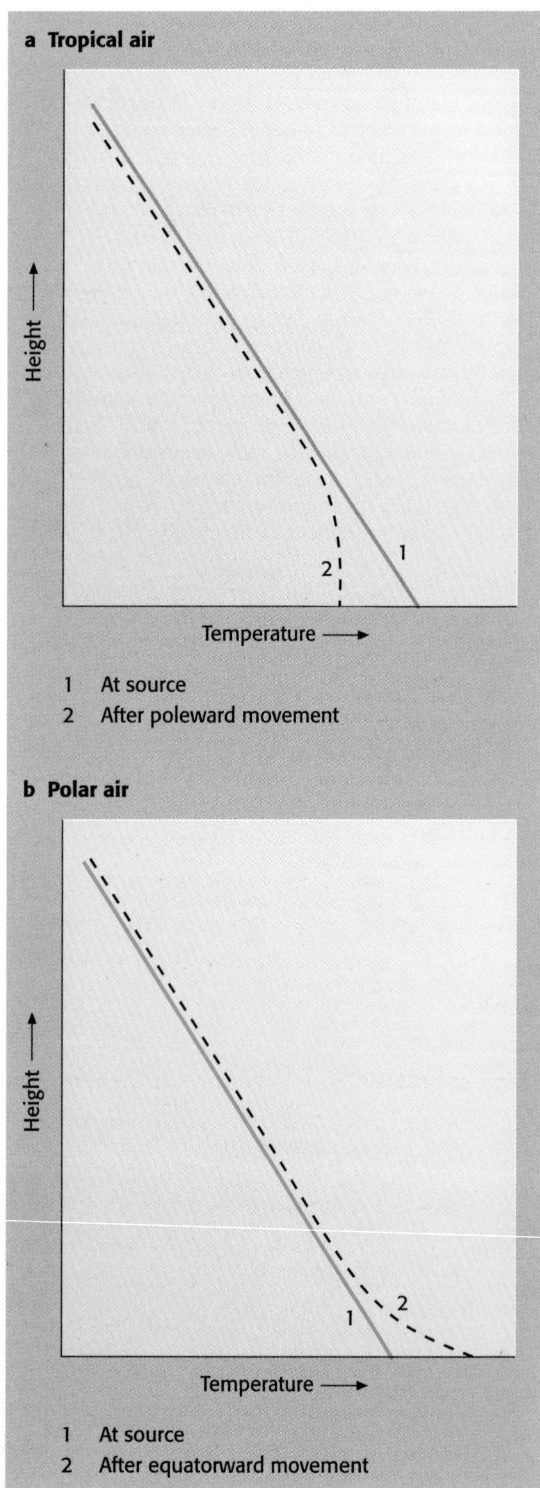

Figure 3.22
Change in air mass temperature with movement

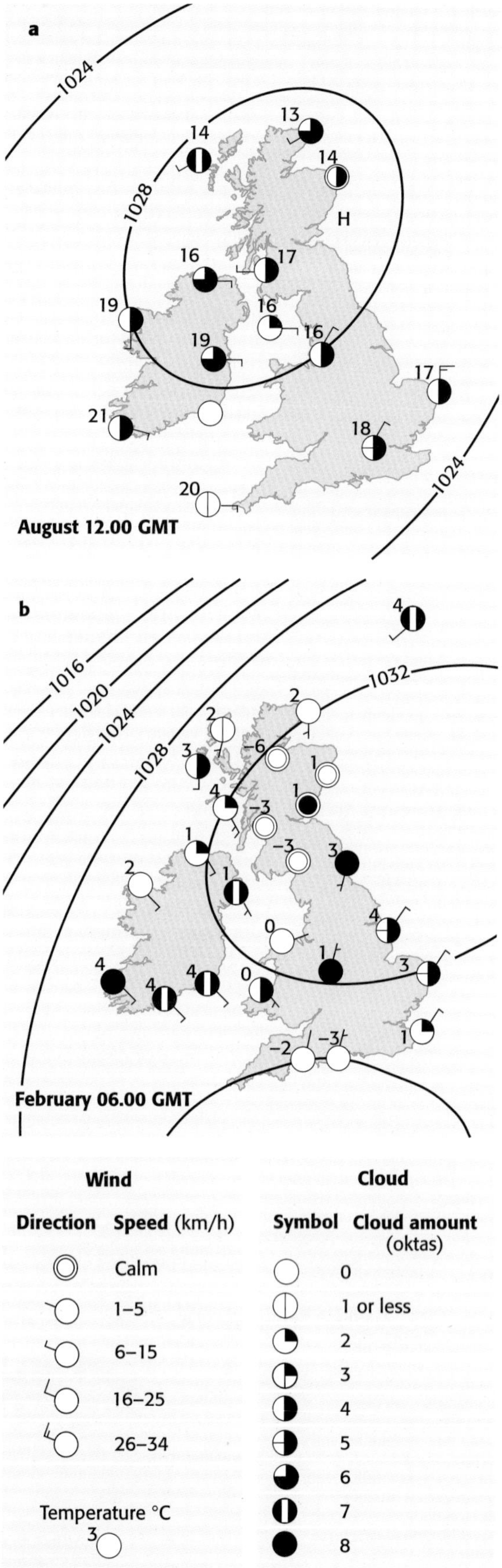

Figure 3.23
Anticyclones over the British Isles in **a** summer and **b** winter

Activity

1 Examine closely the weather associated with the two anticyclones shown in Figure 3.23. Draw up one list of the features that both anticyclones have in common and another of the differences between them. How far can the similarities be explained by reference to the general nature of anticyclones, and the differences by reference to the source of each air mass?

2 Variability in a set of figures – e.g. temperature or precipitation – can be summarised using the coefficient of variation, *V*. Thus if one place experiences more variability in its weather, the value of *V* will be higher than for a location where conditions are more constant. *V* first requires the calculation of standard deviation and is then given by the following formula:

$$V = \frac{\text{standard deviation}}{\text{mean}} \times 100\%$$

Select three different places where you think variability in the weather will be markedly different – perhaps Manchester, Moscow and Lagos. Research the monthly average figures for temperature and precipitation for each place and work out the values of *V*. When you have completed the calculations, attempt to explain your findings by reference to the number and characteristics of the main air masses that influence the weather of each location.

3 At the latitude of the British Isles the volume of the atmospheric energy transfer (Figure 3.12) is very large and accounts for the vigorous and varied weather experienced. Referring to a series of weather maps of a depression (cut from a newspaper or similar source), describe how the weather will vary with time at a location on the ground which experiences a sequence of warm front, warm sector and cold front. What will vary most: precipitation, temperature, wind speed or wind direction?

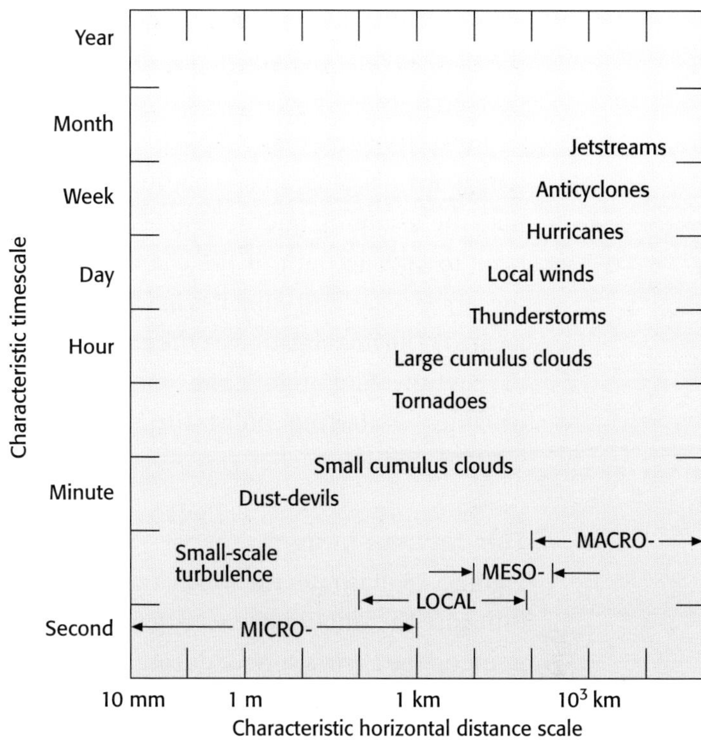

Figure 3.24 Climatic scales in terms of time and distance

and its capacity to store the energy received from the Sun during the day. The greater the storage capacity, the larger will be the amount of energy available for release during the night to offset the cooling that occurs as energy in the air above the road is lost to the atmosphere, and to space by Earth radiation. In effect the surface layer and sub-surface of the road store and release energy like a hot-water bottle or night storage heater.

However, the amount of energy received by the road from the Sun will depend on the road's relationship to the landscape. A road on a south-facing slope may well receive more solar energy than a road facing north. Such landscape or topographical considerations are at the meso-scale. Finally, whether or not there is solar radiation in any quantity to be stored on a given day will depend on the amount of cloud, and this is a large-scale or macro- consideration. If steps are to be taken to reduce the risk of surface icing, then all three scales need to be taken into account. Deeper road foundations collect more heat energy for subsequent release. Exposure to the Sun may need to be maximised, perhaps through the removal or thinning of nearby hedges and trees.

Climatic scales can be viewed rather like Russian dolls – the smaller-scale effects can develop only so far as they are allowed by their larger-scale counterparts. This is a very important point for geographers because it suggests that the study of micro-climates will always need to take account of the characteristics of the larger-scale 'host' climates in which they are located. The investigation of the characteristics of daytime and night-time energy budgets provides a starting point for smaller-scale weather studies.

The daytime budget

Figure 3.25 illustrates the six key transfers which influence the amount of energy gain or loss at a point on the Earth's surface during the day. This basic model assumes a horizontal surface with a grass-covered soil layer. Some of these transfers will already be familiar to you from the study of the Earth–atmosphere system.

1 **Incoming solar radiation** is the main energy input and will be strongly influenced by the amount and type of cloud. Figure 3.26 illustrates this relationship for various cloud types and different angles of the Sun. For example, when the Sun is low in the sky, nimbostratus cloud permits only about 5 per cent of the solar radiation striking it to pass, giving an energy receipt on the ground of about 50 watts/m^2. When the Sun is at a high angle, about 13 per cent of the incident solar radiation is passed and gives a ground heat input in the order of 160 watts/m^2.

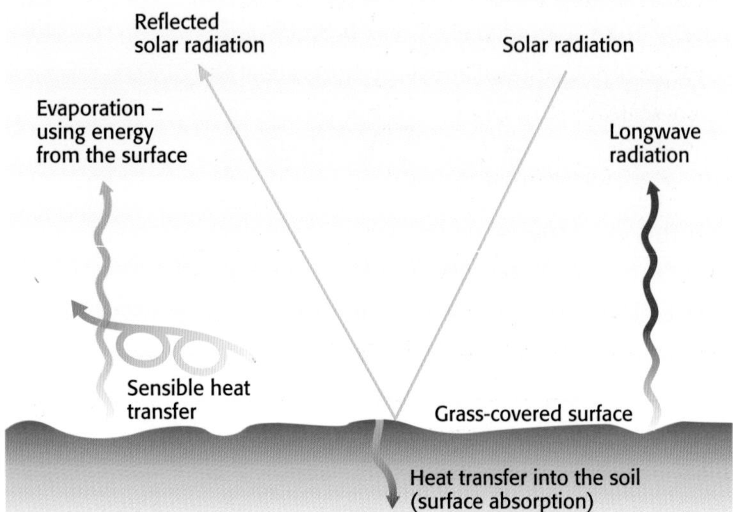

Figure 3.25
The local energy budget at a point on the Earth's surface during the day

2 **Reflected solar radiation** The fraction of the solar radiation reflected will vary greatly with the nature of the surface. Theoretically surfaces can reflect any fraction of the solar radiation they receive, from all of it to none. The degree of reflectance is expressed either as a fraction on a scale of 0 to 1, or as a percentage. This fraction is referred to as the **albedo** of the surface. Grass, the surface in the simple budget model, has a value of 0.25, reflecting 25 per cent of the solar energy received. Values of the reflection coefficient for common surfaces are given in Figure 3.27. The amount of reflection is very important since the smaller the amount that is reflected, the more there is available for heating the surface.

3 **Surface absorption** Energy arriving at the surface is available, at least potentially, to heat the surface. However, the nature of the subsurface plays an important role. If the surface can conduct heat rapidly into the lower layers of the soil, its temperature will be low. If the heat is not carried away quickly it will be concentrated at the surface and result in high temperatures there.

4 **Latent heat (evaporation)** It has already been shown in Figure 3.9 that the turning of liquid water into vapour consumes a considerable amount of energy. When water is present at the surface, a proportion of the incoming solar radiation will be used to evaporate it, and so will not be available to raise local energy levels and temperatures.

5 Sensible heat **transfer** This term is used to describe the movement of parcels of air to or from the point at which the energy budget is being assessed. If relatively cold air moves to the point, energy may be taken from the surface, creating an energy loss. If warm air rises from the surface to be replaced by cooler air, a loss will also occur. This process is best

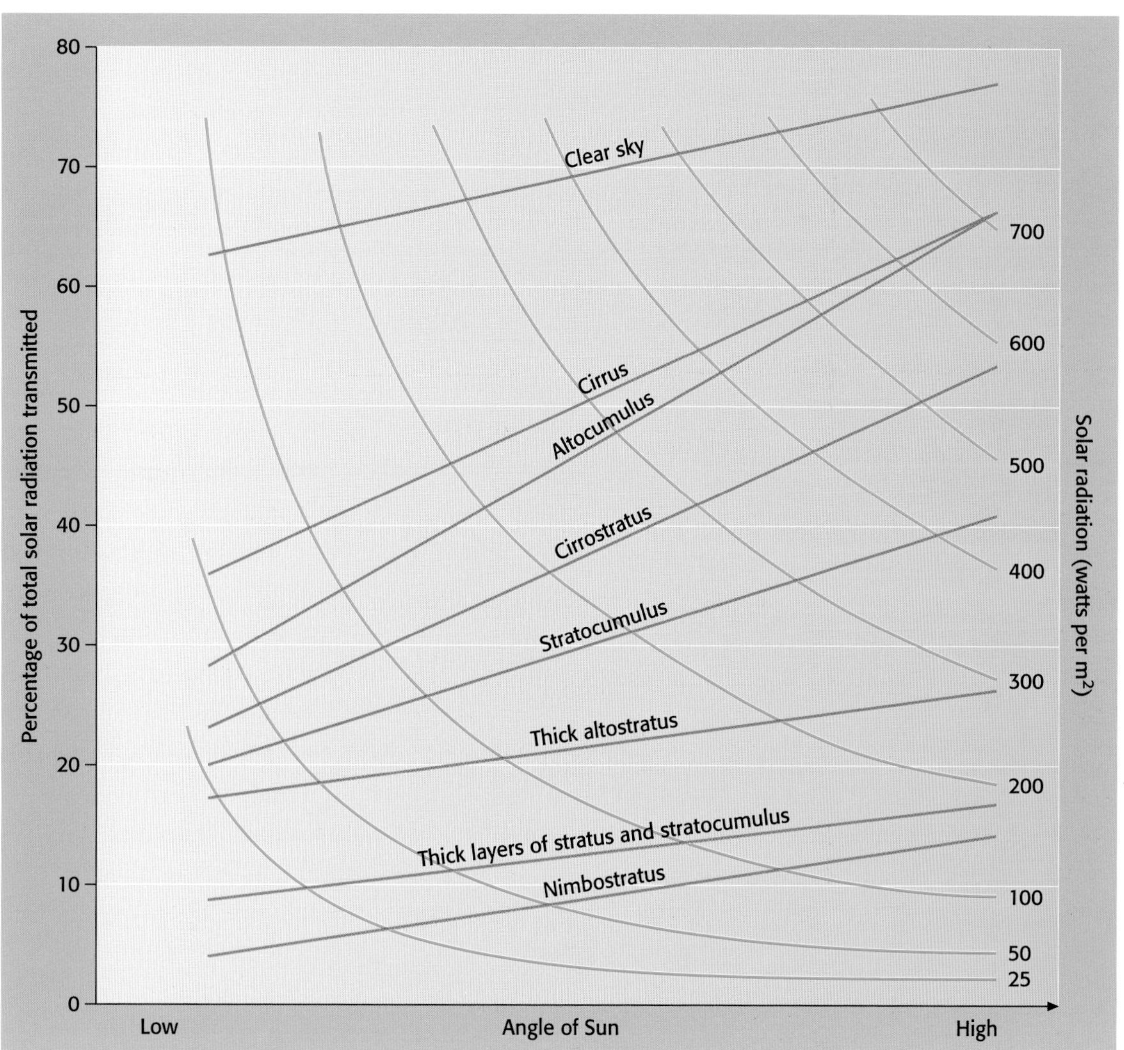

Figure 3.26
Solar radiation transmitted by different types of cloud

described as **convective transfer**, and during the day it is responsible for removing energy from the surface and passing it into the air.

6 **Longwave radiation** is emitted by the surface and passes into the atmosphere and eventually to space. There is also a downward-directed stream of longwave radiation from particles in the atmosphere. The difference between the two streams is known as the **net radiation balance**. During the day, since the outgoing stream is greater than the incoming one, there is a net loss of energy from the surface.

The general relationship between these six processes is represented by a simple budget

Surface or object	Albedo (% solar radiation reflected)
Fresh snow	75–95
Clouds (thick)	60–90
Clouds (thin)	30–50
Ice	30–40
Sand	15–45
Earth and atmosphere	30
Mars (planet)	17
Grassy field	25
Dry, ploughed field	15
Water	10 (daily average)
Forest	10
Moon	7

Figure 3.27
Typical values of albedo for different surfaces

Energy available at surface	=	Solar radiation receipt	−	[Reflected solar radiation	+	Surface absorption	+	Latent heat	+	Sensible heat transfer	+	Longwave radiation]

Figure 3.28
Simple daytime energy budget equation

equation (Figure 3.28). While this equation is likely to be representative of a time around midday, the relative importance of each term will vary throughout a 24-hour period. In Figure 3.29 the values of each transfer derived from detailed measurements over a grass surface are shown for five different times on a clear spring day. This example, which relates to one day's weather conditions only, will not hold true for all states of the weather. The data in Figure 3.30 reveal how some of the budget transfers shown in Figures 3.7 and 3.8 will differ between clear and cloudy conditions.

Time (GMT)	10.33	12.30	15.30	17.30	Night
Surface temperature	16.3°C	17.9°C	13.4°C	7.3°C	5.7°C
Incoming solar radiation	500	540	235	22	Nil
Reflected solar radiation	86	90	51	6	Nil
Outward longwave radiation	134	137	107	81	76
Heat absorbed by soil	40	73	12	-34	-44
Heat used in evaporation	84	88	68	20	16
Sensible heat transfer	157	150	-3	-52	-48

Figure 3.29
Energy budget values for a clear spring day over a grass pasture surface (watts/m²)

The night-time budget

The night-time budget is represented as a simple equation in Figure 3.31 which shows that only four key transfers are involved:

1 **Longwave radiation** During a cloudless night, little longwave radiation arrives at the surface of the ground from the atmosphere. As a result, the outgoing stream is greater and there is a net loss of energy from the surface. Under cloudy conditions the loss is reduced, because clouds return longwave radiation to the surface. A cloud layer is often said to act as a blanket keeping energy in. Common experience shows that with clear skies, temperatures fall to low levels at night and that frost, for example, is likely.

2 **Latent heat (condensation)** At night water vapour in the air close to the ground can condense to form dew because the air is cooled by the cold surface. The condensation process liberates latent heat and supplies energy to the surface, as shown in Figure 3.32, resulting in a net gain of energy. It is, however, possible for evaporation to occur at

Figure 3.30
Variation in budget energy levels between clear and cloudy conditions (watts/m²)

Conditions	High sun, clear	High sun, partly cloudy	Low sun, clear	Overcast day	Clear night
Incoming solar radiation	800	800	80	–	–
Diffuse solar radiation	100	250	30	250	–
Downward longwave radiation	320	370	310	380	270

Figure 3.31
Simple night-time energy budget equation

Energy loss	=	Longwave radiation	+	Sensible heat transfer	–	[Heat supply from soil	+	Latent heat from condensation]

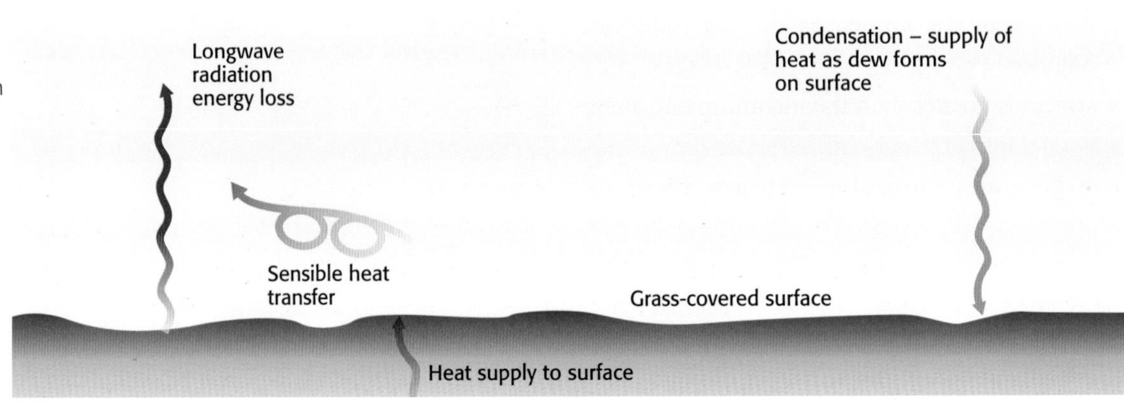

Figure 3.32
The local energy budget at a point on the Earth's surface during the night

night and if it does so on a significant scale, a net loss of energy might be the result.

3 **Subsurface supply** The heat stored in the soil and subsoil during the day can be transferred to the cooled surface during the night. This supply can offset overnight cooling and reduce the size of the night-time temperature drop on the surface.

4 **Sensible heat transfer** Warm air moving to a given point will contribute energy and keep temperatures up. By contrast, if cold air moves in, energy levels will fall, with a possible reduction in temperature.

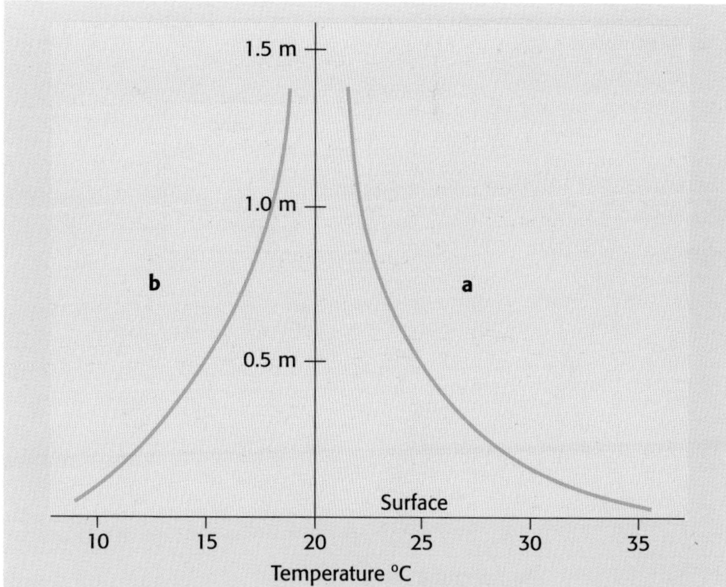

Figure 3.33 Generalised diagram of temperature change with height above a grass surface **a** by day and **b** by night

Air and surface temperatures close to the ground

In order to explain local climates and weather phenomena it is necessary to understand how ground surface temperatures can influence the temperature of the air. During the day the ground heats the air above it through the three transfer processes of radiation, conduction and convection. Energy is radiated from the warmed surface to the air above it, and since the air receives more radiation than it returns to the surface, there is a warming effect. The air close to the ground is also heated by contact (conduction) with the ground, with heat passing from the warmed surface to the cooler air above. At the surface, air moves slowly because of friction with the ground, and there is more time available for contact heating than if the air moved freely. The air immediately in contact with the ground is thus warmed by both radiation and conduction and, as a result of this dual heat input, convection develops and generates rising turbulent eddies. As these eddies move slowly close to the surface, their heat remains concentrated in the vicinity of the surface, although some is passed upwards. Thus the combined effect of all three transfers is that the air closest to the surface is readily heated by the energy transferred to it. As distance from the surface increases, the process is less effective. Measurements above a grass surface on a clear day with little general wind in June result in a temperature distribution of the form shown on the right in Figure 3.33. It can be seen that the reduction in temperature with height – known as the **temperature gradient** – is most rapid close to the ground.

At night the ground surface is cooled by the combined impact of the four night-time budget components (Figure 3.31). Since the air immediately above the surface has a higher temperature, heat initially flows from the air to the ground, so resulting in cooler air. Although the same three transfer processes that operate during the day also operate at night, on a calm, clear night conduction will be very much more important than during the daytime. Just like the day, energy transfers will be most pronounced close to the surface. A typical night-time temperature distribution close to the ground is shown on the left of Figure 3.33.

It is clear from Figure 3.33 that there is a much greater range of temperature close to the ground than higher up. The same general relationship is true for the air above any surface that can receive energy from the Sun and radiate energy to space. In order to record air temperatures that are representative of general conditions over large areas, thermometers must be sited clear of surface zones with their thermally complex and

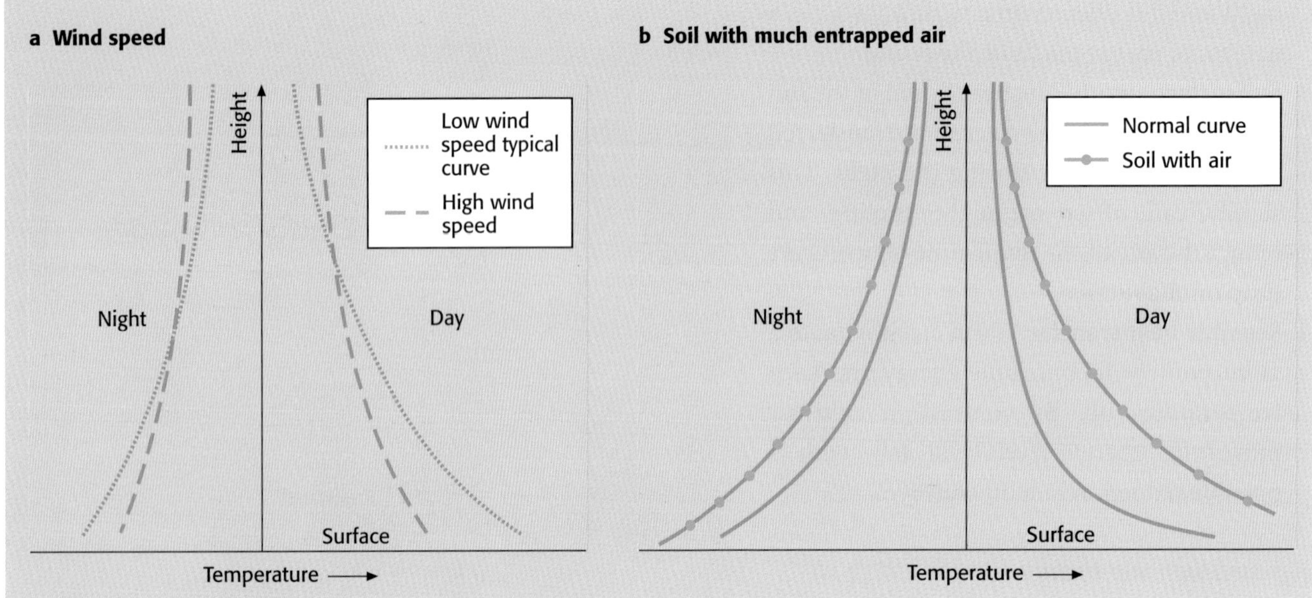

Figure 3.34 The influence of **a** wind speed and **b** soil type on temperatures close to the ground

disturbed patterns of air movement. For this reason, meteorological screens stand at a height of 1.3 m, a position that is safe enough for the production of consistent average data. On the other hand, many of the climates of the thermally disturbed zone close to the ground are of special interest to geographers. The examples given in Figure 3.34 contrast with the grass surface of Figure 3.33 and show the different forms that height–temperature distributions may take under other circumstances. Understanding these relationships is important since changes made to surfaces may change local micro-climates.

Local energy budgets and weather phenomena

Local energy budgets help to explain many weather phenomena. At the same time they can be used to guide the action that may be necessary to mitigate any harmful effects.

Ground and air frosts

Ground frost is a condition that occurs when the temperature of the ground surface, or of other surfaces, falls below freezing point. Visible evidence is the presence of small ice crystals. Since it is at night that ground surfaces lose energy and cool the most, the night energy budget can help to explain the occurrence and patterns of ground frost. All surfaces cool at night and for frost to form the cooling must be sufficient to reduce the temperature of the surface to 0°C. Sufficient cooling is *most likely* when:

- longwave radiation energy loss is high: cloud-free skies and long nights provide the most favourable conditions, allowing the greatest energy loss – the more clear sky that is visible from a given point on the surface, the greater will be the reduction in temperature
- sensible heat transfer is minimised: little or no wind will help ensure that heat energy is not transferred into the area from elsewhere, and that there is little chance of the surface being warmed by incoming air.

Sufficient cooling for ground frost is *least likely* when:

- the amount of heat stored in the sub-surface layers of the ground and available for conduction to the surface is enough to offset the surface energy loss caused by longwave radiation
- condensation occurs at the surface and supplies latent heat
- air movement brings warm air to the location and raises the surface temperature.

Air frost occurs when the air temperature falls below 0°C. Its formation depends on the ground surface also being cooled to, or below, 0°C and on heat being transferred from the air to the ground until the air temperature has fallen sufficiently. The factors influencing the likelihood of air frost are therefore the same as for ground frost, though the need for calm conditions is even more important. Air frost may not be deemed to have occurred unless the air temperature falls below 0°C at the height of the standard meteorological instrument screen, i.e. about 1.3 m above the ground surface. Nevertheless, it may have developed at lower levels nearer the ground.

Preventing frost damage

Frost can be especially harmful to certain forms of agriculture, and of the four transfers that make up the night energy budget it is heat loss through sensible heat transfer which has special significance in causing crop damage. In the first instance, the planting of frost-sensitive crops on sites into which cold air may drain should be avoided. Many hollows in the landscape experience this effect (Figure 3.35) and are best avoided.

Where there is little or no possibility of avoiding vulnerable areas, the night energy budget can guide the adoption of other preventative measures. If the loss of energy by Earth radiation can be reduced, the risk of frost damage is considerably diminished. The simplest, but not necessarily the most manageable, approach is to protect plants with a suitable covering device – plastic cloches, for example. Covers have the effect of placing the cooled surface above the plants and retaining Earth radiation around them.

More extravagant means have also been used to reduce Earth radiation loss. At one time the burning of smoky fuels from smudge pots was widely used to put an artificial cloud in the air above the crop in order to reduce the radiative energy loss. In practice it was difficult to maintain the cloud in the required position and the air pollution consequences are now considered to be unacceptable. An essentially mechanical approach has been to make use of sensible heat transfer by mixing the lower atmosphere with large propellers (wind machines) or helicopters. The object is to bring heat from higher levels down to ground level. An example of the results achieved by this method are illustrated in Figure 3.36, where the use of a carefully located wind machine succeeded in raising temperatures by several degrees. An alternative 'ground-based' method is to water the soil in order to increase its ability to conduct heat from the subsoil to the surface, thus off-setting heat loss. This method has the limitation that the heat reservoir of the subsoil is rapidly exhausted.

Where energy loss through radiation is likely to cause frost, the level of risk can be reduced by screening part of the sky visible from a given point on the ground. For example, Figure 3.37 shows how the Earth radiation loss at the foot of a wall is much less than that of an open site. Gardeners in

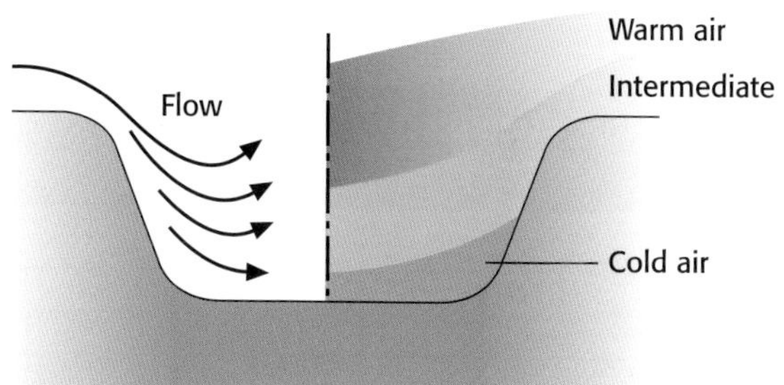

Figure 3.35
Air temperatures in a hollow in the landscape

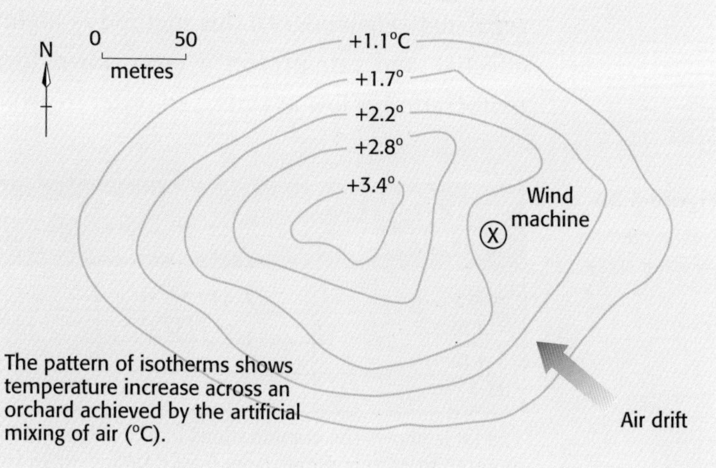

Figure 3.36
Frost reduction by mechanical ventilation

Figure 3.37

The effect of a wall in reducing energy loss through longwave radiation at night

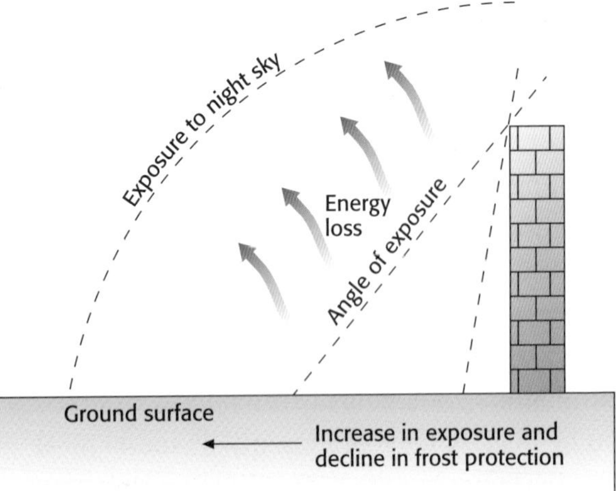

Figure 3.38

Spraying vines with water to protect against frost, in France

Victorian times were aware of this protective measure, and grew sensitive fruit against walls in order to minimise the likelihood of frost damage.

Probably the most effective method of frost protection makes use of the release of latent heat. The technique relies on allowing the temperature of the crops to fall to around 0°C, but no lower, and then spraying them with a fine water mist (Figure 3.38). The spray forms a coating of ice on the plants but, in the process, the release of latent heat which accompanies freezing prevents further temperature drop. Plants do not generally suffer damage until the temperature falls to about –2°C, which means that once the first spray of water has frozen, more spray is needed to keep up the release of latent heat and so prevent the earlier coatings of ice from going below 0°C. Where the frequency of spraying and the spray density are carefully regulated (Figure 3.39), this method is highly effective and can protect a crop down to a temperature as low as –14°C. In order to avoid physical damage to the plants, the weight of the built-up ice has to be carefully monitored.

Frost and ice on road and bridge surfaces

The frequency of frost and ice on roads and bridges can vary substantially, with a much greater risk of both on bridges than on roads (Figure 3.40). Bridges generally lack the energy storage capacity of roads and may be more vulnerable to heat loss by radiation where they are openly exposed to the sky. On stretches of road which face open skies and also occupy relatively sheltered positions, heat loss through Earth radiation can be substantial, with little chance of significant gain from inward sensible heat transfer. Road signs such as the one shown in Figure 3.41 are a good indicator of locations

Figure 3.39

Frost protection by water spray

Spray density (mm per hour)	Interval between wettings (minutes)			
	3	2	1	0.5
< 1.5	-2.5 to -3°C	-3°C	–	–
1.8 to 3.0	-4.5°C	-4 to -5°C	-5 to -6°C	–
3.4 to 4.1	–	–	-6.5°C	-7.5°C
11.3	–	–	–	-9°C

The table shows the combinations of water spray density and wetting frequency required to protect plants from frost damage down to a temperature of -9°C.

prone to pronounced energy loss at night.

Decisions to apply salt to roads are also taken on the basis of heat budget considerations. In Nottinghamshire, for example, where the local authority is responsible for gritting 1800 km of road, a 24-hour weather watch is maintained between October and April. Each application requires 200 tonnes of salt and takes $3\frac{1}{2}$ hours to complete. Overnight frost on cars is not an indicator of the need to salt the roads. Roads retain more of the heat gained during the day than steel, and so do not need salting as soon as frost appears on car bodies. In Nottinghamshire, salt is applied when the road temperature is predicted to fall to 1°C or less within the ensuing three or four hours. Moisture measurements are also important; no ice would form if moisture levels on and close to the road surface were at zero. In practice, of course, zero moisture conditions at low temperatures are highly unlikely, although they can fall to very low levels during a long and settled cold spell.

Figure 3.40
Frost and ice can be a much greater risk on bridges than on a road built over solid ground.

Figure 3.41
The sign (left) warns of road icing where night-time energy losses are high. This stretch of road faces an open sky to the north and is protected to the south by woodland which restricts air movement and reduces the likelihood of sensible heat gain.

Mist and fog

Mist and fog are physically the same; droplets of water in the atmosphere which are so small that they fall only very slowly to the surface under the influence of gravity. The difference between them is that fog droplets are more dense and visibility is lower than for mist. The current official Meteorological Office definitions for mist and fog occurring on land are:

Mist – when visibility is reduced to between 5000 and 1000 m and humidity is 93 per cent or more

Fog – when visibility is reduced to less than 1000 m

Dense fog – when visibility is reduced to less than 200 m.

Air can hold only so much water in the form of vapour. Once that level is reached, the air is described as saturated and the vapour will condense into liquid droplets. The amount of water vapour that air is able to hold depends on its temperature, and is demonstrated in Figure 3.42. At point A, where the air is at a

Figure 3.42
The relationship between air temperature, water content and saturation

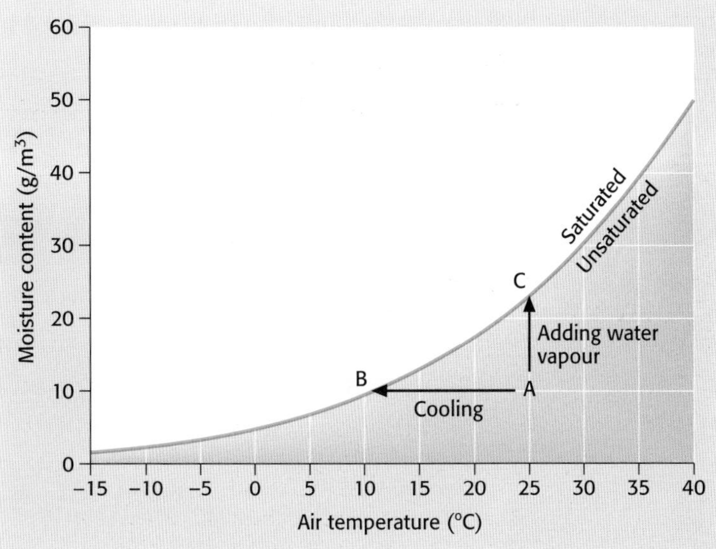

temperature of 25°C and has a water vapour content of 10 g/m^3, it is unsaturated and no fog or mist will be present. If, however, the same air is cooled to 10°C (point B), then saturation will be achieved and fog or mist may develop. Alternatively, holding the temperature steady and increasing the moisture content of the air to 23 g/m^3 (point C) will also create the saturated conditions necessary for mist and fog. The temperature at which saturation occurs is known as the **dewpoint**.

Fog and mist will not always form when saturation point is reached. On occasions small particles of dust, salt and other matter, called **condensation nuclei**, are needed in the air to encourage droplet formation. It is for this reason that fog and mist are more common in cities where the supply of suitable airborne particles is greater.

The problem of reduced visibility on roads owing to mist and fog is an important practical consequence of the relationship between the temperature of the air and its water content (Figure 3.43). Fog is most probable where a stretch of road dips into a hollow where cold air is likely to accumulate. Not only will the temperature be low in such a location; the normal tendency of water to flow downhill is also likely to provide high moisture levels. The most serious problems arise where a heavily used motorway passes through an area where only a small fall in temperature is required to initiate the condensation process and to create a sudden and thick bank of fog. By keeping a watch on temperature change, it is possible to predict the occurrence of mist and fog in these locations and to take measures to restrict traffic flow and speed. Even so, serious accidents continue to occur, and a lack of local-scale energy budget data may mean that warnings of the risk of fog are not issued in time. In any case, motorway routes are not always planned to avoid the most fog-prone locations. Tests of 'intelligent' road studs are now under way in Scotland in an effort to reduce accidents. These studs can detect fog (as well as ice) and change colour when they do so. Further, by communicating with other studs which then change their colour, a warning can be given up to 900 m before the hazard is reached.

Figure 3.43
When fog lies in a valley bottom like this, hazardous driving conditions may be caused by reduced visibility

Dew

Dew is condensation on a surface. It occurs when the air in contact with the surface becomes saturated, usually because the temperature of the surface has dropped sufficiently to cause condensation, as in Figure 3.42. On some occasions, however, dew may form when more moisture is introduced into the air, perhaps by an onshore sea breeze, while the surface temperature remains constant.

Dew can be a useful addition to soil moisture and vegetation in some circumstances. On the lee side of a shelter-belt or hedge, wind velocities will be low and the air will be still. Under night budget conditions there is a strong likelihood of low temperatures, so providing one of the routes for saturation to occur. In very dry areas this process can be an advantage. In other areas where moisture is not scarce, dew may be unwelcome since it can result in damp crops in sheltered locations and lead to a delay in harvesting.

Temperature inversions

As you have seen, air that is warmed becomes less dense than the surrounding air and rises. Like the hot-air balloon, a parcel of air will continue to rise only for as long as it is warmer than the air around it. Once it is at the same temperature it will rise no more. In the case of the hot-air balloon the pilot can use the burner to supply more heat to the air trapped in the envelope and ascent can be maintained. In meteorology, however, there is no ready burner option and once a pocket of air has reached the same temperature as its surroundings its ascent will stop.

In the real world the rising parcel of air will cool at a fixed rate. Nothing changes this rate. The surrounding air presents more of a problem since its temperature at any given height will have developed as a response to how much heating and cooling it has experienced. In the atmosphere the rate of temperature change with height of the surrounding air is described as the 'lapse of temperature' and is termed the **environmental lapse rate**. Normally, once outside the zone very close to the ground, the environmental temperature of the atmosphere decreases steadily with height, largely because the atmosphere is heated from below. Under these conditions a warm parcel of air moving up from the surface will continue to rise as long as it cools at a rate which ensures that it remains warmer than the air around it, i.e. it cools at a slower rate than the environmental lapse rate.

A common source of warm parcels of air is the chimneys of industrial plants; these parcels contain the heat and waste products of industrial processes. The main purpose of chimneys is to release waste gases at a high enough level for them to stay above the surface until they are well diluted by mixing, thereby avoiding contact with buildings and people in a concentrated form. As long as the parcel rises the atmosphere is being used efficiently as a dustbin. Such a situation is shown in Figure 3.44a.

On occasions the environmental air does not cool steadily with height but contains a zone where temperatures increase. This zone is referred to as an **inversion layer**. Under these circumstances, a rising parcel of warm factory air may arrive at this layer at the same or at a lower temperature than the surrounding air. When this happens the factory air will accumulate at the level of the inversion and, if it contains a sufficient quantity of waste particles, it may become thick enough to cut off the Sun's rays and give rise to what is known as the 'dustbin-lid' effect. Where industrial plants are located in valleys, serious reductions in air quality can result from the entrapment of pollutants. Dispersal will be delayed, and the waste will become more concentrated and potentially more harmful. Such a case is shown in Figure 3.44b, which is typical of the smog problem faced by Los Angeles in California. **Temperature inversions** have considerable repercussions for human activity in any circumstances where the atmosphere contains pollutants.

An inversion layer can also occur in valleys where cold, dense air accumulates close to the ground and warm air remains above it. In rural areas a band of mist can often be seen marking the boundary of the inversion (Figure 3.45).

a Normal atmospheric mixing

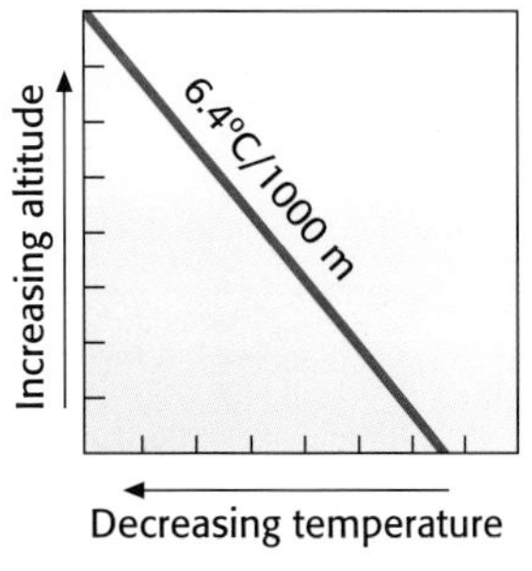

b Inversion layer traps pollutants

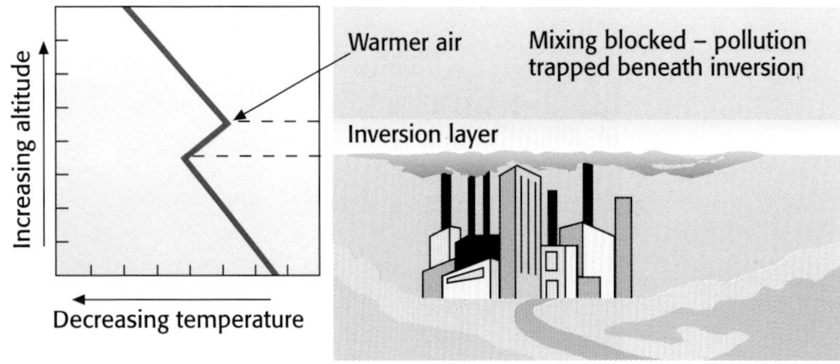

Figure 3.44 Normal and inverted temperature profiles

Figure 3.45
The inversion layer is marked by a band of mist

Activity

Local energy budgets vary considerably between urban and rural areas. Urban areas are well known for their heat islands which are particularly apparent under clear night-time skies. Figure 3.46 shows the extent to which temperatures in urban areas may exceed those in the less built-up surrounding districts, and how there is a link between the strength of the heat island and the population of the urban area. Use this information and refer to the daytime and night-time energy budgets to answer these questions.

1 Using proportional symbols to show the approximate relative importance of each energy transfer, construct daytime and night-time heat budget diagrams for a large urban area and a countryside district.

2 Identify which energy transfers are most significant in creating urban heat islands.

3 Suggest reasons that might account for the difference in the strength of the urban heat island between North American and European towns and cities of the same size?

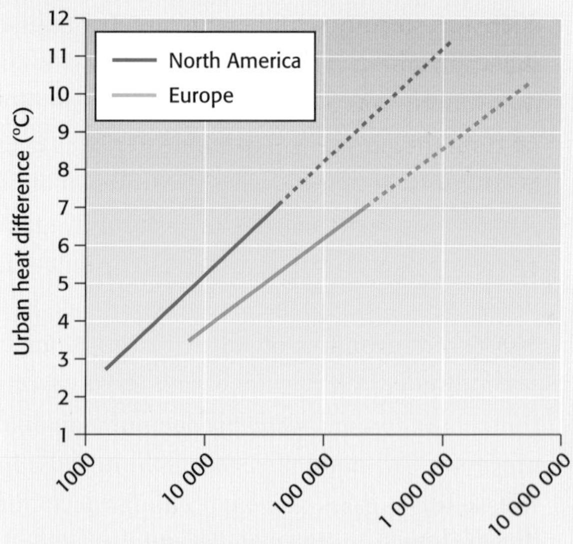

The urban heat island effect is measured in terms of the temperature difference between the urban centre and the districts on the edge of the built-up area. The graph shows the general relationship based on a range of North American and European towns and cities.

Figure 3.46
The relationship between city size and the strength of the urban heat island

4 The lithosphere

Key Themes

- ✔ Tectonic processes and crustal plate movement largely account for the global pattern of volcanic activity and earthquakes.
- ✔ Weathering processes, both physical and chemical, are important landscape-shaping forces which give rise to distinctive landforms in granite and limestone areas.
- ✔ In addition to climate, lithology, structure, vegetation and relief, human activity is exerting an increasingly strong influence on rates of weathering.
- ✔ Slopes are an essential part of the landscape. They are subject to a variety of mass movement processes which can alter their character either imperceptibly or with sudden catastrophic effects.

This chapter is concerned with the tectonic structure of the Earth and the role of weathering and slope development in the shaping of landscape and scenery. While tectonic activity has its origins deep within the Earth, its outward signs are most evident in that part of the globe known as the **lithosphere**, the upper mantle and the crust (Figure 4.1). By contrast, weathering and slope development involve processes found on the surface of the crust alone. Case studies from many parts of the world including Taiwan, Italy, China, Australia and England are studied in this unit.

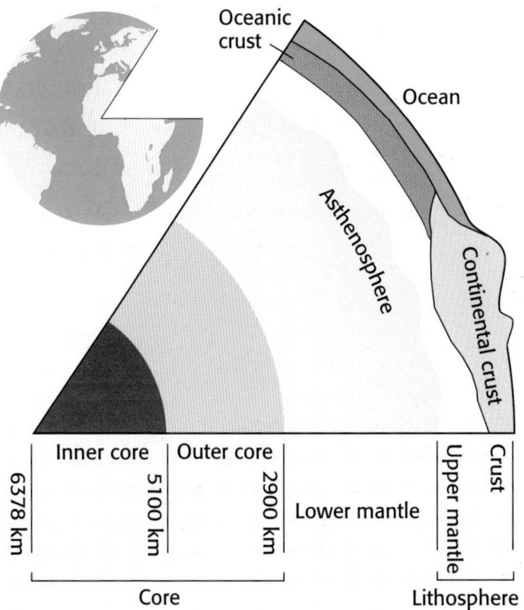

Figure 4.1

The Earth's structure (not to scale)

Earth structure and plate tectonics

The Earth is divided into three main layers: the core, the mantle and the crust.

- The **core**, composed mostly of nickel (Ni) and iron (Fe), is found at a depth of about 2900 km and is thought to be made up of two parts. The outer core is so hot at an estimated 4000–6000°C that it is molten. The inner core, however, is under such extreme pressure from a depth of 5100 km that it is likely to be solid.
- Most of the Earth's mass is in the **mantle** which extends downwards from an average depth of about 50 km to the edge of the outer core. The upper layer of the mantle combines with the crust to form the lithosphere which is rigid but can deform slowly. Beneath the lithosphere lies the

asthenosphere at a temperature of between 1000 and 1200°C. This zone has plastic-like properties which enable it to 'flow'.

- The **crust** is much thinner than any of the other layers, ranging from a few kilometres beneath the oceans to 75 km where it has been formed into mountain ranges. It is divided sharply from the upper mantle by a boundary known as the Mohorovičić discontinuity – the Moho for short. Being relatively cold, the crust is solid and brittle and can fracture. It is divided into seven major and six minor interlocking plates (Figure 4.2). Each plate consists of upper mantle and crust. At any one location, the crust can be **continental** crust, which makes up the land masses upon which we live, or **oceanic** crust which lies under the major oceans. Continental crust is thicker but less dense and lighter than oceanic crust.

Causes of plate movement

The theory of continental drift has long supported the idea of crustal movements on a global scale. Between 200 and 290 million years ago the super-continent of Pangaea was the Earth's principal land mass. Gradually, it broke up to form the continents as we now know them (Figure 4.3). Both geographical and geological evidence suggest the existence of this once massive continent. For example:

- Some of the continents look like pieces of a jigsaw that could have been joined together, such as the eastern coast of South America and the western coast of Africa.
- Fossils of a large reptile, which could not swim long distances, have been found in Australia, Africa and India, which are now separated by the Indian Ocean.
- Carboniferous coal deposits in regions that are now temperate contain plant fossils typical of tropical rainforests. This mismatch suggests that these regions, like Britain, were at one time much closer to the Equator and have subsequently moved.
- Geological structures common to a number of areas suggest that they were once joined. For example, folds resulting from an early mountain building phase are found in the Appalachians of the USA, South Wales and the Urals of Russia.

Figure 4.2
Crustal plates and the types of plate margin

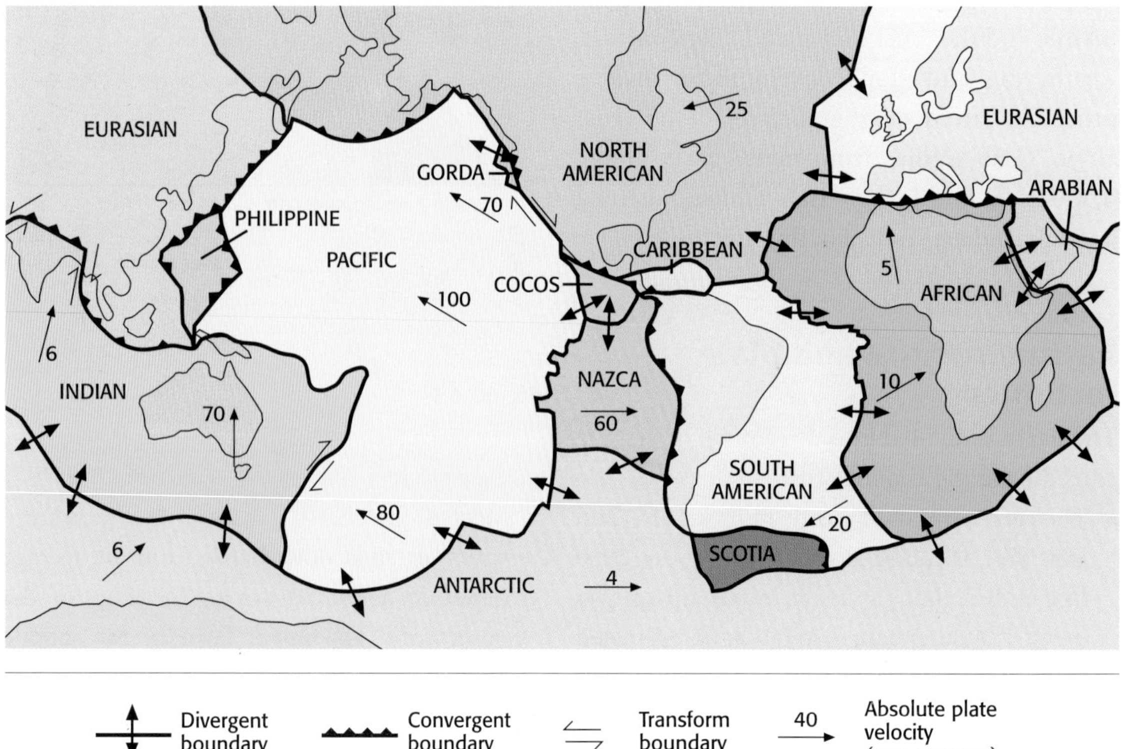

However, continental drift theory did not originally explain how the continents moved. The mechanism behind crustal movement only became better understood once the existence of plates had been established. It is now thought that convection currents largely within the asthenosphere, and driven by heat exchange between the core and the upper zones of the Earth, provide the necessary force for moving the plates. Seismic waves passing through the mantle have been used to map these currents. Colder, denser material sinks into the mantle and warmer, less dense material rises and spreads laterally. It is this lateral movement in the upper mantle that causes the crustal plates to move, usually at speeds of a few centimetres per year (Figure 4.4). In addition, it is likely that as the edges of some plates are reabsorbed into the mantle, or subducted, they pull the rest of the plate along, a process called **slab pull**. Where new plate material is formed along the mid-ocean ridges, **ridge push** occurs as the rising and intruding material forces the plates apart.

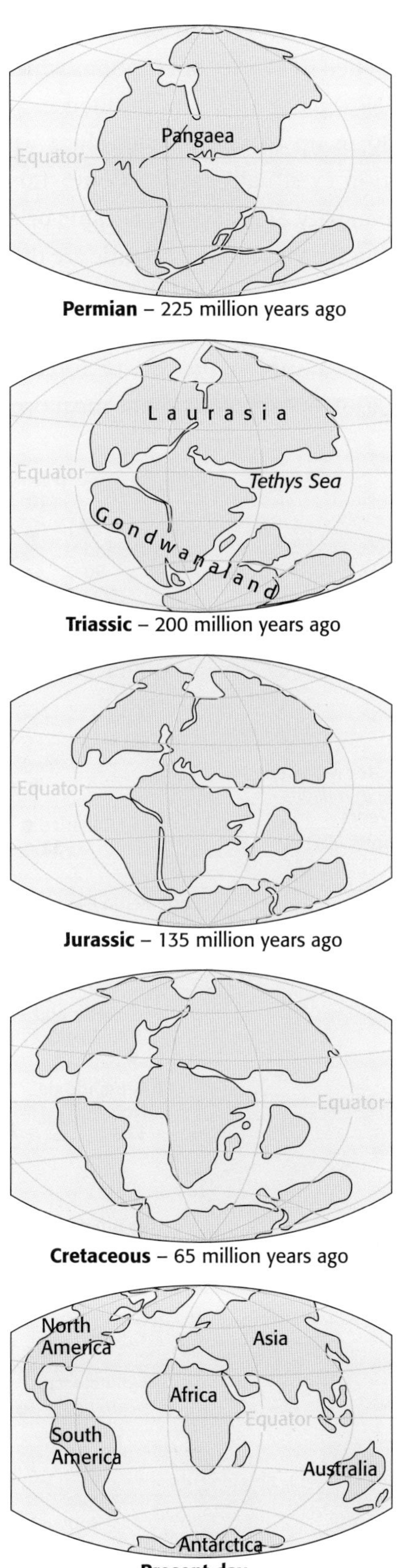

Figure 4.3
The break-up of Pangaea and the drift of the continents

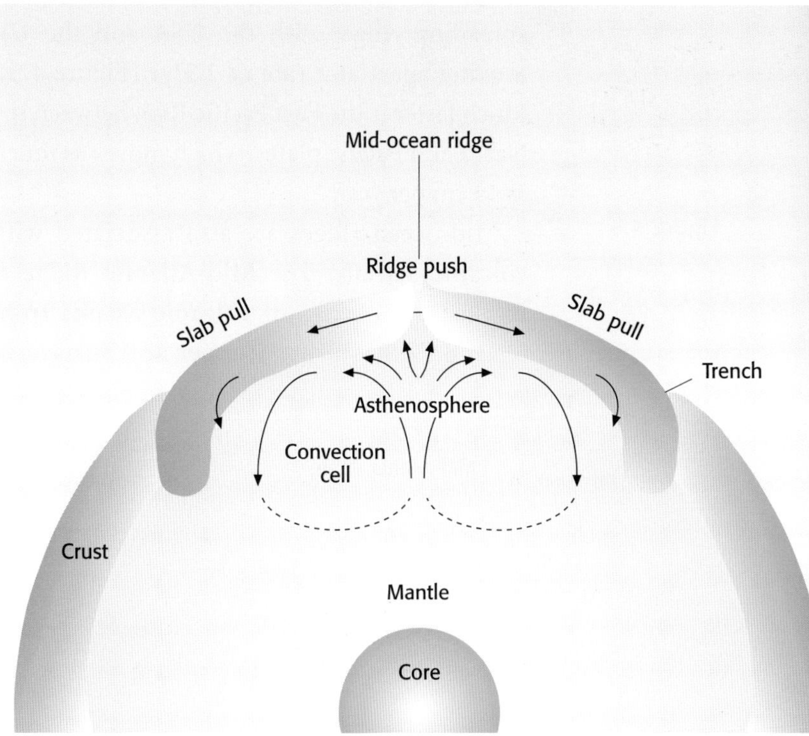

Figure 4.4
The plate-moving mechanism

Plate boundaries

Plate boundaries fall into three broad categories – constructive, destructive and transform – although they may be known by several different names.

Constructive boundaries

Constructive boundaries are also known as **divergent** or **extensional** boundaries. Where rising convection currents force two plates apart, the release of pressure on the asthenosphere causes it to become molten and to rise. As a result the crust spreads as new lithospheric material is created. Where this process occurs beneath oceanic crust, the expanding molten rock forms mid-ocean ridges. Approximately 10 km^3 of new oceanic crust are formed in this way each year. The ridges cover a combined distance of 74 000 km and include the world's highest mountains. The best known example is the Mid-Atlantic Ridge which, as it name implies runs, down the middle of the Atlantic Ocean separating the North and South American plates in the west from the Eurasian and African plates in the east. This is a slow-spreading ridge, with the USA and the UK moving apart at a rate of 2.5/yr (Figure 4.5). Much faster is the East Pacific Rise, between the Nazca and Pacific plates, which moves as much as 14 cm per year.

Mid-ocean ridges are also associated with volcanic activity. The Mid-Atlantic Ridge is marked by a series of volcanic islands from Iceland, with nearby Heimaey and Surtsey, in the North Atlantic, to Tristan da Cunha in the south. The island of Surtsey was formed from the sea bed in a series of eruptions which began on 8 November 1963 and resulted in a growth of 130 m up to sea level within a week; the eruption eventually finished on 5 June 1967. The majority of islands of volcanic origin now flanking the ridge in the Atlantic are thought to have formed along it and to have moved east or west as the ocean floor has spread (Figure 4.6).

Where a similar process of forced crustal separation occurs on land, the most prominent

Figure 4.5

Cross-section through the Mid-Atlantic Ridge and adjoining plates

6000 km
Continental slope
Mid-Atlantic Ridge (volcanic islands)
Continental rise
Halifax, Nova Scotia, continental shelf
Rise
Sea level
Dakar, Senegal, continental shelf
0
2000
4000
6000
8000
Metres
Flanks
Crest
Flanks
Continental margin
Ocean-basin floor
Mid-oceanic ridge or rise
Ocean-basin floor
Continental margin

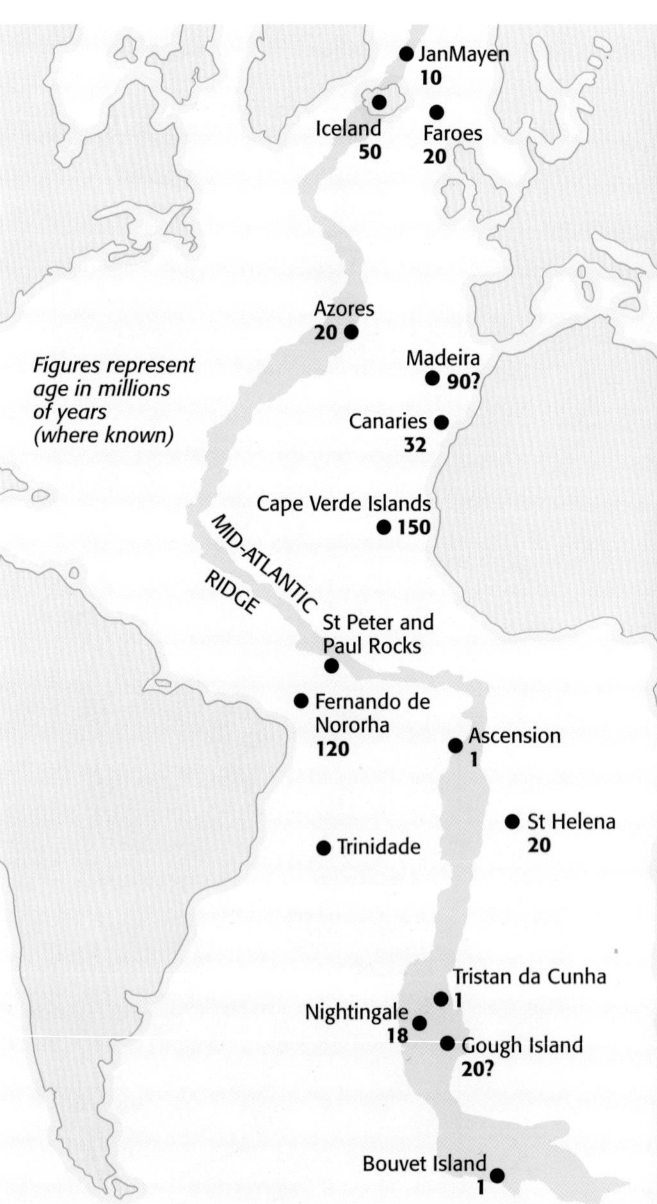

Figure 4.6

Islands of volcanic origin in the Atlantic Ocean

feature is the development of rift valleys as a section of the crust appears to give way and sink (Figure 4.7). Not all rift valleys are formed in the same way and new crust is unlikely to form unless the separation is part of the global movement of plates which allows sufficient 'room' for the new material. In Africa, the East African Rift System is a complex of rift valleys linked to the spreading ridge between the African and Arabian plates along the Red Sea and the Gulf of Aden (Figure 4.8). In parts of the East African system, no spreading is occurring and the valley has filled with sediment whereas the Red Sea is widening slowly. Volcanic activity is also a part of rifting. Mount Kilimanjaro (Figure 4.9) in Tanzania, and Mount Kirinyaga in Kenya are good examples of where new material from the asthenosphere has reached the surface although no active spreading is taking place. Well to the north, some geologists believe that further spreading of the Gulf of Aden could allow the Indian Ocean to flood in and follow the eastern arm of the rift valley, to leave the Horn of Africa as an island.

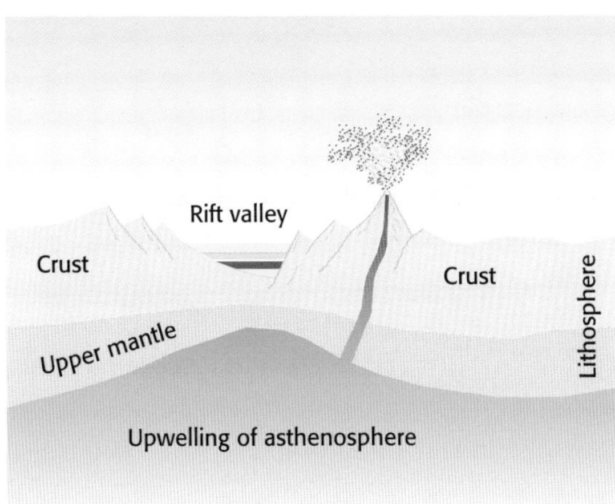

Figure 4.7
Rift valley formation and volcanic action resulting from upward movement of the asthenosphere

Destructive boundaries

These boundaries are also known as **convergent** or **compression** boundaries. There are three types:

1 **Continental–continental** When two continents meet in a collision zone, neither is readily reabsorbed into the mantle because both are relatively light and buoyant and resist downward movement. The outcome is

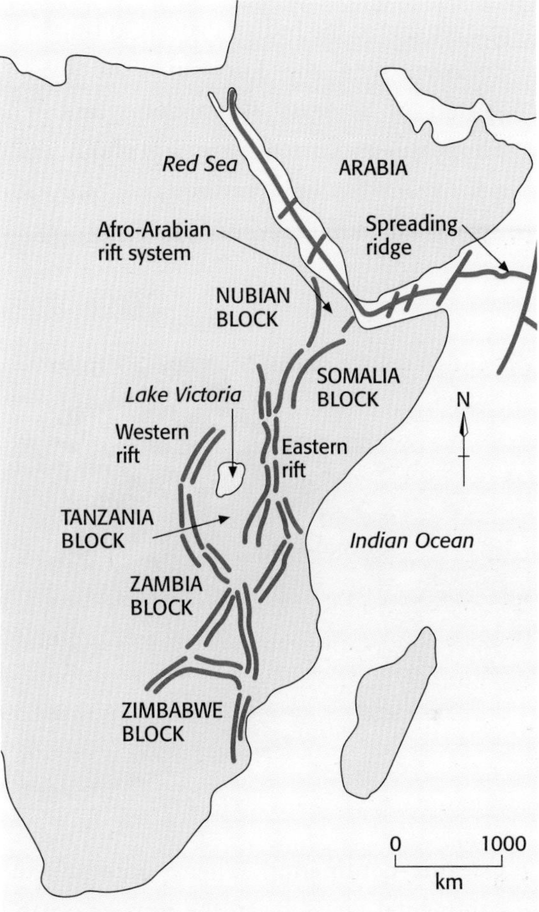

Figure 4.8
The East African rift system

Figure 4.9
Mount Kilimanjaro

that both continental masses become crumpled and compressed together to form fold mountains (Figure 4.10). The Himalayas, the highest continental mountains in the world, have been formed by the slow (18 mm per year) northward movement of the Indian Plate, resulting in its collision with the Eurasian Plate over a period of at least 80 million years. The Himalayas are currently rising at about 5 mm per year. Shallow earthquakes are also associated with this type of plate margin.

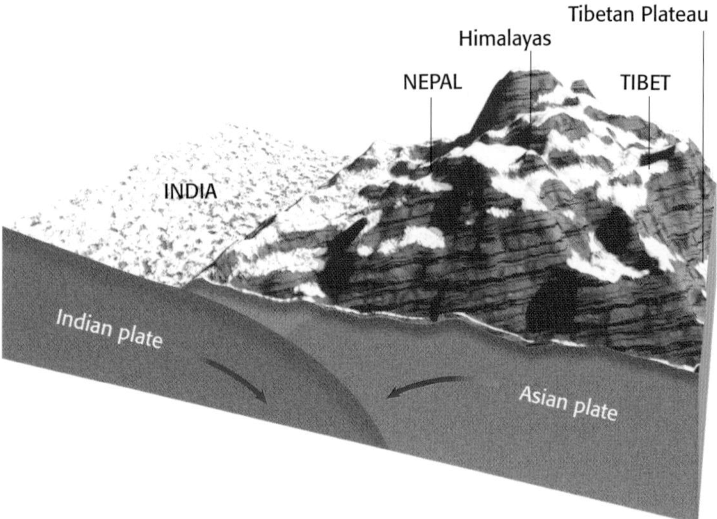

Figure 4.10
Formation of fold mountains at a destructive plate margin – the Himalayas

2 **Oceanic–continental** When oceanic and continental plates meet, the heavier oceanic material sinks below the lighter continental plate in what is called the **subduction zone.** One example is the Nazca plate which is moving eastward and being subducted beneath the South American plate. These zones are commonly marked by a long, narrow trench in the ocean floor and, where the overriding plate is uplifted, by a chain of fold mountains such as the Andes along the western edge of the South American plate (Figures 4.2 and 4.11). Strong, destructive earthquakes are associated with this type of movement and may occur near the surface or as deep as 700 km. In June 1994 an earthquake of magnitude 8.3 on the Richter scale occurred 320 km north-east of La Paz

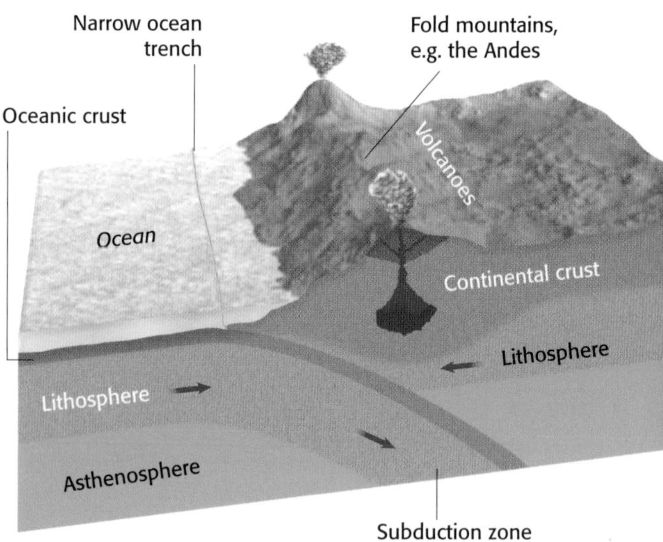

Figure 4.11
Oceanic–continental convergence showing the subduction zone

in Bolivia but, on that occasion, its focus was at a depth of 636 km and little surface damage resulted. Volcanic activity is also likely to be a feature of subduction zones. Molten material from the subducted plate works its way back through the continental plate, perhaps under considerable pressure, to create volcanoes or lava flows. The volcanoes of the Andes, including Nevada del Ruiz, Cotopaxi and Chimborazo for example, owe their origins to this process.

3 **Oceanic–oceanic** When two heavy oceanic plates converge, the sinking plate will exert a strong dragging force creating a pronounced trench. The world's deepest ocean trench, the Marianas Trench, marks the subduction zone between the Pacific and Philippine plates. Part of the Marianas Trench cuts almost 11 000 m into the Earth's crust – compare this dimension with Mount Everest which rises 'only' 8854 m above sea level. At oceanic boundaries, frictional heat is high, giving rise to abundant molten magma which arrives at the surface to create a string of volcanoes following the curved line of the trench. The resulting series of volcanic islands is known as an **island arc** (Figure 4.12). Examples are the Japanese Ryukyu Islands, the Kuril Islands and the Aleutian Islands.

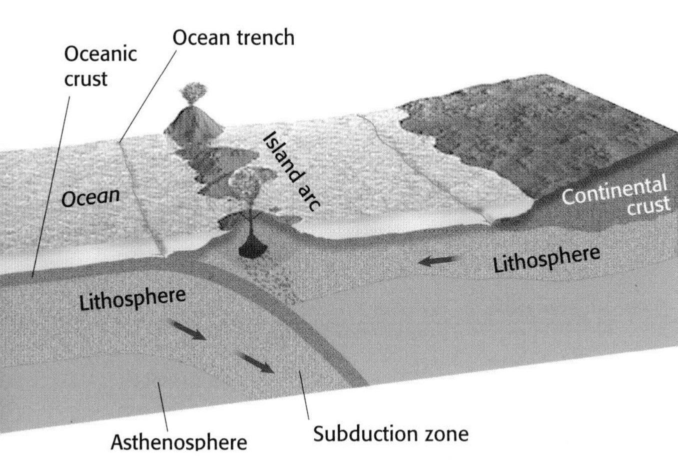

Figure 4.12

Oceanic–oceanic convergence with ocean trench and island arc

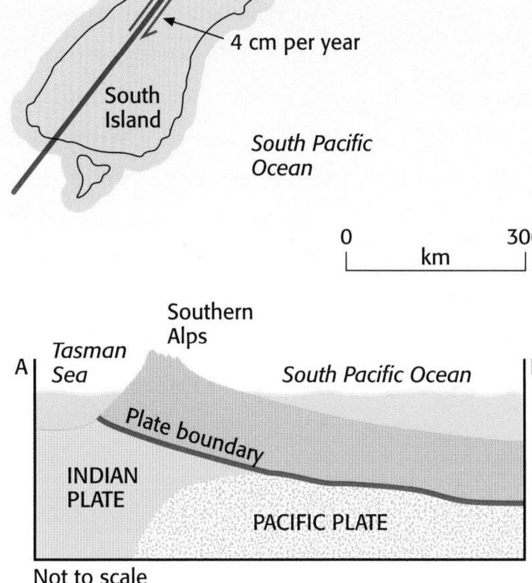

Figure 4.13

The boundary between the Pacific and Indian plates in New Zealand

Transform boundaries

At some plate boundaries, the dominant form of movement is sideways, with the plates slipping past each other. These boundaries are called **transform** or **slip** boundaries. A good example occurs in New Zealand where the Pacific plate moves south-west against the Indian plate at about 4 cm per year. There is also a strong degree of compression, or convergence, with the Pacific plate riding up and over the Indian plate to create the steep westward-facing slope of the Southern Alps (Figures 4.2 and 4.13). The boundary is also marked by a series of volcanoes.

Plate boundary hazards – earthquakes and volcanoes

The global distribution of earthquakes and volcanoes largely mirrors the pattern of plate boundaries, making such regions hazardous zones in which to live. An earthquake is a vibration of the Earth's surface caused when energy is suddenly released through the dislocation of segments of the Earth's crust. At destructive plate boundaries, where the crust is subjected to strong bending forces, it will break and suddenly move to a new position when its strength is exceeded. This sudden movement generates shock, or **seismic**, waves which travel outward from the point where the energy was released, known as the **focus**. Most damage will occur at the **epicentre**, the point on the Earth's surface immediately above the focus. Figure 4.14a shows the relationship between the focus and epicentre, and also the four types of motion created by seismic waves. Earthquake magnitude, or strength, is measured on the **Richter scale** (Figure 4.14b). This scale is logarithmic, which means that each point represents a tenfold increase in the amount of energy involved. 1999 was 'the year of the earthquake', with major tremors in Colombia, India, Turkey,

Taiwan, Mexico and California leading to more than 20 000 deaths and many thousands of injured and homeless people. The ever-increasing death toll associated with earthquakes is due not only to their size but also to the growth of urban areas in earthquake-prone parts of the world, which has increased the potential number of victims.

In order to improve our understanding of earthquakes, important new research is being carried out on the San Andreas fault system which marks the well-known transform boundary between the North American and Pacific plates in California. Geologists are now planning to drill deep into the fault in an attempt to find out if gases and fluids rising from the Earth's interior act to reduce the frictional hold of one plate on another, thus allowing small releases of energy to trigger large earthquakes (Figure 4.15). The Turkish earthquake which killed 17 000 people in August 1999, was the result of sideways movement along the North Anatolian fault which forms a part of the junction between the Arabian and Eurasian plates.

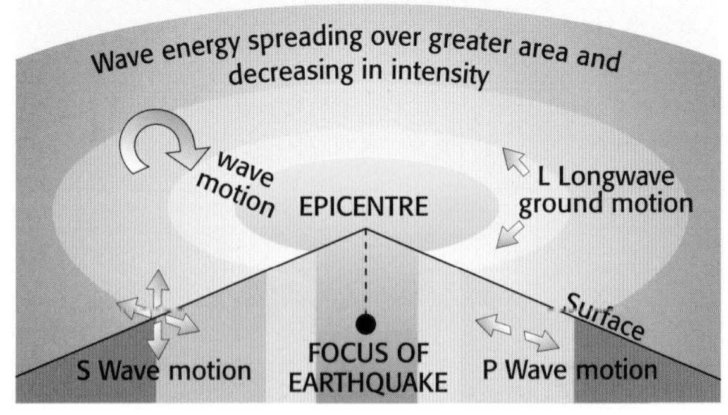

a Features of an earthquake

P = primary waves
S = secondary waves
L = long waves

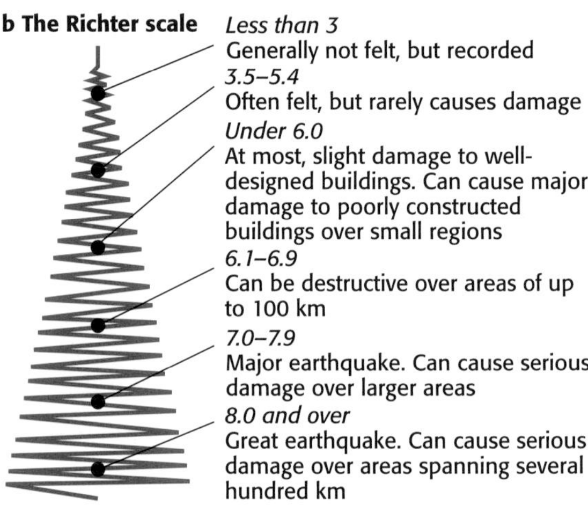

Figure 4.14

Earthquakes, and how they are measured

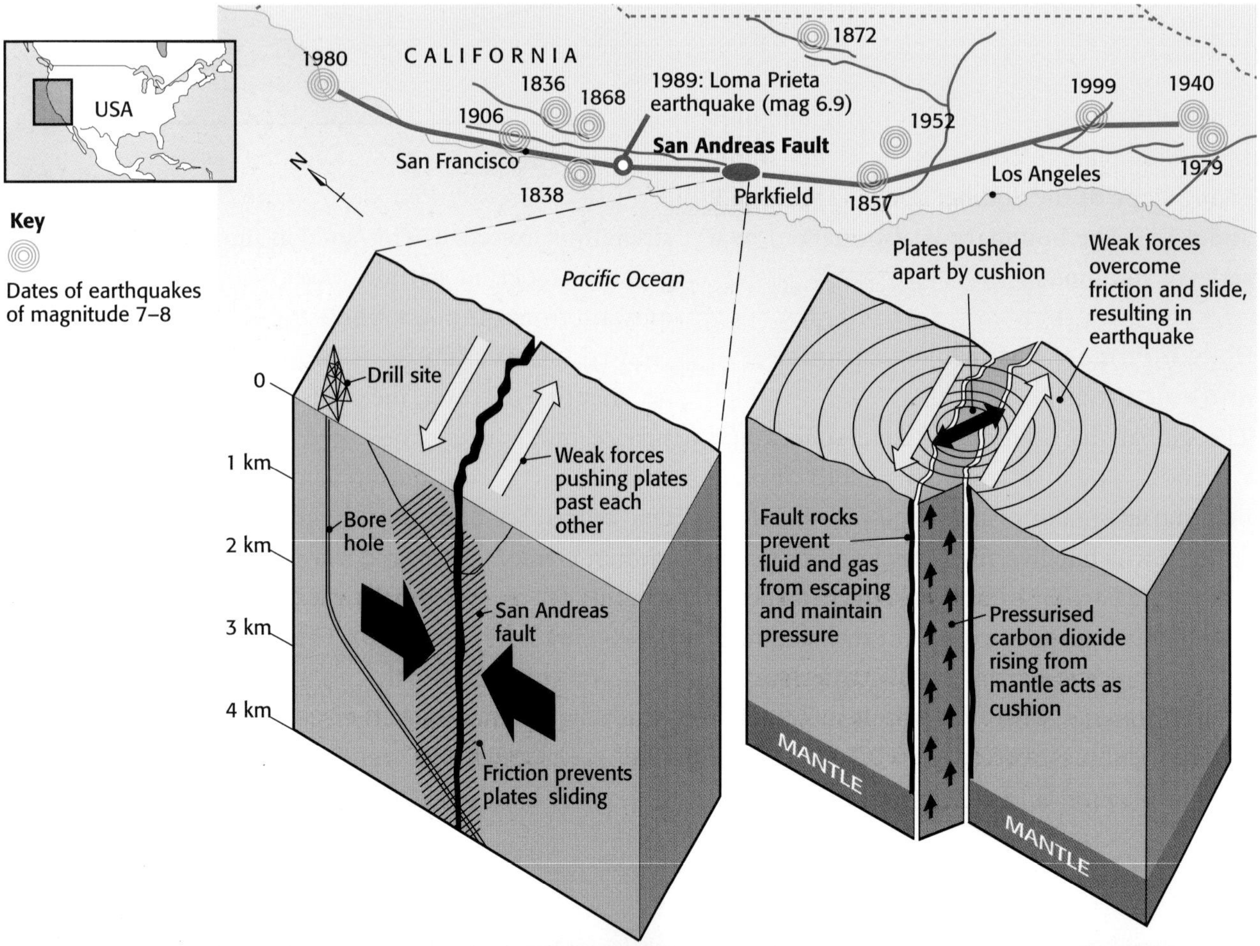

Figure 4.15

Experimenting with the San Andreas fault, California

Case Study: The Taiwan earthquake, September 1999

Taiwan is located on the 'Ring of Fire', the series of plate margins which encircle the Pacific Ocean to create one of the most active earthquake zones on Earth. Taiwan is on a destructive plate boundary where the Philippine and Eurasian plates move towards each other at speeds of up to 7 cm per year (Figure 4.16). Since a major shock recorded in 1935, the country has experienced many thousands more earthquakes, the majority detectable only by sensitive equipment. In March 1999 a warning was issued of potential earthquakes in excess of 7.0 on the Richter scale, and in September the long period of relative calm came to an abrupt end when a sudden movement of the plates, causing them to move briefly at speeds of up to 8000 km/h, released a tremendous amount of energy.

An earthquake of magnitude 7.6 on the Richter scale struck central Taiwan, near Taichung, on 21 September 1999. A number of tall buildings collapsed and many more were damaged. Roads and bridges were torn up, and power and water supplies were cut to 5 million people. Many aftershocks, including one of 6.5 on 26 September, caused further buildings to collapse. Approximately 80 000 people were left homeless; 2100 people were killed and almost 9000 were injured. More buildings would have fallen and broken up as they did so, but for Taiwan's strict building codes (Figure 4.17).

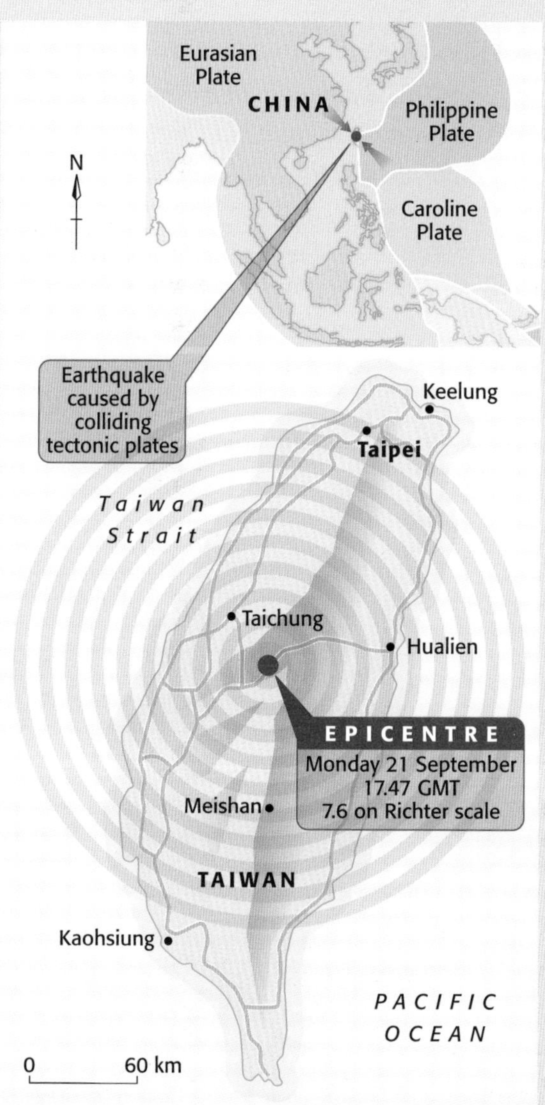

Figure 4.16
Taiwan – teetering on the Ring of Fire

Figure 4.17
Earthquake damage in Taiwan, September 1999

Case Study: Volcanic eruption, Mount Etna, Sicily

Volcanic activity is associated with constructive plate boundaries because the crust is stretched and faulted, and with destructive boundaries where plate edges fracture and melt as they are subducted into the asthenosphere. In both cases hot material is able to find its way to the surface, sometimes causing earthquakes in the process, which can warn of a pending eruption.

Mount Etna in Sicily (Figure 4.18) is on a destructive margin where the African plate is moving northwards towards the Eurasian plate. It is Europe's most active volcano, with four summit craters and a large number of parasitic (subsidiary) cones on the sides of the main cone. Since 1971 there have been six major eruptive phases: April to June 1971; January to March 1974; August 1979; September 1989; December 1991 to February 1993; and, most recently, September to November 1999. The latest phase began on the 4 September 1999 with lava fountains jetting to heights of 1500 m from the Voragine crater. Airborne volcanic material – **pyroclasts** – reached the east coast of Sicily, a distance of nearly 20 km. Matters then calmed down until 5 October when smaller lava fountains were observed erupting from the North East and Bocca Nuova craters. Vigorous eruptive activity continued, with volcanic bombs being hurled several hundred metres, and by 17 October the volume of lava was so great that a portion of the western rim of the Bocca Nuova crater collapsed, causing lava to pour down the western flank of the volcano. Towns in the area were put on alert for a possible evacuation and on 27 October a lava flow cut local roads and tracks at distances up to 6 km from the summit of Etna. Forest fires were started and came within 9 km of the town of Bronte, itself some 15 km from the summit. By the end of November, the eruption was still continuing.

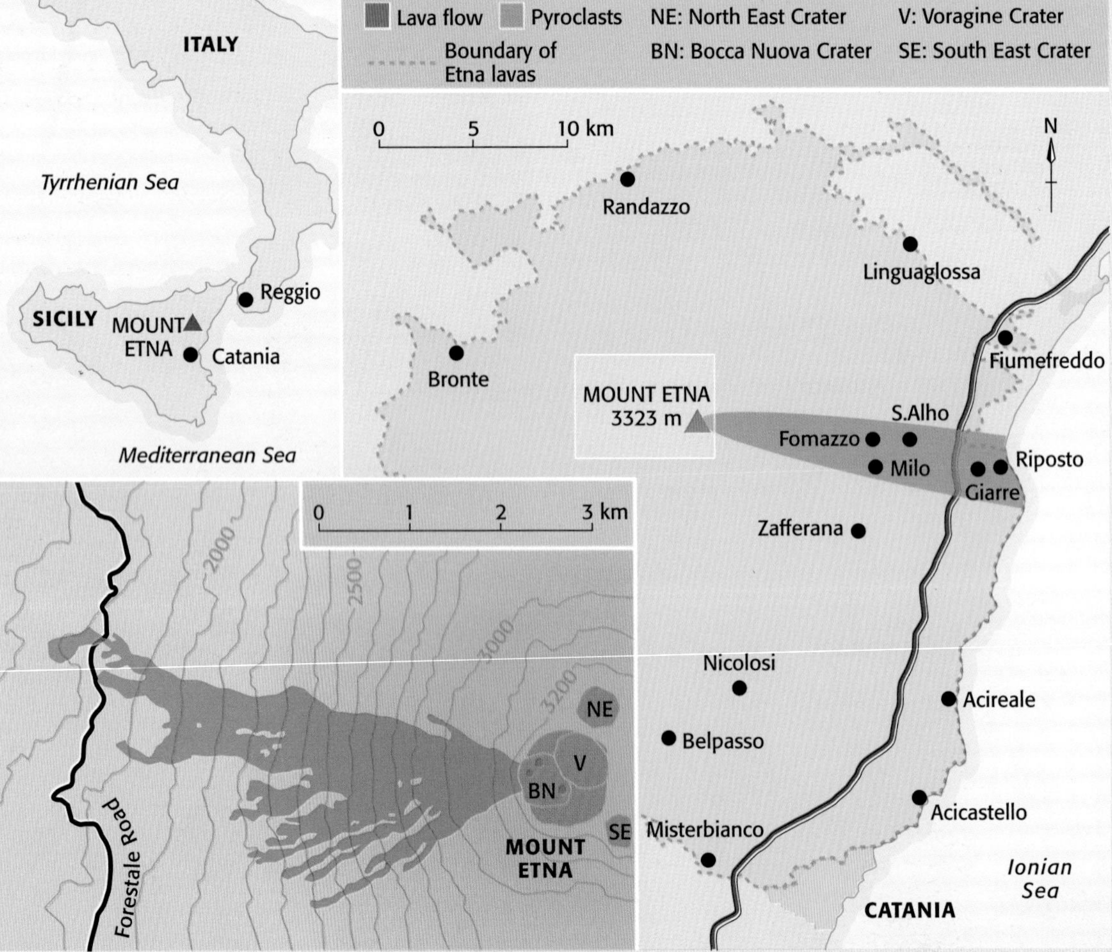

Figure 4.18 The Etna eruption, autumn 1999

Activity

1 Study Figure 4.19, which is a satellite image showing parts of South-east Asia and the western Pacific Ocean. Using a detailed atlas map to help you, identify the following locations on the satellite view:

- Kyushu, Shikoku, Honshu and Hokkaido (Japan)
- Sakhalin Island and the Kamchatka Peninsula
- South Korea
- China
- Kuril Islands and Kuril Trench
- Ryukyu Islands and Ryukyu Trench
- Marianas, Izu Bonin, Japan, and Philippine Trenches.

2 Prepare an outline map of the satellite image and mark on and label the features you have identified. To what extent does the satellite image help our understanding of plate movement? Refer to Figure 4.2 when preparing your response.

Weathering processes

Weathering

Weathering is the breakdown of rock at or near the ground surface when it is exposed to air, moisture and organic matter. Unlike erosion it occurs *in situ* (in place) and the resulting rock particles are only slightly displaced. Weathering processes are typically divided into two broad categories: physical and chemical. Although one category may well predominate in a given area, it is rare for one to occur without the other.

Physical weathering

Physical weathering (or mechanical weathering) involves the physical breakdown of rock first into larger blocks and eventually into grains or individual mineral crystals. There will be little or no chemical change. The general term for this breakdown into small particles is **granular disintegration.** It is most likely to occur in areas with limited vegetation cover, such as high mountains and hot or cold deserts. Although seven types of physical weathering can be identified, they often occur together and, as a result, their influences are not always easy to separate.

Figure 4.19
Satellite image of South-east Asia

1 **Freeze–thaw**, or frost shattering, occurs when there are fluctuations of temperature above and below freezing point. Water collects in cracks in the rock, and when the temperature drops below 0°C it freezes and expands by 9 per cent. The pressure created by this expansion – especially where cracks have become sealed – results in the progressive weakening of the rock and its eventual failure. The frequency of freeze–thaw cycles is important in controlling the rate of this form of mechanical weathering. Thus daily freeze–thaw cycles experienced during the winter in cool maritime regions are more effective than the greater but less frequent temperature cycles encountered in cold continental regions. For the same reason, freeze–thaw is a common process at high altitudes, giving rise to slopes of frost-shattered material, or **screes**, below the most exposed rock faces.

2 **Heating and cooling**, or insolation weathering, results from the thermal expansion and contraction of rock in response to rising and falling temperatures. It occurs during the daily cycle of heating and cooling and sets up stresses in the rock that cause it to disintegrate, perhaps with an explosive crack. It occurs predominantly in hot deserts where a lack of cloud cover results in a pronounced difference between peak daytime and nighttime temperatures, possibly in the order of 30–50°C. There is also evidence that it occurs during bush fires.

Within rocks such as granite, colour differences in mineral crystals have been thought to cause them to expand and contract at different rates, encouraging disintegration into individual grains. However, this type of weathering has not been successfully reproduced in the laboratory in the absence of water vapour, suggesting that alternate heating and cooling alone is not sufficient.

3 **Wetting and drying**, or slaking, occurs when rock is periodically wetted and then dried. Minerals such as montmorillonite, which make up clay rocks, expand greatly when wetted and contract on drying out. As with freeze–thaw and insolation weathering, the stresses which arise from repeated expansion and contraction cause the rock to disintegrate. Slaking commonly occurs in the intertidal zone of coastal areas where wetting and drying occur on a frequent and regular basis.

4 **Exfoliation**, or spheroidal weathering, stems from the fact that rock, in general, is a poor conductor of heat. Under warm conditions, rock surfaces heat up and expand more than the main body of material lower down. The eventual outcome is that the surface layers split off, or **spall**, from the lower layers, sometimes in the form of slightly curved sheets resembling the layers of an onion. In consequence, this process is also known as **onionskin weathering** (Figure 4.20). It is common in regions with little rainfall and high temperatures, and is particularly evident on intrusive igneous rocks such as granite. Signs of exfoliation can also be seen in bricks and masonry, including gravestones.

5 **Crystal growth**, or salt weathering, results from the growth of crystals of salts, such as sodium carbonate and magnesium sulphate, within spaces in a rock. It can be caused when saline water enters voids in the rock and evaporates; the growing crystals then prise the rock apart. It is particularly effective in semi-arid areas where salt solutions dry quickly, but can also occur in coastal regions. Bricks and concrete are vulnerable to salt weathering in temperate areas.

6 **Pressure release**, or dilation, is an unusual type of physical weathering. Unlike the previously described processes it is not caused by elements of the weather. It occurs either when erosion removes a heavy

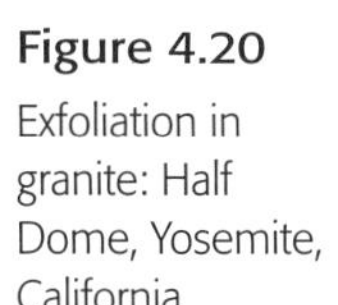

Figure 4.20
Exfoliation in granite: Half Dome, Yosemite, California

covering of rock (overburden), or when huge ice sheets melt at the end of a glacial period. The removal of great weight allows the rock below to expand, producing sheet joints, or pseudo-bedding planes, parallel to the ground surface. These joints may then encourage further weathering (Figure 4.21).

7 **Organic action** consists of the breaking up of rock by plant roots and burrowing animals. Roots tend to exploit existing cracks and lines of weakness and, as they thicken, they exert increasing pressure and cause rocks to fracture. Building foundations are at risk from the roots of larger trees and may be undermined. Burrowing animals can also break apart partially weathered rock, exposing it to further weathering.

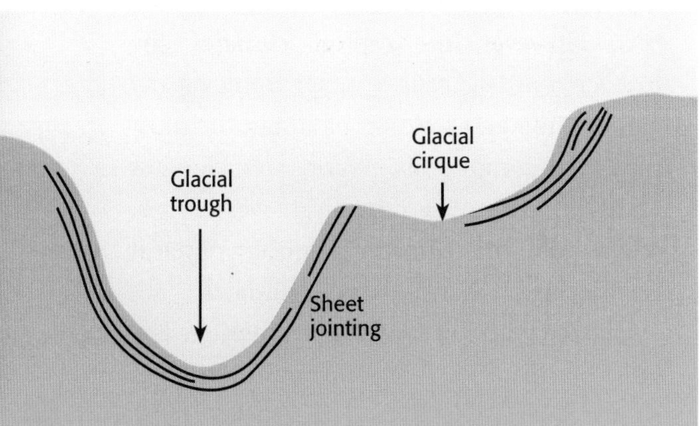

Figure 4.21
Sheet joints formed by pressure release

Chemical weathering

Chemical weathering involves the decomposition of minerals and arises from the modification of the chemistry or the crystalline structure of rocks. It is most common in warm, humid climates with a dense vegetation cover. Rocks that have been attacked by chemical weathering have a dull, pitted appearance. Carbonic acid, produced by carbon dioxide dissolving in rainwater, is the major chemical weathering agent:

$$H_2O + CO_2 \leftrightharpoons H_2CO_3 \text{ (carbonic acid)}$$

Further carbon dioxide will be absorbed if the rain percolates through organic rich soil.

Chemical weathering can be divided into six main types and, as in the case of physical weathering, each type is unlikely to occur in isolation from the others.

1 **Hydrolysis** is the most common chemical weathering process. Carbonic acid releases hydrogen ions from water which then combine with certain minerals in rock, causing the latter to disintegrate. This process is common in rocks that contain the mineral feldspar, such as granite. The end-products of feldspar weathering are clay minerals, such as kaolinite. Sodium, potassium and magnesium ions are removed in solution and the relatively inert quartz grains are left behind, a process known as **kaolinisation.**

2 **Hydration** occurs when water is absorbed into the crystal structure of certain minerals and causes chemical changes. For example, anhydrite (a form of calcium sulphate) absorbs water to become gypsum, which is a very soft mineral. Apart from chemical changes, the absorption of water may also cause rocks to swell, creating stress and leading to physical weathering.

3 **Carbonation** is a process that occurs most commonly in regions with limestone geology. On contact with calcium carbonate (the main component of limestone), carbonic acid creates calcium hydrogen carbonate, also known as calcium bicarbonate:

$H_2CO_3 + CaCO_3 \leftrightharpoons Ca(HCO_3)_2$

As calcium bicarbonate is readily dissolved in water, it is quickly removed, leaving behind only the clay and quartz impurities of the limestone. Carbonation may also occur in sedimentary rocks, such as sandstone, where the rock particles are cemented with a calcite mortar.

4 **Solution** Unlike calcium carbonate, certain minerals in rock require no chemical reaction to be soluble. For example, halite (rock salt) will readily dissolve in water.

5 **Oxidation** Some minerals in rocks react with oxygen dissolved in water to form oxides or hydroxides. This process most commonly occurs in rocks containing iron. Iron in its ferrous form (Fe^{2+}) is changed through oxidation into its ferric form (Fe^{3+}) leading to the collapse of its molecular structure. The more common name for iron in its ferric form is 'rust'.

6 **Chelation** Lichens and decomposing organic matter in soil (humus) release organic acids. These organic acids attack certain minerals in the rock, releasing iron and aluminium ions which can then be transported away by water. The process of release is called chelation, and the organic acids are known as chelating agents.

Factors influencing rates of weathering

It will be clear from the preceding descriptions of the various weathering processes that a considerable number of factors determine the rate at which weathering occurs.

- **Parent material** The solubility and stability of the chemical components of the parent material are very important. Some minerals weather quickly while others, such as quartz, are stable and resistant to breakdown. The structure of the rock is also crucial. Joints and bedding planes act as routes for weathering agents such as water, acids and tree roots.
- **Climate** Heat generally speeds up chemical reactions, with a rise of 10°C producing at least a doubling of the reaction rate. Conversely, carbonation is more rapid in cooler climates because carbon dioxide is more soluble in water at low temperatures, although the process ceases altogether below 0°C. However, in tropical climates the heavier rainfall causes rapid removal by carbonation and solution of all but the most insoluble compounds. Warm wet climates tend to encourage chemical weathering, whilst cold dry climates promote physical weathering. Warm dry climates are associated with low levels of weathering. The link between climate and weathering is shown diagrammatically in Figure 4.22.
- **Availability of moisture** The amount of available water influences the rate of both

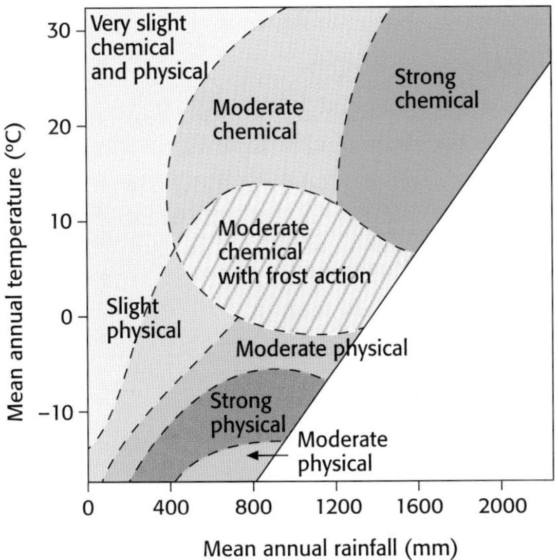

Figure 4.22

The relationship between climate and weathering

chemical and physical weathering. Sufficient water for weathering can be available in seemingly arid areas, for example close to oases, along the coast, in irrigated areas and in the form of dew.

- **Biological activity** Burrowing animals, such as ants and rabbits, turn over soil and expose it and the underlying rock to more chemical weathering. Tree roots can prise apart rock by penetrating joints and exerting a destructive pressure as they grow.
- **Regolith removal** The removal of **regolith** – the surface accumulation of unconsolidated material including the products of weathering – exposes fresh material to weathering. Mass movements and various agents of erosion can lead to the rapid removal of the regolith on steep slopes, but on gentle slopes and in the bottoms of valleys or basins the situation is different. Here, accumulated weathering products are likely to protect the underlying rock from further weathering.
- **Aspect** The direction in which a slope faces affects the temperatures it will experience. In the northern hemisphere south-facing slopes receive more insolation and are much warmer than north-facing slopes. In winter, these slopes may experience a regular, perhaps daily, cycle of temperatures above and below freezing, thus encouraging freeze–thaw action. Some north-facing slopes may never rise above freezing in winter, in which case the effect of freeze–thaw weathering is minimised. Vegetation cover may also vary with aspect, being typically denser on south-facing slopes. In contrast, the impact of chelation and root action will be lower on north-facing slopes.
- **Time** Weathering generally occurs at rates in the order of a few millimetres per hundred or thousand years. Clearly, a very long period is required to build up a significant thickness of weathered material, but the process can be much more rapid under certain circumstances, especially on prominently exposed rock features and on the facades of buildings.
- **Human activity** Atmospheric water is naturally slightly acidic with a pH of 5 to 6 (pH 7 is neutral). However, since the start of the Industrial Revolution, the pH in polluted areas has dropped to an average of 4 and measurements as low as 2.4 have been recorded in some areas where the air is heavily polluted. Sulphur dioxide and NO_x emissions from sources such as motor vehicles, power stations, coal fires and industrial processes are responsible. These substances produce sulphuric and nitric acids in the form of acid rain, which has a number of environmental effects, including the acceleration of the chemical weathering processes of hydrolysis, carbonation and solution. Probably the most evident indication of the impact of human activity on weathering is to be seen on buildings, especially those made of limestone. Increasing volumes of pollutants result in the deterioration of the stone to the point where decorative features become indistinct and complete blocks require replacement once the surface finish has been weathered and break-up begins (Figure 4.23). Individual bricks are similarly affected and turn soft as they absorb moisture.

Figure 4.23

Weathered and disintegrating masonry

Other forms of human activity also contribute to accelerated weathering. Heavy trampling of the land in areas also exposed to vigorous erosion – whether by people, domesticated animals or vehicles – helps to break up rock surfaces and to increase their susceptibility to weathering. Careless planting of trees may also result in weakening of the bedrock, its subsequent fragmentation and damage to foundations. Agricultural practices are known to lead to an increase in the amount of organic matter in the soil, thereby encouraging the process of chelation. The disturbance of the soil through excessive ploughing may also expose the underlying rock to additional weathering.

Weathered landscapes

Weathering can be responsible for creating distinctive landscapes in certain rock types, notably limestone, chalk and granite.

Limestone scenery

The most distinctive weathered landscape is that associated with limestone which contains at least 80 per cent calcium carbonate. It is called **karst** after the area of Kras near the Adriatic coast of Slovenia. The study of this area formed the basis for much of our knowledge of limestone landscapes.

Limestone is a sedimentary rock with horizontal bedding planes formed as it was laid down in layers under shallow tropical seas. Vertical joints in conjunction with the bedding planes give the rock a blocky structure. It is this structure and its chemical composition that make limestone very susceptible to weathering. Several distinctive features are produced both on and below the surface as the joints and bedding planes are widened through the processes of carbonation and solution (Figure 4.24).

Surface features

In arid and temperate regions limestone surfaces are not usually heavily vegetated because carbonation does not leave behind a sufficient thickness of mineral fragments to form the basis of a soil. Further, the lack of surface drainage restricts plant growth. The resulting bare surface is termed a limestone pavement (Figure 4.25). The 'paving slabs' that make up the pavement are known as **clints** and the fissures between them are **grikes**.

Depressions are common on limestone surfaces. They are caused by solution and the settling associated with underground cave systems. **Dolines**, also known as **shakeholes** or

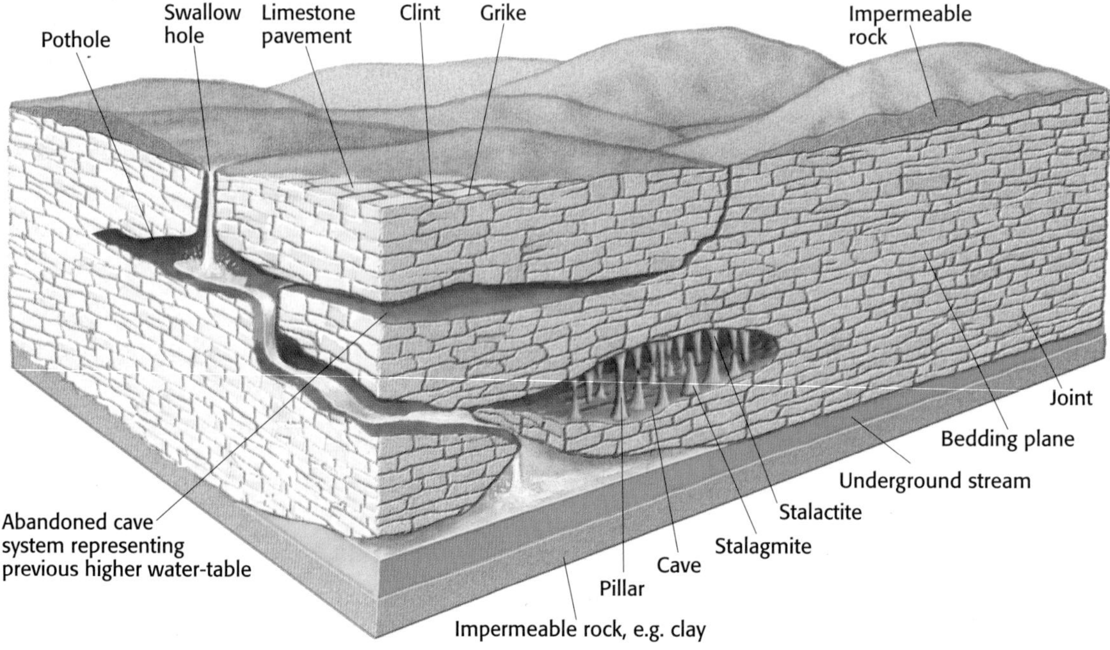

Figure 4.24 Features of limestone scenery

Figure 4.25
A limestone pavement

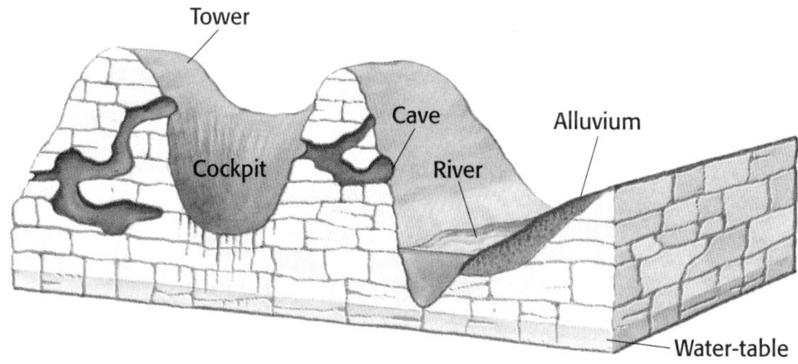

Figure 4.26
Cockpit karst

sinkholes, are roughly circular depressions that may be 2–100 m deep and 100–1000 m across. Water often collects here before it drains through the rock. More extensive depressions with typically flat floors and steep sides are known as **poljes** and are often located where limestone comes into contact with a less permeable rock. Poljes can be dry all year, contain **ephemeral streams** or be continuously wet, depending on the height of the water-table below the surface.

In tropical limestone areas a landscape of depressions separated by small residual hills is called **cockpit karst**. Examples occur in Jamaica and south China (Figure 4.26). The hills, called **hums** or **towers**, are the remnants of the former land surface. They are characterised by fewer joints, which has made them less vulnerable to weathering and, as a result, they have not been lowered as rapidly as the surrounding rock.

Subsurface features

Over a period of time, grikes are widened by carbonation until streams disappear down them. They are then termed **swallow holes** or **swallets**. At lower levels, carbonation encouraged by percolating water enlarges bedding planes and joints to create lengthy systems of underground tunnels and vertical potholes, which help to account for the lack of surface drainage in karst areas.

At depth, tunnels or **potholes** may be enlarged to form caves where, in places, the carbonation reaction may be reversed. As air in caves tends to have a low carbon dioxide content, it absorbs some of the carbon dioxide dissolved within percolating water, causing calcium carbonate to be deposited. Where water seeps uninterrupted for a long period of time from pores in the cave ceiling, thin fingers of calcium carbonate, called **stalactites**, will develop. However, not all the calcium carbonate will be deposited on the ceiling. Some will collect on the floor below and gravity will ensure that the resulting **stalagmite** grows to be a broader feature than its partner stalactite. If the two features eventually join together they create a **pillar** or **column**.

Water flowing down through limestone eventually reaches an impermeable rock below. An underground stream then flows at this junction until it is able to flow to the surface, where it is termed a **resurgent stream** or **karst spring**. A good example in France is the River Douix, a headwater tributary of the River Seine (Figure 4.27). The flow rate of this resurgent varies from 600 litres/second under dry conditions to 3000 litres/second in wet periods.

Figure 4.27
The source of the River Douix, Châtillon-sur-Seine, France

Case Study: The karst landscape of Guangxi, China

Over 1.2 million km^2 of China is exposed karst (Figure 4.28). The karst landscape of Guangxi (Guangzhou) province in southern China is one of the nation's most photographed sites, and the most spectacular karst topography on Earth.

There are three reasons why karst scenery is so well developed in southern China:

- The carbonate rocks attain a thickness between 3000 and 10 000 m.
- Owing to geological stability, it is estimated that carbonation has been active in parts of this region since before the Cretaceous period, more than 136 million years ago. The current solution rates in Guangxi Province may only be lowering the surface by less than 0.3 mm per year, but they have been doing so for a very long time.
- The tropical vegetation cover introduces biogenic carbon dioxide into the soil via plant roots and bacterial decay. This process is regarded as more important in the production of karst than atmospheric carbon dioxide.

Groups of residual hills are separated by depressions producing the distinctive cockpit morphology which the Chinese call *fencong* (Figure 4.29). A karst form common in the Guilin area of Guangxi is the peak forest or *fenglin* where relict towers up to 200 m high are separated by flat plains (Figure 4.30). As in other karst areas, there is a notable lack of surface drainage. In central Guangxi Province there are several main rivers, but a lack of tributary streams. Over 1000 underground streams have been detected flowing through cave systems in this area. The extreme efficiency of these underground drainage systems can lead to problems for the local population. Southern China's annual precipitation is between 1000 and 2000 mm, but 60–80 per cent of it is concentrated in the period May to August. Rapid loss of this rain underground often leads to drought conditions on the surface.

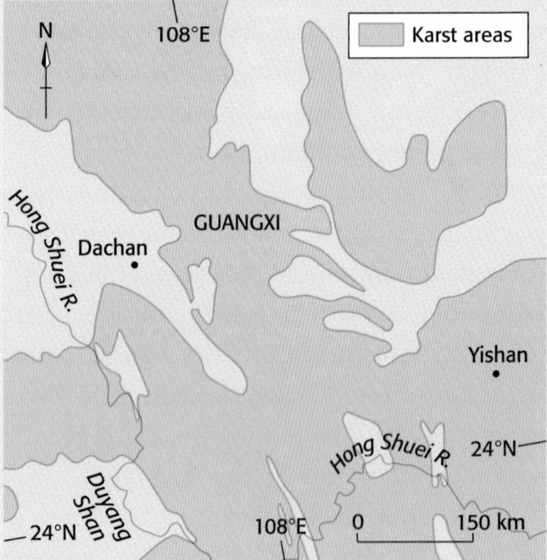

Figure 4.28 The karst region of southern China

Figure 4.29 *Fencong* landscape, southern China

Figure 4.30 *Fenglin* landscape, Guilin

Chalk scenery

Chalk is a type of limestone that does not develop karst scenery. Although the examination of calcium carbonate levels in chalk streams demonstrates that carbonation occurs at a faster rate than in some other limestones, the rock structure is not strong enough to support the formation of underground tunnels and caves. Instead it forms a distinctive landscape of rolling hills and vales, which is known as **downland** in southern England (Figure 4.31). Chalk scenery is also associated with rock folding and the development of **escarpments** or **cuestas** which have steep scarp slopes and gentle dip slopes (Figure 4.32). However, these features are more a product of erosion than of weathering.

As with limestone scenery, there is little surface drainage on chalk. **Dry valleys** are common features, and the size of these suggests different climatic conditions in earlier times. Several hypotheses have been put forward to explain their formation:

- Higher sea levels at the end of the last Ice Age resulted in higher water-table levels and surface streams. Later, as sea level fell, the water-table also dropped, causing the valleys to become dry.
- The freezing of water in rock pores during glacial periods caused the chalk to become impermeable and allowed surface drainage to develop. Later, as temperatures rose and the ice melted, the chalk once again became

Figure 4.31
Chalk landscape in southern England

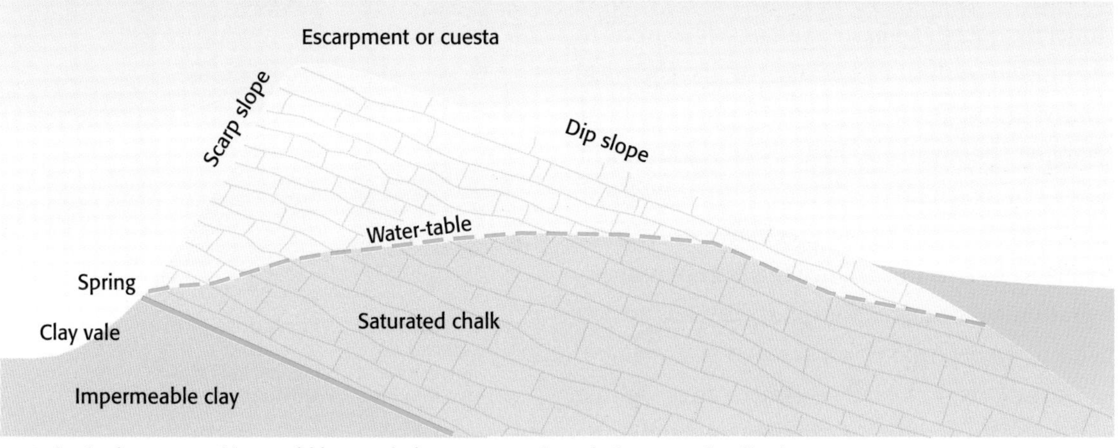

A rise in the water-table would be needed to create surface drainage on the dip slope.

Figure 4.32
A typical chalk escarpment

permeable causing the surface streams to disappear, leaving dry valleys behind.

- The streams and their valleys developed on an overlying layer of impermeable rock. This layer was removed by a combination of weathering and erosion, resulting in the valleys being gradually superimposed on the underlying permeable chalk.
- Surface drainage developed during periods of significantly higher rainfall than at present. When the rainfall decreased the water-table dropped, leaving behind dry valleys.

Other characteristic features of chalk downland are **springs** associated with seasonal streams, or bournes. **Bournes** flow when the **water-table** is high and meets the surface; they dry up when the water-table drops below the surface (Figure 4.33).

Figure 4.33
A clear channel extends several hundred metres upstream of the remains of the footbridge and is occupied when the water-table rises under wet conditions.

Granite scenery

Granite is a crystalline intrusive igneous rock formed when magma is intruded into the Earth's crust. It is typically composed of at least three minerals: quartz, feldspar and mica. It is prone to chemical weathering because of its chemical composition. Both mica and feldspar can be changed chemically by hydrolysis. Kaolinite, or china clay, is an end product of feldspar hydrolysis. Montmorillonite, another clay, results from the hydrolysis of mica. Once this granular disintegration has occurred the quartz crystals are left behind as a deposit known as **gruss** or **growan**.

Granite is a heavily jointed rock which weathers to produce a distinctive landscape dotted with bare stacks of rounded blocks 5–10 m in height, called **tors**. They are considered to be relict features – that is, remnants of a former higher land surface. The most widely accepted theory of tor formation rests on the chemical weathering of the joints beneath a layer of regolith during a warm humid interglacial period. Where the joints were closely packed, weathering was effective in breaking down the granite altogether. Where they were widely spaced, the joints were simply enlarged, leaving behind formations of rectangular blocks, or core stones, some more loosely packed than others. The subsequent removal of the regolith layer by solifluction during periglacial times resulted in the exposure of a landscape consisting of upstanding rock masses (the tors) separated by shallow depressions (Figure 4.34).

Granite is generally regarded as an impermeable rock, although the joints do allow some water to penetrate. As a result, granite areas are typified by high-density drainage patterns (Figure 4.35) and if they receive a high annual rainfall, marshland is likely to be widespread.

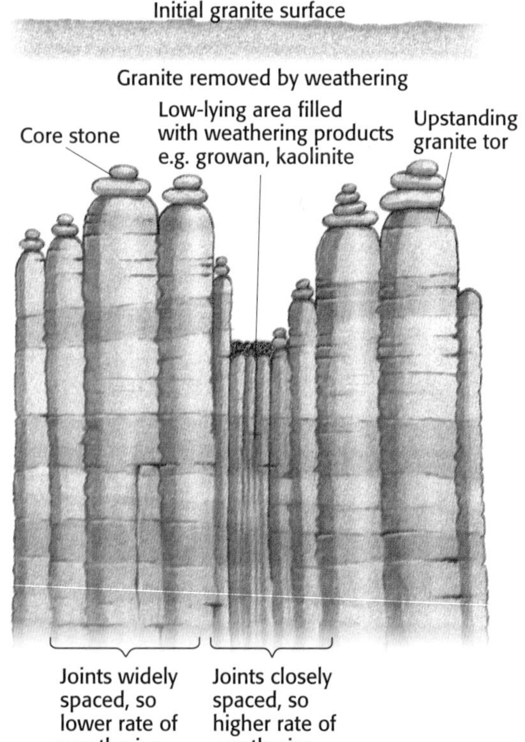

Figure 4.34
Formation of tors

Case Study: Granite scenery, Victoria, Australia

Dartmoor is a much-quoted example of granite scenery but there are many others around the world. Mount Buffalo National Park in north-eastern Victoria, Australia is just one example. It consists of 11 000 ha of rugged, rocky plateau (Figure 4.35) and a mass of blue-black granite, which makes up Mount Buffalo itself and rises 1350 m above sea level. The granite is thought to be Devonian, approximately 350 million years old. Pronounced physical and chemical weathering has occurred along joints in the granite and, as on Dartmoor, it appears that areas with dense joint patterns have been weathered to a greater degree than those with less dense jointing. This process has created clusters of roughly rounded boulders separated by areas of lower relief. The boulders form a number of tors which have been given names reflecting interpretations of their shape, such as the Sarcophagus, the Sentinel and the Cathedral (Figure 4.36).

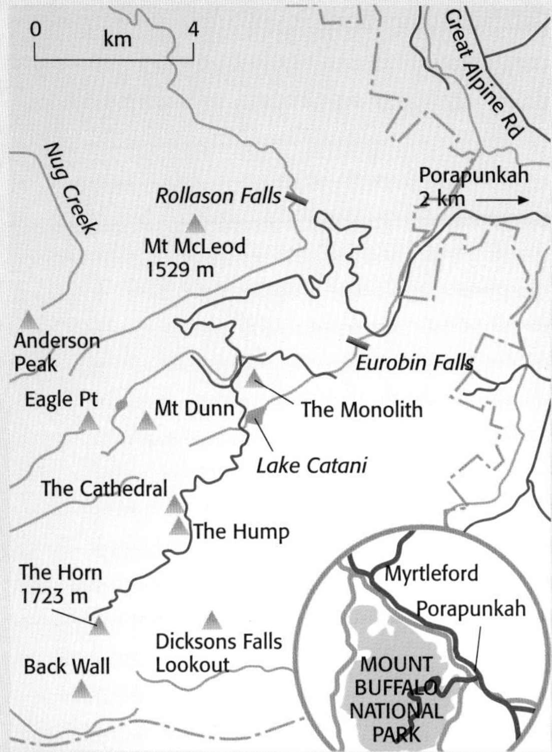

Figure 4.35
Mount Buffalo National Park, Victoria, Australia

Figure 4.36
The Cathedral Tor, Mount Buffalo National Park, Victoria, Australia

Activity

1 Visit a well-established graveyard or cemetery. Find gravestones of different rock types, for example limestone, sandstone, slate, marble, granite. Compare stones of broadly similar ages and attempt to answer these questions:

a Do some tombstones seem to have weathered more than others? Make rubbings of the writing on gravestones. Is some writing sharper, i.e. less weathered, than others?

b Has the rock surface lost its shine? Is there evidence of spalling, pitting, etc.? Are lichens growing on them, possibly causing chelation?

c Does aspect seem to have had any impact on the level of weathering?

d How do sedimentary, metamorphic and igneous rocks compare in terms of their resistance to weathering?

2 **a** Take a close look at hand specimens of limestone and granite, noting differences in colour, chemical/mineral composition, crystal structure and hardness.

b Prepare diagrams to show which weathering processes will have most impact on outcrops of granite, limestone and chalk in a temperate climate.

c For each of granite's constituent minerals, annotate the diagram to explain how it will be weathered.

Slope development and slope processes

Slope systems and slope form

Rather like ecosystems and river basins, slopes can be regarded as systems, with their own **inputs, processes and outputs**. As Figure 4.37 indicates, these factors are usefully divided into those that act on the surface of the slope and those that act beneath it. Slopes receive inputs of solar energy from the sun and kinetic energy from falling rain and the wind. They also receive mass inputs, such as rainwater and meltwater, weathered material, and organic material from vegetation. Under the influence of gravity, slopes also possess stored potential energy because of the difference in height between the top and bottom. Human activity may also have a significant impact on slope inputs and outputs.

Slope form is a function of many influences, including rock structure, climate and a wide range of weathering and erosional processes. Some slope forms are relatively simple, perhaps reflecting a single dominant influence. Others are more complex, suggesting the interaction of several active factors. An examination of many slopes will reveal a number of more or less distinct elements, which are shown in Figure 4.38. These elements form the basis of the description and analysis of slopes but they may not be equally evident on all occasions. Different combinations of angle and curvature create a wide range of slope forms – these are illustrated diagrammatically in Figure 4.39.

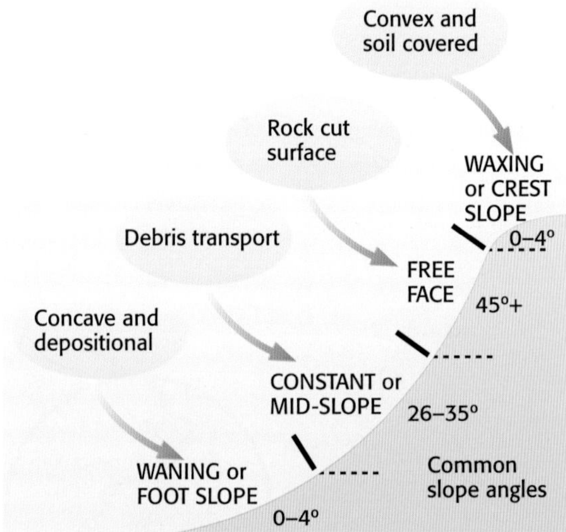

Figure 4.38
The main slope elements and their characteristics

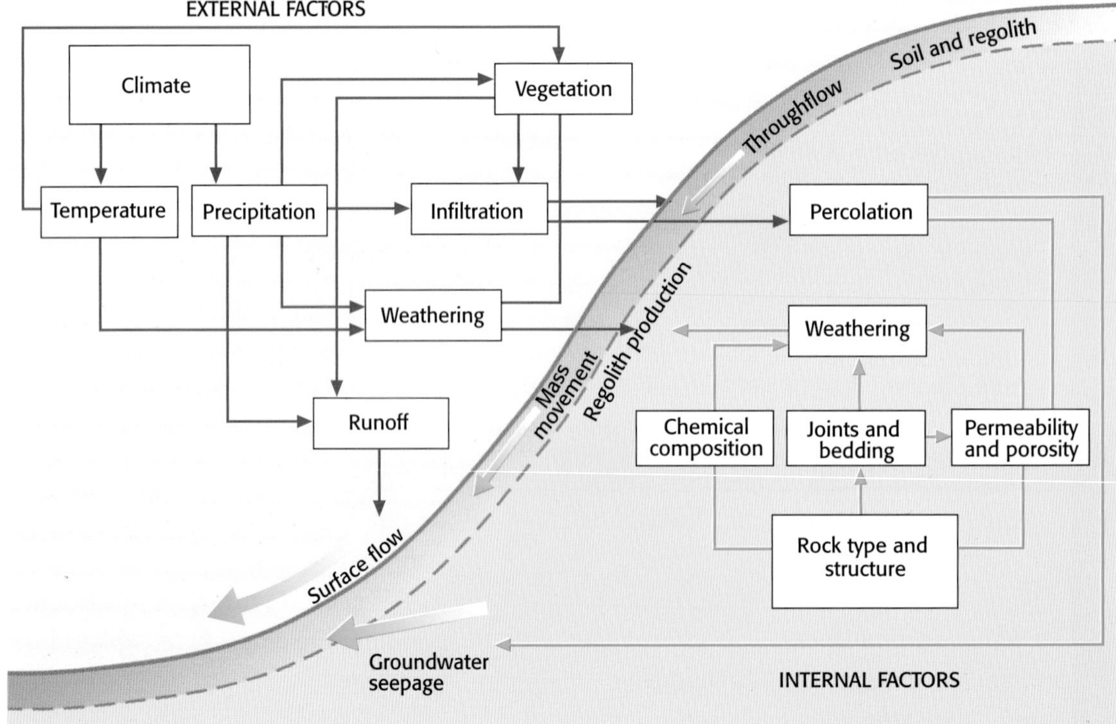

Figure 4.37
Key components of the slope system

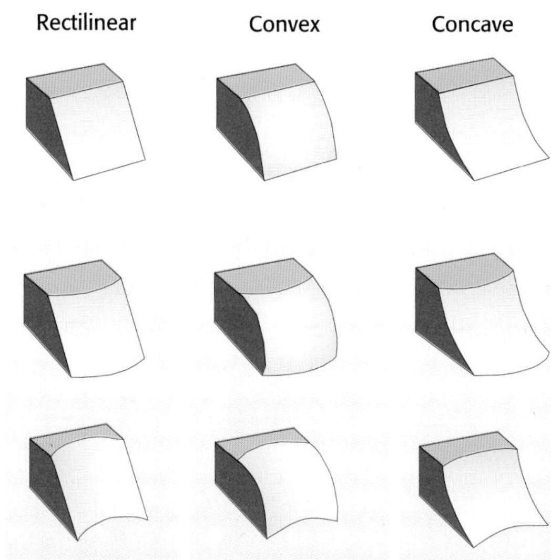

Figure 4.39
Basic slope forms in profile

A range of natural slope forms, and how they might change over time, is shown in Figure 4.40. Each form exhibits a different profile which reflects the history of its creation and subsequent development. Few slopes conform exactly to these rather idealised models because circumstances are rarely the same everywhere. Forceful tectonic movements may create pronounced landscape features with steeply-angled slopes reflecting new rock structures, such as the sides of rift valleys, whereas a gentler folding of sedimentary rocks may give rise to an undulating landscape with mild slopes. With the passage of time, however, the impact of climate, soil, vegetation and human activity may well obscure the influence of **lithology**. The build-up of soil and

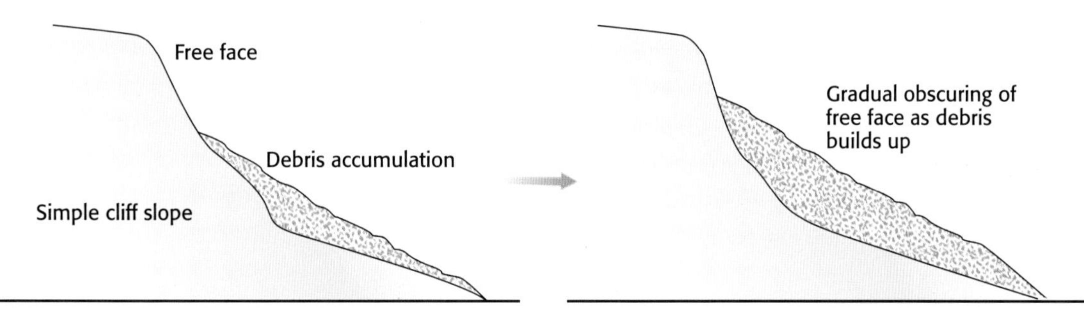

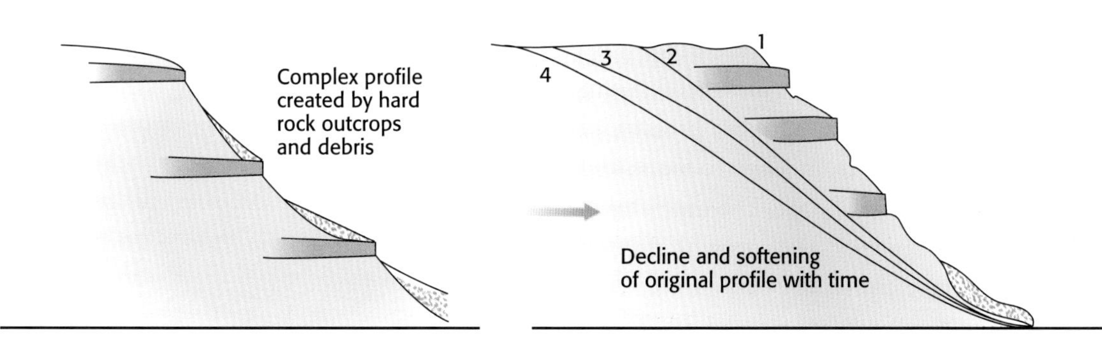

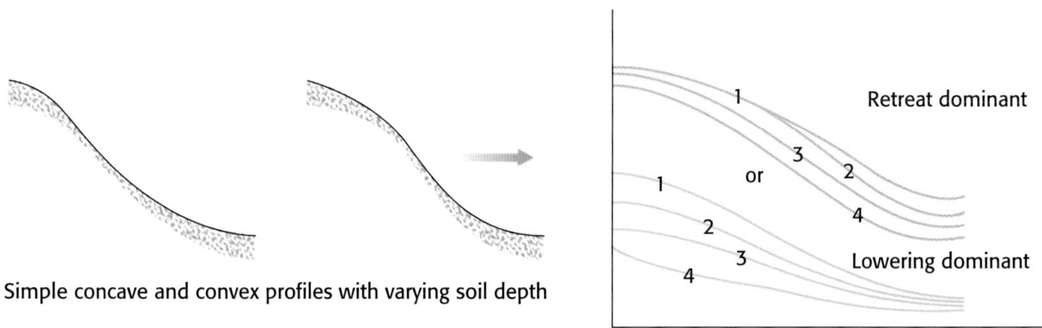

Figure 4.40
A range of slope forms and how they might change over time

debris will bring about a change in the profile, and climatic conditions will have a strong bearing on the impact of the external factors depicted in Figure 4.37. The maintenance or removal of vegetation cover may also be important, especially in relation to the short-term behaviour of the processes that act on the surfaces of slopes. In this instance, human activity is likely to be a key factor.

Slope processes

Every slope can tell a story of weathering and transport, which are the key slope development processes. As you have seen earlier in this unit, weathering can occur in a number of ways and results in the creation of a regolith layer which is subsequently removed downslope by one or more means of transportation. According to their geology, structure and location, individual slopes will experience their own particular range of weathering processes and, consequently, the production of regolith will vary from slope to slope. Where slopes are artificially modified, natural processes may be held up or – perhaps with disastrous effects – accelerated.

Transport processes control the removal of the weathered material and create the slope outputs. Running water (either as surface wash or in channels), ice action and mass movements may all play an important part, though in different proportions from slope to slope and over different periods of time. The build-up of material at the foot of a slope will depend greatly on its angle, the nature of the rock material, and the vigour of the weathering and transportation processes. Substantial accumulations of relatively coarse material at the foot of steep slopes are known as **talus** or **scree**, and typify many coastal cliffs and mountain faces below the **free face**. In other cases, fine material may gradually build up to give an area of gentle relief and fertile soil. Eventually, the efforts of weathering and transportation will combine to cause the slope to change its appearance. It may become lower and gentler or it may retain its original gradient and retreat across the surface of the land, a process known as **parallel retreat**. Slopes only change their appearance dramatically if the inputs and processes acting on them alter suddenly and create a new set of weathering and transport circumstances, such as at Holbeck (page 114) or Beachy Head (page 113).

Mass movement

Mass movement, or mass wasting, is the movement of weathered particles downslope under the influence of gravity. With some exceptions mass movement is also related to climatic conditions (Figure 4.41). It is, however, difficult to categorise types of mass movement because they overlap so much in terms of the processes involved, speed of movement and the slope angles on which they occur (Figure 4.42). None the less, they are commonly grouped into three main types: heave, flows, slides and falls.

Heave

Heave is a slow form of mass movement. It occurs particularly when there are alternating periods of freeze and thaw. During freezing, water in the regolith expands and causes individual soil and rock particles to heave upwards in a direction perpendicular to the ground surface,

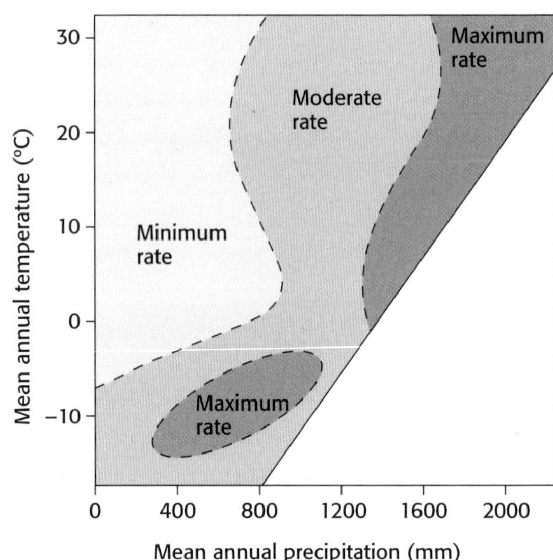

Figure 4.41
The relationship between climate and mass movement

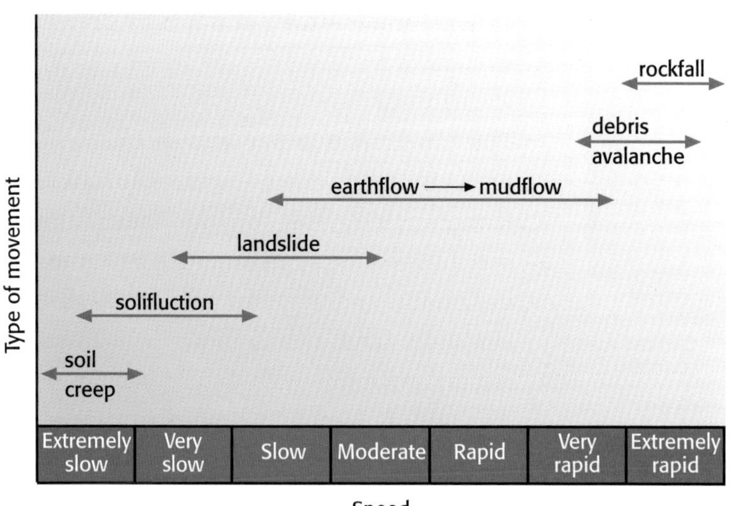

Figure 4.42

Types and speed of mass movement

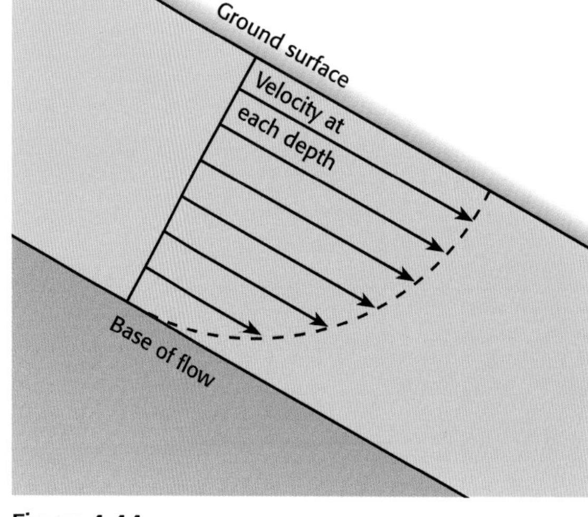

Figure 4.44

The flow process

from position 1 to position 2 on Figure 4.43. On thawing, gravity ensures that the disturbed mass of material is unable to return to its point of origin but it will move a small distance downslope, to position 3. Heave can also occur when clay minerals in the regolith swell on wetting and shrink on drying.

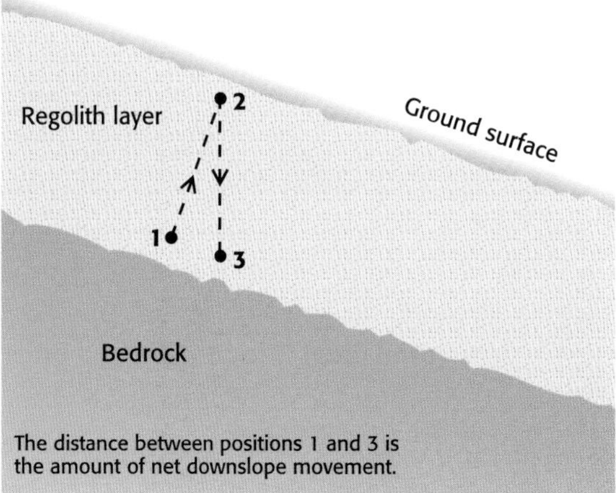

Figure 4.43

The process of heave

Flows

Flow involves the internal disruption of material. The surface layer, which contains smaller more rounded particles, moves fastest while the rate of movement decreases with depth as the particles become larger and more angular (Figure 4.44). Four types of flow have been recognised.

1 **Soil creep** This is the most widespread form of flow but it is extremely slow. It occurs at a rate of less than 1 cm per year and it is continuous rather than catastrophic. One or more of several processes can cause the individual particles of soil or fine regolith to move downslope:
   - lubrication by rain
   - expansion and contraction caused by freeze–thaw (frost creep)
   - burrowing by animals
   - thermal expansion and contraction.

   Soil creep typically takes place on slopes of 5° or more, with little or no vegetation cover to hold the soil together. Step-like features 20–50 cm in height, called **terracettes**, are invariably created (Figure 4.45). They are often enlarged by grazing animals, which use them as tracks across slopes. Other features associated with soil creep include:
   - bent tree trunks
   - fence posts angled downslope
   - torn road surfaces and turf
   - walls damaged by the upslope collection of soil.

2 **Solifluction** This process is a slightly more rapid form of flow than creep, although it is still classed as very slow. It commonly occurs in cold climates and can occur on very gentle slopes. The regolith becomes saturated with

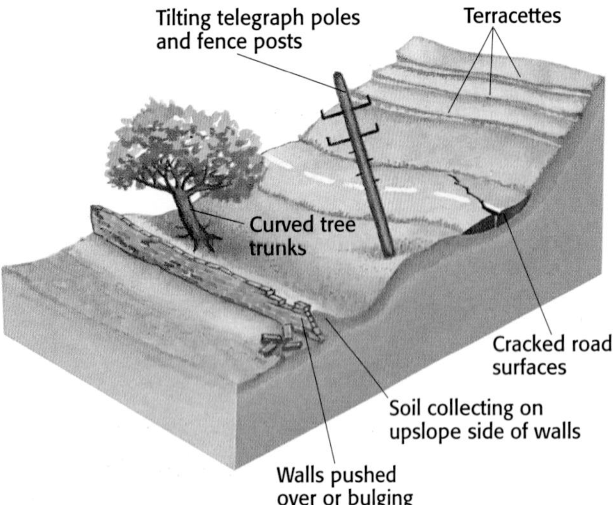

Figure 4.45
Features associated with soil creep

water and then moves downslope at a rate between 10 cm per year on the surface and 10 mm per year at depth. In **periglacial areas** the regolith may be heavily lubricated during a seasonal thaw and it then moves downslope over the frozen subsoil, or **permafrost**. In this case it is referred to as **gelifluction**. Features typically associated with this type of flow are **solifluction lobes**, which are rounded tongue-like features up to 50 m wide, and **head**, a mixture of clay and sand formed in valleys and at the foot of cliffs.

3 **Earthflow (debris flow)** This type of flow occurs on slopes of between 5° and 15°. The rate of flow is moderate to rapid, being between 1 mm per day and 1 m per second. The movement can produce features such as flow tracks of over 100 m in length, but it may not be fast enough to break the vegetation. Earth flows are thicker in consistency than mudflows (see below), having a lower water content, and are common in humid areas where the regolith is deep. A mass of earth is fluidised as a result of a rapid input of water; it then slips suddenly, leaving behind a concave, crescent-shaped scar and a convex bulging toe or lobe below. Earthflows may be caused by:
- spells of heavy rain
- snowmelt
- **basal undercutting** of slopes by streams
- landslides
- earthquakes.

The San Francisco Bay area of California is prone to debris flows (Figure 4.46). In early January 1982, half of the mean annual precipitation of approximately 540 mm fell in 32 hours and triggered over 18 000 shallow landslides and debris flows which swept rapidly downhill with little warning. They damaged at least 100 homes and killed 15 people; the total cost of repairing the damage was $66 million.

Figure 4.46
Debris flow 1982, San Mateo County, California

4 **Mudflow (mudslide)** Mudflows are similar to earthflows but are thinner in consistency. They have a higher water content and often a high proportion of clay particles. They are very rapid, flowing at over 1 km per hour. Mudflows sometimes transport large weathered rocks, which move to the front of the lobe and which can then dam valleys. Mudflows may be found downslope of an earthflow, where the more saturated material has travelled further. They are likely to occur:
- in mountainous areas after heavy rain
- in periglacial areas at the time of maximum summer thaw

- on the slopes of erupting volcanoes where water is provided by melting snow and condensing steam, along with ash particles.

In May 1998 mudslides near Naples in Italy killed 350 people. After days of heavy rain, torrents of mud from Mount Sarno buried six towns under 3 m of debris. The movement was made worse by underground springs lubricating regolith from below. The spread of urban areas, and the cutting down of trees, are thought to have increased the risk in an area already known to be in danger of mass movement (Figure 4.47).

Flows associated with volcanic eruptions are often referred to as **lahars**. In May 1980, Mount St Helens in the USA erupted violently. Superheated ash melted the snow and glaciers which had previously covered parts of the volcano. The resulting lahars travelled at 25 km/h, sweeping trees, houses and bridges before them. Nearly 220 km of river channel were affected. Mud-lines left behind on trees showed that the lahars were 5–6 m deep. Over 200 homes and more than 300 km of road were destroyed (Figure 4.48).

Figure 4.47

Mount Sarno, Campania, May 1998

Slides

Slides do not suffer internal disruption. The material moves in one block with the surface moving at the same rate as at depth (Figure 4.49). There are three main types of slide.

1 **Landslide (landslip/rockslide)** Landslides occur in regions of pronounced relief when a mass of rock or earth moves downslope quite rapidly under the influence of gravity and there is little or no associated flow. Lithology may play an important part, especially in the case of rockslides, which can be either joint or bedding plane controlled and may travel at

Figure 4.48

Damage by a lahar, following the eruption of Mount St Helens, USA

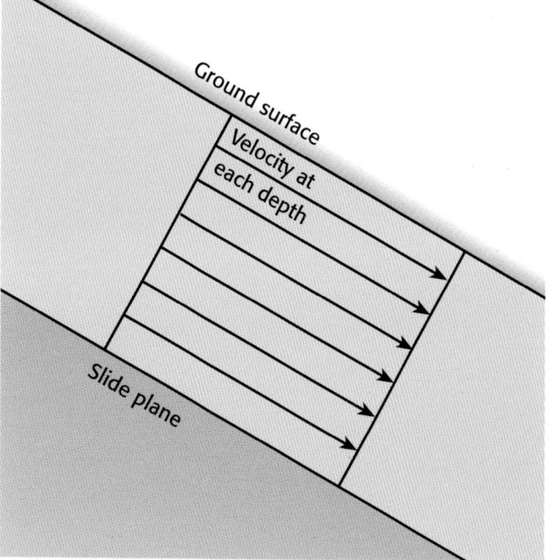

Figure 4.49

The slide process

speeds of between 1 mm per day and 10 m per second (Figure 4.50). Some rock structures are more unstable than others. Joints will allow water to move through the rock, possibly lubricating layers or blocks and causing slides. In 1993 a landslide caused the spectacular loss of a hotel in Scarborough (see page 114).

2 **Rotational slump (rotational slip)** Rotational slumping is characterised by the movement of a mass of weathered material along curved shear planes. It is likely to occur when weathered material becomes saturated with water and gains weight. While some groundwater will undoubtedly seep out at the foot of the slope, much of it will serve to lubricate the lines or planes of movement. Rotational slumps are marked by the tilting back of the slumped mass which commonly exposes a steep curved scar behind and pushes out a toe in front. Often a series of rotational slips will occur, initially causing the slope to gain a stepped profile which later may be covered with landslip debris.

Slumps can occur in areas of homogenous rock but they are more likely where permeable materials, such as sands, overlie relatively impermeable rocks such as clay. Several rotational landslips have occurred over the years along the southern coast of the Isle of Wight, where porous chalk and Greensand overlie a layer of Gault Clay (Figure 4.51).

3 **Debris/rock avalanche (cataclysmic rock-slide)** These movements occur when the stresses on a potential sliding surface exceed any resistance to movement. This situation can be caused by:

- slope undercutting
- the accumulation of snow or sediments
- increased pore water pressure indicating saturation
- the growth of ice crystals
- a trigger event such as an earthquake.

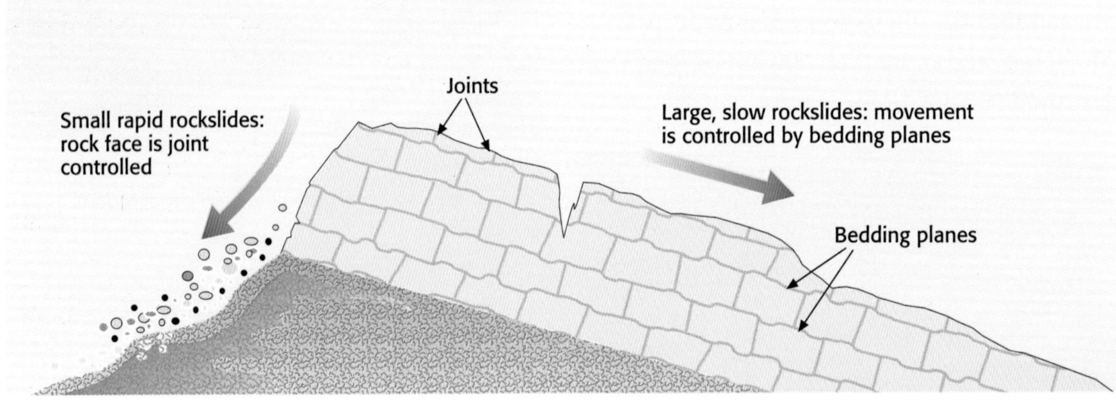

Figure 4.50
Rock structure and landslides

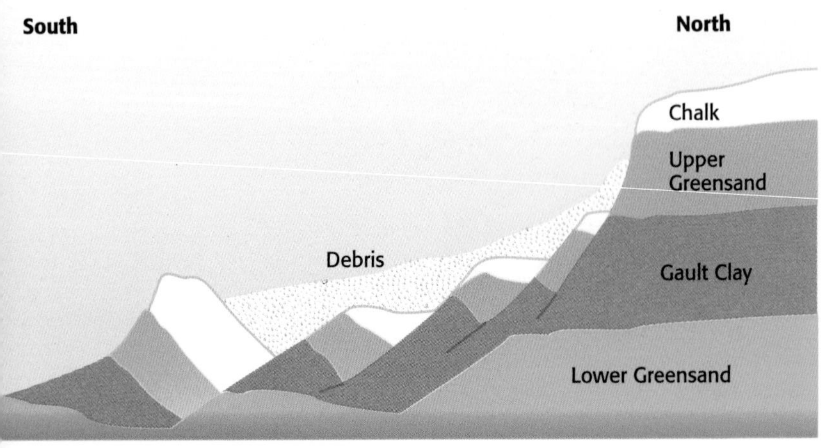

Figure 4.51
Rotational slipping on the south coast of the Isle of Wight

Debris avalanches are extremely rapid, moving at between 1 and 100 cm/s. However, they can reach speeds of more than 400 km/hr for two reasons:

- air trapped beneath the rock fragments acts to increase the rate of movement rather like a hovercraft cushion
- acceleration is increased with the aid of the energy released by the falling and fragmenting pieces of debris.

In Peru in May 1970, an avalanche of ice, snow and rocks buried the towns of Yungay and Ranrahirca beneath the slopes of Mount Huascaran, killing 20 000 people. A mass of approximately 50 million m^3 of glacial ice and rock, moving at an average speed of 160 km per hour and with a front of 1000 m in width, travelled a distance of 17 km. The avalanche was triggered by an earthquake which registered 7.7 on the Richter scale.

Rockfalls

Rockfalls are relatively rare and extremely rapid, occurring on slopes of more than 40°. They are made up of individual blocks, moving at speeds from 1 m/s to more than 100 m/s and may be caused by:

- extreme weather in mountains
- pressure release
- storm action on cliff faces
- earthquakes.

Broken fragments fall or bounce to the foot of the slope forming a scree or talus slope and leaving a nearly vertical free face above. In January 1999, one of a long series of rockfalls at Beachy Head, Sussex, resulted in a single cliff retreat of 17 m. Between 50 000 and 100 000 tonnes of chalk fell, producing a **talus slope** on the wave-cut platform. The talus was 150 m in length, almost reaching the old lighthouse (Figure 4.52). Individual blocks of rock were up to 4 m across and the collapse endangered the more recent Belle Tout lighthouse above. It was subsequently moved, in its entirety, 30 m away from the new cliff edge, at a cost of £250 000. It is unlikely to be the last move for Belle Tout, as these cliffs retreat at an average rate of 0.5 m/yr.

Figure 4.52 Rockfall at Beachy Head, Sussex, January 1999

Case Study: Mass movement – the case of Holbeck Hall Hotel

In June 1993, Holbeck Hall Hotel in Scarborough, North Yorkshire, hit the national headlines. A landslip began in the early hours of 4 June, with the hotel's lawn dropping by 15 to 20 m. Forty guests were evacuated at 7.30 am and shortly afterwards the materials moving downslope pushed the sea wall at the base of the cliffs onto the beach. By 8 pm the hotel was teetering on the new cliff edge. The following evening the collapse of the north-east wing of the hotel was shown on television (Figure 4.53). The Holderness cliffs, south of Scarborough, are the fastest-eroding coastline in Europe and are prone to landslips – the Holbeck cliffs had already suffered a major slip in 1912. The cliffs are composed of alternating layers of sands with gravel and clay. It is likely that heavy rain in spring 1993 penetrated the layers of sand and gravel, lubricating the junctions with the clay and wetting it heavily. Subsequent hot weather was sufficient to dry the clay, causing it to crack and to initiate the slide (Figure 4.54).

Following the loss of the hotel, work began on stabilising the cliff. Bulldozers graded the lobe of slumped material into an even slope. In December 1993 a semicircle of large boulders was placed around the base of the lobe (Figure 4.55). However, this was not the end of the incident. In January 1995 large cracks appeared on the top of the Holbeck cliffs, and were taken as evidence that movement was continuing. It is likely that the millions of tonnes of material that had moved in 1993 were continuing to settle.

Although coastal mass movements are often associated with the undercutting of cliffs by the sea, this was not the case with the Holbeck cliffs, as their base had been protected by a sea wall.

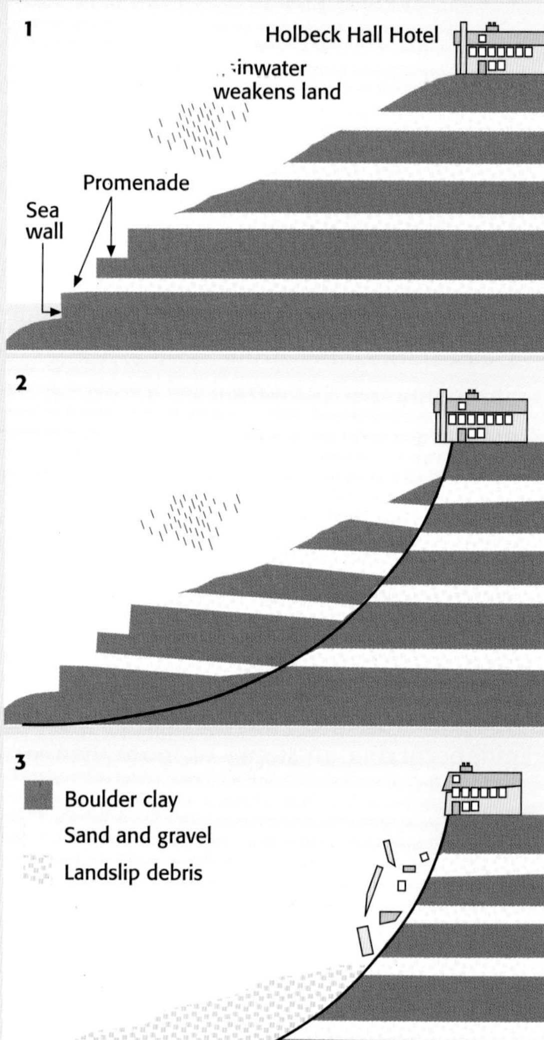

Figure 4.54
The stages of the Holbeck Hall Hotel landslip

Figure 4.53
The landslip below the hotel

Figure 4.55
The site of the landslip after restoration work

Activity

1 Mass movements can be categorised by their speed and the amount of water involved (Figure 4.56). On a copy of Figure 4.56, add the following labels next to the appropriate dot:

- soil creep
- solifluction
- landslide
- mudflow
- debris avalanche
- earthflow.

2 Copy and complete this summary table of mass movements. Some of the information you need will be found in this chapter, but you may need to refer to other sources as well.

Form of mass movement	Heave		
Speed	Slow		
Slope angle			
Causes			
Effects			
Associated features			
Examples			

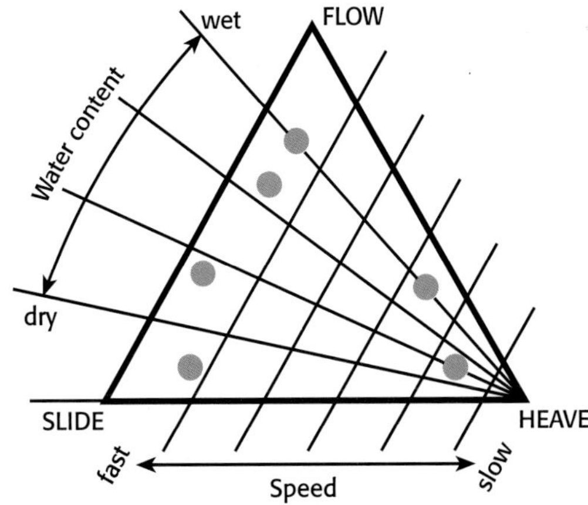

Figure 4.56
The relationship between speed of mass movement and water content

Slopes and human activity

Given that all landscapes are made from a combination of different slopes, it is not surprising that they tend to be treated as passive features – at least, that is, until they become a problem or give rise to a spectacular event. Very few areas of land are flat. Across the Great Plains of the USA, 7 per cent of the land is classified as level; the remaining 93 per cent consists of slopes of varying degree. Further, the human eye is easily deceived by slope angles. For example, a slope of 18° sounds quite mild, but is the same as a gradient of 1 in 3 (or 33%), the normally accepted limit for cars. A gradient of 1 in 24 is the equivalent of a slope of $2\frac{1}{2}$°, while 1 in 25 (just over $2\frac{1}{4}$°), is the normal limit for motorways in Britain. Figure 4.57 is a view of one the approach-roads to High Wycombe in Buckinghamshire. The slope – steep enough to warrant a vehicle escape lane – looks much steeper than its actual overall gradient of about 1 in 14, or just over 4°.

Figure 4.57
Downslope approach to High Wycombe, Buckinghamshire

In some cases, the influence of slopes on human activity is easier to see. In the Champagne region of France, for example, land use is strongly influenced by the orientation and angle of slopes, which play a major part in determining the location and extent of the vineyards (Figure 4.58). The steepest mountain slopes have an aesthetic appeal to people, attracting tourists and supporting a wide variety of recreational activities such as climbing (Figure 4.59), mountain biking, skiing and hang gliding. Where pressures on the land are high, making it necessary to use the steepest land, the modification of slopes often provides spectacular scenery, as in the case of the famous Ifugao rice terraces in the Philippines (Figure 4.60).

In their steeper forms, slopes present a potential hazard if they are not managed with care. The rising demand for land, whether for new homes, farming, or industrial and commercial development often results in steeply sloping land being brought into use when it might better be left in its natural state. Certain thresholds are common in land use planning, and experience suggests they are exceeded at some peril (Figure 4.61).

Figure 4.58
Cultivated and carefully managed slopes in the Champagne region of France

Figure 4.59
Slopes in demand for recreation

Figure 4.60
The Ifugao rice terraces in the Philippines

Some forms of construction can create hazardous slopes. The sides of road and railway cuttings and embankments need to be set at appropriate angles and may need artificial measures to maintain them safely (Figure 4.62). The weight of buildings also needs to be taken in consideration. Heavy buildings on the edges of even relatively gentle slopes can show signs of downhill movement, and even small constructions can cause slopes to become unstable, requiring heavy engineering work to preserve their stability. Rotational slip can be a problem: for example, on the Isle of Wight, retirement bungalows in Upper Ventnor are thought to have created instability and the owners are concerned that they may soon be living in Lower Ventnor! Similarly, vibration caused by commercial vehicles can also trigger slope movements.

In farming, slope angles combined with altitude (and other factors such as rainfall, temperature and soil) play an important part in determining the agricultural capability of the land. While steep slopes at low altitudes may offer greater potential than at high altitudes, the limits they impose on the use of machinery remain the same (Figure 4.63).

Soil erosion on agricultural land may develop into a serious problem where the influence of slope is not taken into consideration (Figure 4.64). Soil erosion is a process which, once started, tends to reinforce itself. In the language of systems (see Figure 4.37) it is not a self-limiting process regulated by negative feedback, but one where positive feedback works to make the situation worse. It can only be stopped by external intervention. Plant roots

Gradient	Limits to use
$< \frac{1}{2}°$	Poor drainage and liable to flood if low-lying; positive drainage measures needed.
$\frac{1}{2}-2\frac{1}{2}°$	Appears flat, usable for a wide variety of intensive human activity with the minimum of site preparation, e.g. crop growing, playing fields, residential areas, transport.
$2\frac{1}{2}°-6°$	Easily managed slopes suitable for informal movement, e.g. housing, shopping areas.
6°	Appears steep; unfavourable for roads in urban areas, especially during winter snow and ice. Unsuitable for most field games.
$8\frac{1}{2}°$	Upper manageable limit for normally loaded goods vehicles over a sustained period.
11°	Upper working limit for sustained ploughing operations.
14°	Limit of surfaces that can be mown by machine.
18°	Upper limit for normal cars; land developed only under extreme pressure.
> 26°	Liable to erosion in humid climates without terracing or thick vegetation cover.

Figure 4.61
Slope gradient and human use

Figure 4.62
A managed slope in a potentially hazardous situation

Land class	Elevation (metres)	Gradient	Key characteristics
1	< 150	< 7°	Few limitations to use
2	151–230	7–9°	Minor limitations, crop choice slightly reduced
3	231–380	9–11°	Crop restrictions, careful management needed
4	381–450	11–14°	Pronounced crop restrictions
5	451–530	15–24°	Restricted use – pasture, forestry, recreation
6	531–610	25°	Severe limitations – rough grazing, forestry
7	> 610	< 25°	Very severe limitations, hard to deal with

Figure 4.63
Limitations on agricultural use of slopes

have an important binding effect on soil and softer sedimentary rocks. Roots may anchor material which would otherwise be easily dislodged, and they may even prevent shallow landslides. Trees normally have a beneficial influence on slope stability. Where tree-covered and grass-covered slopes are subject to the same destabilising conditions, such as exceptionally heavy storm rainfall, the occurrence of sliding and slumping is nearly always greater on the grassy area.

Figure 4.64 Serious soil erosion

Finally, it is not only natural slopes that require management. A number of primary and secondary industries, such as china-clay quarrying and iron making, produce large spoil heaps with steeply sloping sides. These artificial slopes need careful stabilisation with a full understanding of how loose material takes up a natural angle of rest and how this angle may change under wet conditions. Where this knowledge is not properly applied, potentially serious hazards arise. The death of 147 people in Aberfan in South Wales in 1966 resulted from the instability of an artificially created slope (a coalmine spoil heap). Since that event, spoil heaps in the UK have been reduced in steepness and, in some cases, vegetated and reclaimed for other uses.

Case Study: Caracas, Venezuela, December 1999

A spectacular illustration of the consequences of disregarding the behaviour of slope systems occurred in the vicinity of Caracas in Venezuela in December 1999. Unexpectedly heavy rainfall swelled the mountain streams, which turned to mud-laden cascades as they overflowed their banks and spread great quantities of fast-flowing water across the hillside slopes of Mount Avila, on the northern tail of the Andes adjacent to the city of Caracas and its urban region. Over the years, the progressive removal of the vegetation cover on these slopes, in response to the need for more building land and space for temporary dwellings, meant that the floodwater had little difficulty in removing the soil and transporting it as a massive mudflow which swept away buildings, damaged roads and blocked the normal water courses. Up to 20 000 people are thought to have been killed, and 200 000 made homeless. Nearly one-third of Venezuela's population of 23 million people live in the Caracas area, more than half of them in shanty towns. Many of the victims had migrated to Caracas to escape depressed living standards in the countryside, but it was not only their temporary houses that were destroyed. Permanent and substantial buildings were engulfed, such was the intensity of the event and the strength of the forces involved (Figure 4.65).

Figure 4.65 Buildings and vehicles engulfed by mud in the town of La Guaira north of Caracas, Venezuela, December 1999

Population: pattern, process and change

KEY THEMES

- Population distribution worldwide reflects the complex interaction of physical, economic, social, political and demographic factors.
- Population change is a function of fertility, mortality and migration. Small changes in the percentage growth rate may disguise the very large numbers of people involved.
- Migration is a response to a wide variety of factors. While international migration is predicted to decline in the future, steadily increasing rates of internal migration are presenting the less economically developed countries with major social and economic challenges.
- Sustainable local development is an important Agenda 21 principle designed to help the world as a whole cope with the global increase in population.

The global picture

On 12 October 1999 the Secretary General of the United Nations, Kofi Annan, welcomed the world's 6 billionth inhabitant, at a maternity clinic in Sarajevo. This symbolic gesture marked the doubling of the world's population since 1959, when it stood at 3 billion. Current forecasts suggest that the world's population will continue to increase by 78 million people each year (the equivalent of three babies born every second) until it reaches around 9 billion in the year 2050 (Figure 5.1). After that, experts are predicting a decline, but it is by no means certain.

Differences in population growth are marked around the world. Today, 95 per cent of babies are born in the poorest countries, where the 'average' woman has 5.5 children. In the most economically developed countries of Europe, North America and Japan the situation is very different. Just to maintain the current population levels, women need to have 2.1 babies each, but in Japan the average is now 1.4 while in Spain it is as low as 1.15. According to a recent report, the population of Japan will be just 500 people in the year 3000 if the current birth rate does not increase!

The global future

It is estimated that planet Earth can support many more billions of people, but only if a better balance is achieved between the distribution of people and the distribution of resources needed to sustain them. Rising numbers of people inevitably put more pressure on the environment – hence the importance now being attached to **sustainable development** at both global and local scales. Sustainable development is defined as 'development that

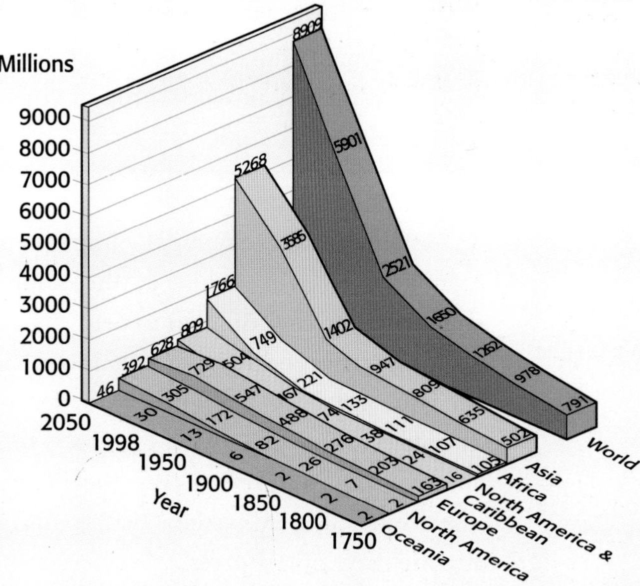

Figure 5.1 The world's population growth, 1750–2050

meets the needs of the present generation without compromising the ability of future generations to meet their needs'. The importance of the local dimension was stressed through the **Agenda 21** initiative developed in Rio de Janeiro at the 1992 United Nations Conference on Environment and Development – the widely publicised Rio or Earth Summit. Agenda 21 argues that sustainable development is both a local and a global process because development is as much the result of work done by local people as by national governments. Local governments are considered to be important in Agenda 21 because they:

- consume resources
- act as a force for change
- act as a role-model for other organisations
- provide information and services
- are important in planning and development
- are important local decision-makers.

Activity

1 Contact your local government offices to find out the local Agenda 21 proposals for your area.

2 Evaluate these proposals against your views of how local resources might be better used.

3 Prepare a brief list of the main worldwide resource issues which you consider to arise from the planet's growing population. Keep these issues in mind as you work through your geography course.

Sustainable development implies rising standards of living while at the same time managing the environment to help ensure that its long-term productivity is maintained. It is an issue for both developed and developing countries. All people, however much they are limited by poverty, have the scope to contribute towards the better use and maintenance of resources.

General patterns of population distribution

There is a wide range of physical and human factors that influence population distribution and **population density**. The major physical influences include climate, soil, altitude, relief and rivers. The location of economic resources, employment opportunities and energy resources are the principal human factors.

The main concentrations of population are mostly on the edges of the continents. For example, 75 per cent of the world's population lives within 1000 km of the sea, and 67 per cent within 500 km of the sea. Coastal sites have long been important for trade, although coastal populations are rarely uniformly distributed but are localised at ports and other favoured sites. Some islands are very densely populated, for example Britain, Japan, and the Philippines, whereas others such as Corsica, Borneo, Tasmania and Iceland are sparsely populated. Similarly, some countries in continental interiors are densely populated, such as Rwanda and Burundi, while others are sparsely populated, for example the interior of the USA and the Russian Federation.

Altitude and relief

Population numbers and density generally decline with altitude (Figure 5.2). Over half the world's population lives between sea level and an altitude of 200 m – an area that accounts for

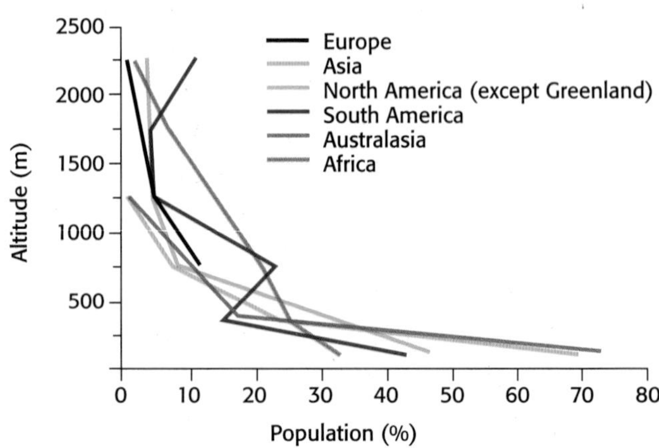

Figure 5.2
The vertical distribution of population, by continent

only about a quarter of the world's total. Over 80 per cent of the world's population lives between sea level and 500 m, occupying just over 50 per cent of the world's total land area.

The reasons for the decline in population with increasing altitude are numerous. They include:

- the substantial reduction in air pressure and oxygen, which makes it dangerous for people (the highest human habitation is at about 5200 m in the Andes)
- cold wet conditions and poor thin soils make farming difficult
- inaccessibility
- difficulties in erecting buildings
- sickness at high altitudes, headaches, nausea and even bleeding from the nose and ears.

In tropical areas, however, high altitudes may be attractive – for example, people have found it easier to live at high altitudes in tropical areas such as the White Highlands of East Africa, the Ethiopian Highlands and the high Andean plateaus of Ecuador. There are also some major towns at high altitudes, for example La Paz at 3640 m, Mexico City at 2355 m and Quito at 2850 m. For comparison, the highest town in Britain is Buxton, at 305 m!

Relief has other effects: steep slopes, exposure and ruggedness restrict access, habitation and cultivation. These disadvantages can be overcome by technical innovations, but dense settlement is rare in upland areas. Large mountainous regions, especially in the middle and high latitudes, are usually barren, such as the plateau of Inner Asia. By contrast there may be abrupt changes in population density where mountains change to plains, such as on the western edge of the Rockies. On a smaller scale this transition can be seen on the edges of Dartmoor in the UK. It is especially noticeable in mountainous countries such as western China and Japan, where the amount of low-lying land is limited and is inevitably densely peopled.

Valleys generally lead to zones of high population density, especially in upland areas such as the Scottish Highlands and Tasmania. **Aspect** in valleys is also important. In the northern hemisphere, south-facing slopes are more attractive to people because they are warmer; the opposite is true in the southern hemisphere (Figure 5.3).

Figure 5.3 In mountainous areas, people prefer to build settlements on south-facing slopes (in the northern hemisphere) because they receive more hours of sunshine: this is a village in the Dolomites in Italy

Rivers attract people because they are sources of water, fish, minerals and fertile soils, and also act as transport routes. Where there are obstacles to transport, towns may grow up at fords, ferry-points and bridges. Many important towns have river sites, including bridging points, heads of navigation, confluence sites and defensive sites. Rivers are especially attractive where they pass through deserts, such as the Nile. On the other hand rivers can discourage settlement where they are infested with insects, where flooding is regular, or where the valley is simply too narrow and its sides are too steep.

Climate

Climate has a direct influence on human distribution and also an indirect influence through soils, vegetation and farming. Climatic unsuitability accounts for many of the most sparsely populated and uninhabited regions of the world. The way in which climate affects individual people is known as **biometeorology** (Figure 5.4). Nevertheless humans are able to adapt to different climates, especially with the help of technology. Perhaps the most extreme example of this ability to adapt is the human habitation of Antarctica (Figure 5.5).

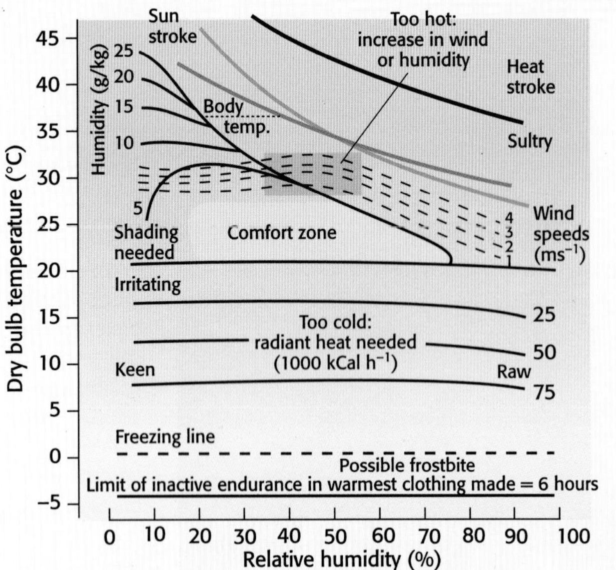

a The comfort zone surrounded by zones of discomfort and danger within the range of climates experienced on Earth.

Impossible environment	Limit of work of moderate intensity	Limit of light sedentary activity

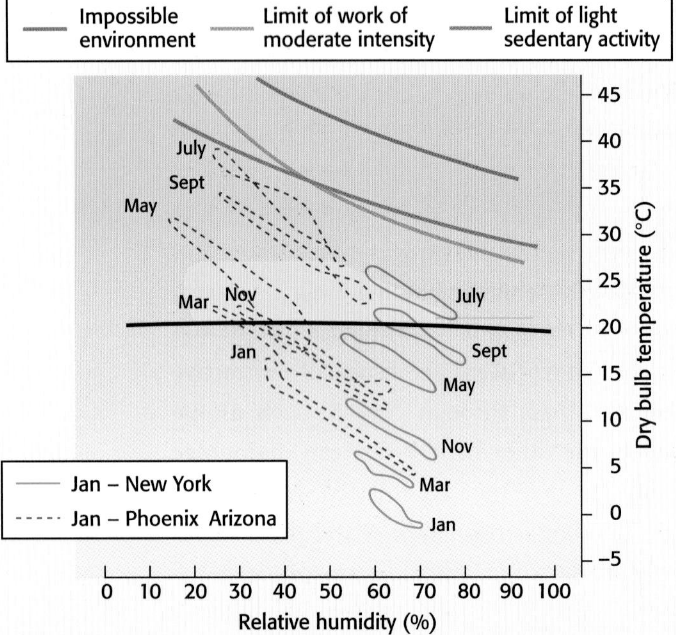

b Examples: New York and Phoenix USA

Note how the climates of New York and Phoenix fall outside the comfort zone in most of the six months plotted.

Figure 5.4

Biometeorology: the human relevance of climatic ranges

However, there is no such thing as a 'climatic best'. Humid tropical environments offer rapid vegetation growth allowing multiple cropping, and people generally require less shelter and clothing, but not all people find it easy to live in these conditions. Cold climates are generally much less suitable for human habitation. The long polar nights and low levels of insolation in summer make the environment difficult. High latitudes in the northern hemisphere account for 10 per cent of the total land area of the world but are occupied by less than one-thousandth of the world's population. In fact over 16 million km^2 of the Earth's surface is too cold for crop growth. Nevertheless there is increasing permanent settlement in high latitudes. Modern technology and increased demand for mineral resources has led to a steady increase in the number of people living in cold and potentially harsh environments, especially within the Russian Federation where major cities exist north of the Arctic Circle. On close inspection, however, it is apparent that these cities rely heavily on resources from warmer regions.

Figure 5.5

A British Antarctic Survey base

Dry conditions can also deter settlements. Deserts cover 20 per cent of the Earth's surface, but are inhabited by less than 4 per cent of the total population. The main population concentrations occur where water is available in oases and river valleys. Semi-arid areas support somewhat higher population densities, although where irrigation is developed population density may rise substantially.

Soils and vegetation

Soils are closely related to factors such as climate and vegetation. Fertile soils such as those in the deltas and river valleys of South-east Asia and along the Nile have always attracted people. Other productive soils include black earths, volcanic soils, and brown forest earths. By contrast, infertile soils such as podsols do not support many people because they cannot readily sustain agriculture on a sufficiently productive level.

Vegetation affects populations in varying degrees, and the attractiveness of vegetation may change over time with the development of a country. For example, the Prairies of America presented different possibilities to native American Indians in the past, compared with wheat farmers in the Russian Steppes during the 20th century. Similarly, marshes along the Mediterranean coastline were once malarial wilderness areas but have now been drained and are fertile agricultural regions supporting a dense population.

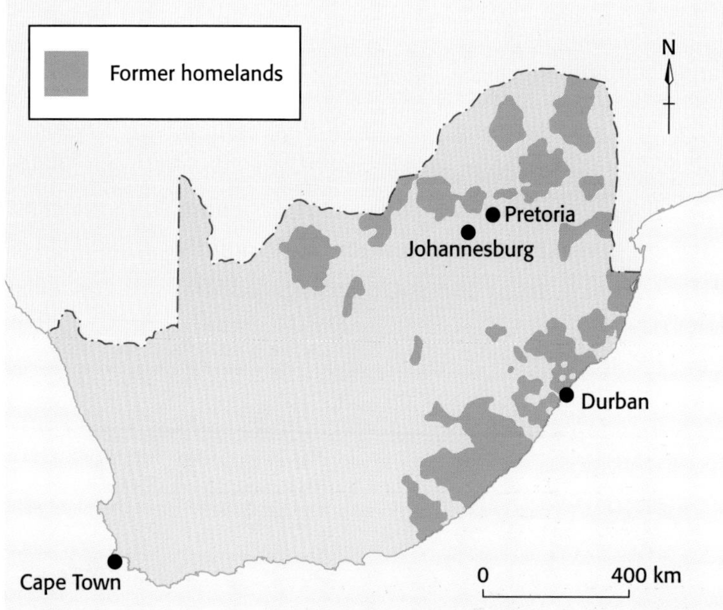

Figure 5.6 South Africa's former homelands

Minerals and energy resources

Minerals and energy resources are a great attraction, especially where the ability to organise their efficient exploitation is well developed. The location of coal deposits has influenced sites of industries and settlement, especially in the case of the UK. Traditionally it has been much easier to move people and other resources to the coalfields than to transport the coal itself. In comparison, non-energy resources have influenced the location of people to a much lesser extent, although in South Africa the location of gold and diamonds at Johannesburg and Kimberley respectively has been an important factor in the distribution of the population.

Agriculture

Agricultural systems and techniques also influence population distribution. In farming societies some high-yielding crops allow dense population concentrations, whereas livestock economies are usually associated with relatively sparse populations. Wheat farming in the Prairies supports a low density of population, whereas rice in the Asian delta regions supports a high population density.

Some population distributions, however, can only be explained in terms of **historical and social factors**. In Northern Ireland, for example, the relative distribution of Catholics and Protestants at a regional scale that we see today reflects in part the colonisation of Ulster in 1601 and the gradual but limited westward movement of Protestants. Similarly the distribution of the Black population in South Africa reflects the apartheid policy whereby Black people were removed from urban areas and forcibly relocated in the so-called homeland areas (Figure 5.6).

Figure 5.7 shows the global distribution of population. The most densely populated areas include the river basins of Asia, industrial Europe and North America; the sparsely populated areas include deserts, tundra, rainforests and mountains. More than half the world's population lives in South-east Asia, and most are farmers who depend on intensive, irrigated rice cultivation. Similar situations exist on a smaller scale in the Nile valley, in Java and in the Philippines. Dense populations in these regions are a product of 'sun, rain, alluvium and irrigation'. Population densities here are also rising as a result of falling death rates. Settlement in Mediterranean areas of Europe is also densest in the valleys where there is some flat land, some irrigation and supporting intensive farming.

To a limited extent only do the dense populations in Europe and the north-east USA reflect the suitability of these areas for farming. The growth of large towns began in Britain, spread to Europe and later to North America. Coalfields became the largest industrial centres and rapidly drew people from the surrounding countryside. However, as industry changed, and especially as it become increasingly foot-loose, employment opportunities have become more widely spread and the pull of the traditional manufacturing areas has declined. Clusters of population are now more numerous and widespread, well illustrated by the satellite image of Europe at night (Figure 5.8).

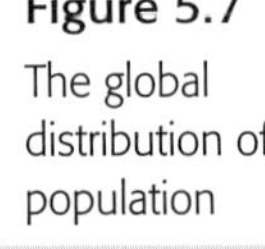

Figure 5.7 The global distribution of population

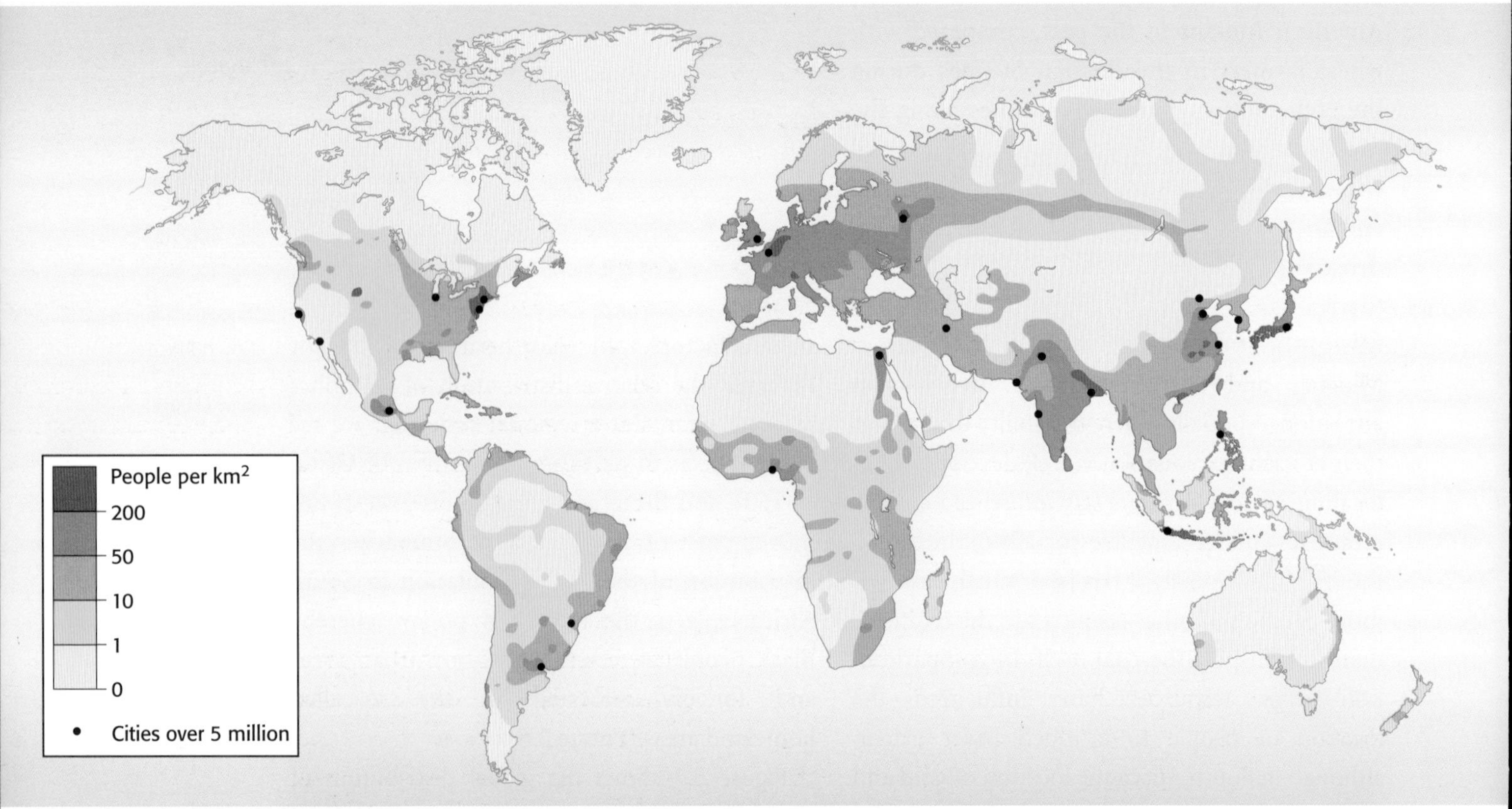

Figure 5.8 Satellite image of Europe at night

Population density

Population density is a measure of the number of people living in a given area. Calculating population density presents several problems, because census information can vary greatly in quality. First, establishing the exact number of people living in an area is often difficult, especially in such locations as rainforests, deserts, shanty towns and so on. Further, there may be problems in deciding the exact extent of the land to be included in the calculation – for example, intertidal districts are not counted in some regions.

Population density is commonly expressed in the form of the **arithmetic density**, which is simply the total population of an area divided by the total amount of land to give the number of persons per unit of area, usually square kilometres. While the arithmetic density has the merit of being simple to calculate, it is best suited to small areas where little variation in density is encountered. Applied to large regions or whole countries, it may bear little or no relation to the actual densities found at specific locations on the ground. An alternative is the **physiological density**, which relates the total population to the area of arable land. However, the usefulness of this measure is questionable unless it can be shown that all the people concerned are supported by the food grown on the amount of land used in the calculation. A similar measure is that of **agricultural density**, which relates the total rural population of an area to the amount of agricultural land within it. Here again there are problems. Not all rural populations are involved in agriculture while in countries such as China and Israel many farming people live in small towns and are not counted as rural inhabitants. The different results provided by these three measures are illustrated in Figure 5.9.

On a smaller scale, **residential density** is often applied to urban areas and relates the number of people living in the urban area to the amount of residential land. Finally there is the optimum population density measure or the **ecological optimum** – the density of population that can be supported by natural resources without destroying them.

Activity

1 Complete the data table, Figure 5.10, by working out both the arithmetic and the physiological densities for the remaining 12 countries of the European Union.

2 On copies of the outline map of Europe (Figure 5.11), use the dot map technique to plot the arithmetic density and the physiological density of each country.

3 Describe and compare the pattern of population density shown in both maps.

4 In the light of your general knowledge of the geography of Europe, which measure do you consider to be the most realistic? Do you think that a map of agricultural density would have been of any greater value?

Area	Arithmetic density	Physiological density	Agricultural density
World	36.20	329.40	192.40
Australia	2.00	34.60	4.60
New Zealand	12.20	709.30	115.60
USA	25.40	124.80	32.20
Bulgaria	83.10	222.10	69.70
Italy	188.50	630.29	130.30
UK	240.06	985.83	66.10
India	231.50	451.00	336.00
Netherlands	375.67	1693.44	126.20

Figure 5.9 Three population density measures: the world and selected countries

Figure 5.10

Population and land area in the European Union

Country	Population (millions)	Total land area (km²)	Arithmetic density (persons/km²)	Arable land area (km²)	Physiological density (persons/km² arable land)
Austria	8.1	83 859		14 028	
Belgium	10.1	30 518		9 372	
Denmark	5.3	43 080		24 996	
Finland	5.1	338 147		21 447	
France	58.6	543 965		179 452	
Germany	82.0	356 718		118 235	
Greece	10.6	131 626		22 745	
Republic of Ireland	3.7	70 273		10 561	
Italy	56.8	301 316	188.50	90 117	630.29
Luxembourg	0.42	2 586		584	
Netherlands	15.6	41 526	375.67	9 212	1 693.44
Portugal	9.9	92 345		22 938	
Spain	39.2	506 000		140 918	
Sweden	8.8	449 110		26 467	
UK	58.6	244 110	240.06	59 442	985.83

Figure 5.11

The European Union

Population change

There are three key components to population change – **fertility** (births), **mortality** (deaths) and **migration** (movement). Together, births and deaths account for the natural increase or decrease in the size of a population. Migration creates a growth or decline through the arrival or departure of people. At the present time, the world's population is growing at a rate of 1.33 per cent per year. Do not be misled by small percentage figures which may seem incidental: a rate of just over 3.2 per cent means that a country's population will double in 23 years. Figure 5.12 gives rates of growth for several defined regions of the world. The rates may not seem to vary much, but the picture is quite different in terms of the number of extra people involved. Note how many extra people are represented in each of the regions by a growth of just 0.1 per cent.

Fertility

Fertility is one of the main determinants of population growth. It is subject to long-term and short-term changes, and can be influenced by a number of factors, including social, economic, political, psychological and physiological factors. The **crude birth rate** (CBR) is defined as 'the total number of births in a single year divided by the total population and multiplied by 1000'. It is easy to calculate, and the data are readily available (Figure 5.13).

Region	Population (millions)	Annual growth rate (%)	No. of extra people after 1 year (millions)	No. of people represented by a growth rate of 0.1% (millions)
More developed regions	1182	0.28	3.31	1.18
Less developed regions	4719	1.59	75.03	4.72
Africa	749	2.37	17.75	0.75
Asia (excl. Japan)	3585	1.38	49.47	3.59
Europe (incl. Russian Federation)	729	0.03	0.22	Below 0.1%
South & Central America, Mexico & the Caribbean	504	1.57	7.91	0.50
North America	305	0.85	2.59	0.31
Oceania	30	1.30	0.39	0.03

Figure 5.12 Population growth rates for world regions, 1998

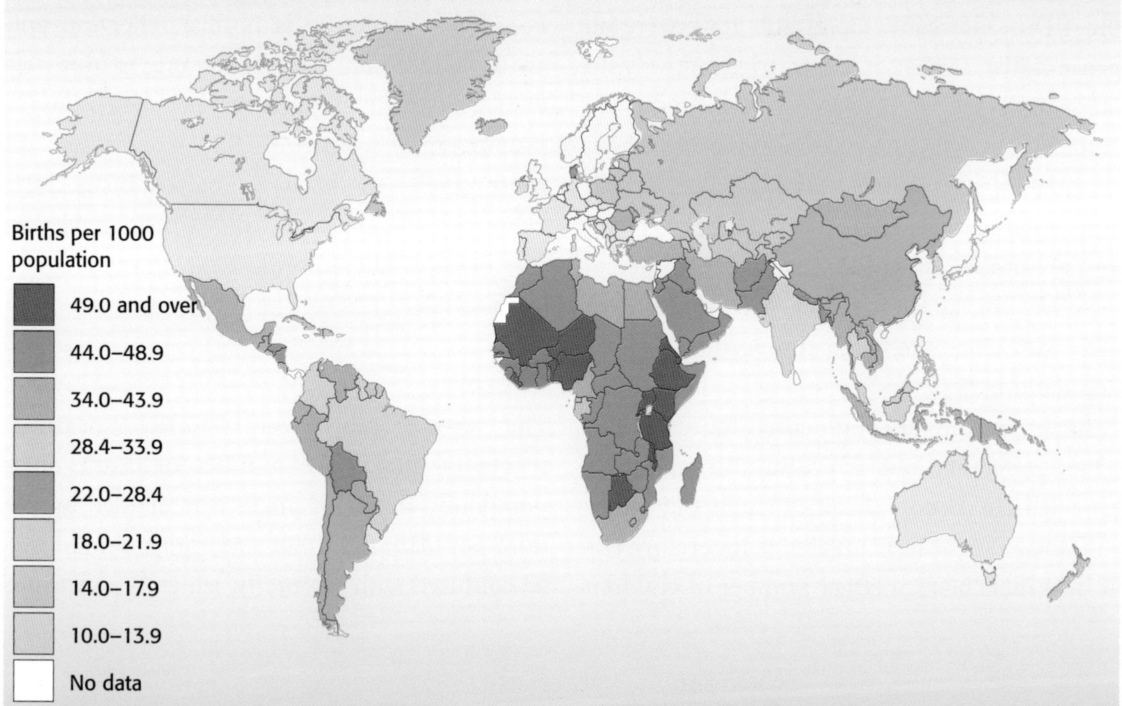

Figure 5.13 World birth rates

However, as its name suggests, the CBR is not a refined measure. For example, it does not take into account the age and sex structure of a population, and would not be very suitable for comparing a new town with a youthful population and a high birth rate, with a retirement area for elderly people where a low birth rate would be expected.

In order to make more informative comparisons between different countries and areas, more precise measures are required such as the **standardised birth rate** and the **general fertility rate.** The standardised birth rate evens out the age and sex characteristics of a particular population by comparison with a hypothetical standard population, and is usually lower than the crude birth rate. The **general fertility rate** is the number of births per 1000 women aged 15 to 45. This measure may also be used to derive the general fertility rate for women in particular age bands, e.g. aged 20–24, 25–29, and so on.

Birth rates are influenced by many factors. There are strong correlations between the state of the economy and the birth rate. Periods of economic prosperity are often linked to an increase in family size whereas in periods of economic downturn there may be a decline in the birth rate, especially when unemployment increases. Political factors are also influential. In the 1930s, Germany, Japan and Italy were all **pro-natalist** – that is, they tried actively to increase the size of their populations. In the late 20th century, countries such as India and China adopted strong **anti-natalist** policies which were intended to reduce population growth. For a number of years, Australia operated a selective immigration policy with the aim of increasing the size, and composition, of its population.

Birth rates are also influenced by social and religious factors, but not always as might be expected. In Hindu society (where the father will not go to 'heaven' unless his funeral pyre is lit by a male heir), a larger number of children helps to ensure a male heir. Although birth rates are often assumed to be high in Catholic countries (and low in Protestant countries), this is very much a simplification. Across Europe, Catholic countries such as Italy, France and Ireland all have low birth rates whereas some Catholic countries in the developing world, such as Mexico and Brazil, have higher birth rates. It is certainly true that strongly religious communities tend to be pro-natalist. Islamic countries, whether they are oil-rich (Saudi Arabia) or not (Bangladesh), have birth rates that are among the highest in the world. In addition, female literacy has an important bearing on the birth rate. Countries that have a high level of female literacy tend to have a low birth rate, and vice versa. Literacy and education are important because they empower people. Education gives people the ability to choose whether they have a large family or not. Women are more likely to have jobs and greater control over their own destiny, including the number of children born to them.

Physiological factors and population structure also have an influence. Populations with the worst levels of health and the lowest levels of nutrition generally have the largest families, a situation which leads to a vicious circle of poverty, high infant mortality rates, low life expectancy but high levels of fertility. Population structure is both a reflection and an influence on the birth rate. Countries with a youthful population, i.e. with a larger proportion of women of child-bearing age, are more likely to have a higher birth rate. Countries such as Japan, which have an increasingly elderly population, have a lower birth rate.

Mortality

The **crude death rate** (CDR) measures mortality, and is the number of deaths in a population during a single year divided by the total population x 1000. (*Mortality* should not be confused with *morbidity*, which is a measure of the occurrence of illness.) As with the crude birth rate, the CDR has its shortcomings. For example, it does not take into account the overall age structure of a population. In order to overcome such difficulties the **standardised mortality rate** (SMR) or **age-specific mortality rate** (ASMR) are the preferred statistics, as they record the total number of deaths per 1000 people of a given age. The **infant mortality rate** (IMR) is one of the most important standardised mortality rates and is defined as 'the number of babies per 1000 live births who die before they reach their first birthday'. It is one of the most widely used statistics of development. Highly developed countries invariably have a low infant mortality rate, whereas those with a high IMR (for example Afghanistan, Mozambique and Rwanda) generally exhibit a low level of development (Figure 5.14).

Factors affecting the death rate

The main factors that affect the death rate include nutrition, standard of housing, access to clean water, hygiene, and levels of well-being. Not only does the death rate vary from country to country, but within a single country there may be variations reflecting differences in social status, occupational structure and place of residence. In Britain, for example, people in the least prosperous **socio-economic groups** are far more likely to experience serious illness than those in the better-off categories who, in turn, are more likely to make greater use of medical facilities, in particular private health care. The **inverse care law** states that 'those who are most ill generally receive less treatment and those who do not need the treatment have it available to them'. This 'law' operates on local, national and global scales.

Variations in the cause of death vary from country to country, from area to area, and over time. People in less economically developed countries are much more likely to experience **infectious diseases**, leading to high infant mortality and high crude death rates. Infectious diseases are those that can be passed from person to person, and include cholera, tuberculosis, malaria and gastro-enteritis. They are generally linked to low incomes, poor

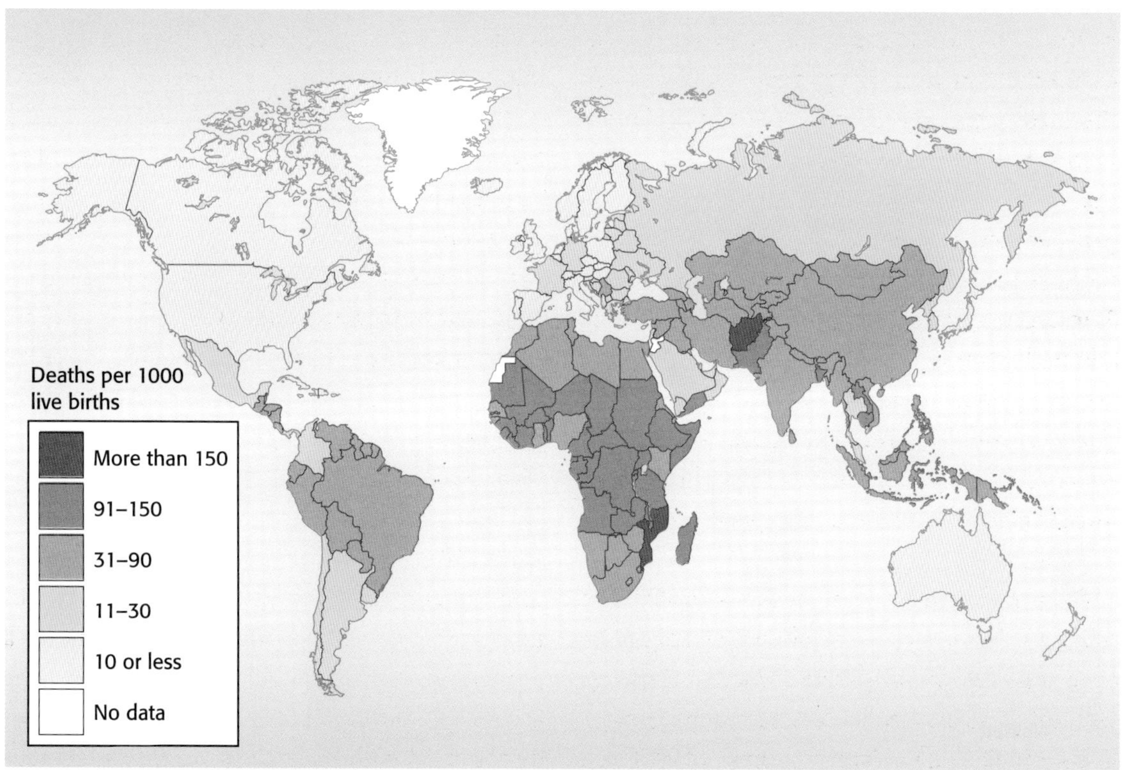

Figure 5.14 World infant mortality rates

standards of diet and housing, poor hygiene, overcrowded conditions and contaminated food and water. As a country develops, and there are improvements in water and food supplies, housing conditions and so on, infectious diseases tend to decline. In highly developed countries, people are affected less by infectious diseases and more by **degenerative diseases** such as strokes, heart attacks and cancers, perhaps brought on by high levels of stress or by a polluted environment in urban areas. Nonetheless, where degenerative diseases are prevalent, death rates are generally lower than where infectious diseases are the main cause of death.

The balance between infectious and degenerative disease may also vary between rural and urban areas. In the rural areas of developing countries, where access to medical facilities is severely limited, infectious diseases are more common. In the urban areas of both developing and developed countries, stress related disease is more likely, although in the shanty towns of the less economically developed regions, the combined impact of stress related and infectious diseases is likely to be felt. Overall, the change from a largely infectious pattern to a largely degenerative pattern is referred to as the **epidemiological transition**

The world pattern of death rates

The world map of death rates (Figure 5.15) shows that there are high death rates in Africa, parts of Latin America and South-east Asia, and much lower rates in Europe, North America and Australasia. The overall trend, however, is that death rates are declining rapidly throughout the world, and variations in the death rate from country to country are much less than variations in the birth rate. Hence variations in the birth rate are much more important in explaining world population growth than variations in the death rate.

The demographic transition model

Differences between birth and death rates may lead either to population growth or to population decline. However, since the 19th century the main trend in population change

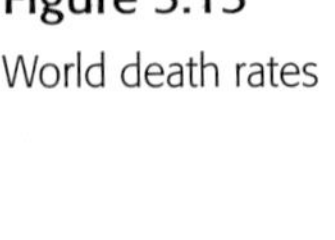

Figure 5.15
World death rates

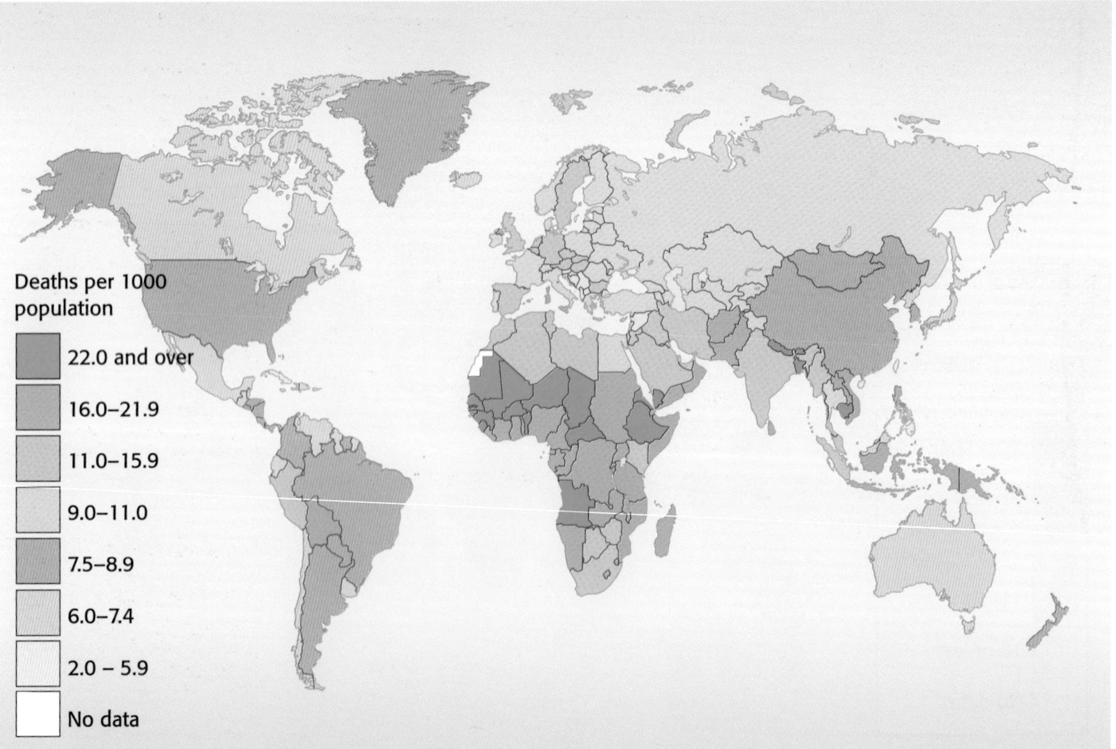

has been for death rates to fall, followed by a fall in the birth rate, leading to a rapid increase in population. For example, in 1950 the world's population was approximately 2.5 billion people; it reached 5 billion in 1987 and 6 billion in 1999.

The **demographic transition model** shows the change in birth rates and death rates over time (Figure 5.16). The model generally recognises four stages, although a fifth has now been identified. In the **first stage** the birth rate and death rate are high and largely cancel each other out. Population fluctuates for short periods and growth is limited. In the **second stage** the death rate declines but the birth rate experiences little change, creating a period of rapid growth. In the **third stage** the birth rate begins to drop and the death rate reaches a low level; population growth continues but begins to slow down. In the **fourth stage** both the birth rate and death rate are low with small fluctuations; population growth is limited and in some years it may decline. The **fifth stage** that has been identified relatively recently is in countries with an ageing population where the death rate has shown signs of increasing and the overall population has begun to decline. Countries such as Japan have reached this stage.

The model was first put forward in descriptive form in 1929 by the American demographer Warren Thompson but it was not until 1945 that it became widely recognised, when Frank Notestein linked population change to socio-economic development and identified the four stages described above. Notestein assumed that decreases in mortality were the direct consequence of improvements in food supply, the standard of living and the general standard of health, but that downward changes in birth rate (fertility) would occur more slowly in response to these improvements, thus creating a growth in population until such a time that the demand for a higher standard of living reduced the demand for children. He did not take account of other factors, such as the changing status of women, increased levels of education, and the declining hold of traditional cultural values. He did not foresee the fifth stage of a stable low birth rate and rising death rate resulting in a population decline.

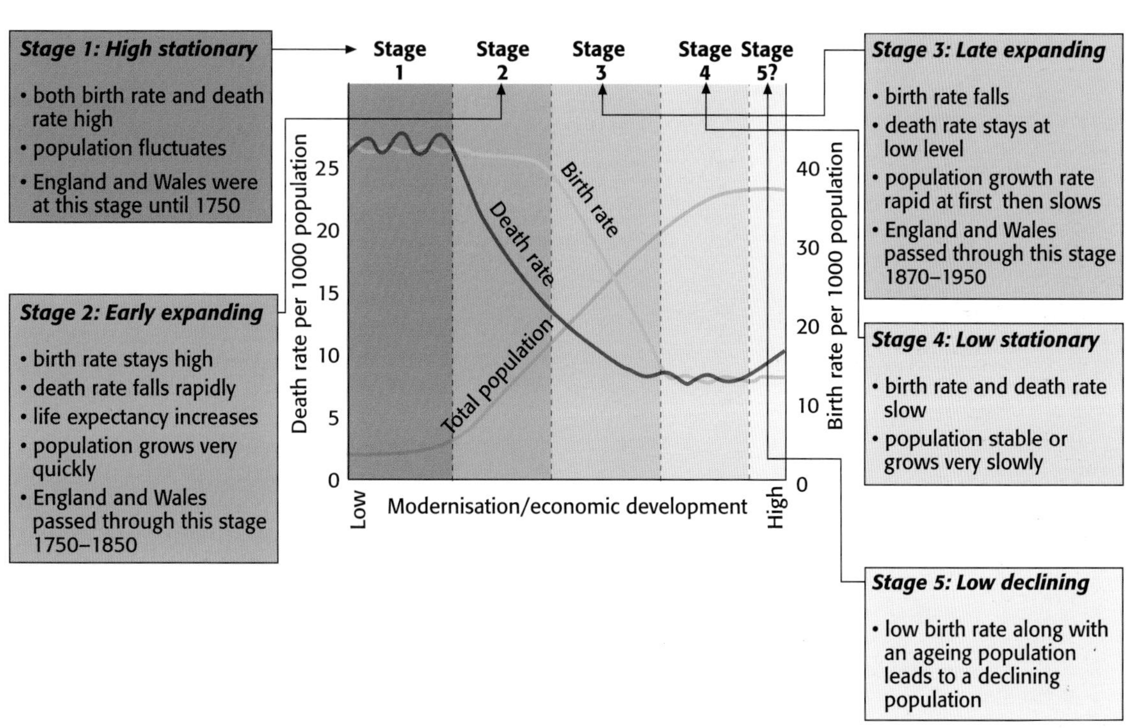

Figure 5.16 The demographic transition model

Limitations of the demographic transition model

Thompson's and Notestein's thinking on demographic transition was heavily influenced by research in the 1920s and 1930s which examined the rapid rise in the population of 18th- and 19th-century Europe. It is now clear that their theories were constrained by a number of factors, including the availability of accurate data. There also remains the whole question of whether it is safe to assume that what happened in Europe at one period of time would necessarily occur elsewhere in the world at a later date (Figure 5.17). Even where demographic trends appear similar, the causes may be different, especially between distinctive social and cultural traditions. Unexpected developments may also occur. In India, for example, population growth has slowed ahead of predictions. The general fertility rate in Uttar Pradesh, the most populous state, has unexpectedly dropped from 4.8 to 4.0, and for the country as a whole the goal of two children only per family looks as if it will be reached in 2011 and not 2016 as originally anticipated. Hence, using the demographic transition model to predict population change in countries around the world may not prove to be a reliable proposition.

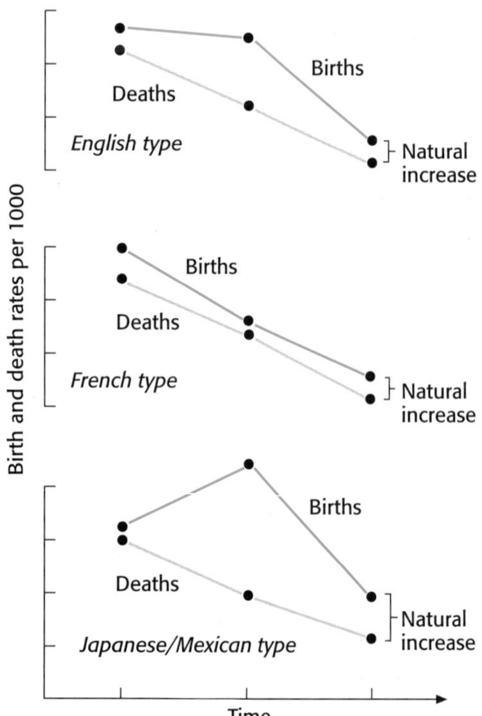

Figure 5.17 Types of demographic change

Population composition and characteristics

Age composition

Population composition encompasses the age, gender, marital status, household size, occupational status, nationality, language and religion of a population. In the main geographers study variations in age, gender, ethnicity and occupational structure, but cultural and religious variations are also important. For example, many of the world's conflict zones are in areas where there are differences in ethnicity or religion.

Population characteristics can be divided into two main types:

- physical or genetic characteristics, such as sex and race
- social or acquired characteristics, such as class, occupation, marital status, religion.

Age structure is concerned with the relative proportion of people in each age group. Commonly, three groups are distinguished: the elderly (60+ years), adults (20–59), and the young (0–19). The main global contrasts are that in western Europe approximately 15 per cent of the population are elderly and less than 30 per cent are young. In North America there is a higher proportion of young people (35–40 per cent) but fewer in the elderly category (about 10 per cent). The broad picture in developing countries is that up to 50 per cent of the population are young and 5 per cent are elderly.

Population pyramids are widely used to show the age structure of an individual country's population (Figure 5.18), while triangular graphs (Figure 5.19) are useful for comparing the age composition of the populations of different countries. A range of

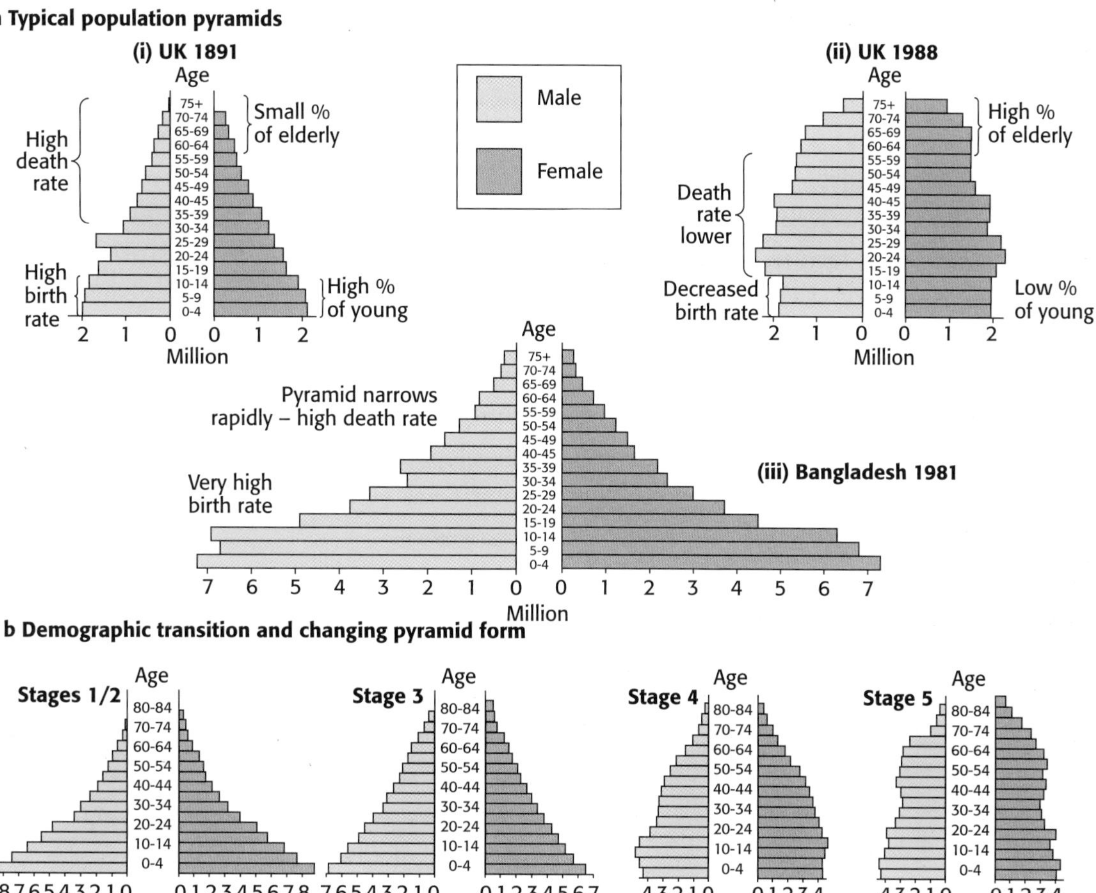

Figure 5.18
Population pyramids

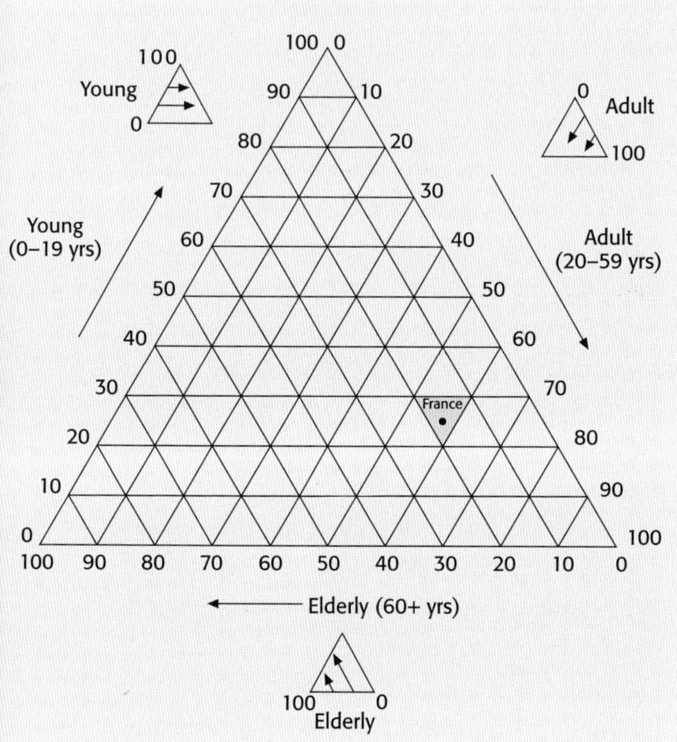

Figure 5.19
Triangular graph

age indices is also sometimes used. **The old age index** is the number of elderly as a proportion of the adult population, while the **dependency ratio** is the number of elderly and the number of young as a proportion of the adult population. In general terms, developed countries have a high proportion of elderly people whereas developing countries have a high proportion of youthful people.

Population pyramids

Although there are subtle differences between the population pyramids of different countries, three broad types are evident. The **stationary pyramid** reflects an unchanging pattern of fertility and mortality which produces a regularly tapering pyramid, e.g. the UK in 1891 (Figure 5.18a(i)). By contrast, the **progressive pyramid** shows a high birth rate and a high death rate, resulting in a pyramid with a very wide base and a rapidly tapering top, e.g. Bangladesh in 1981 (Figure 5.18a(iii)). The **regressive pyramid** is one that reflects a declining birth rate and a low mortality rate. It has a narrowing base but relatively straight sides, e.g. the UK in 1988 (Figure 5.18a(ii)). As well as revealing long-term changes in fertility and mortality, population pyramids also expose the short-term effects of factors such as war, migration and epidemics. Figure 5.18b links changing pyramid shape to the stages identified in the demographic transition model.

Activity

1 Plot the data provided in Figure 5.20 on a copy of Figure 5.19; France has been plotted for you as an example.

2 Describe the distribution of dots on the graph – is it even or clustered?

3 What underlying factors might explain the distribution and clustering of the dots on the graph?

Country	Young (%)	Adult (%)	Elderly (%)
France	26	57	17
Belgium	29	56	15
Sweden	29	55	16
UK	29	54	17
Australia	38	52	10
Russian Federation	36	55	9
Japan	40	52	8
USA	38	50	12
Ghana	48	46	6
Brazil	52	44	4
Bolivia	55	40	5
World average	44	48	8

Figure 5.20

Age composition of selected countries

Gender composition

Regional and national variations occur in gender composition. In general, gender differences are more noticeable amongst the elderly. For example, the number of women aged over 75 in the UK is double the number of men. In many countries women tend to live longer than men, perhaps due to differences in the nature of their work, lifestyle and concern for their health; for instance, women tend to consume less alcohol and smoke fewer cigarettes.

In the past, the number of male births was generally greater than the number of female births by a ratio of about 105 to 100 but the high infant mortality rate, especially of males, quickly cancelled out this differential. In some African countries the male to female ratio was 90:100 by the age of 1 year, whereas in developed countries it often took until the mid-teens before the male to female ratio was more even.

However, with improved health care the number of male deaths is decreasing and the ratio of males to females has closed to around 103:100. However, in some societies the position of women is very much inferior to that of men. In South-east Asia it is estimated that there are some 70 million missing women. Because of the low social standing of women many parents are selectively aborting female foetuses. Although the practice is illegal, it is thought to be widespread in parts of India and China. In surveys in clinics in Bombay it was found that out of 8000 abortions, only one was of a male foetus.

Migration also influences the male to female ratio. There are some environments that attract a large number of males but not females. In the past, for example, this included areas where natural resources were suddenly and vigorously exploited, as in the Klondyke gold rush in the 1840s. More recently it has been found that in parts of Silicon Glen in California the number of males far outnumbers the number of females (Figure 5.21). Not only are areas with energy resources favoured by males but so too are urban areas, perhaps resulting in a higher concentration of females in rural districts. However, as the status of women in society improves, more women are likely to move to urban areas and so the gender differences should become less marked.

As Jane Austen noted, 'a man in possession of a good wife must be in want of a fortune'. The 1999 annual conference of the organisation American Singles, which normally matches potential partners on the Internet, was held in the town of Palo Alto in the heart of Silicon Valley. Silicon Valley is the destination for men from all over the world who work in the software engineering and information technology industry. According to the organiser of the event, workers in Silicon Valley 'are every mother's dream'. They are stable, well-educated and wealthy; some have millions of dollars and nobody to spend it on. There are now 5400 more single men than women in Silicon Valley. The trouble is, they tend to be frequently confronted by girls.

The convention can only improve on the 1998 convention which was held in Alaska (the land of the rugged outdoor type), another place where men outnumber women. Unfortunately it opened on the first day of the hunting season, when all the red-blooded males were out in the bush shooting.

Figure 5.21
Male/female ratio in Silicon Valley

Occupational structure

Occupational structure refers to the size and sex composition of the working population. In developing countries the active population generally accounts for about 30 per cent of the population, compared with 50 per cent in developed countries.

Variations in occupational structure commonly arise from differences in the level of female education and employment. Male employment typically ranges from 50 to 70 per cent of the population, whereas female employment ranges from 1 to 50 per cent. In rural areas a large number of women work, although this may not be recorded as part of the occupational structure. In some societies, for example some Muslim countries, very few women work, whereas in socialist countries over half the women work. In developed countries, as a result of compulsory education and enforced retirement, the working or active population may be reduced in size.

Ethnic composition

An **ethnic group** is a group of people who are distinguished by a common characteristic or set of characteristics related variously to race, nationality, language, religion or other cultural features. All people belong to an ethnic group of one type or another, whether through inherited racial characteristics that cannot be changed, or through cultural attributes that may be open to change. An ethnic minority group is simply a particular ethnic group which happens to be in the numerical minority in any country or region. All countries, to a greater or lesser extent, have ethnic minorities. In Britain, for example, the Irish, Black Caribbean and the various Asian communities comprise the main ethnic minority groups.

Britain is increasingly becoming a **multi-racial society**, owing to a rapidly ageing white population and a small but expanding ethnic minority sector which now makes up about 5 per cent of the country's total population (Figure 5.22). In general, about 20 per cent of the white population is under the age of 15, compared with the ethnic minorities which represent over 30 per cent in this age group. Whereas the white birth rate has fallen from 2.3 to 1.8 children, the overall birth rate amongst the ethnic minorities is 2.5. In some families from Pakistan and Bangladesh it is over 4.6. The number of elderly people, who are predominantly white, has risen by 16 per cent to about 10.6 million since 1971.

Figure 5.22
The main ethnic groups in Britain by age, 1991

Ethnic group	Population	Age breakdown (%)				
		0–15	16–29	30–44	45–59	60+ years
Black Caribbean	456 000	24	30	19	19	8
Indian	793 000	29	25	25	14	7
Pakistani	486 000	44	23	20	11	2
Bangladeshi	127 000	46	26	15	11	2
Chinese	137 000	25	28	29	13	5
Others	683 000	No data				
All ethnic minority groups	2 682 000	34	26	22	13	5
White	51 805 000	19	21	21	17	22
Total	54 487 000	20	22	21	17	20

Activity

1 Construct a pie chart to represent the ethnic composition of the UK's population in 1991.

2 Using a bar chart of suitable proportions, plot the age composition data given in Figure 5.22 in order to show the differences among the main ethnic groups.

3 Briefly describe the main features of your two graphs and, on the basis of what you have studied so far, suggest how the proportion of people from ethnic minority backgrounds is likely to change in the next two decades?

Migration

Migration is the permanent or semi-permanent movement of people, involving a change of home as well as social relations. It does not include commuting, tourism or nomadism. Migration varies in terms of the cause, the distance travelled and the period of time over which movement takes place. Some migrations are **internal** while others are **international**; some are voluntary and some are forced. It is also a selective process. For example:

- the majority of migrants tend to be young adults
- international or long-distance migrants tend to be male
- females are more migratory over short distances
- single people or childless couples are more migratory than couples with children
- professional people are more migratory over long distances than unskilled workers.

Models of migration

E. G. Ravenstein's **law of migration** is one of the earliest models of migration. He was writing in the late 19th century and, as with most models, it is possible to find examples that will back it up as well as contradict it. Ravenstein's key observations, which still hold true in many cases, included:

- most migrants move only a short distance and often in a series of steps from village to town, town to city
- migration occurs mainly from agricultural to industrial areas, and the largest commercial and industrial centres receive most migrants
- the flow of migrants decreases with distance
- migrants who travel further tend to go to large cities
- people living in rural areas are more likely to migrate than those living in urban areas
- females are more migratory than males within their own country of origin
- each migration has a counter or returning flow
- the volume of migration increases with increasing technological and industrial development.

Later models have tended to seek more precise measures and have been mathematical in nature. The **inverse distance law** devised by Zipf in 1946 claimed that migration was inversely proportional to distance, and sought to quantify Ravenstein's observation that distance is a barrier to movement and that long-distance migrations would require extremely strong pulling forces. Zipf's work gave rise to the more sophisticated **gravity model** which took the size of places into account through the simple equation:

$$m = \frac{Pi \times Pj}{Dij^2}$$

where

m is the volume of movement or migration

Pi is the population of town or region 1

Pj is the population of town or region 2

Dij^2 is the distance between them squared.

The model suggests that the larger the towns the greater will be the volume of movement between them, but, at the same time, the impact of increasing distance – sometimes called the **friction of distance** – will be to reduce movement.

A further refinement of the thinking behind the gravity model was made by Stouffer (1940) in his **theory of intervening opportunities.** He stated that the number of people going a certain distance is directionally proportional to the number of opportunities existing at that distance and inversely proportional to the number of intervening opportunities. Stouffer's proposition is a useful idea, although it is hard to measure and not always easy to envisage because it implies a freedom of movement and choice that may not be typical of the reality faced by the majority of people. The sorts of opportunities that Stouffer had in mind, whether at the destination location or 'on the way', included jobs, housing and quality of life.

All these models rest on a number of assumptions, often based on particular events which may or may not be repeated. Such assumptions include ideas about the frictional effect of distance; that movement is not impeded by, for example, political barriers; and that there are ample opportunities to act as incentives to migration. However, not everyone is able to move equally freely. Those who are educated have more opportunities than those who are not, while people from certain ethnic groups may find opportunities denied them, and they may not feel welcome in some districts. Family ties and financial commitments, such as mortgages, may also act to stop people from moving.

One of the models now most widely used is that devised by Everett Lee in 1966. His **push–pull theory** states that there are a number of factors that 'push' migrants out of some regions, just as there are a number of factors that 'pull' them into others. Push factors include low wages, poverty, famine, unemployment and environmental disasters. By contrast, attractions act as pull factors. They may be real or just perceived; what somebody thinks exists is often far more important than what actually exists. Pull factors include good job opportunities, good schools, good houses and a wide variety of social activities and facilities. Hence the perception of what a place is like and the opportunities it has to offer is vital in understanding why people move.

International migration

The global pattern of international migration and its causes is a complex one. Over time, movements of people have been triggered by a wide variety of events including colonisation following exploration, political and social unrest, religious persecution, natural hazards such as drought, coastal flooding, volcanic eruptions and earthquakes, and the search for a more prosperous and secure life. In recent times, major phases of migration have stemmed largely from political, social and cultural change. For example, the division of the Indian subcontinent into Pakistan and India in 1947 resulted in about 6.5 million Muslims leaving India for Pakistan, while approximately 5.5 million Hindus and Sikhs moved into India from Pakistan. The migration of Jewish people to Israel both in 1948 and again in the late

1980s when the USSR relaxed its rules on emigration, is another illustration.

Some of these large-scale movements fall into the category of forced migrations, especially at the start; others have gathered momentum as events have unfurled. Forced migrations receive more public attention and are commonly associated with war and attempts by some countries to remove whole ethnic communities – the process known as **ethnic cleansing**. In some parts of the world, refugees comprise the majority of migrants; for example the conflict in Rwanda in 1994 displaced upward of 2 million people, 25 per cent of whom were classified as refugees. Overall, it is estimated that Africa has approximately 30 per cent of the world's refugees. In Europe, unrest in the Balkan states of Bosnia and Serbia has seen large numbers of people being forced to cross international boundaries, and many will undoubtedly consider looking further afield within the continent for their future life.

The migration of individuals and small groups of people is more likely to be prompted by **economic incentives** than by any other pressures. These migrations, which rarely make the headlines, are largely voluntary in nature, although the 'push' factor of unemployment in one country may be regarded as a strong force causing people to move against their will. The USA continues to attract large numbers from Central America, Mexico and South-east Asia. Within Europe, citizens of the EU are entitled to search freely for employment in any member country, and since the collapse of communism there have been major relocations of people formerly living within the countries of eastern Europe. Taking the globe as a whole, the number of international migrants is forecast to increase by 2–4 million per year for the near future. The largest industrial democracies regard international migration as a manageable global challenge using trade, investment and aid as levers to even out the balance of push and pull factors among different nations.

Approximately 125 million people live outside the country of their birth or citizenship, a figure which accounts for about 2 per cent of the world's population. In terms of numbers of people, migration affects developing and developed countries alike. Half the world's migrants live in the developing world, especially in those countries that are rich in natural resources. In several Middle Eastern countries, for instance, migrants make up the greater part of the labour force. Few places in the economically developed world are untouched by migration. A good example is the town of Gütersloh in Westphalia, northern Germany (Figure 5.23). In 1995, Gütersloh (population 82 000) had a total of 10 000 immigrants, consisting of 97 different nationalities. The largest groups of immigrants were from seven countries:

Turkey	3600	Greece	1600
Yugoslavia	800	Spain	700
UK	500	Italy	400
Poland	300		

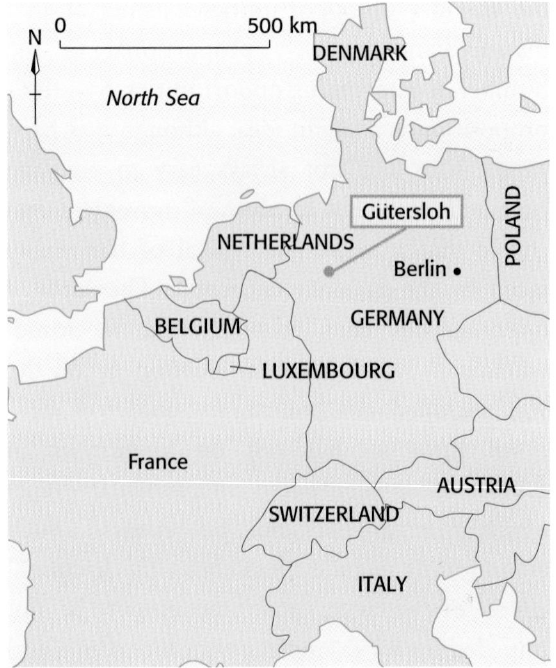

Figure 5.23
The location of Gütersloh, Germany

The town has very good road and rail links with the major cities of northern Germany, including Berlin, and is the base for several manufacturing firms such as Miele. While some of the migrant population, notably the Turkish group, arrived in response to West Germany's post-war efforts to recruit semi-skilled labour, numbers from elsewhere in the EU and beyond continue to grow.

Measuring international migration

International migration can be measured in terms of the total number of people involved or in relation to the existing population of a particular country through the **net migration rate** (NMR). The NMR is the number of migrants per 1000 of the population at a given date, usually close to mid-year. A positive figure means more in-migrants (immigrants) than out-migrants (emigrants); a negative value means more people have left than have arrived.

A survey conducted in the mid-1990s showed that 60 countries of the world had a positive balance. Eighty-six countries were recorded as having a net loss of people and 43 as experiencing no significant net gain or loss.

Activity

Figure 5.24 lists the net migration rates for 24 selected countries, together with their total population.

1 For each country:

a calculate the actual number of net migrants involved

b research the causes of the migration balance in the five countries at the top and the five at the bottom of the table.

2 Evaluate the usefulness of the net migration rate as a measure of international migration. Suggest how it might be improved.

Country	Net migration rate (per 1000)	Total population (millions)
Bosnia & Herzegovina	56.51	3.25
Liberia	38.39	2.60
Qatar	26.64	0.67
Kuwait	24.14	1.80
Afghanistan	19.90	23.74
Israel	6.12	5.53
Canada	6.10	30.34
New Zealand	3.12	3.60
USA	3.10	267.90
Russia	2.38	147.30
Germany	1.87	82.00
UK	1.32	58.60
Italy	0.27	56.80
South Africa	0.09	42.20
Brazil	−0.03	167.60
India	−0.08	966.70
Japan	−0.37	125.70
Bangladesh	−0.73	125.34
Ireland	−1.49	3.70
Cuba	−1.54	10.99
Guyana	−16.42	0.71
Grenada	−16.50	0.95
Trinidad & Tobago	−19.31	1.13
Dominica	−24.04	0.67

Figure 5.24

Net migration rates for selected countries (latest available data, 1995–98)

Case Study: The population of the UK

The present-day population structure of the UK is fairly typical of a developed country with a long history of **capitalist economic growth** and in which the economy has now reached a post-industrial stage. Unlike some younger economically developed countries, such as Australia, and many of today's developing countries, the UK has never implemented a formal comprehensive population policy designed either to expand or to limit its population. From time to time indirect financial incentives have encouraged young people to have families, and immigration from Commonwealth countries was encouraged in the mid-1950s in order to meet rising demands for labour.

For much of this century, **socio-economic forces** have been the essential determinants of the country's population size, structure and location. These forces have created marked variations in the rate of change and in the spatial distribution of people. On the regional scale, for example, the population of Northern Ireland has grown by some 17 per cent since 1961, whereas in Scotland it declined by 1 per cent between 1961 and 1997. Over half the population now lives in cities of more than 100 000 people, although these urban areas account for just 6 per cent of the total land area of the UK (Figure 5.25).

Figure 5.25
UK population distribution, 1991

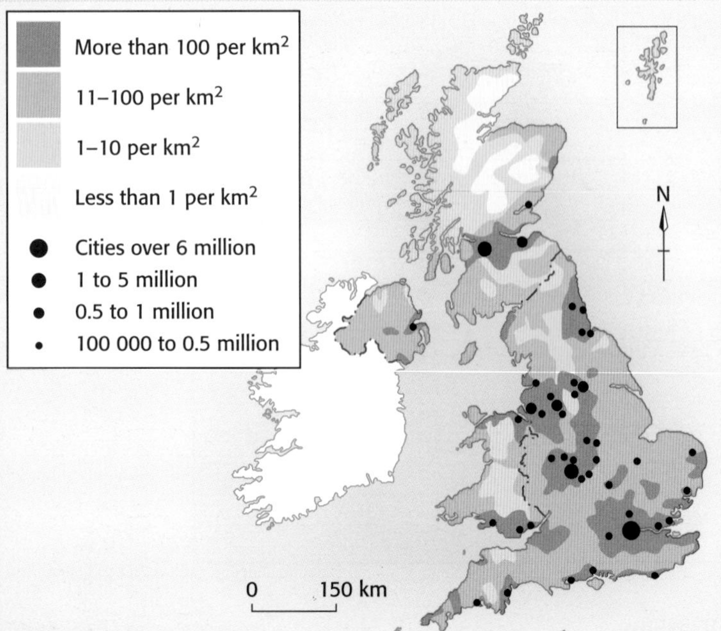

Some regions – London and the South East, for instance – have attracted many people from other parts of the country, especially the young, leading to wide variations in the distribution of the youthful population across the country. Younger people are increasingly living in urban areas and older people in rural areas. In parts of Northern Ireland the youthful population accounts for 28 per cent of the population whereas in parts of Dorset, the Isle of Wight and Edinburgh, this group comprises less than 18 per cent. On a smaller but no less significant scale, the increasing separation of workplace and residence has resulted in the growth of suburban areas on the edges of the main urban centres. These districts contain a high proportion of the very young, and of middle-aged people.

Variations in **gender and social class** are also readily apparent in the UK's population. As Figure 5.26 shows, larger proportions of men occupy the professional, intermediate and skilled manual categories, whereas women predominate in the skilled non-manual and partly skilled groups. This pattern reflects the large number of women in certain occupations such as clerical and secretarial work, as well as the fact that women often take part-time service jobs that fit in around the needs of their children.

In total, the UK's population is now about 59 million. Since the mid-1960s about three-quarters of the overall population growth has been the result of **net natural change** – the difference between births and deaths. The remainder can be accounted for by migration.

	Males %	Females %
Professional	7	2
Intermediate	27	24
Skilled non-manual	11	30
Skilled manual	28	7
Partly skilled	14	16
Unskilled manual	5	5
Other	9	16
Total (100%)	18.7 millions	17.1 millions

Figure 5.26
Population of working age, by gender and social class, UK 1998

Age and gender: structure and trends

Figure 5.27 traces movements in the number of UK births and deaths since 1901 and projects them to 2021. The graph shows the major impact of the two World Wars on the birth rate and, to a lesser extent, on the death rate. There was a noticeable drop in births during the First World War followed by a sharp increase soon afterwards. The birth rate fell again during the 1920s and stayed low during the depression of the 1930s. After the Second World War the number of births increased, creating a post-war baby boom. There was a secondary peak at the start of the 1960s, after which the number of births fell continuously, reaching a low of 680 000 in the late 1970s. A rise in the 1980s was followed by a fall in the 1990s. Since the 1930s the number of children born per woman has declined steadily. In addition women are having children later. In 1937, women on average had had 1.9 children by the time they were 30, but by 1967 this figure had declined to 1.3. In comparison with the number of births, variations in the number of deaths have been markedly less, although the fluctuations from year to year are still important. The death rate for males is higher than for females, who have a higher life expectancy. Figure 5.28 shows the crude death rate for males and females in different age groups for selected years.

Figure 5.29 illustrates the age and gender structure of the UK's population at the end of the 20th century. The peak (A) in population numbers comprises people in their early 50s and is a consequence of the post-Second World War baby boom. The higher peak of those in their 30s (B) is accounted for by the boom of the 1960s. On the other hand the very low number of people in their 20s (C) reflects the reduced birth rate of the late and middle 1970s.

The two dominant themes in the UK's population at the end of the 20th century are an increase in the elderly population and an overall fall in the number of children. Thus, overall, the UK's population can be described as ageing. In 1961 approximately 12 per cent of the population were aged over 65 and 4 per cent were aged over 75. In 1997 these proportions

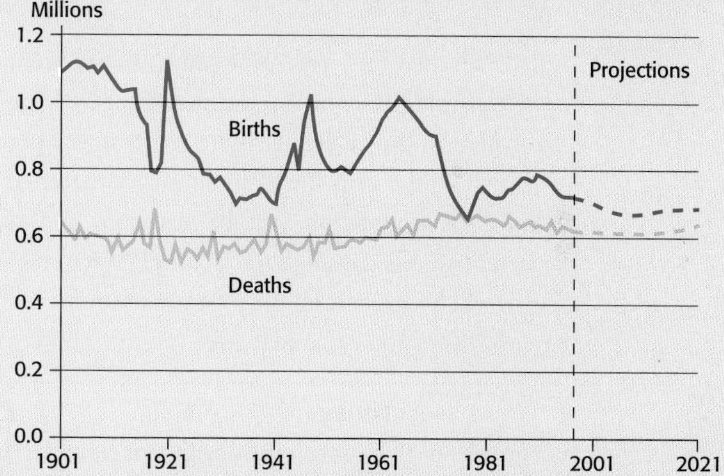

Figure 5.27 Birth and death rates in the UK, 1991–2021

	Under 1	1–15	16–34	35–54	55–64	65–74	75 and over	All ages	All deaths (thousands)
	Death rates per 1000 in each age group								
Males									
1961	26.3	0.6	1.1	5.0	22.4	54.8	142.5	12.6	322
1981	12.7	0.4	0.9	4.0	18.1	46.4	122.2	12.0	329
1997	6.5	0.2	0.9	2.8	11.9	34.0	104.3	10.4	302
2021	3.0	0.1	0.9	2.4	8.4	25.2	86.5	10.8	333
Females									
1961	18.2	0.4	0.6	3.2	11.0	31.6	110.4	11.4	310
1981	9.5	0.3	0.4	2.5	9.8	24.7	90.2	11.4	329
1997	5.3	0.2	0.4	1.9	7.2	20.7	84.4	11.0	331
2021	2.2	0.1	0.3	2.0	5.0	15.2	69.8	10.1	314

Figure 5.28 UK deaths by gender and age: 1961, 1981, 1997 and 2021

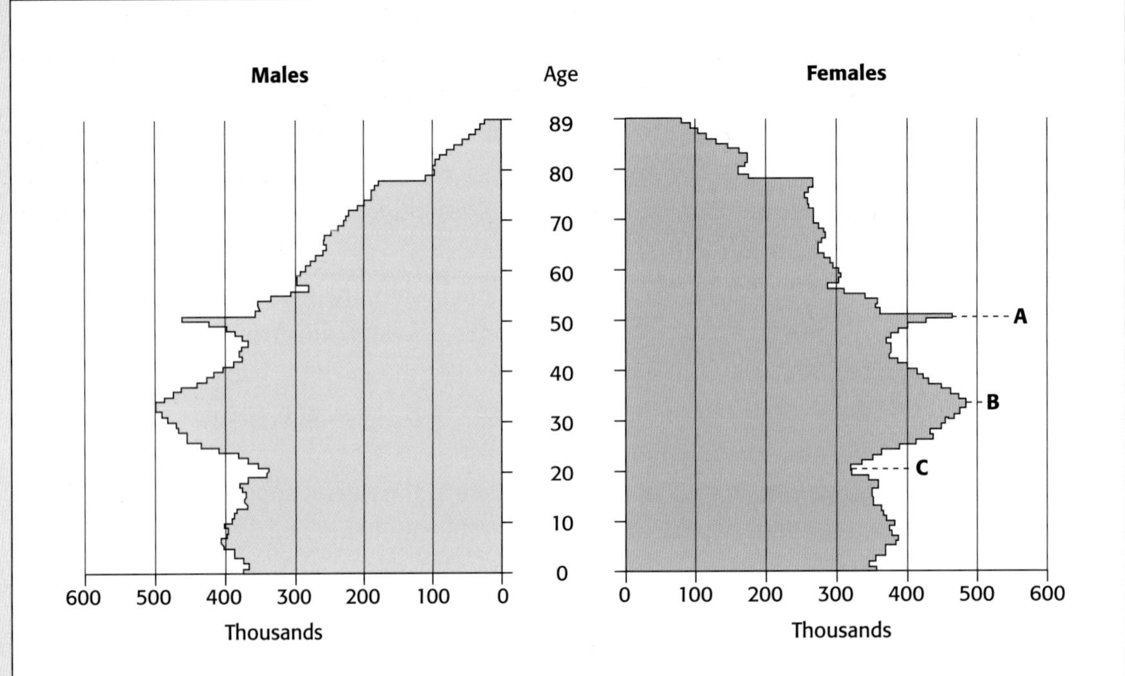

Figure 5.29
UK population by gender and age

had reached 16 per cent and 7 per cent respectively. By contrast the percentage of the population under the age of 16 fell from 25 per cent to 20 per cent. By 2040 about a quarter of the UK's population will be over 65, and if current trends continue the number of 65-year-olds will be larger than the number of under 16-year-olds in about the year 2016 (Figure 5.30).

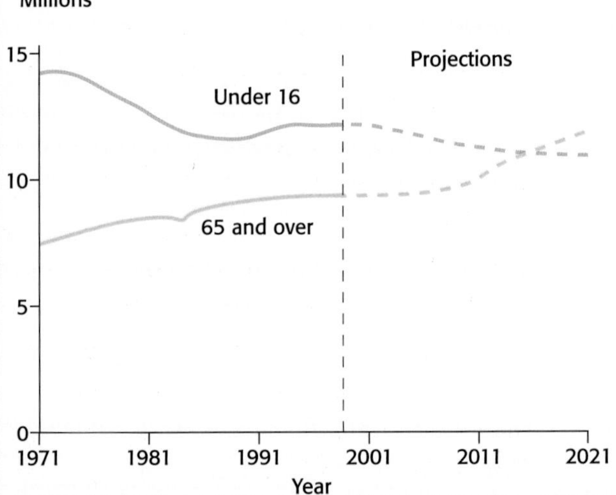

Figure 5.30
The dependent population, UK 1971–2021

Activity

1 Draw a bar graph, with separate but adjacent bars for males and females, to show the data given in Figure 5.26. Describe and explain the pattern of employment that you have shown.

2 Using the data in Figure 5.28, draw a line graph to show the variations in the death rate for males and females in each age group for 1997.

3 Describe and attempt to explain how the death rate for males and females changes between the first year of life and age 75 and over. Draw attention to the groups with the highest and lowest death rates.

4 Compare the data for 1961 with that for 1997 and that projected for 2021. Describe the overall trend. Is it what you would have expected?

Migration

Migration in the UK has operated at two distinct levels:

- people moving in and out of the country – **international migration**
- people moving within the country – **inter-regional migration.**

The net effect of international migration in Britain from 1901 to 1997 is illustrated in Figure 5.31. Almost half of the UK's ethnic minority residents live in London. They generally have a young age structure and in the case of the Bangladeshi population, 45 per cent is under the age of 16. Within the various ethnic groups children under the age of 16 are much more likely to have been born in Britain, whereas their parents are more likely to have been born overseas. This is especially true of the Indian population – 96 per cent of those under the age of 15 were born in Britain and only 1 per cent of those aged over 35 were born in this country.

Inter-regional migration within the country has been extremely complex, yet two dominating features have emerged:

- most migrants proceed only a short distance and so most inter-regional migration has been between adjacent regions
- where migrants move to a more distant region it is likely to be either London and the South East (for employment opportunities), or the South and South West for retirement.

From the 1960s to the early 1980s London lost up to 100 000 people each year owing to migration. Since the mid-1980s the trend has been reversed and London has been attracting migrants. Of those who leave London, up to two-thirds move to adjacent regions such as the South East or East Anglia, whereas those who move into London come from all parts of the UK, and many are from overseas. Figure 5.32 summarises the position in 1996/97.

Urban areas in the UK are also increasingly typified by relatively local migrations. Offsetting the concentration of younger people towards the centre, a greater proportion of people in the 5–14 and the over-45 age groups is to be found in the suburbs. The suburban concentration of these two groups reflects the tendency of many people with growing families to move away from the central districts in response to the perceived need for a more spacious residential environment – a process known as counterurbanisation.

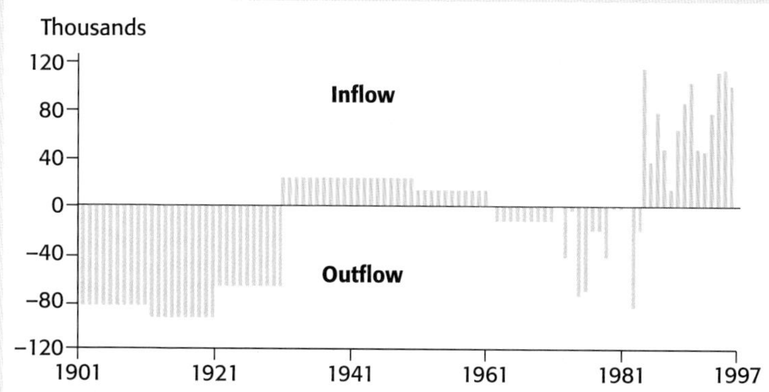

Figure 5.31
Net international migration, UK 1901–97

Activity

1. Complete the three *net migration* columns in Figure 5.32 by subtracting the numbers of people leaving London from those entering it. Use a plus (+) sign to show a gain and a minus sign (–) to show a loss.
2. Describe the age distribution of the inter-regional migrants entering and leaving London and suggest reasons for the variations you have identified.
3. Describe the age distribution of London's international migrants. Does it have any features in common with the age distribution of the inter-regional migrants?
4. Prepare a table to show the main push and pull factors accounting for migration to and from London by the various age groups within the two categories of migrants.

Age group	Inter-regional migrants		Net inter-regional migration	International migrants		Net inter-national migration	Overall net migration
	entering London	leaving London		entering London	leaving London		
0–15	16.1	36.8		7.2	4.7		
16–24	66.1	45.0		38.1	9.6		
25–44	70.3	92.0		35.9	34.5		
45–65	11.0	27.2		3.3	3.9		
65+	5.1	16.4		0.4	no data		
All ages	168.6	217.4		84.9	52.7		

Figure 5.32
Migration to and from London, by age 1996/97 (thousands)

Case Study: The population of China

With a total in 1998 of 1 262 817 000 people, China's population accounts for over one-fifth of the world's total. Prior to the creation of the People's Republic of China in 1949, the population was approximately 540 million. Improvements in the standard of living and health conditions after 1949 led to a decline in the death rate and an increase in the birth rate. By the first population census in 1953 the total number of people had risen to 601 million. Subsequent censuses recorded 723 million people in 1964, 1007 million in 1982, and 1160 million in 1990 (Figure 5.33).

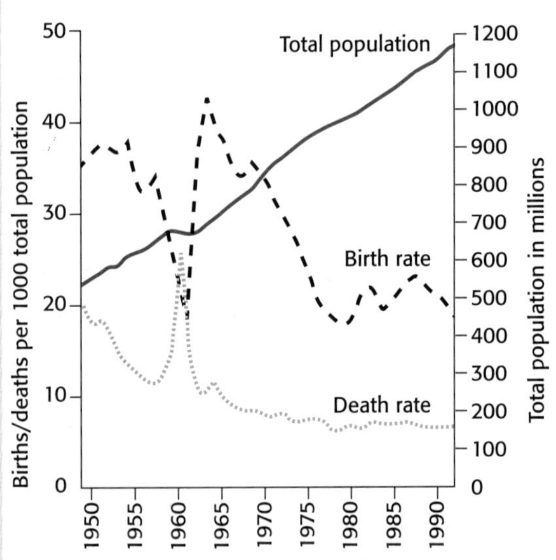

Figure 5.33

China: change in total population, birth and death rates since 1949

Population distribution and density

China's population density has increased rapidly since 1949. In mid-1953 it stood at about 60 people per km^2. By 1963 this figure had risen to 75 people per km^2, and by 1982 to over 107 people per km^2. It is now put at 128 persons per km^2. Globally, China ranks high in terms of population density. It is much higher than that of Egypt, Mexico, the USA, Brazil or the Russian Federation, but lower than Japan, Germany and India. In broad terms, the south-east accounts for 43 per cent of the country's total area and 94 per cent of the total population while the north-west has 57 per cent of the land but only 5.9 per cent of the population. The population densities of the sparsely inhabited regions such as the Mongolia–Xinjiang region with 11 persons per km^2, and the Qinghai–Tibet region with 3 persons per km^2, rank higher than those of Canada and Australia.

Population distribution is very uneven in China accounting for substantial variations in density. Density gradually declines from 375 people per km^2 within 200 km of the coast to less than 20 people per km^2 at a distance of 1000 km inland. One-third of the population lives within 200 km of the coast on a tenth of the country's total land area, and 60 per cent of the population lives within 500 km of the coast on a quarter of the land area. Fifty per cent of China's land area is located more than 1000 km from the coast and contains less than 10 per cent of the population. Further, China's population is mainly concentrated in the comparatively low-lying and flat areas. The low-lying plains and areas with a height of less than 500 m account for a quarter of the area but 80 per cent of the population. By contrast, plateaus and high mountains over 2000 m above sea level account for a third of the area but only 2 per cent of the population.

Population growth is changing the distribution of China's population. For example, growth in the coastal regions is lower than in the inland areas where plans for rapid development are being implemented by the government. The building of strategic inland bases for the national defence industries, railways in the south-west and north-west, the relocation of factories, universities and colleges, and the migration of peasants organised by the state, are all allowing interior centres to grow more rapidly than the coastal centres.

The three population pyramids (Figure 5.34), show the structure of China's population for 1953, 1964 and 1982. The pyramid for 1953 can be divided into two sections, above and below

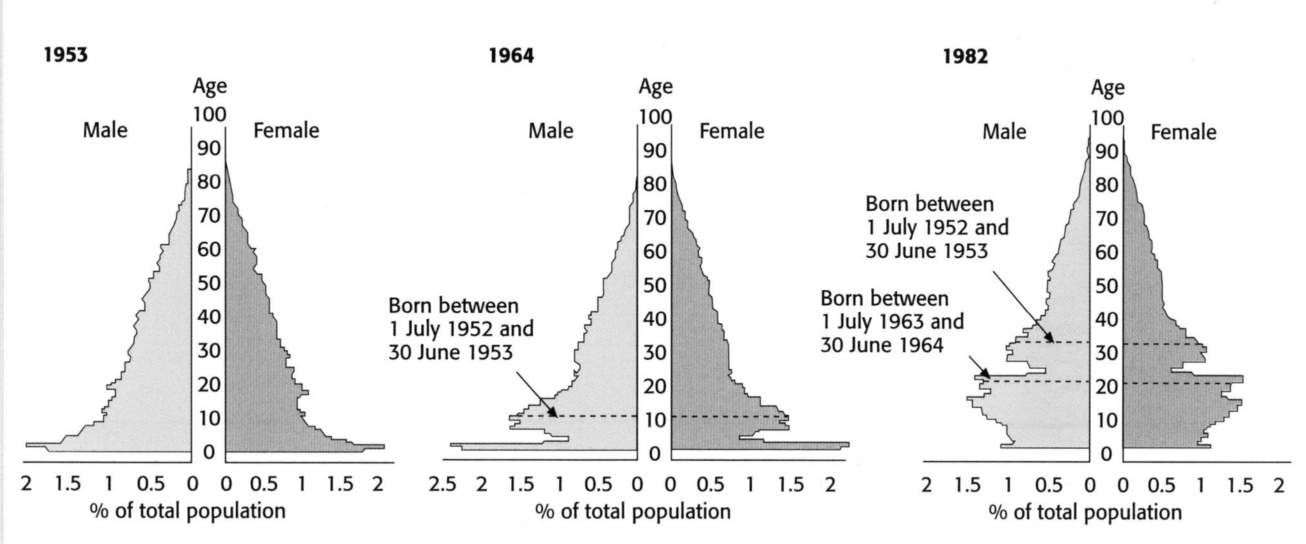

Figure 5.34 China: population pyramids for 1953, 1964 and 1982

the 3-year-old age band. The upper part shows an age composition characterised by high birth rates, high death rates and low population growth: the demographic characteristics of China before 1949. The lower part of the pyramid reveals the rapid population growth which followed the founding of the People's Republic. The narrowing of the pyramid coinciding with the band for 4–16 year-olds was caused by 12 years of war and conflict between 1937 and 1949. The pyramid for 1964 shows progression from 1953; it can also be divided into two parts, this time split by the 11-year-old age band. Above 11 years, the pyramid mirrors its 1953 counterpart, while the lower part continues to show high birth rates and rapid population growth. The sudden narrowing of the pyramid at the 2–4-year age band reflects the national economic difficulties encountered between 1959 and 1961. In the 1982 pyramid the 1953 structure pattern is evident above the 29-year age band, while below the 10-year age level, the lower birth rate stemming from the impact of the birth control policy adopted by China during the 1970s is evident.

Changing birth and death rates

China's birth and death rates for selected years between 1949 and 1997 are listed in Figure 5.35. The rise in population growth between 1950 and 1957 reflected the sustained high birth rate but rapidly falling death rate of the new Republic of China. Prior to 1949, in semi-colonial, semi-feudal China, both rates were high; by 1957 the death rate had virtually halved. The Great Leap Forward in 1958, whereby Mao Zedong attempted to convert China into an industrially based economy within five years, brought major problems and greatly affected living standards. As a result, the birth rate declined from 1958 to 1961 while the death rate rose, leading to a fall in the pace of population growth between these years.

The year 1962 saw a return to high birth rates, which were maintained until the early 1970s. During the same period the death rate continued to decline. After this period, however, there was a change from the pattern of high fertility and low death rates to one of low fertility and low death rates. In 1972 the birth rate was 30 per 1000; by 1980 it had dropped to 18 per 1000. At the same time the death rate continued its decline, dropping slowly from between 7 and 8 per 1000 in the early 1970s to 6 per 1000 in 1980. Throughout the 1980s the birth rate remained around the 21 mark but during the 1990s it dropped further, reaching 16.57 in 1997. The death rate has also continued to fall, hovering around 6.5 since 1992, due in part to improvements in maternal

Figure 5.35

China's birth and death rates: selected years 1949–97

Year	Birth rate	Death rate	Natural increase
1949	36	20	16
1953	37	14	23
1954	38	13	25
1956	32	11	21
1958	29	12	17
1960	21	25	–4
1961	18	14	4
1962	37	10	27
1963	43	10	33
1964	39	12	27
1966	35	9	26
1968	36	8	28
1970	33	8	25
1972	30	8	22
1974	25	7	18
1976	20	7	13
1978	18	6	12
1980	18	6	12
1982	21	7	14
1984	18	7	11
1988	21	7	14
1990	21	7	14
1992	18.20	6.60	11.6
1994	17.70	6.50	11.2
1995	17.12	6.57	10.55
1996	16.98	6.56	10.42
1997	16.57	6.51	10.06

Rounded values except for recent years

and child health care which have reduced the infant mortality rate to a level below that of many developing countries.

There are two major reasons for the slowing of population growth in China. The first is the result of deliberate **government policy**; the second the impact of **rising living standards**.

Population policy

In the early 1970s the Chinese Government decided to implement an extensive family limitation policy, which continues to this day. When the policy was first introduced, China's population was about 900 million people with a rate of increase in the order of 2.2 per cent, or about 20 million new mouths to feed each year. The overall aim was to stabilise the country's population at 1.2 billion by the year 2000 and, in the longer term, to reduce it to 700 million by 2010. This figure, China believes, is the optimum size, given the country's resources.

Family planning policies have included encouraging later marriage, and hence later childbirth; contraception; compulsory sterilisation; forced abortion; and a draconian one-child policy. In addition, China has implemented social insurance systems designed so that people with fewer children pay less taxes – a major incentive to have fewer children. In practice, the one-child policy applies mainly to the majority Han Chinese and not necessarily to the ethnic minorities, of which there are 55 groups making up 8 per cent of the total population. The policy has been relaxed where the first child was a girl, and women living in rural areas have been allowed a further child, but only after an interval of several years. Families with only one child have been given better houses, better education and better employment prospects than those which had two or more children.

The policy has succeeded, to an extent. As the fertility rate has dropped, so the rate of population growth has declined to between 0.9 per cent and 1.4 per cent (different authorities give different figures) from its much higher level of 2.2 per cent in the 1970s. However, the impact of the policy has been uneven. It has met most success among the urban populations where other pressures and incentives not to have children, such as the lack of accommodation, are greater than in rural areas. Away from the larger, more industrialised cities, the policy has been less successful. Many rural households continue to have two or three children. There has been widespread criticism of the policy, not only from foreign critics but also from internal dissidents; it has also introduced a new problem to China –spoilt, overweight 'little emperors'. However, had China not embarked on this programme of family planning it is estimated that there would have been at least an extra 250 million more Chinese people born between 1970 and 1990.

Rising standards of living

Figure 5.36 compares the growth in China's population with **gross national product** (GNP). It can be seen that the reduction in the rate of population growth during the 1990s was accompanied by a noticeable rise in GNP. As in other countries, the impact of greater economic prosperity has been to reduce population expansion, but the numbers of people involved are still great. Improving educational standards has also had some impact on the birth rate. For example, 80 per cent of the total population was illiterate or semi-illiterate in 1949, compared with about 20 per cent at present, and there is a marked link between the educational level of women and the number of children born to them (Figure 5.37).

Since the creation of the People's Republic mortality rates have been declining, to the extent that China is now a low-mortality developing country. Not only has the death rate come down but the causes of death have also changed (Figure 5.38). In the early part of the 20th century, infectious diseases accounted for nearly two-thirds of all deaths; strokes, heart attacks and cancers were not clearly classified in statistics. Now these 'Western' diseases account for almost two-thirds of deaths in cities and over half the deaths in rural areas. Infectious diseases, by contrast, have dropped out of the major ten causes altogether.

Future prospects

There is little doubt that the task of controlling population growth in the future will remain difficult. Past fluctuations in birth rate will continue to haunt the Chinese authorities. The relaxation of family planning controls has already led to an increase in population in some parts of China. In the agricultural areas where manual labour is the main form of labour, there is still a need for children. China continues to face two major challenges. The first is the ever larger scale of the total population despite the downturn in the rate of growth. The second is poverty and allied social problems, which are summed up in Figure 5.39.

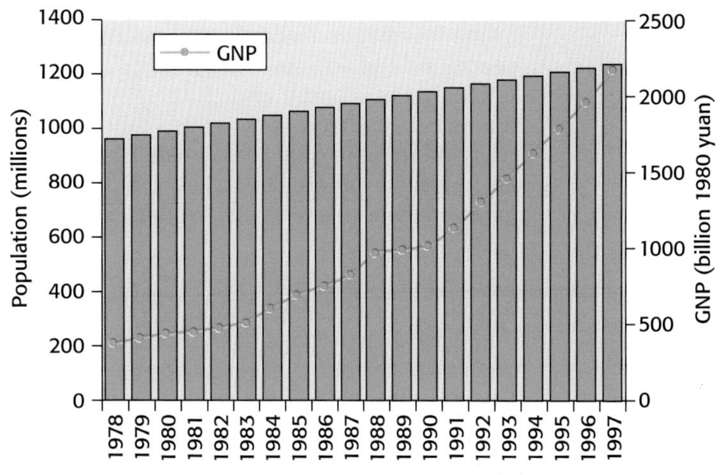

Figure 5.36

The growth in Chinese population and GNP, 1978–97

Education level	Fertility rate per 1000	Average no. of births per female
University	42.18	1.15
Senior middle school	63.88	1.23
Junior middle school	67.43	1.44
Primary school	86.25	2.02
Illiterate	94.50	2.44

Figure 5.37

Women's education level and births

1934 All China		% deaths
Respiratory disease		23.5
Diarrhoea and enteritis		12.2
Other fevers		11.5
Wasting diseases		8.3
Other gastro-enteritic diseases		7.6
1982	**China's cities**	**Rural China**
Cerebral vascular disease	22.3	15.4
Heart disease	21.0	23.7
Tumours	20.6	15.3
Respiratory disease	8.7	11.4
Digestive disease	4.4	5.6

Figure 5.38

Principal causes of death in China, 1934 and 1982

Figure 5.39

From *The Guardian*, 2 September 1999

China faces a hard truth

China has begun to confront poverty in the seamy side of society – including AIDS and trafficking in women and children –with an openness which international aid experts said was unthinkable only a few years ago. There are serious problems to tackle – in deprived areas education and health are desperately in need of attention.

The Rural Health System is falling apart, says one aid adviser. Village-level medical workers aren't paid, and those in the townships get only two-thirds of their proper salaries. Doctors attempt to over-prescribe because they can collect fees directly from the patient instead of doing preventive work.

But aid experts say they are encouraged by Beijing's new sense of energy. Beijing now admits that poverty is far more widespread than previous statistics indicated. Nearly 300 million Chinese, or almost a quarter of the population, are now admitted to be at risk, and most of these are women and children. It is also tackling the previously unmentionable subject of rural lavatories, which in 90 per cent of peasant homes were, until recently, just an open hole in the ground.

China is less defensive about how it appears and much more open about its problems, says Mark Hereward, Planning Officer for the United Nations Children Fund (UNICEF) in Beijing. The Ministry of Public Security wants help in solving the really difficult questions, such as how to deal with babies being taken away and returned later to families who then disown them, says Mr Hereward.

Chinese anti-poverty programmes have focused until recently on a set list of rural counties, mostly in the backward, western areas of the country. Beijing claims to have reduced the numbers of seriously poor from 80 million to 40 million in the past five years, but the list was flawed: some counties falsified the figures to qualify for aid, while others were too proud politically to apply. Now Beijing has accepted a much wider definition of poverty, agreeing with UNICEF that there is a large constituency of deprived people who have lost out in the economic reforms of the past 20 years. The figure of 300 million is based on World Bank minimum income guidelines.

China's ministry of foreign trade and economic co-operation has shown a new attitude in talks with UNICEF – 'they tell us quite recently', says Mr Hereward, 'that not all poverty is in the west of the country. They encourage us to look at the urban poor and at problems for children of migrant peasants. The campaign for sanitary latrines in the countryside has introduced simple technology and routines of hygiene to reduce disease from lavatories. The goal is to ensure that 50 per cent of rural households have adequate sanitation by the year 2005. This would leave China still well behind Thailand and the Philippines but ahead of Cambodia and Vietnam.

China is also more willing to face up to the huge disparities in under-5 mortality. Shanghai suffers 9 deaths per 100 000, the same as any industrialised country. In the western regions of Xinjiang this rises to more than 70, and in the remote mountainous areas in Sichuan Province this figure may reach 300, a level comparable with that in sub-Saharan Africa. UNICEF's new strategy is to emphasise gathering good information and statistics as essential for identifying where the real problems lie. By the end of the year there should be one person in each of the 2000 plus counties that make up China, gathering data on children.

Migration in China

China's internal migration accounts for some of the largest and most important **rural-to-urban** migrations in the world. The main pattern of movement is from less developed parts of the country to the more prosperous cities, especially in the south east and, in particular, Beijing.

When the Communist Party came to power in 1949, China's urban population was about 70 million, or 13 per cent of the total population. From 1949 to 1970 most population migration took place in rural areas, with the majority of migrants moving from densely populated rural areas to sparsely populated frontier zones. Some also migrated to work in the construction industry and in the mines. However, the overwhelming purpose was the peopling, exploitation and consolidation of China's frontiers.

After the death of Chairman Mao in 1976, China introduced a 'socialist market economy system' and began to modernise its agriculture, industry and technology, and to develop new trade links. The government also loosened its grip on the distribution of population through household registration. Migration patterns changed accordingly.

One of the first systematic surveys of migration in China analysed data for the years 1982–87. It reached three main conclusions. First, that population migration increased between 1982 and 1987 compared with earlier estimates. Between 1982 and 1987, 'official' migrants numbered nearly 3 per cent of the population (over 30 million people!). Second, the direction of migration changed. Most migrants moved from rural areas to cities, and during the same period urban areas grew at the expense of rural areas by some 13 million people. By 1982, 20.5 per cent of the population was classified as urban, and by 1996 the figure stood at 31 per cent; in 1953 it had been 13.3 per cent. Third, most people migrated from inland provinces to coastal areas; a smaller proportion migrated to factories and mines in inland regions. Of the 30 million migrants, 79 per cent stayed within their own province; the other 21 per cent were involved in inter-provincial migration.

Provinces that gained migrants included Shanghai, Beijing, Hebei, Shandong, Jiangsu, Guangdong, Tianjin, Liaoning, Hubei and Ningxia. By contrast, Heilongjiang, Inner Mongolia, Xinjiang and Gansu, which used to attract migrants, lost people during the 1982–87 period.

The most popular destination is Beijing. Within the city certain regions attract migrants from different parts of the country. The suburb of Dahongemen, for example, contains over 400 000 people from Zhejiang province in south-east China and is referred to as 'Zhejiang village'. Another is Xinjiang village, containing Muslim Chinese from the west of China.

The 1990 census revealed that these trends were continuing. Between 1985 and 1990 the population officially moving to other cities, provinces or overseas was 3 per cent. The great majority of migrations were internal, and 81 per cent involved moves within or to urban areas. Fewer than 18 per cent were moves to rural areas, and of these only 5 per cent were new residents to rural areas – the others were moving from one rural area to another.

Since 1979 over 100 million people have left rural areas for urban areas where overpopulation is putting a strain on housing, education and health, and on services such as water and electricity. Most of the migrants are young and have moved in search of employment in the construction industry, factories, textile sweatshops, and in the service occupations. However, working conditions are often poor, and wages are low. Many migrants send a large part of their wages home as remittances, in order to support their families in rural areas.

Activity

Study Figure 5.40, which shows regional variations in migration in China, 1990.

1 Using a copy of Figure 5.41, draw a choropleth map (density shading) to show the level of net migration in each region.

2 Identify the five regions that experienced the most in-migration and the four regions with the most out-migration.

3 Consulting an atlas and any other suitable resources, suggest reasons why the nine regions you have identified experience the highest levels of in- and out-migration respectively.

Region	Proportion (%) of China's 100 million internal migrants	
	Entering from other regions	Moving to other regions
North		
Beijing	6.13	1.13
Tianjin	3.51	0.98
Hebei	0.78	1.10
Shanxi	0.96	0.80
Inner Mongolia	1.13	1.32
North-east		
Liaoning	1.29	0.68
Jilin	1.01	1.38
Heilongjiang	0.96	1.71
East		
Shanghai	4.87	1.11
Jiangsu	1.23	0.86
Zhejiang	0.79	1.53
Anhui	0.61	0.96
Fujian	0.97	0.74
Jiangxi	0.59	0.72
Shandong	0.73	0.63
Central South		
Henan	0.57	0.67
Hubei	0.75	0.64
Hunan	0.41	0.40
Guangdong	1.84	0.40
Guangxi	0.37	1.74
Hainan	2.08	1.74
South-west		
Sichuan	0.42	1.21
Guizhou	0.61	0.95
Yunnan	0.64	0.74
North-west		
Shaanxi	0.94	1.02
Gansu	0.70	1.17
Qinghai	2.36	2.22
Ningxia	1.67	1.19
Xinjiang	2.19	1.78

The migrant population in Tibet has not been enumerated.

Figure 5.40

Population movement in China, as indicated by the 1990 census

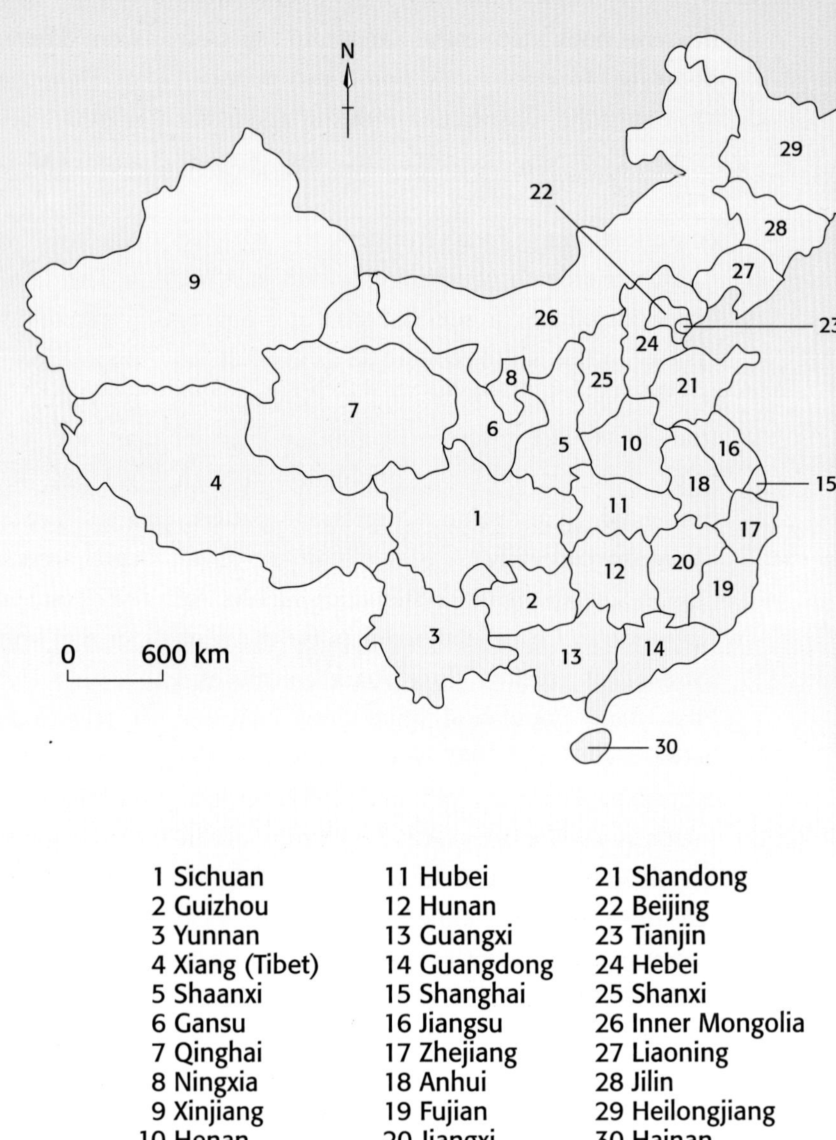

Figure 5.41

The administrative divisions of China

6 Rural settlement and population change in MEDCs

Key Themes

- ✔ The location of rural settlements is influenced by a range of physical and human factors, but the part each plays is highly unlikely to remain constant over time.
- ✔ Rural settlements can be arranged into a hierarchy according to the services they provide; these hierarchies are subject to change, both in terms of population and economic functions.
- ✔ While the predominant migration trend in the more economically developed countries of the world is now from bigger to smaller settlements, the more remote rural areas still experience depopulation.
- ✔ Pressure for more building – especially for more homes – often leads to disputes about the relationship between town and country in the rural–urban fringe.

Rural settlements – change and development

In the more economically developed countries (MEDCs) a relatively small percentage of the population lives in rural settlements – that is, in isolated houses, hamlets and villages. Others live in small market towns within what most people would still consider to be a rural landscape. However, definitions of terms such as 'urban' and 'rural', and even 'town' and 'village', differ between countries. In Canada, a settlement is considered to be rural if it has fewer than 1000 inhabitants, but in Switzerland communes of up to 10 000 people are classified as rural.

In 1988 the Commission of the European Communities recognised that rural areas across Europe were not only places where people lived and worked (largely in agriculture) but that they also served society on a much wider front, especially for recreation. In response, EU policy on rural areas has evolved from giving support through the Common Agricultural Policy to farming alone, towards achieving a balance between support for farmers and for the development of rural communities as a whole. So while direct support for farmers still takes up 50 per cent of the EU budget, other strategies aimed at revitalising rural areas are also in place. The EU further recognises that while policies are needed to arrest decline in remote areas, it is also necessary to address problems of rapid change in the more accessible rural areas. Figure 6.1 shows the distribution of rural problem regions across the EU where economic diversification is regarded as essential to relieve over-dependence on agriculture.

This chapter traces the evolution of rural settlement patterns and examines how broader economic and social trends have changed the nature of life and the environment in the countryside.

Rural settlement – process and patterns in England

Rural settlements vary in size and shape as well as in the pattern of their distribution. Some rural areas are dominated by quite large and well-defined **nucleated settlements**; others by a **dispersed settlement** pattern of isolated farmsteads and small hamlets (Figure 6.2). As Figure 6.3 shows, nucleation is characteristic of lowland

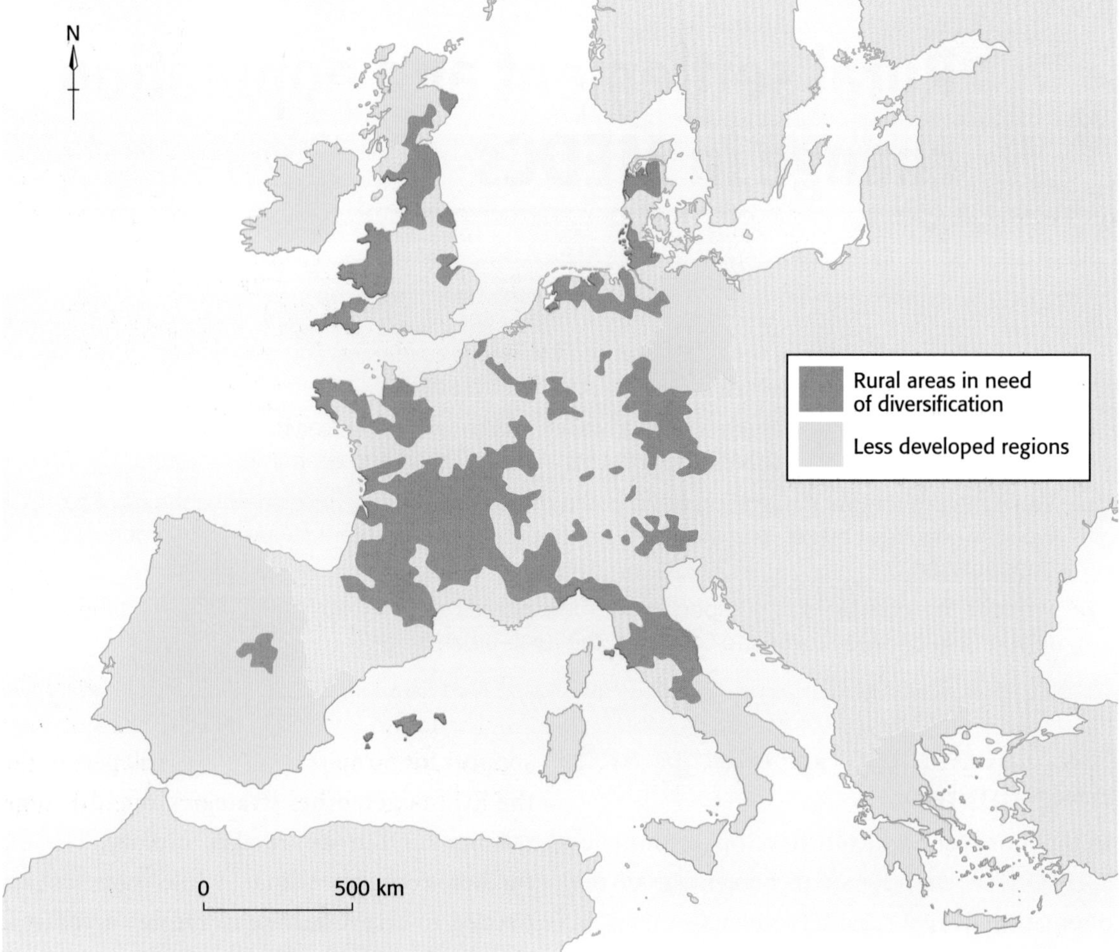

Figure 6.1
EU rural areas in need of economic diversification

Figure 6.2
Contrasting types of rural settlement:
a a nucleated settlement
b an isolated farmstead

areas of Britain, while dispersal tends to be the common pattern in upland environments. Factors encouraging nucleation:

- **Physical influences:** fertile land supports a high population density, and encourages the development of large villages. Alternatively, nucleation might occur around a scarce resource, such as a dry site in an otherwise marshy area as in the case of Ely in the Fens of eastern England.
- **Cultural influences:** the Anglo-Saxon settlers tended to farm large, open fields in communal groups, sharing plough and oxen teams. It made sense to locate together in the middle of the cultivated area (Figure 6.4), although later enclosure of land on the edge of the cultivated area could lead to the dispersal of settlement as outlying farms were established.
- **Settlement evolution:** some new villages have been created in more recent times.

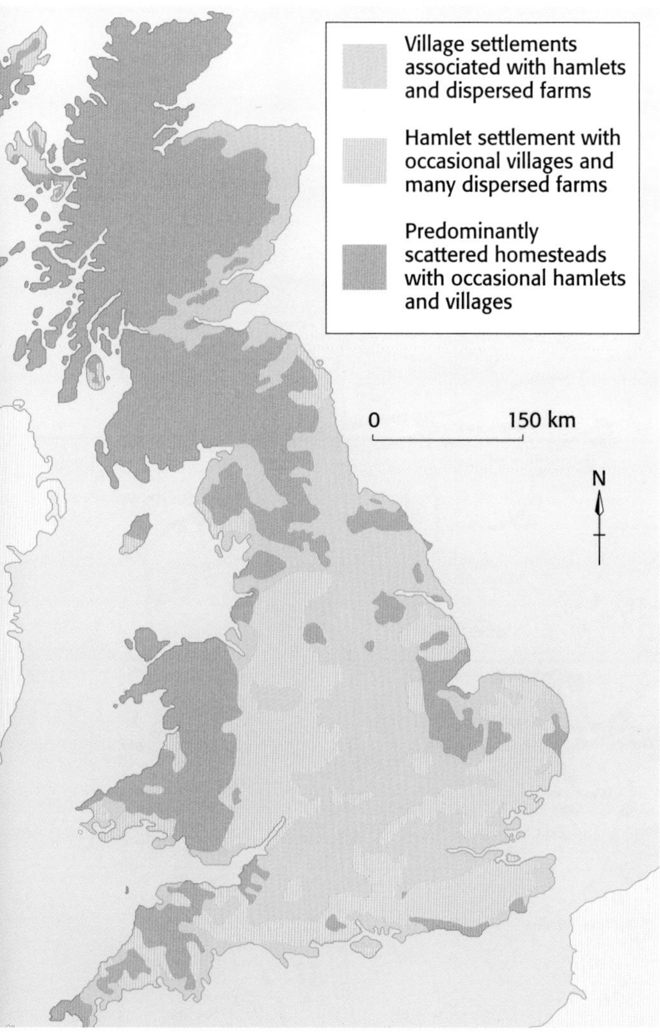

Figure 6.3
Rural settlement patterns in Britain

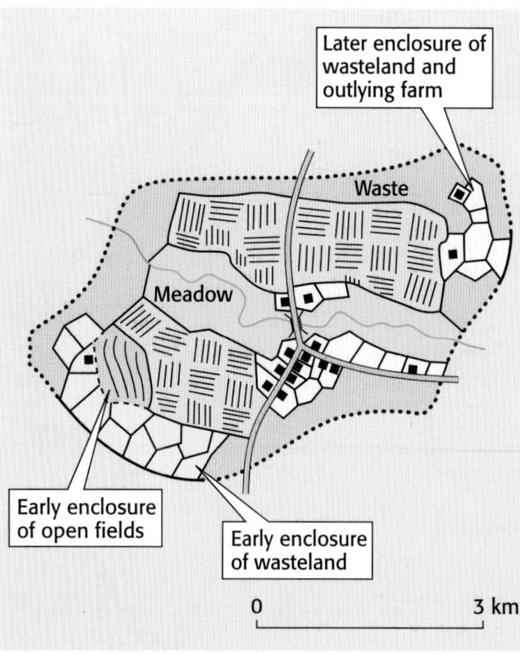

Figure 6.4
Model of a typical Midland nucleated village

County Durham has a very complex **settlement hierarchy**. The earliest settlement took the form of agricultural villages, with a greater density in the south and east where the land is lower and more fertile. However, in the 18th and 19th centuries the exploitation of the coalfield created a whole new network of settlements (Figure 6.5). Mining communities grew up around each pit-head and were found mainly to the north and east of the county.

Factors encouraging dispersal:

- **Physical influences:** dispersed settlement occurs in upland areas where poor soils and a short growing season can only support a low population density (Figure 6.6).
- **Cultural influences:** in 'Celtic' areas (such as Wales and parts of south-west England) the inheritance system of tyddyn meant that farms were split up between sons on the death of the father. Each son might then go off and establish his own farmstead.
- **Settlement evolution**: as **population pressure** increased in fertile areas, individuals or families might be forced to move on to less favoured land, clearing piece by piece and setting up isolated farmsteads.

Evidence of settlement evolution

Maps and aerial photographs provide evidence that settlement patterns change over time, with new settlements being added to historic patterns. By this means a very complex pattern emerges, reflecting a host of influences.

- **Iron Age settlement**: evidence of pre-Roman habitation includes hill forts (Figure 6.7), tumuli (small mounds, often marking burial chambers), stone circles, and other relict features, which are marked in italics on OS maps.
- **Roman settlement**: the Romans left their mark on the landscape with the remains of roads and villas. Place-names (e.g. towns ending in –chester or –caster) also suggest a Roman origin.

Figure 6.5

The settlement pattern around Trimdon in County Durham

© Crown Copyright

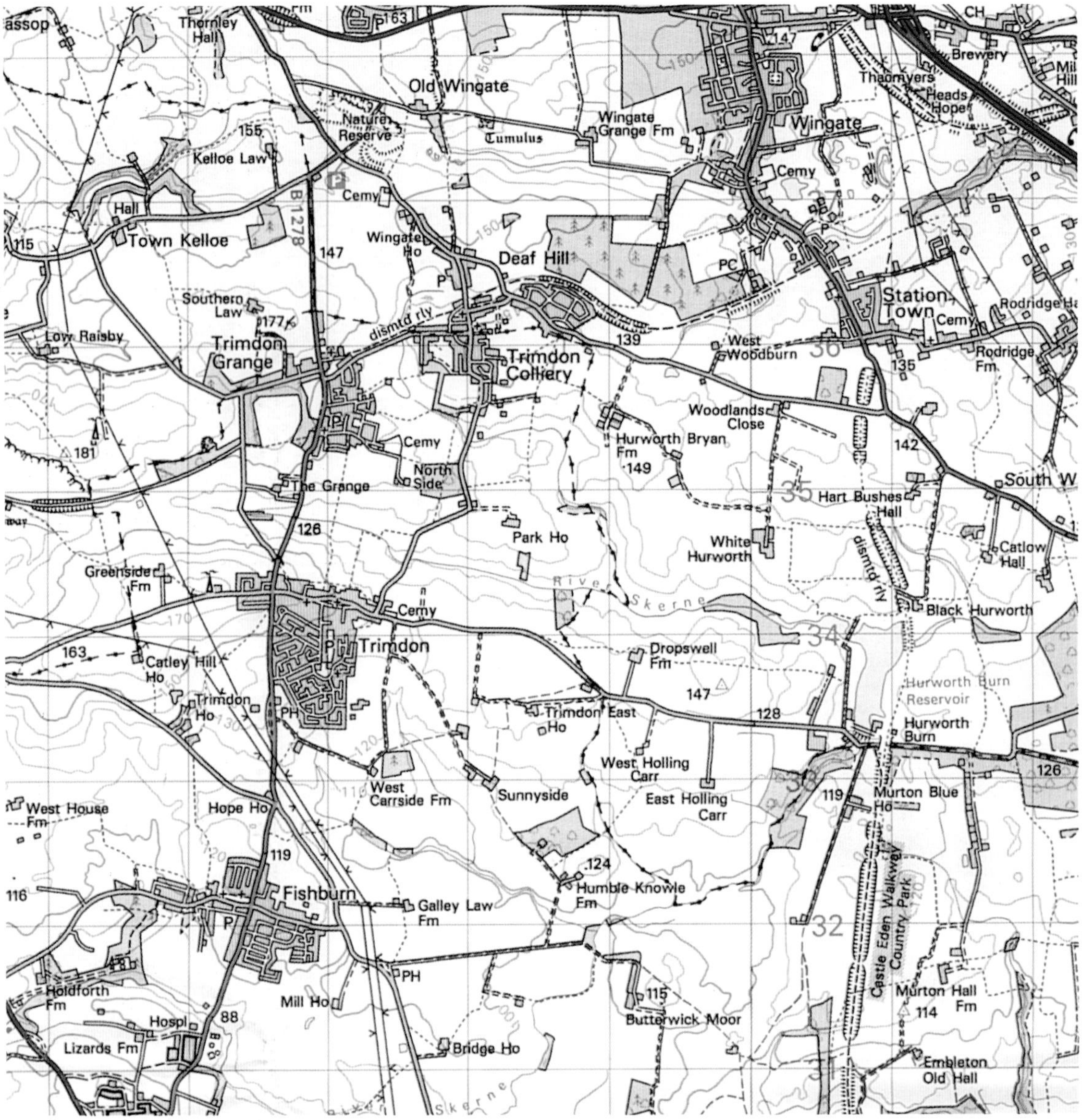

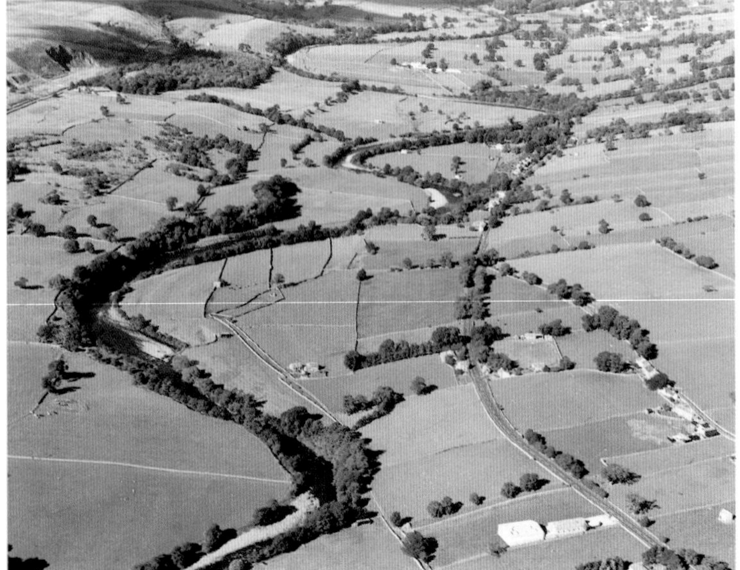

Figure 6.6

Dispersed settlement in Teesdale, County Durham

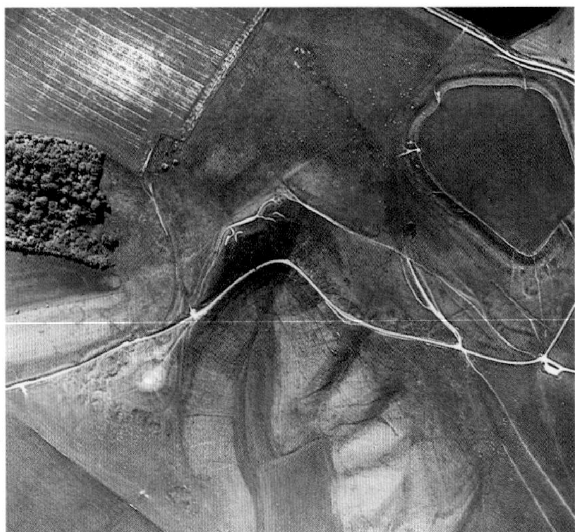

Figure 6.7

Iron Age hill fort at Uffington, Oxfordshire

- **The Anglo-Saxons:** most villages in England date from the Anglo-Saxon folk migration into England from AD450. It is possible to trace stages in the creation of settlements (Figure 6.8), because earlier sites have names ending in –ing, –ham, and –ton (e.g. Wilton); while later clearances of less favoured areas tend to be denoted by place-names ending in -field, -ley, -wold or -den (e.g. Tenterden).
- **Scandinavian incursions after AD800:** these led to a new phase of village settlement in eastern England. Place-names ending in –by (e.g. Grimsby), –thorpe (e.g. Scunthorpe) or –holme suggest a Scandinavian origin.
- **Settlement desertions:** almost all the villages in England today had already been established by the time of the Domesday Book survey of 1086. However, many of the villages in existence in the Middle Ages subsequently disappeared (Figure 6.9). One piece of evidence for this would be a church, standing in isolation rather than in the midst of a village. Such cases, common in East Anglia, might arise from the migration of a village away from its original site (Figure 6.10), or through the depopulation of a village, possibly as the result of plague (Figure 6.11). Another possibility is the gradual shrinkage of a hamlet into an isolated farmstead.

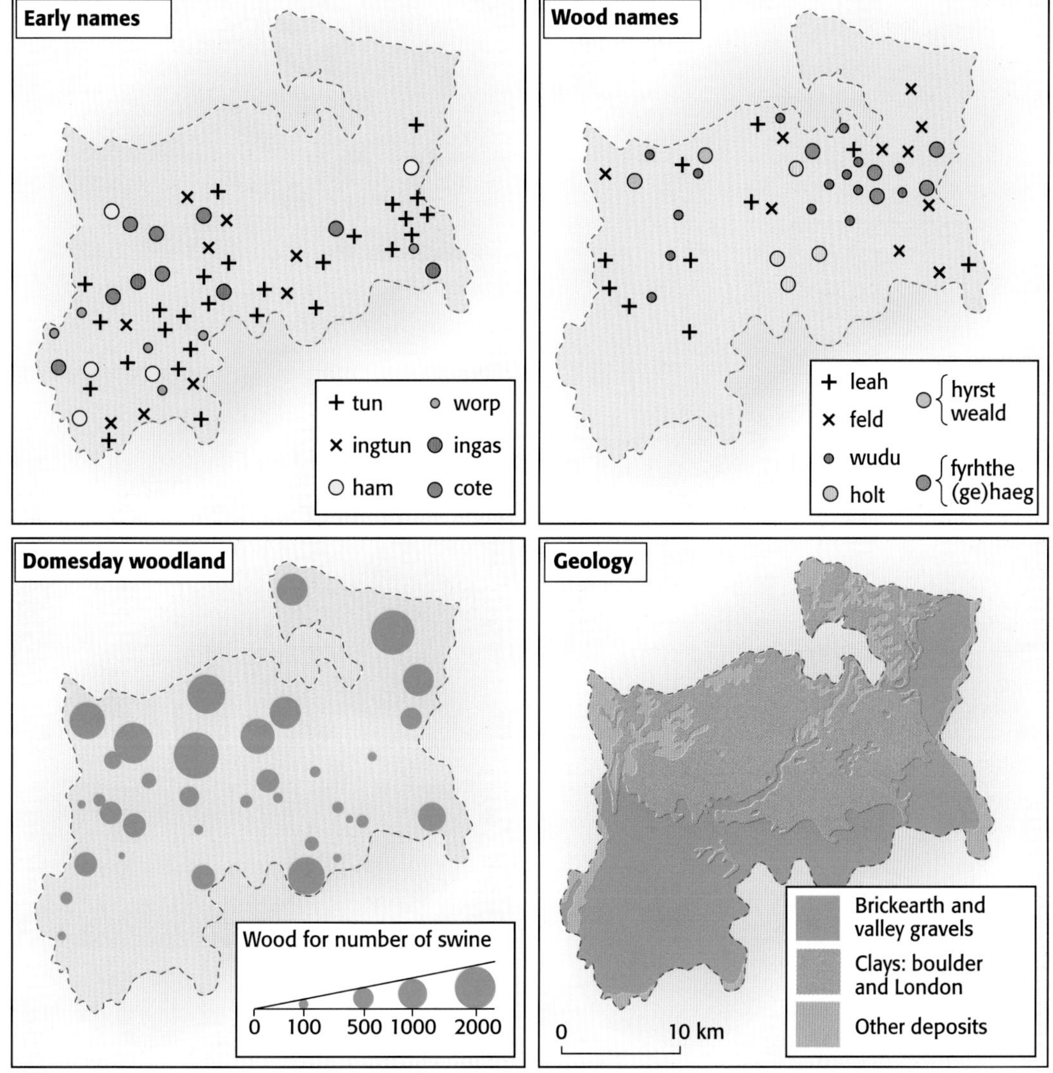

Early place-names occupy more favoured sites in the south on lighter soils close to the River Thames. Later place-names suggest woodland clearance in the heavier soils to the north.

Figure 6.8 Place-names as evidence of settlement evolution in Middlesex

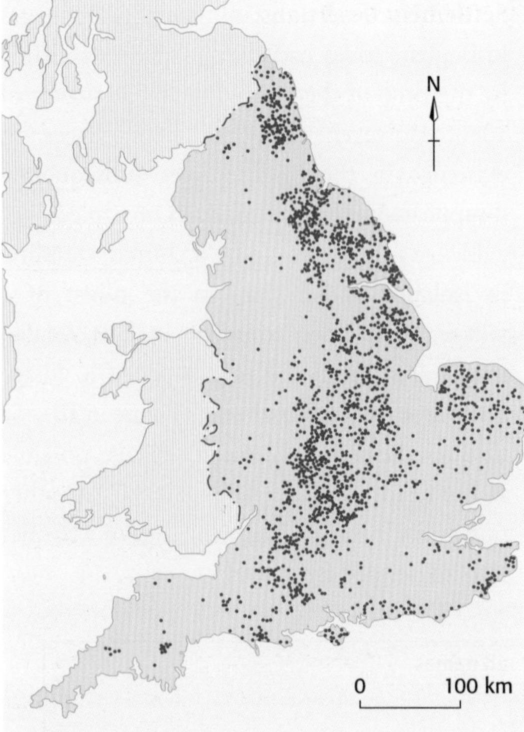

Figure 6.9

Deserted medieval villages in England

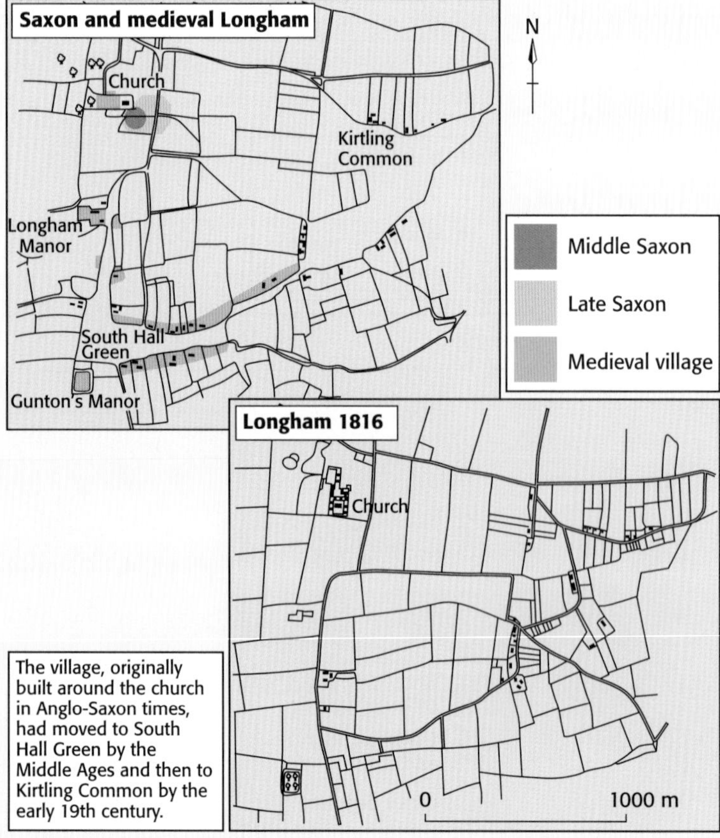

Figure 6.10

Village migration at Longham, Norfolk

- **Modern changes:** some villages have been intentionally added to the landscape for a particular purpose. These villages tend to show evidence of planning. Examples include pit villages in coalfield areas, and planned villages, such as Milton Abbas in Dorset, built by landlords to house estate workers in the 18th century (Figure 6.12).

Figure 6.11

A shrunken village: Knapwell, Cambridgeshire

Figure 6.12

The planned village of Milton Abbas, Dorset. The model village, built 1786/87 and consisting of pairs of thatched cottages, was located along a dry valley to make it invisible from the nearby family mansion built by the Earl of Dorchester

Case Study: The evolution of settlement patterns in south Oxfordshire

There is evidence of Iron Age and Roman occupation in south Oxfordshire (e.g. Dor*chester*), but most of the existing villages were established by Anglo-Saxon migrants (Figure 6.13). The earliest Anglo-Saxon villages were located in open country close to the Thames and its tributaries – places like Stadhamp*ton* and Gor*ing*, for example. Nucleated settlement associated with open field agriculture thus characterised these fertile lowlands.

At first, settlers avoided the chalk uplands of the Chilterns which were less fertile and had little surface water. However, as population pressure increased, individuals or family groups moved onto these higher areas, clearing piecemeal and establishing dispersed farmsteads. Some grew into hamlets (e.g. Ips*den*, Nuf*field*), but they remained dependent on the bigger villages down in the vale. For example, Stoke Row originated in 1435 as a daughter settlement of North Stoke. The size of the hamlet was limited by the lack of water. A well dug in the 19th century had to be more than 120 m deep. The hamlet did not have its own church until 1848.

The area has seen changes to its settlement pattern. Nuneham Courtenay was moved by a landlord who was keen to redesign the park around his stately home. New settlements have also been added and others expanded to provide more homes. Berinsfield originated in the 1960s as a new village planned to house squatters occupying an old airbase, who had been made homeless during the war. RAF Benson is to all intents and purposes a new village superimposed on the landscape, housing military staff.

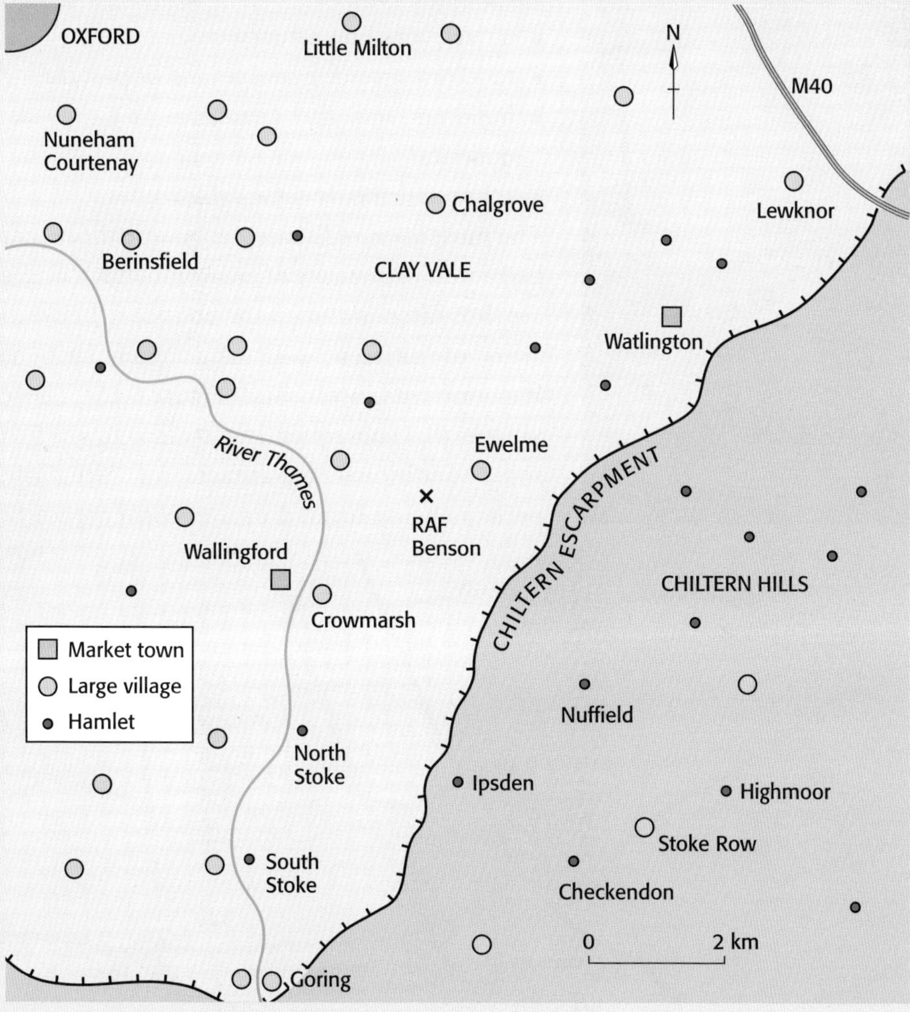

Figure 6.13
South Oxfordshire: the physical setting

Settlement location

When settlements were originally established by the Anglo-Saxons, they tended to be small and self-sufficient. Decisions on where to locate settlements were made on the basis of imperfect knowledge, and perceptions of the environment were influenced by the cultural background of the settlers.

Site and **situation** are the two key aspects of location.

Site

Desirable physical features of a site:

- good for defence
- water supply
- free drainage
- flat land
- shelter.

Figure 6.14 Eton Wick, Berkshire

However, new settlers in unfamiliar locations would have had to guess about the likely impact of local hazards such as large flood events. Here an additional, human factor becomes important – **hazard perception**, which refers to the ability to assess the long-term potential of a site. The site of Eton Wick in Berkshire, shown in Figure 6.14, demonstrates the need to strike a balance between access to a supply of water and the need to avoid the risk of flooding.

New settlers might also be attracted by some types of site, and repelled by others. Anglo-Saxons, for instance, avoided sites with Roman remains, believing them to be haunted – a culturally-perceived quality.

Situation

The features of a settlement's situation are essentially concerned with access to resources and facilities, such as:

- a river, coastline, estuary, etc.
- food resources, e.g. arable land or pasture
- building and fuel resources, e.g. woods, quarries
- other settlements via suitable routes.

The most favoured settlements were those that had access to a variety of environments. Villages are thus often found on the boundary between areas of different soils and relief, such as Welbourn in Lincolnshire (Figure 6.15). Those villages that subsequently grew into towns had some additional advantages of situation, perhaps being located on the convergence of

Figure 6.15 Welbourn, Lincolnshire. Scarp-foot villages often have a water supply from springs, good communications, and access to a variety of environments.

important routes which encouraged the development of a trading community (Figure 6.16).

Unlike the site, the situation of a settlement can easily change over time. Examples include:

- improved transport, perhaps where a new motorway brings a village within commuting distance of a large city (Figure 6.17)
- pit closures in a coal-mining area which undermine the economic foundation of a village.

Figure 6.16

The Goring Gap where the River Thames passes through the Chiltern Hills on the Berkshire/Oxfordshire border. Goring-on-Thames occupies a convergence zone where transport routes pass through the Gap.

Figure 6.17

The village of Lewknor adjacent to Junction 6 on the M40 in Oxfordshire

Settlement morphology

Economic, social and historical conditions influence the form, or morphology, of villages (**village morphology**). The basic classification of **settlement morphology** is twofold:

- **Nucleated villages** – these may take several forms. An irregular form is likely to result from the haphazard growth of a hamlet. By contrast, green villages have grown up around a central open space (Figure 6.18), and grid-iron villages have usually been planned from scratch, e.g. a pit village.
- **Linear villages** derive their shape from the positioning of buildings along the sides of the main road running through the settlement (Figure 6.19). Such a linear

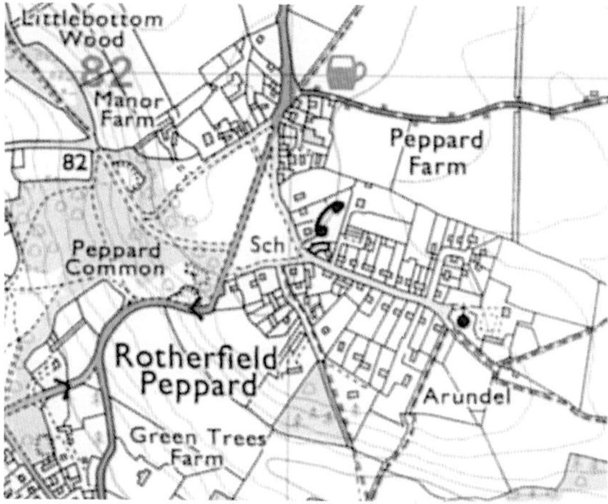

Figure 6.18

Rotherfield Peppard: a 'green' village near Henley-on-Thames. The village green would have been used originally to keep animals safe at night – it is now used as a cricket pitch.

Figure 6.19

Great Shefford, Berkshire. This village was originally linear, following the line of a narrow valley. Not only would it have been easier to build in the valley bottom, but access to water would also have been better. More recent development has been free of these traditional constraints.

pattern is likely to develop under certain conditions, especially:

– along a major transport route
– in hilly areas with narrow valley floors
– along narrow ridges of higher land
– along raised banks in fenland areas.

More recently, the influx of people from the city – either commuters, home-workers or retired people – has led to the growth of **metropolitan villages** (Figure 6.20). The character and form of these settlements tends to reflect their new-found purpose. Typical features are:

- the conversion of property, e.g. post offices turned into homes
- infilling: new houses built between existing houses
- accretions of occasional new buildings on the edge of the village
- ribbon development along roads out of the village
- large planned additions, such as estates of similar houses.

The actual form of a growing village might well be influenced by planning decisions. New growth might be concentrated in a small number of selected villages or, in green belt areas; infilling might be preferred and ribbon development not permitted.

Figure 6.20 Growth and morphology of a metropolitan village

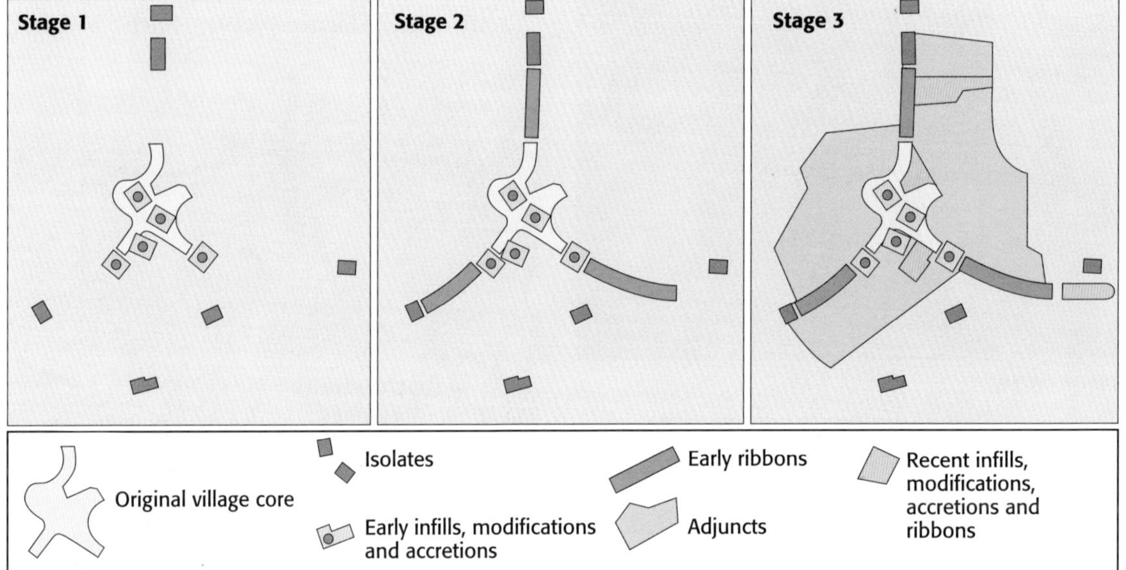

a Possible stages of morphological evolution of a suburbanised village

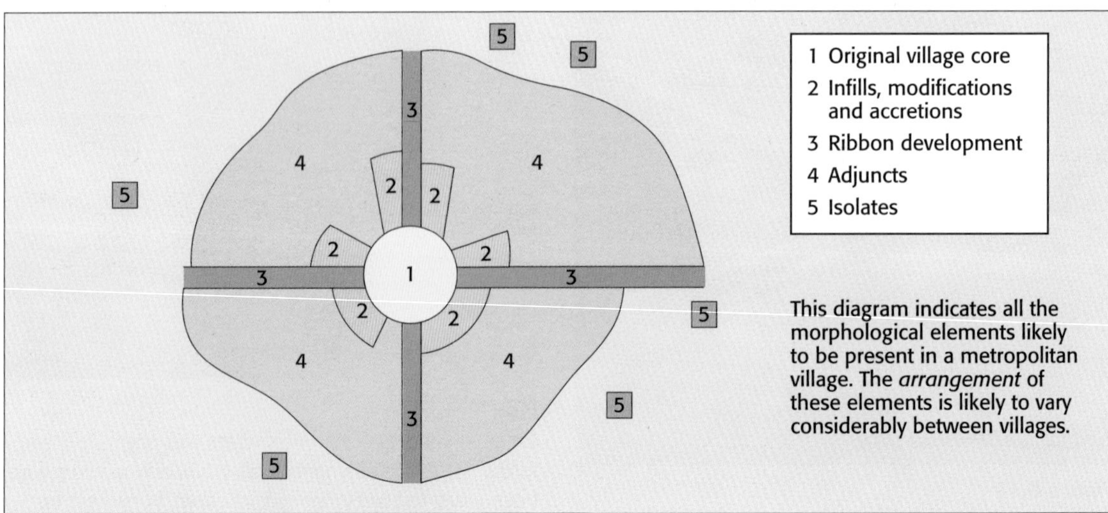

b Metropolitan village: morphological features

Case Study: Chalgrove, Oxfordshire

Chalgrove is a large, long village (Figure 6.21). It originated as a linear village surrounded by open fields and occupying a site which avoided the most flood-prone areas on the right bank of a stream. The form of the village reflects the history of its growth (Figure 6.22). Initially, houses were built along the original road to Oxford, reflecting the situation of Chalgrove. After a long period of stagnation, the population grew very rapidly from under 1000 people in 1961 to just over 3000 by 1996. In response, infilling in the form of large new housing estates has taken place in the area between the village core and the more recent bypass.

CHALGROVE CP
Hampden' Monumen
Chalgrove Field
1643
Manor Farm
Moat
Mill
PO
64
Langley Hall
ngley Field Farm
Sch
Chalgrove

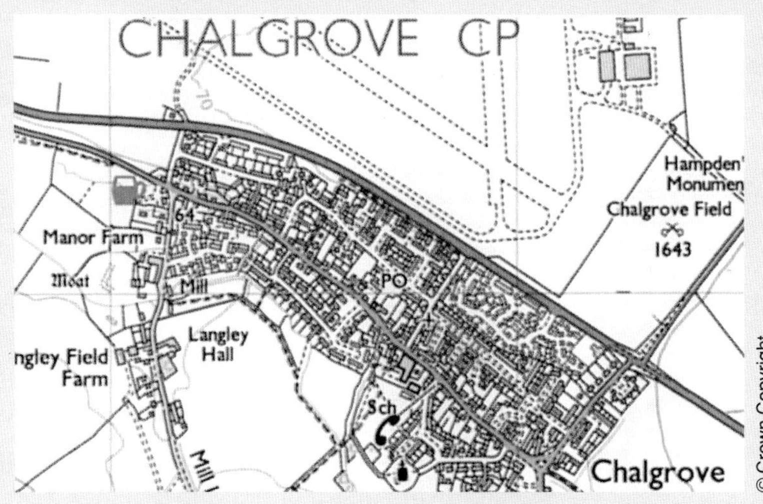

Figure 6.21

Chalgrove, Oxfordshire

Village core
B480 to Stadhampton and Oxford
Subsidised housing: council housing with infilling by housing association
1970s lower-cost housing: grid-iron street pattern, 2–3 bedrooms
1980s higher-cost housing: variety of styles, culs-de-sac, 4 bedrooms
B480 to Watlington
To Warpsgrove
1960s low-cost housing: grid-iron street pattern, 2–3 bedrooms
High Street
Mixed development
1930s semi-detached housing
1990s high-cost housing: new units and conversions
Mixed development
N
0
100 metres

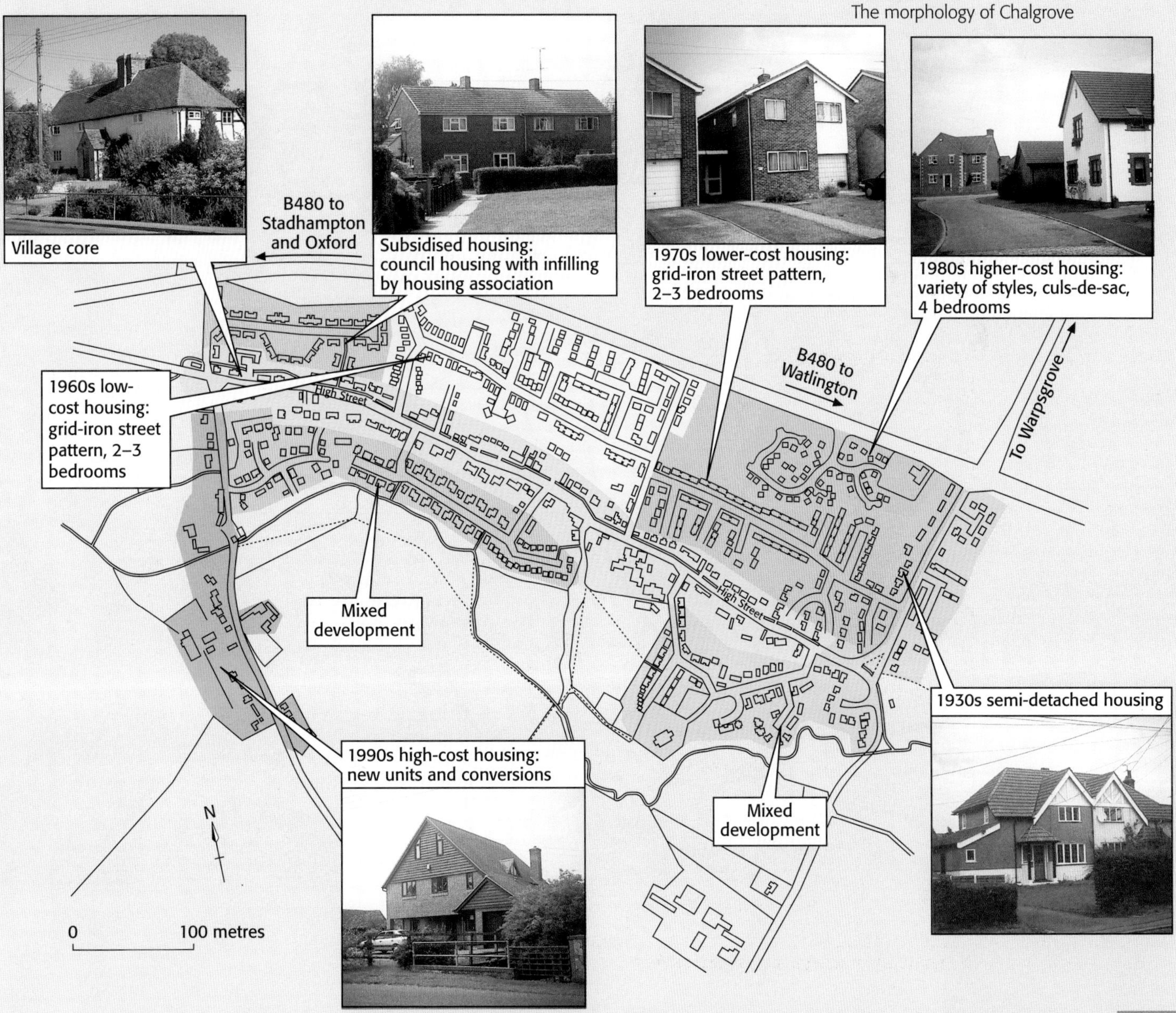

Figure 6.22

The morphology of Chalgrove

Activity

1 Study Figure 6.23, which shows the area to the south of Shaftesbury in Dorset.

a Compare the settlement patterns on either side of the A350 road.

b Suggest reasons for the settlement pattern found to the east of the road.

c Suggest two site and two situation advantages of Fontmell Magna.

2 Examine Figure 6.24, showing the form of the village of Ferryhill in County Durham in the 1960s. Originally a linear agricultural settlement, the 19th century saw the opening of a colliery and the grafting on of terraced housing for the workers. Additions in the 20th century included an area of lower-density council housing. Study the map closely and try to identify the three main stages in the growth of Ferryhill. Prepare a simple sketch map, marked Stages 1, 2 and 3, to demonstrate the growth pattern of the village.

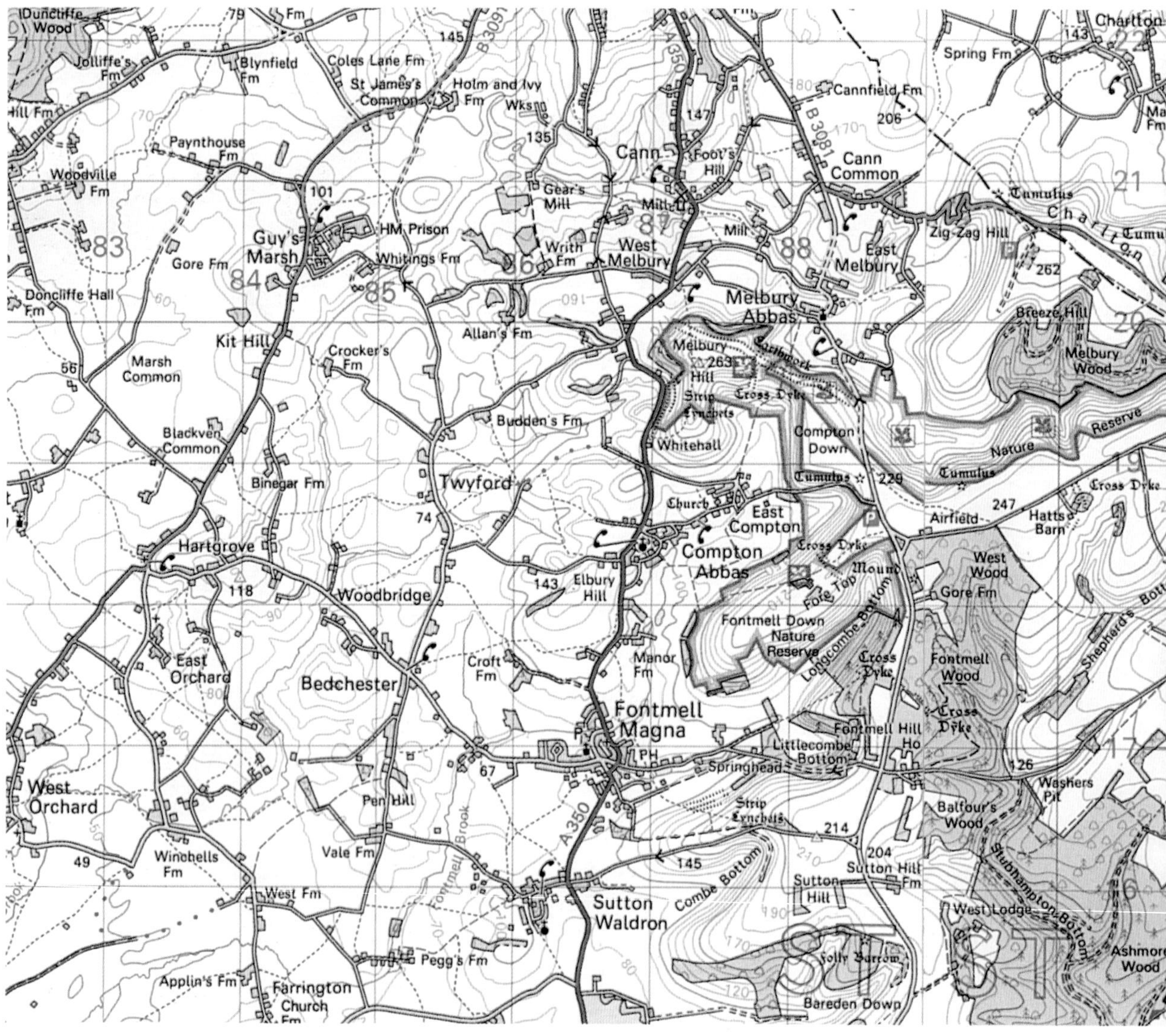

Figure 6.23 The area around Fontmell Magna, Dorset

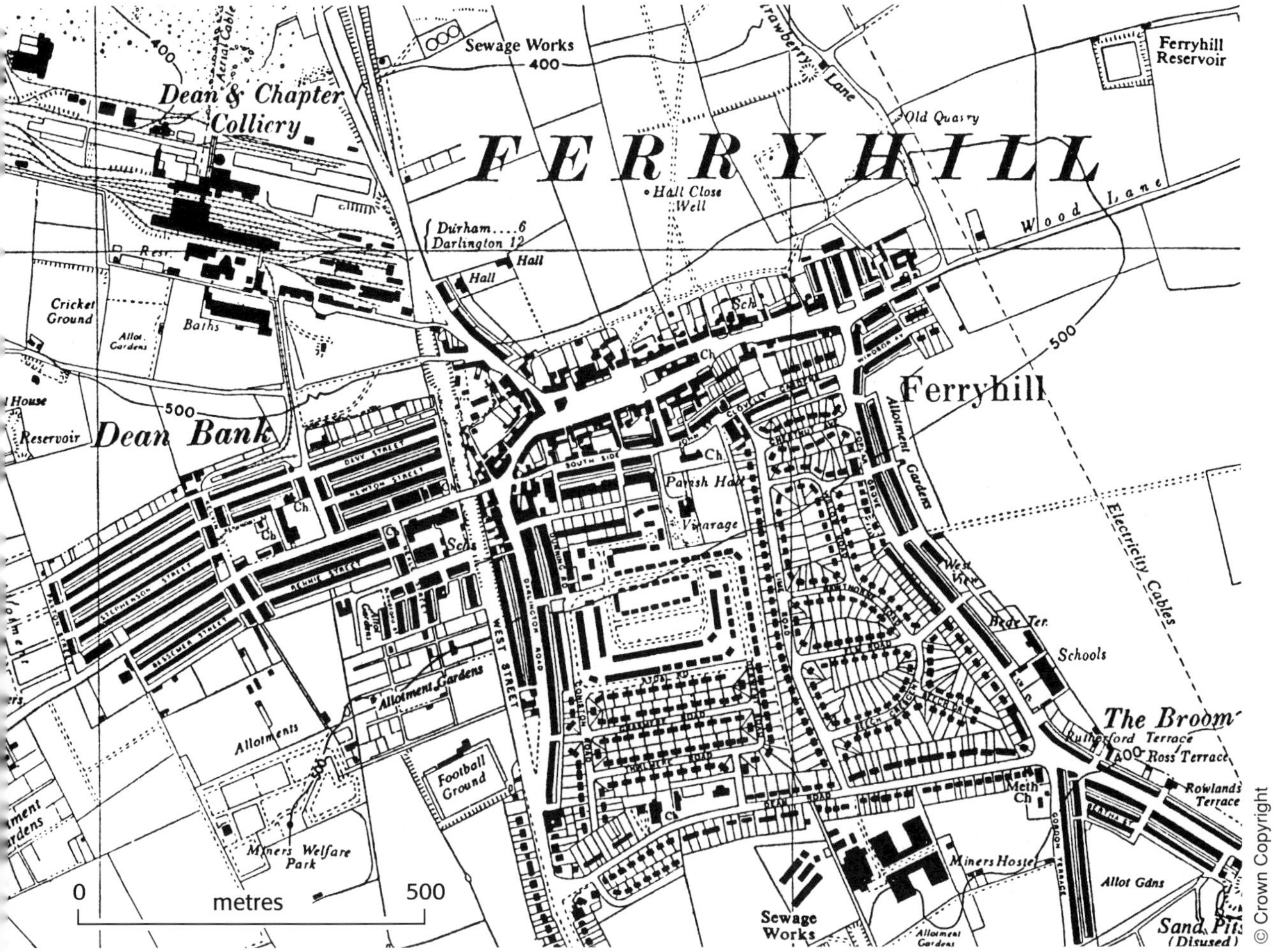

Figure 6.24
The morphology of Ferryhill, County Durham

Hierarchies of settlement

Villages are not just concentrations of people, they are also centres for the provision of goods and services. In this way they have an economic function as a **central place**. Typically, people use the village shop (Figure 6.25) to buy items such as newspapers or fresh groceries. These are **low-order goods** for which people will travel only a short distance in order to buy them. The distance people are prepared to travel is known as the **range** of the good or service.

Whether a village sells particular goods or services depends on the level of demand for them. The minimum number of people required to create sufficient demand for a service to be provided is known as the **threshold** population. The threshold population for low order goods tends to be small, but even so, many villages fall below the minimum required. In England, the threshold for a general store tends to be about 300 people; for a primary school it is about 500.

Figure 6.25
A typical village general store selling low-order goods

Higher-order functions, such as more specialist shops supplying **higher-order goods**, or secondary schools, need more custom – or a higher threshold population – to make them viable. As they also have a greater range, they are concentrated in larger villages or small towns (Figure 6.26). Each larger, or higher order, centre will serve several smaller settlements. The result of these differences in order is the emergence of a rural service **hierarchy**, with many small centres providing low order goods and a smaller number of higher order centres providing more specialist goods and services.

Figure 6.26

A larger shopping centre serving a wider market area

Given that higher order services need a bigger threshold population, it is not surprising that there is usually a clear relationship between the number of services provided and the size of settlements (Figure 6.27). However, there are exceptions. Some towns have more functions for a special reason, perhaps because they are tourist centres. Others have fewer functions because their residents are commuters who use facilities in nearby bigger towns. At the village level, not all villages are service centres in the traditional sense. Villages that grew up around collieries in areas such as County Durham sometimes had very limited service provision. Even where village populations are growing, services are being lost because people are prepared to travel further to do their shopping, thus reducing the profitability of small shops and the viability of some services, such as schools, banks and post offices.

In view of the fact that population alone is not a completely reliable measure of a centre's

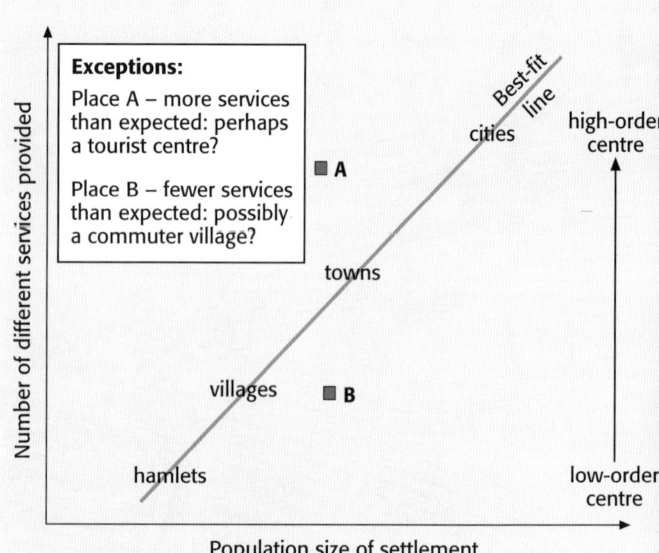

Figure 6.27

The relationship between population and number of services

importance in terms of the services it provides, geographers sometimes use the term **centrality** to measure a settlement's significance as a service centre. One way to do this is to find out what proportion of the retail and service sales in a central place is accounted for by people living outside the central place. The more a place meets the needs of people from outside its immediate area, the greater is its centrality. A good example is Clark's Shopping Village in Street, Somerset. This small town has a more significant service function than its population size would suggest (Figure 6.28).

Changing settlement hierarchies

Rural settlement hierarchies can be studied in terms of both population size and service functions. Both are likely to change over time, and the relationship between them can change dramatically for several reasons. In some rural districts, where county councils have to provide for big increases in population, one option is to minimise the impact on the rural environment by concentrating most of the growth in one place. Projected rapid growth in north Hampshire is thus due to be focused on a

Figure 6.28

Clark's Shopping Village, Street, Somerset

new settlement with up to 5000 houses at Micheldever Station.

Planned growth or decline

In the 1960s and 1970s, planners in several counties adopted a strategy of concentrating services in a few **key settlements**, while restricting development elsewhere. This policy enabled some villages to retain their services because they continued to serve other less favoured settlements. In other words, they continued to have access to a population above the threshold needed to maintain their services. In Lincolnshire, certain villages were chosen to provide low order goods and services to up to six surrounding villages; and in Wiltshire, pressure on small village schools has led to a policy of concentration on area schools that serve around five villages.

Durham's rural settlement hierarchy

After the Second World War, with coal-mining in decline, and the economic basis of the pit villages collapsing, Durham County Council took a radical step. In its Structure Plan, villages were given a designation A to D, according to their viability. One-third were designated D villages – essentially a death warrant – because the Council planned no new investment in them (Figure 6.29). Although the plan was revised in 1964, it was too late for many villages, which had simply ceased to exist.

Figure 6.29

A Durham 'D' village. In 1972 this settlement was literally on the point of collapse.

Case Study: Oxfordshire

Oxfordshire is a largely lowland county with a clear hierarchy of settlements in terms of population size (Figure 6.30). It is also relatively self-contained, with 87 per cent of its residents working within the county boundary. Oxfordshire is a classic **city region** with employment, higher-order shopping and other facilities centred on the county town (Figure 6.31). The city and its region are closely interdependent (Figure 6.32). The city of Oxford (120 000) is the hub of the transport network, and accounts for a third of the county's jobs, of which nearly half are held by commuters from outside the city.

The city is ringed by commuter settlements, such as Abingdon. Further out there is a network of small market towns, such as Wallingford. Each market town serves the surrounding smaller towns and villages.

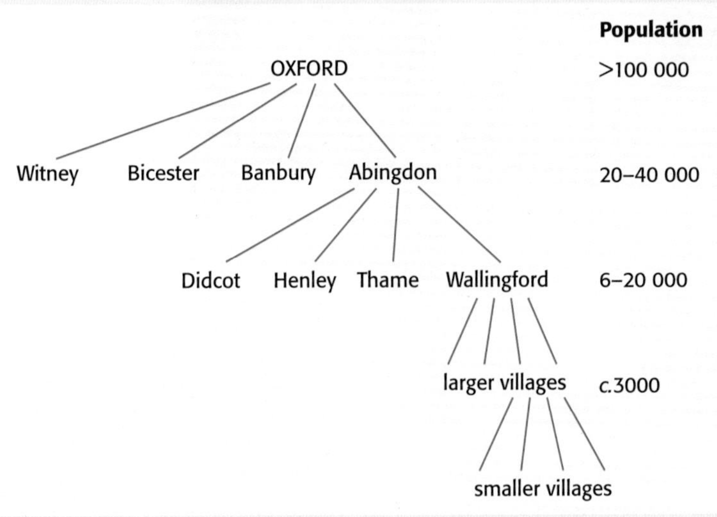

Figure 6.30
The settlement hierarchy in Oxfordshire

Figure 6.31
The city of Oxford

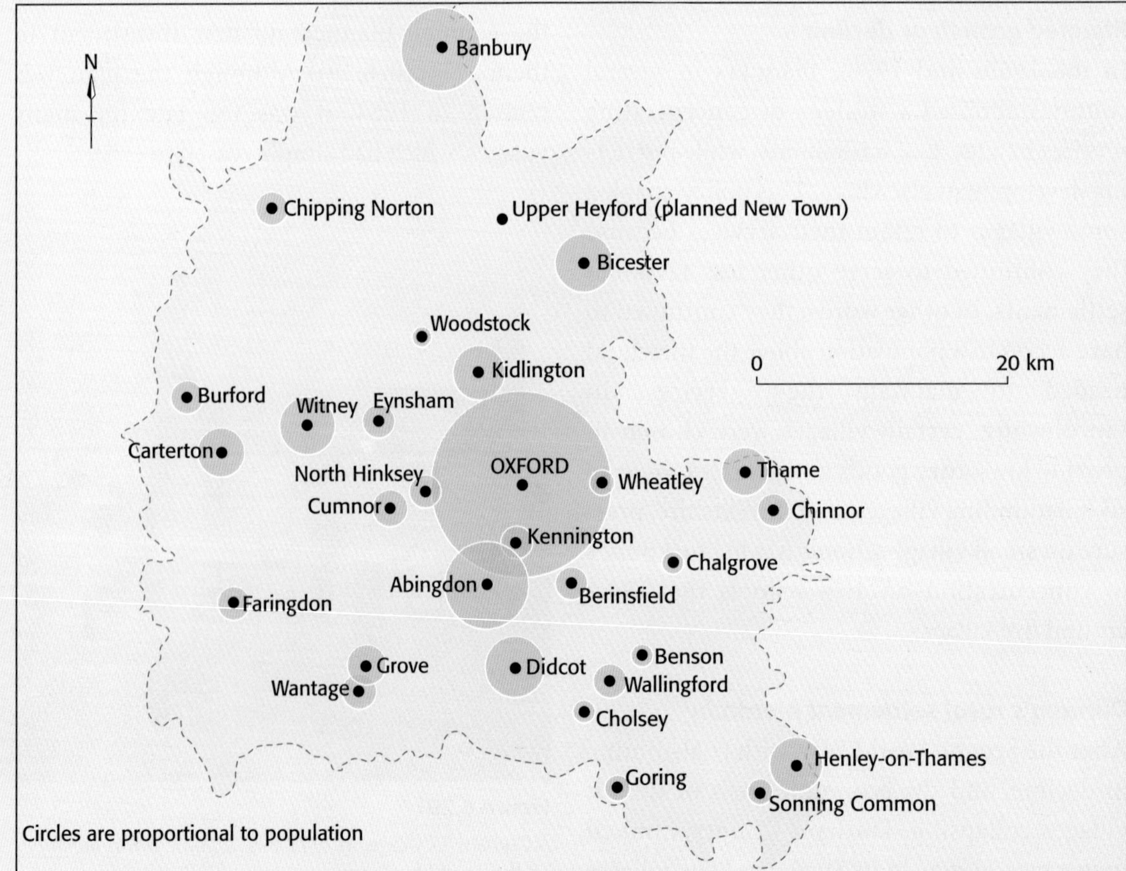

Figure 6.32
The main settlements of Oxfordshire

Activity

1 Study Figure 6.33.

a Describe and explain the general relationship between population and size of shopping area.

b What services do you imagine might be found in Abingdon, Witney and Bicester which are not available in the smaller towns?

c In what sense is Banbury exceptional among the market towns of Oxfordshire? Using Figure 6.32 and a suitable atlas map, suggest a possible reason why.

d Didcot appears to have fewer services than its population would warrant. Try to explain why.

2 Study Figure 6.34, which details the shops, bus services and schools located in the smaller settlements in the area surrounding Wallingford (see Figure 6.35 on page 169). Is it possible to identify a hierarchy of service centres? How many levels does it have?

a Devise a graphical way of showing the relationship between population and number of services.

b Estimate the threshold population figures for the following services:

- post offices
- small supermarkets
- electrical goods shops.

c Which service appears to have little relationship to population size? Can you suggest a reason?

d Crowmarsh appears to have relatively few services considering its population size. From Figure 6.35, can you suggest a reason?

e Compare Watlington and Woodcote. In what ways are they (i) similar and (ii) different? How might the differences between them be accounted for?

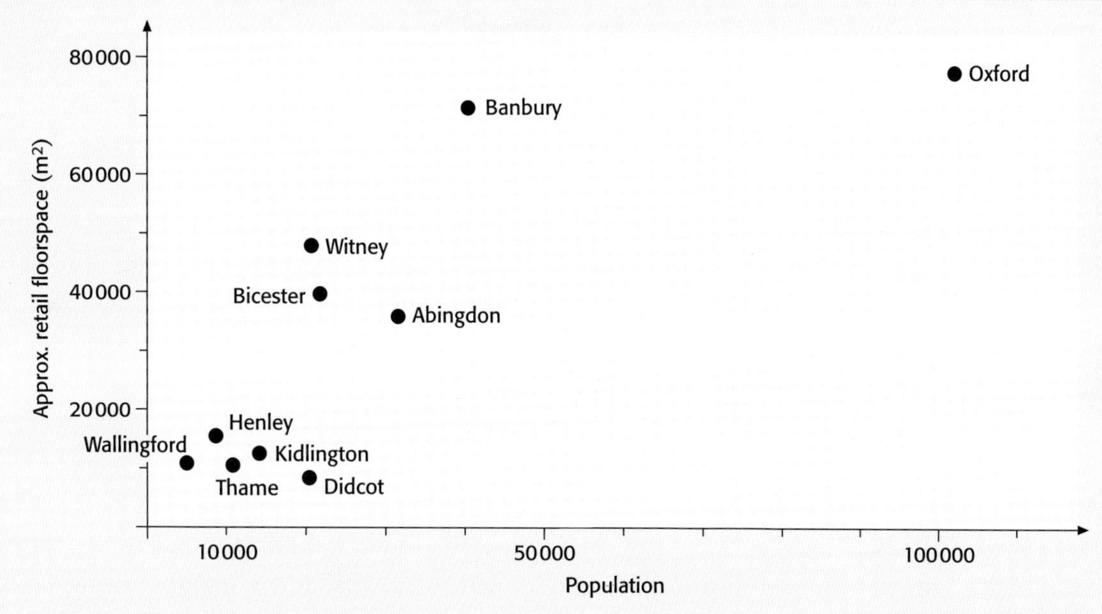

Figure 6.33

The relationship between shopping centre size and population in Oxfordshire towns

Figure 6.34

Settlements and services in the Wallingford area

Parish	Population 1991	Public house	PO/General store	Daily bus service	Primary school	Secondary school	Small supermarket	Supermarket	Fresh food	Chemist	Hardware	Bank	Library	Electrical goods
Wallingford	6503	✓	✓	✓	✓	✓	✓	✓	✓	✓	✓	✓	✓	✓
Benson	3716	✓	✓	✓	✓		✓		✓	✓	✓			
Chalgrove	2832	✓	✓	✓	✓		✓		✓	✓				
Woodcote	2565	✓	✓	✓	✓	✓	✓							
Watlington	2462	✓	✓	✓	✓	✓	✓		✓	✓	✓	✓	✓	
Crowmarsh	1454	✓	✓	✓	✓									
Warborough	996	✓	✓		✓									
Ewelme	869	✓	✓	✓	✓									
Stadhampton	718	✓	✓	✓	✓									
Stoke Row	640	✓	✓	✓	✓									
Checkendon	555	✓	✓	✓	✓									
South Stoke	526	✓	✓	✓	✓									
Nuffield	393													
Rotherfield Greys	342													
Highmoor	329			✓										
Ipsden	318		✓											
Drayton St Leonard	243	✓												
Brightwell Baldwin	192	✓												
Britwell	187	✓												
Berwick Salome	163	✓												
Newington	137													
Cuxham	137	✓		✓										

Changes in the regional hierarchy

Planning decisions are set to change Oxfordshire's settlement hierarchy. Beginning in 1991, Oxfordshire County Council has been required to make provision for up to 37 000 new houses by 2006. An earlier plan had called for a new country town to be built at Stone Bassett, on the M40 east of Oxford. It was intended that the population should reach 16 000. This plan was strongly opposed by local residents and was rejected by the Government. But the problem has not gone away, and attention has now switched to a disused airbase at Upper Heyford where there are plans to create an entirely new urban centre. In the South Oxfordshire District, where 8500 new houses are needed, it is intended to put around 5500 of them in the town of Didcot. The argument for this plan is that the **infrastructure** already exists, and growth would protect the thresholds needed to maintain the existing services in the town. It would also protect many smaller settlements from the impact of substantial growth.

Population change in rural areas of MEDCs

Rural–urban migration and depopulation

In the early 19th century most rural areas in England and Wales experienced population growth, reflecting natural increase as death rates fell while birth rates remained high. At the same time, the Industrial Revolution stimulated the growth of towns, and a major turning point occurred around mid-century. The 1851 census recorded, for the first time, that more people lived in towns than in rural areas. As migration

Figure 6.35

The area around Wallingford

to towns increased and birth rates started to fall, the balance tipped further, and between 1861 and 1901 the rural population actually declined despite the continued rapid growth of the total population. The reason was simple: out-migration exceeded natural increase in large parts of rural England. Many villages shared the experience of Pyrton in Oxfordshire, which grew through natural increase until the mid-19th century, but then experienced **rural depopulation** (Figure 6.36). Many villages simply shrank in size and even disappeared (Figure 6.37).

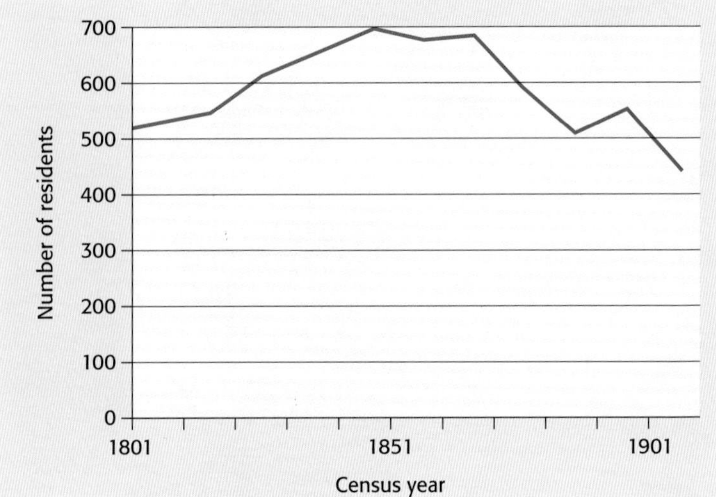

Figure 6.36

Population change in Pyrton, Oxfordshire

Figure 6.37

A shrunken settlement in Shropshire

Depopulation was largely the result of out-migration, with people leaving for the towns. Two sets of factors encouraged migrants to leave:

- **Push factors**
  - **Job losses in agriculture:** enclosure, mechanisation and the decline in agricultural prices in the last decades of the 19th century all contributed to unemployment.
  - **Lack of alternative employment opportunities in rural areas:** mass-produced goods from urban factories undermined traditional rural industries.
  - **Lack of marriage opportunities:** in small villages, the lack of eligible potential partners was a very real issue for young people.
- **Pull factors**
  - **Opportunities for better jobs and higher wages** in industries and service activities in the growing towns: wages in general were higher than in agriculture.
  - **The prospect of training and higher education:** as a result, young people with 'get up and go' often got up and went.

Continued urbanisation in Europe

In Europe as a whole, strong urbanisation tendencies still prevail (Figure 6.38). The percentage of the population living in urban areas has risen from just over 50 per cent in 1950 to about 75 per cent at the start of the 1990s. In France alone, the rural population fell from 38 per cent in 1960 to 22 per cent in 1980. Although rural depopulation remains a problem in the more remote, mountainous districts of Europe, the rural–urban migration process has gone into reverse in many areas. Where poverty once drove people to emigrate from the more hazardous and insecure areas, or at least to seek seasonal employment in the more productive lowlands, such regions are now regarded as highly desirable, at least by tourists and the owners of holiday homes (Figure 6.39).

N

Countries with falling rural populations 1975–2000

0 500 km

Figure 6.38
Rural depopulation across Europe. 'Rural population' is defined as those people living in dispersed settlements and villages.

Figure 6.39
A once-disused farmhouse in Normandy, France, now converted into a holiday home for in-migrants from urban areas

Rural change in Italy

Traditionally, migrants have left the less-developed south of Italy to form the labour force in the big factory towns of the more developed north. Those who did not go north went west, to the USA. Between 1951 and 1971, 4 million people moved out. In recent decades this process has been reversed, and much of the south has experienced repopulation. But the process has not reached the remote mountainous interior of the Italian peninsula, where conditions are arduous. Reduced support from the European Union's Common Agricultural Policy, and the abolition of the Cassa per il Mezzogiorno, the development agency for the south, have resulted in continued depopulation of these environmentally harsh areas.

Case Study: Aliano, Basilicata

Aliano is a hill-top village in the 'deep south' of Italy. It has suffered a long history of out-migration, fuelled partly by high birth rates, the desire to escape poverty, and the chance to earn higher wages in the north. For many years the population remained close to 2000, reaching a peak of about 2200 in 1951 before declining to 1600 in 1981. More recently, there has been some tendency for migrants to return and settle back in the village, but this has served only to add to the ageing structure of the population. Local changes have also undermined life in the village. The draining of the lowland areas, and the construction of fast new highways in the valleys, has drawn people away from the hill-villages. The population pyramids (Figure 6.41) show the selective impact of continued out-migration, leaving a population dominated by older age groups and females. The expectations of young people cannot be met in the village: few schoolchildren want to become farmers – they aspire to better-paid jobs which can only be found in the towns.

Figure 6.40
A hill-top village in southern Italy

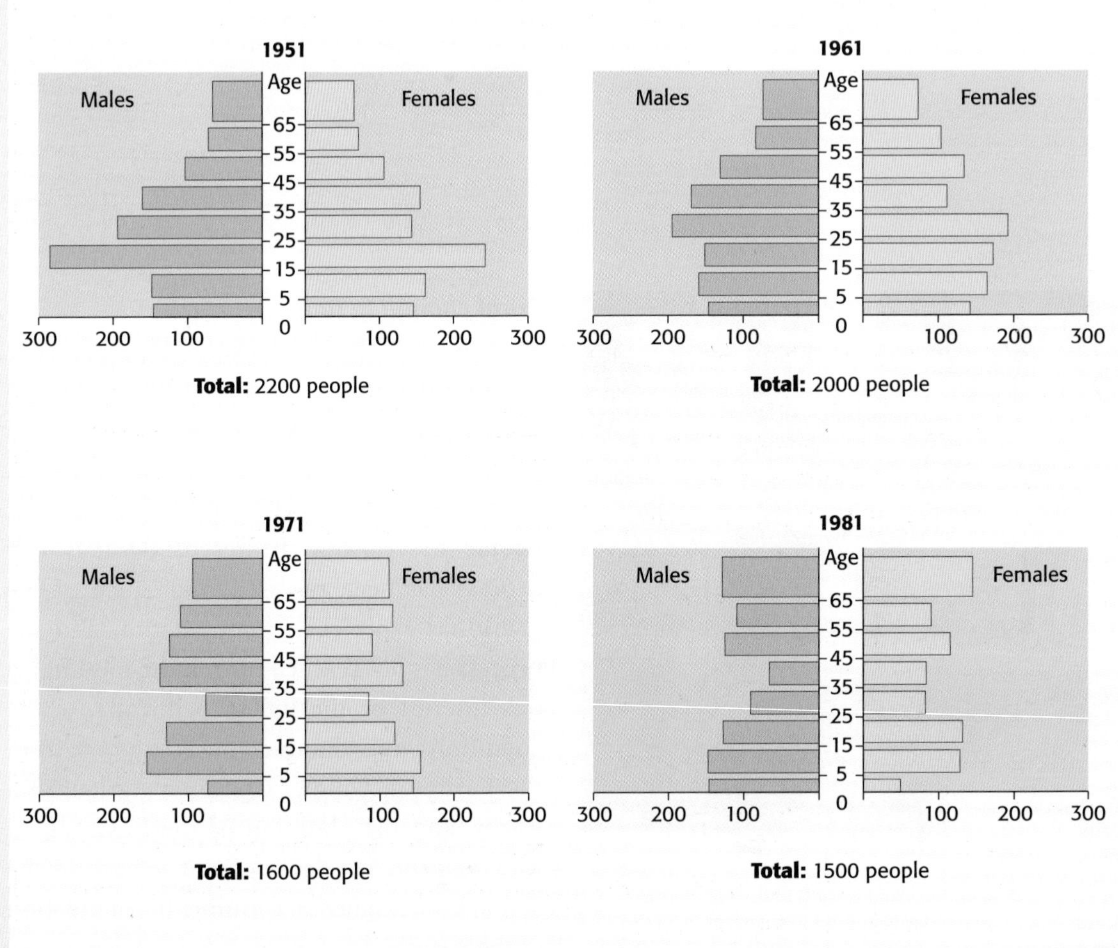

Figure 6.41
Population change in Aliano, 1951–81

Rural change in eastern Europe

During the communist era, urbanisation made less of an impact on the countries of eastern Europe than on those in the west, and the rural share of the population tended to be higher. In Hungary, for example, 47 per cent of the population was rural in 1980, compared with 34 per cent in Italy and 22 per cent in France. However, since the late 1980s and the entry of the former Communist Bloc countries into the global capitalist economy, the removal of state support for agriculture and the arrival of large agribusiness firms has put increased pressure on rural economies. The bright lights of the cities are also showing signs of leading to accelerated rural depopulation. In Hungary the rural proportion of the population now stands at 33 per cent and is predicted to fall to 21 per cent by the year 2025.

Activity

1 Describe and explain the changing population structure of Aliano from 1951 to 1981.

2 Read the following extracts taken from Harry Clifton's book *On the Spine of Italy, A Year in the Abruzzi* (1999, Macmillan) which present a picture of a village high up in the Abruzzo Mountains, in central Italy.

'Although the village had a normal population of about ninety, the return of emigrants from America had swollen it to three hundred for the (summer) season.'

'... an abandoned house, once the home of the parish priest when it was still worthwhile for the diocese to keep a priest in so tiny, high and remote a village.'

'... its windows looked over the road to what had once been a schoolhouse. Now, the children were bussed to a neighbouring village.'

'At this time, there was no shop in the village. Twice a week, at eleven in the morning, a travelling grocery driven by a man named Mario arrived. To get to our village from the neighbouring one, he had to describe a huge loop up valley around the ravine...it was the only way into the village.'

On the basis of what you have studied and read so far, evaluate Figure 6.42 as a model of the impact of rural depopulation. Are there any other problems not addressed by the model that are likely to result from the demographic changes experienced by villages like Aliano?

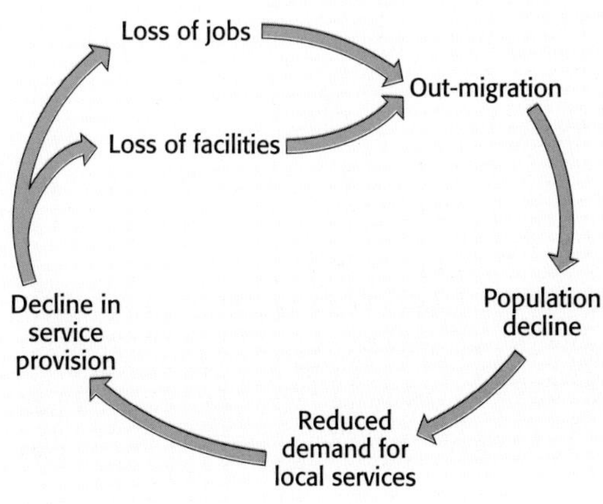

Figure 6.42
The vicious circle of rural depopulation

3 Select a former east European communist state and using an atlas map, attempt an initial prediction of which regions will experience most rural depopulation in the coming decades. Put your prediction to the test by gathering as much relevant population data as possible. Conduct your research using sources such as the various UN statistical volumes, CD-ROMs such as Encarta, Internet searches and data published by the country itself.

Rural poverty: a hidden problem

In 1998 Dorset County Council published a report highlighting rural poverty. The Council's point was that in a county that is widely regarded as affluent, there is a significant proportion of poorer people scattered thinly across the area, with small pockets of severe deprivation in both urban and rural districts. A survey in Scotland found that rural areas had a higher proportion of people earning less than the official 'poverty wage', and it is estimated that 25 per cent of the rural population in England is in poverty.

The Government's White Paper on Rural England in 1996 also pointed the finger:

> *'Rural poverty must be spoken about, and its causes and consequences discussed, if perceptions of a rural idyll are to be corrected and hidden pockets of poverty sought out and relieved.'*

Case Study: Rural decline in St John's Chapel, Weardale, County Durham

St John's Chapel is a marginal agricultural village at the head of Weardale in the northern Pennines (Figure 6.43). Originally, it was a medieval hunting stop, and then grew as a lead-mining centre from about 1600. The population of the village itself is about 442, which also makes it marginal in terms of thresholds for service provision. The population of the ward, which includes outlying hamlets, has been fairly stagnant for 30 years, but this masks considerable selective out-migration which has made its mark on the population structure (Figure 6.44).

On the surface, St John's Chapel is a very attractive place to live. It is quiet, with few of the problems that cause stress in modern city life – pollution, crime, high house prices and a lack of space. The quality of life for most people in such an area is high. But below the surface, it is possible to identify a pocket of relative deprivation, comparable in many ways with inner cities, except that the scale is much smaller. Male unemployment is 17 per cent and 21 per cent of households do not own a car. Such figures suggest a pocket of poverty that is masked by overall statistics for rural areas. Poverty in rural areas arises in large part from the decline in agricultural employment, made worse recently by reductions in support from the state and by reduced demand for some

Figure 6.43
St John's Chapel, Weardale

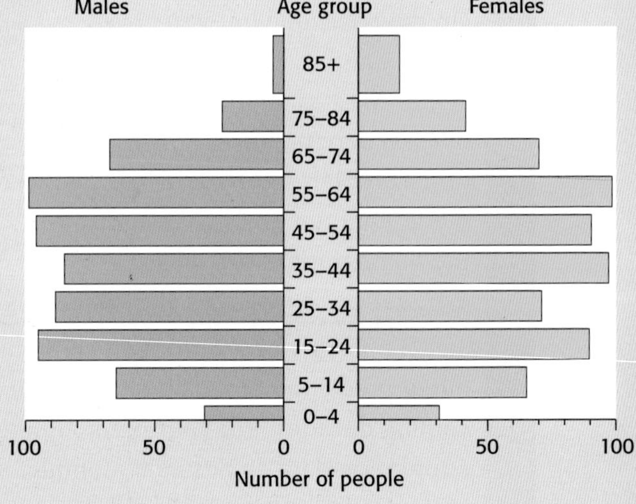

Figure 6.44
Population structure of St John's Chapel, 1991

foods as a result of health scares. Combined with a lack of alternative employment opportunities, this decline is made still harder by the remoteness of the area, and by the cost of transport to facilities elsewhere. For the residents of St John's Chapel, the nearest secondary school is 14 miles away, the nearest library 22 miles, and the nearest swimming pool 14 miles – which is fine if you have a car...

The response of many people has been to leave. One man in his thirties commented:

'The young move away to jobs. Of seventeen in my class, five went to London, two to Harrogate, one to Cambridge, one to Scotland. Of the three left in the village, two are unemployed. My advice to the young is get training and get out. The Dale is a dead end, there is no future and no jobs.'

Out-migration leads to a vicious spiral of decline, and a loss of services. As one elderly resident put it:

'The loss of families is really frightening. It spells the end of the local school and of the bus service. We are like a stack of dominoes, if one bit goes it all falls over.'

In 1980 there were 160 children in the village; now there are 38. While out-migration is a positive strategy for those who move, it leaves those who remain behind even worse off. It is estimated that 25 per cent of people living in the countryside in Britain are in poverty and are trapped by a network of disadvantages which add up to **social exclusion**. The lack of social facilities and employment opportunities, coupled with the high cost of transport, ties people into a hopeless situation (Figure 6.45).

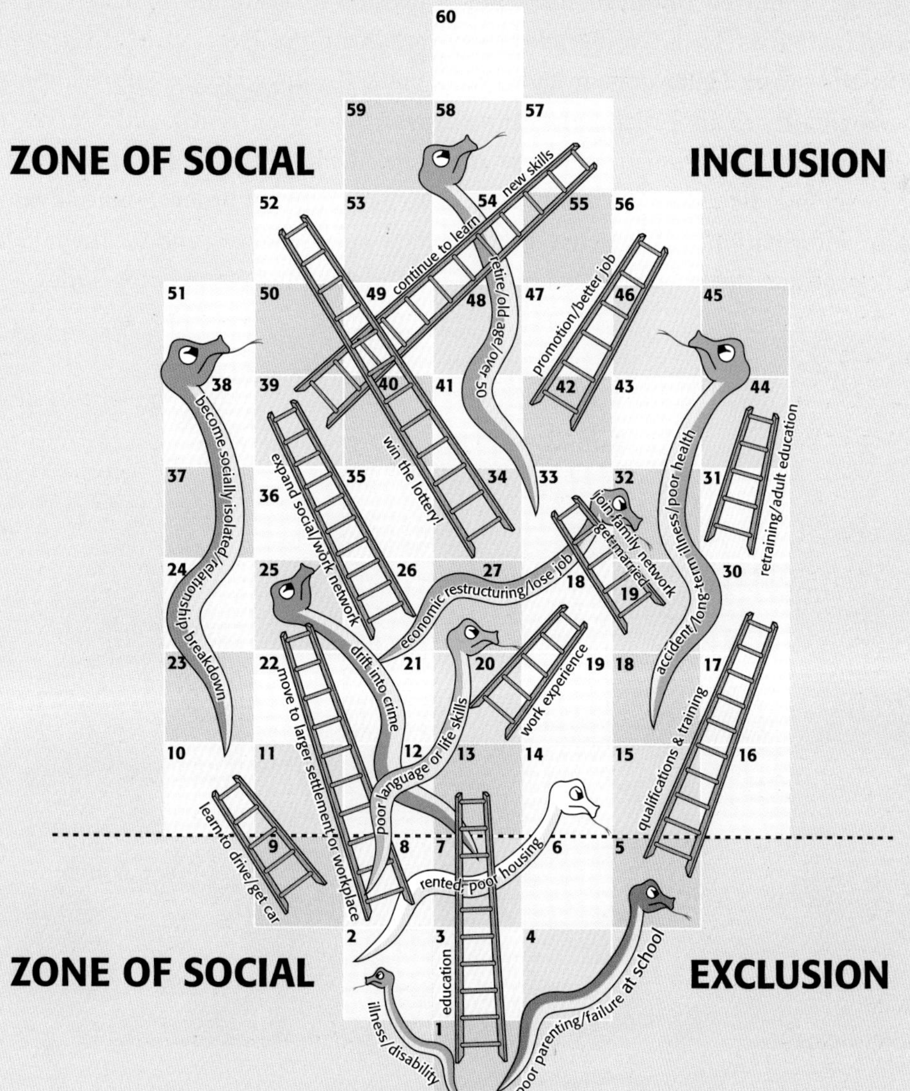

Figure 6.45
The processes of disadvantage in rural areas

Activity

1 What evidence is there from Figure 6.44 that St John's Chapel has suffered out-migration? Try to identify the age groups involved.

2 In what senses are poor people in the countryside doubly deprived, compared with poor people in the city?

3 Look closely at Figure 6.45, which shows the processes of disadvantage in rural areas. Write a paragraph explaining how disadvantages early in life can lead to more permanent social exclusion.

Case Study: High-tech solutions to rural decline? The West Durham Rural Network

Information and communications technology (**ICT**) is seen by many people as a unique opportunity for rural areas to overcome their most basic disadvantage – remoteness. Modern technology has removed the need for many office-based activities to be undertaken in urban locations – work can be done from home or from small offices in isolated locations (Figure 6.46). But the sophisticated use of computers to handle and transmit large amounts of information, making use of the Internet, depends on the existence of an information superhighway consisting of fibre-optic cables. This technology allows more rapid data processing, and the use of video and interactive computer services. If rural areas are going to take advantage of the information revolution to eradicate the **friction of distance**, they need first to be linked to the information superhighway, which currently only serves the bigger settlements. Other requirements are for people to be trained in order to take advantage of the new opportunities, and for them to have access to Internet and computer facilities.

Figure 6.46 Information technology in a rural setting. Software companies like the one in this building are often small, and with few overheads they can operate from residential areas.

In 1997 a consortium of 26 organisations representing both the public and the private sector put together a **Rural Challenge** bid based on the idea that technology could be used to benefit rural communities. Computers and telecommunications technology could be used to improve competitiveness and enhance services in rural areas. The organisations involved included parish councils, telecommunication companies, the police and local health and education authorities (Figure 6.47). The four main aims of the scheme were to:

1 Extend the information superhighway infrastructure beyond the urban areas by laying broadband cables to connect several of the bigger villages. This should enable businesses in these villages to take advantage of high-speed voice, video and data services.
2 Extend public access to the superhighway through providing computer facilities in public buildings, with open access.
3 Establish learning centres providing training for local people, to allow them to take advantage of new job opportunities.
4 Make public services more accessible, enhancing the social advantages of new technology. Two examples of this aspect are giving Internet access to the Careers Service in order to provide up-to-date information on job openings (local people can even post their CVs on the network), and virtual policing. People in remote communities often feel isolated and vulnerable, and are acutely aware of the lack of a visible police presence. The scheme plans a video-kiosk link in villages, so that local people can talk directly to someone in the police station, which may be located miles away.

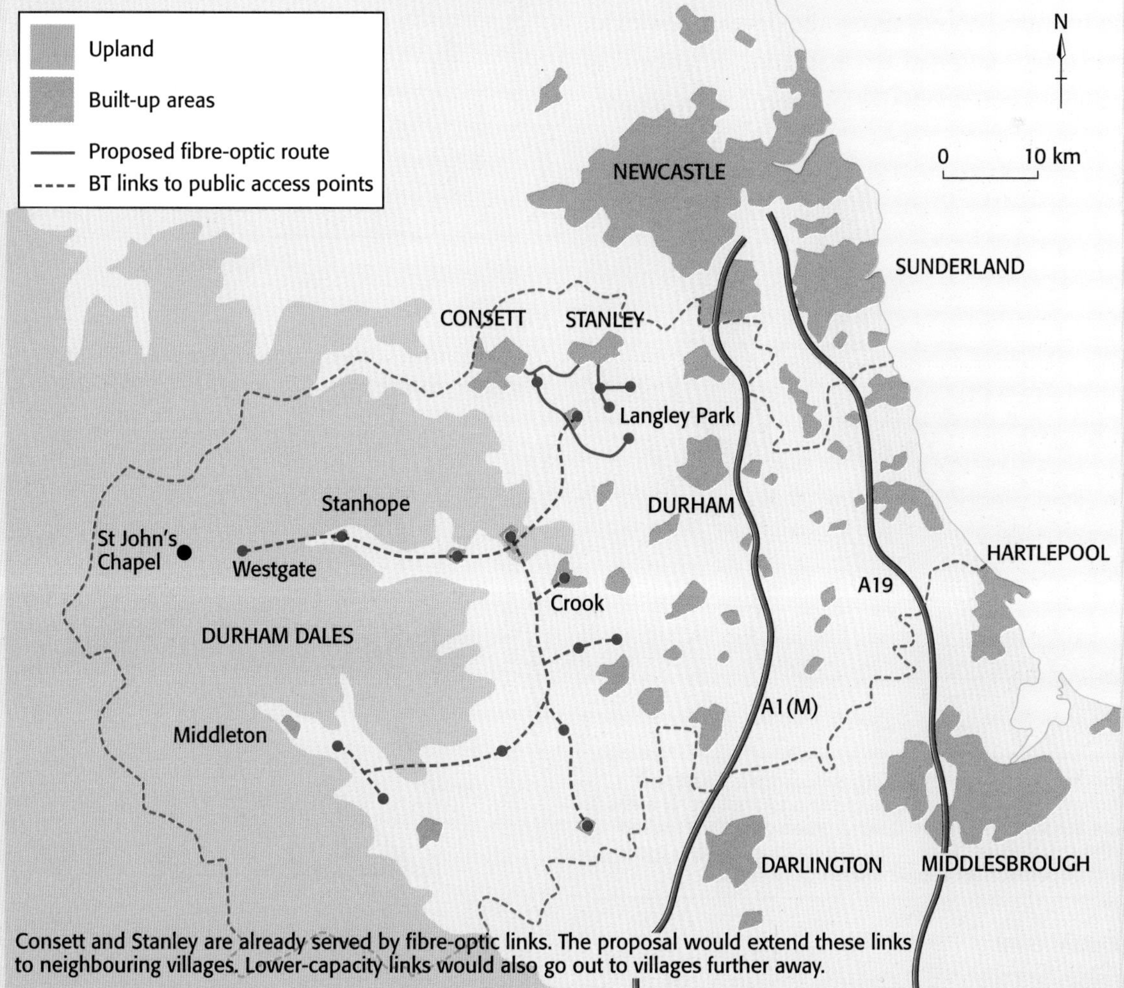

Figure 6.47 The West Durham Rural Network

Not all rural dwellers benefit equally, however. The Rural Challenge scheme focuses on the West Durham Rural Development Area, and targets the area between Consett and Durham City, in particular. Here, the population density is fairly high and the old pit villages tend to be bigger and closer together than in the more remote upland areas to the west where, arguably, the need is even greater. In the event, it was not thought viable (i.e. profitable to the telecommunications companies involved) to extend the infrastructure into the very remote rural areas with the lowest population densities.

Urban–rural migration and counterurbanisation

In almost all developed countries, the proportion of people living in urban areas is rising and, in this sense, the developed world continues to become more urbanised. But hidden within this trend lies a remarkable phenomenon, known as **counterurbanisation**, representing a reversal of long-established trends (Figure 6.48).

The phenomenon was first noted by US geographers in the 1970s, but it quickly spread to Europe. Indeed, across the developed world, censuses revealed a negative relationship between settlement size and population growth, which is summed up in Figure 6.49. The biggest cities appeared to have gone into decline, while smaller towns and rural areas grew rapidly. The overall trend in France is revealed by Figure 6.50, and the effect on the ground in Brittany is well illustrated by Figure 6.51.

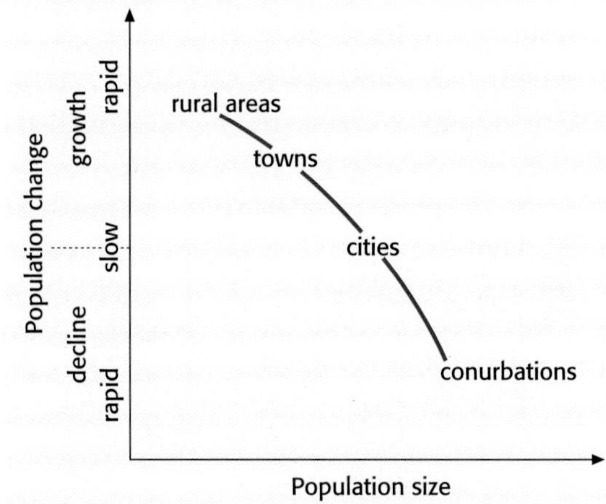

Figure 6.49
The relationship between population size and rate of population change

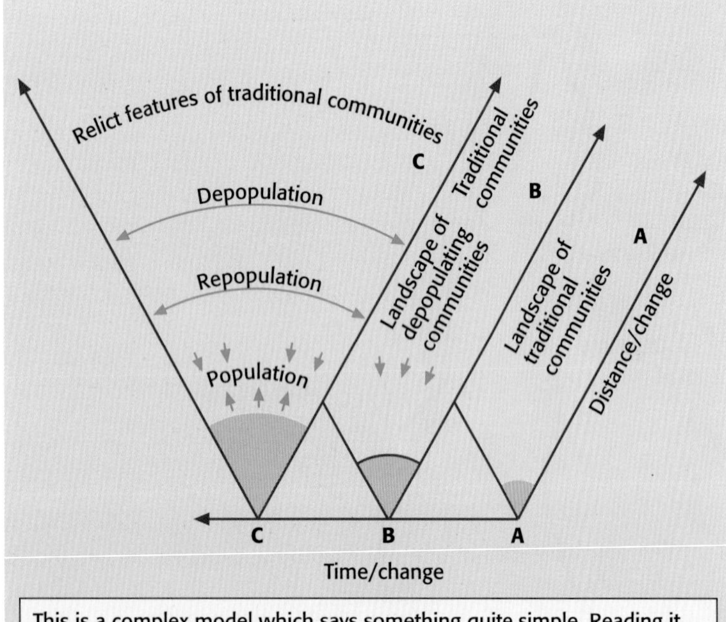

Figure 6.48
Lewis and Maund's model of rural population change

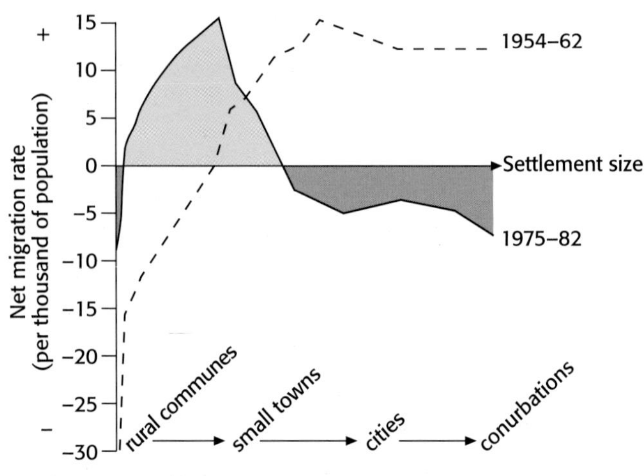

Figure 6.50
Counterurbanisation trends in France

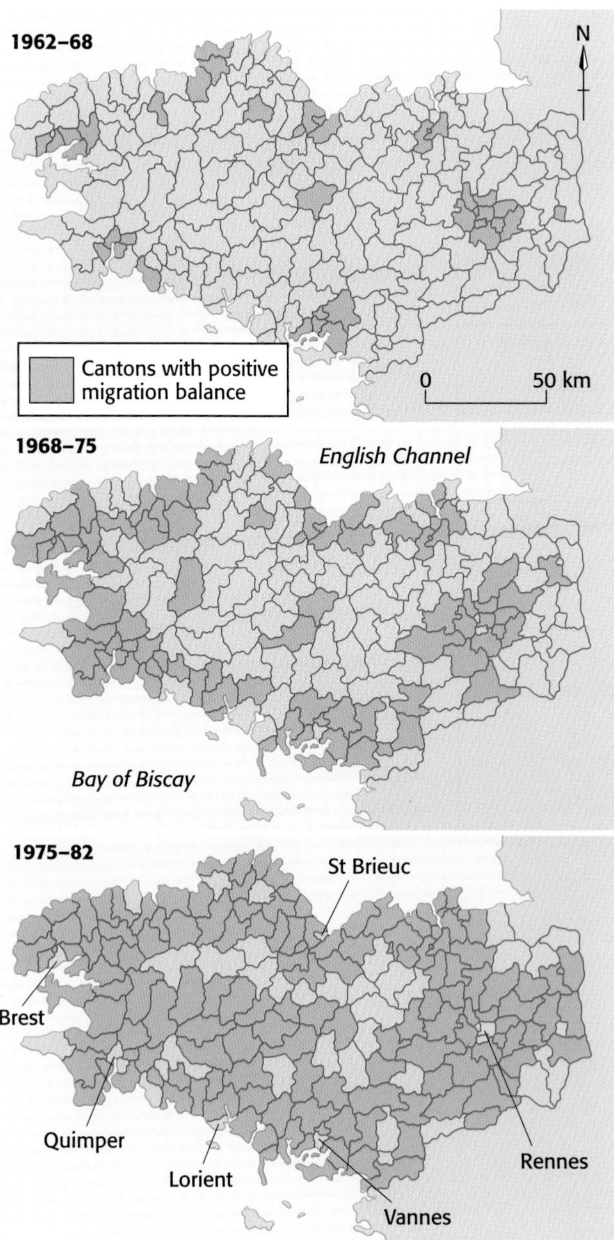

Figure 6.51

Counterurbanisation penetrates interior Brittany

However, early predictions about the imminent demise of big cities have proved to be premature in the light of subsequent trends. During the 1980s the counterurbanisation trend diminished, and was replaced by a more complicated pattern. Not all rural areas continued to grow; most grew more slowly than before and some large cities reversed their decline, beginning what some have called an **urban renaissance**.

Counterurbanisation in England and Wales

Given that Britain's total population has grown only very slowly, the marked shift of population seen over the last few decades must have been due almost entirely to migration. Even the traditional pattern of depopulation in the more remote rural areas has been reversed, or at least slowed up. Although considerable population turnover continues, out-migrants are now more than balanced by people moving in. Growth has been fastest in villages and small towns in rural areas (Figure 6.52). Figure 6.53 shows that in the 1980s the process slowed down somewhat. Hidden within these gross figures is the apparent revival of at least some of the conurbations. London started to grow after 1985, reversing 44 years of population decline.

Figure 6.52

New housing estates are grafted on to small towns like Mere in Wiltshire

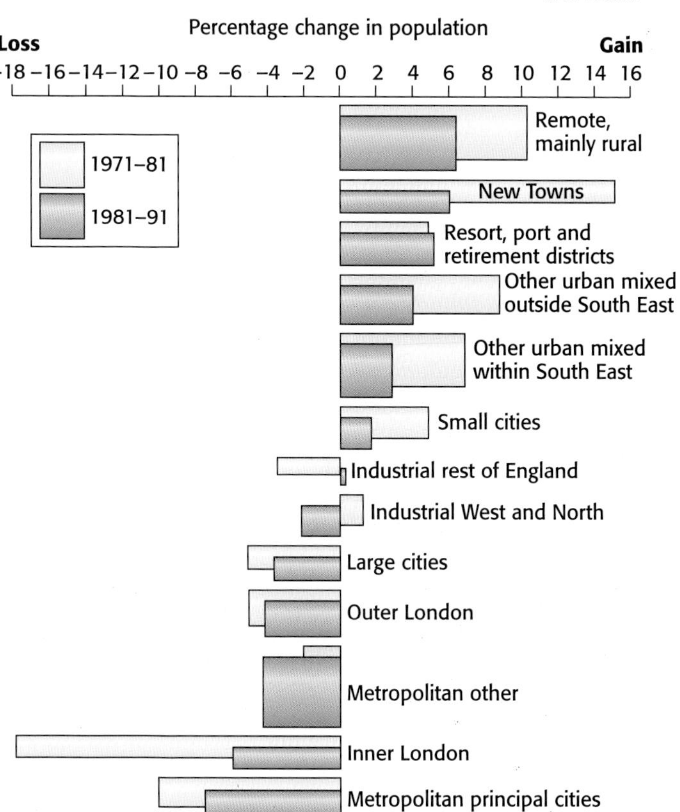

Figure 6.53

Population change by type of area, England and Wales

Activity

1 Compare the two maps in Figure 6.54 and describe how the pattern of population changed across England and Wales during the two decades.

2 What might explain the rapid growth of Shropshire and Hereford & Worcester (on the border with Wales)?

3 What special factors might explain the growth of counties along the south coast of England?

4 Why do you think the counties nearest to London have not grown as rapidly as those further out?

5 Now examine Figure 6.55. To what extent do the data confirm that counterurbanisation is currently the dominant process in population growth?

6 Read the text in Figure 6.56.

a What changes to the counterurbanisation trend are predicted in the article?

b What reasons are offered for the change?

c Why are some cities unlikely to benefit?

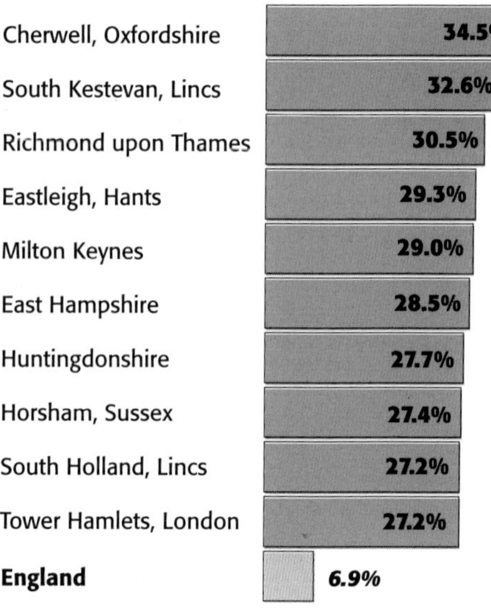

Figure 6.55

England's fastest-growing populations, 1996–2021

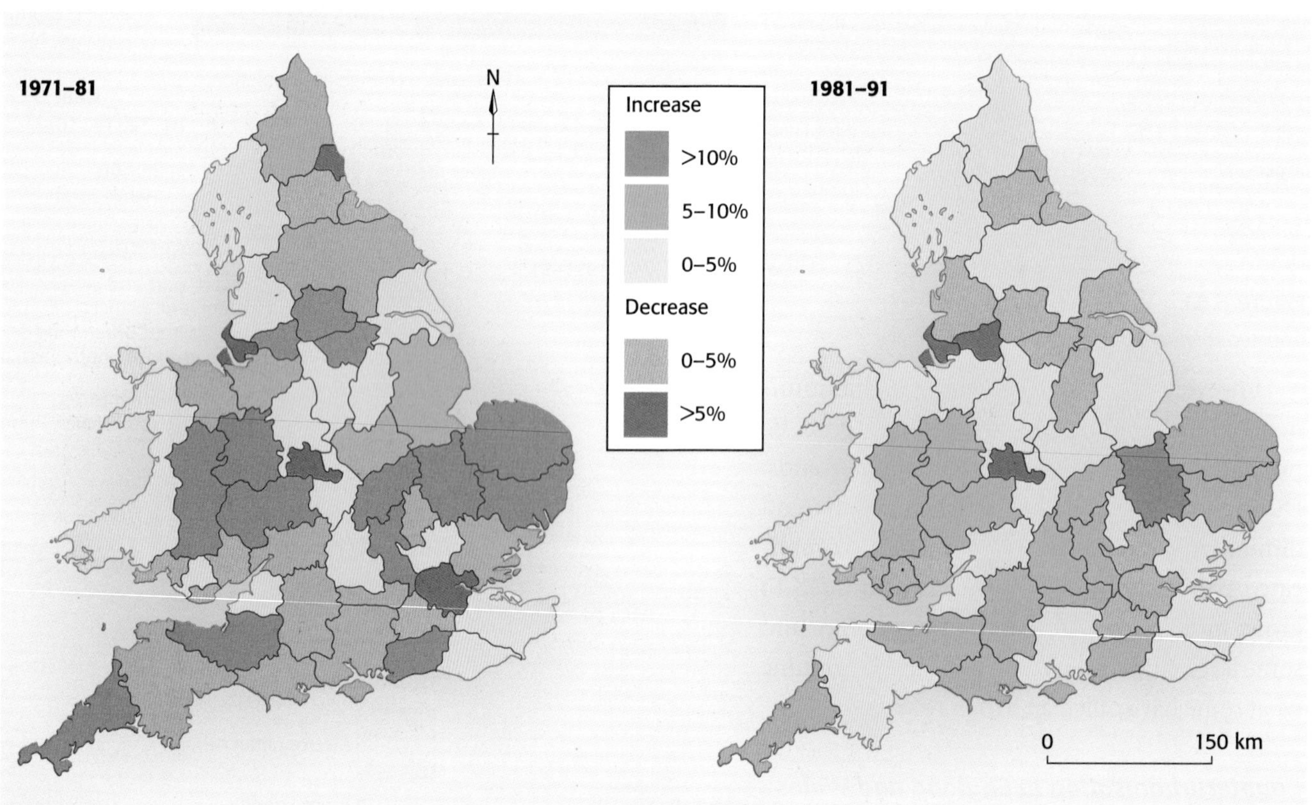

Figure 6.54

Population change in England and Wales, 1971–81 and 1981–91

Mothers will lead race back to town

Supercities will boom while commuter havens and urban centres rooted in the past go bust, a new report predicts

by David Harrison

WORKING mothers will lead a middle-class march back to the cities, which will become Britain's most desirable places to live and work.

A generation of thirtysomething 'nest-builders' will turn its back on market and commuter towns because of the problem of 'time squeeze' – too much time spent travelling and not enough with their children, according to a report published this week.

But the choice will be limited to a small group of 'world cities' emerging over the next few decades which will offer the best housing, schools, transport and nightlife.

The 'supercities' will include Cardiff, Glasgow, Edinburgh, Manchester and Leeds. But Birmingham, Liverpool, Exeter, Bristol, Sheffield and Newcastle face steady decline because they are 'rooted in the past'.

The 'premier league' conurbations will prosper and become 'regional capitals'. Their growth will drain life out of affluent market towns and resorts such as Harrogate and Brighton.

The report says that London is Britain's only true world-class city, but half a dozen others are 'embryonic'. Their boom will be fuelled not only by economic success but also by changing working patterns, international appeal and a government commitment to urban renewal.

The most dramatic change will be the demand from working mothers, couples, singles and friends sharing for easy access to work in cleaner, greener cities with good schools and public transport and modern homes.

But as world cities rise, so other, less competitive urban hubs will fall. The North East will not improve without a 'serious remarketing' of Newcastle, the report says. Liverpool's poor image had contributed to the weak economic performance of Merseyside, despite its many attractions.

Smaller towns and market towns will also suffer, losing the middle classes who demanded good public services, used local shops and pushed up property prices. Towns such as Brighton and Cheltenham will be hit hard unless they act quickly.

Others could suffer mixed fortunes. Guildford in Surrey may lose commuters to London, but its proximity to the capital could attract jobs.

The report highlights a contrast between the fortunes of the Yorkshire cities of Leeds and Sheffield. While Leeds has developed modern sectors like financial services, Sheffield has failed to replace defunct, traditional industries and is locked in a struggle for survival, depicted in the film The Full Monty.

The statistics tell the story: Leeds is home to 9 of the top 500 companies, Sheffield 1. Leeds has 27 big foreign investors, Sheffield 19. Private-sector employment has soared by 41.1 per cent in Leeds in recent years, nearly four times the Sheffield figure. Small businesses, seen as the firms of the future, employ 26 per cent of Leeds' working population, nearly treble the number in Sheffield.

Figure 6.56 From *The Observer*, 12 April 1999

The causes of counterurbanisation

In order to understand and analyse the reasons why people move to rural areas and smaller towns, it is necessary to establish the types of people who move.

- **Retired people:** they are no longer tied to cities, and may be attracted by lower house prices in rural areas.
- **Long-distance commuters:** these are people who still work in urban areas but who can afford the high costs of commuting by taking advantage of increased personal mobility (car ownership) and improved transport links (motorways, electrified main rail routes).
- **People working for firms based in rural areas:** the counterurbanisation trend closely mirrors the urban–rural shift of employment (Figure 6.57). Jobs have been lost more rapidly in cities, and rural areas

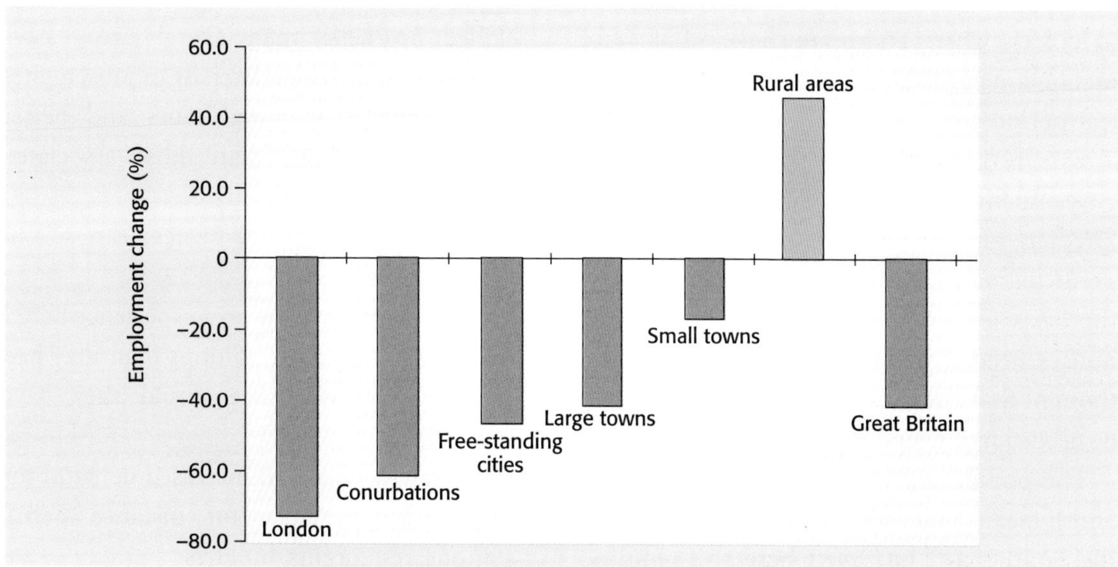

Figure 6.57 Employment change in manufacturing by area, 1960–91

Figure 6.58
Small-scale industry in a rural setting: Clun, Shropshire

have experienced recent economic growth. People have moved out to take up the expanding employment opportunities there (Figure 6.58).

- **People working from home:** an increasing number of people have turned away from working in offices and now take advantage of information and communications technology to work from computer terminals at home. The technology also now exists to replace centralised telephone call centres with people answering queries from their homes.

The process of decentralisation of both people and employment has been encouraged by Government, sometimes indirectly and not always intentionally. Green belt policy halted extensive suburbanisation, and people have responded by 'leapfrogging' the green belts and moving into rural areas beyond. Controls on the growth of jobs in London encouraged firms to look elsewhere. Policies to choke off pressure on London and other conurbations in the post-war period also saw the establishment of New Towns in rural areas. In the past few decades, government planning has been based on the 'predict and provide' principle, whereby predicted population movements are taken as the basis for estimating the number of new houses needed in each county. In total, it is thought that almost 4 million new homes will be needed in England by 2021 (Figure 6.59).

The population movement from North to South means that most of the pressure falls on the South East, but even here the required supply of new housing greatly exceeds the rate of growth of population. The reasons are numerous but in broad terms an increased number of new houses is required as more people choose to live alone rather than as members of a larger household and because, in general, people are living longer.

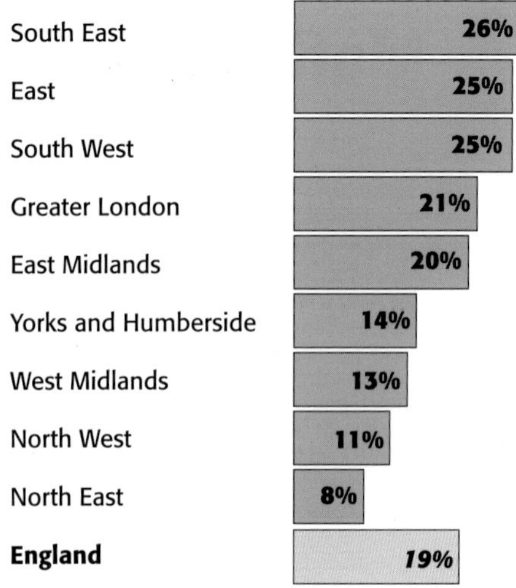

Figure 6.59
Projected household growth, 1996–2021

Counterurbanisation: threat or blessing?

For rural areas experiencing population growth through counterurbanisation, there are benefits, but also problems.

Benefits

1 The prospect of local employment for less skilled workers: many rural areas have experienced a greater diversity of jobs, higher wages, shorter working hours and better working conditions than those associated with traditional rural activities.
2 Landowners and house-owners can sell at higher prices.
3 Those moving into the area experience better living and working conditions than they had in the city. (Why else would they have moved?)
4 New arrivals create an increased demand for some rural services, for instance petrol stations, restaurants, builders.

5 Newcomers are often motivated to improve the local environment, through renovation and conservation.

Problems

1 The increased cost of housing is a double-edged sword: local people on low incomes might not be able to afford to buy houses in the area. Furthermore, second homes in rural areas reduce the number of dwellings available to local people. Villages in Cornwall and Devon, and also those in National Parks, tend to have a large proportion of their houses empty for much of the year.

2 Some services are lost: less mobile residents (the old or those without cars) depend on local services like schools and shops, yet these are in decline.

3 There may be a loss of the traditional rural character: some rapidly growing villages are more like characterless suburban islands set within a sea of fields (Figure 6.60).

4 Social tension: incomers often have very different priorities from those of local people. Their ideal of rural tranquillity might not square with the local farmer's need to make a living.

5 Traffic congestion on small rural roads – in the next 35 years, road traffic in Bedfordshire, for example, is estimated to grow by 265 per cent.

6 Loss of areas traditionally used for recreation (Figure 6.61).

Figure 6.60
New housing on a greenfield site

Figure 6.61
From *The Times*, 18 December 1999

The fight goes on in Dorset

RESIDENTS of Fernham in Dorset are continuing their four-year fight for a 40-acre stretch of land to be granted village green status.

Planning permission has been granted for 151 homes to be built on the land, known as Poor Common, despite the fact that it has been used as a public recreation area for over 20 years.

Concerned residents formed the Friends of Poor Common group in 1995 and applied for village green status for the land.

Their application was rejected in 1996 on a legal technicality. Although the judge conceded that the Common was used for recreation, he ruled that an absence of organised games on the land meant that it did not fulfil the requirement of being used for 'sports and pastimes'.

But in the wake of a similar case at Sunningwell, Oxfordshire in June this year, residents of Fernham are now optimistic that they stand a fighting chance of winning at the appeal hearing.

A recreation area in Sunningwell was granted village green status after the judge ruled that sports and pastimes are one and the same thing, and can be interpreted as anything from walking the dog to children's games.

Hundreds of Fernham residents have supported the campaign, which has continued despite difficulties in raising enough money to cover court costs.

'We have had to pay for all legal costs and luckily we had a very sympathetic solicitor who treated it as a cause célèbre,' says Marjorie Kerr, secretary of the Friends of Poor Common. 'We have raised money through collections, car boot sales and a barn dance, and through people promising regular monthly donations.'

Housing developers Bryant Homes purchased the land after planning permission had been granted. They stand to lose if the residents win the case, as it is illegal to build on a village green.

But the developers remain determined. They have already fenced around the area, chopped down trees and started to clear the land in preparation for building work.

'Of course Bryant are optimistic about the outcome,' said a Bryant Homes spokesman. 'How can a County Council that has already given you authority to build then change its mind once building has started?'

He has faith in a legal system which, pre-Sunningwell, had always made it difficult for village greens to be established. 'It's all down to the lawyers now really,' he said.

The final decision will be made on 9 February 2000.

The limits to counterurbanisation

Counterurbanisation is a much more complex process than is sometimes imagined. In south Oxfordshire, for instance, most growth has taken place not in villages but in country towns, such as Thame (Figure 6.62). If counterurbanisation is the predominant trend, most people would have moved to Thame from larger places, especially Oxford or London. In a survey of 150 people conducted in 1998, only 5 per cent had been born in Thame, confirming that in-migration had indeed been the cause of the town's growth. Of the migrants, 55 per cent came from larger settlements. The rest came from settlements no bigger than Thame, and 12 per cent had moved to Thame from local villages.

As part of the survey, people were asked whether they supported plans for a new housing development in the town. Of those people who had lived in Thame for less than 10 years, 21 per cent said Yes, 61 per cent were against and 18 per cent replied 'Don't know'. Of those who had lived in the town for more than 10 years, 36 per cent were in favour, 53 per cent against and 12 per cent did not know.

Figure 6.62
Thame: a thriving market town

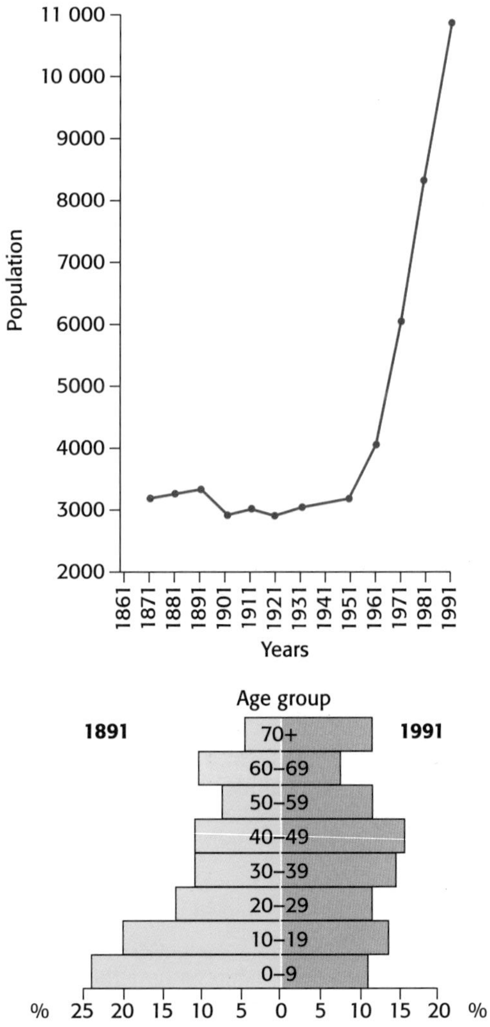

Activity

Study the graphs showing the population growth and structure of Thame (Figure 6.63).

1 In 1891, Thame's population pyramid had a broad base, suggesting a high birth rate. How then might the fact that total population was hardly growing at all be explained?

2 In 1991, Thame's population was growing rapidly, yet its pyramid had a very narrow base. What was causing the total population to grow?

3 To what extent does this study confirm the importance of counterurbanisation?

4 What reasons would you expect people to give for moving from larger settlements to Thame?

5 Who do you think is likely to move from a village to Thame? Why?

6 Which group of people stood out most strongly as being opposed to the new housing development? Why do you think this might be?

7 Can you suggest any reasons why longer-standing residents might be marginally more sympathetic to new development in their town?

Figure 6.63
Population growth and structure of Thame

Rural social change and service decline

Growing and declining rural areas share a number of significant social changes which together have greatly changed the nature of the countryside:

- decline in the number of agricultural jobs and the development of agribusiness (large-scale farming as a profitable business)
- increase in the size of the rural middle-class (including commuters, home-workers, second-home owners, retired people)
- loss of control by traditional landowners
- greater mobility through increased car ownership and better roads
- improved infrastructure and quality of housing
- reduced rural isolation.

A recent survey by the Women's Institute found that in the last ten years of the 20th century, more than a thousand village shops had closed, and most rural communities now lie within ten miles of a supermarket.

Many people are now more mobile and do not need local shops. If they work in towns, they might shop there too, before leaving for home. Bigger shops can charge lower prices, because they benefit from economies of scale. Freezers have made it possible to do 'big shops' once in a while, further reducing the need for daily access to local shops. Figure 6.64 shows the decline in selected services in Wiltshire villages. The concepts of range and threshold can be used to explain why the number of food shops has fallen more than the number of post offices and schools.

Similarly, in south Oxfordshire many parishes are now without key services:

43 per cent do not have a shop
51 per cent do not have a primary school
81 per cent have no doctor based in the parish
74 per cent do not have a daily bus service
51 per cent do not have a post office.

Remedying rural decline

South Oxfordshire District Council's 1999 Rural Action Plan proposed several measures to help reduce rural decline. Small firms are being encouraged to locate in rural districts, and several forms of support for shops have been introduced, including:

- rate relief for post offices and shops in villages
- support through the Village Shops Development Scheme
- business advice to shopkeepers
- resisting pressure from developers to convert rural shops and pubs into houses.

Financial support for non-profit-making rural bus services has also been proposed under a Rural Transport Partnership Scheme.

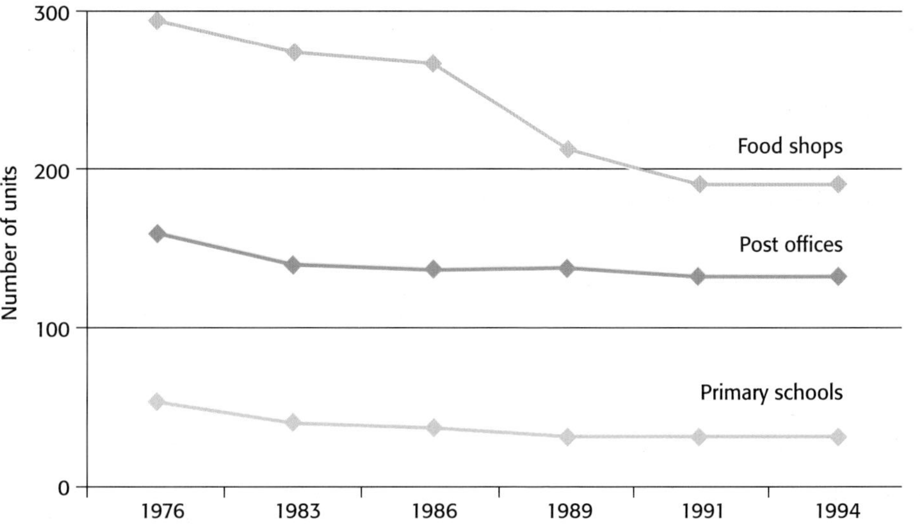

Figure 6.64 Changes in selected village services, Wiltshire 1976–94

Case Study: Population change in south Oxfordshire

The population of south Oxfordshire grew by 32 per cent between 1961 and 1971. From 1971 to 1981 the rate slowed to 2 per cent only to pick up to 7 per cent between 1981 and 1991. Counterurbanisation has been uneven in its nature and impact. Most of the growth has been concentrated on the market towns, including Henley, Wallingford and Thame. Thame itself grew by 132 per cent between 1961 and 1991. Some villages also grew rapidly, but a quarter of the villages actually lost population.

Why did some villages grow and others decline?

A number of factors together help to explain the pattern illustrated in Figure 6.65:

1 **Accessibility:** settlements on good transport routes or close to large towns had an advantage. Ipsden, in the Chilterns, is served only by single-track roads and has no daily bus service.

2 **Land ownership pattern:** 'closed' villages, dominated by a single landowner (sometimes described as 'estate villages'), tend to grow less rapidly. The main landowner in Ipsden prevented rapid development in the village.

3 **Settlement size:** larger villages have tended to grow faster, mainly in response to planning priorities. The South Oxfordshire Local Plan (1993) stressed that most development should take place in settlements where a reasonable infrastructure and range of services already existed. In practice, this policy has favoured growth in the districts nearer Oxford, which were dominated from medieval times by large villages, such as Chalgrove.

Figure 6.65 Population change in south Oxfordshire, 1961–91

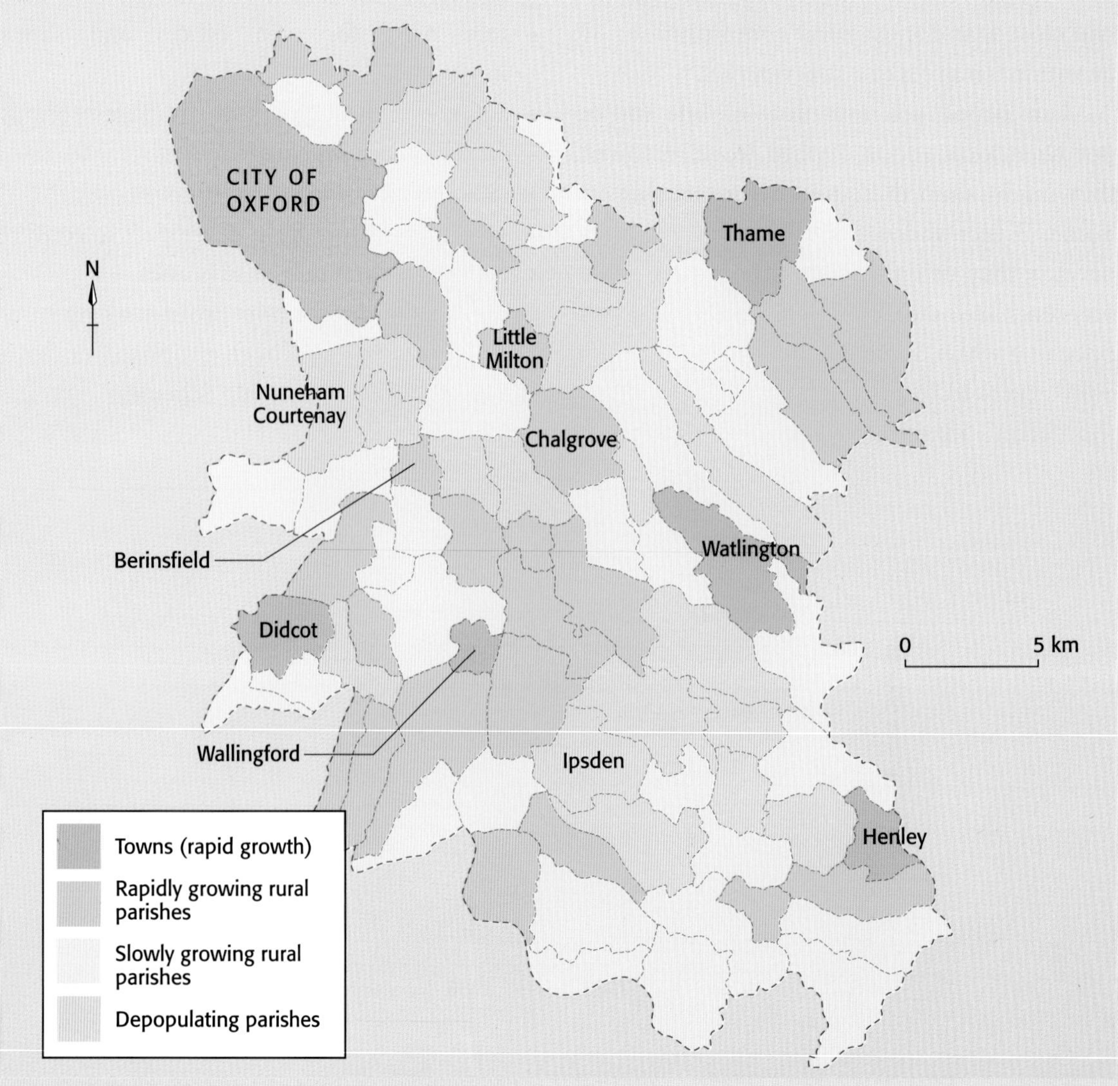

4 **Planning constraints:** the green belt around Oxford has discouraged growth in order to prevent urban sprawl on the outskirts of the city. Thus settlements like Nuneham Courtenay have failed to grow. To the south-east, the Chiltern Hills are an Area of Outstanding Natural Beauty (AONB), and growth has been constrained in order to conserve the landscape and the character of existing settlements. The outcome is that most new growth has been decanted into the Thame – Didcot axis (Figure 6.66).

The combination of all four factors has operated to cause depopulation or at least stagnation in some villages, and rapid growth in others. Ipsden has stagnated because of its inaccessibility, the dominance of a single landowner, and its location in the AONB. Since it has remained small, it is less likely to grow in the future. By contrast, Chalgrove, always a big

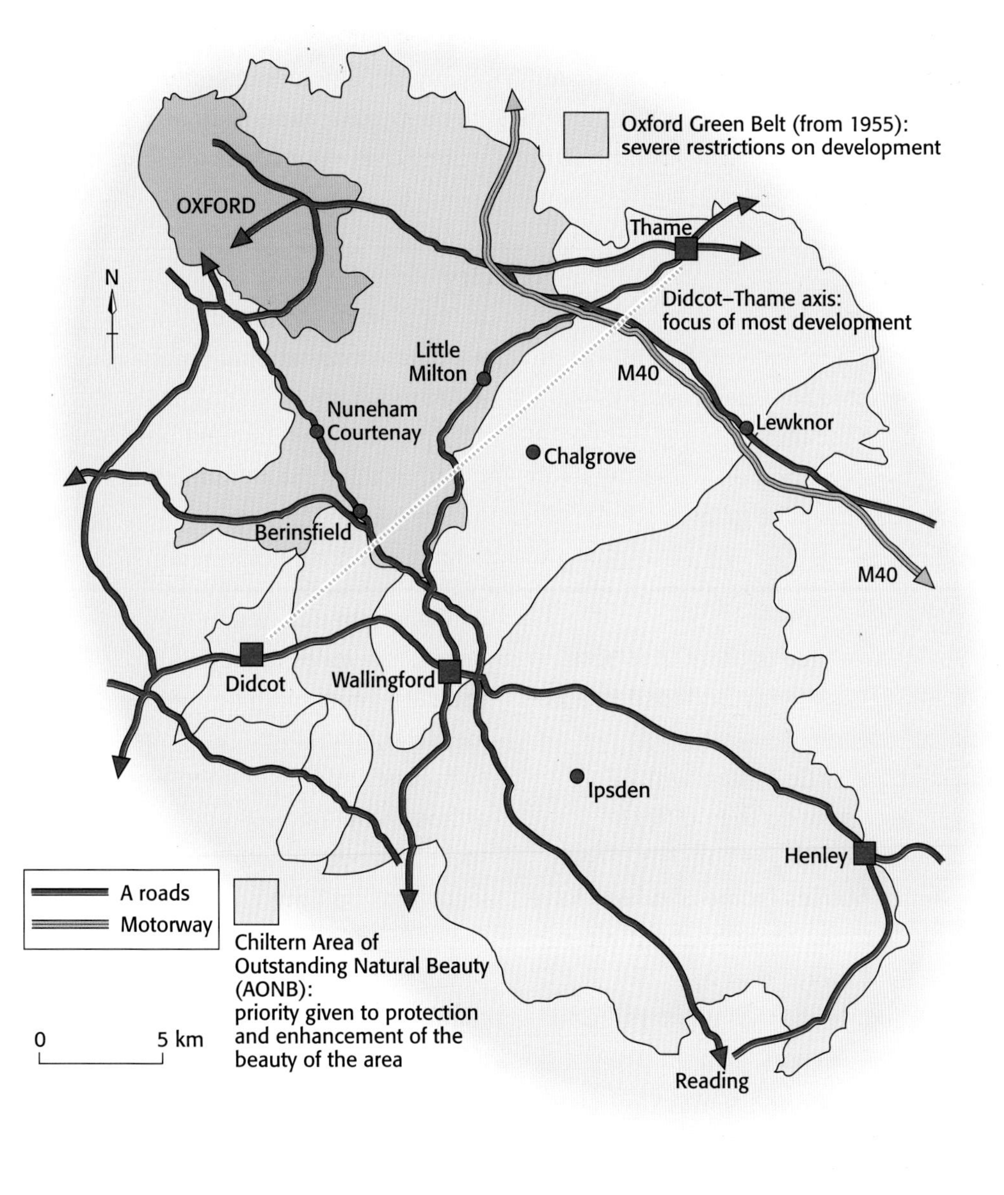

Figure 6.66 Planning opportunity zones in south Oxfordshire

village, is easily accessible by road and the finger of fate is pointed very firmly in its direction.

Like most villages Chalgrove lost population in the late 19th century owing to enclosure and the mechanisation of agriculture. Unlike some of the other south Oxfordshire villages, the population of Chalgrove has grown extremely rapidly since the early 1970s, essentially turning it into a **metropolitan village**.

The resulting problems have been largely social. Suburban estates have been grafted on to the village core. The new residents lead essentially urban lifestyles, contrasting with the small surviving group of old-established village residents. Now, only 4 per cent of Chalgrove's working population are employed in agricultural or related activities and about 50 per cent commute to work outside south Oxfordshire. Today's workers are more mobile (more than 90 per cent of households own at least one car), working and shopping in urban centres, and less dependent on local services. They are relatively affluent (40 per cent have professional or managerial jobs) and tend to be unsympathetic to modern farming practices, and most prone to NIMBYism – the 'Not In My Back Yard' opposition to further development. Their lives cause them to look out beyond the village – indeed the very layout of the streets in the 1980s housing area reflects this perspective. The road connects to the bypass; there is no direct road link to the village centre (look back at Figure 6.22).

Activity

1 Study Figure 6.67.

a Describe and account for the shape of the pyramid for Chalgrove.

b Describe the impact of counterurbanisation on the village of Chalgrove under the following headings:

- Population structure
- Social/occupational structure
- Morphology (see the earlier section on Chalgrove's morphology, page 161).

c What does the pyramid suggest is happening to the population of Ipsden, and how might it be explained?

2 Study Figure 6.68.

a What evidence is there that both Nuneham Courtenay and Ipsden are 'closed' villages?

b Compare Little Milton with Chalgrove. How do they differ?

c One of the villages consists largely of council houses (some of which have been sold to the tenants), built after the Second World War to accommodate manual workers from Oxford. It is thus atypical in being essentially a working-class commuter village. Which village is it?

d Nuneham Courtenay is a 'closed' village only a few miles from Oxford. It was built in the 17th century, the houses are almost identical, and there has been little subsequent development. However, although the population has not grown, there has been major social change. As the leases expired the estate owner, an Oxford college, sold off some houses at market prices. Use these details to help you write a paragraph analysing the profile shown in the table.

Rural regions – the future

A White Paper on Rural England, published in 1995, recognised the problems of the countryside, especially the loss of services, the lack of jobs, and the lack of affordable housing. But it also identified a real dilemma – how to encourage rural development while still conserving and protecting the environment and the special character of rural areas. The White Paper called for business rate relief for small shops, subsidies for rural bus services, and restrictions on the right to buy council houses.

Support for rural areas in England comes in five ways:

1 **Rural Development Areas:** these are those rural areas with the worst economic and social problems which qualify for grants towards improving employment (e.g. by building new industrial estates or renovating redundant buildings), stimulating tourism, supporting transport, extending training opportunities and conserving the environment.
2 **Rural Challenge:** grants take the form of prizes that reward imaginative and effective schemes to tackle specific problems. The last round was held in 1998, and the schemes are scheduled to wind up in 2001. In total, 23 schemes were offered up to £1 million each over three years.
3 **EU funds**, through the European Regional Development Fund or other Structural Funds and Community Initiatives.
4 **Specific targeted strategies**, e.g. the Rural Transport Partnership Scheme (aimed at preventing the decline of rural bus services) and the Village Shop Development Scheme, both of which are administered through the Countryside Agency.
5 **Funds to voluntary organisations:** the government delegates funds to voluntary organisations, like ACRE (Action with Communities in Rural England). Money is spent on supporting local initiatives for **sustainable development**. The Millennium Fund has given £10 million towards a scheme to build or renovate village halls across the country.

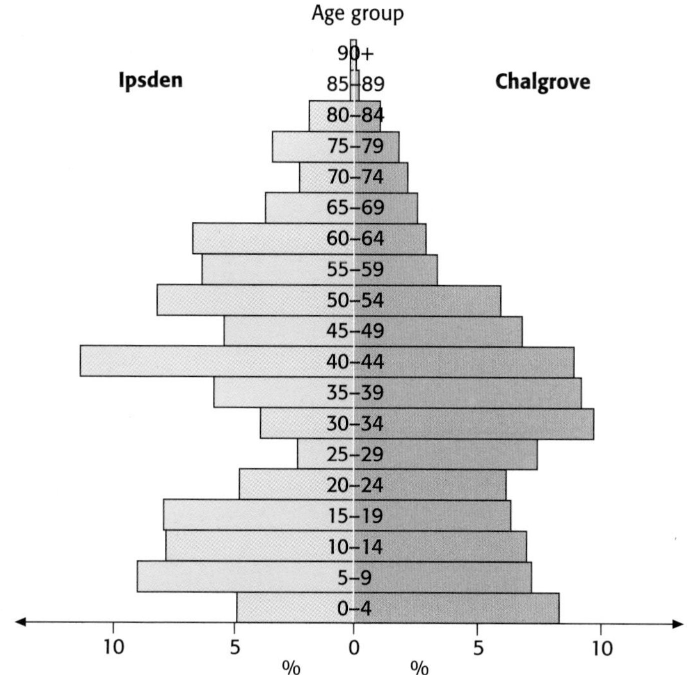

Figure 6.67

Contrasting population structures: Ipsden and Chalgrove, 1991

	Nuneham Courtenay	Berinsfield	Little Milton	Ipsden	Chalgrove
Population change 1991–2001	Decline	Decline	Decline	Decline	Growth
% aged 0–15	12	26	24	23	25
% aged 60 +	31	10	16	20	10
% unemployed	4.1	8.4	6.1	4.0	3.0
% households with no car	24	25	12	9	9
% owner-occupied	46	51	68	50	81
% managers or professional workers	45	21	52	41	42
% commuters	75	48	66	29	45

Figure 6.68

A comparison of five south Oxfordshire villages

Figure 6.69 summarises the pattern of government support for rural areas in England.

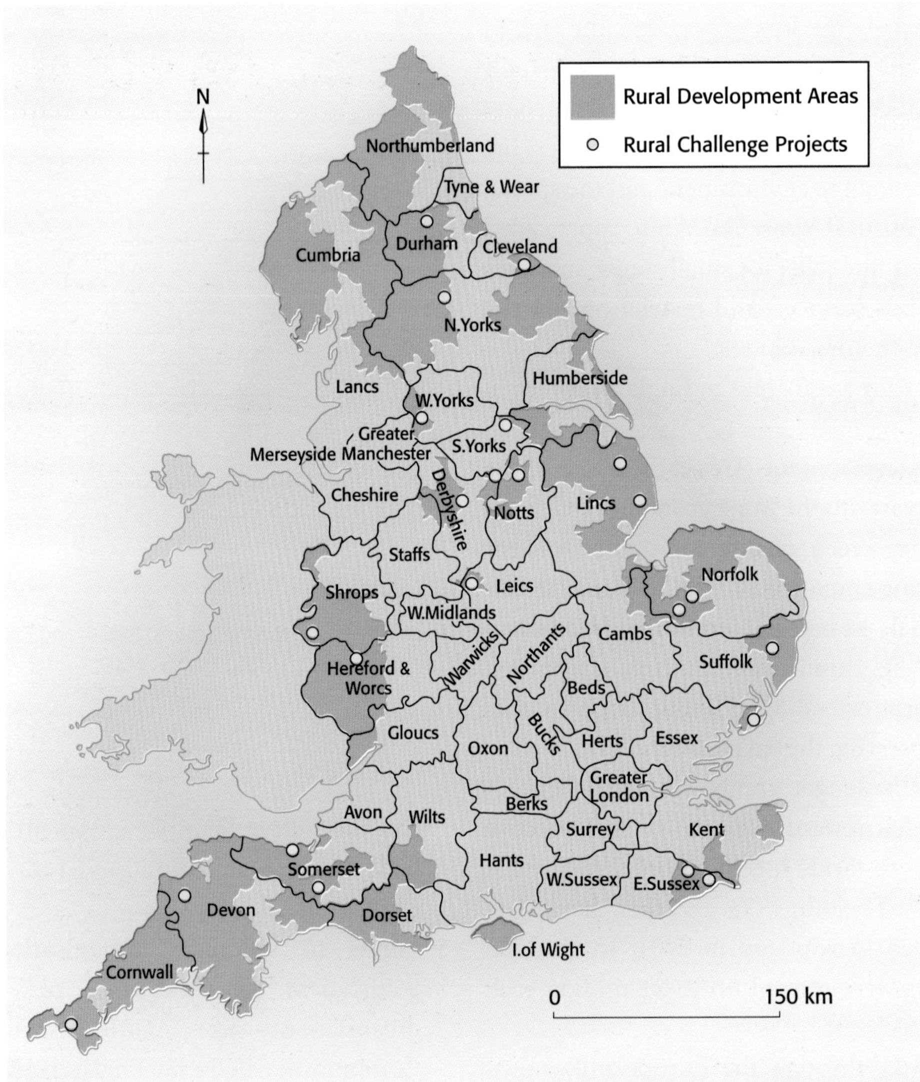

Figure 6.69
Government assistance for rural areas in England

7 Contemporary urban growth in MEDCs

Key Themes

- ✔ Suburban growth is caused by a combination of the pull of the suburbs and the push of the city.
- ✔ The process of suburbanisation is entering a new phase, with offices and businesses now leaving the centres of cities.
- ✔ Rapid urban growth creates social and environmental problems, including sprawl, pollution, congestion, and problems of water supply and waste disposal.
- ✔ Planning responses to the problems of urban growth vary in terms of their attitude to the quality of urban life and the environment.

Growing and declining cities

In the more economically developed countries (MEDCs) of the world, about 75 per cent of people now live in urban places (Figure 7.1). The trend since the 1970s, however, has been for people to move out of cities into rural areas, but this pattern of **counterurbanisation** (see Chapter 6) hides significant variations between cities. While older industrial cities often continue to decline, many small and medium-sized cities, as well as some larger metropolitan regions, are increasing in size and population. In the UK, for example, towns and cities traditionally based on heavy manufacturing or port industries are losing people. Examples shown in Figure 7.2 include Glasgow, Liverpool and Middlesbrough. By contrast, places such as Milton Keynes, Leeds, Oxford and Cambridge are booming in both jobs and people. After three decades of decline, London's population is also growing – by 7 per cent between 1981 and 1996.

A similar pattern can be found in North America, western Europe and Japan. Large metropolitan regions are enjoying steady economic and demographic growth, including the world's major metropolitan regions, or

Figure 7.1
The urban landscape, home to half the world's population

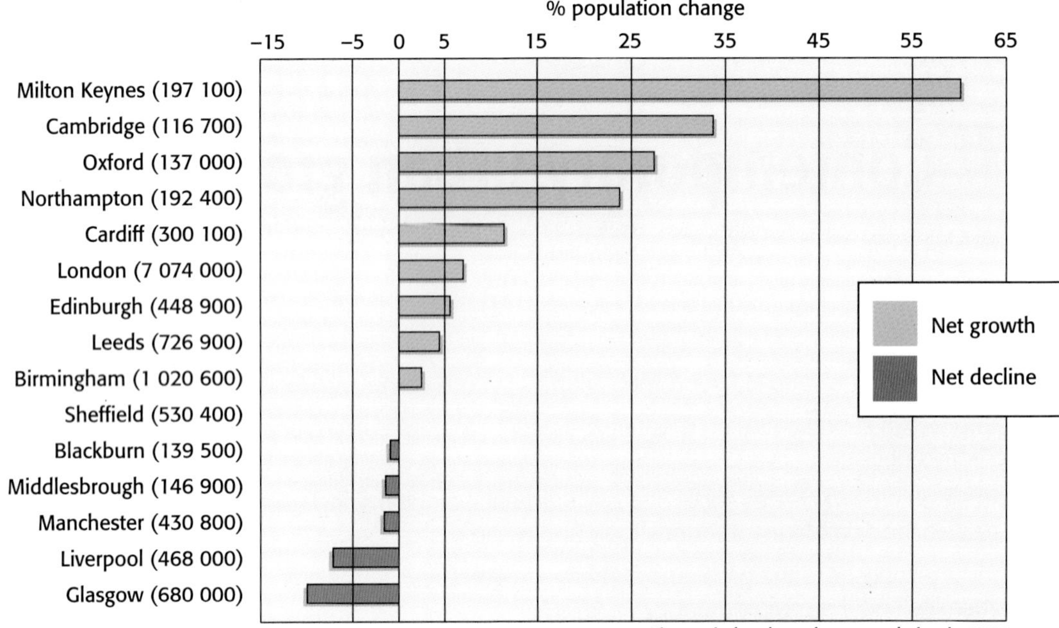

Figure 7.2

Patterns of growth and decline in selected British towns and cities, 1981–196

	Activity
1	Figure 7.3 shows a selection of 30 US cities together with their populations in 1990 and 1998. Calculate the population change between 1990 and 1998, in numbers and as a percentage.
2	Experiment with arranging the cities in different orders using both sets of data. Are any patterns evident?
3	Figure 7.4 shows the location of these cities in the USA. Plot the percentage change figures onto a copy of the map, using suitable proportional symbols. Describe the pattern that emerges and suggest reasons for it.

global cities, such as Tokyo, Paris, New York and Los Angeles. Many smaller cities associated with new industries in high-technology and financial services are expanding rapidly in regions such as Mediterranean France and the US Southwest.

City	Population 1990	Population 1998
Atlanta	393 929	403 819
Austin	472 020	552 434
Baltimore	736 014	645 593
Boston	574 283	555 447
Buffalo	328 175	300 717
Charlotte	419 558	504 637
Chicago	2 783 726	2 802 079
Cleveland	505 616	495 817
Dallas	1 007 618	1 075 894
Denver	467 610	499 055
Detroit	1 027 974	970 196
El Paso	515 342	615 032
Irvine	110 330	136 446
Houston	1 786 691	1 654 348
Kansas City	151 521	141 297
Las Vegas	258 877	404 288
Los Angeles	3 485 557	3 597 556
Miami	358 648	368 624
Milwaukee	628 088	578 364
New York	7 322 564	7 420 166
Orlando	164 674	181 175
Philadelphia	1 585 577	1 436 287
Phoenix	988 015	1 198 064
Portland	485 975	503 891
St Louis	396 685	339 316
San Bernardino	170 036	186 402
San Francisco	723 959	745 774
San Jose	782 224	861 284
Seattle	516 259	536 978
Washington DC	606 900	523 124

Figure 7.3

Patterns of growth and decline in selected US cities, 1990–98

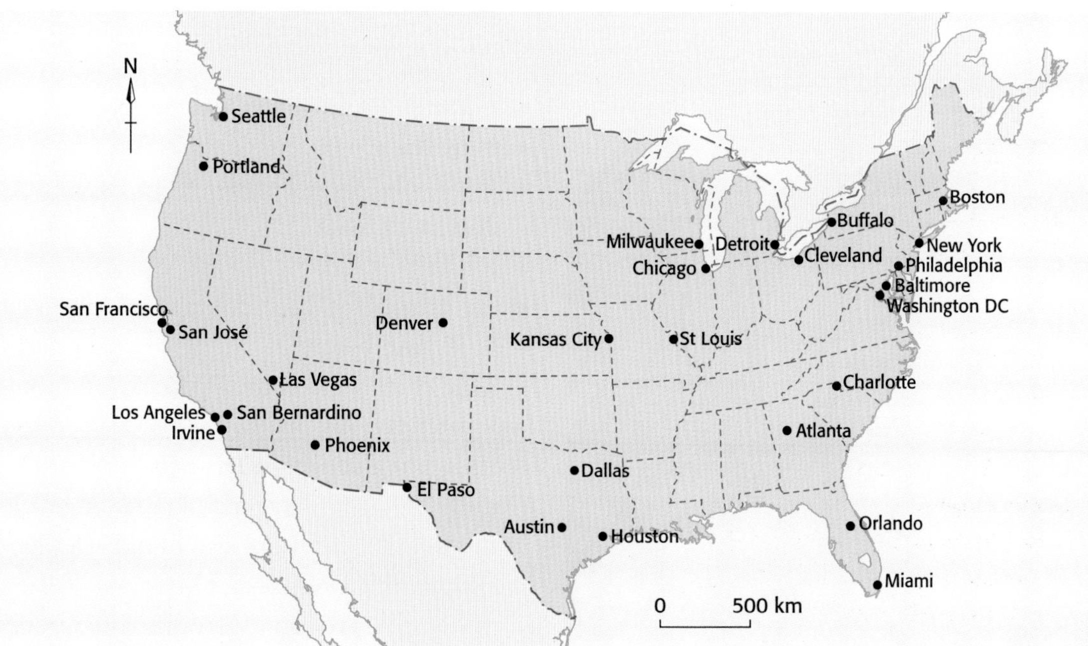

Figure 7.4
Location of selected US cities

Centre and suburbs

The new skyscrapers and waterfront developments in large cities throughout the MEDCs show that much of the new growth is concentrated in the centre of cities. Here, offices, shops, hotels, restaurants and other leisure facilities are appearing in once rundown and unpopular areas. London's Docklands and Barcelona's old port district are good examples.

While the centres of growing cities tend to build upwards, their edges rapidly spread outwards creating **suburbs** mainly consisting of housing rather than factories or offices (Figure 7.5). These usually have lower population densities than city centres.

The first real suburbs in Britain started in the mid-19th century, when wealthier families moved out of the crowded and dirty city centres to new and more pleasant districts. Edgbaston in Birmingham is a good example of an early suburb. These families could afford horses and carriages to take them back into the city for work and shopping. Over the next century and a half each new transport revolution was accompanied by a new phase of suburban growth, each one adding a ring onto the existing city. First trams, then underground railways and finally the car made it possible for people to live at a distance from where they worked. The suburban dream was for families to own their home with a garden, send their children to good schools and escape from the congestion, dirt and crime of the cities (Figure 7.6).

The oldest suburbs, and some of those built between the 1930s and the 1950s, are now in decline themselves. The physical deterioration

Figure 7.5
A residential suburb in Sydney

Figure 7.6
Typical interwar 1930s suburban development in Britain

of buildings, outward migration, unemployment and other signs of urban decline are spreading within the inner suburbs.

Edge cities and growth corridors

The latest phase of suburbanisation differs from previous ones. As well as the spread of houses and factories, shopping centres, offices and the headquarters of large companies are now moving into the suburbs. Connected by new systems of motorways, these new suburban districts are part of a much greater deconcentration of the functions of large cities than ever before.

Geographers have tried to find new terms for this process, such as **exurban growth**. The American writer Joel Garreau has defined a new feature of urban growth which he calls **edge cities**. He dates their beginning as some time in the early 1980s when, for the first time, there were more office buildings outside US cities than in their central business districts.

There are five defining elements of an edge city:

- more than 500 000 m^2 of office space
- more than 56 000 m^2 of shops
- more jobs than bedrooms, i.e. it is not a dormitory town
- residents perceive it as a single place
- the urban landscape doesn't look like a city of 30 years before.

Edge cities are commonly found on motorway intersections on the far borders of large centres, but also within large cities themselves (Figure 7.7). They have mainly been identified in the USA, but they are also found elsewhere, for example La Défense and Marne-la-Vallée in Paris, North Sydney, Australia, and around Toronto and Seoul.

The British geographer Peter Hall has suggested that new suburban centres and fast-growing towns are often strung out along major transport routes to form **growth corridors**. His examples include the M4 corridor in Britain, the E-4 Arlanda airport corridor north of Stockholm, and the Dulles Airport corridor outside Washington DC.

The combination of new suburban growth, edge cities and growth corridors has expanded the geographical limits of many metropolitan areas. Hall has identified, 'a pattern of extremely long-distance deconcentration stretching up to 150 km from the centre, with local concentrations of employment surrounded by overlapping commuter fields, and served mainly by private car'.

Figure 7.7
A typical edge city: Riverside, USA

The causes of suburbanisation

As cities have grown they have needed to find room for more people by spreading outwards as well as growing upwards (Figure 7.8). Some of the causes of suburbanisation have been operating for over a century, while others are newer. Suburban growth involves decisions made by families, companies, developers and governments. There are factors which pull people and businesses to the suburbs and others which push them out of the city (Figure 7.9).

The causes of suburbanisation work together. As more offices and industries move to the suburbs, so people have to follow them to find work. And where people are located, shops, restaurants and leisure facilities follow. Employers sometimes choose to locate in suburbs because they know that there are good workers there; for example, businesses doing routine office work are attracted by the presence of working mothers with a good education and relevant skills.

Governments also play a role. They decide the land tax system which makes it more attractive for developers to start on new land rather than re-use old land. In the UK, VAT is charged on house repairs but not on new development. Governments also fund and build the transport networks which make it possible for people to move to the suburbs. London's M25, the boulevard périphérique around Paris, and the interstate highway network in the USA all encourage suburban expansion.

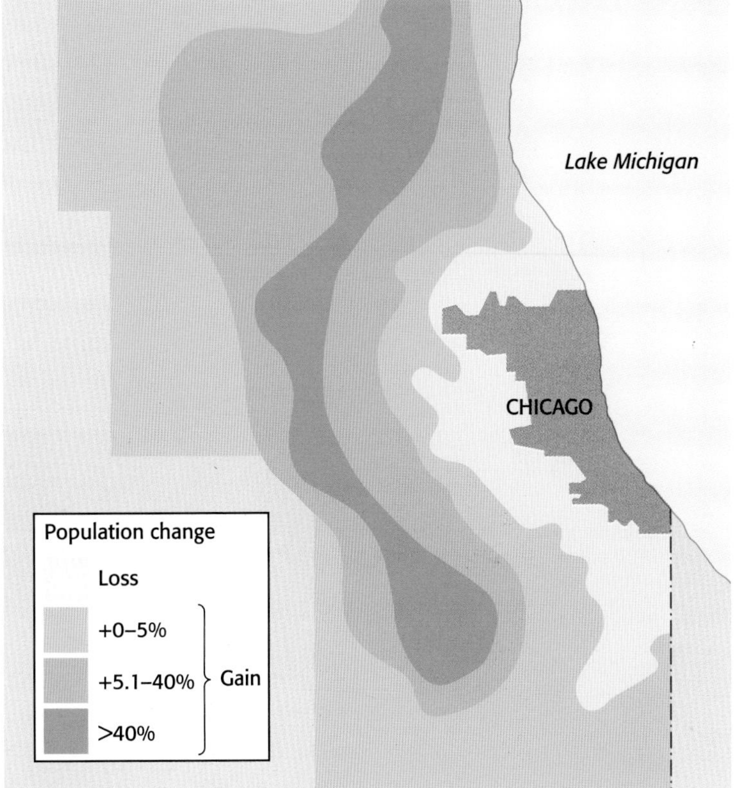

Figure 7.8

Suburbanisation in Chicago, 1970–90. In this period the population of metropolitan Chicago grew by 4 per cent but the amount of land used for housing increased by 46 per cent.

Figure 7.9

Push and pull factors

	Push out of the city	Pull of the suburbs
Families	• Older housing in crowded areas with less garden space • Congestion, pollution, noise • Fears for family safety • Few or restricted job opportunities	• New, low-density housing with modern facilities • More open space • Better schools and services • Large, pleasant shopping centres • Safer neighbourhoods • More job opportunities
Companies	• Old and cramped buildings • Congestion • High rents for land and services • Shortages of skilled workers	• Cheaper and more plentiful land for expansion • New buildings with adequate car parking and space for computers, new cabling and air-conditioning • Skilled workers • Access to new roads, airports and rail networks
Developers	• Expensive land • Costs of clearing sites and cleaning up chemical or toxic waste from industry • High taxes on repairing old buildings	• Cheaper land for large developments • Financial incentives offered by suburban authorities

Case Study: Los Angeles

Few places grew so much and so fast in the 20th century as Los Angeles (Figure 7.10). From a population of 100 000 in 1900 it reached 15 495 000 in 1996. The urban area has spread so far from the original centre of the city that it now covers large parts of four surrounding counties – Riverside, San Bernardino, Orange and Ventura. Altogether the built-up area extends over 86 000 km^2. To travel from the north to the south of the region, a distance of 200 km, would take over two hours at least (Figure 7.11).

Since its beginnings as a Spanish colonial town in 1781, Los Angeles has grown from a site by the Los Angeles River towards the coast, across mountains and out into the desert. The first suburbs were built in the 1920s and 1930s along electric railway lines. Suburbs such as Vernon were based just on industry, Maywood on affordable housing for industrial workers, and Lynwood was for better-off families. In the 1950s and 1960s car ownership increased enough to open up suburbs further away in the San Gabriel and San Fernando Valleys.

The new suburbs developed in the 1980s. Riverside and San Bernardino counties doubled their populations in the 1980s and 1990s as the demand for affordable suburban housing intensified. The new suburbs also included edge cities such as Irvine, Anaheim and Ontario Airport. Industries such as computers, aerospace, medical technology and tourism provided the jobs. Huge shopping malls opened in the 1980s, starting with South Coast Plaza.

Meanwhile the older suburbs entered into decline as heavy industries closed. In many places the existing inhabitants were replaced by immigrants from Mexico, East Asia and Central America. In fact, people born in Los Angeles are leaving the region and the population is only growing because of new migrants, who now make up 27 per cent of the population.

Figure 7.10
Metropolitan Los Angeles, viewed from space

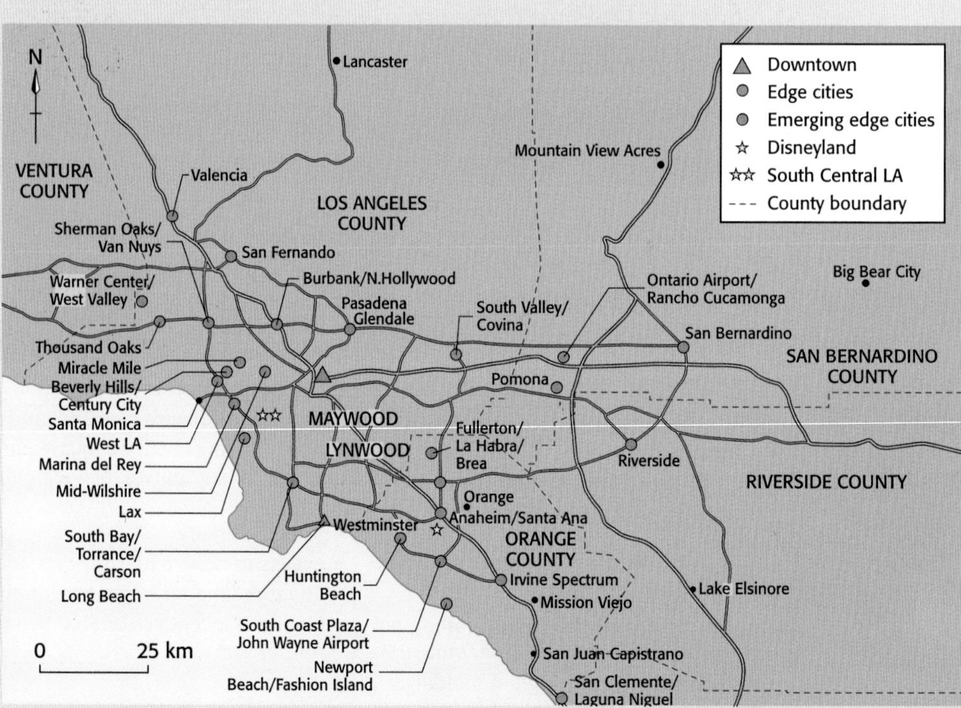

Figure 7.11
Los Angeles metropolitan region

Problems caused by urban growth

The problems of urban decline were first noticed in the 1960s, since when governments have introduced many policies to prevent unemployment and restore the social and physical health of inner cities. But since the 1980s there has been a new set of problems associated with growing populations and suburbanisation, including, in particular, sprawl, congestion, pollution, water supply and waste disposal.

Urban sprawl

The US Department of Housing and Urban Development defines **urban sprawl** as:

> *'a particular type of suburban development characterised by very low-density settlements, both residential and non-residential; dominance of movement by use of private automobiles; unlimited outward expansion of new subdivisions* [developed blocks of land] *and leapfrogging development of these subdivisions; and segregation of land uses by activity'.*

Private houses, modern offices, shopping malls and highways all consume large amounts of land. In the case of new suburban US office developments, for example, 60 per cent of a plot of land is designated as space for car parking. Room also has to be found for recreation and leisure facilities such as golf courses and sports stadia.

Suburban building prevents the use of land for other purposes, including farming and recreation. It may also threaten natural habitats such as wetlands, desert and forest, and exert negative impacts on the environment, for example by altering the hydrological properties of river catchments. In North America and Australia there is usually more flat open land

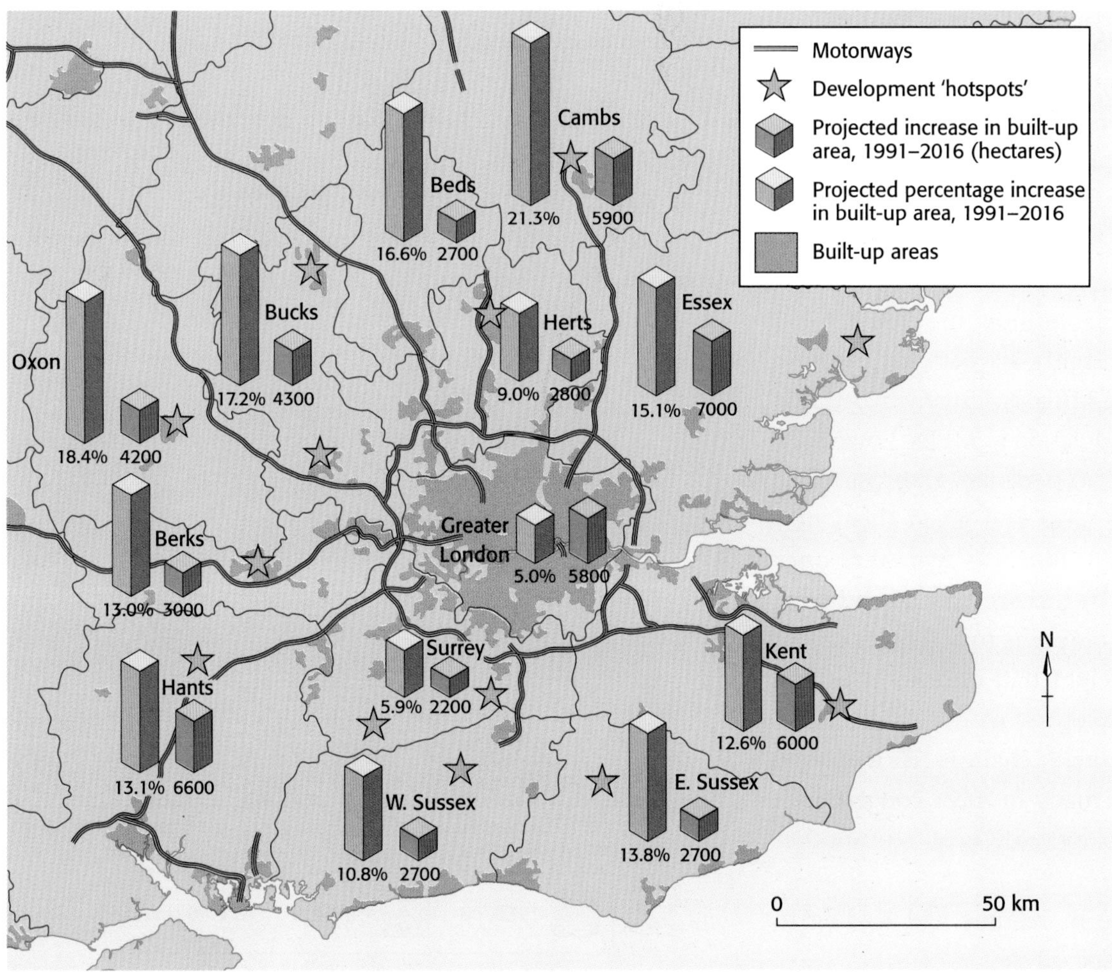

Figure 7.12 Sprawl in south-east England

around fast-growing cities than in Europe, which helps to explain why the levels and extent of suburbanisation are usually higher in North America than in Europe. Even so, regions such as south-east England are under intense pressure from developers (Figure 7.12). At the same time, the buildings and services in inner urban areas which people are leaving are going to waste. Schools, hospitals, parks and other public facilities are not being used to their full extent.

Commuting and congestion

Urban sprawl tends to increase commuting by private car for two reasons. First, in the suburbs people generally live further away from their places of work. Second, new suburbs are often beyond the reach of public transport systems such as London's Underground or San Francisco's Bay Area Rapid Transit network. Another problem is that rail and underground systems are usually designed to take passengers in and out of the centre of cities, but many people want to travel between suburbs. By contrast, people living in the central areas of big cities tend to use public transport the most.

The number of vehicles on the world's roads increased from 53 million in 1950 to 460 million in 1994. Eighty-six per cent of those vehicles are in the MEDCs. Usually two-thirds or more of the population in MEDCs own cars. The revolution in personal transport has changed people's lives and given them new freedoms to travel. Journeys that were once taken on foot or by bus are now taken by car instead, for example going to and from school (Figure 7.13). Freight that once went by rail now goes by road.

The cost of these changes is increased congestion on the roads. In effect, congestion is the delay imposed by vehicles on one another and it leads to:

- journeys taking more time and leading to frustration among drivers
- slower journeys for goods and delivery vehicles, costing companies more in wages and fuel
- increased air pollution from slow or stationary traffic
- blight in city centres from too many vehicles clogging the streets.

In the UK, the facts about traffic tell their own story:

- There are 27 million vehicles on Britain's roads.
- The total distance covered by all cars in a year is over 360 billion km.
- Since the 1970s the average distance travelled per person per day has increased by almost 75 per cent to 29 km.
- Journeys by car make up 86 per cent of the total distance travelled; buses and coaches make up only 6 per cent.
- Two-thirds of journeys are for shopping or leisure; one-fifth for work.
- Cycling has declined to only 2 per cent of journeys.
- One-third of British households do not have a car.
- Car travel is twice as high in the outer South East as it is in London – an average of 7000 km per driver per year, the highest in the country. London has the lowest average car travel per year in the country.

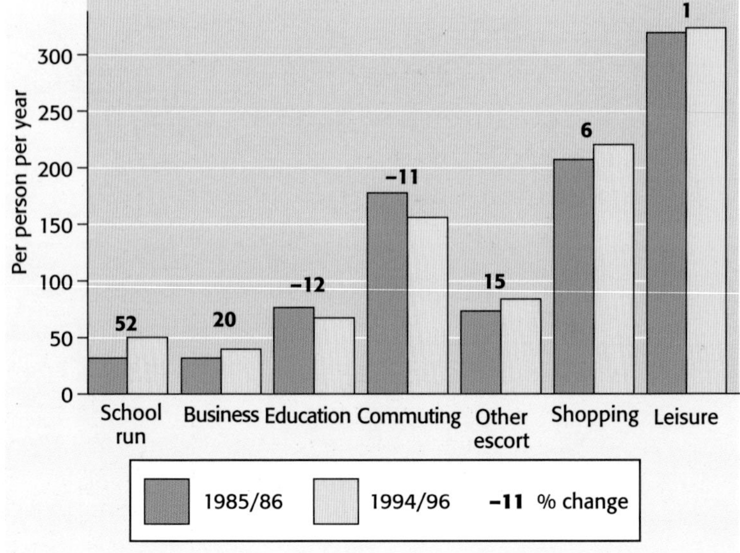

Figure 7.13 More journeys to school. The graph shows the number of journeys taken for different purposes and how they changed between the mid-1980s and the mid-1990s.

Activity

National travel surveys rely on personal travel diaries kept by individuals. The table, Figure 7.14 is adapted from such a survey:

1 Make out a copy of the table for a whole week or fortnight, including weekends.

2 Before you start, prepare an approximate estimate of the total distance you travel each week (or fortnight) and how much time you spend travelling. Remember that even walking a short distance counts as a journey, and return trips should be counted as two separate journeys, for example going to and from the shops.

3 When you start your diary, for each day enter the total distance travelled for each journey in the appropriate box under the 'Purpose of travel' column. If your trip had more than one purpose, enter the data in the most applicable box. Under the 'Method of travel' column enter the total time spent travelling by each method you used.

4 At the end of your survey, work out and then present the following information using suitable graphs or charts:

- the total distance travelled and the total time spent travelling
- how your total distance and time were divided among the various purposes and methods
- for each method of travel, the relationship between distance travelled and time spent travelling
- the proportion of your journeys where you experienced congestion.

5 What limitations did you encounter in using this method of data collection? Would it be good enough for national surveys?

Journeys	Purpose of travel					Method of travel					Travel		Travel time	Estimated distance
	School	Shopping	Visiting people	Entertainment & recreation	Other	Walk	Cycle	Bus or train	Car	Other	Alone	With someone		
Monday														
1														
2														
3														
4														
5														

Figure 7.14
Personal travel diary

Air pollution

Air pollution in cities and suburbs is not caused by traffic alone. Factories, waste incinerators and power plants also produce pollutants. But vehicles do contribute substantial proportions of many pollutants, as Figure 7.15 reveals. For example, a quarter of the UK's emissions of carbon dioxide, one of the main greenhouse gases, is produced by motor vehicles.

Although pollution features prominently in the news it is easy to forget that in the cities of MEDCs levels of many pollutants are falling. Pollution from lead and sulphur dioxide is now generally at safe levels for health and the environment (Figure 7.16). Lead levels have fallen because of the introduction of unleaded petrol, which became compulsory in the EU in 2000. SO_2 levels are lower because of the closure of many old factories and the introduction of clean technology in power plants. By contrast, in cities in the LEDCs, such as Mexico City, the levels of urban air pollution are often much worse. The main problems in cities of the MEDCs now come from ozone and particulates. Particulates are tiny particles that people can breathe in. Some people are more likely to suffer from the effects of air pollution than others. Young children, the elderly and people with breathing difficulties are most at risk.

Traffic generates a cocktail of pollutants, each of which can have its own harmful effect on health and the environment. Many contribute to respiratory or breathing diseases such as asthma. Others can have a toxic effect, poisoning the blood system and leading to heart disease. Sulphur dioxide and nitrogen oxides also contribute to acid deposition which, in cities, is a cause of building stone decay. Ozone is formed by chemical reactions in the urban atmosphere involving exhaust pollutants such as unburned hydrocarbons and volatile organic compounds. It is one of the elements in photochemical smog, which causes poor visibility over cities.

Figure 7.15 The main air pollutants and their effects

Pollutant	Proportion coming from vehicles	Effects
Sulphur dioxide (SO_2)	4%	Respiratory diseases; acid deposition
Nitrogen oxides (NO_x)	Over 50%	Respiratory diseases; acid deposition
Ozone	Indirectly	Respiratory diseases; damage to crops and forests
Particulates	14–50%	Respiratory diseases
Carbon monoxide (CO)	70–90%	Toxic
Lead	1%	Toxic
Volatile organic compounds (VOCs)	30–40%	Cancer

City	Sulphur dioxide	Particulates	Airborne lead	Carbon monoxide	Nitrogen oxides	Ozone
London	Low	Low	Low	Above guideline	Low	Low
New York	Low	Low	Low	Above guideline	Low	Above guideline
Los Angeles	Low	Above guideline	Low	Above guideline	Above guideline	Serious
Moscow	No data	Above guideline	Low	Above guideline	Above guideline	No data
Tokyo	Low	Low	No data	Low	Low	Serious
Mexico City	Serious	Serious	Above guideline	Serious	Above guideline	Serious

Figure 7.16

Urban air pollution in large cities. The table shows whether cities are above or below the World Health Organisation guidelines for air pollution. 'Serious' means that levels are double or more what is considered to be safe.

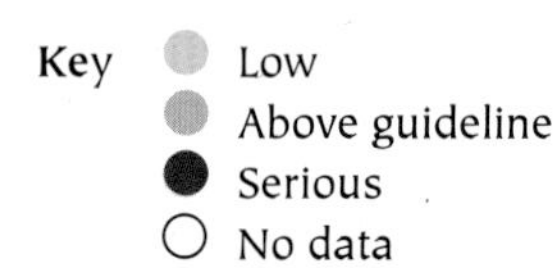

Case Study: Congestion and pollution in Los Angeles

Los Angeles has perhaps more vehicles per person than anywhere else in the world, and the toughest air quality regulations in the USA. Nevertheless, it still suffers from the worst urban air pollution of any MEDC city. In California there are over 25 million vehicles and 32 million people. Construction of an underground rail network began in the 1980s but it has few lines and does not reach the suburbs. Only around 4 per cent of people use public transport to travel. The rest go by car, resulting in a staggering 182 million km of travel per day for the area's residents. Although the average journey to work is only 25 minutes, many people travel up to 100 km a day. Sometimes there are traffic jams in both directions on highways. The cost of delays and fuel are estimated at $920 a year for each driver in Los Angeles County and $1100 in Riverside and San Bernardino.

Although air pollution from cars has been cut by tough laws for emissions, the continued growth in population and cars means that the air quality remains dangerously poor. Pollutants from cars and factories become trapped in the Los Angeles basin, hemmed in by mountains and with only weak winds (Figure 7.17). High levels of sunshine contribute to the formation of photochemical smog from the chemicals released by pollution. On average there are over 100 days a year when ozone levels in Riverside and San Bernardino exceed national standards for health. The effects on health are a cause for serious concern. In 1996, 5873 deaths caused by particulates were recorded. The annual cost to the region's hospitals of respiratory diseases and cancers related to air pollution is as high as $10 billion.

Figure 7.17

Air pollution in Los Angeles. The topography of the Los Angeles region causes pollutants to be trapped beneath a layer of air, giving rise to smog.

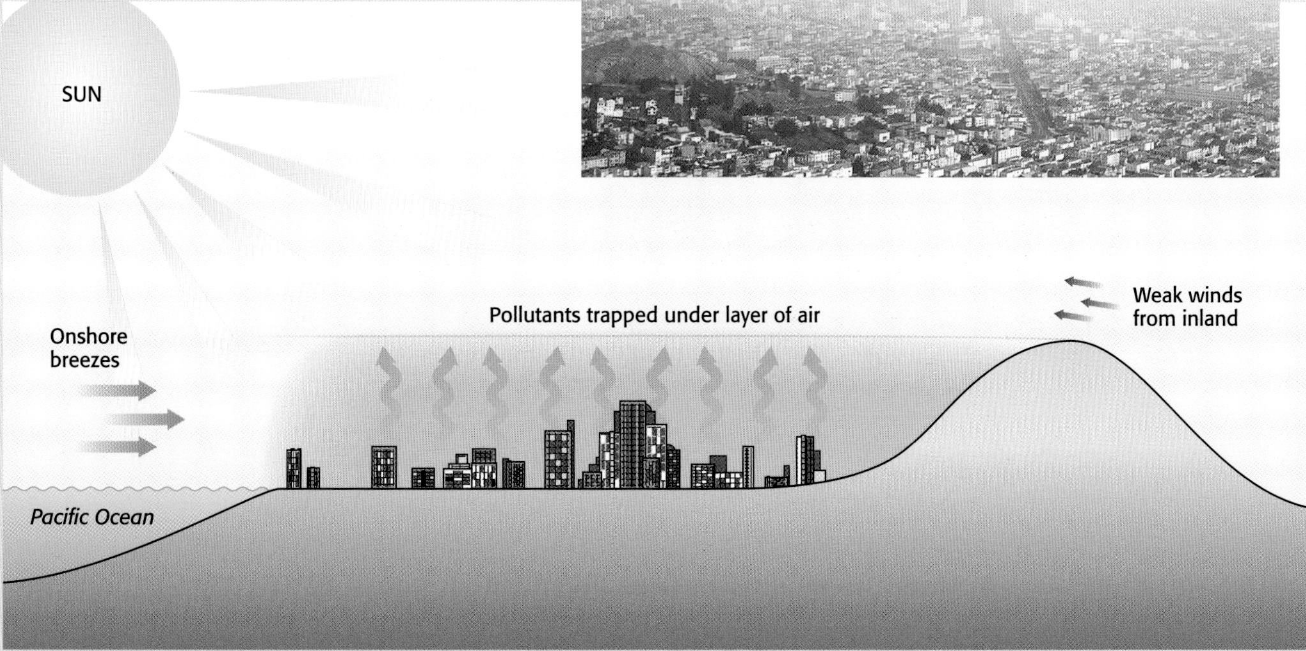

Water supply

Cities in MEDCs are thirsty places. Industries and power plants use more water than households, but household use is increasing because of the nature of modern lifestyles. Lawns, gardens, washing machines and dishwashers all consume a lot of water (Figure 7.18). People living in the suburbs often use more water than city-dwellers, partly because of the greater incidence of lawns, gardens and swimming pools. In the drier regions of the USA these uses account for up to 80 per cent of domestic water consumption. In Australia it is reckoned that high-density neighbourhoods use only two-thirds the amount of low-density suburbs. Even in cities with similar standards of living, the amount of water used may vary greatly (Figure 7.19). North American and Australian cities tend to use much more water than European cities.

There are two main sources of water for cities: fresh water and groundwater. Sources can either be local or distant. Groundwater sources are common in US, Australian and Spanish cities. Although it is fairly straightforward to withdraw groundwater, excessive use may have adverse consequences for the environment, including:

- aquifer depletion, e.g. Tucson, Arizona
- ground subsidence, e.g. Tokyo
- intrusion in coastal cities, e.g. San Francisco
- depletion of surface rivers and streams, e.g. south-east England.

If there is insufficient water locally it must be brought from afar by constructing reservoirs, dams, aqueducts and canals. Transporting water over long distances involves expensive engineering projects, and the further it travels the more is lost through seepage and evaporation (Figure 7.20). While the demand for land from suburban and exurban building makes it difficult to find sufficient space for reservoirs near urban areas, environmental groups often object to new reservoirs in the countryside.

Waste disposal

Waste products may be either solid, such as paper and packaging, or liquid, such as sewage or industrial waste. In MEDCs, city households usually contribute around three-quarters of all solid waste. Changing lifestyles have resulted in both more waste per house, and different types of waste. In the USA domestic waste has risen by 50 per cent since 1900. In earlier times ash and coal dust from fires was the main household waste product. Nowadays a larger range of items is thrown away (Figure 7.21), and in

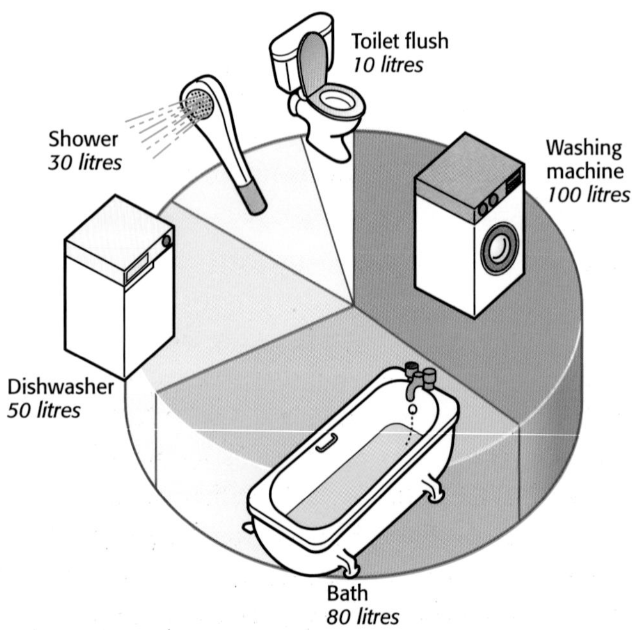

Figure 7.18
Water use in the average UK household (4 people)

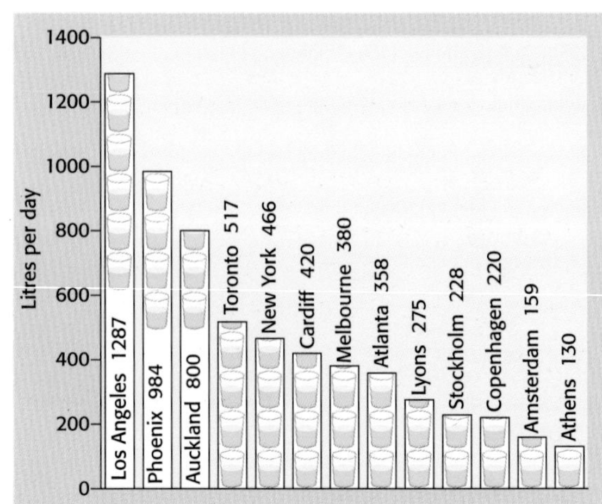

Figure 7.19
Water use per person in MEDC cities

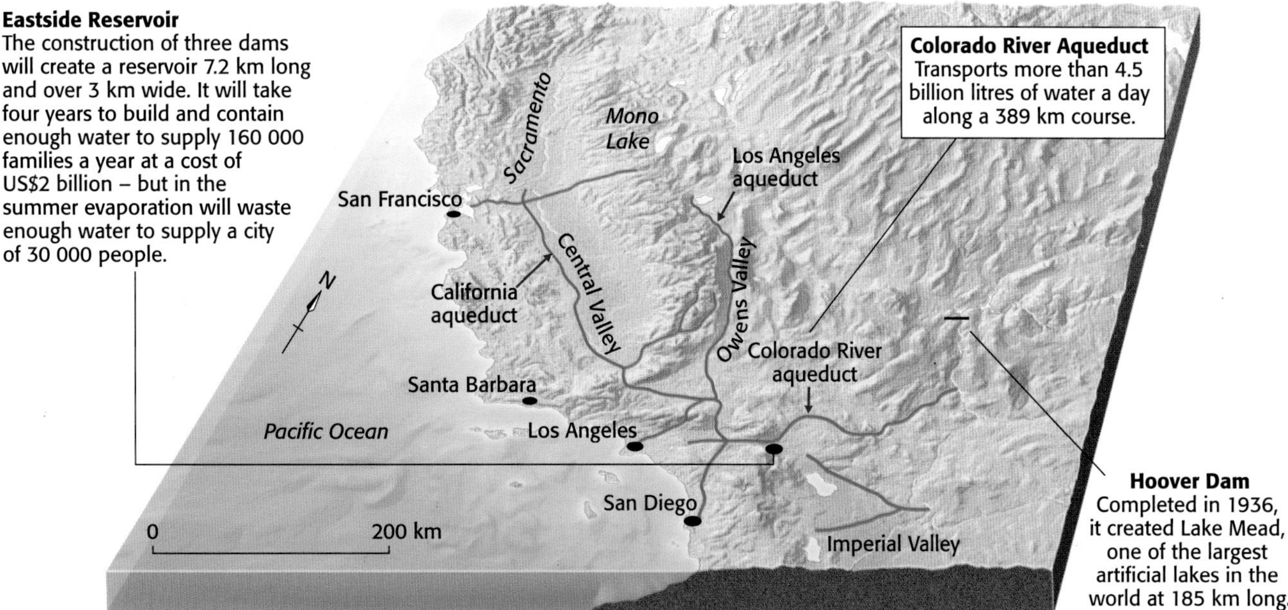

Figure 7.20

Water for Los Angeles

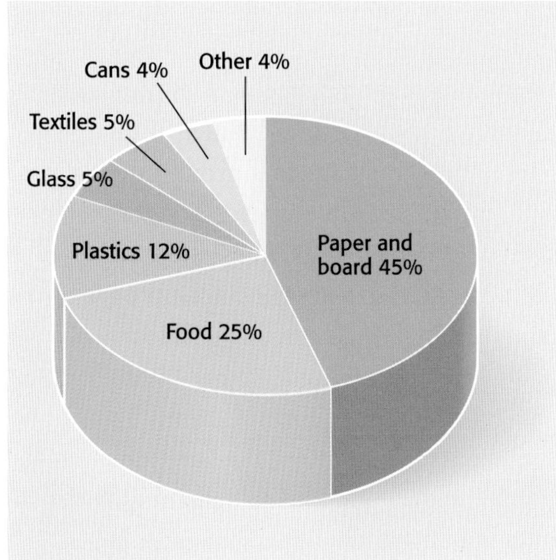

Figure 7.21

The main types of household waste in US households

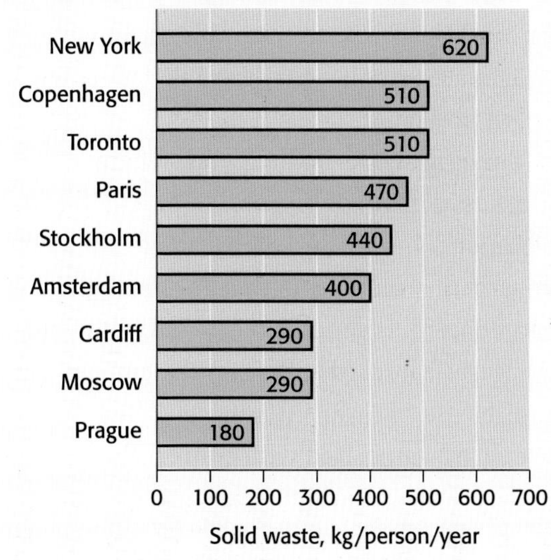

Figure 7.22

Solid waste in MEDC cities

much greater quantities. The amount of rubbish varies greatly between different countries (Figure 7.22), while affluent lifestyles are increasingly associated with more waste than in the past.

There are three main ways of disposing of solid waste:

- landfill
- incineration
- export.

Burying waste in landfill sites is the most common means of disposal in North America and in most European countries (Figure 7.23). Eighty-four per cent of the UK's municipal waste is dealt with this way – 20 million tonnes a year. The main problems are the danger of groundwater contamination from seepage, and the lack of suitable sites. Few people want a tip near their home, so as cities spread out the number of potential sites diminishes. Closed

Figure 7.23
A landfill site at Hempsted, near Gloucester

full sites pose an environmental threat and further limit the available land for expansion. Around New York, for example, there were 294 sites in 1986 but it is predicted that there will be only 13 by 2006.

Burning waste in incinerator plants is the most usual form of disposal in Japan, Belgium, Denmark, Greece and Switzerland. An advantage of this method is that the resultant heat can be used to generate electricity. But unless the waste is burned at the correct temperature it can release harmful chemicals, called dioxins, which are associated with cancer. Not surprisingly, few householders want a waste incinerator in their neighbourhood. In US cities they have often been located in poorer districts occupied by ethnic minority populations. Many neighbourhood groups have organised opposition to them – one example is the successful battle against the Los Angeles City Energy Recovery Project (LANCER) in an African-American neighbourhood of Los Angeles.

Many cities now export waste over long distances, either to rural areas in their own countries or abroad. New York sends much of its rubbish to the southern states, while Mexico and some Asian countries earn revenue from handling waste from the MEDCs.

Planning responses to the problems of urban growth

Each of the main problems of urban growth has its own set of planning responses. However, it is unlikely that attempts to tackle one problem in isolation from the others will succeed. Attempts to develop 'integrated policies', such as the joint planning of land use and transport, for example, are now more common.

Sprawl

There are three main approaches to the problem of urban sprawl:

- designating areas where no development is allowed
- channelling population growth to selected towns or cities
- increasing urban densities through 'compaction' or 'consolidation'.

Urban sprawl has been seen as a problem since the 1930s. At that time many cities adopted planning laws to block development in designated areas while concentrating growth on planned new towns. London and Moscow, for instance, established green belts. These were zones 8–16 km wide surrounding the built-up edge of the city, within which urban development was normally not allowed. Other British cities, including Glasgow, Birmingham, Oxford and Manchester (Figure 7.24), have green belts. London also channelled settlement growth into eight new towns just beyond its green belt. Other cities, such as Paris and the Ruhr conurbation in Germany, have created large green wedges or zones in order to limit sprawl (Figure 7.25).

Green belts and new towns served their purpose, but many planners now believe that new solutions are needed for the latest phase of surburban and exurban sprawl. One alternative is the idea of the **compact city**. This approach involves making better use of the land within cities and increasing urban population densities. Amsterdam adopted this idea in 1978, and the UK's Urban Task Force Report in 1999, entitled 'Towards an Urban Renaissance', recommended a 'compact and well-connected city'. Among the features of compact urban planning are:

- increased density, from 20 dwellings per hectare to 35–40
- mixed land use patterns with homes, workplaces and shops close together to reduce the need for travel
- homes, workplaces and services co-ordinated with public transport routes
- clusters of small settlements along major rail corridors.

Stockholm's suburban satellite towns are an example of compact settlements located on rail routes. Potential clusters in the UK might include a corridor between Welwyn Garden City (Hertfordshire) and Peterborough (Cambridgeshire), or from Folkestone to Ashford in Kent.

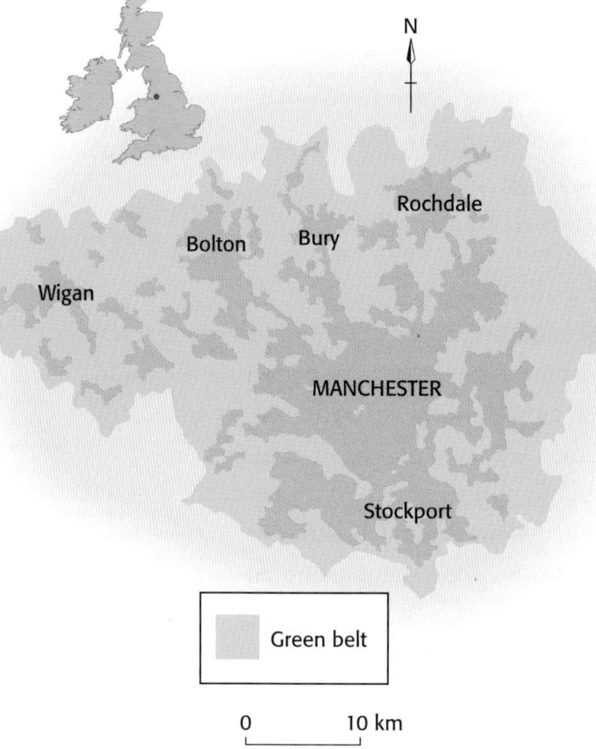

Figure 7.24
Greater Manchester's green belt

Figure 7.25
A green wedge area in Paris, designed to limit urban sprawl

Congestion

There are many possible planning responses to reducing congestion (Figure 7.26), and these can be grouped under two main headings:

- Policies to restrain use of cars and trucks.
- Policies to promote alternatives, such as public transport (buses, tram, rail), cycling and walking.

Policy	Example
Quotas limiting the number of vehicles licensed	• Singapore
Restrictions on access in space	• Oslo charges tolls on cars entering the city centre
Restrictions on access in time	• Athens allows cars into the city on alternate days depending on their licence plate number
High Occupancy Vehicle (HOV) lanes restricting use to vehicles with two or more occupants	• Los Angeles has 480 km of HOV lanes • Amsterdam • On trial in Leeds
Electronic road pricing to charge drivers for using roads at peak times, using roadside monitors to identify and track vehicles	• Trials in Singapore and Cambridge
Park and Ride to encourage drivers to enter towns by bus	• Hull, Oxford, Chester, Cambridge
Parking restrictions in the centre to limit long-stay parking	• Cambridge, Oxford
Pedestrian-priority zones (home zones) using traffic calming (humps, narrow lanes) and low speed limits	• Hanover's 30 km/h zones • Netherland's Woonerven scheme
Pedestrian-only zones	• Common in MEDC cities
Car-free residential areas	• Bremen, Germany

Figure 7.26
Policies designed to reduce city congestion

Traffic flows may also be better managed by encouraging off-peak travel or by the sophisticated co-ordination of traffic signals.

Governments have found that policies to restrain car use fail unless there are adequate alternatives. These include:

	Example
• Mass transit systems using fixed routes.	New York Metro Dublin suburban railways; Manchester Metrolink light rail system
• Public transport with bus lanes and bus priority lanes at traffic lights.	Oxford's Transport Strategy Leeds bus guideway (Figure 7.27)
• Cycle path networks.	Delft, Netherlands (Figure 7.28).

Public transport systems work best where travellers can buy multi-modal tickets (for bus, rail and underground), when fares are kept low, and when routes and times match their needs. Public transport use varies considerably between cities (Figure 7.29), suggesting that city governments could do more to encourage it. The experience of many cities suggests that while such policies can prevent an increase in congestion, they rarely lead to a decrease in car use.

Figure 7.28
Cycleway in Delft, Netherlands

Air pollution

Planning responses designed to reduce traffic and congestion should also reduce air pollution, although industry and energy generation require separate pollution controls. There are also different approaches to cutting the amount emitted by individual vehicles:

- policies aimed at conventional petrol-powered vehicles and fuels
- policies encouraging alternative vehicles and fuels, aimed at the long and medium term.

Figure 7.27
A bus guideway in Leeds

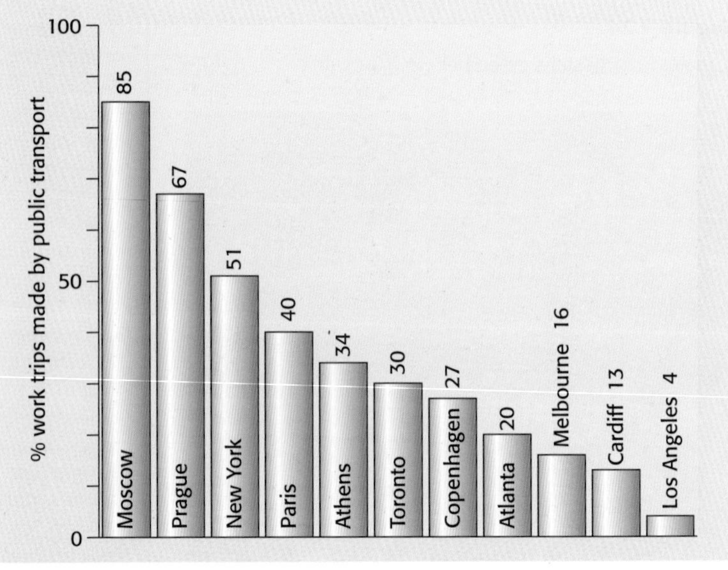

Figure 7.29
Use of public transport in MEDC cities

Policies for conventional vehicles and fuels usually involve setting increasingly tough emissions standards for new vehicles, designed to meet targets for air quality in a city or country. The European Union sets standards for its member countries. Vehicle producers, oil companies and drivers will know in advance what standards are required. Reducing emissions may involve one or more of a number of technological changes:

- Improvements in engine performance to ensure the cleaner and more efficient use of fuel. *Examples:* random roadside smog checks in the UK; regular annual inspections in California.
- New technology to burn fuel more efficiently or remove harmful chemicals after combustion. *Example:* catalytic converters, introduced in the USA in 1977.
- Developing cleaner fuels. *Examples:* European Union ban on leaded petrol from 2000 or Southern California's introduction of low-VOC reformulated petrol under the 1990 Clean Air Act.
- Encouraging drivers to replace inefficient old cars with new ones. Example: Singapore's financial incentives.

In the past two decades such policies have been successful in holding down air pollution in cities, especially in recent years (Figure 7.30). In the future, further reductions will require the development of alternative vehicles and fuels:

- Low emission vehicles (LEV) using alternative fuels such as Liquified Petroleum Gas (LPG) or combinations of petrol-engines and batteries.
- Zero emission vehicles (ZEVs) using fuel cells to generate electricity by combining hydrogen and oxygen, with water as the only 'exhaust' product. Ford intends to have its first ZEV on the road by 2005.

Vehicle makers are developing new technologies but they know that the first alternative vehicles will be costly and they do not know whether there will be a market. In 1995 Southern California set standards requiring 2 per cent of vehicles on the region's roads to be ZEVs by 2003, with the proportion rising to 10 per cent in later years. Manufacturers are therefore assured of a market in advance, encouraging them to invest in researching the technology.

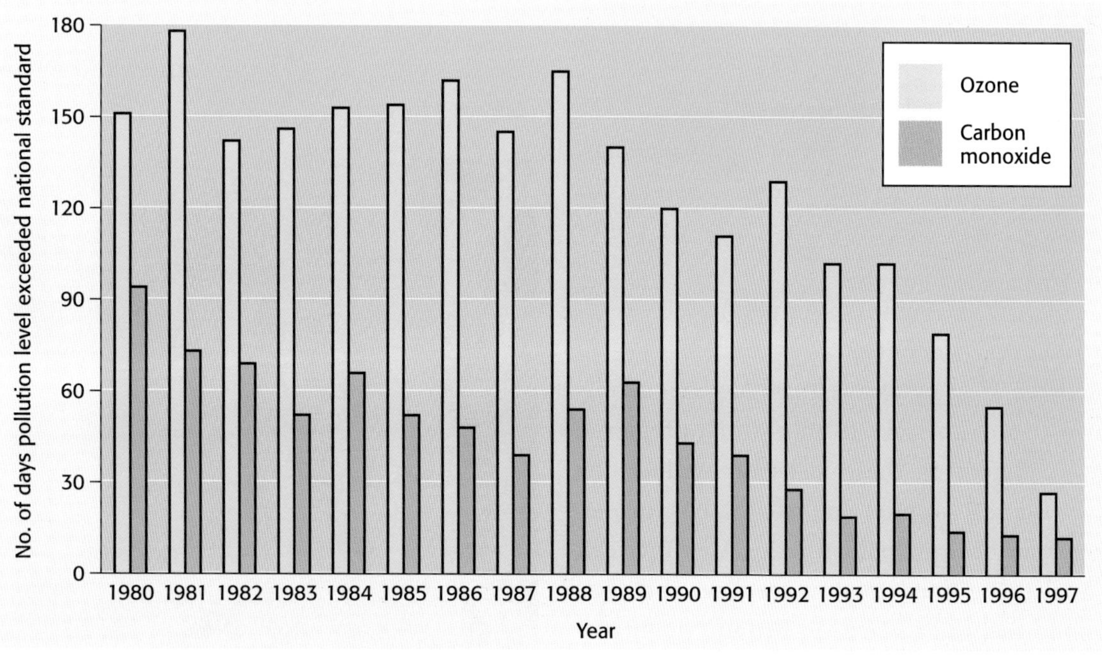

Figure 7.30
Air quality in Los Angeles, 1980–97

Case Study: Zürich, Switzerland

Zürich is one of Europe's wealthiest cities, the largest in Switzerland and the country's financial and banking centre. The metropolitan area has grown to over 1.1 million. Despite the growth in its wealth, Zürich has succeeded in persuading its citizens to chose public transport over the car.

The main motivation for its transport strategy was Switzerland's clean air laws introduced in the 1980s. The decision was made to plan for an actual reduction in traffic, the first of its kind by a European city. From 1988 onwards Zürich set out a number of transport goals:

- a reduction in on-street parking from 61 000 to 51 000 places by 1990
- the development of a Veloroute Network, with over 300 km of cycle track separated from the main traffic routes
- improvements in the bus and tram system with priority lanes and traffic lights (Figure 7.31)
- the development of 400 km of suburban railway network (S-Bahn) with radial and 'spoke' lines – each of the 40 stations is linked to the cycle network
- the establishment of a single transport authority for the whole region – the Zürich Transport Association – offering multi-modal tickets, uniform fares and a co-ordinated timetable.

The transport planners have also ensured that virtually everyone lives close to a bus stop, tram stop or S-Bahn station. They have managed to increase the proportion of journeys taken by public transport to three-quarters, one of the highest in Europe. The volume of car traffic has not grown.

Figure 7.31
Part of the tram system in Zürich, Switzerland

Water supply

Apart from increasing the supply of water by building more dams, reservoirs and aqueducts, there are also policies to reduce demand for water. There are two main kinds of policy response:

- reducing waste and consumption
- re-using waste water.

In urban areas up to one-third of water supply is lost through leaks from old or unrepaired pipes. Repairing these leaks can reduce the need for new supplies. In the USA, Los Angeles water authorities paid for the All American Canal to be lined to stop seepage, and thus gained the water saved. In Britain, the privatised water utility companies have been obliged by the regulatory authority, OFWAT, to adopt a rigorous policy of leak prevention and repair (Figure 7.32).

Figure 7.32
Leakage from the water mains in Britain

Water consumption may fall in the urban areas of MEDCs because industries using a lot of water, such as brewing, are closing down in cities. Nonetheless, consumers can also be encouraged to use water more wisely, for instance by introducing water metering. A metering trial in the Isle of Wight led to a 20 per cent drop in water consumption. Redesigned toilets and showers can save up to 80 per cent of the water currently used. Savings in gardens are also possible by changing to plant species that use less water. In the arid south-west USA, new houses are as likely to feature cactus gardens as traditional grass lawns.

Finally, water used for one purpose may be re-used for others rather than flushed away. In Tucson, Arizona, for example, domestic waste water is recycled for aquifer recharge, use in cooling systems and on golf courses. Recycling water is a national policy in Israel, where 30 per cent is re-used. A good example of waste water processing being used to create power can be found in the Thames valley. Here, Thames Water has opened two generators powered by the sludge derived from processed sewage. The amount of 'green' electricity generated is sufficient to provide heat and light for about 35 000 people.

Waste disposal

There are three main ways of reducing the amount of solid waste requiring disposal:

- re-using materials
- recovering or recycling materials
- preventing waste.

Many items can be re-used rather than thrown away. For example, glass milk bottles are used on average 24 times each in the UK. Supermarkets may encourage shoppers to re-use plastic carrier bags.

Other materials can be recycled or recovered. This approach is particularly suitable for paper products, glass and cans. While the amount of recycling is partly dependent on technology, it is mainly a function of national or local laws and initiatives requiring, or encouraging, recovery. Considerable differences in these arrangements explain why the rates of recycling vary so much from country to country (Figure 7.33), and, in the case of England, from district to district. In Buckinghamshire, for example, Chiltern District Council (35 500 households) provides for the collection of household plastic waste, whereas the neighbouring Wycombe District Council, with a substantially greater number of households (59 000), does not.

Germany (Figure 7.34) has led the way in the European Union, with tough regulations introduced in 1991 requiring manufacturers to be responsible for recovering waste packaging. Berlin pioneered the use of separate bins for different kinds of household waste – paper, glass and cans. British cities have also adopted the idea. Since 1994, the European Union has set targets for recycling which all member countries must meet. Many US states require newsprint to contain 40–50 per cent recycled

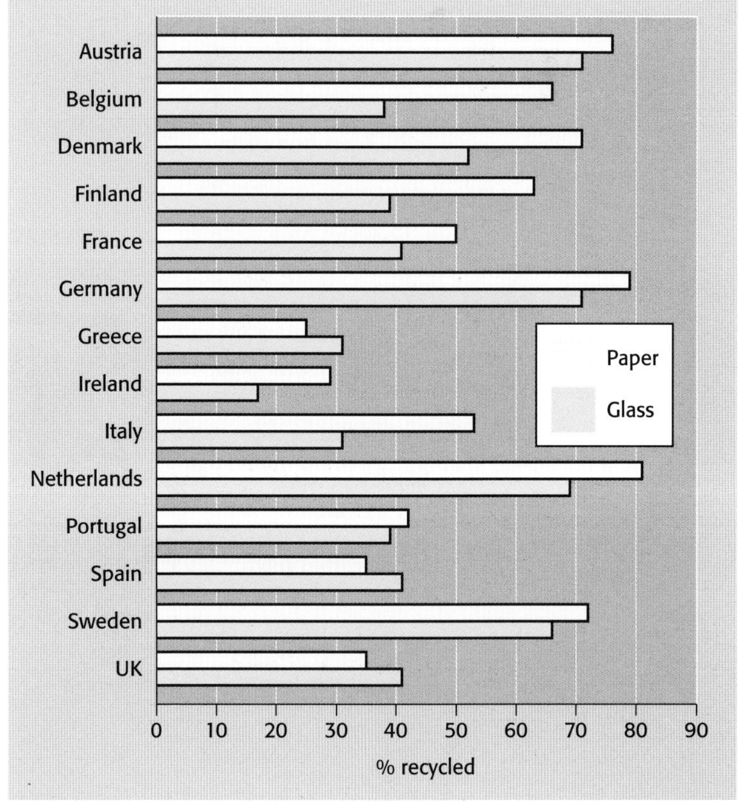

Figure 7.33
Recycling rates for paper and glass in Europe

fibre. Consumers and businesses can also be given financial incentives to re-use and recycle material. Germany, Denmark and Sweden, for example, require returnable deposits on plastic bottles.

Most MEDCs have greatly increased the amount recycled in the past 20 years. But in the longer run the answer to waste disposal may lie in a combination of prevention, changed attitudes and modified lifestyles, if rising levels of consumption are to result in less waste (Figure 7.35).

Figure 7.34
Municipal recycling site in the Bavarian Forest National Park

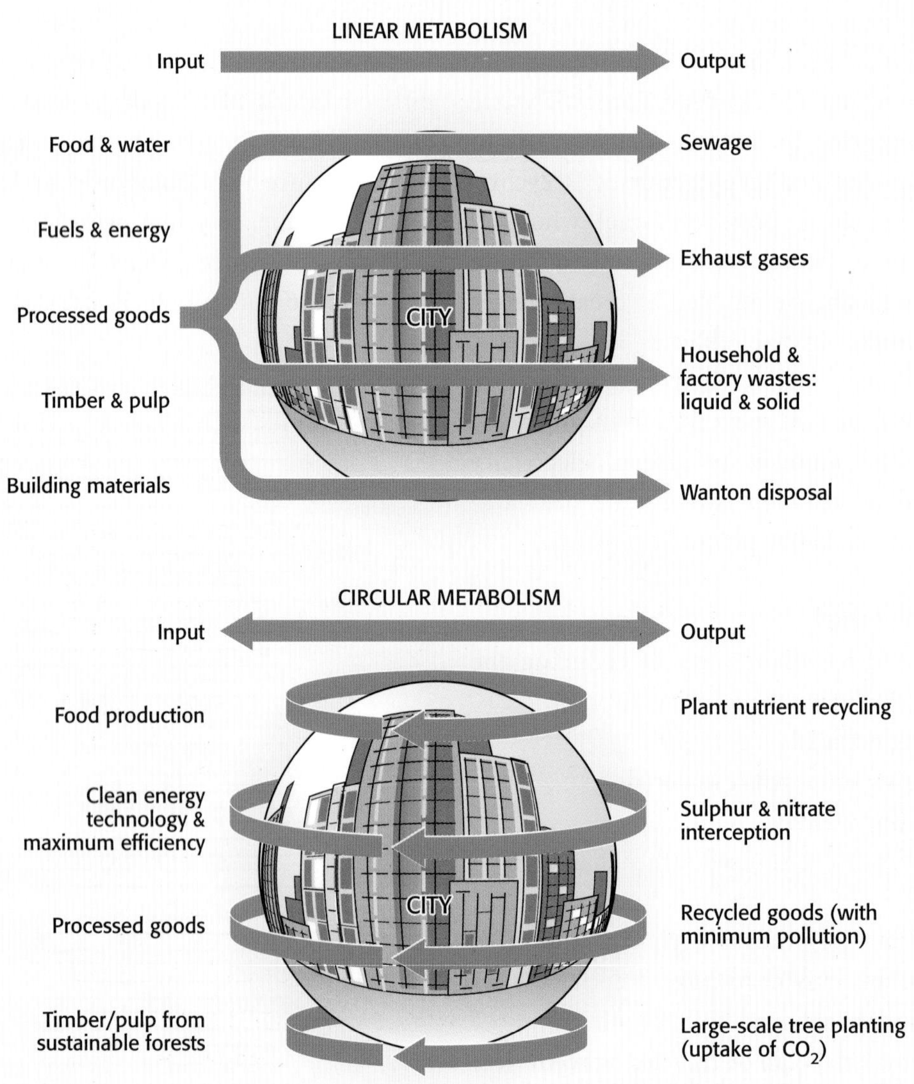

Figure 7.35
Linear and circular metabolisms of the city

Activity

Planning England's urban future: the sustainable city

- *The problem:* In 1999 the Department of Environment, Transport and the Regions (DETR) projected that England would require 3.8 million new households between 1996 and 2021. As noted in Chapter 6, the main cause of this increase will not be population growth but the rise in the number of smaller households.
- Where will these households go? The DETR intends that 60 per cent will be added to existing urban areas on so-called brownfield sites, in contrast to undeveloped areas or greenfield sites. Environmental groups say that 75 per cent should be in brownfield areas. Developers and builders want a figure nearer 40 per cent.

Task

On the basis of the issues raised in this chapter, hold a class discussion around the following questions:

1. What are the main issues involved in deciding where new houses should be located?
2. Should governments tell people and businesses where they can locate?
3. What proportion of households should be in greenfield and brownfield sites?
4. How can these targets be met by planning?
5. What are the regional aspects of the issue?

The following facts may help your discussion; you may be aware of others:

- 11 per cent of Britain's land surface is urbanised.
- Each year 250 000 people choose to leave British cities and only 160 000 choose to move to them.
- The National Land Use survey found that there is enough vacant land in cities for 2.5 million medium-density homes, but much of this land is in northern cities.
- Newcastle has 7000 empty dwellings.
- Eighty per cent of future demand will be from single-person households.
- At current rates, 30 per cent of the South East will be built up by 2050.

When you have completed your discussions, select a residential area you know well. Imagine that the number of dwellings is to be increased by about 15 per cent. Write a series of statements in favour of, and against, the proposal. Estimate how much growth might be accommodated without significantly altering the environment of the area, and without putting undue strain on the local infrastructure and existing services.

8 Contemporary urbanisation in LEDCs

Key Themes

- ✔ The highest rates of urbanisation occur in the less economically developed countries of the world.
- ✔ The perceived advantages of one particular city may result in an above-average level of inward migration sufficient to create a 'super' or primate city far larger than all the other urban centres in a country.
- ✔ Despite the problems of living in a rapidly expanding urban area where the infrastructure and facilities cannot keep pace with the growth in population, the quality of life is often considered to be superior to that in remote rural regions.
- ✔ Population pressure and declining agricultural resources in rural areas combine to increase the pace of urbanisation in many developing countries.

Urbanisation in developing countries

This chapter is concerned with the processes responsible for urban growth in less economically developed countries (LEDCs), and the social and economic implications for the cities themselves and for the surrounding rural areas. During the last 50 or 60 years the highest rates of **urbanisation** have been in the less developed regions of the world. This trend is illustrated in Figure 8.1, which not only compares levels of urban population among the continents since 1950 to the present day, but also shows the further growth expected by the year 2030. In 1970, one in four people living in the LEDCs were urban dwellers; now the figure is about two in every five. At 75 per cent, the proportion of urban dwellers in Latin America is already close to that in Europe and North America, while in Africa and Asia urban growth during the first 30 years of the 21st century will result in a further 1900 million people becoming urbanised.

One increasingly important aspect of urbanisation in the LEDCs is the way in which urban populations are becoming concentrated in a relatively small number of **megacities** – that is, cities with over 10 million people. Figure 8.2 compares the growth of these cities from 1975 to 2015. As the graphs show, the development of megacities is very much a feature of Asia, where particularly high levels of natural increase and inward migration have underpinned a huge expansion of the urban population.

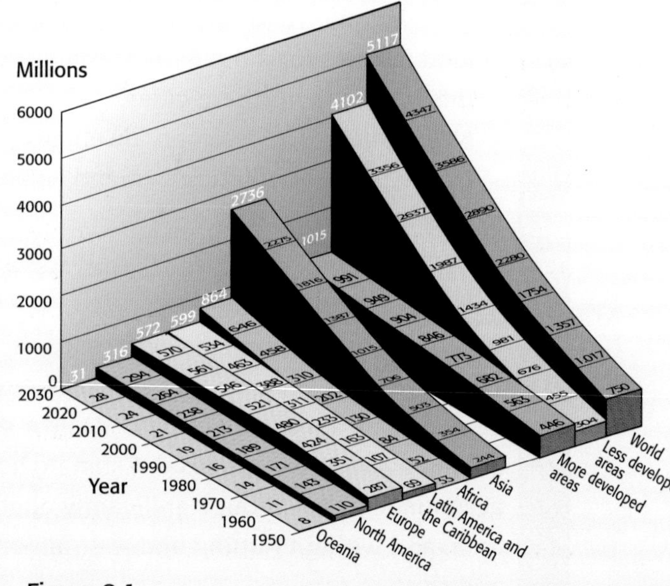

Figure 8.1
Worldwide urban populations, 1950–2030

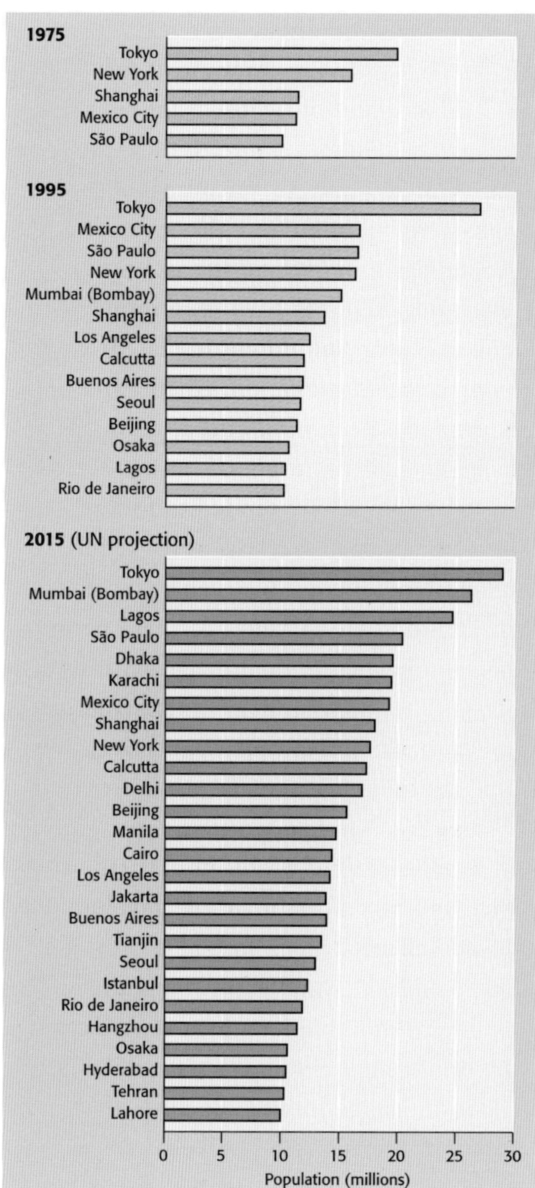

Figure 8.2
The growth of megacities, 1975–2015

Rural–urban migration in LEDCs

Large-scale migration from countryside to city is a feature of many developing countries. Relatively poor economic and living conditions in the country, perhaps coupled with environmental deterioration (Figure 8.3), or displacement through resettlement and large-scale development projects which upset traditional patterns of life, act as powerful **push factors** causing people to leave rural areas in search of a better life. At the same time, it is the large urban areas that exert the most pull. Typical **pull factors** are perceptions of greater wealth, better occupational opportunities and higher living standards, all of which are more likely to be found in larger rather than smaller towns. Quite often one particular urban area is the target of most migrants, leading to the creation of a city which far exceeds all others in terms of its population and physical size. These cities are known as **primate cities** simply because of their dominance. The study of one example – Mexico City – forms the major part of this chapter.

Figure 8.3
Seriously deteriorating environmental conditions in the Sahel. Drought is turning this farmer's fields into deserts (Burkino Faso).

Declining rural fortunes

Although large urban concentrations in LEDCs may be crowded, and living conditions in some districts may leave a lot to be desired, the resource base of the city is far more capable of supporting large populations than that of the rural regions. In fact, national population pyramids of developing countries are often more typical of population structures in rural districts than in the urban areas, thus adding to the pressure on the countryside. Figure 8.4 compares the population structure of Mexico City with that of the country as a whole; the narrower base of the urban pyramid indicates a substantially smaller number of children.

In the developing world the most pronounced impact of **population pressure** in rural areas is on the natural resources of soil, water and forests. These resources are not always as renew-

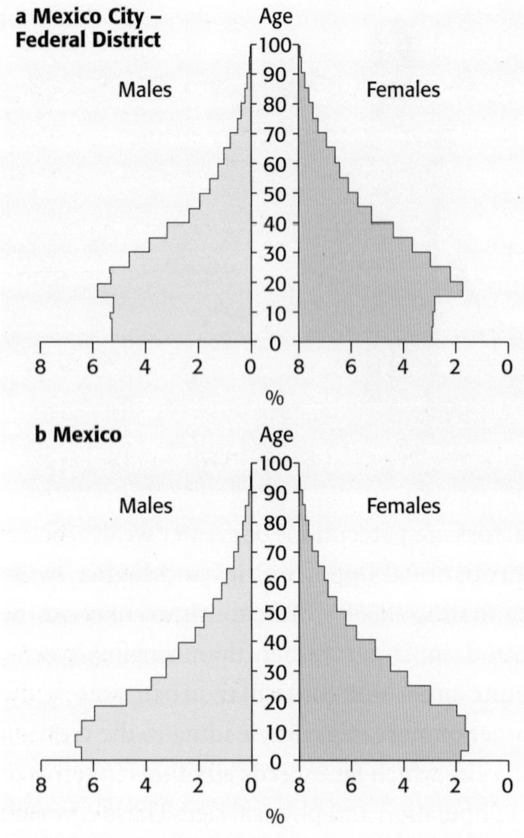

Figure 8.4

Population pyramids for Mexico City and Mexico, 1990

able as they are claimed to be. It is estimated that about 75 per cent of rural dwellers in the LEDCs live in ecologically fragile areas. Poverty obliges them to exploit limited resources to the full, leading to overgrazing, overcropping and the overcutting of woodland. Once productive land is readily lost. In India, for example, about 26 000 km^2 of land (an area equivalent to a country the size of Rwanda) have been lost to agriculture through erosion, salinisation and waterlogging brought about by the over-intensive use of farm land. An expanding rural population also means that existing land is divided into ever smaller plots. In many LEDCs, the majority of farms are now less than one hectare in size and can no longer support a family. As a result, marginal land is pressed into use which may require the destruction of forest cover. In India, Pakistan and Bangladesh, more than 30 million rural households now have no land at all. The Food and Agriculture Organisation (FAO) of the UN estimates that 65 per cent of the land that is now usable for cropping in Asia, Africa and Latin America will be lost by the year 2100.

Ironically, schemes designed to improve life in rural areas, and to encourage people to remain in them, often have the opposite effect. In some parts of Africa, for example, rural regeneration schemes have been implemented (Figure 8.5), but sometimes too late to reverse the march of desertification. Where export crop schemes have been introduced, reductions in soil fertility and the abandonment of anti-erosion practices have tended to follow. Their long-term impact has been to reduce the number of local people who can be sustained by farming and hence to trigger further migration. Other approaches have also met with limited success. The provision of infrastructure – schools, roads, health centres and electricity – has not automatically made rural areas more attractive but it has added to the cost of living there, and heightened problems of rural poverty.

The substantial growth of **development-induced schemes** has also had a pronounced impact, displacing rural populations and further encouraging movement to the towns. According to a World Bank review, up to 100 million people worldwide were moved against their will between 1985 and 1995. Hydro-electric and water conservation projects have been largely

Figure 8.5

Farmers in West Africa are shown how to conserve precious water resources by building small stone terraces to trap rainwater

Figure 8.6

A large industrial site in India that required the displacement of local people

responsible for this exodus, and it is estimated that between 1 and 2 million people are displaced annually as a result of such schemes. Unknown numbers are relocated as a result of forestry, mining, park development and the building of transport corridors and industrial plants (Figure 8.6). In India, approximately 20 million people have been displaced by development projects since 1950, and in China the figure is put at 10 million. For developing countries, particularly those with rapidly growing populations, a balance has to be achieved between national development projects and the costs of resettlement and continuing urban growth.

The attraction of urban areas

Despite the well-publicised disadvantages of life in the megacities of the developing world – poor housing in shanty towns, water and power shortages, and pollution – people from rural areas appear to find them irresistible. The fact is that these cities are highly active places with relatively strong **formal** and **informal economies** which create far more wealth than can ever be generated in the rural regions. The concentration of physical infrastructure (water supply, roads, power, etc.) and social facilities (education and health facilities, etc.) plays a major role in the growth of productivity. This growth could not take place if attempts were made to disperse such an infrastructure throughout the country, because of the high costs involved. Moreover, large urban concentrations create a substantial market for agricultural production and thus have the potential to stimulate rural development. However, the gap between urban and rural productivity, already wide in most LEDCs, continues to grow and the likelihood of rural areas finding themselves at a permanent disadvantage is high.

Urban areas now generate between 60 per cent and 80 per cent of the Gross National Product (GNP) in developing countries. Further, the higher the level of urbanisation, the higher is the GNP per capita of the entire population. Figure 8.7, based on 52 developing countries, illustrates this relationship. Although the degree of correlation is modest, and there are noticeable exceptions, the general trend is clear, especially above the 30 per cent level of urbanisation. In the light of this relationship, urbanisation assumes great significance as a tool of economic development. It is attractive to urban and rural dwellers alike, and is unlikely to be curtailed regardless of any attempts to develop the economies of rural areas.

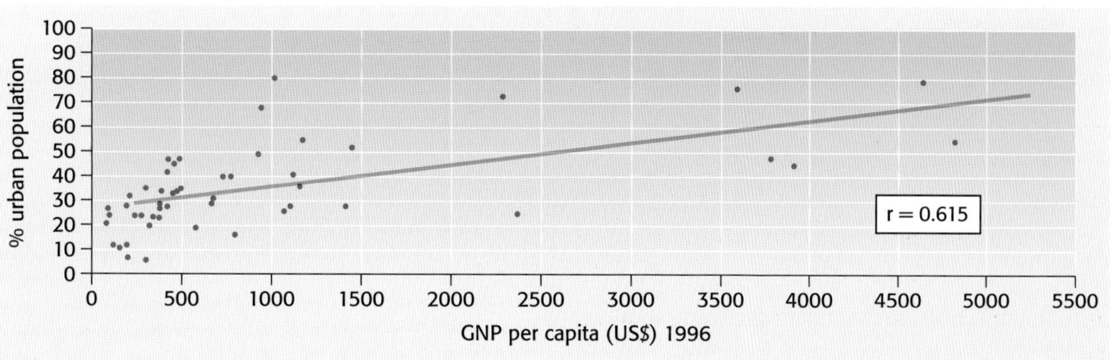

Figure 8.7

Levels of urbanisation and GNP per capita. The graph is based on 52 developing countries in Africa, Latin America and Asia.

Case Study: Urban growth and urbanisation in Mexico

The rate of population and urban growth in Mexico during the 20th century was epic. Before 1860 the total population grew only at a slow rate but after the dismantling of many large religious and civil land holdings by the reform laws of 1859, it increased steadily to 13 million by 1900. For much of the 20th century, a growth rate of nearly 2 per cent resulted in the population reaching 81 million people in 1990 and 97 million by 1997.

This overall growth in population has been accompanied by a remarkable concentration of people in urban areas. Until 1910 there was little internal migration in Mexico, mostly because of the dominance of the hacienda system which kept workers virtually bound to the farms on which they were employed. Following the Revolution of 1910, a new constitution was introduced which further revised the rules of land ownership and allowed people to move around the country. Many migrated to the cities and towns, setting off the intense rate of urban growth which continues to this day.

The association of urban dwelling with economic prosperity accounts for the high rate of urbanisation in Mexico. In the urban areas there are higher levels of education, literacy, vehicle ownership and access to telephones, whereas in the rural areas the population is considered to be marginalised. Urban areas provide higher salaries, more services and more employment, including employment for females, whereas the rural areas have higher dependency ratios, higher fertility rates, more households with lower incomes and more households without electricity and immediate access to toilets.

From 1930 there were large increases in the urban population in all the Mexican states (Figure 8.8), especially in the state of Mexico and the nearby states of Queretaro and Tlaxcala as

Figure 8.8 The states and main cities of Mexico

well as in Baja California. Although this urban increase was initially due to migration, many of the migrants were young and the urban population rose further as a result of natural increase. In the last half of the 20th century, Mexico's urban population expanded nearly six times, from 13 million in 1950 to 73 million in 1997. Over the same period, the rural population increased by only one-third, from 17 million to 23 million. Today, 50 per cent of Mexicans live in cities of 50 000 or more people, and over 76 per cent of the population is classed as urban.

Figure 8.9 illustrates these trends in percentage terms since 1900, but despite the level of change, the *pattern* of urban growth has altered little. Today, the **geographic concentration** of population and economic activity is one of the most remarkable aspects of modern Mexico. A major urban axis occupies a narrow band across central Mexico from Puebla de Zaragoza to Guadalajara, with the greatest concentration of people and industry in Mexico City, which has consistently attracted the largest number of rural migrants to make it the leading urban centre in Mexico.

In addition to this central urban zone, important urban centres are also to be found on the US–Mexican border. These towns and cities have strong economic links with neighbouring US cities, and through the North American Free Trade Agreement (NAFTA) they have become major centres of economic growth. The *maquiladora* 'twin plant' programme has acted as an important catalyst for economic development and urban growth, especially since the 1980s. The **maquiladora industries** are those where intermediate materials produced on the US side of the border are processed or assembled on the Mexican side and then returned to the USA for subsequent sale. The border location is popular with US companies because labour, particularly migrant female labour, is plentiful and wages and taxes are low. The number of maquiladoras and people employed in them has increased substantially over the years. In 1968 there were 79 such firms employing 17 000 people. By 1988 the number of firms had risen to 1400 employing nearly 370 000 workers. In 1999 there were more than 3000 twin plants which between them provided 1 million jobs.

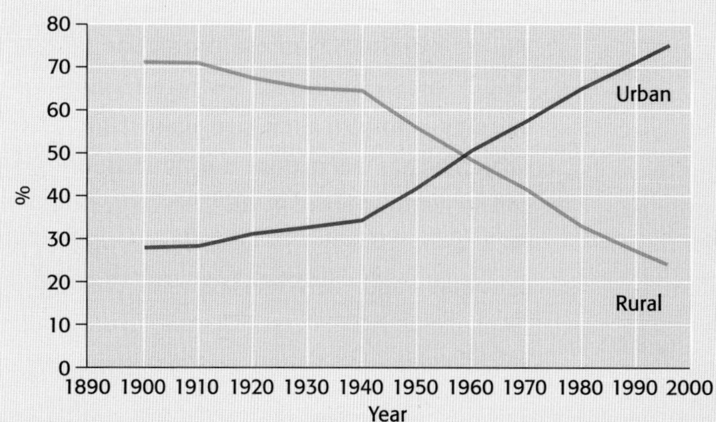

Figure 8.9
Changes in the balance of urban and rural population in Mexico, 1900–90

During the 1980s both the Mexican and US border cities grew more rapidly than other urban centres in either country. Mexican cities in the border region grew by 42 per cent compared with a national average of 22 per cent; their US counterparts grew by about 25 per cent compared with 10 per cent nationally. The Mexican sectors of these cities have also tended to grow at a faster rate than the US parts, reflecting the continuing concentration of economic growth along the border and demonstrating Mexican dependence on the USA for investment and employment.

Nevertheless there are some differences between the states of the border regions. Population growth in Baja California, for example, has been above average because it acts as the main channel for Mexicans intending to enter the USA, and it has benefited from its proximity to the large and prosperous regional economy of California. By contrast, growth in the state of Tamaulipas has been at a much slower rate because it is located in an economically depressed region adjacent to the south Texas border.

The Mexican urban hierarchy

Most countries exhibit an **urban hierarchy** where one primate city, possibly the capital, is the leading centre in terms of economic wealth and growth, services and cultural and political status. A useful way of examining the relationship between the major towns and cities of a country is to plot their size against their rank order, as has been done for four developing countries on Figure 8.10. The largest city of each country exhibits a different degree of primacy. Lagos in Nigeria shows the highest level, being more than six times larger than the second city, while Jakarta is a little more than three times the size of Indonesia's second city.

The growth of Mexico City

Mexico City is located in a high-altitude basin at 2200 m, surrounded by mountains reaching above 5000 m. Two corridors located to the

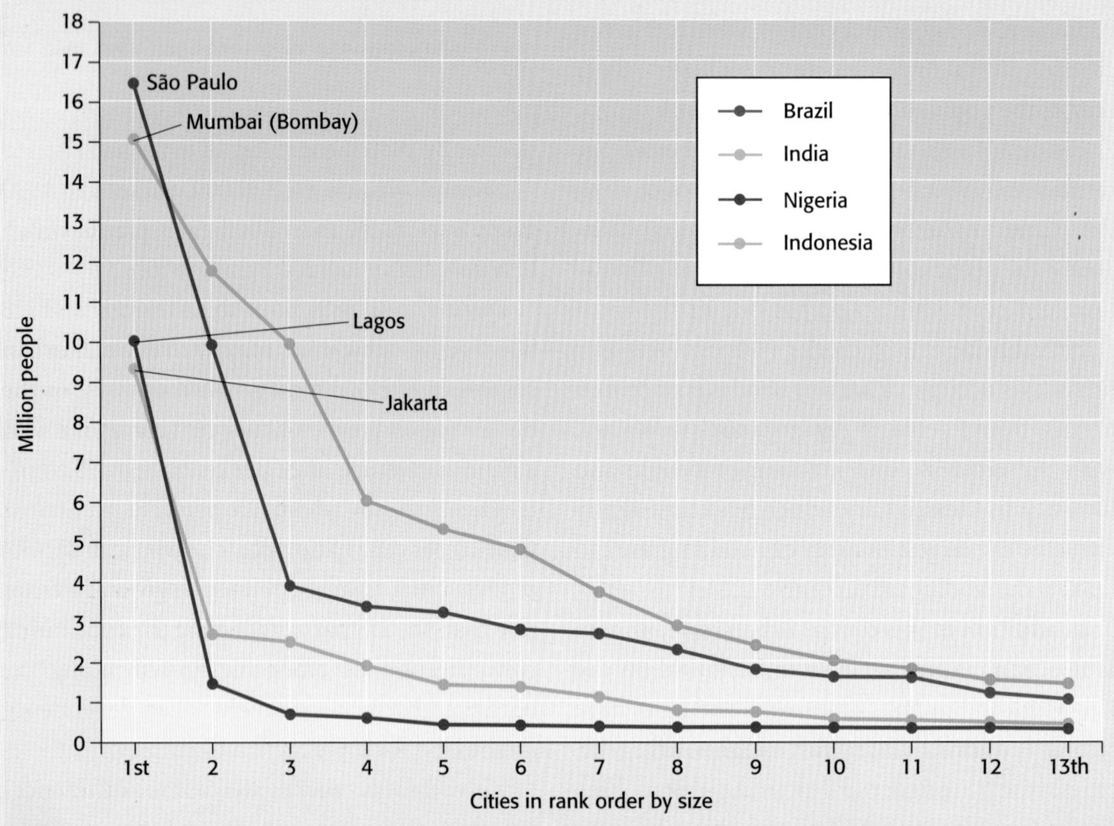

Figure 8.10 The urban hierarchy of four developing countries. The graph shows the 13 largest cities in each country.

Activity

1. Referring to Figure 8.11, and using proportional shading, represent the population density data for each of the Mexican states on a copy of Figure 8.8.
2. On your map, locate the main cities listed in Figure 8.12. For each one add a proportional bar showing the size of the city.
3. Describe the relationship between the overall distribution of population in Mexico and the location of the main urban centres. Is there any apparent relationship between density and the location of the main towns and cities?
4. On a copy of Figure 8.10, plot the points for each city listed in Figure 8.12, and draw in the line.
5. How does Mexico compare with the other developing countries shown on Figure 8.10 in terms of the relationship between its principal city and other urban centres? Can you offer an explanation for the differences and similarities among the five countries?

State	Population density (persons per km^2, rounded values)
Aguascalientes	166
Baja California	30
Baja California Sur	5
Campeche	11
Chiapas	49
Chihuahua	11
Coahuila	15
Colima	90
Durango	12
Guanajuato	143
Guerrero	45
Hidalgo	103
Jalisco	76
Mexico City (Federal District)	5487
Mexico State	552
Michoacan	67
Morelos	290
Nayarit	33
Nuevo Leon	55
Oaxaca	35
Puebla	136
Queretaro	104
Quitana Roo	18
San Luis Potosi	35
Sinaloa	43
Sonora	12
Tabasco	71
Tamaulipas	32
Tlaxcala	219
Veracruz	94
Yucatan	36
Zacatecas	18

Figure 8.11

Population density of the Mexican states, 1995

City	Population
Mexico City*	15.15
Guadalajara*	2.87
Monterrey*	2.56
Puebla de Zaragoza*	1.27
Toluca de Lerdo*	0.82
Ciudad Juarez	0.79
Leon	0.76
Tijuana	0.75
San Luis Potosi	0.69
Torreon	0.68
Zapopan	0.67
Merida	0.60
Cuernavaca*	0.54

* Figure applies to the entire urbanised area

Figure 8.12

Population of the 13 largest cities in Mexico (millions), 1995

north-east and north-west funnel air to the centre of the city but do little to aid the dispersal of pollutants emitted from the city itself. Much of the built-up area is located upon a former lake-bed which makes part of the city especially vulnerable to land subsidence and to earthquake damage.

Mexico City as a whole – perhaps more aptly known as **Mexico Megacity** – consists of the capital Federal District (which occupies an area of 1500 km^2) and 17 adjoining counties in the state of Mexico. The total metropolitan area is now approaching 3700 km^2 in area, ten times its size in 1940 (Figure 8.13).

Mexico City has been described as an example of **pathological urban development**. Even at the start of the 20th century, Mexico City was the most important city in Mexico, ideally located to attract migrants. It had the most sophisticated infrastructure, the largest consumer market and the greatest concentration of the few industries in existence at that time. It was also the home of the national government. In 1900 Mexico City's population was 344 000 and was growing at an annual rate of 3.1 per cent, largely as a result of migration. Although migration slowed somewhat during the 1930s, there was a fairly constant population increase between 1900 and 1970, the City growing at about 4.6 per cent per year – that is, doubling every 15 years or so. Today the Federal District has a population of 10 million, while estimates vary from 15 million to 20 million people for the population of the metropolitan area as a whole. It is certainly close to one-sixth of the total population of the country.

Mexico City's importance relative to the country's other urban centres has changed noticeably over time. In 1803 Mexico City was only twice as large as the second largest city which was then Puebla. By 1900 it had become 3.4 times larger than the next city which was then (as now) Guadalajara. It is now more than five times larger than Guadalajara.

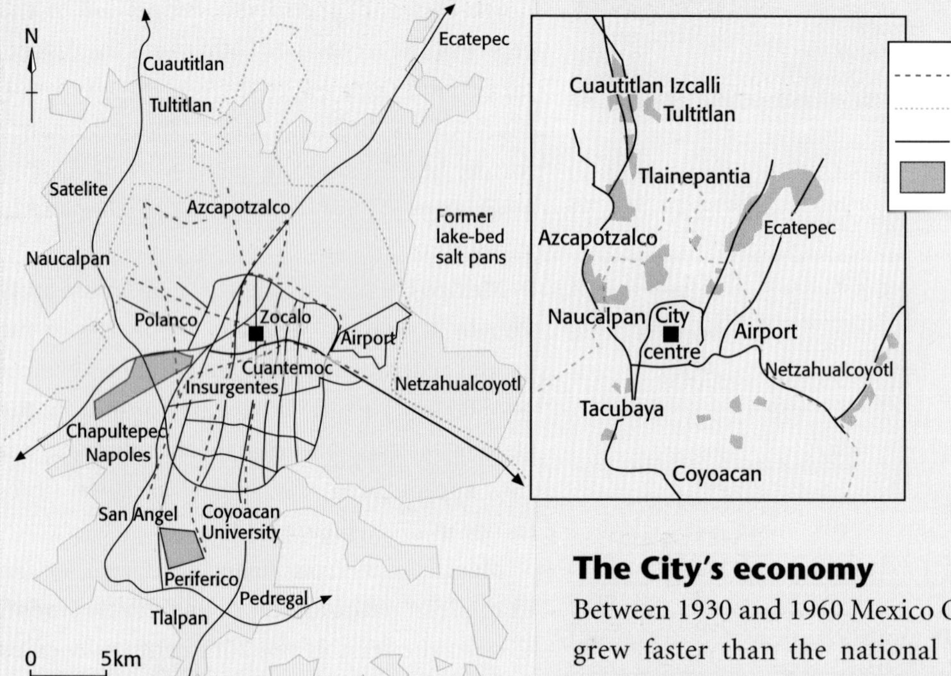

Figure 8.13
Mexico City – the urban area and key industrial concentrations

The role of migration

Migration has played a major role in the growth of Mexico Megacity. Most people came from the central and southern regions of the country (Figure 8.14), many making journeys of only 150 km. Net migration into the state of Mexico grew substantially from about 1 million during the 1960s to close on 3.5 million during the 1980s (Figure 8.15a), largely undeterred by the earthquake of September 1985 which killed more than 10 000 people. Many new arrivals sought land on which to build their homes, and since land was increasingly scarce in the Federal District, they turned to the surrounding area, particularly to the north of the Federal District in a rapidly growing and now very large industrialised zone. One million people moved out from the Federal District during the 1980s as space became short and the central city environment declined (Figure 8.15b), thus adding to the sprawling growth of the metropolitan area. Today, it is estimated that 2000 people arrive in the city each day despite attempts by the Mexican Government to stem migration to the urban areas by decentralising industry and opening up new farmlands through irrigation and land reform.

The City's economy

Between 1930 and 1960 Mexico City's economy grew faster than the national economy and transformed the city's industrial base. Growth stemmed largely from the city's rapidly expanding population but also from increased productivity and the broadening of the urban economy to encompass a range of manufacturing and service industries beyond the traditional food and textiles. The government's attempt to develop import substitution industries (ISIs) also proved a boost for industry. Today the megacity is the industrial, financial and retail centre of the country, generating more than one-third of Mexico's wealth.

The most important products of Mexico City's economy are metal goods and machinery, chemicals, petrochemicals, food, drink and tobacco. The main services are wholesale and retail commerce, specialised professional and technical services, and hotel, restaurant and leisure services.

The distribution of the major economic activities is varied. The **industrial sector** is mostly in the northern part of the Federal District in huge industrial zones, especially Azcapotzalco and Ecatepec (Figure 8.13). Ecatepec, which is the largest single industrial complex in Mexico, occupies a vast site close to the city centre. Industry located on the semi-urban periphery tends to be textiles, clothing, food, drink and tobacco. The

commercial and **service sectors** of the city's economy are firmly concentrated in the old city centre where they have been traditionally located.

Employment and labour

Mexico City has about 6 million workers, of which males outnumber females by two to one. Employment opportunities in the city centre are especially attractive to skilled female workers because there is a greater proportion of **service occupations** there. However, there are sharp gender differences in the employment market, and the activity rate for females at 37 per cent is half of that for males, and much lower than the 70 per cent female activity rate typical of the USA. When the increasing number of female workers is coupled to the rising number of people of working age across the country as whole, the Mexican labour force is estimated to be rising at about 1 million

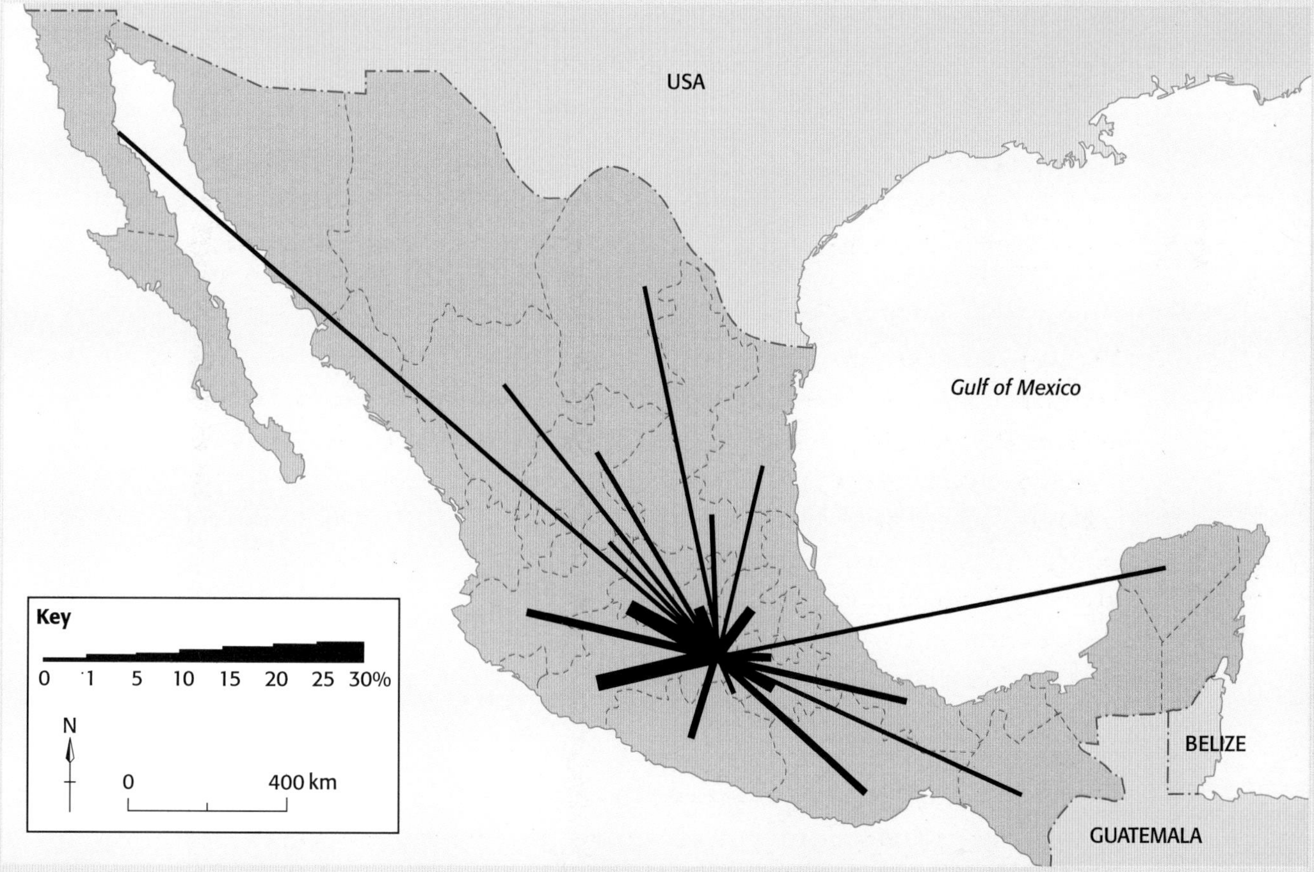

Figure 8.14
Flows of migrants to the Mexico City region during the 1970s

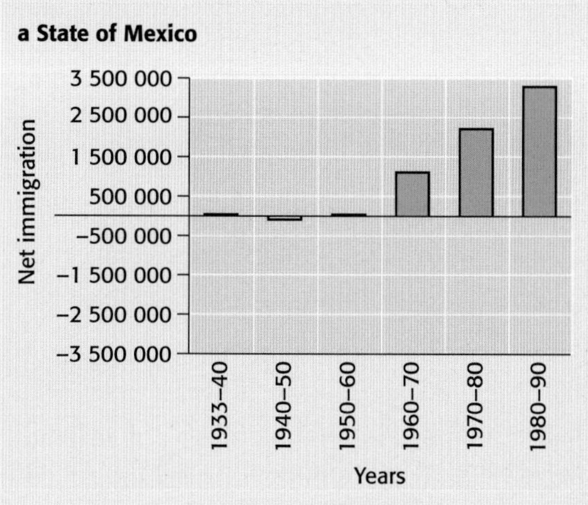

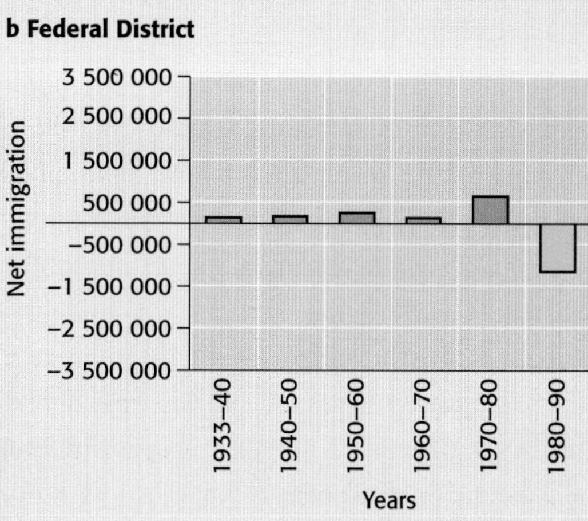

Figure 8.15
Net migration to **a** the state of Mexico **b** the Federal District of Mexico City

people per year. Much of this increase will occur in Mexico City where the availability of a productive and inexpensive labour force (relative to the USA and other developed countries) will further attract multinational corporations to the region.

The spatial structure of Mexico City

Mexico City conforms to a reasonable degree with the model of Latin American cities put forward by Ford (see Figure 9.3 on page 229), which should be compared with the actual structure of the city shown in Figure 8.16.

The **traditional urban core is** characterised by:

- a high population – nearly 5 million people – but which is declining relatively slowly (by about 8 per cent between 1970 and 1990)
- a low ratio of men to women
- good housing conditions – less than 7 per cent of houses lack a toilet
- good economic prosperity – 79 per cent are owners, employers or salaried workers; less than 2 per cent unemployment
- a low proportion of indigenous people – less than 1 per cent.

In many respects the urban core of Mexico City (Figure 8.17) resembles the cores of cities in MEDCs. **Population density** is high but with some deconcentration as increasing numbers of people move out. Housing is generally good and the level of economic prosperity is relatively high. There is a strong concentration of commerce, financial power and communications in the geographically small central business district (CBD), a feature which is typical of many megacities. The areas of highest social status form a distinct wedge with ready access to the CBD which, again, is suggested by the Griffin and Ford model.

Surrounding the core in a broadly concentric fashion are three zones (A, B and C on Figure 8.16), two of which are densely populated. Their characteristics are as follows.

Zone A

- a large population of almost 6 million
- a high population growth rate; the population doubled between 1970 and 1990
- a fairly even gender ratio
- sound housing quality – 16 per cent lack toilets and 17 per cent have their own septic tank or open flow
- reasonable economic prosperity – 71 per cent are home-owners or employers or salaried workers; 2 per cent unemployment
- a small indigenous population – less than 1 per cent.

Zone B

- a large population of about 4 million people
- modest population growth of about 3 per cent between 1950 and 1970
- a fairly even gender ratio
- sound housing quality – 17 per cent lack a toilet

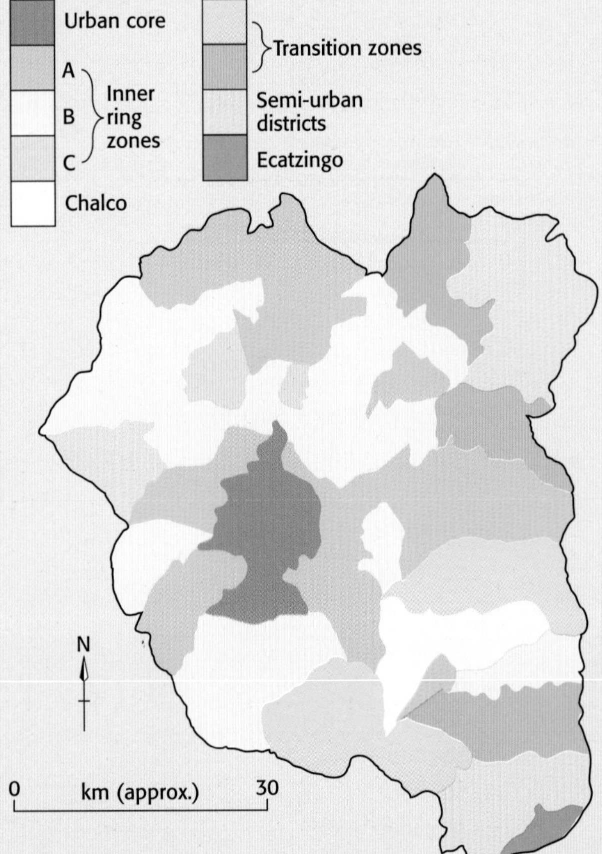

Figure 8.16
The structure of Mexico City

- reasonable economic prosperity – 70 per cent are home-owners or employers or salaried workers; 2 per cent unemployment
- a small indigenous population – 1 per cent.

Zone C

- a relatively small population, less than 500 000
- population growth of 10 per cent between 1970 and 1990
- a fairly even gender ratio
- good housing quality – 4 per cent lack toilet, 4 per cent have own septic tank or open flow
- good economic prosperity – 94 per cent are home-owners, employers or salaried workers; 2 per cent unemployment
- a very small indigenous population.

Adjacent to this ring in the south-east is the Chalco area which is often described as the most impoverished area of Mexico City. It developed as a result of in-migration after 1950, and lacks many public utilities and amenities. It is characterised by:

- a relatively small population of about 300 000 people
- an even gender ratio
- fair housing quality – 17 per cent lacking toilets, 13 per cent depend on septic tank or open flow
- modest economic prosperity – 67 per cent of workers are home-owners, employers or salaried workers; 2.4 per cent unemployment
- a high indigenous population – 3 per cent.

Further away from the centre, to the west, north-east and south-east of the city, are the **semi-urban peripheral districts.** In the north-east and south these areas are separated from the inner ring by transition zones typified by:

- relatively low populations of about 120 000 people
- high population growth – 60 per cent between 1970 and 1990
- a relatively even gender ratio
- poor housing quality – 32 per cent without toilet
- modest economic prosperity – only 8 per cent are home-owners, employers or salaried workers; 2 per cent unemployment.

Figure 8.17
Mexico City CBD

The semi-urban districts themselves have many rural characteristics but by virtue of **urban sprawl** are classified as being part of the Mexico City conurbation. Typical features of these areas are:

- low populations – about 100 000 people
- high population growth – up to 80 per cent between 1970 and 1990
- an even gender ratio
- poor quality housing – nearly 50 per cent lack toilets and 16 per cent depend on septic tanks, or open flow; 16 per cent lack running water
- high use of wood and coal for fuel
- limited economic prosperity – 38 per cent are home-owners, employers or salaried workers; 3 per cent unemployment
- low indigenous population – less than 1 per cent.

In fact, the semi-urban districts are more impoverished and worse off than Chalco, although it is the latter that persists in the public mind as being the worst poverty zone within Mexico City. While many of the earlier temporary settlements (*ciudades perdidas* or 'lost cities') situated nearer the city centre have now become established districts (Figure 8.18), the most recent squatter settlements are located on the steep upland areas towards the boundaries of the metropolitan area where it is particularly hard to provide even the basic services such as a piped water supply. The Ecatzingo district to the extreme south-east is one such case, located on rough terrain next to the huge Orcanic mountain. The level of **urban deprivation** is high and housing quality in such districts is very poor (Figure 8.19).

Environmental problems facing Mexico City

Mexico City and the surrounding area suffer from most of the environmental problems that beset large and rapidly growing urban areas in developing countries. The Vallé de Mexico has lost 99 per cent of its lakes, 75 per cent of its woodlands and 71 per cent of its rural land to urbanisation. It is estimated that up to 44 per cent of housing in Mexico City is overcrowded with over 6.3 persons per household, and many dwellings lack basic services such as water, sewerage and electricity. Apart from housing quality, the region's main environmental problems include those relating to water supply, land subsidence, waste disposal and air pollution.

Water supply

Mexico City uses about 60 m^3 of water per second. The groundwater supply is based on the Mexico City aquifer, but this source is close to crisis and about one-third of the city's water now has to be pumped in at great cost from outside the area (Figure 8.20). Long-distance pumping is not only expensive but the risk of loss through leakage is high, and it also reduces water availability in the supply region. There are many environmental problems associated with the supply and use of water. Even as early as 1900, subsidence of the land had been linked to the abstraction of water. Parts of Mexico City subsided by as much as 7 m between 1940 and 1985, and on the city's fringes the annual rate of subsidence is now between 15 and 40 cm. In turn, land subsidence has led to increased problems of flooding during the wet season, including overflows of the wastewater system.

Waste products

Water quality in the Mexico City region is steadily decreasing. Wastewater from Mexico City is carried through an open sewage canal called The Grand Canal (Figure 8.21), and by a deep transmission system known as the Emisor Central. Sewage in the Grand Canal is completely untreated, and at its destination it is used as a fertiliser to irrigate 5500 ha in the state of Mexico and 80 000 ha in the state of

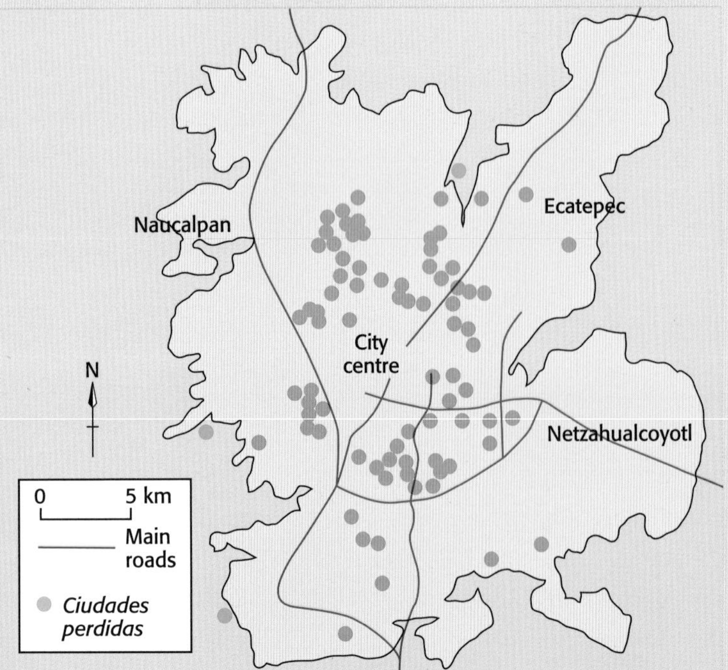

Figure 8.18
The distribution of *ciudades perdidas* ('lost cities') in Mexico City

Figure 8.19
Poor-quality housing in the Santa Fe district of Mexico City

Hidalgo. The high concentration of the nation's industrial production in the area means that there is also a major problem in disposing of hazardous waste. Currently, over 90 per cent of it is released into the sewerage system, and there is evidence that the main aquifer is being polluted – that is, the water supply is being contaminated at source. Serious human health problems are being attributed to the poor water quality, including diarrhoea (especially in infants), cholera, and diseases triggered by exposure to toxic waste.

The problem of solid waste disposal is equally acute. In 1992 over 8000 tonnes of solid waste were generated every day in Mexico City. Large quantities go uncollected. Of that which is collected only about 25 per cent is placed in legal landfill sites at the city's edge (Figure 8.22). Some open-air sites have had to be closed in recent years and the challenge for the future is to provide landfills of sufficient size and quality to accommodate the huge volume of waste generated across the entire urban area. The hope is that new landfills will adhere to higher sanitary standards and help to reduce the impact of uncovered and untreated solid waste on air and water pollution. A programme designed to develop treatment plants for solid waste has made only a very slow start.

Air pollution strategies

Air pollution has developed into a serious issue in Mexico City during the last 20 years. Levels of ozone exceeded safe levels on 71 per cent of days in 1986 and 98 per cent of days in 1992. Pollutants, half of which originate from unburned liquefied petroleum gas used for cooking and heating, are readily trapped in the high-altitude basin. Numerous strategies to control Mexico City's chronic air pollution have been devised, but their implementation has been limited:

- lowering the sulphur content of oil and fuel
- retrofitting buses, vans and trucks to burn natural gas
- limiting carbon monoxide emissions from vehicles
- increasing the use of unleaded fuel and equipping cars with catalytic converters
- restricting commuter traffic, including an extension of the 'no driving today' programme which bans cars from being driven one day per week
- a ban on new industries regarded as potentially polluting
- reducing industrial emissions
- relocation of over 200 foundries and steel mills

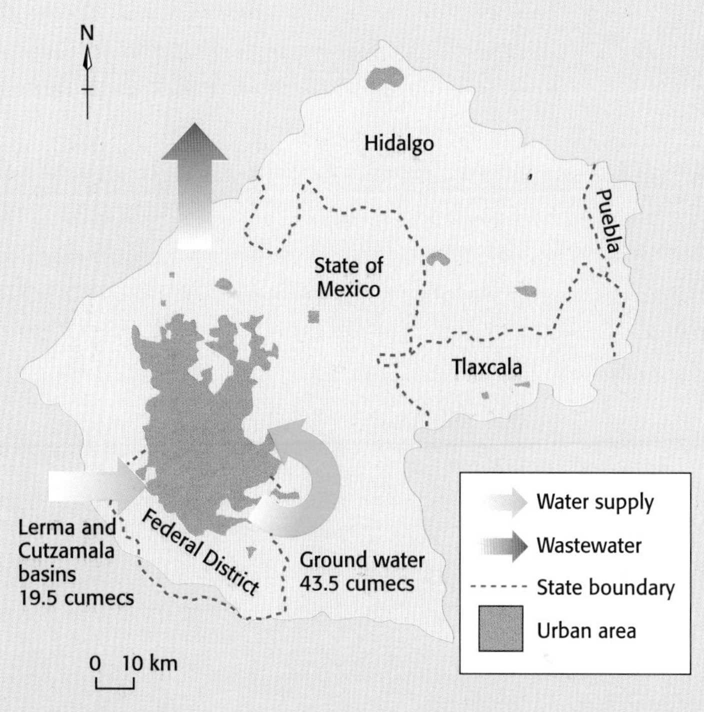

Figure 8.20
Water flows into and out of Mexico City

Figure 8.21
Polluted water in the Grand Canal, Mexico City

- closure of certain buildings and restricting vehicle use during high-pollution periods.

In spite of all these strategies, air pollution has intensified in the area (Figure 8.23). The answer appears to lie in longer-term solutions which have yet to be put into practice, such as a change in the economic basis of the city from polluting industries to service industries, the development of more efficient air pollution control technology, and a programme of reforestation intended to take advantage of the natural ability of plants to clean the atmosphere.

Figure 8.22
Garbage at the city edge

Activity

1 This chapter focuses on Mexico City as an example of a major urban centre within a developing country. Other such centres are shown on Figure 8.2. Select a city from the UN projection graph for the year 2015, and carry out a detailed investigation of :
- its rate of growth
- causes of growth
- environmental problems and challenges
- the contribution it makes to the economy of its country.

2 Write a brief comparison of your selected city and Mexico City, drawing attention to any features they have in common and to any key differences.

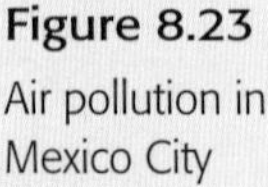

Figure 8.23
Air pollution in Mexico City

9 Urban land use and population patterns in cities

KEY THEMES

- ✔ The internal structure of cities is neither random nor exactly the same everywhere.
- ✔ Similar land use patterns are identifiable because the processes that shape urban growth are much the same in most parts of the world.
- ✔ Urban land use patterns may originate from economic and spatial factors but they are likely to be modified by political and cultural influences.
- ✔ Patterns of segregation within cities may be observed in housing types, family status, income and ethnicity, but most neighbourhoods are socially mixed

Urban land use patterns in MEDCs and LEDCs

Cities contain many different types of area, each with its own land use, for example residential, industrial, office and retail. The geographical distribution of these areas is never random, but neither is it exactly the same in every city. There are similar but not identical land use patterns in all urban areas. Cities also vary according to the physical layout of their streets, buildings, parks and so on – their **urban morphology**. Again, there are often common patterns in the structure and shape of cities.

Similar urban land use patterns can be identified in many different cities because the processes that shape urban geography are similar in both MEDCs and LEDCs. The main processes are economic in nature, but cultural and political forces may also have a considerable influence.

Economic processes and patterns

Economic processes involve the buying and selling of land and buildings in the **urban land market** (Figure 9.1). Different users, such as families, offices or supermarkets, have different needs and preferences for how much land or space they want and whereabouts in the city they want it. They make these decisions within the limits of how much they are willing – or able – to pay. Not every location in an urban area is equally desirable. It is possible to identify five key factors which influence how users find the locations that best meet their needs:

1 **Centrality** In theory the city centre is the most accessible location. Shops, businesses or services which need to attract large numbers of customers may therefore choose central locations. The high demand for space in central areas pushes up property and land prices, so that only the largest or most profitable businesses can afford to locate there.

Figure 9.1 The urban land market in operation in China

2 **Accessibility** After the centre, the most accessible locations are found beside major transport routes. Being close to a major road or rail route is particularly important for the delivery of supplies and for those individual people who rely on public transport rather than private cars.

3 **Mobility** Some families have cars and some do not. Those with cars may choose to live further away from where they work. People who rely on public transport may opt to live closer to their workplaces to cut down travel time and cost.

4 **Proximity** Some urban land uses may deter or repel others – polluting factories, for example. Businesses or families that can afford it may, therefore, distance themselves from uses they do not like.

5 **Clustering** Similar land uses tend to cluster together. For example, shops benefit from one another's customers and families generally choose to live among people who are similar to themselves in terms of income and lifestyle.

Urban land use models show the effect of these five factors on urban land use patterns. Three well-known models, typical of MEDC cities during the industrial era, are shown in Figure 9.2. They differ from each other because they attach a different degree of importance to each of the factors involved. They also reflect the urban morphology of the places on which they were based at the time they were devised, as does the much more recent model of the Latin American city (Figure 9.3).

Urban land use models are not intended to be an exact fit for every city. Changes in the nature of urban growth since the 1970s in particular are altering cities so that they now look less like these models. City centres are becoming more congested, and ring roads make suburbs more accessible. New business districts are located in the suburbs to escape the crowded centres. With more people owning cars, including people in the LEDCs, differences in mobility are becoming smaller and of less significance. The closure of many polluting factories makes old industrial districts less repellent and more attractive to

Figure 9.2 Urban land use models

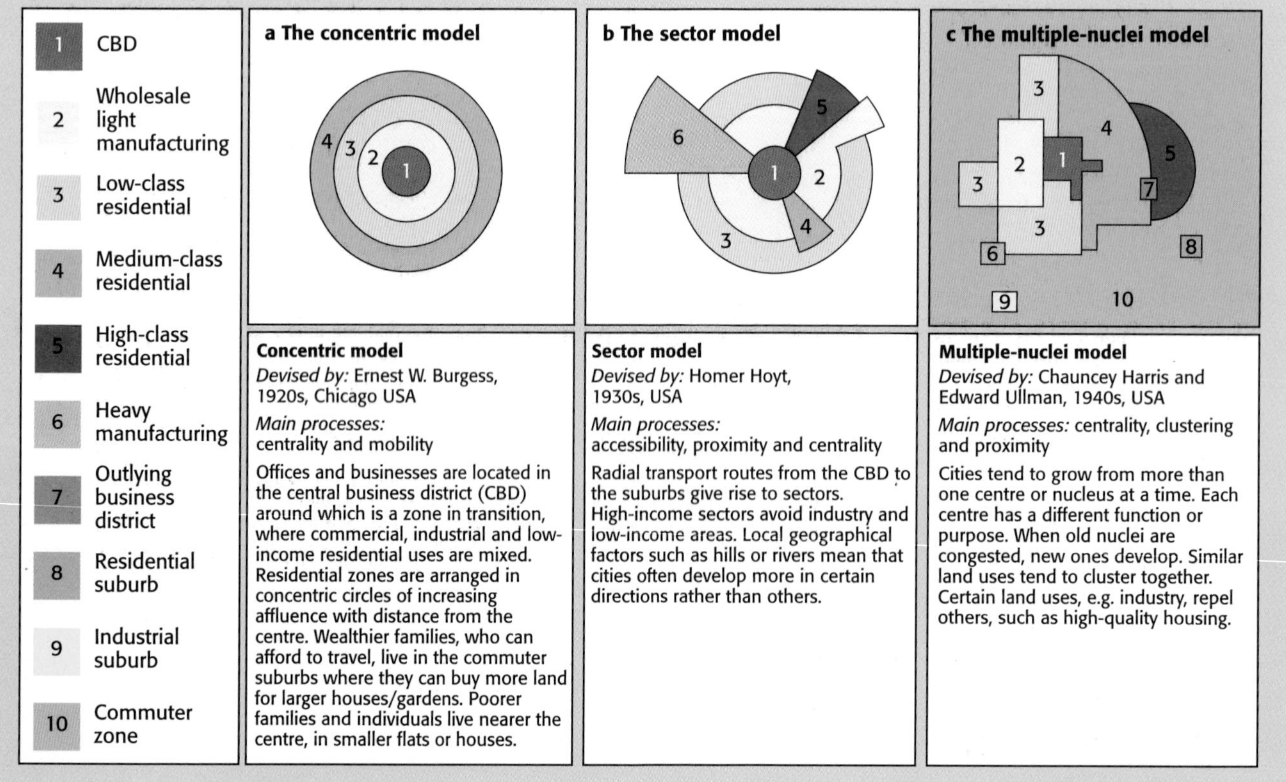

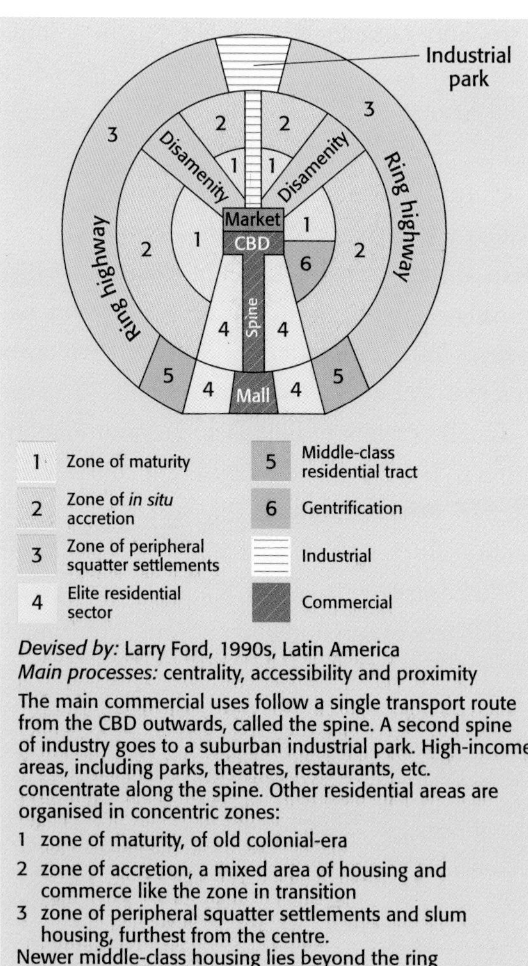

Figure 9.3

The Latin American city

offices or to wealthy residents. Although the five factors may create change in new and sometimes unpredictable ways, cities do not suddenly change overnight, which is why older patterns remain visible for long periods.

Political processes and patterns

Under certain circumstances political forces may outweigh economic processes. Governments, both national and local, make land use decisions in the public interest, which would not come about through the buying and selling of land and property on the open market. They decide where to locate schools, hospitals and public services, and they may create **green belts**, parks and zones free from certain types of development. Some of the morphological differences between urban areas in Europe and North America, for example, arise because European governments generally play a more active role in restricting development.

Governments may also build housing for those families who are unable to buy or rent privately. Many European cities, for example in France, Sweden and Hungary, have huge public housing developments in their suburbs. The *grands ensembles*, as these developments are known in Paris, were built from the 1950s onwards to meet the growing demand from city dwellers and rural migrants for better-quality housing (Figure 9.4). This action has led to the reverse of the concentric ring model, which has lower-income zones in the suburbs. In Hong Kong and Singapore, two densely populated city-states, the majority of housing is planned and built by the government.

In some cases, the land use pattern of whole cities may be determined by governments rather than by the decisions of families and businesses. In theory the government made all land use

Figure 9.4

Public housing in Paris, 1990

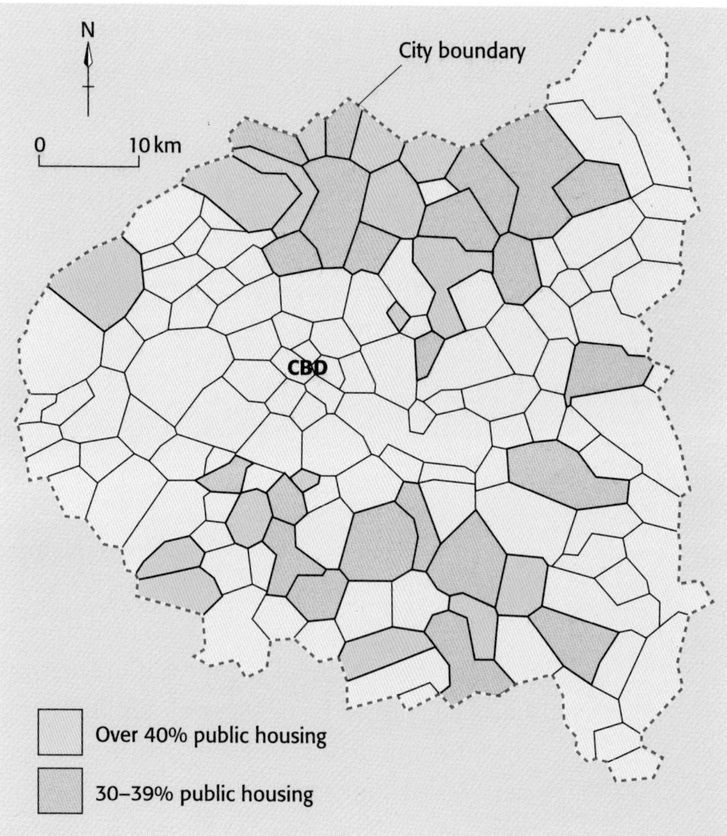

decisions in socialist or communist cities. Land and property could not usually be bought and sold by private individuals. Socialist governments were committed to the equal provision of shops, services, and dwellings. For these reasons, centrality was less marked, and more equal importance was attached to accessibility and mobility. In reality the cities of the former Soviet Union and eastern Europe – and of socialist LEDCs, such as Havana in Cuba – did not completely reflect these ideals, partly because private ownership of flats and houses continued to exist. Until the early 1990s, visitors to Moscow, for example, would have seen that there was no real central business district with tall office buildings. In fact, building heights appeared to be more or less the same everywhere. Offices, factories and shops were more spread out, often closer to where people lived. Commuters and shoppers used buses or the underground railway. Almost everyone lived in flats rather than houses, with little or no observable differences between richer and poorer areas. Moscow is now changing, with more cars, shops and private apartments, but the old socialist city structure is still readily visible.

Cultural processes and patterns

The third major influence shaping urban land use patterns and city morphology are cultural factors, including the history and traditions of people in different parts of the world. The cities of ancient civilisations, for example, were laid out according to how societies saw the universe, or *cosmos*. Traces of these **cosmological cities** can still be seen throughout Asia – in Beijing, for example.

The Ancient Greeks and Romans planned their cities with grid-iron street layouts. This plan was carried throughout the world by European colonisers, for example to the Latin American cities established by the Spanish Empire. From the European Renaissance onwards, urban planners added long, straight avenues connecting monuments. This plan can be seen in London, Paris and St Petersburg, as well as in colonial cities such as New Delhi (Figure 9.5). Often these straight roads contrast markedly with the narrow, winding streets of the medieval districts.

Cultural influences are also seen at a smaller scale in the street patterns and layouts of residential areas (Figure 9.6). For example, British families tend to want gardens and detached houses much more than other European families, many of whom live in apartments.

Finally, certain buildings and monuments are often so highly valued by different cultures that they are preserved even as the city changes round them – Buckingham Palace in central London and the Imperial Palace in Tokyo are good examples. Places of worship and national monuments also frequently occupy central positions in cities.

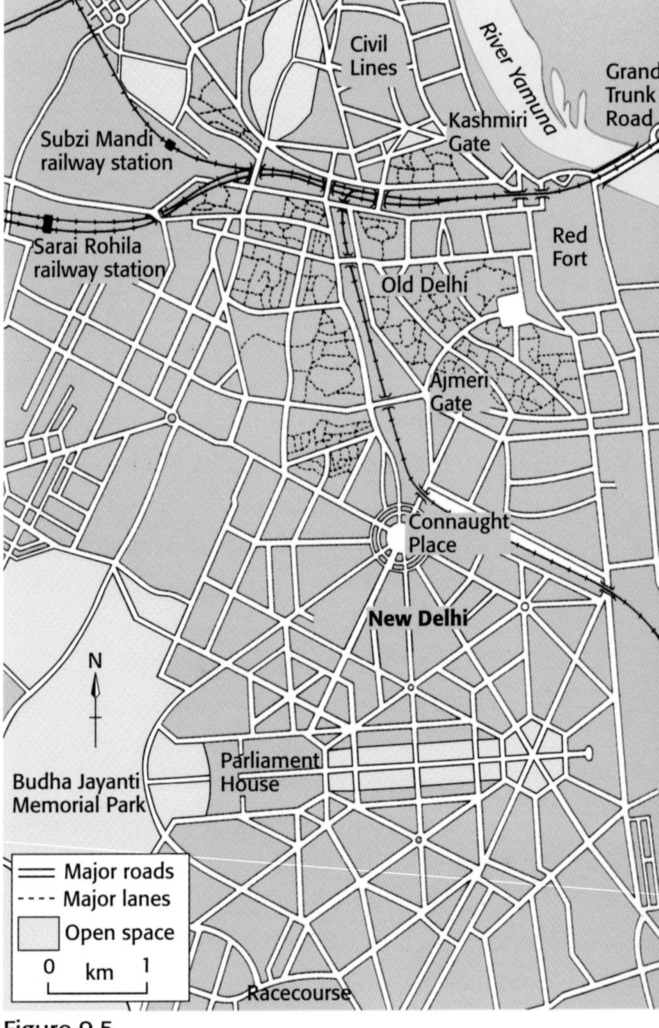

Figure 9.5
Urban morphology: Old and New Delhi

Figure 9.6

Street patterns from around the world

a Traditional Middle Eastern, e.g. Kuwait's old city
Narrow irregular streets and alleys provide little public space in residential areas. Houses have small courtyards to give privacy and protection from heat, dust and noise.

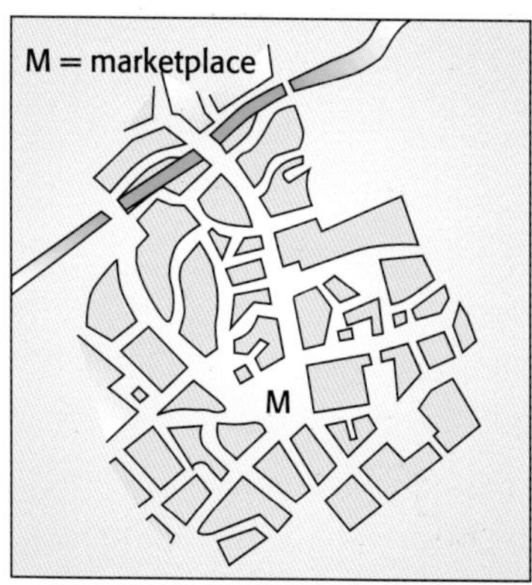

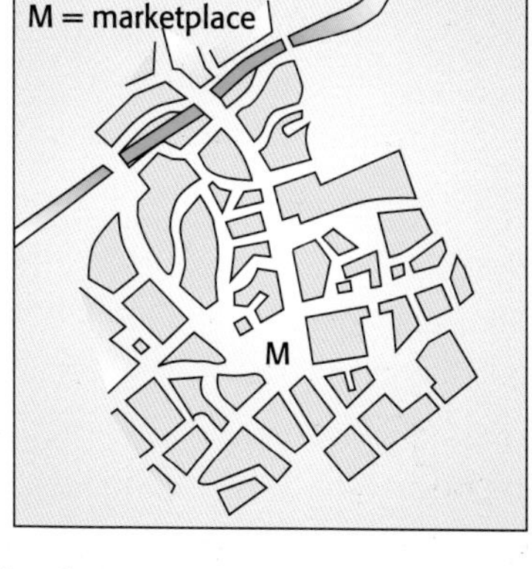

b Medieval Europe, e.g. Bruges in Belgium
Irregular narrow streets with marketplaces and town squares. Steets in medieval towns often followed natural features such as contours or rivers.

c 19th-century terraced housing, e.g. former mill towns of northern England. Workers in the industrial city lived in small terraced houses; better-off workers had small gardens. Note the intensive use of space to cram as many houses into one area as possible.

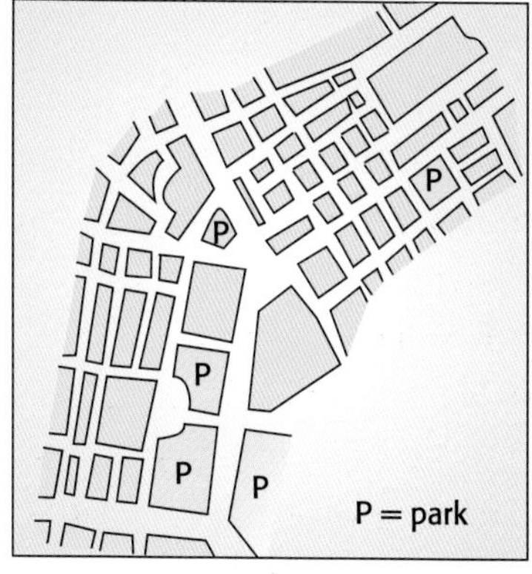

d 19th-century planned district, e.g. Ringstrasse, Vienna
Before the age of the automobile, Europe's middle classes lived in large apartments near the centre of cities. Wealthier families lived in apartments facing the street, while servants and poorer families often lived behind them where it was darker.

e 1950s American suburb
Gently curving streets, detached houses, large gardens and parks give a feeling of space and comfort, with plenty of space for cars. This layout was adopted all over Europe.

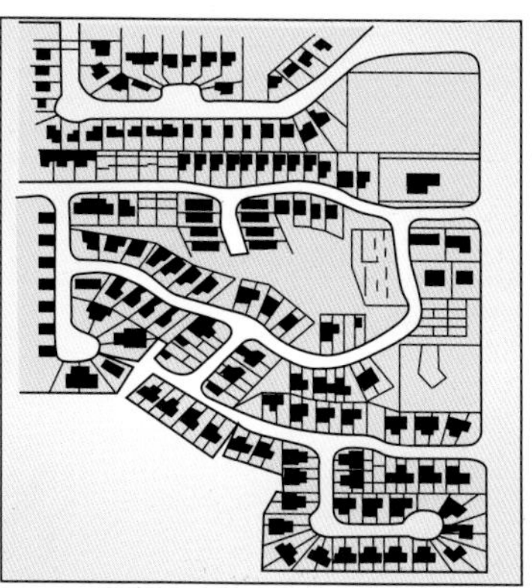

f Modern 1970s suburb
The use of the cul-de-sac and looped roads reduces the amount of through traffic and makes residential streets safer and quieter. Semi-detached houses set back from the road are common.

Case Study: Beijing

Beijing (Figure 9.7) has been the capital of China, with brief interruptions, since 1270. It was founded under the Mongols and then flourished under the Ming and Qing Dynasties. Today it has a population of over 10 million.

The Ancient Chinese designed their cities to represent the cosmos. The sacred centre of the world was where the Emperor reigned. His palace was inside the Forbidden City, surrounded by walls. Ordinary people were not allowed in. In turn this City was surrounded by the Imperial City, where courtiers and nobles lived. It also had walls, and the gates passing through them were carefully aligned with the points of the compass. The Imperial City was entered from the south, through Tiananmen, the Gate of Heavenly Peace. Surrounding the palace there were temples and altars, placed so as to preserve the harmony of the cosmos – for example, the Altar of Heaven was to the south, the Altar of Earth to the north. Beyond these walls the ordinary people lived in a maze of alleys, called *hutong*. Temples and courtyards were dotted throughout the old city.

The last Chinese Emperor gave up the throne in 1912 and after 1949 a Communist government took power. Although the Communists rejected imperial ways, they did not destroy the Imperial City. Instead, they enlarged Tiananmen Square and built the national parliament, the Great Hall of the People, beside it. The great Communist leader, Mao Zedong, was buried nearby. Thus the centre of political power in China has remained in the same place for over 700 years.

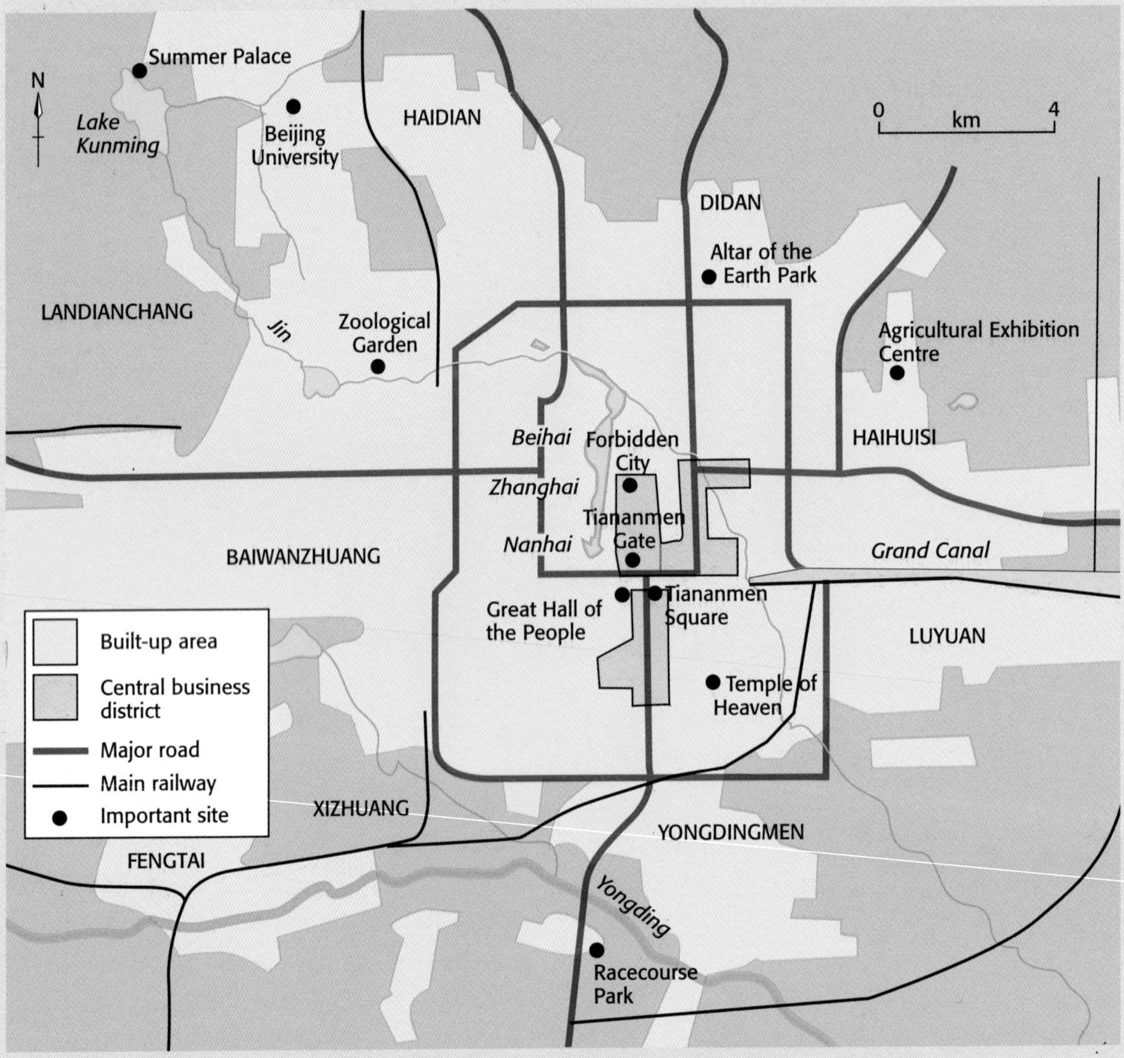

Figure 9.7
Beijing: cosmological city

	Activity Examine a 1:25 000 OS map of a part of a British city of your choice.
1	Identify any major industrial, commercial or other non-residential zones on the map.
2	Identify the main areas of 19th-century terraced housing and 20th-century suburban housing. Which type of housing is closest to the industrial or commercial zones?
3	For each type of housing, select one area and work out the approximate number of dwellings per hectare.
4	What evidence on the map is there of any planned public housing?
5	Can you detect the main influences which appear to have shaped the morphology of the area of the city covered by the map? Look for clues in the physical geography of the area.

Population distribution and density

Cities are places where people both live and work. Different areas are likely to be dominated by one or the other of these activities, as shown by the three models in Figure 9.2. The census counts upon which geographers depend for mapping urban populations are taken at night-time. They record where people eat, sleep and socialise. A daytime count would show the city's inhabitants spread out in shops, offices and schools, where they mix more with strangers than with acquaintances. Therefore the mapping of population in cities is not like the mapping of plants or soils – people move and mix. This simple point should be remembered when studying the distribution of people within urban areas.

The best measure of population distribution in cities is **population density**, which is:

- the number of people in a given area, measured in persons per hectare or square kilometre (km^2)

Population density should not be confused with **overcrowding**, which is:

- a measure of the number of people per room in a dwelling (in the UK, overcrowding is said to occur when there is more than one person per room, excluding kitchens).

Although they are related, these two measures are not quite the same. Large, densely populated cities, with many people living in multi-storey or high-rise buildings, are not necessarily overcrowded. Overcrowding is more a result of poverty, when families cannot afford large enough dwellings for everyone to have a room each, and floorspace per person is limited (Figure 9.8). Population or residential density also varies within cities, sometimes as much as it varies between them. In MEDC cities, population and building density is usually low in the CBD, rising in the zone in transition and the rest of the city, then lowest in the suburbs (Figure 9.9). In LEDCs, if there are peripheral squatter settlements, densities remain high on the outskirts. In general, LEDC cities are more densely populated than MEDC cities, although European cities are more densely peopled than North American and Australian urban areas (Figure 9.10).

The number of people living in particular areas of a city also changes over time. Three main types of population change in established built-up areas are evident:

1 **Abandonment:** when an area suffers from high unemployment, high crime and poor living standards, people may leave in large numbers. Examples include the inner-city areas of Chicago, Detroit in the USA, and Manchester and Newcastle in Britain.
2 **Subdivision:** large family houses are divided into flats for single people, to create multi-occupancy dwellings. Subdivision occurs in the zones in transition of most MEDC cities, and in old colonial districts of LEDC cities.

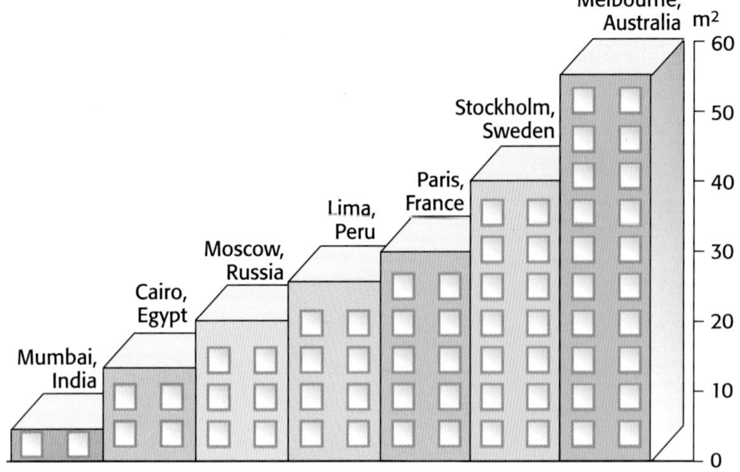

Figure 9.8

Average floorspace (m^2) in seven cities

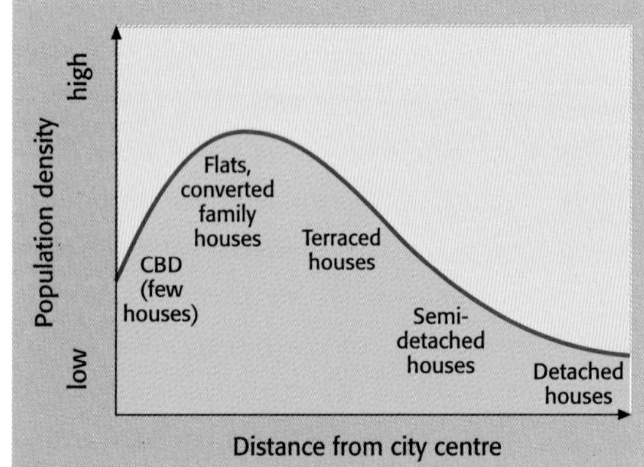

Figure 9.9

Population density in a typical MEDC city

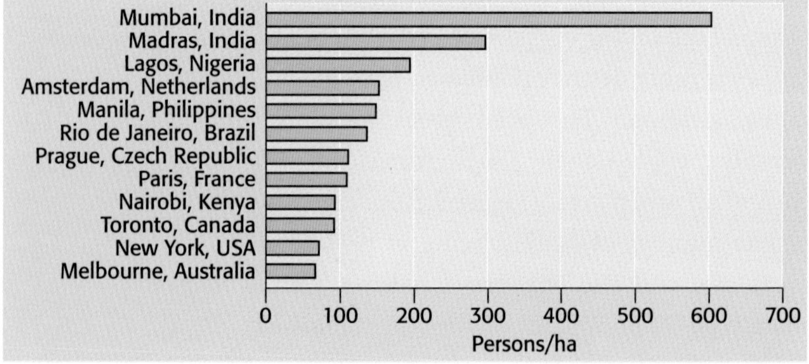

Figure 9.10

Urban residential density

3 **Gentrification and displacement:** economically prosperous individuals and families move into areas which were either formerly occupied by less well-off people or are characterised by subdivided dwellings. Sometimes the neighbourhood's old residents are forced out and replaced by smaller households, in which case the residential density falls. The Lower East Side of New York and the East End of London are good examples.

Activity

This activity explores how population density, overcrowding and population change are related and vary within the city. Figures 9.11 and 9.12 refer to wards in Leeds, the third largest city in Britain.

1 Calculate the population density for each ward in persons per hectare. Decide how best to group the density data, and map them on a copy of Figure 9.11. Is a spatial pattern evident, and is it what you might expect? Are there any anomalies? How do your figures compare with densities in any other cities you have studied?

2 On your map, write in the percentage of overcrowded houses for each ward. To what extent do the wards with the highest and lowest levels of overcrowding correspond with areas of high and low population density? What is the nature, if any, of the relationship between population density and overcrowding?

3 Calculate the number of movers for each ward as a percentage of the population. Identify the wards with the highest and lowest levels of population turnover. How far do they correspond with areas of high and low density and overcrowding?

4 Using Figure 9.9 as a model, construct three generalised graphs for Leeds to show changes in population density, overcrowding and population change with distance from the city centre (regard Ward 8 as the centre). Different groups of students should choose different directions from the centre. What are the similarities and differences between the graphs, and what are their limitations as models?

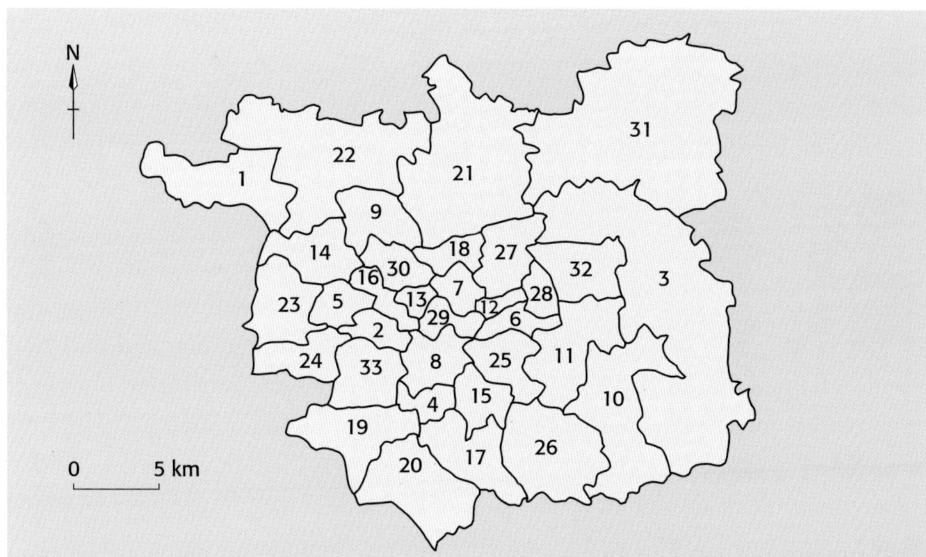

Figure 9.11
Leeds wards

Figure 9.12
Leeds: demographic data by ward, 1991

No.	Ward	Area (ha)	Population 1991	% overcrowded households*	Movers**
1	Aireborough	2084	24 633	0.8	1905
2	Armley	539	20 623	2.2	2227
3	Barwick & Kippax	8114	22 461	1.1	1492
4	Beeston	437	17 262	2.5	1767
5	Bramley	649	21 389	2.2	2026
6	Burmantofts	481	18 736	2.6	2241
7	Chapel Allerton	456	21 984	3.5	2371
8	City & Holbeck	985	20 754	3.6	2972
9	Cookridge	1110	21 161	0.7	1294
10	Garforth	2897	23 499	0.8	1403
11	Halton	1908	21 502	0.7	1333
12	Harehills	261	21 297	6.0	2398
13	Headingley	274	16 073	3.3	4197
14	Horsforth	1153	21 080	3.3	1624
15	Hunslet	750	14 802	2.6	1156
16	Kirkstall	477	19 104	2.0	2432
17	Middleton	1497	17 977	2.4	1565
18	Moortown	539	20 342	1.1	1492
19	Morley North	1660	22 170	1.4	1804
20	Morley South	2144	25 301	1.6	2490
21	North	4829	21 031	0.7	1566
22	Otley & Wharfedale	4300	23 108	0.9	1615
23	Pudsey North	1377	22 597	1.2	1577
24	Pudsey South	934	21 192	1.6	1465
25	Richmond Hill	940	20 066	2.8	1837
26	Rothwell	2295	19 944	1.1	1255
27	Roundhay	1157	21 092	1.2	1753
28	Seacroft	428	18 983	2.9	1627
29	University	484	17 348	3.9	3513
30	Weetwood	706	16 618	1.2	1758
31	Wetherby	7641	24 656	0.6	2108
32	Whinmoor	1258	19 010	1.8	1340
33	Wortley	1222	22 927	1.8	1802
	Leeds	**55 046**	**680 722**	**1.9**	**63 444**

*Overcrowding = percentage of households with more persons than rooms

**Movers = number of people who moved to the area in the preceding year

Hong Kong Special Administrative Region of China is one of the most densely populated and richest city-regions in the world (Figure 9.13). It is home to 6.7 million people, which is smaller than London, but London covers 50 per cent more land. In Hong Kong, because of the large areas of hills, parks and farmland, almost everyone is packed into only 15 per cent of the region's 1042 km^2. Flat land is so scarce that over 30 km^2 has been reclaimed from the seas and rivers. In the most built-up districts, such as Mong Kok, there are 1165 people per hectare living in high-rise apartment blocks built close together. The average person has just 7 m^2 of floorspace each.

The causes of this situation lie in a combination of history, demography and economics. For over 150 years Hong Kong was a British colony, with a thriving economy based on trade, manufacturing and, more recently, on banking, electronics and tourism. Immigrants and refugees from mainland China arrived in huge numbers throughout this period, while rates of natural increase were also high. This growing population, which doubled between 1940 and 1960, was crammed into the part of the colony around the harbour over which Britain had permanent control. Immigration, legal and illegal, remains high.

In the 1950s, 300 000 people lived in shanty towns on the hillsides. To relieve crowding and **congestion**, the government planned nine new satellite towns in the New Territories. Now over 40 per cent of Hong Kong's citizens live in these high-rise **new towns**, which are well-provided with shops and services. They have planned densities of over 300 persons per hectare, which is high by international standards.

Since Hong Kong returned to Chinese rule in 1997 its economy has continued to grow. It is now a vital part of the larger Pearl River delta region, which includes Shenzhen's factory complexes. Planners expect the population to increase to between 7.5 and 8.1 million by 2011, placing even more pressure on housing as well as on water, waste and sewerage systems.

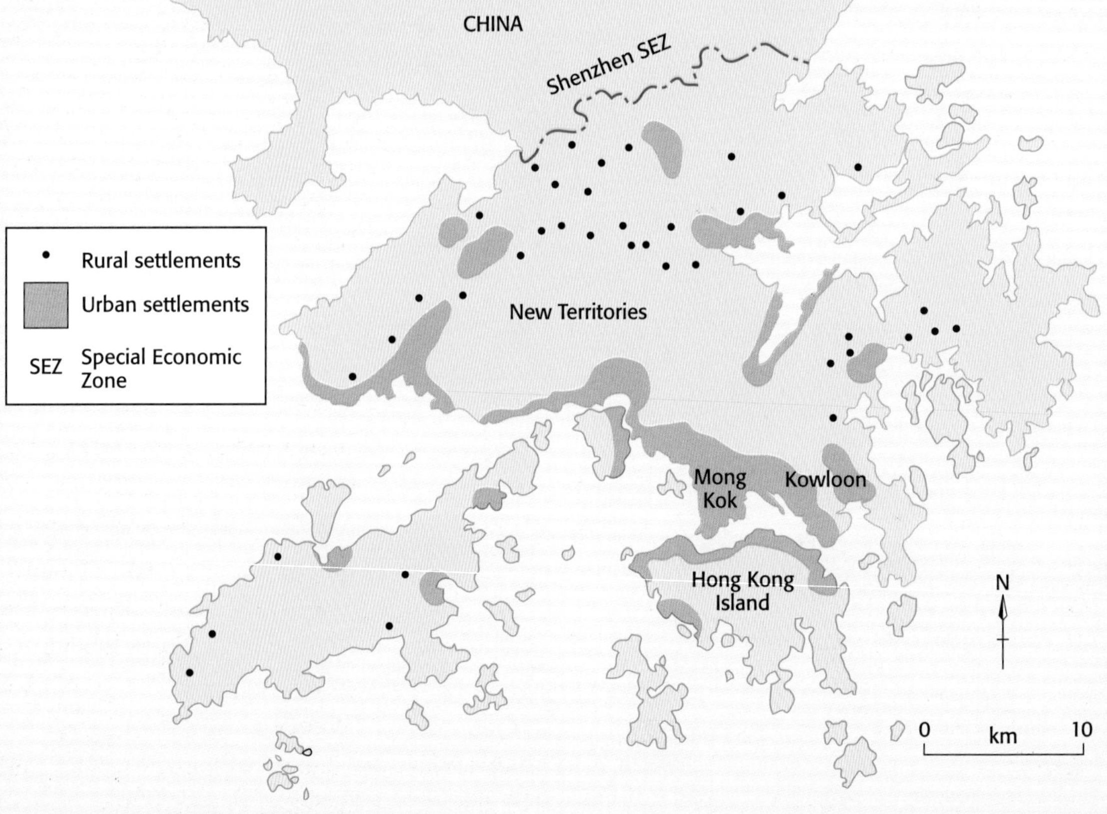

Figure 9.13
Hong Kong Special Administrative Region

Spatial segregation

Cities are not only divided into residential and non-residential areas. Within residential districts people are not geographically distributed at random; there are clear patterns of what is called **spatial segregation**. Segregation refers to the fact that socio-economic classes, family types, **ethnic groups** and lifestyle groups tend to live in different neighbourhoods. There are at least three key dimensions to spatial segregation:

- **Mixing:** the extent to which social groups are distributed evenly or unevenly throughout the city relative to one another.
- **Concentration:** the extent to which particular social groups are concentrated in specific districts, such that they may form the majority of the people living there. Sometimes concentration is also referred to as **ghettoisation**.
- **Centralisation:** the extent to which social groups are found close to the centre of a city, or further out in the suburbs.

Patterns of segregation arise from the interaction of many factors in the city. The main factors are the working of the urban land and housing markets, the location of work and the impact of planning regulations and laws. Patterns of segregation also reflect tens of thousands of decisions taken by individuals and families about where they want to live (Figure 9.14).

The main actors in the urban land and housing market include governments, planners, landowners, developers, builders, gatekeepers and managers. '**Gatekeepers**' and '**managers**' are institutions or businesses that control access to housing, such as building societies or Council housing offices.

Reason	Home-owners	Renters
Bigger or better dwelling	27%	15%
Closer to workplace	8%	22%
Move to a nicer area	16%	6%
Marriage/cohabitation	6%	3%
Divorce/separation	8%	10%
Other reasons	35%	44%

Figure 9.14
The main reasons for moving house in the UK

Actor	**What they do**
Government	– Decides the balance of private and public housing (Figure 9.15) – Sets interest rates to make borrowing for house purchase more or less attractive (Figure 9.16)
Landowners	Decide whether to release land for development, how much to charge for it and what to build there
Developers	Look for land to build on and try to finance building schemes, especially large, profitable ones
Planners	Decide where building can and cannot take place, e.g. green belts; also set building standards
Builders	Build houses, often in association with developers
Private gatekeepers	– Banks and building societies decide to whom they will lend and in what districts of the city they will or will not encourage house purchases – Estate agents help match buyers and sellers – Landlords decide to whom they will rent their properties
Public gatekeepers	– Local authority housing offi cers assess applicants for public housing according to need and suitability as tenants; they draw up waiting lists and then allocate applicants to properties when their turn comes
Individuals or families	Choose where to live and whether to rent or buy

Country by income category	Owner-occupation	Public housing	Unauthorised (i.e. squatters)
Low-income countries	33%	13%	64%
Middle-income countries	59%	14%	20%
High-income countries	51%	13%	no reliable data

Figure 9.15

Private and public housing throughout the world

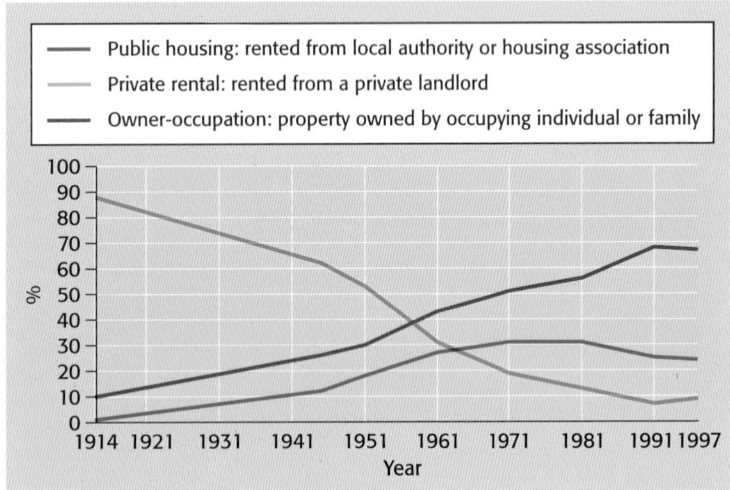

Figure 9.16

Housing in the UK, 1914–97

From the point of view of the individual or family, choice is made within an already existing set of circumstances and constraints, such as the type, cost and location of dwellings. Other constraints may result from discrimination by one or more of the actors. Examples include:

- banks and building societies being more willing to lend money to men than to women, or to white people rather than black people
- banks deciding not to make loans for purchases in run-down areas of the city (known as '**redlining**')
- landlords refusing to rent to people they do not like, possibly on the grounds of ethnicity or lifestyle, for example.

Housing types and tenure

Over time, planners, developers and builders combine to produce the city's housing stock. As dwellings are usually built in clusters of similar age and quality, they give rise to distinctive housing areas. The main types of dwelling are:

- detached houses standing on their own land, usually the most expensive and desirable
- semi-detached houses (or duplexes in the USA), sharing one wall in common
- terraces (row houses or townhouses in the USA), built immediately next to one another in rows
- apartments, or condominiums if owned rather than rented, in purpose-built buildings
- flats in houses, sometimes called bedsits, after a large house has been subdivided into individual units
- shanty or self-built dwellings (common in LEDCs).

In the UK today, around half of the country's households live in detached or semi-detached houses, and most of the rest live in terraced houses. By contrast, apartments and flats are more common in mainland European and North American cities, and in Latin American cities. A country's stock of dwellings will also change over time. As society becomes richer, so developers and builders respond by producing more properties for the better off while, at the same time, properties originally built for the wealthy may be taken over by less well off groups as the rich move on up the housing ladder; this process is called **filtering**. A third of Britain's current stock of terrace houses was built before 1919 for so-called working-class families. Slightly more than half the stock of detached houses and nearly two-thirds the stock of flats have been built since 1964 (Figure 9.17).

Type of housing	Date of construction				All
	Before 1919	1919–44	1945–64	1965 or later	
Detached	17	14	17	52	100
Semi-detached	10	28	33	29	100
Terrace	32	20	18	31	100
Flats and maisonettes	5	10	26	59	100
All dwellings as % total stock 1997	19	20	23	38	100

Figure 9.17

Trends in housing construction in the UK (percentage figures)

Shaping residential patterns

Families and individuals wanting to buy property generally look for detached and semi-detached houses; flats and apartments are more commonly rented. The overall outcome of preferences such as these is that a close spatial association emerges between type of dwelling and form of **tenure** (Figure 9.18). In Leeds (Figure 9.19), the generally older terraces are found more in the centre of the city, along with flats, where public and private renting is more usual. Detached and semi-detached houses are more suburban, and commonly associated with home-ownership. However, almost all districts of Leeds have a mix of housing types and tenures. In any case, areas exclusively of one tenure, or of one house-type, are rare in Britain, partly because public housing includes a mix of flats and terraces, and can be found throughout the urban area. Compare Leeds with Robson's model of the British city, which is based on different forms of tenure (Figure 9.20).

People's choices are also influenced by three personal characteristics: income, family status, and ethnicity.

Income

The choice of what house to buy or rent, and in which neighbourhood to live, is greatly affected or determined by individual or family income. Buying a house usually involves the use of savings as well as loans, the latter being more easily obtained by better-off families. In MEDCs, governments generally provide income support, rent subsidy or other forms of assistance to lower-income families. Spatial segregation by income can be seen in at least three different ways in MEDC cities:

- **In zones or sectors** where high-, middle- or low-income households are concentrated, as reflected in the urban land use models. In Leeds for example, there is a high-income sector from Roundhay in the centre out to the north-eastern suburbs (Figure 9.21). The central wards, many of which have levels of

Type of tenure	Detached	Semi-detached	Terraced	Flats	All
Owner-occupation	26	36	26	12	100
Public housing	0	26	32	42	100
Private rental	13	18	29	40	100
All tenures	22	32	28	18	100

Figure 9.18

Tenure and housing type in England, 1997–98 (percentage figures)

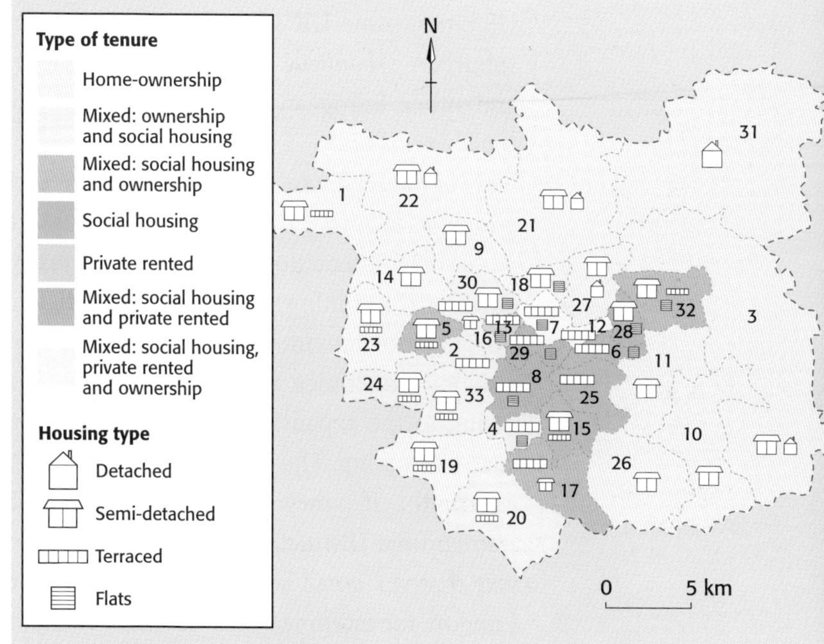

Figure 9.19

Tenure and housing type in Leeds, 1999

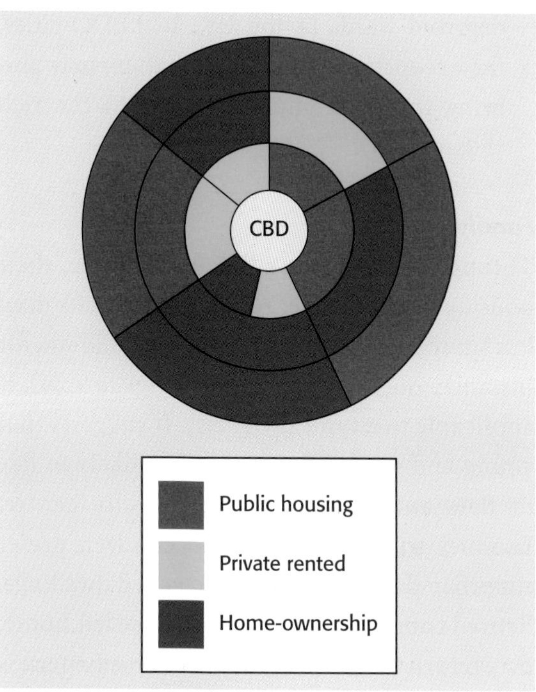

Figure 9.20

Robson's model of the British city

unemployment above 10 per cent, have lower average incomes.

- **In areas of extreme poverty** where the poorest people are concentrated in the worst housing, and rich and poor families are strongly separated (Figure 9.22). Such areas are associated with **social exclusion** – a combination of poverty and powerlessness. Although the prime example is the **ghetto** of US cities, some UK housing estates and the suburban *banlieue* estates in France and other European countries also exhibit social exclusion.
- **Through social precipices**, where rich and poor live in physical proximity but without close social interaction. The centres of many cities are becoming gentrified, with richer people moving in while poorer people remain. Sometimes the rich are super-rich owing to the expansion of highly paid jobs such as banking. The poor may be very poor, especially if they are newly arrived immigrants. Distinctions of this magnitude give rise to small-scale segregation. Inner London, for example, is the wealthiest area in Europe, but it contains 14 of the 20 most deprived wards in the UK. In LEDC cities, the occupation of land by squatters may also bring the poor physically close to the rich (Figure 9.23).

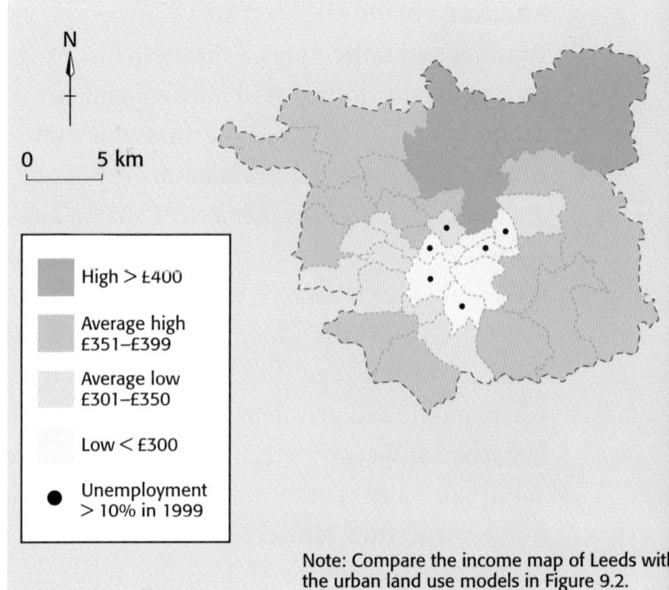

Figure 9.21
Income in Leeds: average household weekly income

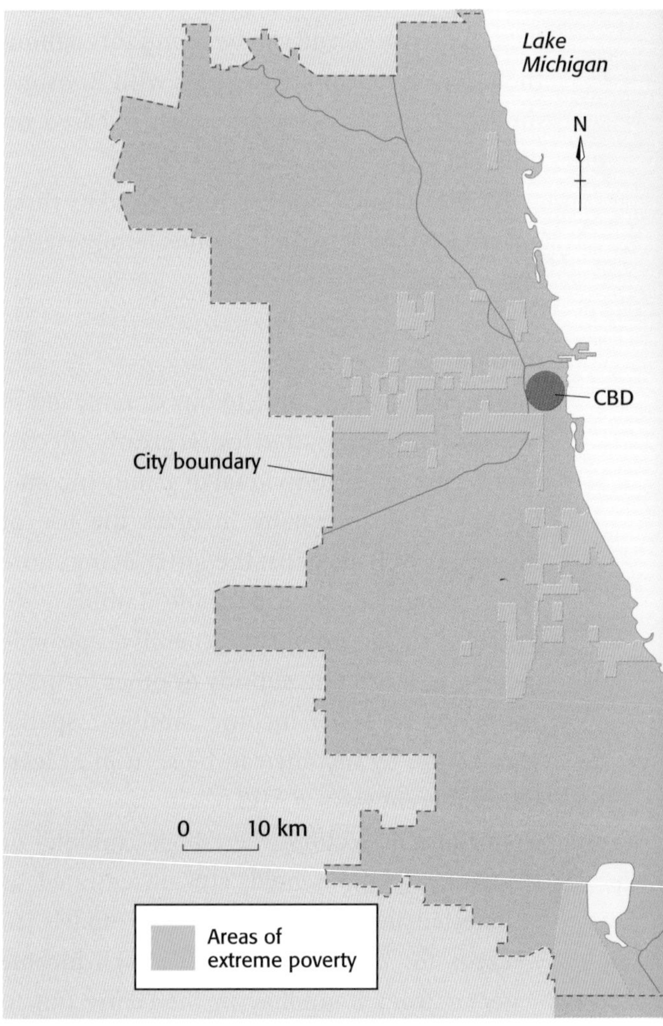

Figure 9.22
Areas of extreme poverty in Chicago, 1990

Family status

Throughout a person's life, or life cycle, their housing needs change. Young single adults need less space than families with young children, for instance. Burtenshaw's model (Figure 9.24), is applicable to a typical UK city. It suggests that young and single adults are more likely to live in flats and apartments in the city centre. Families with two adults and children prefer suburban detached or semi-detached dwellings. Retired couples, whose children have left home, may return to the inner suburbs. This pattern is evident in Leeds to some degree (Figure 9.25), but it should be remembered that almost all

Figure 9.23
Wealth and poverty side by side in Mumbai, India

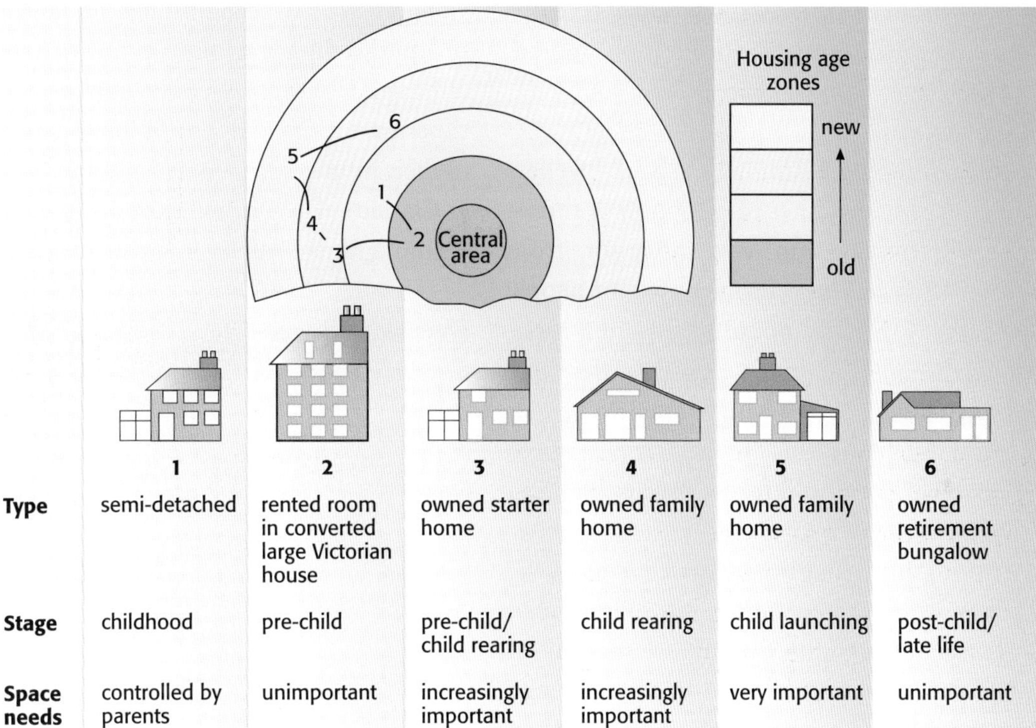

	1	2	3	4	5	6
Type	semi-detached	rented room in converted large Victorian house	owned starter home	owned family home	owned family home	owned retirement bungalow
Stage	childhood	pre-child	pre-child/ child rearing	child rearing	child launching	post-child/ late life
Space needs	controlled by parents	unimportant	increasingly important	increasingly important	very important	unimportant

Figure 9.24
Family life cycle moves in the British city: Burtenshaw's model

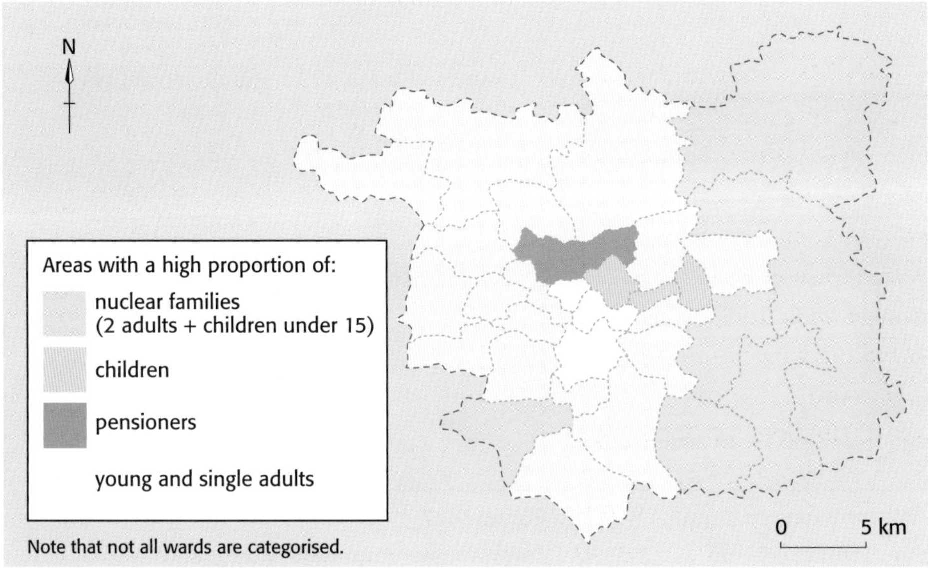

Figure 9.25
Leeds: family status

neighbourhoods have a mix of households and families.

Changes in family and personal life are sometimes visible in the social geography of the city. UK household types have changed over the past 40 years or so (Figure 9.26). With more lone adults, young and old, later marriages, and fewer families with two resident parents, the demand for housing is changing. In the city centres, apartments and condominiums for young, single, urban professionals are spreading rapidly. In the inner suburbs housing developments are often aimed specifically at the retired.

Ethnicity

Ethnic differences among urban dwellers largely arise from either colonisation or immigration (from within a country or from abroad). The mixing within the city of people from diverse regions or countries often highlights the social and cultural differences between them. At the same time, exchanges between different ethnic groups may give rise to new or hybrid cultural forms such as bhangra music or balti food.

Ethnic groups may be segregated in all of the three ways described earlier – that is, spread unevenly throughout the city, dominant in particular neighbourhoods, or concentrated near the centre. Such segregation comes about through a combination of choice and constraint, or positive factors supporting segregation, and negative factors forcing it upon people against their will (Figure 9.27). Compared with US cities, European cities have experienced large-scale immigration more recently. With minority ethnic communities often only one or two generations old, the paths of spatial integration, or non-integration, which they follow can be shaped by government policies affecting the balance of positive and negative factors.

There are five recognisable models or paths of **spatial integration** (or non-integration) although, in reality, any one ethnic group may experience more than one of them as the weight of their influence changes over time:

- **Classic US immigrant model:** poor immigrants settle in low-cost housing in the

Household type	% of all households 1961	1995
One person under pensionable age	4	12
One person over pensionable age	7	15
Two or more unrelated adults	5	6
Married couple, no children	26	25
Married couple, 1–2 dependent children	30	20
Married couple, 3 + dependent children	8	5
Lone parent, dependent children	2	7
Others	18	10

NB: dependent children are those under 16 or aged 16–18 and in full-time education.

Figure 9.26

Types of household in Great Britain, 1961–95

Negative factors	Positive factors
Legal restrictions on residence, e.g. • Jewish ghettos in medieval Europe • apartheid system in South Africa • refugees in some European countries	Maintenance area of of social contacts • friends and family • informal job contacts • marriage partners
Discrimination in housing • by private landlords • by local authorities • by gatekeepers, e.g. redlining	Commercial centres • special shops and services catering for ethnic groups, e.g. halal food stores • tourist attractions, e.g. Chinatowns
Discrimination in jobs • workers trapped in centre of city by low-paid service jobs	Cultural practices • Places of worships, e.g. mosques • schools providing special languages • radio, TV and newspapers
Real or perceived threat of violence • physical attacks and harassment	Political power and representation • ethnic concentrations in one or more electoral districts make it easier for a member of that group to be elected to office

Figure 9.27

Factors causing ethnic spatial segregation in MEDC cities

zone in transition (port of entry), form distinct ethnic clusters or urban villages and, over time, secure better jobs, learn the language and move outwards, becoming less segregated. *Example:* Chicago, 1880–1950

- **European immigrant model**: poor immigrants are housed by the government in suburban estates where, because of lack of jobs and discrimination, they suffer social exclusion. *Example:* Paris
- **US ghetto model:** faced with powerful discrimination, including the threat of violence, an individual group becomes heavily concentrated in one area where it forms the vast majority of the population. This model applies widely to African-Americans. Equivalent areas occupied by Mexican-Americans are called *barrios*, the term used for Hispanic neighbourhoods in US cities. *Example:* East Los Angeles
- **New immigrant model:** middle-class or professional immigrants settle in suburban **ethnoburbs**, where they invest in businesses and property and may form their own economic enclaves. *Example:* Monterey Park, Los Angeles
- **Colonial elite model:** in LEDCs, where the colonising power establishes a new district around a fort or business area and residences are physically separated from the local people. *Example:* Mumbai (Bombay), India

Figure 9.28 shows the ethnic minority and high-income areas of Los Angeles. In most cities, segregation by ethnicity is much more pronounced than that by income or family status. Most cities and neighbourhoods are socially mixed, especially if the daytime distribution of people – people at work, leisure or shopping – is taken into account.

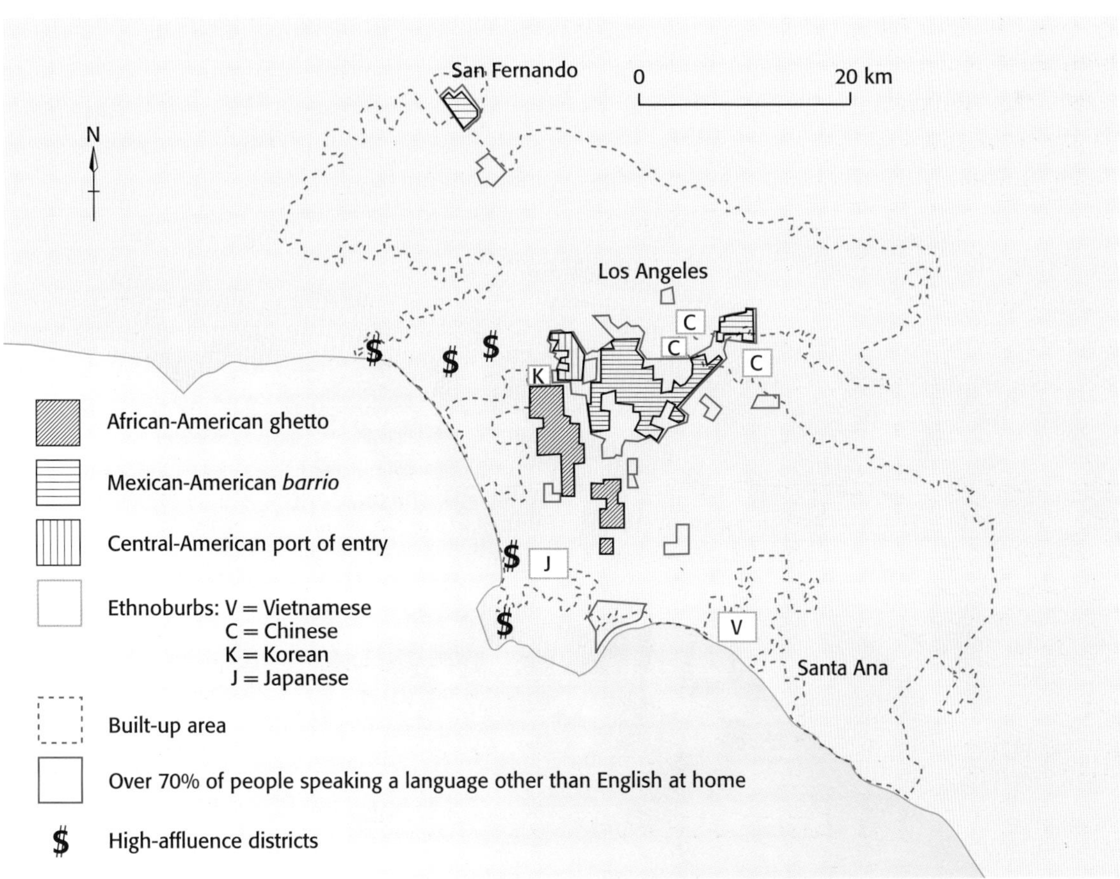

Figure 9.28
Ethnic minority areas in Los Angeles

Case Study: Ethnic segregation in Leeds

Leeds is an 'average' British city, so far as migration and ethnic groups are concerned (Figure 9.29). In the 18th and 19th centuries, workers from Scotland and Ireland were attracted by jobs in the textile and engineering industries, and there is still a distinct Irish community in the city, kept going by continuing migration since the 1960s.

After the Second World War there were new arrivals, first from the Caribbean then from countries in South Asia – India, Pakistan and Bangladesh – and also from China and Africa. As in other British cities, these newcomers settled near the city centre where there was cheap rented accommodation and plenty of jobs on offer. But wherever they lived, they were in a minority. In 1991 there was only one ward where a minority ethnic group formed more than a quarter of all the residents.

Further, each group tends to have its own neighbourhood within the central area (Figure 9.30) – Indians and Black Caribbeans in Chapel Allerton and Pakistanis in Harehills ward, for example. Harehills was also home to 45 per cent of Bangladeshis in 1991. These neighbourhoods are where places of worship, shops, travel agents and restaurants cater for the different communities.

In recent years, the Indian and Black communities have begun to disperse into the suburbs. Indians from Leeds and nearby Bradford are settling in west Leeds. They have the highest rates of home-ownership. Black Caribbeans are more likely to live in public housing. Pakistanis, who also have high rates of home-ownership, remain close to the centre. The most isolated group are the Bangladeshis. There are many parts of Leeds where there are no Bangladeshi families. They were the only group not to become less segregated between 1981 and 1991.

In 1996 just over 6 per cent of the total population of Leeds (726 000) was recorded by the census as belonging to a minority ethnic group. Among the various ethnic communities there are many who continue to suffer from the disadvantages of the inner city, for example unemployment, racism, and poor-quality housing. But there are also some who have moved to the suburbs and climbed in socio-economic terms, as predicted by the classic US immigration model.

Figure 9.29

Leeds City Market supplies a range of food items for the different ethnic groups who live in the city

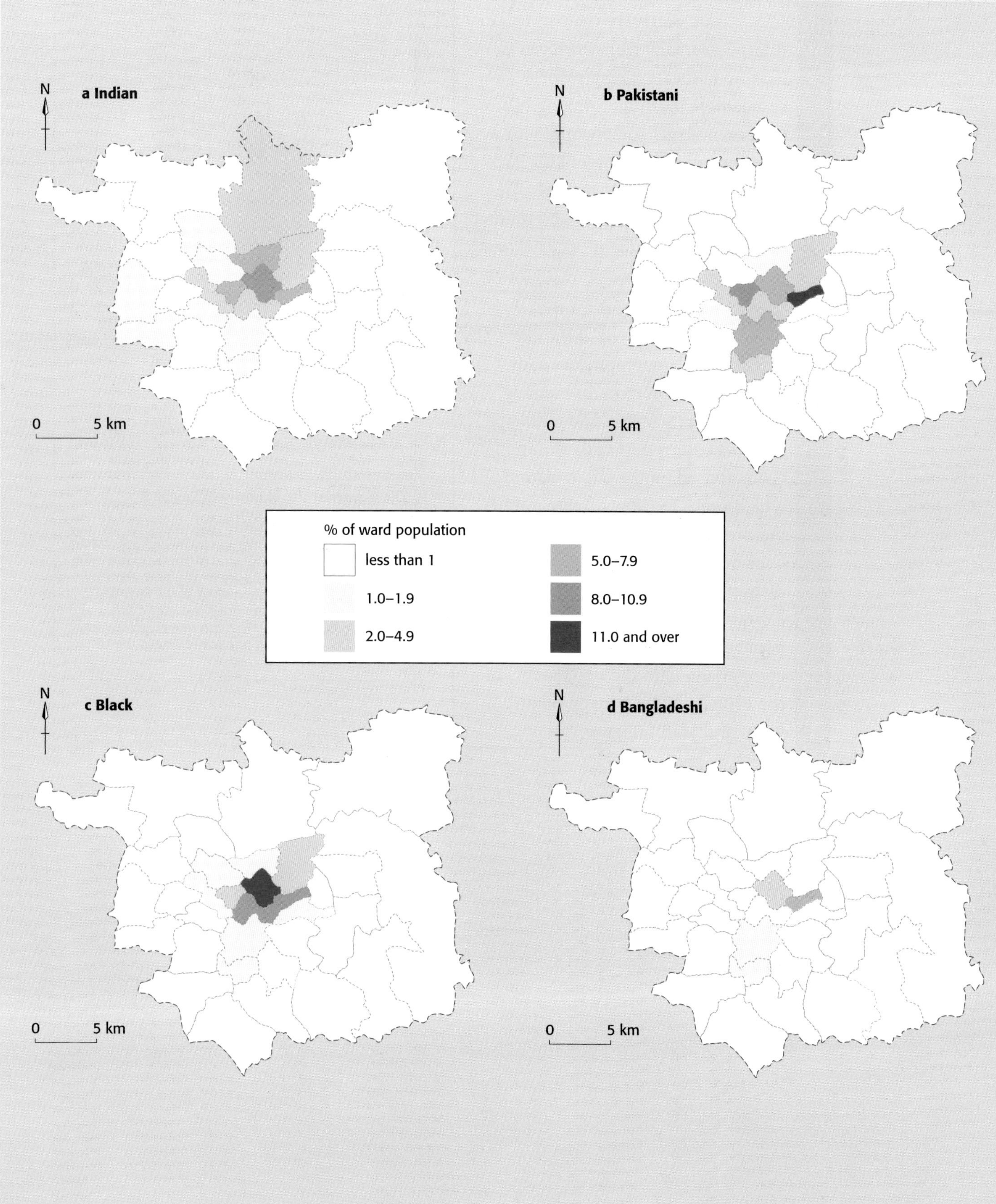

Figure 9.30
Distribution of minority ethnic groups in Leeds

Activity

1 A large company from overseas is looking to locate a new plant somewhere in Britain. Among other factors, it wants somewhere with a good housing environment for its workers. Write a brief resumé of housing quality in Leeds, and predict the changes that might occur across the urban area over the next 20 years.

2 Write a concise report for the personnel department of the company on the social geography of Leeds, including information on housing, income, family status and ethnicity. Support your report with a map of Leeds (based on the city's wards) which seeks to show an integrated picture of how the factors you have considered currently combine to create districts with distinct socio-economic characteristics. As an aid to writing your report, consider Leeds in comparison with the two models of the British city by Robson (Figure 9.20) and Mann (Figure 9.31).

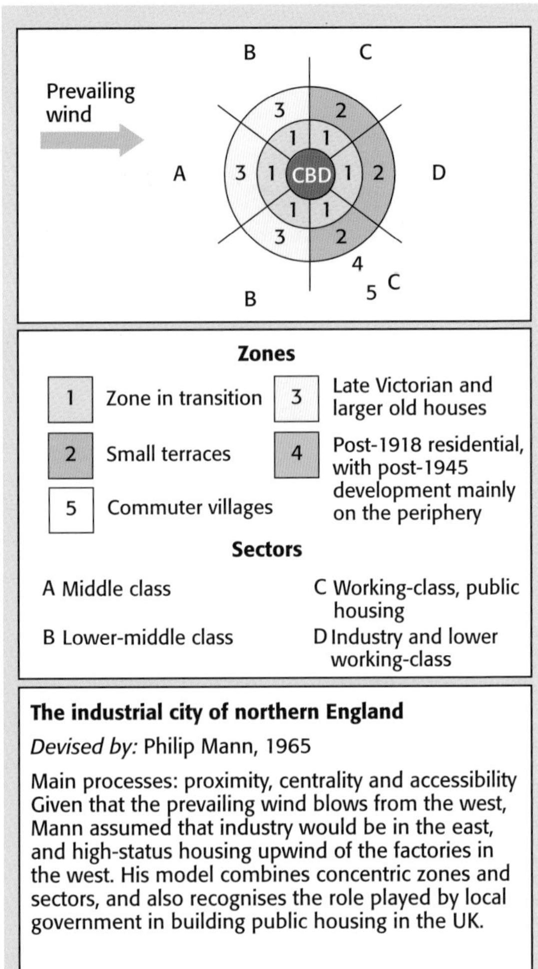

Figure 9.31
Mann's model of the industrial city of northern England

10 A guide to geographical investigation

Module 2682 of OCR's Advanced Subsidiary GCE in Geography, Specification A, requires you to carry out an investigation into a topic from physical, human or environmental geography, the last involving a theme that combines both physical and human elements. For this task you will need to identify a question that can be answered through geographical enquiry. The chances are that you will wish to base your investigation on a topic arising from the areas of geography that you have studied so far, i.e. Modules 2680 and 2681, the Physical and the Human Environments. The investigation must be framed to explore a question at the local scale, and lead to a report of no more than 1000 words divided into five separate sections. This unit provides some suggestions for a successful study and is itself divided into the five sections of the report. Although the sections are useful organising tools, do not let them tie you down too much in the early stages. As you plan your investigation you may need to revise earlier intentions as your ideas become more sharply focused. In the course of the planning phase, you will also need to give thought to your personal health and safety while carrying out the necessary fieldwork. You should make an assessment of likely risks and discuss them with your teacher.

1 Identifying the question

The nature of geography means there is – quite literally – a whole world out there to investigate. You may be set a 'teacher-led' investigation, or you may choose your own. If planning your own study, consider the following points carefully.

- **What are my main interests?** Landforms, hydrology, settlement, urban growth, weather or ecosystems? If you are undecided, look through the topics in this book and rank them according to your level of interest. You should aim to choose a topic from one of the higher-ranked subjects.
- **Are there any issues or conflicts that could be examined?** Although you may choose a topic from either physical or human geography, such as river processes or rural settlement patterns, there are extra angles to examine if the river is a source of potential flooding for a new housing development. Studies that integrate different aspects of geography can be more challenging but more rewarding too. Local newspapers are a good source of ideas for this type of study, but you could also talk to people who live in the area, and contact local government offices or pressure groups.
- **How accessible are the suitable locations?** Make a list of the localities within easy reach of your home, or the home of a friend or relation. You could end up with a surprisingly wide range of interesting locations, so give some thought to the necessary transport arrangements, especially if several visits (at different times of day, for example) are likely to be necessary. You may also need to think about obtaining permission to visit some locations in order to collect data.
- **What can I measure?** You should bear in mind that time for data collection will be limited. Thus, while a study of ecosystem change in your home area might appeal, you

will not be able to collect suitable data in one day and then claim to have a basis for describing long-term changes. Data always needs to be reasonably representative, both in terms of the scale of the topic 'on the ground', and in time. For further ideas, see the section below on planning data collection.

- **What am I aiming for?** Have a clear idea in mind of the purpose of your study. Are you setting out to test an idea or hypothesis, to examine the relevance and applicability of a geographical model or rule, or to probe the environmental aspects of a local development such as new houses, woodland clearance, a new road, etc.? Do not embark on a study that is so complex that you risk becoming lost in a maze of conflicting sources of information, or where an excessive number of techniques could hinder the progress of your investigation. Try to resist being side-tracked by interesting, but marginal, lines of enquiry. None the less, make sure your chosen topic has enough substance within it to enable you to demonstrate your skills of data collection, presentation, analysis and evaluation. You should talk to your teacher about the kind of study that will be manageable yet deserving of good marks.

2 Developing a strategy

The quality of your planning will have a big influence on the quality of the outcome. As a start, attempt to decide the sort of questions you could ask, and whether it would be appropriate to adopt an hypothesis to be tested through your fieldwork. In making up your mind, consider the following questions:

- Does my intended question have a focus that is sharp enough to underpin a clear line of enquiry?
- Will it be easy to stay focused on the main theme of the study?
- What methods of field investigation are manageable in the time available?
- What kind of information will be required – published documents, numerical data, pictorial and satellite images?
- What information data sources will I use – primary (self-collected data), secondary, or both?
- How straightforward will it be to collect reliable data, especially reliable primary data?
- How will the investigation be ordered, i.e. what is the sequence in which each step will occur, and what are the possible completion dates?

Building a background picture

In order to develop a clear idea of the scope of your investigation, it is important to read around the topic and to gather any supporting material to which you might want to refer at a later stage. You may also need to make contact with people who could supply you with information. You will need to think about:

- how well the topic fits into your existing knowledge of geography
- the sources that might help you, e.g. textbooks or journals like the *Geographical Review*
- geographical processes, systems and models that might be relevant to the study
- the availability of computing resources to help you analyse data
- using the correct geographical terminology and reporting 'language'.

3 Collecting the data

Planning data collection

Detailed planning at this stage will save a lot of time and help avoid frustration later on. Not all the information you use need necessarily be numerical, but a good proportion is likely to be of that type, so will require thoughtfully planned collection. The golden rule is to be clear in your mind about the purpose the data will serve, i.e. what question or questions they will help you to answer. Once this aspect is clear, the collection of data and their subsequent analysis will fall into place. Remember that some of the most interesting aspects of geography are the least measurable, for example ecological value, environmental quality, and public perceptions and attitudes towards new developments. You can usually 'measure the unmeasurable' by creating your own system of scoring linked to a numerical scale. Decide what the relevant criteria are and then score them on a numerical scale. As long as your system is consistent and unambiguous, you will have little difficulty in using it to generate useful information. Figure 10.1 illustrates a simple example of a scoring system.

Shopping Quality Score	
Location	
Score 1 2 3 4 5 (5 = high)	
Range of goods	....
Price of goods	....
Ease of parking	....
Shopping hours	....
etc.	
Total	......../20 (or more)

Figure 10.1

A scoring system for measuring shopping quality in different locations

Figure 10.2 suggests a range of themed questions, and the kinds of data collection techniques that might be used to answer them. Note how the same or similar techniques can be applied to many different questions. The important point is always to choose a data collection technique that is well matched to the nature of the information you are seeking to gather; do not feel obliged to use a wide range of techniques simply to show that you know about them. However, you may well find yourself using more than one technique if your study demands it.

Collecting data can be made smoother and more reliable if you follow the simple preparatory steps set out below.

Figure 10.2

A checklist of questions and techniques

Questions you could explore	Possible techniques
URBAN STUDIES	
Is parking adequate? Can the town cope with more traffic? Are traffic levels hindering economic development? Does the town need a bypass/park and ride scheme, etc.?	Car park capacity survey
Do traffic flows vary significantly in different areas? Is traffic a problem? Are pollution levels related to traffic flows? How does traffic influence the environmental quality of the area?	Traffic survey Traffic speed survey Traffic mix survey
What is the value of this area? What is the function of this area? How economically successful is this area? How vulnerable is this area to ... (development/noise/etc.)? How will pedestrianisation influence ...? To what extent does tourism influence the town?	Land use survey Land value survey
What is the environmental quality of this area? How does the quality of the environment reflect ...? How will the area be affected by ... (new development, etc.)?	Environmental quality survey Noise and litter survey Vandalism/graffiti survey
Does housing quality vary, and why? Is housing quality affected by the ...? How successful is the current environmental improvement policy ...?	Housing stock survey Building quality survey
How do people perceive ... (quality, etc.)? What opinions are being expressed about ... (proposals, etc.)?	Questionnaire
How accessible is the area? How popular is the area? Is this an appropriate location for a new ...?	Pedestrian survey Accessibility survey

Continues overleaf

Questions you could explore	Possible techniques
ENVIRONMENTAL STUDIES	
What is the ecological value of this habitat?	Species survey (bird/butterfly count, etc.) Transect or quadrat survey Environmental quality survey Environmental index Habitat survey
What is the recreational value of this habitat?	Questionnaire People activity survey Visitor density survey Pedestrian flow survey Landscape evaluation Recreational index
What are the threats to this environment?	Pollution survey Trampling survey Erosion survey Questionnaire Noise survey Vulnerability index
How effective is the management of this area?	Questionnaire Management map and/or index Land use survey Habitat survey
LANDFORM STUDIES	
What processes are active in the river?	Lateral erosion survey Discharge survey Landform survey Water quality survey
Is erosion or flooding a problem?	Land use map Erosion map Questionnaire
How important is the river for recreation?	Questionnaire People activity survey Visitor density survey Pedestrian flow survey Landscape evaluation Recreational index Beach quality index River quality index
How important is the river for ecology?	Species survey (freshwater/saltwater) Transect/quadrat survey Environmental quality survey Pollution survey Environmental index Habitat survey Beach quality index River quality index

Pilot and trial runs

Pilot and trial runs help to ensure that your intended methods of data collection will actually work in the real world. Questionnaires that made so much sense to you may prove ambiguous and confusing to other people, and the criteria for scoring environmental quality may not be entirely relevant when you are on site. These problems can be avoided through small-scale trials. Half an hour extra spent on piloting a draft questionnaire may more than repay itself in the time saved later on.

Sampling design

In order for your findings to represent reality, you will need to be confident that you have gathered enough data and that the material has been collected objectively. Care in designing your sample will help you meet this requirement and avoid unnecessary work.

- **Sample size** – 'as much as possible in the time' is a useful rule but it has to be balanced with regard for quality. For example, an environmental quality survey based on ten criteria will produce more information than one based on fewer items. However, a smaller and more accurate data set may be preferable to a larger but cruder set of measurements. As a rule of thumb, less than 30 of anything should be avoided because it provides too little information for statistical tests to work satisfactorily, especially where subdivisions of the data are involved. For example, 30 measurements from a total of 5 different locations would not be enough to underpin reliable conclusions about differences among those sites.
- **Sample method** – there are three commonly used sampling methods. **Random** sampling is the most risky and is best avoided. True random sampling is worked out with reference to random number tables but the temptation is to choose whatever data comes to hand most easily, e.g. 'I asked whoever came along'. This approach is *not* random and must be avoided. **Systematic** sampling is generally more effective. You may generate your own system, for example sampling plants at every 10 m, or asking every 5th person. On balance, the best approach is probably to gather a **stratified** sample. This is 'intelligent' sampling in that it takes account of underlying patterns. For instance, if 65 per cent of the population of a retirement town consisted of pensioners and you were using a questionnaire to investigate the facilities for the over-60s, you would need to ensure that your sample included about 65 per cent of people over 60 years of age. On the other hand an investigation into the need for a skateboard park might deliberately sample predetermined numbers from younger age groups rather than an even distribution of all the age groups in the area. The most important aspect of a stratified sample is your justification for its bias in favour of certain groups or conditions. Do not overlook a combination of stratified and systematic sampling, which can be doubly effective.

Recording data

You can greatly improve the quality of your data collection by preparing detailed data recording templates, or recording frames, beforehand. It is not the time to be thinking about how best to write down the data you are gathering when you are out in the cold, rain or sweltering heat. A general model for a data collection template is given in Figure 10.3.

Figure 10.3 Model data collection template

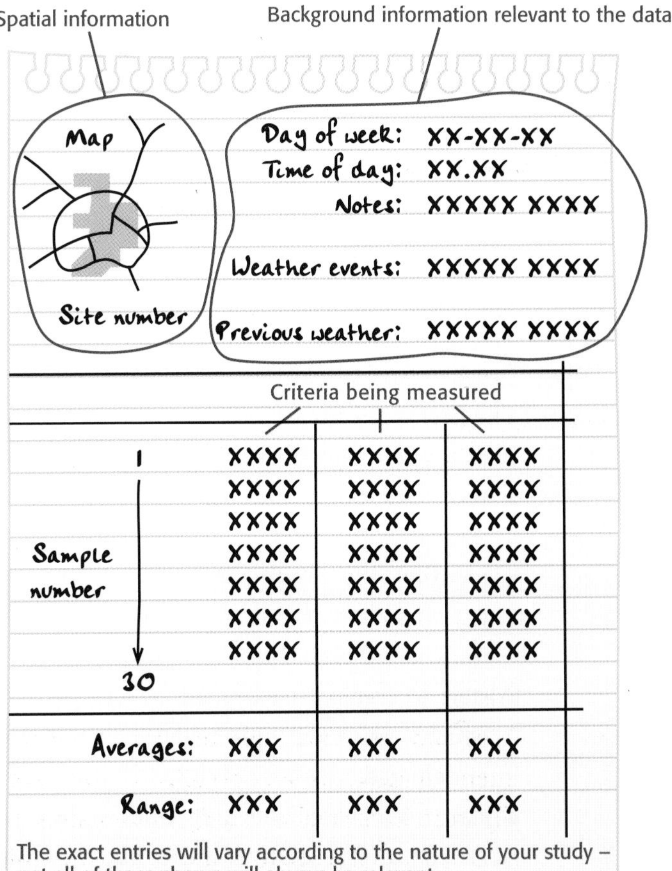

However, be prepared to modify the template – you may need to collect other data that you did not anticipate to be necessary during the planning phase. In some cases, you might prepare an outline map and record the information on it at the locations where it was gathered. This approach is useful if you want to keep an eye on emerging spatial patterns as the investigation progresses in the field.

Finally, although not a part of the collection process, you should give some thought at this stage to the techniques you will use to analyse the data once it has been collected. Thinking about this aspect of the investigation will also help you to firm-up your ideas about the type of data you need in order to support a well-focused study.

4 Analysing, evaluating and interpreting the data

Once you have assembled all your data, the interesting part begins. It is also the dangerous part when a large amount of data can look daunting and lead you down the wrong pathway. If you have collected your data according to plan, and you are clear how the material is to be used to provide answers to the questions you are investigating, then few problems should arise when it comes to organisation and analysis.

Data organisation

The first step is to arrange and display the data in a manner that will enable you to:

- spot and point out the key patterns and trends
- identify the anomalies – the expected patterns that failed to show up or the unexpected ones that turned up as surprises
- start to explain the key trends and patterns, which you will probably have already anticipated
- start to explain the anomalies, which are nearly always due to unpredicted 'other factors'.

In order to display your data, a wide range of graphical techniques is available, a selection of which is shown in Figure 10.4. The key rule is to select the most appropriate technique for the job in hand. You need to be especially certain that it will show what you want it to show in a clear and readily understood way. To demonstrate skill in these techniques you will need to use them in ways that are appropriate, consistent, accurate and well executed. Some examples of good and poor practice are given in Figure 10.5. Note that a combination of techniques can be very effective, such as a map accompanied by annotated photographs or bar charts, showing the situation at specific locations.

Data analysis

The use of specific statistical techniques will help you to probe your data for particular relationships and enable you to answer questions with greater confidence. Some of the most useful techniques are outlined here, but you will need to consult a specialised text on statistics in geography for more details. Using a computer- or calculator-based statistics package will make the work easier, but you must be clear about what each technique is telling you about your data. The computer will not help you to understand the message in the results. Quite often, it is a good idea to show your data graphically and to present the results of a particular statistical technique alongside the graph as confirmation of the message.

Descriptive statistics

Descriptive statistics enable you to give a picture of the typical or average situation. The mean, mode and median are common measures. The **mean** is simply the average value of a set of data; the **mode** is the most commonly occurring value; and the **median** is the middle value when all the items of data are arranged in rank order. Of these three measures, the mean is probably the most useful, especially when

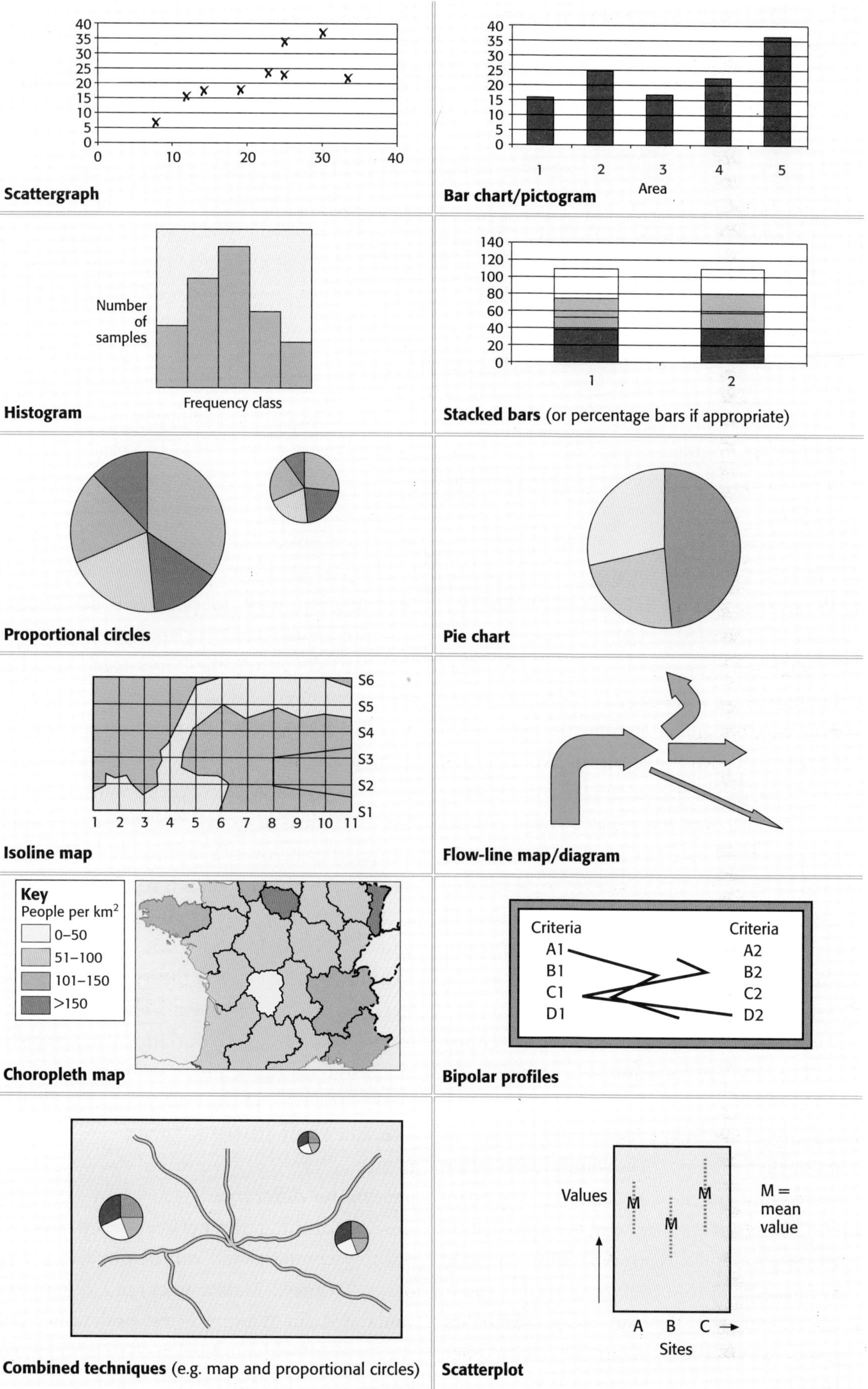

Figure 10.4 A range of graphical techniques

Figure 10.5

Graphical techniques – good and poor practice

Skill area	Good practice	Poor practice
Appropriateness of chosen technique	Scattergraph showing the relationship between two factors, e.g. noise levels and distance from a road for 30 sites.	Separate graphs that do not link the two factors being measured, e.g. one bar chart for distance (with 30 bars) and one for noise (again with 30 bars).
Consistent application	Using the same method at several sites, e.g. stacked bar charts for measures of environmental quality at locations A to F.	Using different types of chart for each location, e.g. a stacked bar for location A, pie charts for B and C, and percentage bars for D, E and F.
Accuracy and execution	Careful use of scales and accurate construction, e.g. proportional circles drawn to a clear and sensible scale.	Proportional circles sketched in by eye, with segments roughly estimated.

data sets overlap or when there are many values. It provides answers to such questions as:

- Which area of the town has the highest average environmental quality?
- Which beach has the highest average wave height?
- Which age group is most positive about the new scheme?
- Which street has the highest noise levels?

The mean itself may not tell you much beyond its actual value, but it may provoke further questions. Much will depend on what you were expecting. If there is an unexpectedly large difference between the means of two, or more, sets of data, you may need to take your analysis further to discover the reasons. Close values might also require deeper enquiry. The mean is a useful starting point for more sophisticated measures but it can be deceiving. Few people, for example, actually earn the *average* income for the UK; most earn an income either greater or less than the average.

More useful descriptive statistics are the range and the standard deviation. The **range** is the maximum value minus the minimum value; it is helpful in giving an impression of the spread of values within a data set. The **standard deviation** is more subtle and measures the average amount of departure, or variation, from the mean within a data set. It is especially useful when two sets of data have similar mean values, and you need to find out if, and how, they vary within themselves. Typical use of the standard deviation is in providing answers to such questions as:

- Which area of the town has the most varied environmental quality?
- Which beach has the biggest variety in wave height?
- Which age group has the most consistent views about the new scheme?
- Which street has the biggest variation in noise levels?

An illustration of the standard deviation is given in Figure 10.6. The larger the value of the standard deviation, the larger is the variation within the data set, and vice versa.

It is often worth going a little further and comparing the standard deviation with the mean in percentage terms. This value, known as the **coefficient of variation** (V), is a tidy way of expressing the overall level of departure from the mean within a data set. You can then make statements like, 'The coefficient of variation shows that there was a lot of variation in people's opinions about the issue – nearly 70% variation around the mean.' The formula for V is simply the standard deviation divided by the mean and multiplied by 100%. The value of V for Precinct 1 in Figure 10.6 is 25.8% and for Precinct 2 only 10.0%.

Testing for difference

Testing for difference between sets of data (or making comparisons) can be done in several ways. Two well-known tests are Chi-squared, and the Mann-Whitney U test. Both tests generate 'answers' which have to be tested for significance using suitable tables. The Chi-squared test is best used with frequency data, i.e. actual counted values, rather than percentages.

The Mann-Whitney U test is a test of difference between the medians of two sets of data, and can be used where you are uncertain whether there are clear differences between each set, e.g. to see if the responses obtained from different groups of people (or people in different areas, perhaps) were significant or merely chance variations. The test starts out by assuming that both sets of data are alike and then seeks to establish if it is safe to accept this assumption or whether it should be rejected. As the test makes use of rank positions (from lowest to highest), not actual measurements, it can be used for any data once they have been put in overall rank order. A worked example is given in Figure 10.7.

To complete the test, the *smaller* value of U must be checked for significance – that is, to see whether the differences between the sets of data could have occurred by chance or if they are real. To carry out this check, you need to refer to tables of critical values of U. A small section of one table is reproduced in Figure 10.7, and shows that for the given example where $n_x = 6$ and $n_y = 5$, the critical value is 5. Where the calculated value (6.5 in this case) is greater than the table value, the two sets of data cannot be considered to be significantly different. Where the calculated value is equal to or smaller than the table value, then the two sets of data can be considered to be significantly different. Thus the difference between the counts of plant species in the soil areas of the worked example cannot be regarded as significantly different, despite initial appearances.

Figure 10.6

Standard deviation: a worked example

Quality ratings for two shopping precincts were collected and the standard deviation was calculated for each data set using the following formula:

$$\sigma \text{ (standard deviation)} = \sqrt{\frac{\sum x^2}{n} - \bar{x}^2}$$

where

$\sum$ means the sum of

$\bar{x}$ is the mean value

n is the number of items in each set of data.

Shopping Quality Ratings			
Precinct 1		Precinct 2	
n = 9		n = 12	
Rating (x)	x^2	Rating (x)	x^2
7	49	9	81
8	64	10	100
11	121	9	81
12	144	9	81
9	81	11	121
10	100	10	100
14	196	11	121
13	169	9	81
6	36	9	81
$\sum x = 90$	$\sum x^2 = 960$	11	121
		12	144
		10	100
		$\sum x = 120$	$\sum x^2 = 1212$
$\bar{x} = 10$		$\bar{x} = 10$	
$\sigma = \sqrt{\frac{960}{9} - 100}$		$\sigma = \sqrt{\frac{1212}{12} - 100}$	
$= \sqrt{6.67}$		$= \sqrt{1.0}$	
$= 2.58$		$= 1.0$	

In Precinct 1, 9 people were interviewed; in Precinct 2 12 people were interviewed. Although both sets of data have the same mean value, there is a distinct difference in their standard deviations. The opinions of people in Precinct 1 were much more variable than those in Precinct 2.

Testing for relationships

Testing for relationships is again possible in several ways, all of which work best with larger, rather than smaller, amounts of sample data. The Spearman coefficient of correlation is an easily managed technique which can help to establish if two sets of data are related, e.g. whether one value goes up as the other goes down. It is based on the starting assumption that there is no correlation between the two sets of data being compared. The result will range between –1.0 (a perfectly negative correlation where one set of values goes down at the same rate as the other goes up) and +1.0 (a perfectly positive correlation where both sets of values go up in step with one another). As with the Mann-Whitney U test, the Spearman coefficient uses ranked data, but the sets are kept

Figure 10.7

The Mann-Whitney U test: a worked example

The number of plant species per m^2 was counted using quadrats on two areas of the same type of soil about 1 km apart. The Mann-Whitney U test was used to see if there was any significant difference between the two counts. The test first requires all the data from both sets to be put into one overall rank order; the actual values themselves are not used. Two values of U are required and the smaller is used for completing the test. The formula looks complicated, but is actually a very simple set of calculations:

$$U \text{ (for Soil area X)} = n_x n_y + \frac{n_x(n_x + 1)}{2} - \sum r_x$$

In the table, the data have been ranked from the smallest (Rank 1) to the largest (Rank 11); tied ranks have been split equally.

Number of plant species per m^2 quadrat			
Soil area X (6 m^2)		Soil area Y (5 m^2)	
n = 6		n = 5	
No. (x)	r_x	No. (y)	r_y
14	11	8	7
12	10	7	6
11	9	5	4.5
9	8	4	3
5	4.5	2	1
3	2		
$\sum r_x = 44.5$		$\sum r_y = 21.5$	

$$U \text{ for Soil area X} = \left[30 + \frac{42}{2} - 44.5\right] = 6.5$$

$$U \text{ for Soil area Y} = \left[n_x n_y - U \text{ for Soil area X}\right] = 30 - 6.5 = 23.5$$

Critical values of U at the 0.05 significance level (95% confidence level)

n_x \ n_y	1	2	3	4	5	6	7	8	9	10	11	12	13	14	15	16	17	18	19	20
1																			0	0
2					0	0	0	1	1	1	1	2	2	2	3	3	3	4	4	4
3					1	2	2	3	3	4	5	5	6	7	7	8	9	9	10	11
4				1	2	3	4	5	6	7	8	9	10	11	12	14	15	16	17	18
5		0	1	2	4	5	6	8	9	11	12	13	15	16	18	19	20	22	23	25
6		0	2	3	5	7	8	10	12	14	16	17	19	21	23	25	26	28	30	32
7		0	2	4	6	8	11	13	15	17	19	21	24	26	28	30	33	35	37	39
8		1	3	5	8	10	13	15	18	20	23	26	28	31	33	36	39	41	44	47
9		1	3	6	9	12	15	18	21	24	27	30	33	36	39	42	45	48	51	54
10		1	4	7	11	14	17	20	24	27	31	34	37	41	44	48	51	55	58	62
11		1	5	8	12	16	19	23	27	31	34	38	42	46	50	54	57	61	65	69
12		2	5	9	13	17	21	26	30	34	38	42	47	51	55	60	64	68	72	77
13		2	6	10	15	19	24	28	33	37	42	47	51	56	61	65	70	75	80	84
14		2	7	11	16	21	26	31	36	41	46	51	56	61	66	71	77	82	87	92
15		3	7	12	18	23	28	33	39	44	50	55	61	66	72	77	83	88	94	100
16		3	8	14	19	25	30	36	42	48	54	60	65	71	77	83	89	95	101	107
17		3	9	15	20	26	33	39	45	51	57	64	70	77	83	89	96	102	109	115
18		4	9	16	22	28	35	41	48	55	61	68	75	82	88	95	102	109	116	123
19	0	4	10	17	23	30	37	44	51	58	65	72	80	87	94	101	109	116	123	130
20	0	4	11	18	25	32	39	47	54	62	69	77	84	92	100	107	115	123	130	138

separate. One useful aspect of the coefficient of correlation is that it can be supported by a scattergraph showing the actual values of the data concerned. A scattergraph with the coefficient given alongside make good partners. Together they show the strength of the relationship and its direction. Neither, however, can prove there is a causal connection between the sets of data, i.e. that one actually causes the other to change. A worked example is given in Figure 10.8.

The Spearman coefficient must also be tested for significance. The coefficient value is compared with the allowed 'degrees of freedom' – simply the number of data pairs minus 2. From the significance graph in Figure 10.8c, it is clear that a coefficient of –0.868 with 28 degrees of freedom is highly significant, which means that the correlation is significant and highly unlikely to have occurred by accident.

Data interpretation and evaluation

Once you have organised and analysed your data you should turn to its interpretation and evaluation in order to discover what it is telling you about the topic you have investigated. The most appropriate approach will depend on the nature of the question you have chosen to explore. For example, if you have examined the relevance to your local area of a standard geographical model, it would be appropriate to begin with a factual description of how well your findings support or contradict the model. You may also need to state how much faith can be placed in your statistical data, perhaps by reference to a test of significance (see Figures 10.7 and 10.8). An explanatory description of the patterns of data shown in your graphs will also be necessary.

In broad terms, the following sequence will help you to interpret and evaluate your findings in an orderly manner and will provide you with the basis for the conclusions you draw in the final part of the report:

- describe the spatial distribution of the information you have researched, referring to

Figure 10.8

The Spearman coefficient of correlation: a worked example

Thirty residents living progressively further away from a motorway have been asked to judge noise levels on a scale from 1 to 10 at a given time on a particular date. Their responses are shown in the table (a) and the data have been ranked. The largest value is given rank 1 in each case, and tied (or shared) ranks are split equally. The Spearman coefficient (r_s) is given by the formula:

$$r_s = 1 - \frac{6\sum d^2}{n^3 - n}$$

where d^2 = difference in rank order squared
n = number of pairs of data

The calculation gives a value of −0.868 for the coefficient, i.e. a strong negative correlation. The scattergraph (b) shows the actual data; the (negative) direction of the relationship between distance and noise levels is clearly visible, and you can see that a considerable amount of scatter can be associated with even a strong numerical coefficient. The graph has the advantage of showing up the anomalies, which can then be investigated further.

a

Distance		Noise level	
Metres	Rank	Level	Rank
50	30	10	1.5
60	29	9	4.5
70	28	10	1.5
80	27	8	9
90	26	9	4.5
100	25	8	9
110	24	7	12.5
120	23	8	9
130	22	9	4.5
140	21	7	12.5
150	20	6	15.5
160	19	8	9
170	18	6	15.5
180	17	6	15.5
190	16	5	19
200	15	8	9
210	14	6	15.5
220	13	5	19
230	12	9	4.5
240	11	2	28.5
250	10	4	22
260	9	5	19
270	8	4	22
280	7	4	22
290	6	3	25.5
300	5	2	28.5
310	4	3	25.5
320	3	3	25.5
330	2	3	25.5
340	1	1	30

n = 30 (30 pairs of data) $\sum d^2 = 8397.5$

$$r_s = 1 - \frac{6 \times 8397.5}{26\,970}$$

$$r_s = -0.868$$

b

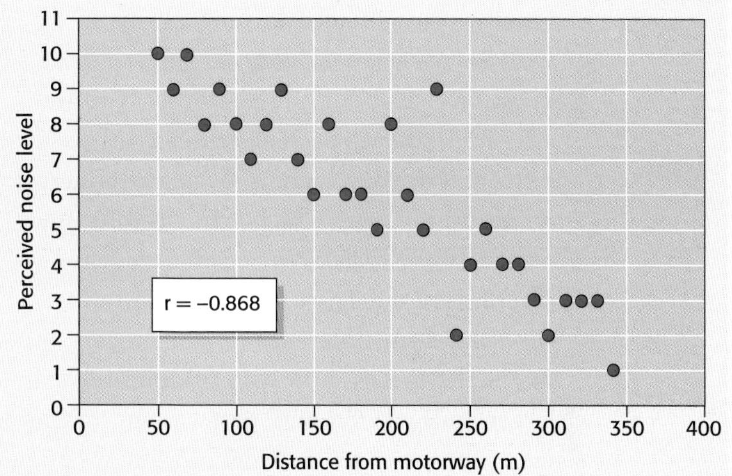

c

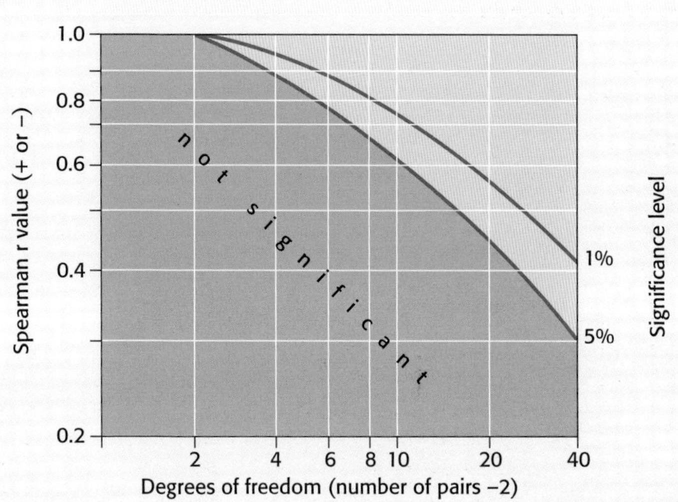

any maps you have prepared in order to illustrate and explain the presence (or absence) of any expected patterns and anomalies

- describe and attempt to explain any differences in the numerical data you have collected, e.g. the number of plant species in one location compared with another nearby, and test apparent differences for their significance
- look further into any relationships in the data that seem to be important – e.g. changes in pedestrian or traffic flow with increasing distance from a central point – and test these apparent associations for their strength and significance.

Finally, you will need to sum up this section with an overview of your findings. Where a question has been posed, or a hypothesis advanced, you will need to state clearly how the outcomes of your analysis reveal patterns and relationships on which conclusions may reasonably be based. Where you have relied on several sets of data, you should point out any similarities and differences. In the process, you might also discuss how your findings relate to larger-scale geographical patterns and/or how they support or refute wider models or issues in geography.

5 Presenting a summary

In this final section of your report, you should draw together all the threads developed during the analysis section, and arrive at a reasoned judgement. Your analysis will probably have produced many 'mini-conclusions' relating to each strand of the topic investigated, and now is the time to use those pieces of evidence to come to a conclusion about the answer to the question you have investigated, or the hypothesis you have tested. There may be a clear answer one way or the other, or you may find it necessary to conclude that no single straightforward answer is possible. Whatever the situation, you must support and justify your conclusion with reference to the evidence you have gathered throughout the investigation.

An important part of the conclusion is an evaluation of the quality of your work. This aspect is often misunderstood, and optimists write 'I have enjoyed doing this and feel it is a good project' while the pessimists write 'I could have done much more'. The evaluation is not designed to test your personality but your grasp of reality. You should describe clearly those parts of the investigation that went well and gave good-quality information. Likewise you should describe your reservations about the methods you used and the limitations of the data collected. It is also helpful to note how you might redesign the project if you were to repeat it, and to draw attention to any further lines of enquiry that could be followed. Remember, a geographical investigation invites you to research something new, to make links between ideas, and to support your geographical intuition with hard facts.

Glossary

Advection fog Fog caused by condensation of water vapour when air passes over a colder surface.

Agenda 21 The initiative of the 1992 UN conference in Rio de Janeiro designed to foster local-scale projects that support sustainable development.

Albedo The proportion of solar radiation reflected back by a surface – as in the 'Earth's albedo'.

Allogenic succession A succession where the stimulus for change is external to the ecosystem, e.g. a flood.

Annual hydrograph A graph showing average river flows over the year.

Anticyclone A slow-moving and large area of high atmospheric pressure giving relatively clear skies and calm weather.

Aquiclude A relatively impermeable rock layer which defines the boundaries of an aquifer.

Aquifer A relatively permeable rock layer which can store water.

Asthenosphere The zone beneath the lithosphere where rock is heated close to melting point and in which convection currents 'drive' continental drift.

Autogenic succession A succession where the stimulus for change is internal, i.e. gradual soil improvement.

Basal undercutting The undercutting of the foot of a slope by an erosive force such as a stream or the sea; also known as *sapping*.

Baseflow The movement of water through rocks deep underground.

Basic cations or bases Elements such as calcium, magnesium, sodium or potassium, all forming important plant nutrients in soil.

Bedding plane The junction between each bed or layer of a sedimentary rock; the term is also used to describe the junction between different sedimentary rocks.

Biomass The total dry weight in kilograms of living matter – trunks, branches, stems, leaves – measured at one point in time in a given area, usually a square metre.

Biome Large-scale ecosystem; some may cover several continents (e.g. rainforest).

Birth rate The crude birth rate is the number of births in a single year per 1000 of the population. More refined measures are the standardised birth rate and the general fertility rate.

Bourne An intermittent or seasonal stream, usually found in chalk areas, the length of which varies according to the height of the water-table.

Brown earth A soil type developed under deciduous woodland and improved pasture, free draining and with moderate acidity.

Catena A sequence of soils developed across a slope and underlain by the same parent material.

Cation exchange The process by which cations are exchanged between a plant root and clay/humus particles.

Cation exchange capacity (CEC) The number of cations on the surface of mineral and humus particles available for root uptake.

Central place A place that provides goods and services to people in the surrounding area.

Centrality A measure of the relative importance of a centre in terms of the number of services it provides, and its accessibility.

Chelation The chemical weathering process whereby organic acids (chelating agents) derived from humus attack selected minerals in the rock.

Chemical weathering The decomposition of rocks by chemical activity including hydrolysis, hydration, carbonation, solution, oxidation and chelation.

City region A regional centre, together with the surrounding smaller towns and rural settlements linked to it by commuting, shopping and recreation flows.

Clay–humus complex Mixture of fine clay particles and humus to which cations are attached.

Climatic climax community A community of plants in equilibrium with its regional climate and soils. All ecological niches are filled and no further development will take place.

Closed village A village dominated by a single landowner; sometimes called an estate village.

Compact city A city where houses, offices and shops are located close together.

Condensation nucleii Particles in the atmosphere which attract moisture and accelerate the process of condensation.

Congestion The delay imposed on vehicles by one another.

Contour ploughing Ploughing around a hill rather than up and down its slopes.

Cosmological cities Cities planned in harmony with cultural interpretations of the universe or cosmos; found in the oldest urban civilisations.

Counterurbanisation The process of population decentralisation whereby larger settlements lose people while smaller settlements in rural areas and on the city margins increase in population.

Cover crop A crop grown to protect the soil from erosion.

Crumb structure Small peds, about 1–5 mm in size, associated with loam soils.

Death rate The crude death rate is the number of deaths in a single year per 1000 of the population. More refined measures are the age-specific mortality rate and the infant mortality rate.

Deciduous plants Trees and shrubs that shed their leaves during the dry or cold season.

Demographic transition model A model of the change in birth rates, death rates and overall population size over time, usually linked to the process of economic development.

Dependency ratio The ratio of elderly (over 65 years) and young (under 15 years) people to the total adult (15–64 years) population.

Depression An area of low atmospheric pressure developed on the polar front marked by a warm and cold front and warm sector.

Dewpoint The temperature at which a body of air becomes saturated with moisture.

Dispersed settlement A rural settlement pattern dominated by isolated farmsteads and hamlets.

Ecological pyramid A graphic representation of the numbers and/or biomass and/or energy in each trophic level of a model ecosystem.

Ecosystem A community of living and interdependent organisms linked by the exchange of material and the flow of energy.

Edge cities New urban developments, mainly in the outer suburbs and centred on businesses and offices.

Eluviation The physical movement downwards of particles from the upper to the lower horizons of free-draining soils.

Environmental lapse rate (ELR) The rate of temperature change with height in the atmosphere; not to be confused with the rate of temperature change experienced by a rising parcel of air.

Ephemeral stream A temporary stream, often seasonal in nature, which flows only when torrential rainfall or high groundwater conditions occur.

Epicentre The point on the Earth's surface immediately above the focus of an earthquake.

Epidemiological transition The change from a pattern of mainly infectious to degenerative diseases.

Escarpment An outcrop of titled rock strata with a steep (scarp) face in one direction and a gentle (dip) slope in the other.

Ethnic group A group of people distinguished by a common characteristic or set of characteristics related variously to race, nationality, language, religion or other cultural features.

Ethnoburb A residential and business district formed in the suburbs by better-off immigrants.

Eutrophication Water chemically enriched with nutrients.

Evaporation The process by which liquid water transforms to gaseous water vapour.

Evapotranspiration The combined effect of evaporation (physical process) and transpiration (biological process) in moving water from the soil store back to the atmosphere.

Falling limb The declining curve on a hydrograph. The shape of this curve reflects both the catchment area water stores and the shape and relief of the basin.

Filtering The process by which housing built initially for wealthy families passes down to poorer families over time.

Flood hydrograph A graph showing the response of river flow to a single rainfall event.

Focus The point at depth in the Earth's crust where the dislocation of rocks occurs to create an earthquake.

Food chain A simple model showing how energy flows through an ecosystem.

Food web A collection or matrix of food chains.

Free face A steep and mainly bare rock face exposed to active weathering and erosion.

Friction of distance The idea that increasing distance serves to reduce the volume of communication and activity between places.

Gatekeeper An organisation or individual controlling access to housing.

General circulation The global pattern of atmospheric movement.

Ghetto A segregated district where one particular social group is dominant.

Ghettoisation The process of over-concentration, usually as a result of outside forces, of a single social group in a defined residential area.

Green belt The area around a city where development is prevented by law.

Greenhouse effect The warming of the atmosphere caused by the entrapment of longwave radiation energy.

Gross primary production The amount of plant tissue created by photosynthesis, including the energy used for respiration measured in kg/m^2/year.

Growan On Dartmoor, an accumulated mass of sandy fragments derived from the chemical decomposition of granite.

Growth corridors New settlements lying close to major transport routes.

Gruss A deposit made up of tiny flakes which results from the chemical breakdown of granite.

Halosere A series of communities that occupy a saline environment.

High-order goods Goods that are high in price but are bought only occasionally. People are generally prepared to travel further to buy them.

Humidity (relative humidity) The moisture content of a body of air expressed as a percentage of the total amount of moisture that could be held at the same temperature.

Humus Leaf litter and faecal material which has completely decomposed so that no original structures are visible.

Hydrograph A graph showing the change in river flow with time.

ICT The combination of information and communications technologies, harnessing computer power with new developments in telecommunications, including fibre-optic technology. It allows data of all kinds to be transmitted faster, in greater volume, and used in an interactive way.

Illuviation The accumulation of clay-size particles in the B horizon of soil (removed by eluviation from the A horizon).

Infiltration The process by which water on the surface moves into the soil store.

Infiltration excess overland flow Water flowing on the surface as a result of intense rain exceeding the soil's infiltration capacity.

Infrastructure The term used to describe the basic facilities and services available to a given area, e.g. roads, water and power supplies, communication and waste disposal systems.

Interflow A 'semi-deep' flow of water in the unsaturated zone above the regions where baseflow takes place.

Inter-tropical convergence zone (ITCZ) The zone of rising air and associated low pressure broadly coincident with the Equator.

Inverse care law The 'law' that states that those who are most ill generally receive less treatment, and vice versa.

Inverse distance law The 'law' that states that migration is inversely proportional to distance.

Jetstream A wind blowing at about 12 km above the Earth's surface with average speeds in the order of 250 km/h and a maximum of 500 km/h.

Joint A crack or parting within a mass of rock caused by stresses such as contraction on cooling, shrinkage on drying out, or the release of overlying pressure.

Karst The term used to describe limestone scenery and its features, including cockpit karst.

Key settlements Villages in which planners try to concentrate investment and services in order to maintain thresholds and ensure the survival of at least some rural services.

Lag time The time between the peak of a rainfall event and the peak of a storm hydrograph.

Latent heat Heat in a hidden form which changes the nature of a substance. When ice turns to water and when liquid water is converted into water vapour, latent heat is locked up. When freezing and condensation occur, latent heat is released.

Leaching The removal down the soil profile of organic matter and minerals in solution.

Legumes Plants that are capable of fixing atmospheric nitrogen using bacteria which live in their root nodules.

Lithology The character of rocks.

Lithosphere The rocks of the Earth's crust and upper mantle.

Low-order goods Goods that are low in price and bought regularly. People will generally only travel short distances to buy them.

Mantle The layer of high-density rocks lying between the Earth's crust and the core.

Maquiladoras Foreign-owned factories located on the Mexico–US border to take advantage of cheap labour from Mexico.

Mass movement The collective term used to describe the transport of weathered material on slopes without the action of running water. It includes heave, flow, slides and falls.

Mechanical weathering The decomposition of rock through physical processes, including slaking, exfoliation, pressure release and the action of salt crystals and plant roots.

Metropolitan village A village within commuting distance of a city which has grown rapidly and is no longer socially or economically 'rural' in character.

Migration The movement of people to a permanent or semi-permanent new place of residence in response to push or pull factors. Internal migration ocurs within single countries; international migration involves the crossing of national borders.

Moder Humus intermediate in nature between mor and mull; derived from deciduous litter.

Mohorovičić (Moho) discontinuity The junction between the Earth's crust and the upper mantle.

Monoculture Planting the same crop on land every year.

Mor Fibrous, poorly decomposed, acidic humus derived from conifer needles and heathland plants.

Mull Soft, black, crumbly, nutrient-rich humus derived from decomposing grasses.

Net primary productivity The amount of plant tissue created by photosynthesis minus the energy used up for respiration, measured in kg/m^2/year.

New town A planned urban settlement usually designed to take people out of large cities.

Nucleated settlement A rural settlement pattern dominated by large villages.

Omnivore Organism that eats both animals and plants, the choice being controlled by what is available.

Open system A system where inputs and outputs can vary independently between the system and its surrounding environment.

Overcrowding A measure of the number of people per room in a dwelling.

Overland flow Water flow across the surface of the land.

Ozone layer The layer in the atmosphere between 55 km and 15 km above the Earth's surface where ozone (O_3) is concentrated.

Pangaea The super-continent which broke up eventually to form the continents of today.

Peat Undecomposed plant remains which accumulate in anaerobic conditions to a depth of 30 cm or more.

Ped A natural soil structural unit consisting of many soil particles held together by natural glues.

Percolation The process by which water in the soil store moves down to deeper groundwater stores.

Periglacial area An area found on the edges of ice sheets and glaciers, in high latitudes such as the tundra of Asia and North America and at high altitudes. Permafrost is frequently present.

Pioneer community The first group of plants to occupy a site.

Pipeflow A rapid movement of water in subterranean channels (pipes) in the soil. Common in peaty soils.

Plagioclimax community A plant community that is permanently prevented from reaching its climax state by human activity.

Plant succession The replacement of one plant community with another on a given site without any change in external environmental conditions.

Plate boundaries The edges or margins of crustal plates which may be constructive, destructive or transformational in nature.

Platy structures Horizontal peds about 1–10 mm across, associated with clay soils.

Podsol A soil with an ashen layer and distinct horizons subject to podsolisation.

Podsolisation The removal in solution of iron and aluminium down the soil profile by organic acids.

Polar front The junction between cold polar and warm tropical air along which depressions are generated.

Population density The arithmetic population density is the number of people living in a given area, measured in persons per km^2 or in hectares. Variations relating to available resources and the amount of agricultural or residential land are also used.

Population pressure The relationship between the population of an area and the local resources at its disposal, especially the capacity to produce food.

Precipitation Atmospheric moisture in the liquid or solid forms of rain, sleet, snow, hail, frost and dew.

Primary consumers Organisms that feed directly on producers.

Primary producers Organisms that create plant tissue from inorganic substances.

Primary succession The plant communities that occupy a site that has not been previously vegetated.

Primate city A city that is vastly larger than all the other urban centres in a country and which enjoys a higher rate of economic growth.

Psammosere A series of communities that occupy a sand dune complex.

Pyroclasts Airborne volcanic rock particles which, when they fall back to Earth and are deposited, make up pyroclastic rocks.

Range The maximum distance people are prepared to travel to obtain a particular good or service.

Recharge The process by which water in an aquifer is replenished.

Recurrence interval A statistical average relating to the timing between events of a given size (e.g. floods). The bigger the flood the longer the recurrence interval.

Regolith A layer of disintegrating weathered rock material overlying the bedrock.

Resurgent stream A stream that emerges from underground, usually at the base of a limestone outcrop.

Richter scale The logarithmic scale used to measure earthquake intensity.

Ridge push The upthrust action of rising convection currents in the Earth's mantle creating mid-oceanic ridges.

Rising limb The initial rising curve on a flood hydrograph. The steepness of the curve depends on the intensity of the rainfall and the character of the basin.

Runoff Water flow generated by a rainfall event (or, in some regions, by snowmelt).

Rural Challenge A government scheme for funding rural development projects.

Rural depopulation The decline of population in rural areas; it could be the result of an excess of deaths over births, or of net out-migration.

Salinisation The movement of salts up the soil profile by capillary action.

Saturated overland flow Overland flow in those parts of the drainage basin that have become saturated so water cannot soak into the soil.

Secondary succession Plant communities forming on sites that have formerly been vegetated.

Sensible heat The heat of a substance as measured by its temperature; the heat that can be sensed or felt.

Sere A complete succession from pioneer to climax community on one site.

Settlement evolution Changes in the settlement pattern over time.

Settlement hierarchy Settlements ranked according to their relative importance. Criteria can be population size, number of services, or size of sphere of influence.

Settlement morphology The shape, layout and structure (i.e. pattern of land use) of a settlement.

Settlement pattern The type of settlement found in a particular area.

Site The area of land occupied by the buildings of a settlement.

Situation The location of a settlement in terms of access to other settlements and to resources beyond the site.

Slab pull The down-dragging action of descending convection currents in the Earth's mantle creating oceanic trenches.

Social exclusion The idea that a minority of people is excluded from the benefits of society by virtue of poverty, powerlessness, unemployment, lack of mobility, or lack of qualifications.

Solar radiation Electro-magnetic radiation emitted by the sun and consisting mainly of visible light, ultraviolet and infrared rays.

Spatial integration The process by which a segregated social group becomes mixed with the rest of the population.

Spatial segregation The distribution of different social groups in different neighbourhoods.

Stemflow The movement of water from interception storage (on vegetation) to the soil store via plant stems or tree trunks.

Storm hydrograph See *flood hydrograph.*

Stratosphere The layer of the atmosphere above the troposphere – that is, extending a distance of more than 50 km above the Earth's surface.

Strip cultivation Alternating strips of crops often arranged at right-angles to the prevailing wind or parallel to a slope.

Subsere community A community that is prevented from reaching its climatic climax by an arresting factor.

Suburbs Low-density, mainly residential areas built on the outskirts of towns and cities.

Surface runoff Water flowing across the surface. May include either *saturated overland flow* or *infiltration excess overland flow.*

Sustainable development Development that meets the needs of the present generation without compromising the ability of future generations to meet their needs.

Talus slope A sloping surface made up of accumulated angular fragments of rock debris produced largely by weathering.

Temperature inversion An atmospheric condition in which temperature increases with height, often caused by cool denser air sinking to ground level and leaving warm air above.

Tenure The way someone occupies property, e.g. renting or owning a house.

Threshold The minimum number of people (or size of market area) needed to keep a service in business.

Throughfall The movement of water from interception storage (on vegetation) to the soil store by dripping from vegetation.

Throughflow The movement of water horizontally through the soil and subsoil.

Tor A prominent outcrop in granite marked by angular blocks of rock separated by distinct vertical and horizontal joints.

Transmissivity The rate at which water can move through an aquifer.

Transpiration Movement of water from the soil store back to the atmosphere as a result of biological processes in plants.

Trophic level A group of organisms that have the same method of feeding or way of obtaining their energy.

Tropopause The junction or boundary between the *troposphere* and *stratosphere.*

Troposphere The lower part of the atmosphere, 12 km in depth on average.

Urban hierarchy The classification of urban areas according to a given measure such as population size, built-up area and the nature and number of services available.

Urban land market The term used to describe all the processes and actors involved in the buying and selling of urban land and property.

Urban morphology The physical layout of streets, buildings, parks, etc. within a built-up area.

Urban renaissance The recent reversal of population decline experienced by some big cities.

Urban sprawl The uncontrolled spread of built-up areas into the countryside.

Urbanisation The process of urban growth and development. It can be applied to the expansion both in the number and the size of towns and cities.

Village morphology The shape, layout and structure of a village.

Water balance graph A graph showing the relative balance of precipitation and evapotranspiration throughout the year.

Water-table The variable upper surface of the saturated zone in permeable rocks.

Watershed The boundary formed by the highest points between one drainage basin and the next.

Wavelength The distance (L) between the crests of successive waves in any energy stream.

Weathering The breakdown and decay of rocks *in situ* creating a layer of waste rock known as the *regolith.* Weathering can be mechanical, chemical or biological.

Xerosere A plant community that occupies a very dry environment.

Index

Note: Page numbers for glossary definitions are in **bold**

Acknowledgements

We are grateful to the following for permission to reproduce photographs:

Art Directors/Trip 4.25, 4.62, 7.7, 7.25, 9.23; Associated Press 4.17; John Bailey 3.40; Penni Bickle 7.6; British Antarctic Survey 5.5; Chalgrove Local History Group 6.22 (all); James Davis Travel Photography 1.2, 1.11, 2.2a, 7.1, 7.5; Earth Images Picture Library 5.8; Eye Ubiquitous 7.31; Frank Lane Picture Agency 1.52b, 3.6, 4.47; Geophotos/Tony Waltham 1.28, 2.2b, 4.20, 4.23, 4.29, 4.30, 4.48, 4.53, 7.10; Geoscience Features 1.13,1.14, 2.13, 2.14, 2.16, 2.17, 2.26; Clive Hart 2.23, 2.24, 3.45, 4.27, 4.33, 4.51, 4.57, 4.58, 6.39; R. Glassock (1992) *Historic Landscapes of Britain from the Air*, CUP, plate 53, p.113, 6.11; John Heseltine Studios 6.40; ICCE Photo Library/Rob Cousins 3.43; Leeds City County Council Photographic Department 7.27, 9.29; David Lowther 6.29; MEPC 6.28; Garrett Nagle 5.3; Philip Nixon 6.43; Photoair Ltd 6.2, 6.6, 6.7, 6.14, 6.16, 6.17, 6.19, 6.31; Planet Earth Pictures 4.31; Radiation Services Branch, Langley Research Center, NASA 3.10a and b; Rex Features 4.52, 4.65; T. Rowley (1978) *Villages in the Landscape*, Orion Press 6.12; Science Photo Library 4.19; Scope/Plassant 3.39; Lynne Shandley 4.36; Shropshire County Council/Watson and Musson (1993) *Shropshire from the Air*, Shropshire Books, p.75, 6.37; Peter Smith Photography 4.55; Kevin Stannard 6.25, 6.26, 6.46, 6.52, 6.58, 6.68; Still Pictures 1.7, 4.9, 4.59, 4.60, 4.64, 6.60, 7.17, 7.23, 7.28, 7.32, 7.34, 8.3, 8.5, 8.6, 8.17, 8.19, 8.21, 8.22, 8.23, 9.1; Topham Picturepoint 4.28; Peter Walker 2.8; US Government Geological Survey 4.46.

We would like to thank the following for permission to use their material in either the original or adapted form:

1.4 T.E. Graedel & P.J. Crutzen *Atmosphere, Climate and Change* 1995; 1.16 adapted from R.C. Ward *Principles of Hydrology* Mcgraw-Hill; 1.17 P. Thran *Agroclimatic Atlas of Europe* Elsevier 1965; 1.28 based on Marsh & Davies 1983, quoted in Bishop & Prosser *Water Process and Management* 1995; 1.30 NERC 1998 (in *Groundwater – Our Hidden Asset* Earthwise Publication; 1.31 K. Hilton *Process and Pattern in Physical Geography* 1979; 1.36 adapted from Itchen Data File © Environment Agency 1999; 1.46 adapted from D. Wheeler and J. Mayes *Regional Climates of the British Isles* 1997; 1.48 Institute of Hydrology; 1.51 K. Gregory & D. Walling, *Man and Environmental Processes* 1981; 1.52 Katharine Jackson 1996; 2.4 after Dowdeswell *Hedges and Verges* 1987; 2.20 B. Clayden 'Soils of the Exeter District' in *Memoirs of the Soil Survey of England and Wales*, Sheet 32, 1971; 3.2 adapted from T.J. Chandler *Modern Meteorology and Climatology* Nelson 1972; 3.4, 3.5, 3.7, 3.8, 3.15, 3.44 adapted from R.W. Christopherson *Geosystems* Prentice-Hall 1999; 3.22 adapted from N. Horrocks *Physical Geography and Climatology* Longman; 4.2, 4.7, 4.8, 4.39 adapted from M.A. Summerfield *Global Geomorphology* Longman 1991; 5.2 J. Staszewski, 'Vertical distribution of world population', *Geographical Studies* 14, 1957, Polish Academy of Sciences; 5.4 R. Barry and R. Chorley *Atmosphere, Weather and Climate* 1998; 5.25 G. Nagle, *Geography through Diagrams*; 5.26 Labour Force Survey, Office for National Statistics; 5.27, 5.29, 5.30, 5.31 Office for National Statistics, Government Actuary's Department; 5.39 *The Guardian* 2 September 1999; 6.3 and 6.9 B.K. Roberts, *Rural Settlement in Britain* 1979; 6.4 J. Everson & B. Fitzgerald, *Settlement Patterns* 1969; 6.8 H.C. Darby (ed.) *A New Historical Geography of England before 1600* 1976; 6.10 T. Rowley *Villages in the Landscape* 1978; 6.20 W. Hornby and M. Jones *An Introduction to Settlement Geography* 1991; 6.22 Chalgrove Local History Group (R. Jacques *et al*) *Chalgrove: an Oxfordshire Village* 1990; 6.41 R. King and J. Killinbeck 'Carlo Levi, the mezzo-giorno and emigration', *Geography* Vol.74, Geographical Association 1989; 6.44 and 6.45 Durham County Council; 6.47 West Durham Rural Networks Bid Document 1992; 6.48 G. Lewis & D. Maund 'The urbanisation of the countryside, a framework for analysis' *Geografiska Annaler* 58B, 1976; K. Dean 'Counterurbanisation continues in Brittany' *Geography* 71, Geographical Association 1986; 6.53 & 6.54 G. Lewis 'Rural migration and demographic change' in B. Ilbery (ed.) *The Geography of Rural Change* 1998; 6.56 Extract from *The Observer*, 12 April 1999; 6.57 adapted from D. North 'Rural industrialisation' in *The Geography of Rural Change* Longman 1998; 6.61 Extract from *The Times* 18 December 1999; 6.63 Geography Department, Eton College; 6.65 D. Spencer 'Population growth and change', University of Reading Discussion Paper No.9 1992; 6.69 Rural Development Commission 1993; 7.2 *Philips Geographical Digest 1998/99*; 7.3 US Bureau of Statistics; 7.12 Department of Environment, Transport and Regions; 7.13 Transport Trends 1998; 7.16 UNEP/WHO, *Urban Pollution in Megacities of the World* 1992; 7.21 *US Abstract of Annual Statistics 1999*; 7.22 & 7.29 World Resources 1993; 7.30 Air Quality Board, State of California 1999; 7.33 Eurostat; 8.9 INEGI Estadisticas Historicas de Mexico, 1992; 8.13 & 8.19 S. Morris 'Mexico City – urban issues' *Geofile* 306, 1997; 8.14 F. Slater (ed.) *People and Environments, Issues and Enquiries* 1986; 8.15 INEGI Estadisticas Historicas de Mexico, 1994; 8.21 National Research Council, Academia de la Investigation Cientifica, Academia Nacional de Ingeniera, 1995; 9.4 INSEE 1990 census; 9.5 D. Drakakis-Smith *The Third World City* 1997; 9.8 World Resources 1993; 9.10 World Resources 1998/99; 9.14, 9.16, 9.17, 9.18 *Social Trends 1999*; 9.15 UN Centre for Human Settlements 1996; 9.19, 9.21, 9.25, 9.30 Leeds City Council; 9.24 Burtenshaw 1983; 9.26 *Social Trends 1997* 9.28 R. Waldinger and M. Bozorgmehr (eds) *Ethnic Los Angeles* 1996.